I HAVE SEEN THE FUTURE

I HAVE SEEN THE FUTURE

A LIFE OF LINCOLN STEFFENS

PETER HARTSHORN

COUNTERPOINT
BERKELEY

Library of Congress Cataloging-in-Publication Data
Hartshorn, Peter, 1956–
I have seen the future : a life of Lincoln Steffens / by Peter Hartshorn.
p. cm.
ISBN 978-1-58243-807-8
1. Steffens, Lincoln, 1866–1936. 2. Journalists—United States—Biography. I. Title.
PN4874.S68H37 2011
070.92—dc22
[B]
2010031495

Jacket design by Ann Weinstock
Interior design by www.meganjonesdesign.com
Printed in the United States of America

COUNTERPOINT
1919 Fifth Street
Berkeley, CA 94710

www.counterpointpress.com

Distributed by Publishers Group West

10 9 8 7 6 5 4 3 2 1

TO CRISTINA

Contents

INTRODUCTION

In his later life, he was at times shunned, ridiculed, and blacklisted. One of the most well-known journalists in America, a man whose counsel was sought for years by presidents, congressmen, governors, labor leaders, and machine bosses, he often found himself unable to interest publishers in his work. Still, at the age of sixty-five, Lincoln Steffens could reflect on a career marked by both brilliant successes and utter failures with the comment, "My story is of a happy life—happier and happier."

Indeed, it was a happy life, and Steffens made it so by looking outward, examining everyone else's life more than his own. He developed an uncanny and impressive knack for getting influential people in both government and the corporate world to tell him their stories even when they hardly knew him. "He cultivated the 'big fellows' and always knew what was going on," Upton Sinclair observed of Steffens. And their stories told the journalist what he most desired to know: how things worked. Politically, economically, and socially, Steffens questioned everything. Why were people rich or poor? Successful or helpless? Praised or ignored? What he learned in his search would shock the nation: Democracy in America was decidedly undemocratic, and equality of opportunity a myth, and much of it deliberately so. Too often in the halls of power, corruption and graft came before law and order. How could this happen in Christian America, of all places? he wondered. So Steffens purposely sought the message of Jesus in the most obvious settings—Sunday morning churches, across America—but found no hint of actual Christianity. Tirelessly, he looked elsewhere for explanations, investigating and pondering why his own country, which worshipped freedom and God, had created a social system that clearly did not favor the majority of people, and how it might yet save itself.

Steffens saw that in order to approach the truth—not the newspaper accounts, the editorials, the inflated and self-serving rhetoric of politicians and bosses, but the actual essence of the matter itself—it was continually necessary for him to unlearn much of what he had come to know as facts as taught through schools, books, and the other usual means of education. "For every illusion I lost," he would say, "I gained a new and better—illusion." And it was this intriguing, endless process of unlearning, of considering all sides and asking countless questions of people, no matter how high or low their rank, to try to "see it" whole and clear, that gave Steffens much of his happiness.

Throughout his life, he had an almost childlike wonder over how much more there always was to comprehend and how problems might be solved, which meant that he was keen to hear all views. His willingness to consider a range of opinions, as well as his capacity for self-doubt, are apparent in a warm letter that Steffens, then forty-six, sent to his young nephew Clinton before a trip to Europe:

> Europe is east, not west, but I find that I often go east when I think I'll go west. Maybe that will happen to you sometimes. And sometimes again . . . I get ready to go somewhere and don't go at all. This is an interesting world we live in, you and I. . . . It goes round and round, and it twists us round and round, and I suppose we shall not any of us know where we are going till we find out where it is going. I wish you'd help me to discover that,—when you grow up.

For Steffens, his eventful life would be full of discoveries that fascinated him while at times stunning his fellow citizens.

I

BOY ON HORSEBACK

STEFFENS'S EARLIEST MEMORIES were those of a carefree child on horseback, eagerly exploring the farmlands, cattle ranches, and vast, open spaces of the Sacramento Valley. Such freedom, Steffens often said, was ideal for a boy with a wide imagination and an insatiable desire for explanations of nearly everything he observed, two personal traits that he nourished with enthusiasm throughout his life.

The fortunate son had quite different beginnings from his parents, who met in the chaotic post-gold-rush days in San Francisco. His mother, Elisabeth Louisa Symes, was born in England and, as a young girl, moved to New Jersey, where she grew up in Hoboken to be a seamstress. Trapped on the East Coast, she understood that she would not easily find what her heart desired: "She not only knew that she . . . wanted a husband; she acknowledged it to herself and took steps to find one," Steffens recounted. Barely a decade after the start of the gold rush, it was painfully obvious to Louisa, as she was called, that most of the eligible young men had gone west, which is where she set her sights, sailing with one of her sisters to San Francisco, via the isthmus crossing, in the early 1860s. Practical, intelligent, and quite shrewd in her approach, Louisa found her man (after swapping dates with her sister) at her first boardinghouse in San Francisco.

One of sixteen children, Joseph Steffens was first raised on a farm in eastern Canada before his family headed west in a wagon and settled in Illinois. Better suited for school and business than the physical demands of farming—his father called him "the scrub"—Joseph attended a seminary and a commercial college before working as a teacher and a clerk. By the summer of 1862, at the age of twenty-five, he had saved enough money to join the line of fortune seekers bound for California. Traveling for weeks on horseback in a wagon train, he finally reached California in late summer and soon found work as a bookkeeper for the firm of Fuller and Heather, importers of paints, oil, and glass. Three years later, Louisa and he were married.

Their first child, Joseph Lincoln Steffens, named after the father and the president and called "Len" or "Lennie" in the family, was born on April 6, 1866, in the Mission District of San Francisco. Three sisters, Louise ("Lou"), Dorothy ("Dot" or "Lottie"), and Laura, followed, and the children would grow up in comfort, as Joseph Steffens had succeeded so well in business that soon after the birth of his son, he was offered a quarter interest in a branch store of Fuller and Heather in Sacramento. So the family set off for the state capital, where young Steffens's "conscious life" began at the family's new home on Second Street.

To a young, curious boy, Sacramento in the 1870s offered no limit of entertainment. Not far from the Steffens house was the Sacramento River, where vessels of all kinds—steamboats, cargo ships, and passenger boats—passed by the gazing boy in an endless, magical flow, while back in the city, a tapestry of Western life recalling the bustle of the gold rush era left an indelible impression on the young Steffens. He remembered seeing Mexican cowboys known as *vaqueros* and belled mule trains "ringing into town," as well as miners and steamboat men, who reveled in drinking, gambling, and fighting. Steffens's youthful mind was "snapping wide-eyed shots" of the rough scenes, while stories of men getting "rich, broke, or shot" filled his head.

He imagined himself as "a gun-playing, broncho busting vaquero," although his dreams of machismo and adventure were often undone by his long, soft curls of blond hair that brought ridicule from other boys, who called him a sissy or worse. His mother, however, adored his cute appearance and would not hear of touching his head with a pair of scissors, no matter how much he pleaded with her. It was only after some of the boys had cornered Steffens one day and stuffed horse droppings in his mouth that his father got him to a barber shop and solved the problem, much to his doting mother's chagrin.

Steffens's growing independence as a child brought on other challenges as well and, on one very memorable occasion, introduced him to the world of sex. At six or seven, Steffens built a tree hut, where he liked to hide as a spy, an Indian, or an army scout and watch all that happened below, which often was disappointingly little. One day, an older boy appeared and climbed up into Steffens's private space. Steffens shrank from his look. "I didn't know why," he recalled in his autobiography, "but there was something queer in it, something ugly, alarming." The boy reassured Steffens, only to start discussing and then exhibiting a sex act. "It was perverse, impotent, exciting, dirty—It was horrible." Steffens ran all the way home, and when his mother touched him fondly, the boy shrieked and closed himself in the bathroom, washing his hands and his face repeatedly. His father finally coaxed him out, but the little boy would not let anyone near him, as all signs of affection "meant something dirty." Still, he could not shake the new, mysterious allure of sex, which intensified when a servant girl in the house, he conceded, "taught me more."

Many years later, he judged that the shocking experience with the boy had "a light to offer" as he grew up. While admitting that he was "not an expert on sex," Steffens noticed that men separate romantic love and "animal sensuality," observing in a letter to a friend that some men "cannot love fully a refined woman (their wife, for example) and so seek out now and then some gross creature who represents what sex is to them; a rather dirty, loose thing of vice. I was started off in this direction by that first experience of mine which coupled dirt and disgust, a sort of horror of fascination, with my image or sense of love." A more appropriate direction, however, would elude him for decades. By all accounts, including his own, Steffens never fully grasped the sensitive nuances of intimacy until late in life, and his own inadequacies in numerous relationships with women would reflect both his natural self-indulgence and his stunningly tactless behavior.

What Steffens as a boy loved most of all was horses. On rainy days at home, he would grab a chair and ride it as fast as any vaquero. Even more fun was begging a driver in the street to let him ride and actually hold the reins for a moment, which became a regular thrill for the boy until his mother, terrified by such a risky sport, gave him his first good spanking. Still, Steffens's love of horses was genuine. His greatest pleasure as a boy came with the freedom he gained a few years later, when he learned to ride on his own across the wide, open stretches of the Sacramento Valley.

The Steffens family soon moved again, to a slightly larger home on H Street. There, Steffens discovered that the switch line on the railroad was no less fascinating than the great river had been. Freight trains with long lines of boxcars stirred the boy's interest in the wider world. Sometimes they arrived covered by fresh snow, a sight Steffens had viewed only on the distant Sierra peaks. What lay beyond those white peaks? he wondered, as he gazed at the endless trains. He hung around the station, eagerly collecting whatever bits of information he could from the railway workers.

While Steffens was keen to know more about the world outside Sacramento, he had scant interest in his own schooling in spite of strong encouragement from his parents, who regretted their own limited education and were determined that their children would have a far different experience. Steffens entered school—"that Terror"—with great reluctance and was not surprised to find that it did little but obstruct his adventurous future: "It interfered with my own business, with my own education." Steffens's teachers evidently agreed with him, keeping him back a grade.

Years later, he could not remember learning anything in grammar school except how to read aloud from a teacher he adored until she crushed his infatuation by announcing her engagement. It was, in fact, only his love of reading that truly fired his youthful imagination. He raced through books on the heroics of Napoléon, Richard the Lionheart, and Byron, pretending to singlehandedly reenact their glories while valiantly riding his beloved pony.

Meanwhile, rapid change was occurring around Steffens. Sacramento itself grew steadily away from its frontier past as a haven for gold miners and gamblers to a more respectable and prosperous town attractive to farmers and practically minded, upwardly mobile businessmen such as Steffens's father, who looked upon himself as an organization man. Joseph Steffens's fortunes rose with the town (he would go on to become vice president of the California National Bank of Sacramento, president of the Sacramento Chamber of Commerce, and owner of a winery), and when Lincoln was in grammar school, his father moved the family yet again, this time "uptown" to a larger house. Steffens now, for the first time, had his own room, but was far more intrigued by what lay behind the spacious, new home: a stable, where Steffens's father let him have a stall all his own. The boy took this as a very hopeful sign that the next Christmas might bring him a horse as well.

Unfortunately for Steffens, his father was known not for extravagance but for prudence. He would not commit to buying any horses in the near future and commented that even the empty stall brought up the value of the property, not at all what his eager son had hoped to hear. Having already pestered his grandfather, his father, his father's business partners, and "everybody that had anything to do with horses," including God, to make the next Christmas special, Steffens had his heart set on a pony. The sight of the empty stall only frustrated him to the point that even a gift of high riding boots, he told his father, would not be enough. "All I want is a pony," he insisted. "If I can't have a pony, give me nothing, nothing."

Christmas finally arrived. When Steffens and his three sisters dashed out of their beds and down the stairs, only the girls found piles of presents. For Steffens, there indeed was nothing: no pony, no gifts. Heartbreak led to indignation for the boy. His sisters tried to console him, but he just waved them away, retreating to the pony stall, where his mother found him crying on the ground. Hardly able to bear it herself, she excoriated her husband before returning to the house, where the family, minus one boy, endured a miserable breakfast.

Steffens passed a tearful hour or so on the front steps before spotting a man coming down the street on a pony with a brand new saddle. His spirits rose momentarily until the man, checking the home addresses, continued on down the street past the despondent child. Steffens was in tears again when he heard a voice call out about a boy named Steffens, and the man then mumbled something about being late after getting drunk and fighting and a trip to the hospital—but Steffens saw only the horse, a magnificent, bay pony with a black mane and tail and a white star on his forehead. Joseph Steffens's practical joke had gone much too far, but the boy, finally, had his cherished pony. Later, his father asked him if it had been the best or the worst Christmas, and Steffens answered both. "It covered the whole distance," he recalled, "from brokenhearted misery to bursting happiness—too fast. A grown-up could hardly have stood it."

Steffens wasted no time in learning to ride. He treated the pony with deep love, often spending more time on the pony's care than his own, and some of his happiest memories of childhood were his long rides alone, outside Sacramento, where he explored the wide countryside and foothills. "Now I could ride . . . to—anywhere, I thought. The whole world was open to me. I need not imagine it anymore, I could go and see," he wrote. The freedom that his parents allowed him at an early age gave Steffens experience and confidence that would later prove enormously beneficial to him in his success as a muckraker, and the story of his Christmas pony would become an endearing chapter in his acclaimed autobiography.

The time spent on his own also taught him the beauty of solitude. He passed many hours playing in his own imagination, which, he later acknowledged, became "the most active faculty of my mind. . . . I learned to like to be alone, and that pleasure I come back to always, even now."

On his horse, Steffens saw and learned a great deal, sometimes taking in far more than he anticipated or wished, which is exactly how he discovered the shady business of horse racing at the county fairgrounds. Naturally drawn to a place where horses were the center of attention, Steffens became a regular visitor, often hanging around the stable of a young, black jockey named Smoke. Steffens quickly gained the trust of other jockeys and trainers, who used the boy to ride some of the trotters. It was rugged work for no pay, but Steffens was determined to make the most of his opportunity and rode as much as four to five hours a day, his reward being a trackside seat at most of the races.

All of the trackside talk of winning and losing ultimately led to a moment of painful disillusionment for the young Steffens. Around the stables, Steffens had heard talk of "fixed" races and wondered what the word meant, only to be answered by jeers from the others. It fell to Smoke, by now a true friend, to explain to the boy the importance of rigging the outcomes and, hardest of all for him to believe, the holding back of horses when they most wanted to sprint. "I could cry—I did feel tears in my eyes whenever such a thing happened," he wrote. After watching his father lose money on a fixed race and Smoke get fired for pulling back his horse (while not betraying the white men who instructed him to do so), Steffens had seen enough of the track. He adored horses far too much to accept such wanton unfairness.

What perhaps bothered him most—and what he remembered vividly years later—was the role played by the "suckers," or the enablers of the deceit, described by Steffens as "the outsiders that bought in the road and bet on the races—blind." He saw that his father, who wagered with friends on the favored horses and knew nothing of what Steffens had learned, was a sucker. "I did not care for suckers," Steffens sadly concluded. He never ceased loving his father, but having experienced Joseph Steffens's parental manner, unkind Christmas joke, and gullibility at the track, the son had shed any illusions over the exceptional wisdom that a boy supposes his father has. His father made money—and lost it—the same as many other men did, and it was his money, and the money of all the other suckers, that fueled the immorality.

Another perplexing moment for Steffens was his introduction to the world of politics by a friend, Charlie Marple, who would be serving as a page in the upcoming session of the California legislature. With bored detachment, Marple explained to an astonished Steffens the routine activities of a politician's world: how agreements were reached, jobs were offered, salaries were set, committees were formed, and leaders were named, all in secrecy and all in the name of democracy. Steffens, not yet over the notion of fixed races, could hardly accept such revelations, even after Marple and he went on to pass many intriguing hours witnessing the daily commotion of the legislature. He saw that the legislature wasn't what his father, his teachers, or his history books had described. It was a mysterious process to Steffens. "And Charlie took it as it was; my father took it as it seemed to be; I couldn't take it at all," he recalled.

It was a paradox that would later propel Steffens to travel the world, to pursue the most powerful politicians and profiteers, to nervelessly pose vital questions, in search of an explanation. The early days in the California State Assembly instilled in Steffens a fascination of power and its inevitable, corrosive effects, but without burdening him with the cynicism that seemed to afflict nearly everyone else. And it was a critical moment of unlearning that he would experience repeatedly, for he now saw with his own eyes that good people and bad people were often the same people.

Independent and most comfortable living in his own imagination, Steffens as a growing boy was already moving away from his family's influence in search of the outside world and how it worked. He certainly felt affection toward his parents, who provided love, stability, and, wisely, enough freedom for the boy to escape regularly on his pony and indulge his curiosity. Joseph Steffens, who hoped that his son ultimately would follow him into business, was a stern but not unfair father, and when it was necessary, he punished Steffens, on occasions with a whip—"he did it very seldom, but he did it hard when he did it at all." Steffens's mother preferred a milder approach to discipline and "often smacked" the boy. Much more frequently, though, she smothered her only son with worried affection, aware that every day, he was slipping beyond her reach, but she was reluctant to let him go. Later he observed, "My father's way was more appropriate. It was hard." But Steffens's comment applies only to the punishment; his father was prone to long, eerie silences, cementing a certain distance between father and son that the boy never felt toward his more gregarious and supportive mother. As a husband and lover, Steffens would later display similarly unsettling behavior that cost others dearly.

Of his three sisters, Steffens thought little, even though all of them shared his love for the pony and helped him to care for it. Obsessed by his own passion for horses and exploration, he did not think of his sisters as anything other than girls living in the same house. "I had never considered my sisters," he acknowledged. Yet, he had a deep gratitude that eventually grew into a sincere and sustained love for his whole family.

As he approached adolescence, Steffens seemed to need the company of other children far less than he required both his own privacy and the attention of adults. His solo rides took him farther and farther from home, eventually becoming entire days that he spent roaming long stretches of countryside, befriending others—a bridge tender, a fireman who kept horses, a Chinese farmer, a cowboy—who admired the boy's independent spirit and boundless curiosity. On one of his longest journeys, more than seven miles out, he met a family that had almost as much need for Steffens as he had for them. The Neelys lived in a white cottage on an eighty-acre ranch that featured a windmill;

a large, unpainted barn; a vineyard; and, of course, a sizable number of horses, all of which became a special childhood memory to Steffens. When he first approached, Steffens found himself gawking at the ranch from the gate when he suddenly realized that Mrs. Neely was staring hard into his face, expecting an explanation from him. His straightforward answer—that he was looking for someone to feed both his pony and him—must have touched Mrs. Neely, for she took him in and stuffed him with food. A childless, strong-willed woman, Mrs. Neely treasured the boy's arrival and, along with her husband, gave him a hearty welcome. Steffens was not sure why they took such a liking to him, but he knew he would return whenever possible. A boy's life "is one long search for people who have some insight," he later wrote, and the Neelys, Steffens discovered, had much to offer. Eventually, he rode out to the Neely ranch so often that his father wryly suggested that he live at the ranch and visit his family occasionally.

Mrs. Neely had an unshakeable religious faith that she tried, unsuccessfully, to instill in the young boy by encouraging him to be a minister, practically mesmerizing him with her passionate retelling of the biblical story of the Creation. Steffens had attended church dutifully with his family and though he believed in God, he found church, like school, "a mere matter of the dull routine of life." In college, he would pray for Mrs. Neely as she lay on her deathbed, yet he understood the truth of the matter. "Mrs. Neely never knew that I took to drink and, from the broad road to the pulpit, turned off into the narrow road to hell," he admitted. Steffens's early moral struggles would never leave him; so much of his later work, while hardly a form of proselytizing, bears the mark of a man gripped by the interplay of right and wrong, determined, like a scientist, to understand it all.

"I became a drunkard as I had been a knight, a trapper, and a preacher, not for long and not exactly with my whole heart, but with a large part of my imagination," he recalled. In fact, alcohol made Steffens ill and he hated drinking. Yet all the schoolboys, of course, saw drinking as a competition that only the weak failed, so Steffens dutifully persevered. To Joseph Steffens, however, education was paramount, and he saw his son as a little more than a budding profligate, so in 1881, the father had him transferred to St. Matthew's Hall, a military academy in San Mateo.

At fifteen, Steffens was delighted to be going away to school. Bent on learning "soldiering" and reading voluminously on Napoléon, Steffens performed so well in the new school that he soon was named cadet drillmaster, a challenging position, given that the other boys loathed everything about wearing a uniform, performing drills, and following orders. They hated being there and naturally scorned drillmasters.

In such a hostile environment, Steffens's own school life, predictably, again collapsed. Bored in class; unskilled in baseball, football, and other popular sports, which set him apart from the main student body; and homesick for his horse and his old Sacramento gang of friends, Steffens grew miserable and, not surprisingly, found trouble. After narrowly escaping punishment for one infraction, Steffens, unrepentant, joined a keg party in a field and later staggered back to campus, where he was singled out for twenty-two days of solitary confinement in the guardhouse. The punishment was a deliberate one-day increase over the longest confinement ever given to a student. Yet the stiff punishment did not bother Steffens at all—he spent the entire time with his head in books. But the purposes of the school were served, for Steffens's experience in the guardhouse changed him in ways that no sermon or beating could have. His voracious reading included blunt portrayals of how alcohol destroyed lives. "It showed me," he admitted, "so that I never forgot, not only the waste and the folly, but the vanity of drinking. . . . I never could enjoy drinking after that."

The drinking punishment, however, did much more than teach him a lesson—it awakened his mind, always active but too often in a self-centered, insincere, and conceited manner, to much greater challenges of intellectual development and self-awareness that far surpassed the boyish games and pranks he had found so appealing. Steffens eagerly read books on Spencer, Darwin, and, hardest-hitting of all, war. The title of the war book later escaped him, but not the message. "That book . . . told as a story of idiotic waste the history of all the wars in the whole story of man," he recalled. He reached a "tentative but emancipating" conclusion that adults he had respected were mostly "ignorant fools." If he wanted to learn anything, he felt, he had to find enlightened teachers and, even then, look out for himself.

For the first time, he was determined to use school for the serious purpose of unearthing the truth, or at least making his best effort to do so. "I was not to be put off any longer with the appearances of things. I meant to know, really, and I had no doubt that some of those professors really knew the truth."

Joseph Steffens approved of his son's punishment and did not visit him until it was nearly completed. Sensing that this might be a critical point in the boy's development, he offered his son some stern words about the "posings" and the "bunk" the youngster always seemed to prefer. "That's poppycock," he warned his son. "It does no harm in a boy, but you'll soon be no longer a boy, and there are a lot of men I know who are frauds and bunkers all their lives. . . . It's up to you to choose your chance."

The boy, who had already understood the wisdom of his father's words on the matter, might have drawn closer to his father after their talk but for the rest of what he had to say. Unknown to Steffens, his father, in his first flush of anger over the drinking incident, had taken the unforgivable step of selling the boy's horse. The news crushed Steffens, who could barely finish their conversation. Joseph Steffens, too, understood that he had crossed a threshold and caused pain that no apology could heal. The boy had treasured the horse, his second, devoting all the care and love that he had to give, and it is clear from Steffens's autobiography that the horse had long been his best friend. Now, it was gone forever. With the sudden loss of his horse and the knowledge that his father was responsible, Steffens moved farther away from his parents' influence into a new world of books, learning, and ultimately unlearning, and into a future that he wanted to meet very much on his own terms.

Steffens certainly had taken an intellectual turn for the better by the time he departed San Mateo—he had been editor of the school literary journal and published a poem in the *Sacramento Record-Union*, but at eighteen, he was far from adequately prepared for college. As he was unable to pass the Greek, Latin, and other entrance exams at the University of California at Berkeley, his application was rejected, a blow that his father blamed on himself for having steered his son to the wrong school. Later, however, Lincoln Steffens came to realize that the problem was not his father's doing and did not lie in the selection of any particular college: The right school for him did not exist. Instead, he observed, colleges attracted young men who were dutiful, memorized what teachers required of them to learn, and questioned nothing. They were the men the world was made for. While he at times envied them, he was more often glad he was not among them. "Their own motives were foreign to me: to beat the other fellows, stand high, represent the honor of the school," he recalled.

Joseph Steffens, himself very much a man of duty and of the system (as the Republican candidate, he nearly won the 1884 mayoral race in Sacramento) remained adamant that his wayward but obviously bright son obtain a good education, and eventually Steffens was enrolled in a private school in San Francisco. For Steffens, eager to learn and explore his new surroundings, the school proved a blessing. He walked the hills and the coastline of the city with the same enthusiasm and determination that he had felt throughout his days of riding across the Sacramento Valley, always observing, imagining, seeking out not the familiar but the new. And his perceptive tutor, Evelyn Nixon, an

Oxford-trained classicist, gave Steffens the push he most needed. "Go to, boy. The world is yours," he asserted. "Nothing is done, nothing is known. The greatest poem isn't written, the best railroad isn't built yet, the perfect state hasn't been thought of. Everything remains to be done—right, everything."

Infused with Nixon's love of classics and inspired by the endless encouragement to see the world afresh, Steffens thrived in his new environment, stimulated to the point that he felt he now knew virtually nothing and had to make up for years of sloth and ignorance. Most invigorating of all to him were the Saturday evening discussions that Nixon held with an eclectic group of Oxford and Cambridge friends. The tutor was convinced that the engaging evenings would challenge Steffens, which indeed was the case. The wide-ranging and often heated exchanges carried on well into the night, covering religion, politics, philosophy, poetry, and other topics, all fascinating to the young Steffens. As the wine flowed freely and the air grew thick with smoke, the men, intellectual giants to Steffens, debated with passion but also with civility and respect. He called it "my preparation for college."

The most penetrating lesson he learned from all the hours of lively conversation was objectivity. Steffens observed that these highly educated men focused only on the outside world, never mentioning or apparently even thinking of themselves. Humbled, Steffens saw that the days of imagining himself as a Byronic hero or a knight or any other of his favored poses were finished. The Saturday night debates "established in me the realization the world was more interesting than I was." It was a creed that later would send him—well prepared—down a remarkable road of muckraking.

The practical effect of Steffens's year in San Francisco was that he was admitted, barely, into Berkeley in 1885. Berkeley at the time was a small, recently established university with a true Western flavor—Steffens used some of his free time to shoot quail among the bushes lining the campus. In his class, there were about one hundred students, mostly boys. But his fellow students, and the classes they took, were no threat to Steffens's expectations. After the animated Saturday evenings in San Francisco that he had so thoroughly enjoyed, Steffens had looked forward to Berkeley, where he anticipated being part of an atmosphere of thought, discussion, and scholarship. Dejectedly, he discovered "there was nothing of the sort."

Instead, Steffens found an academic desert. Teachers oversaw rigid, formal classes, where questioning—practically Steffens's greatest pleasure—was done not by the students but by the teachers in what amounted to private conversations with themselves. The college boys, Steffens saw, were "specialists in football, petting parties, and unearned degrees." So Steffens did not fault the professors for their academic approach. "The professors' attitude was right for most of the students who had no intellectual curiosity," he wrote. "They wanted to be told not only what they had to learn, but what they had to want to learn— for the purpose of passing." Steffens did concede that professors would help a student with initiative once they had recovered from the shock of discovering such an individual, leading him to wryly conclude, "It is possible to get an education at a university. It has been done; not often." Overall, dissent was nil at Berkeley. "I was the only rebel of my kind," he lamented.

Still, Steffens may have protested too much. As bleak as the situation appeared, Steffens, following a circuitous route, had advanced to college, and he did benefit at least marginally from the experience. He joined the prestigious fraternity Zeta Psi, where he made a close friend in fellow student Frederick Willis. As a junior, Steffens served as class president. Of most importance, he found that he truly enjoyed the study of history.

Being at that age when a mirror was essential, Steffens also took a greater interest in his physical appearance. Barely five and a half feet tall, he was hardly an imposing figure, a limitation he tried to correct by growing a mustache, which he carefully curled and waxed, and keeping his hair stylishly short. And while Steffens probably was not a regular at the Berkeley petting parties, he entered a relationship with a fellow student, Etta Augusta Burgess. The young woman's presence would provide Steffens with significant relief as well as regret—far more of the latter for the unfortunate "Gussie," as Steffens called her—until well into middle age. She was a language and music student who hoped to sing operatically, and her aim with Steffens, two years older, was marriage. Steffens enjoyed spending time with Gussie and may have even had a serious infatuation with her, but marriage, at that point, was clearly not his objective. Yet, Steffens's way with women was that a yes or a no response often meant "maybe" or was simply a word to deflect the matter into the vague future. In this spirit, Steffens allowed himself to become secretly engaged to Gussie shortly after his graduation in 1889, the first example of his recurring irresponsibility toward women once they had shown a serious interest in him.

Steffens graduated after passing the courses he liked—history, literature, philosophy, and political science—and bluffing his way through math and science, finishing at the bottom of his class with an overall grade average of C plus. Regardless, he looked forward to more education, but not in America and not in classes that encouraged napping more than diligence. What he desired was a return to the Saturday nights of intellectual fervor that he had cherished in San Francisco.

His passion, he saw, was in ethics. He was less interested in what was happening in the world than in *why* it was happening, and he hoped to gain much greater insight into the natural laws that must, he felt, determine human behavior. German universities, with their reputation for shaping disciplined intellects and where the emphasis was not on the money-earning side of education, seemed an appropriate place to start, and thousands of well-to-do American students, some more academically committed than others, had already made their way over in recent years.

To finance such a plan, Steffens would need to continue his reliance on his father, who certainly was in a position to help. Joseph Steffens by then had become a highly successful businessman who moved easily in influential circles, counting among his close friends Albert Gallatin, manager partner of the hardware firm owned by railroad barons Collis Huntington and Mark Hopkins. Two years earlier, the senior Steffens had purchased Gallatin's Victorian home on the corner of Sixteenth and H streets. The palatial estate (with six Italian marble fireplaces) became a historic building when he later sold it for more than $30,000 to the state of California, which made it the official governor's mansion. Earl Warren and Ronald Reagan would live there, Franklin Roosevelt and John Kennedy would stay overnight, and for the reform-minded journalist Lincoln Steffens, the family home recast as the seat of power in California would be one of many settings in which his campaign for justice unfolded over a long career.

At the moment, however, Joseph Steffens, not surprisingly, balked at his son's ambitious—and expensive—plan. Germany was just a detour, he believed. Moreover, he had made what he thought was the reasonable assumption that his son would take control of his successful business once he earned his degree. Steffens's mind, predictably, was in a far different place. Fully supported by his mother, Steffens was determined not only to extend his education but to do so in science and philosophy, impractical fields of study that held little interest for his father. Much more painful to Joseph Steffens, though, was hearing his son insist that he would never go into business, no matter what the circumstances. In a desperate effort to keep Steffens at least inside California, Joseph Steffens offered to buy him a San Francisco newspaper and set him up as a journalist.

But the young man would not be swayed. Sadly watching his dream slip away, Joseph Steffens accepted the inevitable and agreed to provide the money for Steffens's trip abroad, apparently for the profitless goal of becoming an intellectual.

2

TO THE CONTINENT AND BACK

AFTER AN OCEAN voyage of eleven days during which he used his crude German at every opportunity, Steffens, eager to see the world and uncover its hidden truths that he was certain existed, arrived in Hamburg in early August 1889. Within a few days, he had moved on to Berlin, where he would be attending the elite University of Berlin and living in a small room near the campus. Classes, though, would not resume until the fall, so Steffens took advantage of his free time to pursue his interest in art.

Ever since childhood, Steffens had wanted to "understand and feel painting," and he had taken some drawing lessons in high school. But he knew that he was very much an untrained observer, so in Berlin he set out to educate himself. Depending heavily on the art criticism of John Ruskin as a guide, Steffens avoided the fate of having to rely on his own "natural and unsound taste." Alone, he visited the art galleries for an hour or two each day, carefully observing whatever work caught his eye, and he found that his taste changed dramatically. "I could see and enjoy lines, designs, and even forms, while color combinations came to have as much meaning for me as a chord of music," he noted. But it was hard work. "A gallery is like a library. I was trying to read all the books at once."

The opening of school provided one of Steffens's first instructive lessons regarding the German mind-set. Having "nothing but scorn" for degrees (although he reported with some pride to his sister Lou that people addressed him as "Herr Doktor"), seeing them as merely another flaw in the typical university system that encouraged not "inquiry and research into the unknown" but "learning (and teaching) of the known," Steffens nevertheless followed the rules at the start. He declared himself a candidate for a doctorate in philosophy, with additional study in art history and economics. Yet when he registered at the university, Steffens discovered that his struggles at Berkeley had been unnecessary—all the clerk cared about was his American passport. His bachelor's degree, as the clerk pointedly informed him, was worthless in Germany. "He despised my degree as much as I did his, and I was hurt," Steffens recalled.

But the academic freedom that Steffens found at the university was precious. "I did not have to work, no one knew or cared whether I heard my lectures or played my time away." Many students chose the latter route, and Steffens joined them a few nights a week at a café poker table, but most of his energy went into his education, particularly his main courses of History of Philosophy, Greek and Latin Art, and Hypnotism. Immersing himself in German, he read voraciously and attended every lecture that seemed to be of value, regardless of the subject. He gladly reported to his sister Lou his pleasure in working steadily and feeling a sense of accomplishment. It was the kind of academic life he had dreamed of at Berkeley. He was determined not to waste it.

Steffens's enthusiasm for his new life abroad is evident in the torrent of letters he sent to his family and to Fred Willis, his Berkeley friend. Writing long, opinionated letters of several thousand words, sometimes on a daily basis, Steffens commented on the most minute details of German culture (rocking chairs were "very scarce" in Berlin) and of his own practical concerns ("both my woollen shirts are dirty"). He benefited from the cheap cost of student life abroad. But what fascinated him most were the German people. He admired their emphasis on family time and their ability—unlike Americans—to discuss serious topics other than work. In short, living well was certainly the best revenge for Germans. Steffens noted with admiration, "Sunday evening they are more tired than on any other night, only they are better and happier." In a lighter moment, he remarked that if Americans would clean their streets and Germans would take a bath, both sides would benefit.

Later, he must have given his parents, particularly his father, something of a jolt with his unabashed comparison of Germans and his countrymen, already flashing his impatience with the crude American embrace of business while barely hiding his disdain for his own parents' lifestyle. He declared that common sense was on the German side. Americans strived for carriages and horses, magnificent homes, and other luxuries to keep up with "the richest men who have empty heads" and no wisdom concerning money. German merchants, on the other hand, were more classically trained and valued conversation "with men (not dunces) and women." Steffens noted the pleasure of seeing a German banker leisurely pondering a few paintings after dinner, unlike an American who "must work to keep him contented."

Steffens, who had shown little regard for his own teachers at Berkeley, was also struck by the esteem given to German professors. "Of all the privileged classes [in Germany], the intellectual is the most unquestioned," he observed. There was no honor too high, no token of respect too good for German teachers, according to Steffens, and they were granted the broadest freedom of thought.

From his barrage of letters to his family (he wrote hurriedly and nearly illegibly, claiming that it disguised his poor spelling), it is clear that Steffens needed not only to share his experiences with them but also to gain a measure of empathy. This was particularly true in the case of his father, whose priorities clearly were not Steffens's but whose respect Steffens dearly sought. Steffens, in fact, wished to travel with his father through Europe the following summer, probably with the intent of nudging open his father's mind on the value of an education in the arts. Even his long-neglected sisters were now receiving stern but sincere instructions from their brother on how to read George Eliot and play Liszt. (They hardly needed academic guidance from Steffens, though. All three sisters would attend Stanford, and Dot and Laura followed Steffens for studies in Germany, with Dot receiving a doctorate signed by the kaiser.) "You can scarcely realize the joy I felt to hear from home," he told Lou. Part of his keen interest obviously resulted from lingering homesickness, but it was also true that for the first time, Steffens genuinely appreciated his family.

Steffens's most revealing letters were those to Fred Willis. Before his time abroad, Steffens was an eager, probing, but still unsure young man with an almost romantic desire to develop his mind. But now, while still questioning and digging endlessly to uncover a practical philosophy of how to live, he openly shouted his findings with a certainty that must have struck some, surely including Willis, as condescending if not brash. Steffens started writing to Willis in August 1889, shortly after his arrival in Germany, and easily confided his most personal thoughts, particularly those of constant self-assessment that dominated his mind. "I know, too, that my intuition is not sound, for it is not an outgrowth of a strong intellect" was a typical comment from Steffens at the time. Yet he ran into an unfortunate problem when he understood that while he wanted to live strictly for himself in his pursuit of the beautiful, he conceded that he most likely would not become a philosophy teacher or a literary type. He would go into business, he imagined, and succeed well enough to retire after a few years to "a life of study and thought." (Steffens's views of the future, like those of many intellectuals, were a bit short on accuracy. He never went into business or retired early, and in December, he told Willis, "I am inclined to think the history of Germany from now on will resemble England's—be a constitutional, peaceful development.")

Willis thrilled Steffens by matching his intensity if not his self-absorption. "Your letter came yesterday—and such a letter," Steffens once replied. "I cannot describe to you the pleasure it gave me, for it made me feel like a girl in love." Within three years, though, they would part dramatically in their philosophical approaches. Steffens, by then all of twenty-six, was so certain of his conclusions—"I think I am as nearly the materialist everyone denies the existence of, as ever was known"—that with pleasure and a sizable dose of immodesty, he informed Willis, an increasingly devout student of philosophy, of the widening divide while leaving no doubt as to which of them was heading in the proper direction.

The Berlin days were a heady time for Steffens, who witnessed royal visits by the Austrian emperor Franz Josef and Czar Alexander III of Russia, regularly patronized the city's art galleries, and attended concerts of Beethoven, Haydn, Wagner, and Strauss. His practice of German was so dedicated that after two months in Berlin, he reported to his father that he had not spent three hours speaking English and in fact was devoted at the moment to a fifteen-volume history of Greek philosophy. On Thanksgiving, he attended a lavish dinner for 450 Americans at the Hotel Kaiserhof, where the orchestra played dance music while "the Americans whirled and hopped and reversed as only Americans can." The fact that he now had the time he needed for reflection and the pursuit of his studies gave him a huge boost. "I have enjoyed a bliss I never knew before," he told Willis. Europe quickly came to mean a satisfying life of culture, reason, and pleasure, one that Steffens would return to for much of his adult life.

Although he enjoyed Berlin, Steffens's restless mind inevitably began looking elsewhere for new challenges. By late September 1889, Steffens already had informed his father of his wish to move on to the University of Heidelberg and study under the noted Hegelian philosopher Kuno Fischer. While Steffens conceded that his Berlin professors were devoted and bright, they were nevertheless teaching him useless information, namely, philosophical facts. It was time to move on.

What had not changed at all for Steffens was the old matter of Gussie, his fiancée, who was stuck in Berkeley wondering about her future while Steffens was chasing his own dreams in Europe. To force the issue, she went in desperation to Steffens's parents in January 1890 to divulge the secret of their engagement, which understandably was not greeted with cheer by the astonished

Steffens household. Steffens received a solid upbraiding in a letter from home. On February 23, he wrote to Willis, explaining in detail his real-life ethical dilemma. The "foolish" girl had loved him, and Steffens, admitting his own guilt in the matter, had simply gone along with the relationship, aware that he did not share her attachment. After becoming engaged, Steffens had asked her if she could wait several years before marriage (she agreed), all the while continuing the deception because he could see no other way out. "What do you think?" he asked Willis.

Willis's response was irrelevant, as Steffens soon had broken off the relationship "in as gentle a manner as possible." She released him "without a word of reproach," Steffens later wrote, as if it had been merely a perfunctory matter for her. The "end," though, became instead a lengthy pause, ultimately leaving Gussie with a heartache that Steffens did not share.

In the spring of 1890, Steffens's education resumed in Heidelberg. His best friend at the time was an art history student, Johann Krudewolf, who shared Steffens's devotion to study. Unlike Steffens, Krudewolf was a sensitive, rather sickly young man, yet Steffens held him in the highest regard, proudly telling Willis that Krudewolf had a "brilliant young mind" and already had been "published with success." The two friends reveled in their freedom as students, using some of their ample time to explore nearly every part of Germany, Steffens probably leading the way. Often accompanied by Krudewolf, Steffens managed to travel through Bonn, Cologne, Frankfurt, Mainz, Coblenz, and other cities, the Black Forest, and parts of the Alps. It was a young man's experience that forged a lasting bond between the two. Later in the year, they were joined in Heidelberg by a Berkeley acquaintance of Steffens's, Carlos Hittell, who had already spent seven years in Munich as an art student and fit in comfortably with the pair. But the attachment between Steffens and Krudewolf in particular grew so intense that an American friend of Steffens's, Harlow Gale, thought they might have had a homosexual relationship. Steffens was astonished when he later heard of Gale's assumptions, although Krudewolf's sexual leanings were, like much of his personality, a mystery.

Steffens's work in the classroom was far less satisfying. While Professor Fischer was an amiable lecturer whose German struck Steffens as "poetical prose," he no more had the answers Steffens sought than anyone back in Berlin or in Berkeley. "They could not agree upon what was knowledge, nor upon what was good and what evil, nor why," he realized. So Steffens abandoned his study of philosophy because, he reluctantly concluded, "there was no ethics in it."

Steffens needed a new direction. Hittell, the veteran of the group, had been stressing the importance of getting their heads out of books and into the real world of art. Disappointed at the waste of "a couple of good years of conscientious work," Steffens nevertheless understood that his friend was right, and acted. "I must leave the philosophers," he decided, "and go to the scientists for my science of ethics as I must go to the artists for art." The art came first. In the summer of 1890, Steffens, Krudewolf, and Hittell left Heidelberg for Munich, where they hoped to find artists—and insight.

Although he met Hittell's artist friends, Steffens found only disappointment in Munich. Heated discussions over the nature of art at the Blüthe Café, the local hangout for art students, revealed nothing, mainly because most of the young painters in Munich had neither genuine talent nor vision. He had come to Munich to observe painters at their craft and to hear them explain the essence of their work, but instead he found only pretenders who "talked while they worked, told jokes, laughed, poked fun at the model, flirted with her, made love. . . . They were not and never would be artists."

In the winter of 1890, he left with Krudewolf for Leipzig, where both hoped to spend a year at the university studying, again, art history. Still in pursuit of "truth," Steffens also planned to attend the psychology classes of Wilhelm Wundt, a leading proponent of experimental psychology who, Steffens hoped, could aid him in finding "in psychology either a basis for a science of ethics or a trail through psychology to some other science that might lead on to a scientific ethics."

In Leipzig, Steffens and Krudewolf took two rooms in a boardinghouse that featured a practical and certainly more entertaining form of ethics. The other tenants there, Steffens recalled, were "a working-girl who raised a living on her wages by some traffic in the business of love and a regular old street-walker who made love a business." The landlady herself was "a lone, but not a lonely, old widow" who was so intrigued by Steffens's habit of taking a daily bath that more than once, she barged into the bathroom to show a delegation of disbelieving old women the curious ways of her American guest. Steffens hardly minded, though. He was seeking out new experiences and finding them, while at the same time developing his uncanny ability not only to get along with almost everyone who interested him but to engage them in long, intimate conversations that later became the hallmark of his muckraking efforts. The boardinghouse escapades appalled Krudewolf, but Steffens simply made himself at home.

At the university, Steffens again immersed himself in his work, eager and hopeful for the results that had eluded him since his Berkeley days. He performed diligently in the lab, searching for "the facts" that Wundt demanded from his students. Yet, even under the guiding hand of Wundt, Steffens grew impatient. Over time, Steffens saw that Wundt had his facts, while others had their own, contradictory, facts. Only two months into the semester, Steffens was already thinking of departing Leipzig, and each passing week brought only more frustration. Sounding unusually pessimistic, he told Willis that "almost all of the joy" had left his life: His scientific work was "deadening," and he did not know "what to think" of philosophy anymore. Wundt, he felt, had wasted his time. He later observed in his autobiography, "Lightly I say this now, but to me, in the spring of 1891, the conflict of ideas and emotions was a crisis that weighed heavily on me. I had lost time. I had lost myself."

What Steffens now envisioned was a year in France at the Sorbonne to conduct more research, a plan that deeply worried Joseph Steffens, who naturally wanted something to show for his European investment. Earlier, the father had urged his son at least to get a degree in Germany, a formality that served no purpose to Steffens other than "satisfying vanity." In a sharply worded rebuke to his father, Steffens declared that he had no interest in wasting another year on German studies and hoped that his father would "give up the degree business," pointedly noting that only one in a hundred American students there "tries for it." Steffens insisted that his time (and his father's money) would be better spent in France and Italy during the coming year.

Growing accustomed to his son's direct language, Joseph Steffens nevertheless remained concerned about his obvious lack of direction. Still, father and son had remained on generally good terms throughout their separation: Steffens sought his father's opinions and counsel, while Joseph Steffens set aside whatever misgivings he had and kept up his correspondence and, of course, his funding. Both were vital, for as much as the young man wanted to continue to travel and study in Europe, Steffens missed his family—and California—badly. After so much time abroad, Steffens was not yet settled or satisfied in any sense, and his thoughts often returned to the natural splendor of the Golden State. He told Willis that if he could feel the relentlessly cold, damp weather in Germany, he would truly appreciate the "glory of divine beauty" around him at home. "What would I not give for one long, still view of California's colors! You have no idea of the flight a poetical German soul will take at sight of a poor dim sunset which would not receive a second glance from our spoiled Californian eyes," he wrote. At that moment, Steffens could hardly imagine that he would not see his beloved California anytime soon.

Yet, by the summer of 1891, all of Steffens's complaints about his dismal progress, while sincere, occupied his mind far less than thoughts of an American girl who sat behind him in Wundt's class. Her name was Josephine Bontecou, she was ten years older than Steffens, and they were falling in love. Like Steffens, Josephine, well off, had not gone to Europe to pass a few years of youthful frivolity far from home, and she did not make a habit of joining the American crowd at their favorite bars and restaurants. Her main companion was her divorced mother, Susan. They lived together after leaving New York to start new lives—the mother to see the places she had only read of during her long marriage to a prominent New York surgeon, and the daughter to study psychology for the purposes of writing fiction.

Clearly this would be no typical courtship. Josephine, who rejected an offer of marriage from a wealthy German student, did not need a man of means to carry her through life. Already well-traveled and fluent in several languages, she was determined to cultivate her mind and establish her independence as a woman. If marriage came, she wanted to be treated as an equal partner. Her opinions would count as much as her husband's. This was not a recipe for marriage for most men at the time, but Steffens was not disturbed by such concerns and had no objection to her wishes. Recently, he had become enamored with Ibsen and his views on marriage, pointing out approvingly to Willis, "He demands even in that [marriage], at any time, *freedom*,—freedom of choice, to stay or to go, and, not only absolutely, but both for man and for woman." Steffens boldly commented to his mother, "Your remembrance of the sudden breakage of the engagement with G. may lead you to think this is also to be short-lived. And, in fact, it may be."

Steffens found Josephine's mother to be almost as intriguing. "Her mind was alert, keen, and kind, like her eyes; she was really a shrewd woman of the world," he observed, "a woman I understood—the only one, I think." The comment was no jest, as Steffens went on to confide in Mrs. Bontecou more than many men confide in anyone.

The age difference was an obvious issue. Mrs. Bontecou brought it up but wisely did not dwell on it. Krudewolf, jealous of Steffens's new love and angry that their intellectual life together was being overtaken by a "dominating" American woman, lambasted him for his stupidity. Steffens, though, was not thinking of age. Love was now the beautiful challenge in his life.

Coincidentally, both Josephine and Steffens had plans to go on to Paris that summer. With his father's hesitant approval, Steffens looked forward to leaving Germany and beginning his studies at the Sorbonne, while the Bontecous would take a tour of the Alps before Josephine, too, would attend the same elite institution. Their hope was to have a devoted but free-spirited life: They would be engaged without a wedding date (only their parents and Krudewolf even knew of the engagement); they exchanged no pledges, including rings; and each had to feel free to leave the relationship at any time.

Being separated from Josephine, however, was no wish of Steffens's. In a July 1891 letter, he appealed to his mother for approval of Josephine: "From a purely worldly standpoint it will be a good match for me, from an intellectual point of view the best I could possibly hope for, and as for love,—we both love more and more every day, and she is as affectionate as ever I could long for." And, reflecting his ongoing financial dependence as well as his lack of tact, he added, "I suppose I ought to give her a ring some day. This I will leave to you to tell me. Perhaps you would be pleased enough to send me one for her."

By the fall of 1891, Steffens and the Bontecous were in Paris, and all went according to plan in the early days. Josephine and Steffens adopted a lifestyle that made each happy: "Our agreement," he wrote rather pompously to Gale, "gives full liberty for individual development, individual life and pursuit to both of us, and, although we shall comply with all the forms of law and society, we shall reserve absolute freedom of action always." Josephine was working on a novel whose main character, Letitia Berkeley, embodied the liberation she felt with Steffens. Steffens expected her book to "make a noise," while he was finishing his own novel on art life in Munich, telling his father that they looked forward to a literary "double success not very long hence."

Steffens was correct that a dramatic change would occur soon, but it proved to be unrelated to his writing. After only a few weeks in Paris, Steffens informed his father that he would be going to London to buy a suit and visit a publisher. In fact, the three traveled there to allow Steffens and Josephine, with her mother's blessing, to spend the required twenty-one days in England prior to their wedding ceremony, which took place before the Registrar of the Parish of St. Giles on November 4, after which they returned to Paris. Suspecting that his father would put a quick end to his European adventure if he knew of the marriage, Steffens was careful to tell no one of the change.

Yet, like any young husband, he yearned for others' approval of Josephine, particularly from his mother, a wish tenderly reflected in a letter he sent to her three months after the wedding. Her own previous "sweet" letter with its "warm glow of long, silent, but ever active, maternal love" had reminded him of her unconditional love, and he pleaded that she be sure of his love for Josephine as well, insisting that Josephine was a "noble, earnest little woman, and calls out all that is best in me." Still, even with his "darling Mother," he held fast to his secret.

In Paris, Steffens's days were spent mostly among the throngs of students and artists crowded into the "idyllic" Latin Quarter, and he crossed the Seine only to get money from the bank or to see tourist friends. At the Sorbonne, he attended his own courses plus any other lectures of interest. Steffens and Josephine did not shrink from their goal of exercising their intellects. After going to classes, sometimes together, they had dinner before devoting four hours each night to reading and discussing the works of Hobbes, Locke, Hume, and Kant, the last in German; Steffens, already comfortable in German and French, went on to master Italian as well. They allowed themselves only the slightest of intellectual breaks on weekends by visiting art galleries and theaters.

Otherwise, Steffens lived the life of a carefree, curious student abroad—while married. He observed the French intensely ("The French speak French almost universally as few Germans can speak German"), enjoyed the noise of endless debates in the cafés, made friends among the artists, and pondered his always vague future. One thing he now knew for certain: Universities were no place for learning. "Obedient, unquestioning" students, he saw, could get the standard body of knowledge at most universities, but if they had any inclination to get beyond that point, they were on their own. In Paris, he understood that his search ultimately must take him beyond the classrooms and intellectuals and into the world of business and politics to discover "not what thinkers thought, but what practical men did and why."

A two-month tour of Italy with Hittell in the spring of 1892 took them through Turin, Genoa, Pisa, Rome, and Naples, with side visits to Pompeii and Capri. Opinionated as always ("Italy is the worst-governed country I have seen, but even Italy, I think, is better governed than America"), Steffens grew fascinated by the contrasts he observed in cities. "The work of beautifying a city, of keeping it clean, orderly and healthy," he wrote to his father from Rome, "is most admiringly well done in Europe, and that cannot be said of any city in the U.S. except Boston and Washington." Earlier in France, he had commented to Gale, "The fame of cities and the attractions are the consequences too often of the grand opportunities for gilded vice,—and Paris is not an exception." It was a thesis that he would prove over and over again when he muckraked some of the largest cities in America.

Steffens returned to Paris before visiting Krudewolf, who had been ill, for a week in Germany. Steffens found his friend looking surprisingly fit, and they enjoyed their reunion, with Krudewolf speaking of his upcoming art history research in Italy. Krudewolf, however, pointedly asked Steffens how bequests for scholarships were handled in America, as well as questions about his parents and whether Steffens would consider returning to Germany should anything happen to Krudewolf. Caught off guard, Steffens admitted that he expected to be quite busy in the years ahead but would honor his friend's request, if necessary, which satisfied Krudewolf, and the two parted amiably.

At about the same time, Josephine had been ill, Steffens informed his father, from overwork, and was recuperating at a spa in Kissengen, Germany. What Steffens failed to tell his father, who was still unaware that he had a daughter-in-law, was that the blossom had already fallen from the scientifically based romance. In a letter to Gale in the fall of 1891, Steffens, unwittingly, had indicated that all was not well: "So soon as I felt that passion for this woman I respected, there occurred in me no longer any semblance of a desire for sexual intercourse with *any* woman,—not, most of all, with the one I loved. There was no credit in the fact that *I* was true,—there was simply no thought of such things. . . . This seems quite remarkable to me and chiefly because of the effortless submission of passion."

In a long letter to Gale several years later, Steffens, still blinded by science, recounted their troubles more honestly but with a clinician's eye. Steffens and Josephine found themselves drawing apart, he wrote, "in a sad and unaccountable way." Their conversations were less animated, their exchange of ideas less frequent. The assurance of success they felt at the start—"we had acted deliberately and not without a good deal of mutual investigation"—was now shaken and had delivered a "hard blow" to their treasured "rationalism." But by "means of the application of the scientific method"—analysis and diagnosis—they managed to remove the cause of "the worst suffering, mutual reproach." Their experiment in love, they agreed, had started with some incorrect assumptions, most notably the power of rationalism. "The historical method showed that all the while we were thinking we were actuated by intellectual considerations and rational ends, we were driven by the most ordinary impulses of passion, even sensuality," he wrote. Their self-deception, he concluded, was inevitable, and the solution was for both to accept a "relationship of calm and frequently silent friendship." Having rescued themselves from "the first abnormal state of experimental bliss," they entered their new future of marital adventure together, and Steffens, with his illusions of a salvaged and stable marriage intact, planned his final weeks in Europe.

Josephine, once recovered, accompanied her mother to London, where she sought a publisher for her novel. Steffens hoped to join them, his own agenda including reading and writing time at the British Museum and attending the International Psychological Congress. Money to pay for the excursion, as always, was an issue, one that Steffens felt no hesitation in raising—and justifying—by assuring his skeptical father that his devotion to philosophy had not permanently clouded his head or wasted his generous allowance. But Joseph Steffens's doubts are starkly reflected in the inflated measure of earnestness put forward by his son, particularly in a May 1892 letter intended to secure yet more money from his father. Steffens insisted that none of their journeys were "pleasure trips," and they devoted themselves to "observing and studying." He went as far as to say that he could not recall having done anything in Europe "merely for pleasure." With as much spirit as he could muster, he tried to write convincingly of his road from theory to reality, but Steffens conceded the obvious. "I have never felt more self-confident," he wrote, "and yet I have never before so clearly realized the difficulties I shall have to face."

Three weeks later, Steffens, who at twenty-six had yet to see his first paycheck, sent another lengthy and remarkably assured version of the bright future he saw ahead. He noted that he first wanted to enter business life for a reliable source of income as well as an opportunity to observe "American life" in preparation for a literary career to be followed "much later" by a life in politics. Accustomed to his father's support, Steffens was not shy about raising the point for future purposes: "I don't expect you to get me a position, but you know men and institutions, and could keep an eye out for possibilities." He assumed, he wrote, that his father had more doubts than ever about him. Yet, he promised, "In business life I shall be a business man, with never a trace of aught else."

But his studious years in Europe had left Steffens, with his affected goatee or beard, long, striking bangs, and penchant for fine but hardly businesslike attire, looking—and thinking—far more like a high-browed intellectual with a touch of bohemia than a sober man of business. Intuitively, his father suspected as much. Steffens could go to London, but soon he would be coming home to a life of practicality.

In London, Steffens continued to work feverishly on a book-length essay on ethics, which he hoped to have published in New York upon his return in the fall. Otherwise, he passed his time shopping, having "all sorts of fashionable clothes" made for his return to America and his belated "start in life." His taste was not inexpensive: He purchased "morning suits, evening suits, sporting and even business suits, and hats—high, low, soft, and hard, all English, the latest things. There was even a lounge suit and cap for the steamer." He also sported a new beard. On the voyage to New York, Steffens recalled with self-deprecation in his autobiography, "I was a beautiful thing," adding, "I was happily unaware that I was just a nice original American boob, about to begin unlearning all my learning, and failing even at that." Steffens's proud airs aside, his years spent immersed in the life of European cities prepared him well for the urban success he would soon enjoy in America. First, though, came a jolt of reality.

Upon his arrival in New York in the fall of 1892, Steffens quickly grasped his father's assessment of his years of wanderlust throughout Europe and his pursuit of esoteric knowledge. It was not an ambiguous message. "By now you must know all there is to know of the theory of life," Steffens recalled his father writing, "but there's a practical side as well. It's worth knowing. I suggest that you learn it, and the way to study it, I think, is to stay in New York and hustle. Enclosed please find one-hundred dollars, which should keep you till you can find a job and support yourself."

3

MAKING HIS MARK

STEFFENS, WHO HAD not seen his family or California in more than three years, was stunned to learn that he would not be seeing either in the near future. Married, jobless, and nearly exiled in New York, Steffens finally understood the depth of his father's impatience and the plight that he himself had unwittingly created through years of self-indulgence. Josephine urged him to inform his father of their marriage and the need for money (Joseph Steffens later said that he would have helped had he known), but Steffens, his pride stung, vowed to rescue them without any assistance from home. Josephine was livid over his vain stubbornness, although her mother was impressed by his bold reaction.

Having no other option, they stayed in New York to face their entirely unforeseen predicament. Steffens, remembering the rags-to-riches stories of his childhood, would find a job—anything that paid—and support his family as best he could. His brave, new world actually started off well enough. *Harper's Weekly* offered Steffens thirty dollars for "Sweet Punch," a story that he had dashed off in three days about a successful businessman who finds that he has betrayed his ideals in making his fortune. At thirty dollars a week, Steffens projected, he could make a respectable living as a writer. But weeks turned into months, his next story was rejected, and it would be years before magazines would again care about the name Steffens. His literary career would have to wait.

In a stylish coat and top hat, Steffens set out optimistically day after day and answered ads "from an editorship to errand boy." What he found, though, was a cold, urban world far removed from Steffens's comfortable, European life of the mind. Responding to ads from the waterfront, where employers needed help, Steffens entered the squalid workplaces as shopkeepers eyed him in amazement. "But—but do you think you can do the work?" they asked. "It's hard work and—and—are you—qualified? What has been your experience?" When Steffens replied that he had studied at Berkeley, Berlin, Heidelberg, and the Sorbonne, "that seemed to end it," he recalled.

For Steffens, doleful weeks passed as he lurched pitifully from interview to interview. All thoughts of banking and politics were dashed—with no income and Mrs. Bontecou now supporting everyone, Steffens was desperate for work. Finding himself hopelessly adrift in the dead of a New York winter, he conceded the obvious: "My father was right." His writing had not produced any best sellers, his college degrees and fluency in languages had not dazzled any manager behind a desk, and his newfound humility had not gained him any sympathy, even from Josephine. Moreover, he wanted to go home. "I wish I could see you and Mamma," he wrote to his father in November. "It seems rather hard to pause here, but I suppose there is no other way open."

His dreams of self-reliance had turned to despair until, against his own wishes, he finally took advantage of a letter of introduction arranged through his father. An influential California editor, at Joseph Steffens's request, had contacted Robert Underwood Johnson, the respected editor of *The Century Magazine* in New York, who agreed to see Steffens. Soon enough, Steffens was recommended for a position at the *Evening Post* and was invited to attend the Authors Club to meet "the men of the day in literature." The well-practiced ways of the real world, which he had tried so dearly to understand for years across the ocean, were becoming much more apparent to him.

Steffens was hardly starting at the bottom. The venerable *Evening Post* had reported much of America's history. Established by Alexander Hamilton at the turn of the century, the paper took on a crusading zeal as time passed, particularly under activist editor William Cullen Bryant, who arrived in 1829 and remained in control for the next fifty years. Strongly opposed to slavery and in favor of trade unions, Bryant was an ardent progressive and ran the paper accordingly.

When Steffens began working at the paper in 1892, however, it was managed under very different conditions by the esteemed newspaperman E. L. Godkin, who nearly thirty years earlier had founded the weekly journal *The Nation*. As likely to attack Democrats, especially those connected to Tammany, as Republicans, Godkin was an abrasive, fiercely independent editor with no patience, Steffens learned, for "bad government and bad journalism." Yet the *Evening Post* articles, unfortunately for Steffens, were largely conservative in tone and bland in style, and had been since Godkin took over as editor in 1883.

Openly elitist and fully aware that the *Evening Post* was serving a limited audience of urbane, well-heeled readers (circulation never surpassed twenty-five
thousand during Steffens's years at the *Post*, less than one-tenth that of some
competitors), Godkin wrote to a friend that year, "My notion is, you know,
that the *Evening Post* ought to make a specialty of being the paper to which
sober-minded people would look at crises of this kind [municipal mismanage-
ment], instead of hollering and bellering and shouting platitudes like the *Herald*
and the *Times*."

Priced at three cents to distinguish itself from the racy one-cent scandal
sheets, the paper avoided any hint of yellow journalism and demanded factual
reporting, as Steffens ruefully noted: "Reporters were to report the news as it
happened, like machines, without prejudice, color, and without style; all alike.
Humor or any sign of personality in our reports were caught, rebuked, and,
in time, suppressed." Godkin's mantra, "I do not want literature in a daily
paper," kept creativity to a minimum. Steffens himself felt Godkin's wrath over
one of his early stories, which evidently had rather too much color in it, until
he was rescued by his editors. Steffens may have even counted himself lucky
that Godkin noticed him at all. The paper's rank and file considered Godkin
"a remote deity," for what mattered most to him was assuredly not his anonymous staff of reporters but the views expressed on the editorial pages, particularly Godkin's own vitriolic barbs aimed at Tammany grafters and war-happy
jingoists—barbs that left no doubt where the paper stood.

For the moment, though, Steffens did not need to worry about how to write
his articles: He had been given no assignments, a crippling predicament, as he
was paid at a fixed "space" rate. Henry Wright, the city editor, had told him that
he did not need any more reporters and had only taken him on at all, Steffens
thought, with some resentment. So, like many young reporters, Steffens saw his
first days at the paper spent sitting idly in the city room, watching other, more
experienced—and jaded—reporters take turns heading out begrudgingly to
cover stories or hanging around and complaining about their monotonous beats
and grueling hours. As 1892 came to a close, what saved Steffens was his natural
optimism and his recent, painful lessons in survival. His disastrous job search
still fresh in his mind, Steffens was relieved to have his "toe in the door of the
best, or at least the most reliable, paper in New York City," he told his father.

Without griping, Steffens waited for his chance to prove himself, at first
occasionally covering German theater in the city, where his knowledge of the
language and interest in the arts served him well. A significant break came one
afternoon, when he was sent to report the case of a missing stockbroker. Steffens

raced from the office directly to Wall Street, where he located the broker's tight-lipped partner, who at first claimed to know little about it, hoping the inquisitive reporter would lose interest. Steffens persisted, however, with a relaxed, conversational, at times almost whimsical approach, always careful not to judge morally but to listen intently, adopting a probing, congenial interview style that he would perfect over the years to charm everyone, from prostitutes to presidents, into telling him more than the person had intended, and often with gusto, as if the interviewee were pleased to have such an attentive audience. By the time Steffens was finished with the broker, both men had been sitting for some time in a private office, sharing stories about their lives, and Steffens had learned not only that the missing broker was in fact from the firm but also that he had fled with virtually all of its money.

As Steffens filed additional, well-researched stories, taking a more mannered, professional approach to his craft than did his cynical colleagues, his stature at the *Evening Post* improved rapidly. In January 1893, he was already reporting to his father that his work was "regular and constant," and he found Wright, while reserved, to be "one of the fairest, most even-tempered, patient and generous men I ever met." He was a professional journalist—a success, and in New York, the toughest learning ground of all. From this first taste of power, he wrote in his autobiography, "I have never since failed to understand successful men; I know, as I see them, how they feel inside." It was a new life for Steffens, far removed from his days of chasing theories across Europe, and one that he embraced. He told Willis of "the joy I feel on finding myself an active sharer, a busy part, of the noisy, hurried, over-serious life about me in New York. I enjoy this American living, working and running, and I admire this healthy American manhood."

And Steffens, still under his father's considerable shadow politically, adjusted without great difficulty to the *Evening Post*'s conservative style, avoiding topics such as homosexuality and treating prostitution, as prevalent as it was, with a diplomatic touch. He had no great quarrel with Godkin's views supporting small government, personal freedom, and privileges of the wealthy while opposing any efforts at social engineering, stances that not only favored him in the office but, in the eyes of the *Evening Post*, improved his reportage.

Steffens hustled everywhere for news, speaking to businessmen, politicians, policemen, and ordinary people while covering fires, accidents, fights, strikes, and meetings across the city. He did his job so effectively, with canny interviews, careful fact-checking, and an insatiable curiosity for the full story, that soon he was getting plum assignments and had more responsibility than the veteran

reporters had. Best of all, his salary rose with his effort, increasing from a pitiful five to twenty dollars a week and helping him to cope with more than seven
hundred in debt.

What pushed him ahead was his ability to make contacts and convince
them to talk. By being meticulously accurate in reporting and polite in manner,
Steffens gained a measure of respect among the New York power brokers, who
often fed him tips that gave him a decided edge over competing reporters. The
president of the Board of Education, probably noting his formal English attire,
called him "the gentleman reporter." By mid-January 1893, barely a month into
the job, Steffens had already met three former mayors of New York, J. Pierpont
Morgan, the president of Columbia University, and other influential figures in
the city. As such men considered the *Evening Post* an accommodating paper,
they became the type that Steffens not only approached more often but eventually came to admire. He kept up his literary work as well, which got a boost in
February, when *Harper's Weekly* paid him the thirty dollars he was owed for
"Sweet Punch," which had been published in December. Balancing journalism
with his intellectual pursuits was not easy, but he could not resist telling his
father that he soon expected to show that a long and expensive education did
not disqualify a man from a profitable business career. "Years of theory and
science is not inconsistent with practical sagacity, judgment, and success," he
pointed out.

In March, Steffens became the *Evening Post's* regular Wall Street reporter.
It was a move that "dazed" Steffens and left Josephine laughing, but his ambition was in full throttle by then, so he applied himself accordingly. Wall Street
looked upon the *Evening Post* as a trustworthy (and sufficiently boring) paper,
unlikely to create a scandal, aiding Steffens in his efforts to gather the financial
news. Still, it would have been a challenging assignment even for a seasoned
financial writer, for the Panic of 1893, probably the worst of the century, had
paralyzed much of the national economy, giving Steffens a swift education on
markets, graft, and American history.

A major cause of the economic slowdown was the failure of the Philadelphia
and Reading Railroad, once one of the largest corporations in the world. The
railroad declared bankruptcy on February 20, just two months before the
National Cordage Company, the most actively traded stock in the country, went
into receivership, all of which brought down other railroads, banks, and businesses while rural farmers in the South and West continued their own losing
struggle against falling crop prices. In the ensuing chaos, there was an overwhelming demand to redeem notes for gold while frightened citizens pulled their

money from banks: Steffens saw New York's banks alone lose tens of millions in deposits. Unemployment in the United States hit double figures and remained there for the next five years. At the same time, certain American monopolies in steel, insurance, banking, oil, and railroads remained as strong as ever, an inequity that would ultimately result in White House intervention and the meteoric rise of the muckraking press. And Steffens, barely three months into his work at the *Evening Post* and clearly learning on the fly, was covering much of it. "The great Reading failure, the Coal Combination and investigation, the crisis in the Exchange, the gold situation and discussion of a bond issue, the U.S. Book Co.'s failure,—these are some of the events I have had to follow closely and report on," he wrote to Gale.

The crisis, Steffens observed, spread far beyond Wall Street. No one was angrier about the economic collapse than farmers. Feeling squeezed by low prices, high debt, and ruthless bankers, they began to organize and eventually united with protesting laborers and the jobless to form the boisterous Populist Party. The Populists' cries preceded the onset of the more influential progressives, including many friends of Steffens's. The change, though, would not come for another long decade.

From coast to coast, strikes large and small erupted: Between 1891 and 1905, some thirty-seven thousand strikes blanketed the country. Relations between workers and owners were marked by absolute distrust, and power was wielded not by interceding courts but by whichever side could bring to bear the most violent methods of coercion. As owners could call on both their privately funded security forces and the local police (and even a sympathetic judge if necessary), the fight was rarely fair. Among the most notorious confrontations was the 1892 Homestead battle in Pittsburgh, where striking Carnegie steelworkers, angered over a pay cut, fought three hundred police officers and government troops in a clash that left ten dead and scores wounded. The unruffled demeanor of President Grover Cleveland, who chose to remain above the fray and allow the chaotic marketplace ample time to sort itself out, only stoked the fires of public outrage and created favorable conditions for socialists, anarchists, trade unionists, and progressives to attract thousands to their cause. Intrigued by the tumult but far from any inclination toward radicalism, Steffens dutifully maintained his support for the Republican Party while learning economics on the job.

Such was the financial turbulence in the country shortly after Steffens arrived on Wall Street. He did not understand everything he observed, but it was "an opportunity to see giants," and that was the angle he worked to get his stories. Using the same blend of sincerity, curiosity, and patience to gain access to the

Wall Street insiders, Steffens, still a bit wide-eyed, compared the adventure of the panic to sailing through a storm on the bridge with the ship's officers: "The falling, failing banks, railroads, and busted pools of speculators were only the action and scenery of a great drama."

His view from the bridge was most beneficial. Routinely, his connections tipped him off to breaking news, privately informing him that "such and such a railroad or industrial organization was in trouble," and allowing Steffens to prepare the story ahead of time and have it ready for publication at a moment's notice. Steffens's frequent scoops gave the *Evening Post* an air of authority on the economic chaos at a time when anxious readers were paying particularly close attention to the news. He was also not averse to shaping his stories on occasion to favor his sources, and his later success with stocks had its origins in these early days of learning the market from those who dominated it.

Meeting powerful men (and all of the powerful were men), sometimes one on one, gave Steffens an excellent chance to apply his scientific inquiry to the corporate mind, and he did not waste the opportunity. "As a study of moral phenomena or moral facts, my work is the best I could have got," he wrote to Gale. "As a chance to see human nature posing nude, no artist could have found a better occupation."

So Steffens collected a range of facts for his stories, but the fascinating part of his job was to carefully observe these men of means, to understand what motivated them and separated them from the mainstream. His early conclusions were not encouraging, as he found that successful men such as Russell Sage, J. Pierpont Morgan, and George Williams, president of Chemical Bank, "are all, all incapable of logical thought *even in* business matters." The "formula" for their thinking seemed to be that "they simply feel that such a thing will go." They took great risks, paid lip service to the ethics of management, and counted success as "not being *publicly* convicted" for their deeds. "They do not start or finish at the honesty line," Steffens observed.

Morgan was of particular interest to Steffens. Known behind his back as Pierpontifex Maximus, both admired and despised in private and feared by almost everyone, the elusive Morgan worked, as Steffens discovered, plainly in the open. He sat at a large, clean desk in a room with glass sides inviting anyone, including Steffens, to look through and see the great man. But looking apparently was all most people did in his potentially volcanic presence.

After one bold but failed attempt to meet Morgan, Steffens's luck turned one day when his editor gave him an assignment requiring a visit to the bank. Morgan had issued a rambling, one-sentence press release that neither the editor nor Steffens could decipher, so Steffens was dispatched for a clarification. "As brave as I was afraid," he recalled, he approached Morgan's desk and inquired about the statement. Steffens had barely finished asking about the meaning when the imperious Morgan exploded, his eyes glaring and his "great red nose" flashing in Steffens's face. "Mean! It means what it says. I wrote it myself, and it says what I mean."

Steffens found the courage to say that it did not mean much of anything the way it was written. As Morgan grabbed the sides of his chair and looked as though he was going to leap up, Steffens repeated that it was not very good English. Expecting the worst, Steffens instead saw the fire go out of the billionaire's eyes. He leaned forward and, in a much softer voice, asked what was unclear. Steffens suggested that two sentences would improve it, and Morgan had to agree. Not pressing his luck, Steffens then hurriedly returned to his office, later hearing that Morgan had stared at him as he departed, demanding to know who he was and remarking, "Knows what he wants, and—and—gets it."

Over time, Steffens found much of Wall Street oddly understandable, at least from an investor's point of view. He understood that a man such as Morgan made money by selling wisely on the falling market, but also by picking up cheap stock that he could later use to his advantage. Purchasing a railroad at a bargain price, for instance, and revitalizing it could be a hugely profitable venture for Morgan, who stood to make a fortune both as the railroad owner and as its banker. He alone controlled the money. Best of all, Steffens noted, no one questioned it, as it was all "common practice." People discussed it openly as "plain business." Steffens also noted that successful investing was no great mystery and wondered why men seeking money went into any business other than Wall Street. And he included himself. When his writing days were over, he envisioned, "I would go into Wall Street. I would quit working and—make money." To a considerable extent, he did.

Now that Steffens was learning the inner workings of the economic system, he focused on a particular mission, "what the world needs all the time: someone who was not sincere but intelligent." He did go on to find many intelligent men, some of them among the most reviled and scorned—but successful—people in the country, and saw that bad and good often were inseparable, even necessary, qualities in a great person, while pure honesty, particularly the righteous kind that he would find in many shrill reformers, was useless in pushing society forward. For Steffens, it was a lesson in unlearning that lasted a lifetime.

In November 1893, after nearly a year at the *Evening Post*, Steffens was asked by Wright if he was interested in adding the police beat to his work on Wall Street. The move momentarily left him with "doubts and confusion" largely because the paper had never shown much interest in police news, seeing it as a slippery slope to the sensationalism that was splashed across the covers of lesser papers. Dignity, however, was not keeping circulation up, so the *Evening Post* considered running additional crime coverage and saw Steffens as the best candidate for the position, one that would require the reporter to write stories about the seamy side of the city without tarnishing the paper. He later told his father, "That's why they put me at police headquarters,—they wanted to see if I could not write police news in such a way that a dignified journal could print it."

The upgrade was delayed some weeks, with Steffens dividing his days between Wall Street and Mulberry Street, but ultimately, he was named head of a news department and given an office on Mulberry Street, across from police headquarters in one of the toughest sections of New York. He did not underestimate the difficulty ahead. "It is beastly work, police, criminals, and low-browed 'heelers' in the vilest parts of the horrible East Side amid poverty, sin and depravity," he explained to his father. His new weekly salary of thirty dollars seemed hardly enough. (It would rise to thirty-five the following year, the highest rate paid by the *Evening Post*.)

It was Steffens's chance to see firsthand the growing divide in American life, as boatloads of destitute immigrants continued to arrive in cities teeming with the impoverished while the middle class swelled and the wealthiest entrepreneurs, even after the crash of 1893, lived in unimagined comfort. In *Farewell to Reform*, John Chamberlain laid out the scene of fin de siècle America, which many saw as "a delightful way of life," with even the moderately successful "living in their roomy houses set about by lawns and maple trees." Baseball and bike riding grew in popularity. "In brief," Chamberlain wrote, "they enjoyed themselves with the enjoyment of a blessed naivete. . . . But the deeper movements of the nineties were toward an abyss."

Steffens would learn well the compelling reasons why Jane Addams had established the Hull House in Chicago and why so many other urban and rural areas could have done so as well. New York's Lower East Side, Steffens's new beat, was probably the starkest example of America's abyss. Enclosed by the Bowery on the west, the East River, and Houston and Monroe streets to the north and south, tens of thousands of the poor huddled shoulder to shoulder in the gritty tenements and alleyways of the notoriously squalid neighborhoods and suffered lives that were always miserably hard and often very short. A young friend of Steffens's later recalled him "standing at Mulberry Bend, in the heart of the East Side district, and telling me, with tears in his eyes, of the great poor of the city and the crusade to improve their lot."

Dominant among the poor were the desperate but persevering Jewish masses. Having fled pogroms and poverty in Russia, Ukraine, Poland, Romania, and the vast Austro-Hungarian empire, throngs of Jews—nearly one-third of the entire Eastern European Jewish population—migrated across Europe, many crowding aboard ships departing Hamburg, Antwerp, Rotterdam, and Trieste headed for the vague promise of the New World. More than two hundred thousand of these Jews would find themselves eking out livings amid the degradation of the New York ghettos. In one wretched block rivalling conditions of Bombay, nearly three thousand immigrants shared 264 water closets and had not even a single bathtub.

With countless saloons, houses of ill-repute, and gambling dens thriving in the midst of the most decrepit squalor in the city, the crime was as constant as the poverty. Legitimate work often meant the grueling, door-to-door routine of a peddler or, more likely for women, the exploitation of the multiplying garment sweatshops, which in New York City alone soon produced $100 million annually in women's clothing. And death was an unremittent presence. Young and old alike died from tuberculosis, from typhus, or by their own hand. But new arrivals at the city's ports, displaced from their European shtetls and hamlets with a vague hope of finding opportunity abroad, continued to melt into the mass of humanity that was the Lower East Side.

Steffens grew fascinated by the fervent determination of the arriving Orthodox Jews to maintain their old culture of scholarship and religious observance in a Christian land where risk and personal freedom held sway and where, among the dominant hordes of Jews, Christian missionaries roamed freely in hopes of mass conversions only to be greeted with derision or silence. Synagogues, in fact, became the center of life in many East Side neighborhoods. Steffens looked forward to attending the services and reporting on the "mixture of comedy, tragedy, orthodoxy, and revelation" that he observed. Jewish theaters thrived as well with their Yiddish performances. One typical Steffens piece during this time was titled "Yom Kippur on the East Side, Scenes of Devotion and Mockery Among the Poorer Jews."

Perhaps most interesting to Steffens was the timeless story of immigration everywhere—the tension between the old and the new, which he watched with curiosity and chagrin. Jewish elders back in the shtetls of Europe had insisted that America—the land where people who fought their way to the top by any means necessary were revered, while anyone, especially an immigrant, with excessive formal education was likely to be eyed suspiciously—was no place for a Jew. And those Jewish elders had never even witnessed the teeming excesses—the flowing alcohol, the women waving feverishly from their windows to attract another paying flesh mate, the alley brawls, the fathers throwing down a week's pay in a night of gambling, the parents desperately trying to protect their wide-eyed children from the seductive temptations all around—of daily life in the Lower East Side. One Jewish parodist invoked a biblical passage to document what the elders had feared: "Blessed is the man that walketh not in the counsel of scholars, nor standeth in the way of the enlightened, nor sitteth in the seat of the learned. But his delight is money, and in the accumulation of wealth does he meditate day and night." The English language itself threatened the survival of Yiddish, and many Jews simply infused their native language with a generous supply of commonplace English words, a blasphemous development to their elders.

In his autobiography, Steffens poignantly offered his own view of the cultural upheaval, noting that among the Russian and the other European Jewish families was "an abyss of many generations," seemingly stretching from the Old Testament to the present. Examples abounded. Steffens recalled covering a reported suicide and finding young Jewish boys, hatless and bored, sitting outside and smoking cigarettes while their emotionally wrought fathers, draped in black, with tall hats and uncut beards, charged into synagogues in desperation. At times the boys and their fathers exchanged blows until the police arrived and clubbed each side into submission. To Steffens, it was not the flowing blood in such instances that was the tragedy. It was "the tears . . . the weeping and gnashing of teeth of the old Jews who were doomed and knew it. Two, three, thousand years of continuous devotion, courage, and suffering for a cause lost in a generation."

Steffens became so enraptured by the ways of the Jews that for a time, he nearly adopted a Jewish lifestyle. He attended synagogue on the Jewish holy days, fasted on Yom Kippur, and nailed a mezuzah to his office door. "You are more Jewish than us Jews," he was told by friends. Later, Steffens had no difficulty in seeing the folly of "the American who is more French than the French, more German than the Kaiser," but his exposure to Jewish culture allowed him an understanding of the complex Lower East Side, and the understanding gave him a distinct advantage over other reporters.

Through the first months of 1894, Steffens reported largely on strikes, murders, fires, and, occasionally, politics, his stories at times featured on the front page. By far the most significant story concerning the police department, however, was the blatant, entrenched corruption that plagued the department itself, the emerging details of which amused and outraged the public on a daily basis and hastened Steffens's unlearning of the urban ways of business.

The catalyst to the latest outcry over police malfeasance was a man who would become a key ally of Steffens's, the Reverend Charles Parkhurst. Deceiving in appearances—he was a nearsighted, slender, quiet, middle-aged man fluent in Greek, Latin, and Sanskrit—Parkhurst had been using the Sunday pulpit to denounce the New York police and had joined the Society for the Prevention of Crime to counteract the city's own crime fighters. He recalled that shortly after taking up his ministry at the Madison Square Presbyterian Church in New York, he gained a more cynical view of law enforcement: "It dawned upon me that crime was the policeman's stock in trade, his capital, which of course it was to his interest to encourage in order to enhance his personal revenues."

Parkhurst had been headline news in New York ever since a Sunday morning in February 1892, when he astonished his congregation with a scathing assault on the city fathers, particularly the police and their elected enablers, notably Mayor Hugh Grant. Declaring that "every step that we take looking to the moral betterment of this city has to be taken directly in the teeth of the damnable pack of administrative blood-hounds that are fattening themselves on the ethical flesh and blood of our citizenship," Parkhurst looked on the political elite of the city as nothing more than "a lying, perjured, rum-soaked, and libidinous lot" of "polluted harpies." City officials, naturally, rushed to defend themselves. The public works commissioner spoke for many when he rejected Parkhurst's words as the "intemperate ravings of a madman."

To witness the graft firsthand, Parkhurst decided to go undercover, accompanied by a reputable member of his congregation and a private detective. And with his church bordering the city's crime-ridden Tenderloin district, he did not have to travel far. The group spent several evenings in some of the most notorious after-hours establishments in the city, where they watched uniformed police drinking for free in saloons, little girls buying alcohol to bring home, whorehouses with squealing prostitutes grabbing any available man, including Parkhurst at one point, and dozens of streetwalkers begging for business within sight of the Mulberry Street police headquarters. In Chinatown, parents smoked opium with kids. One night, Parkhurst quietly drank a beer at Hattie Adams's bordello, a short walk from his own church, while several dancing girls ripped off their clothes and played leapfrog. Later that night, the three men went on to a "French circus," where the entertainment, Parkhurst declared, was "the most brutal, the most horrible exhibition" he had seen yet. And the police, well compensated for their efforts, stood watch over the whole enterprise.

Now Parkhurst had the evidence he needed, and he wasted no time revealing it from the pulpit before a packed church. Just a month after his first devastating sermon, he once more railed against the "Tammany-debauched town" that was "rotten with a rottenness that is unspeakable and indescribable" and infested by conditions "so coarse, so bestial, so consummately filthy" that the pastor felt the urge to "go out of town for a month to bleach the memory of it out of my mind and the vision of it out of my eyes." And all of the illicit activity, he declared, was in plain sight: "Anyone who, with all the easily ascertainable facts in view, denies that drunkenness, gambling and licentiousness in this town are municipally protected, is either a knave or an idiot."

While there was a hue and cry from police and prostitutes alike, the public seemed more fascinated by the image of a God-fearing pastor in a bordello than by what they already knew was commonplace activity in the netherworld of New York. Hattie Adams defended her establishment by calling Parkhurst "a lecher in ministerial broadcloth." A grand jury convened but made little immediate headway. Other than the imprisonment of a few bordello owners, business continued uninterrupted.

The antics of the police department cried out for scrutiny, even by the staid *Evening Post*. To prevent Steffens's reporting from becoming too unseemly, Wright directed him to avoid the bloody street battles the police fought day after day and focus mainly on the case of Parkhurst, whom Steffens had already interviewed several times for the paper. Wright directed Steffens to cultivate Parkhurst as a source, with Steffens understanding that if he as a reporter employed a diplomatic tone in his articles, the *Evening Post* might address criminal activity to a far greater extent. The new challenge inspired Steffens because just as he had learned that the truth behind Wall Street transactions was not to be found in the newspapers, he suspected that police work would yield a similar verdict. He was eager to enter the world of crime and study it, as he had Wall Street, realizing "that it was possible to think that I knew all about something and yet be an innocent ignoramus."

Steffens found Parkhurst to be a "calm, smiling, earnest, but not unhumorous gentleman." The journalist established the same confidence with Parkhurst as he had with the Wall Street set, and the *Evening Post* was intrigued by what the embattled pastor had to say. Steffens heard stories privately from Parkhurst, later learning much more when the Lexow Committee of the New York State Senate held hearings on why the police were such adept facilitators of corruption. For the moment, Parkhurst's legitimate insights convinced Steffens—and Wright—that Parkhurst was the best source on the scandals.

The challenge for Steffens would be approaching the police department and its superintendent, Thomas Byrnes, renowned as a law enforcer who "filled the upper world with respect and the lower with terror." And any method of confronting criminals, including a particular type of torment—apparently a specialty of Byrnes's—known as "the third degree," was acceptable if the result was a confession. A writer from *Collier's* did not doubt Byrnes's effectiveness: "His very manner, the size of him, the bark in his voice, his menacing shoulders and arms would terrorize the average crook."

New York's well-to-do families particularly admired Byrnes, as he rarely lost a moment in investigating the case of any crime touching the moneyed class. Byrnes, the story went, allowed his personal favorites among thieves to operate safely within the city, but if one of them happened to victimize the wrong family of means, Byrnes would "solve" the case by having the chastened criminal turn over the pilfered goods to the police. And such selective policing benefited Byrnes handsomely: He had amassed a personal fortune of $350,000 by the middle of the decade.

Parkhurst, of course, did believe that corruption flourished precisely because Byrnes was the man in charge and that the superintendent sought to discredit the reverend for peering into the dark, profitable underside of the city. Steffens's task was to uncover the truth.

With "no little dread and a solid foundation of certainty," Steffens ventured to the police headquarters to make his case to Byrnes. He had to wait uncomfortably among a crowd of citizens and journalists jammed in a small outer office before being allowed an opportunity to hand his card to a police official. A belligerent police inspector with a voice, Steffens recalled, "clear and distinct like a pistol shot" wasted no time in humiliating Steffens. "A reporter from the *Evening Post*," Alexander "Clubber" Williams boomed, "here to expose and clean us all out, us rascals." Steffens turned red and sank into a chair, only to hear Williams sneer, "We'll see how long he stays here."

Steffens had good reason to pause, as Williams was Byrnes's chief enforcer, the man who once said, "There is more law at the end of a policeman's night stick than in any ruling of the U.S. Supreme Court." Clubber Williams thrived on violence, having firmly established his reputation years ago by descending upon the worst tenements, beating a few thugs senseless, and heaving their bloodied bodies through saloon windows as a calling card. Steffens's persistence in the office, however, ultimately resulted in a meeting with Byrnes.

After a stiff welcome, the superintendent sternly but diplomatically stated his expectation that Steffens and the *Evening Post* would be fair and, of course, view matters from the police perspective as well—the challenge of protecting lives and property, of the daily strikers and thieves who hated cops, and of all the other dangers faced by men in uniform. Steffens listened patiently, studiously observing the details—the attitude, the speech, the body language—of his subject. Superintendent Byrnes, he concluded, awed people mainly because most never really knew the man, only his reputation. "He struck me as simple," he wrote, "no complications at all—a man who would buy you or beat you, as you might choose, but get you he would." Steffens, increasingly self-confident, made clear to Byrnes his resolve to report the police stories as he found them, no better or worse.

On that note, the meeting broke up and Steffens left the office, retreating through the staring crowd, not quite certain of his latest predicament. The police obviously were already well informed on him, although the source of their knowledge perplexed him. He had hardly left the building when he came upon another reporter, a much older, "shaggy-looking fellow," yelling from an office window above, who possessed precisely the street knowledge necessary for Steffens to master his new post. Jacob Riis, a Danish immigrant who a generation earlier arrived in New York with a sum total of forty dollars and a head full of adventurous, James Fenimore Cooper stories of Indians and buffalo hunting, had found a very different type of adventure among the hardscrabble lives of the city's poor. Despite a tough beginning, including a day's work deep in a Pennsylvania mine shaft and many cold nights sleeping in tenement doorways along the grimy Lower East Side, Riis persevered, finally landing work as a reporter for the *Evening Sun*. There he became a nemesis to the New York police and the Lower East Side slumlords alike. As Steffens noted in admiration, Riis not only got the news, but also cared about it: "He hated passionately all tyrannies, abuses, miseries, and he fought them." No less impressed was Theodore Roosevelt. In 1890, after reading Riis's disturbing, best-selling account of New York's underclass, *How the Other Half Lives*, Roosevelt left a card at Riis's newspaper office: "I have read your book and I have come to help." Indeed, Roosevelt would lead the charge of reform in the Lower East Side several years later.

With his excellent sources, particularly his cagey, young assistant, Max Fischel, Riis was already aware of Steffens's rough start with Byrnes and understood that the new reporter had admirable—and rare—nerve. Shouting at Steffens down in the street, Riis urged him on. "You have started off on top. Stay there," he advised. He immediately befriended Steffens and brought him to the police and health offices, where they witnessed officers hauling a beaten immigrant, an East Side Jew, into the station. Riis berated the officers and insisted that Steffens see how many broken bodies were already in custody, a normal day's tally; through the open door, Steffens could glimpse a row of bruised Jewish men lining the wall across from Clubber Williams's desk. "Many a morning when I had nothing else to do I stood and saw the police bring in and kick out their bandaged, bloody prisoners, not only strikers and foreigners, but thieves, too, and others of the miserable, friendless, troublesome poor," Steffens later recalled.

The Jews, more and more of whom were dropping their stoic acceptance of misery, had begun defending themselves, literally with their fists. Nevertheless, Steffens remained far more interested in understanding than condemning either side, seeing both as pawns in a much larger struggle for power that he had yet to fully comprehend. In any case, the *Evening Post* had no intention of printing stories on police clubbings.

But the labor issue of strikers and scabs that resulted in many of the clubbings was more acceptable, so in November 1893, Steffens started a series of articles on labor conditions—a series that he expected would be "the most exhaustive newspaper work" done on the topic. Still influenced by his university days in the lab, Steffens hoped that his reporting would produce "facts of scientific value" on labor issues in New York. What he learned by observing labor strife, Wall Street, and police behavior, however, was that "newspapers, literature, and public opinion did not picture men and life as they are." The first public caricature he had to debunk—scientifically—was that of Parkhurst.

Through the 1890s, Parkhurst's personal battle against vice kept him very much in the public eye. From the pulpit on Sunday mornings, Parkhurst would announce a new charge of police corruption or repeat an old one. His favorite target was saloons with their profitable habit of staying open after hours and on Sundays, under the approving eyes of police inspectors, while husbands and fathers exchanged their weekly wage for drink before staggering home to their neglected families. Wives, often beaten and always poor, pleaded for relief, which Parkhurst called on the police to provide. Steffens, more than others, reported Parkhurst's claims to the extent that Byrnes, most reluctantly, had to address the matter. As a result, a number of saloons actually kept up a pretense of maintaining regular hours.

The process, though, only further confused Steffens. The saloons appeared to be taking turns in shutting down, almost on a schedule of sorts, while the police ignored the most notorious of the lot. And the more that saloons were shut down, the more anger was aimed at Parkhurst and the *Evening Post*.

Steffens could understand why the police and the politicians were annoyed—after all, they were losing serious graft—but not the "good, prominent citizens" such as bankers, businessmen, and even other clergymen. The answer lay in the mysterious workings of the underworld, to Steffens still a vague, murky place of shadowy figures who seemed somehow to be on both sides of the law. He saw that he needed to get beyond the meetings with Parkhurst and even Byrnes, who controlled the police graft, to the men who wielded ultimate power over the illicit activities.

During his years at the *Evening Post* and beyond, Steffens always viewed reporting as a form of self-education. What he learned, particularly through his Wall Street and police reporting, was what he correctly suspected he had never been taught in college. From powerful New York attorney James B. Dill, nicknamed "the corporation architect," Steffens got a cold but invigorating splash of economic reality when he heard Dill's accounts of "dummy directors" and of how police boards, aldermen, mayors, and governors were all "dummies" for someone, all parties addicted to the ubiquitous graft. And especially in New York, even years after the devastating political cartoons of Thomas Nast and the fall of William M. "Boss" Tweed, Tammany graft dominated public and private enterprise.

Hutchins Hapgood, who spent years as a roving journalist haunting New York's working class and poor neighborhoods and becoming a close friend of Steffens's in the process, captured the essence of the Tammany mystique: "The real thing in Tammany's eyes is friendship. That is the great virtue, and that is why ingratitude is the blackest sin. The common people believe this implicitly, and it is consequently true that Tammany is strong in the hearts of the people."

The current Tammany boss was Richard Croker, who grew up in a poor Irish family of squatters and, like many other immigrant New York boys, fought his way out of the slums as a paid brawler for Tammany and Boss Tweed. Unlike Tweed, who swindled his victims for both profit and sport, Croker was a surprisingly soft-spoken man who prized loyalty and what he believed was Tammany's commitment to the common man, who, after all, was the one keeping Tammany in power with his automatic vote in election after election. And with increasing frequency, these votes were being cast by soaring numbers of immigrants who desperately sought the jobs and other practical help offered by leaders like Boss Croker and his minions. Croker himself, of course, cast the Tammany image as one of loyal, decent people using government to ensure that even the neediest were not forgotten. But he understood how government functioned largely because he made it function. The system worked so well for

Croker, in fact, that he owned a $200,000 home near Central Park and was one of the biggest spenders in the country on thoroughbreds, even though, for the most part, he had held relatively minor appointive positions in city government. Steffens wanted to know the differences between a political boss and a banker boss, so he approached Croker, the expert.

Catching Croker one day as he was departing his Tammany Hall office, Steffens was invited to walk along. In person, the Tammany boss appeared to Steffens as a "sweet-faced" man with "kind" eyes and whose hair, hat, and clothes were "of one tone of dark gray." Croker immediately disarmed Steffens by pointing out that the *Evening Post* was obviously no ally of Croker's and that he would be a fool to confide in Steffens at all. Steffens then agreed to keep their conversation private and came to the point: Why did the city need a Tammany boss when it already had a mayor and city council? Croker quickly enlightened Steffens. It was precisely because there was a mayor, a council, judges, and countless other officials for businessmen to deal with that gave Tammany its advantage, he explained. To businessmen, government was a business, and it was far easier to conduct business with a Tammany boss than a parade of public officials who may be here one year and gone the next. "A business man wants to do business with one man," Croker insisted.

Government was not business but politics, Steffens pointed out. Croker again corrected him: *Everything* is business. And in a voice "hard as nails," Croker asserted that "like a businessman in business, I work for my own pocket all the time."

Croker's insights intrigued Steffens and hastened his unlearning. That so many "good" people could be bought or could silently look away; that "bad" people could be responsible, civic leaders who made government function; that most people, not unlike Steffens, were oblivious to the entire apparatus of power, all made Steffens's young mind whirl in a mix of confusion and excitement. He glimpsed a world where morals, money, and egos clashed daily behind closed doors and in smoke-filled rooms to produce the imperfect but operational world that Steffens, in university labs, European cafés, and hours of solitary thought, had so longed to comprehend. He was determined to see far more, and would do so when the Lexow Committee provided a panoramic view of the lawbreaking that was endemic in New York.

First, though, came the challenge of determining how widespread the graft was and how best to eliminate it. Sensing both the popular will that some action be taken and the political will that the action be as restrained as possible, the state legislature in Albany, according to Steffens, debated how best to control the damage before a sneering public opinion urged on by Parkhurst and other reformers pushed the reluctant body into performing its actual duties. The subsequent political theater reminded Steffens of his youthful experience in the California legislature. "It was the same picture," he observed. The two groups of lawmakers sounded and acted the same, he noted, and now in New York, both the Republicans and the Democrats plotted to control the investigating committee, the Republicans to tar the Democrats, and the Democrats to protect Tammany and silence Parkhurst. The result was that by the start of 1894, there was a pretense of a hue and cry over police misconduct, but where it would lead was the question.

A commission chaired by Senator Clarence Lexow, the personal choice of Senate Republican boss Thomas Platt, known as "The Easy Boss" for his deceptively mild-mannered style, was formed in February 1894 to look specifically into the charges against the New York City police force. Not that public hopes ran high for any startling changes to emanate from the commission's work: One of its members, a Tammany Democrat, openly praised the department as being "singularly efficient," and Boss Platt, who set up the investigation from Albany, was no reformer. His main goal in the police shake-up was to strengthen the Republican presence on the police board, thereby increasing his own patronage, and to capitalize on Parkhurst's thrashing of the Tammany-dominated City Hall by putting his nemesis Croker out of power.

The case against the police was not a hard one to make, as waves of discreet informants were eager to provide the commission with abundant detail of graft. A colorful cast of police officers, victims, politicians, saloon owners, criminals, and businessmen were called forward to reveal the dark secrets of the New York underworld and satisfy the public outcry for some version of justice. As often as he could escape police headquarters, Steffens attended the sensational hearings.

Even though the probe was limited to police corruption, ample entertainment was on display in the courtroom. Upon being asked whether he had ever paid off police, one brothel owner elicited roaring laughter from the spectators when he rolled his eyes and responded, "Oh God, yes." Clubber Williams, after revealing his considerable bank savings (in excess of $300,000), a mansion in Connecticut, and a yacht, was asked how he, a policeman, could afford such luxury on a salary of less than $3,000. Williams replied with a sincere look that he had done well in some real estate deals in Japan. One person who clearly had been paying close attention to the Lexow investigation was Croker, who in May, citing health reasons while fully aware of the likely fate of Tammany in the next election, became the first Tammany leader to go voluntarily into retirement. And as the hearings intensified a month later, he left New York on a "long-planned" trip to Ireland aboard a Cunard liner, to the delight of Platt and to the surprise of everyone else, who had expected Croker, as the *New York Times* put it, to "remain here during the racing season and give personal supervision to his interest on the turf."

One day, however, probably in early summer, Steffens received an unexpected letter that took his mind far from police hearings and the squalor of the Lower East Side. The German consulate in Naples dramatically—and sadly, for Steffens—flung his past in his face. Johann Krudewolf, Steffens's friend from the carefree university days spent crisscrossing Europe, had died of consumption, alone in a Naples hospital, leaving Steffens as executor of his will.

The news stung Steffens not only with grief but with guilt. While his own career had steadily gained momentum in New York, Steffens had continued to receive letters from the sickly Krudewolf. The American had often responded belatedly and with little interest in Krudewolf's "painful labor" in art history research. Reading the letter reminded Steffens that his own letters in those heady days had rarely focused on anything other than his "selfish, healthy interest in my vivid, purposeless life." Even Krudewolf's letters focused largely on Steffens. "Always me: as my mother had always said," he conceded.

Josephine by then had spent sufficient time with Steffens to know that his mother, of course, was correct. Watching Steffens's remorse along with his stubbornness in leaving New York temporarily to deal with Krudewolf's estate in Germany (as he had promised to do), she commented, "You will always be loved more than you love," and Steffens knew it was true. Josephine still bristled at the thought of their early struggle in New York and their financial dependence on her mother, all because Steffens, his pride wounded, would not inform his father of their marriage and ask for the desperately needed money. When Joseph and Louisa Steffens eventually did learn of their son's secret marriage, they immediately offered to help. In exasperation, Josephine merely said, "There, I told you."

But Krudewolf's money was not Joseph Steffens's, so in the summer of 1894 Steffens agreed to perform his duty and sail for Germany with Josephine. Steffens did not believe that the whole affair would amount to much, and obviously, Krudewolf had taken to heart Steffens's offer to help. Tending to his friend's affairs was the proper course of action, Steffens thought, and it might restore some of the goodwill lost between Steffens and Josephine.

Their destination was Lehe, a small seamen's village tucked away along the channel to Bremerhaven, where most passengers caught trains for Bremen and

Berlin. Only the captain and crew had ever heard of Lehe, and Steffens could hardly convince them that he wished to go there. After finally reaching the town, Steffens began to realize that the Krudewolf business was more involved than he had anticipated. First, Josephine and he were received like royalty by the servants at Krudewolf's home. More striking, Steffens learned that Krudewolf had bypassed indignant relatives eager for a share of his estate and left much of it—a total of twelve thousand dollars—to Steffens, without qualifications, with the aim of setting Steffens financially free. Steffens, amazed, wondered why.

For several weeks, Steffens attended to the legal necessities that included various bequests and endowments of parks and schools. But about Krudewolf himself and his odd selection of an absent American to oversee the delicate matter, Steffens heard nothing more than terse, factual statements from Krudewolf's lawyer and servants. Only after much patience could Steffens and Josephine gain their confidence and begin to piece together an explanation of Krudewolf's mysterious act of benevolence.

The reason evidently lay in Krudewolf's difficult relationship with his father, a miserly, impatient man deeply hardened by years at sea, and his stepmother, the sister of Krudewolf's own deceased mother, who had always loved the boy and empathized with his sensitive nature. Herr Krudewolf insisted that his dreamy, imaginative son learn business as an apprentice to a merchant, a future that depressed both Krudewolf and his stepmother, who longed for a life of travel and was fond of envisioning grand openings at theaters and opera houses. Herr Krudewolf focused instead on making, not spending, money.

Johann, though, was an obedient son, so he abandoned his goal of travel and art studies—a life of the mind encouraged by his mother—to appease his stern father, reluctantly but dutifully joining the business world. It was not at all a good fit: The young man, weakened by his labor, caught a cold that damaged his lungs and would later result in his final illness. Following his father's death, Krudewolf finally used a portion of the family money to pursue his dreams, a move that only angered his relatives, who saw him as a fool chasing butterflies and squandering the family fortune.

The story clarified a great deal for Steffens. He recalled—and now understood—Krudewolf's loathing of business and his resentment of parents anywhere who selfishly dominated their children's lives. Krudewolf and his stepmother had been alone among the family in their vision of a life spent freely in pursuit of knowledge and beauty. Through his long and heartfelt conversations with the young Steffens, on his own quest for truth and the son of a man emphasizing the practical side of life, Krudewolf quietly saw his foreign friend as a fellow traveler, a man with an inner light that Krudewolf deeply admired. "Like a thoughtless American," Steffens confessed to Gale, "I recklessly broke through this reserve and won, without caring much for it, his confidence and, as I now see, his love. No one before had cared at all for his hopes, except his mother."

Krudewolf died determined to help Steffens roam as his mind wished, unburdened by the guilt and responsibility that had weighed so heavily on Krudewolf. "Money is not money," Krudewolf had told Steffens, "it is liberty." And Steffens, with his knowledge of Wall Street, invested Krudewolf's money well enough to eventually give himself that liberty and fulfill the final wish of his departed friend.

Steffens and Josephine returned to New York in the fall of 1894. After placing some of his inheritance in stocks, he was confident enough to inform his father, "Now I feel pretty well started toward being a capitalist, and Josephine and I have concluded that it will be safe to go ahead and have a family,—small but contented,—of workers for whatever the world may open up a road to." In fact, Steffens plunged back into his work at the *Evening Post*. There would be no children, and Josephine remained merely an emancipated wife on a clear path toward emotional isolation.

4

ENTER TR

STEFFENS'S LETTERS AT that time show great enthusiasm for the grinding, partisan political battles, both local and national, that held his attention for the next four decades. The ugliness of the police scandals left Steffens, Josephine thought, looking "pegged out," but he assured his father, "I enjoy the situation hugely." He declared that he was neither a Democrat nor a Republican but a "mugwump or independent" who nevertheless planned to vote the straight Republican ticket in November. Not surprisingly, he had written his father from Lehe that he had every intention of remaining with the *Evening Post* and strengthening his status there: "I feel that I have earned promotion and position on the *Post*. As I look back over my record I can see that the rapidity of my advancement was not undeserved. I did some good and original work and I won the *Post* some credit for sound and quick work in all the fields in which they tried me." He envisioned building up a "department of labor news" and personally covering the great strikes and disputes of the time, eventually establishing a foreign news bureau at the paper.

Though he was still in his twenties, Steffens's personal views on labor, immigration, and the underclass continued to reflect his conservative upbringing and the editorial environment surrounding him. In 1893–1894, both the weekly "letter" he submitted for publication in the *Sacramento Daily-Record Union* and his letters to his father illustrate a nativist streak at times exceeding even that of the *Evening Post*. Steffens cautioned on "the disrepute into which the excesses of the strikers had brought our government and our working classes." Unions were havens for the weak, he felt, while New Jersey laborers were "foreigners as ignorant as Chinese, and not one-tenth as shrewd." He never condoned the police beatings of immigrants, but neither did he oppose their absence during the economic hard times: "On the survival of the fittest their departure is good. They rid us of the weaklings of the multitudes." Steffens would later use these same New York experiences to form quite different, if not always consistent, views on the struggle for economic power in America.

In the fall, politics dominated the talk of New York. Amid all the tumult of the Lexow investigation was the matter of selecting the next mayor. Some reform activists on the Republican side, eager to destroy the old Tammany system, tried to entice Theodore Roosevelt into the 1894 race. Roosevelt was certainly in favor of reform and eager to return to an elective position, particularly to eliminate the memory of his defeat in the New York mayoral race eight years earlier. But his wife, Edith, had far less enthusiasm for a political campaign, so Roosevelt, most reluctantly, demurred for the moment. In a bittersweet letter to Senator Henry Cabot Lodge of Massachusetts, though, Roosevelt left no doubt that he yearned for the big stage: "I would literally have given my right arm to have made the race."

Ultimately, after negotiations with a reluctant Boss Platt, reformers settled on William L. Strong, a moderate Republican businessman who was then president of the Central National Bank. He was an ideal "Fusion" choice for mayor, Steffens noted, because "he knew nothing of politics." And although he was born poor himself, Strong now moved in a world far removed from the hellish conditions on the Lower East Side or the other daily troubles of many struggling New Yorkers who had always taken comfort in the belief that Tammany was their safety net. But the widespread assumption was that reform was inevitable and that Strong would cleanse the system and run a solid, practical, businesslike government. Steffens favored reform, too, until it arrived, when he realized that his unlearning was far from complete.

But on election night in 1894, with Superintendent Byrnes issuing strict orders to his captains to foil any Tammany efforts to rig the voting, the people of New York delivered a message to Tammany in the form of a resounding defeat. Reformers and Republicans won races across the city. To many, Parkhurst was the savior of New York, and letters poured in to his rectory from people across America, eager to apply the same cure to their own civic ills. For the moment, at least, Steffens found the election results "eminently satisfactory," encouraged to see that there was "some moral stomach in the community which will expel proven corruption," and he was convinced, he told his father, "that the Republican officers mean to give good service."

The Lexow Committee, meanwhile, was not finished. Following the election debacle for Tammany, courtesy largely of Lexow and Parkhurst, with some notable help from Steffens's work in the *Evening Post*, the commission forged ahead, getting its most explosive testimony from Max Schmittberger, an earnest, diligent precinct captain who became an unwitting star of the Lexow hearings and a good friend of Steffens's. Up to that point, Schmittberger's life had been a version of the American dream—the hardworking German immigrant rising through the ranks on his own sweat and and eventually finding success. By 1890, he was a well-regarded captain on the force. How he came to be so admired was a story that would soon have a profound effect on Steffens's thinking. For the moment, it was Schmittberger's encyclopedic knowledge and stunning honesty that captivated his Lexow audience.

Wearing his uniform proudly, Schmittberger carefully explained the system of graft in all its myriad forms, providing names, dates, amounts, schedules, rules, and many other details. Schmittberger himself was hardly a bystander, admitting that he, too, had been paid off by a steamship company to ignore any small infractions of dock regulations, but he hoped his cooperation might earn him some leniency and save his job.

Most importantly, Schmittberger was privy to the extensive police corruption—"the department is rotten at the top," he asserted—and left the courtroom audience spellbound by his astonishing testimony. The whole, sordid story, filled with money and sex, was a disaster for the police force but a boon for the New York papers. With insatiable appetites for the latest titillating revelations, readers gasped over the shocking headlines that filled front pages and dominated the gossip about the city. Even Steffens, who by then had become a known player in exposing the scandal, was caught up in the frenzy, telling his father on December 15 that his work as a police reporter was giving him "the most exciting strain of nerve." The competition for news on the scandals was an adrenaline rush for Steffens, who raved to his father, "The officials about me are under a heavier strain than I, and 'lies' I have printed are proving true."

Steffens and many others in New York had good reason to be emotionally charged. The graft itself was appalling. Taxpayers gave $5 million a year for the police department to do its job professionally, but another $8 million flowed in from brothels alone, nearly $2 million from saloons, and $60,000 gouged from new police officers themselves. Patrolmen, the lowest on the scale, were required to pay $300 for the job, while anyone interested in becoming one of the city's thirty-five captains was obliged to contribute as much as $15,000 for the promotion. Of course, only the promise of lucrative and ceaseless graft could explain why so many participated in such extortion. Even radical reform could not revive the New York political system. It had to be destroyed.

At least, that is what Steffens, Parkhurst, and the reformers concluded. But at the close of 1894, events began to conspire against them. First, Superintendent Byrnes, whom both Steffens and Parkhurst saw as a key link to years of graft and a man who unquestionably had to be removed, went before the Lexow Committee in late December and received rather lenient treatment. Byrnes was able to speak seemingly as a solid opponent of corruption, a man of principle whose only goal was to enforce the law. Even Mayor Strong was impressed and did not see why Byrnes could not remain in place to implement the critical reforms that lay ahead. Then, after months of shocking testimony, the Lexow Committee's final report—all 10,576 pages of it—dutifully cataloged the criminal acts of the police themselves, damning Democrats and Republicans alike and cooling Platt's excitement for reform, now that Tammany was not the only target. And, for the moment, that was it.

Meanwhile, the prospect of reform at City Hall seemed a disappointing illusion. Steffens looked on in frustration as Strong and his supporters assumed power and negotiated their own deals and favors for one another while Strong, like every mayor before him, was being pressured to appoint one man or another and make promises that he had no hope of fulfilling. "I saw enough of it to realize that reform politics was still politics, only worse; reformers were not so smooth as the professional politicians, and it seemed to me they were not so honest," Steffens observed. Jacob Riis was more philosophical but resigned to the inevitable: "Mayor Strong was always on the side of right, but when he wanted most to help he could not. It is the way of the world." Steffens would not be discouraged, though, telling Gale, "I think I could write a book now on 'immorals' . . . but I cannot stop yet; I must go on seeing more, deeper."

Most reformers kept their focus on police headquarters, where Steffens by now was clearly persona non grata. The day after the election, Clubber Williams sneered at him, "Well, are you satisfied now?" The reformers and the holdovers on Mulberry Street openly despised each other, a tension that could not endure. With Parkhurst routinely lambasting Byrnes and the timid Lexow members, and Steffens maintaining the pressure at the *Evening Post* ("First or last must Byrnes come down," Steffens declared to his father), events quickly placed Byrnes in an untenable position. Giving his father a mix of facts and hyperbole, Steffens, on January 6, 1895, provided the inside story. Claiming that his was "the only voice" raised against Byrnes in the city, Steffens felt vindicated when, finally, one newspaper after another, including his own, called for Byrnes to go. Their cries were joined by a chorus of other powerful players, including the Chamber of Commerce and the Committee of Seventy, a reform group that included the *Post*'s editor, Godkin.

Steffens now also referred to himself as Parkhurst's "advisor." He went on to say that Parkhurst and other reformers had asked Steffens to seek out a military man who could replace Byrnes and provide the strong leadership the police desperately needed. Steffens apparently did speak with several candidates, but found the men "deplorably ignorant of police matters." At the same time, Steffens helped set up a secret meeting between Parkhurst and Mayor Strong at Godkin's house, where the urgency of the police crisis could be addressed. Byrnes was clearly faltering, but not without a struggle.

The level of police corruption exposed by the Lexow Committee called for a strong, determined hand at Mulberry Street headquarters. For years, the police board of commissioners had been filled with loyal supporters of Tammany and Republican bosses and given almost no power. The new mayor would make little headway, reformers knew, unless he appointed an entirely new board. Mayor Strong, ignoring the wishes of Boss Platt, tried to do just that by dismissing two Platt supporters. One of their replacements was the enforcer that Strong had originally sought: Native son Theodore Roosevelt was happy to have the job.

Roosevelt, thirty-seven, was no stranger to New York politics or to the public. Elected in 1881 as the youngest member of the state assembly, the hard-charging Roosevelt, after two terms and numerous confrontations with public officials, was dubbed the "Cyclone Hero of the Assembly" by one newspaper and had left no doubt as to his will to reform government.

Roosevelt's appointment as police commissioner was a theatrical affair that highlighted the boundless enthusiasm he brought to his new task. After being sworn in to office at a City Hall ceremony on the morning of May 6, 1895, Roosevelt made his way up to his new workplace, the dreary police headquarters at 300 Mulberry Street, surrounded by blocks of decrepit tenements in neighborhoods blighted by saloons, gambling houses, prostitutes, thugs, hawkers, flim-flammers, and endless swarms of immigrants. But Roosevelt hardly stopped to notice, Steffens recalled. Jacob Riis, a good friend who had known Roosevelt since the state assembly days, raced down the street shouting the news of the new commissioner's arrival. Soon Roosevelt himself came charging along on foot, yelling out, "Hello, Jake," before dashing up the stairs of police headquarters and waving for reporters to follow him. "Where are our offices? Where is the boardroom? What do we do first?" he roared as he bounded up to the second floor, with an amazed Steffens, who had just been introduced to Roosevelt by Riis on the run, merely trying to keep pace.

After gathering the police board only long enough to take care of the formality of electing him board president and naming committee assignments,

Roosevelt then dismissed the other three board members and pulled Riis and Steffens aside to hear their perspective, a scene Steffens undoubtedly recounted with a generous dose of embellishment and pride. "It was all breathless and sudden," in Steffens's memory, with Riis and Steffens briefing Roosevelt on the police situation, advising him on individual officers, and explaining the customs and rules of the job. "It was just as if we three were the police board, T.R., Riis, and I," Steffens asserted.

Fortunately for Steffens, his relationship with Riis clearly swayed Roosevelt, who in fact had little good to say about the *Evening Post* or Steffens's boss, Godkin. Ten years earlier, Godkin had criticized Roosevelt over his support of James G. Blaine for the U.S. presidency, and the impetuous politician did not take it lightly, returning fire by declaring that Godkin suffered from "moral myopia, complicated with intellectual strabismus."

Riis, conversely, was a hero—very nearly a saint—to Roosevelt, who later hailed Riis as "the man who was closest to me throughout my two years in the Police Department." The admiration was absolutely mutual. In his autobiography, Riis left no doubt as to his regard for Roosevelt: "I loved him from the day I first saw him; nor ever in all the years that have passed has he failed of the promise made then. No one ever helped as he did." Steffens's path to Roosevelt would be cleared by Riis and certainly not by the *Evening Post*. And Roosevelt, eager to jolt the department and leave a mark on the city, knew well that both reporters could provide significant aid.

The lively, twenty-year relationship that developed between Roosevelt and Steffens, reflective of their personalities and ambitions, is somewhat distorted by their own perspectives given years later, after their political leanings diverged rather dramatically. In his lengthy autobiography, Roosevelt failed to even mention Steffens. Roosevelt's words from as early as 1895, however, bely the implication that Steffens was merely a passing face in a prominent man's life. Recommending a police article by Steffens for consideration in the *Atlantic Monthly*, Roosevelt characterized Steffens as "a personal friend" who "has seen all of our work at close quarters," adding, "He and Mr. Jacob Riis have been the two members of the Press who have most intimately seen almost all that went on here in the Police Department. . . . As to Mr. Steffens's competency as an expert I can, myself, vouch."

Roosevelt, understanding that the relationship was more political than personal, astutely chose the moments when he most needed the publicity Steffens could amply provide. The police commissioner was, in fact, very careful and calculating in his use of the press in burnishing his own image among the readers—and voters. His combustible personality alone made him newsworthy on an ordinary day, and his cultivation of the press, pointedly leaking stories to preferred reporters who allowed him to influence much of the day's reporting, only grew in scope until reaching its zenith during his presidency. It was a grand political game of favors given and withheld by Roosevelt, who could praise and mock reporters—Steffens being a prime example—almost in the same breath. Roosevelt and Steffens were not confidants; it is unlikely that Steffens directly swayed Roosevelt's opinion on any substantive issues, but Roosevelt often heard Steffens out and responded at great length both in letters and in conversation. The sheer amount of time and correspondence they shared during the years of Roosevelt's greatest power indicates that Roosevelt did not merely use Steffens as a disposable pawn in his own advancement. He enjoyed his banter with Steffens, a pleasure that would last nearly a decade, until his patience with the muckrakers ran out.

For his part, Steffens deeply respected Roosevelt but at first saw himself as virtually a tutor to the new commissioner in the art of police work. More than thirty years later, in correspondence regarding his autobiography, Steffens acknowledged that while Riis understood the mechanics of police work, Roosevelt did not. "I did feel immensely superior to T.R.," he declared. "He knew nothing and I could not see how he was ever to be taught all that I had to teach him." While admitting that he hoped readers "would laugh and enjoy" his colorful portrayal of Roosevelt's first days on the job, he emphasized the credibility and intelligence of his viewpoint: "I still feel as to cities and politics when talking with an audience as superior as I did when I was instructing T.R. in the A B C of police corruption. I may be modest about human relations and women and astronomy, but I have no inferiority complex on my own subjects."

In fact, Steffens admired Roosevelt nearly to the point of idolatry in his early articles and did not mind leaving the impression that the two were intimates. His later doubts regarding Roosevelt's sincerity toward reform were generally expressed civilly, with an eye toward maintaining the friendship and his access to power. What mattered most was that both men spent sufficient time together to take the measure of one another and, when appropriate, offer critique and assistance, Roosevelt obviously being the greater orchestrator of the action. That their later commentary drifted from the truth does not diminish the extent of their actual relationship.

Reforming the police department was a trying task from the start, but Roosevelt took up the challenge with relish. "I have the most important and corrupt department in New York on my hands," he conceded, adding, "I shall speedily assail some of the ablest shrewdest men in this city, who will be fighting for their lives." Much less swift, unfortunately, were the deliberations of the police board, which consisted of two Republicans and two Democrats, a perfect recipe for gridlock. In his first press conference, though, Roosevelt declared, "The public may rest assured that so far as I am concerned, there will be no politics in the department." All in all, the job fit Roosevelt. "I am glad I undertook it; for it is a man's work," he wrote.

Roosevelt tackled both the poverty and the wayward police simultaneously. Barely a month on the job, he ordered the razing of an appalling row of tenements along Mulberry Bend while diligently rooting out the police officials named by the Lexow Committee as the worst offenders. "When he asks a question," one paper reported, "Mr. Roosevelt shoots at the poor trembling policeman as he would shoot a bullet at a coyote." His efforts, predictably, led to a throng of defenders—businessmen, doctors, lawyers, and priests among them—who insisted to Roosevelt that each of the accused had been falsely maligned. The range of justifications only ignited Roosevelt's fiery wit, Steffens recalled. "Come on, come into my office," he once called out to Steffens, "and listen to the reasons they give for letting bribers, clubbers, and crime protectors stay on the police force and go on grafting on the public."

While some of the protests found a sympathetic ear, the majority failed. Far more significant to Roosevelt was the removal of the worst of the grafters, the two prizes being Clubber Williams and Superintendent Byrnes. Steffens, who had always resented the arrogance and cruelty of Williams, was afforded a special treat by Roosevelt when the moment came for Williams to depart. Williams had returned from vacation soon after Roosevelt's appointment, amid rampant speculation that the police inspector would decide to retire from the force, as others named in the Lexow hearings had done. When reporters besieged him on his first day back at work, however, Williams said he had no intention of leaving under pressure. But Roosevelt wanted Williams out and knew that Steffens had promised Williams that he, Steffens, would outlast the inspector at police headquarters. So on May 24, Roosevelt summoned Steffens to his office, where the reporter sat in the back of the room and watched as Roosevelt called Williams in and, "almost without words," received the officer's resignation. Within ten minutes, Williams was gone, and Roosevelt was waving Williams's resignation to an astonished press.

Byrnes, who had warned Roosevelt from the beginning that he would break the new commissioner, also had no plans to surrender his post. Roosevelt, however, had no doubt that he must go. "I shall move against Byrnes at once. I thoroughly distrust him," he told Senator Lodge on May 18, "and cannot do any thorough work while he remains." Barely a week later, Byrnes was gone, reaching an agreement with Roosevelt that he be allowed to retire quietly on a full pension without facing any charges or penalties.

Steffens, Parkhurst, and many others were thrilled to see him depart as well, although Riis, who had known Byrnes as long as anyone, noted, "We shall not soon have another like him, and that may be both good and bad." Some who believed that the mythical Byrnes had controlled crime like a magician now wondered if the city would fall prey to all manner of illicit behavior without its seasoned superintendent in charge. But Steffens belied this notion: "When Superintendent Byrnes retired that day and walked without good-by to any of us out of his office forever, men stopped and stood to watch him go, silent, respectful, sad, and the next day the world went on as usual." An acting chief was named to replace Byrnes, but it was clear that Roosevelt had taken personal control at police headquarters.

Even Parkhurst found himself dazzled by Roosevelt, surprised at how swiftly Roosevelt had purged the department and apparently restored order. Barely a month after Roosevelt arrived, Parkhurst already felt sufficiently reassured to declare, "We have four commissioners who have no earthly ambition but to do their duty." For the moment, the respect was mutual, as Roosevelt, in a letter to Lodge, characterized Parkhurst as "full of fight" and "a very good fellow." And Steffens, wisely, was on good terms with both.

Roosevelt moved quickly to professionalize the force. The illicit activities of the past he found abhorrent. "The policeman, the ward politician, the liquor seller, and the criminal alternately preyed on one another and helped one another to prey on the general public," he said. He personally took an interest in cases involving charges of police misconduct. At night, with Riis leading the way, Roosevelt would go into the darkest corners of the city, as Parkhurst had, to secretly observe his own officers, who too often were far from their posts and engaged in unacceptable behavior. Steffens was invited along one night by Roosevelt, although the commissioner prohibited Steffens from reporting the experience, possibly to maintain the surprise element in future forays.

What aided Roosevelt immensely in his work was his skill at influencing the newspapers to print what he wished the public to read. Roosevelt chatted incessantly in his office with reporters, especially Steffens and Riis, even more than with politicians, providing colorful anecdotes that resulted in flashy headlines of a bold Roosevelt rocking the department and fearlessly promoting reform. Publicity was as necessary as oxygen to Roosevelt, and he made every effort to ensure that the press portrayed him as the man in charge, practically daring his opponents to question him. His entertaining, midnight escapades earned him accolades from newspapers across the city. To Roosevelt, the numerous caricatures of him stalking the dark city streets in pursuit of corruption were welcome signs of his surging popularity.

Those were intoxicating days for the young Steffens, exchanging gossip with Roosevelt and Riis and having been taken into confidence by the bull-chested chief himself. And there was no doubt that Roosevelt was climbing the political ladder. Riis, in fact, insisted to Steffens that the headstrong commissioner was headed to the White House. Steffens doubted it, but suggested that they approach Roosevelt on the possibility. Roosevelt's reaction was very much in character—an explosion. "Don't you dare ask me that," T. R. blazed at Riis. "Don't you put such ideas into my head. No friend of mine would ever say a thing like that, you—you—" Seeing Riis's stunned look calmed Roosevelt a bit, and he lowered his voice to explain that a politician must never be reminded that he may be president. "It almost always kills him politically," Roosevelt asserted, believing that the politician would lose the very traits that make him a contender. Roosevelt pointedly noted that he planned on doing great things, but he needed a certain isolation to keep his focus. And such a focus might be lost to premature dreams of the White House. "I won't let myself think of it," he declared. "I must not, because if I do, I will begin to work for it, I'll be careful, calculating, cautious in word and act, and so—I'll beat myself. See?"

5

A New Venture

WHILE THE DAILY political intrigue of New York captivated Steffens, it did little to inspire Josephine, who had dwindling interest in Steffens's separate-but-equal philosophy of marriage. In a January 1895 letter to Harlow Gale, Steffens had conceded that he was sinking "more and more deeply" into his life at the *Evening Post* and that Josephine "marks my descent with genuine sorrow and fear." She most likely feared for herself as well, as she watched their marriage fall into a routine of her husband at work, her husband with friends, her husband always the focus. His social life became hers. Possibly worse for Josephine, her literary progress remained nil: She had published a couple of articles in *The Nation*, but other magazines were not interested in work from a feminist, and her novel still struggled to find a publisher.

To resurrect a degree of romance and leisure, Steffens and Josephine moved north with her mother to a large, red, square house in the countryside of Riverdale-on-the-Hudson in May. For the summer, Steffens would be a commuter to his job. At least from Steffens's point of view, it seemed a grand change. He told his mother in early May 1895 that it was doing both Josephine and himself "a great deal of good," implicitly acknowledging that not all had been well domestically.

Settled in their new summer home, Steffens and Josephine enjoyed many "bicycle days" together, riding through the surrounding farmland and estates into the city. One day, they were out from nine in the morning to seven in the evening, covering nearly forty miles—"Both of us now are as brown as peanuts," Steffens reported to his father. One of the people they routinely passed, surprisingly to Steffens, was Captain Schmittberger, the policeman whose Lexow testimony had done so much to undercut Byrnes and elevate Roosevelt to the commissioner's chair. For his efforts, though, Schmittberger had been relegated to patrolling a remote county precinct—"Goatsville," to the city officers—where crime was an event.

As Steffens had been one of the voices calling repeatedly for him to present his startling account in court, Schmittberger initially rebuffed his old acquaintance. The hearings had severely shaken the conscientious Schmittberger. Having always taken the greatest pride in his police work, Schmittberger had a compelling story that he yearned to tell, one that Steffens had not imagined and that would again provide him a lesson in unlearning.

"What a handsome man he is on his fine horse," Josephine had said of Schmittberger upon seeing him. His rugged good looks and his honesty were the two striking features of the officer. While Steffens now listened to Schmittberger's remarkable tale, he understood that it had been these same qualities that initially landed Schmittberger in the midst of the squalid affairs of the New York police department. Put up by Tammany leaders determined to exploit his innocence and his impressive build, Schmittberger was named to the police force, where his obedient ways, as well as his ability to wield a club, made him popular as a "decorative" officer who reflected well on the department. Eventually, he was transferred to tougher beats marked by payoffs and deals largely between prostitutes and police. Unaware of what he had stumbled into, Schmittberger attempted to report the graft only to learn that this, too, was a part of police work. Apparently loyal and dutiful to an extreme, Schmittberger was assigned more and more responsibility of collecting and carrying the money to the point where Byrnes made him a ward man in charge of delivering the cash from saloon-keepers, prostitutes, and gamblers to police headquarters. For years, Schmittberger saw—and facilitated—some of the most spectacular corruption in the city. And when the Lexow Committee asked him about his activities, he simply told them—everything. Steffens wrote, "His testimony was the completest, most appalling of all; his confession summed up the whole rotten business, and yet as he spoke of it to me he looked like a nice big boy caught stealing apples."

The uproar that his testimony created, Schmittberger told Steffens, nearly destroyed him. "You don't know what I've been through. You never had your kids sit silent at dinner, nudge one another on, and so pass the buck to the big boy you always kind of—wanted the respect of, and then had him swallow a lump and blurt out, 'I say, Pop, is it true this stuff they are saying? It's all lies, ain't it?'"

Perhaps feeling guilty over his own role in the sordid affair, Steffens formed a plan to restore the good name of Schmittberger. Roosevelt had been having mixed results in his reform efforts, as resistant parts of the city continued to function much as before, with police enforcing the graft but not the law. Most likely, Steffens thought, Schmittberger could alleviate the problem.

Steffens proposed to Roosevelt that Schmittberger be assigned to a tough precinct, a task Steffens knew Schmittberger would carry out with vigor, given his devotion to his work. "No, no, no!" Roosevelt shouted, fearful of sending the wrong signal to the police on the beat—men whose skeptical gaze monitored his every move. How could he reinstate one of the grafters without risking ridicule? But Steffens, Riis, and Roosevelt had passed many hours discussing the challenges the department faced; Steffens knew the terrain, and Roosevelt listened. With Parkhurst adding his own voice, the commissioner, reluctantly, consented.

Schmittberger went along with the transfer and did not disappoint Roosevelt or Steffens. Starting on the Upper West Side, Schmittberger moved from one corrupt precinct to another, sweeping out the bribers, wiretappers, gamblers, and other lawbreakers with such efficiency that he became known within the department as "the broom." Wherever police corruption presented itself, the commissioners would respond, "Well, send Schmittberger." He proved so effective that he eventually rose through the ranks to become New York's chief of police. Steffens invited him often for dinner, and Roosevelt remained a good friend as well, once sending an encouraging note to his son. At Schmittberger's funeral in 1917, a bouquet of flowers was given by former president Roosevelt.

With Schmittberger's aid, Roosevelt's reform efforts continued through the summer and fall of 1895. Enough officers accepted his message of change to keep the activities of saloons, prostitutes, and gamblers tolerable. But as the popular zeal for reform faded and and some reformers themselves, accustomed to being ignored, had to exercise actual authority, the process fell victim to the same pressures that eventually afflict any political change. Ego clashes and turf struggles led to infighting on the police board, feeding the cynicism of the press and repelling both the public and the officers. Mayor Strong's well-intentioned but feeble attempts at reconciliation proved useless, and Roosevelt, whose reform efforts were admirable but whose blunt manner was a sizable part of the problem, could not prevent the slide of the average officer back to his old habits. For Roosevelt, the effort was a daily struggle yielding mixed results. As he told Steffens, "It worked—a little."

The popularity of New York's efforts at good government became obvious two years later, on election night in 1897, when Tammany, having patiently waited for reform to run its course in New York, returned to power. Much of the public discontent undoubtedly was aimed at Roosevelt. The failure of reform, Steffens wrote, was no longer a mystery: The police were a key element, and despite Roosevelt's efforts, they were not reformers. Steffens noted that unlike himself, police—and most other government officials—had few illusions about human nature and were surprised by unexpected good, not evil. They generally supported Tammany and had little enthusiasm for the previous victory of the reformers. "What counted with them," Steffens admitted, "was their belief that reformers are no better than others."

The experience had taught Steffens that for the political process to operate efficiently, certain "bold, intelligent bandits" were sometimes preferable to a "good" but irrelevant leader like Mayor Strong. It was a lesson that he would later remember while muckraking in America and, too well, in Soviet Russia and Fascist Italy.

Unfortunately for Steffens, the relaxing summer along the Hudson only masked his growing conflict with Josephine. Even the acceptance of Josephine's novel, *Letitia Berkeley, A.M.*, in the fall of 1895 by the Boston publishing house Roberts Bros., an event Steffens felt sure would restore her "old-time confidence," provided merely an illusion of hope. The offer of publication was soon withdrawn. Much worse, after finishing the book, Josephine suffered a breakdown. For years, she had complained unrelievedly in her diary of physical discomfort; indigestion, insomnia, backaches, shoulder pain, vertigo, piles, and depression all plagued her. "It seemed as though she had held herself up by sheer will power till that job was done and then let go," Steffens explained to his father. Although the doctor was treating Josephine for bronchitis, Steffens by now was aware that her ailment was not simply physical. "Something else, something that lies deeper is the matter," he confided, acknowledging that "all her interest in everything is gone." In the letter, Steffens displayed a rare introspective moment filled with severe self-doubt. He admitted that the struggle of life in New York could be "despairing," and although he resisted the temptation of falling into cynicism, he conceded that it was no consolation: "The thought of giving up is sometimes sweet." His own heavy workload at the paper, which he had enjoyed to the point of nearly destroying his marriage, now seemed only an added burden.

The cure for Steffens, as always, was action. In February 1896, Josephine left with her mother for an indefinite convalescence of at least two months in Greenville, South Carolina, prompting Steffens to make a move of his own. He took a room in Greenwich Village, where he hoped to frequent enough restaurants and other local spots "to make some studies of the neighborhood."

To that end, he joined other journalists and artists in an informal dining club known as "The Cloister." The group gave Steffens the stimulating companionship, mostly male, that he had enjoyed so much in Europe but that his marriage did not provide, despite Josephine's being undoubtedly more intellectual and serious-minded than some of the men.

At the *Evening Post*, he continued to chronicle the ongoing turmoil at police headquarters, with the imposing bulwark of Commissioner Roosevelt holding firm against an array of attacks from Tammany, Platt Republicans, and especially the commission itself, most particularly from fellow member Andrew Parker, a man of great political skill and possibly even greater hatred for his boss. On March 24, Steffens wrote an *Evening Post* piece admitting the turmoil: "It is idle to say that there is even a semblance of peace in Mulberry Street. There is war and nothing but war in prospect." Roosevelt himself conceded that he had passed "hours of profound depression" on the job, having been in power not even a year. By summer, as the Republicans nominated William McKinley for the White House and trouble was stirring in Cuba, Roosevelt was privately indicating that an appointment as assistant secretary of the navy would meet with his approval. (After McKinley had secured the presidency in November, Steffens commented to his father, "I have no faith in McKinley as a statesman; he seems weak and lopsided." Roosevelt would come to a similar view.)

When Josephine and her mother returned to New York, the marital issues persisted. In a July 1896 letter to Gale, Steffens, again writing as if he were a psychiatrist analyzing a patient rather than a husband speaking of his wife, implied that the marriage remained stable, even though his own words indicate that Josephine was severely unhappy with the situation. According to Steffens, they spoke less, thought less, and even knew less. Emotion between them was ebbing. "We were not so interested and interesting as we used to be," he admitted. They had settled into intellectual "ruts," and while Steffens believed, rather selfishly, that the situation might improve if they had independent circles of friends, Josephine was "revolted" by the idea. She was discontented with Steffens's "barrenness" to her and blamed the "monotony" of their marriage on his diminished attitude toward her intellectually. In such circumstances, it was not surprising that Steffens inquired about Gussie in a November letter to his Berkeley friend Fred Willis, seven years since he had last seen her.

Steffens's insensitive manner, as well as his pride in his impressive and meteoric rise in New York (he was only thirty), was on full display in another letter to Willis. "I am sorry to say I have been rather contented with my life lately," he wrote, flippantly telling Willis that now his friends had "increased in number and have improved in quality." "Several of them are fine characters and sterling minds," he went on, conceding, "Not all are newspaper men, but the best two or three are." Noting that Willis still lived in Berkeley, the globe-trotting Steffens observed, "I wonder if you haven't been too long in one place. . . . Have you thought about it?"

While he described his own life to his father as "busy, anxious, wearing and dubious,—all agog with the rush of competition," Steffens, aside from his success at the paper, was making significant headway with his other work, both fiction and nonfiction. Over the summer, the reputable Chicago *Chap-Book* had published "Schloma, the Daughter of Schmuhl," a ghetto story of the immigrant struggle for assimilation, in an issue containing a piece by Robert Louis Stevenson. After the *Evening Post* ran "The Tanagra of Mulberry Bend," an Italian story, in November 1896, Steffens received a letter from Henry Holt and Company asking if he had other stories of similar quality, as they were interested in producing a volume of his work. Steffens was thrilled by the initial offer and wrote several New York–based stories for inclusion, although years went by and the project never materialized. A popular juvenile weekly, *Youth's Companion*, boasting publication of wholesome family selections by luminaries, including Andrew Carnegie, Theodore Roosevelt, and Rudyard Kipling, eventually accepted four of Steffens's stories, while *Scribner's* and *McClure's* magazines, much more impressively, would publish three nonfiction pieces in 1897. This was the literary attention he had craved, restoring his old enthusiasm for the writer's life. "I am working in all my spare time now to get my things done as early as possible," he told his father.

It was not until the summer of 1897 that Steffens and Josephine, finally, had a home in which they could socialize with friends—Steffens's, mostly—in style. With Josephine and her mother, Steffens had "spent considerable" to purchase and furnish a spacious apartment at 341 West Fifty-Sixth Street. It featured a library, a parlor, and an entertainment center—the dining room—with its mahogany table, expensive sideboard, European collection of brasses, pewters, and pottery, and a samovar that Steffens had picked up from some East Side Jews. The new home meant that Steffens no longer had to resort to meeting with others in restaurants but could pass long, relaxing evenings enjoying wine from his father's own California winery with his growing number of friends. "Now we are getting up in the world," he proudly wrote his father, a comment that reflected not only his finances but also his literary rise.

In late 1897, Wright became the editor in chief of New York's oldest paper, the *Commercial Advertiser*, and brought with him Steffens as city editor, as well as reporter Norman Hapgood, Hutchins's brother. The change had the initial feeling of a demotion for Steffens; he referred to the venerable *Advertiser* as a "wretched old street-walker" that no longer had any influence in the city. Its circulation was a mere twenty-five hundred. Indeed, a competitor sarcastically dismissed both the paper and Steffens: "The Commercial Advertiser, the good old grandmother of journalism, is still being printed. Why, God only knows. A Mr. Steffens is the city editor. He wears on his chin a little down fuzz he thinks is a beard and he gets $25 a week." Robert Dunn, a young staff reporter who would go on to a colorful career as an intrepid journalist roaming from the Klondike to the Caucasus, described the *Advertiser* building as "a Park Row firetrap" with an office where "the grime of three tall windows gave daylight no chance. Naked bulbs on ceiling cords hung above the long table where men in green eyeshades pushed carbon pencils, with a litter of paper on the floor."

Still, Steffens remained an optimist, and the paper's policy of editorial freedom, in sharp contrast to the *Evening Post*, struck him as the ideal opportunity to go beyond his previous investigative work. "My inspiration," he later wrote, "was a love of New York, just as it was, and my ambition was to have it reported so that New Yorkers might see, not merely read of it; as it was: rich and poor, wicked and good, ugly but beautiful, growing, great." Norman Hapgood, who became the paper's literary and drama critic, agreed completely but acknowledged, "We probably, though by no means certainly, offered to the public more [intelligent] literature than in its daily paper it desires."

"Nobody is more cynical than the confirmed newspaper reporter," Hutchins Hapgood, then one of Steffens's green reporters, observed, echoing Steffens's feelings precisely. Recalling not too fondly his earlier years among the *Evening Post*'s jaded veteran reporters, Steffens followed a simple rule when hiring his new staff: no professionals. He quickly rid the *Commercial Advertiser* of its seasoned reporters—men who had been on the beat to the point that "a murder was not a human tragedy but only a crime"—and screened the new candidates with a careful eye. After one of the classic "professional" types had contemptuously droned on about his unparalleled experience, Steffens cut short the interview and, no doubt with a gleam in his eye, told the startled man to head for the dock and "go on. Don't stop. Keep right on."

What Steffens sought were the fresh eyes of young, educated, curious *writers*, not merely reporters of facts, so he scoured the student ranks of Yale, Princeton, Columbia, and particularly Harvard in search of those who "openly or secretly, hoped to be a poet, a novelist, or an essayist." He favored a style of literary journalism that went well beyond facts, that presented stories people would read precisely because they were focused on real lives—how an individual human being landed in jail, or in the gutter, or in whatever predicament or spotlight made the person newsworthy. "Care like hell," he told his reporters. "Sit around the bars and drink, and pose, and pretend, all you want to, but in reality, deep down underneath, care like hell."

Hutchins Hapgood, who would go on to his own fame as both a writer and a radical, explained that when he put together a story, "I should become identified for the time being with their lives." And this often helped Hapgood to envision what lay over the horizon, always a favorite topic of Steffens. Hutchins recalled, for example, that at the time, the New York art scene was largely conventional. On occasion, he stopped by the studio of Childe Hassam for a glass of wine and a long talk. When Hapgood wrote of the relatively mild impatience Hassam expressed toward the art establishment, Steffens showed his appreciation by featuring the piece on the front page before the other papers got hold of the story and gave it the same treatment.

The result of Steffens's efforts was an eclectic gathering of "utterly inexperienced writers," including Hutchins Hapgood; Carl Hovey (later the influential editor of *Metropolitan Magazine*); William Dean Howells's nephew, who "couldn't spell, punctuate, or keep to the rules of grammar" but "drove words like nails"; and a Tammany reporter with a gift for music. Carefully selected, the reporters were just the types that Steffens had sought, and they did not disappoint him. The *Commercial Advertiser*, as Steffens insisted, developed no singular style. He wrote to his father that his staffers were educated, thoughtful writers with character and ambition, "hand and glove in the conspiracy" with Steffens to make a newspaper featuring "literary charm" as well as daily information. He went as far as to say that they were doing things that had never been done in journalism before. Hutchins Hapgood noted that the success flowed from Steffens's approach: "He was almost incredibly 'fresh' in the sense that he was palpitatingly alive to anything that had any quality or interest in it at all. One of the things that showed his vitality was his quick perception of where the talent of other men lay."

Robert Dunn was one of the Harvard graduates hired by Steffens, whose first words to the new reporter were characteristic: "I'm city editor. Steffens. The paper's got too many Harvard men. They can't report because that's not an art. But some of you know where a sentence ends. Go down to the business office, Dunn. Say you're on the staff and come back here." Dunn's initial impression of Steffens was not encouraging, as Steffens struck him as "pert, conceited, and persnickety over civic reform," but as Steffens spent more time with Dunn, his "fervent, clear personality finally won me," Dunn admitted.

Dunn also knew that Steffens—"a David with a slingshot"—was instrumental in reviving the paper. Against the predictions of many, the *Advertiser* slowly did stabilize, turning a profit within two years and validating Steffens's belief that news did not have to be stale, orthodox, and boring to be fit for a respectable city paper. It proved to be fun as well for Steffens. "There was almost nothing in the course of the day's work," Hutchins Hapgood noted, "that couldn't get a smile from him." He recalled that during lunch and after work, Steffens and the reporters "would have long platonic conversations about style, about life, about art, more specifically about the newspaper and what might be done with it. . . . They were delightful talks; frank, enthusiastic, democratic; full of the contrasts due to the differing personalities of the men. They brought them near together and made them see that under fortunate conditions work is play and play is work; and that both are richly worth while."

Two of the reasons why Steffens was so comfortable in the editor's chair were the invaluable Hapgood brothers, both good friends of his. Like Steffens, they were born into a well-to-do family, but the Hapgood parents made clear to the children their socially progressive views and their opposition to great concentrations of wealth. After attending Harvard, both brothers found their callings in journalism. Norman, cultivated, liberal, personable, but tied far more to duty and work than Hutchins, had quickly found common ground with Steffens at the *Evening Post*. "He is a man," Steffens wrote to Gale, "who has it in him to say effectively anything he may decide to say, and the deliberate work-habit of his mind ensures some sincere and progressive conclusions." Norman's charm captured not only Steffens but Josephine and her mother as well, and he was always a welcome dinner guest.

Hutchins, on the other hand, went considerably farther afield in his thinking and behavior, not that it disturbed Steffens. Picking up his philosophy, Steffens saw, from "artists, bums, and thieves" that he often came upon while roaming the East Side, Hutchins produced insightful articles with a touch of sentiment, particularly on the thriving Jewish life that was all but ignored by other papers. He told empathetic stories of the downtrodden, the artistic, the dreamers—the kind of stories that Steffens encouraged and was eager to print. Hapgood's articles on Jewish life in New York garnered enough attention that he later collected them in his classic work, *The Spirit of the Ghetto*. The book was illustrated by Jacob Epstein, a then unknown but talented young artist Hapgood had discovered in his wanderings about the East Side, highlighting the type of serendipity Steffens hoped for when he set his writers loose in the city.

Hutchins also attracted attention in the office by dating Steffens's rather more hard-headed editorial assistant (and the only female staffer), Neith Boyce, known around the office as being "a very charming piece of congealed ice," Hutchins learned. She had written some *Vogue* pieces that Norman had criticized as too flowery, and Boyce now showed little mercy in cutting the emotion out of Hutchins's work, leaving the young writer suffering, Steffens knew, "like a wounded bird."

Still, a blooming love brightened up the dingy, old office, and Steffens, with a soft spot for both, saw that it had a future, for "Neith Boyce was as romantic in her way as Hutch Hapgood was in his way." They married in 1899 in what was essentially an open marriage (more on Hutchins's part than Boyce's) and went on to establish impeccable bohemian credentials as social and political writers and activists. Their marriage, however, lay bare some raw nerves on the part of Steffens and Josephine. Prone to long silences and a slavish devotion to her work, Boyce was a bit of an acquired taste for some, almost certainly including Josephine. Viewing the pomp and circumstance of the couple's traditional wedding ceremony and most likely unsettled by the reminder of her own years spent so quietly in the shadow of her husband, Josephine remarked cuttingly, "Of course, that way you get more presents." Boyce never forgot the slight, while Hutchins passed it off as the comment of "an advanced woman for the time." Years later, when Hutchins and Boyce moved into a twenty-room mansion along the Hudson left to them by Hutchins's father, Steffens was a frequent guest but thought the house preposterous. Looking at Boyce, he apparently found an explanation, saying, "Well, of course, a picture wants a frame." Still, Steffens and Hutchins remained close for years.

Steffens was particularly satisfied with the paper's popularity among the Jews, who had greatly influenced Steffens since his early days on the East Side. The writings of ardent socialist and novelist Abraham Cahan, a Lithuanian Jew and a good friend of Steffens's who later became the esteemed editor of the world's largest Yiddish newspaper, the *Jewish Daily Forward*, brought a colorful view of the Jewish ghetto's spirit and culture, particularly its thriving Yiddish theater, to the paper's readers. In fact, it was Cahan who introduced Hutchins Hapgood to the Jewish poets, actors, playwrights, and other personalities in the ghetto. Norman Hapgood, a pure intellectual whose interest in the popular theater was minimal, ignored the howls of advertisers who demanded the standard reviews only of Broadway; instead, he routinely featured Cahan's insightful work on Jewish culture at the head of the arts page.

Steffens, who had initially published Cahan's work at the *Evening Post* in 1897, put the novelist in touch with Riis and assigned him to cover Steffens's old police beat, aware that Cahan would adopt a creative, empathetic approach to the sordid news he was sent to cover. When a murder flash came into the office, Steffens would quietly issue his instructions, his point none too subtle but essential. He told Cahan that the details of the crime were less important than what had preceded it. "That man loved that woman well enough once to marry her, and now he has hated her enough to cut her all to pieces. If you can find out just what happened between that wedding and this murder, you will have a novel for yourself and a short story for me," he advised.

But it was Cahan's enthusiasm in leading animated newsroom discussions of radical politics, Russian culture, and ghetto life that fascinated Steffens. "It was a place of constant debate," he wrote. "This may have been Cahan's influence. He brought the spirit of the East Side into our shop." Some of the most heated debates occurred between Cahan and Hovey, who, puffing furiously on his cigar, ridiculed Cahan's insistence that European novels were inferior to those of the Russians, while Steffens, pipe in hand, enjoyed the literary exchange and rarely hesitated to add his own commentary.

Steffens also believed that Cahan's contributions, particularly regarding the "picturesque Ghetto," increased circulation and improved the paper's quality: "The Jews read the *Commercial*, and it broadened the minds of the staff and of our readers." It was no accident that in February 1898, the paper provided extensive, above-the-fold coverage of the Émile Zola trial following his "*J'Accuse*" defense of the beleaguered Captain Alfred Dreyfuss.

In the fall of 1898, Steffens was happy to divert his attention from work to his mother, who made the journey from Sacramento to New York. Steffens found her "changed wonderfully." They spoke at length, particularly on her last night, "a happy evening" for both. As awkward as his own marriage had become, Steffens saw only beauty in the final years of his beloved parents. He wrote warmly to his father, "It is old age, Papa. . . . It is the perfect round of a good life, and the results that are best are those Mamma never dreamed of—they are the ripeness and sweetness of her own character. I remember her, you know, as an anxious, worrying woman who worked much and gave up more. That is all over. She is placid, smooth-faced, restful, quiet and in love with her love."

Steffens continued to savor the human angle in journalism as well, whether it was on the Lower East Side or elsewhere. There was no shortage of national and international news, the most compelling being the Spanish-American and Boer wars that Steffens followed closely, but he was determined that the *Commercial Advertiser* reporters would find a name, a face, an incident, that would personalize the story for readers in a way that some grand strategy mapped out thousands of miles away could not. "The place for a war correspondent to go," Steffens believed, "was not the front, but the rear of a fighting army," and the rear of Theodore Roosevelt's Rough Riders was stationed at Montauk on Long Island. So, on a daily basis, Steffens's writers visited Montauk and reported the Cuban clash through scenes and incidents among the soldiers encamped there.

Since the tumultuous Mulberry Street days, Roosevelt had forged ahead in public life, as Steffens had predicted: Following Roosevelt's resignation from the police commissioner's job in April 1897, Steffens wrote in the *Evening Post*, "The end of the reign of Mr. Roosevelt in the Police Department is not the end of Rooseveltism. That will last long." The next step had been acceptance of President McKinley's reluctant offer of assistant secretary of navy to the rising, brash political star who might conceivably challenge McKinley himself. When the USS *Maine* exploded in Havana Harbor, Roosevelt was eager to dispatch the navy and fumed when McKinley instead carefully pondered his next move, reportedly complaining that the president had "no more backbone than a chocolate éclair." Eager to personally engage the Spanish enemy, Roosevelt organized an unlikely collection of Texas Rangers, sportsmen, cowboys, and other fighters—the Rough Riders—to be prepared when the war arrived, which it finally did on April 25, 1898. Roosevelt immediately resigned from the navy to lead his men into battle.

What bound Steffens and Roosevelt, as before, was a love of the political game. After his dynamic charge up San Juan Hill, Roosevelt returned a war hero and an obvious candidate for the Republicans in New York, who were desperate for a fresh start in the wake of an embarrassing state contract scandal. At Montauk, Roosevelt undoubtedly delighted Steffens when he admitted that he was feeling some pressure to run as the Republican candidate for governor. Steffens insisted that the public would go to the polls to support such a fearless leader, even a Republican, and Steffens naturally looked forward to the exceptional access he would have to the new governor. Roosevelt, sitting on a box in his tent, grumbled in return that he could never get any serious advice from Steffens and preferred to do more thinking.

Although Roosevelt assumed an air of ambivalence, Steffens suspected otherwise. Having observed Roosevelt up close at police headquarters, Steffens felt able to guess Roosevelt's true intentions. "He did not know that day at Montauk, even when he acknowledged that I did, that he meant to be governor of New York," Steffens wrote. It was not long before Roosevelt entered the race.

Steffens and Roosevelt had developed a mutual respect over the years, and the campaign for governor gave each an opportunity to assist the other. In the pursuit of news, Steffens could outmaneuver other reporters with the aid of strategic leaks from Roosevelt, while Roosevelt's political future would benefit from favorable coverage in the *Commercial Advertiser*, which Steffens amply provided in several articles running in late September and October. From his own conversations with the candidate, journalist William Allen White understood that although Roosevelt already envisioned residing in the White House, the politician also conceded that McKinley was due a second term. Until 1904, he could wait, prepare, and, above all, remain in the public eye. The governor's office in Albany would be a suitable resting place for the moment.

Steffens rarely hesitated to tweak Roosevelt when his political judgment seemed shallow, the result often being a reply from Roosevelt "looking as he often looked: as if he had half a mind to beat me up." Such a thought may have crossed Roosevelt's mind at a key moment in the governor's race, over a man both Steffens and Roosevelt loathed: Boss Platt.

Roosevelt, Steffens claimed, was a reformer from the neck up, though the rest of his ample body reflected the brawny style of the Rough Riders. By contrast, Platt, a dignified, old-fashioned power broker whose political days began in the 1856 presidential campaign of frontier hero John C. Fremont, was no reformer at all. Having returned from Cuba as a genuine war hero, Roosevelt had enough support to claim the nomination, but Platt's political influence remained significant, and it was clear that some accommodation between the two would be needed before Roosevelt could emerge as the Republican candidate. What Platt desired was for Roosevelt to recognize Platt's leadership role in the party, particularly regarding consultations over key appointments and new policies. Working with Roosevelt, however straining it may be, was preferable to any Tammany Democrat. The question was whether Roosevelt would agree to meet Platt in some form of negotiation or simply steamroll over him. It was Roosevelt, after all, who had once noted Platt's singular success "in identifying himself with the worst men and worst forces in every struggle, so that a decent man *must* oppose him."

Steffens, never at a loss for opinions, told Roosevelt that he did not have to meet Platt, but would. "Will I? Why will I?" Roosevelt snapped back, annoyed at hearing Steffens of all people correctly guess his own thinking.

"You're a practical man," Steffens explained. And on September 17, the practical Roosevelt, looking "bronzed and a trifle thin," the *New York Times* duly noted, did venture to see Platt at Republican Party headquarters on Fifth Avenue, where a waiting throng in the lobby caused Roosevelt to sneak through the ladies' entrance at the hotel. A compromise, at least for the moment, was agreed to, and Roosevelt emerged after two hours as the Republican candidate for governor. Clearly up for the task, Roosevelt, when asked by a reporter whether he would accept the Republican nomination, sniffed, "Of course I will. What do you think I am here for?"

The Independent Party, having entertained the highest of hopes that Roosevelt would run on its reform ticket, was stunned by his decision and felt a bitter betrayal, while newspapers, including the *Evening Post*, lambasted Roosevelt for aligning himself with Platt, the standard bearer of corruption. Not surprisingly, though, the *Commercial Advertiser* ran a favorable story on Roosevelt's decision, stressing that he had reached it after much deliberation prior to his meeting with Platt. Whether the article was written by Steffens or Roosevelt, or both, hardly mattered— Roosevelt could count on a supportive boost from any paper run by Steffens.

Americans were keen to know more about their dashing war hero and rising political star, with publishers eager to oblige. Frank Nelson Doubleday and Sam McClure had joined forces the previous year to form the publishing firm Doubleday & McClure. Impressed by Steffens's article "The Real Roosevelt," in the December 1898 issue of *Ainslee's*, McClure now expressed his interest in a Steffens biography of Roosevelt. The governor encouraged the work, promising to assist Steffens as much as possible and inviting him for a visit to his Sagamore Hill mansion overlooking Oyster Bay and Long Island Sound. "Since I know Col. Roosevelt so well, and have his consent," Steffens assured his father, "I should be able to write a good life of him,—swift and vigorous; and the man and his story will do the rest." Roosevelt's exuberance nearly overwhelmed Steffens: Roosevelt would lead him on what seemed to Steffens to be a death hike at breakneck speeds through the woods, all the while reciting the details of his life with Steffens gasping for air behind him.

Inevitably, Roosevelt ascended to the governor's office in 1898, benefiting Steffens—and the *Commercial Advertiser*. The governor had a regular schedule of spending most of the week in Albany and returning on Fridays to New York City. Steffens at times met Roosevelt at the station and passed some of the weekend with him before seeing him off to the capitol at the start of the week. "He let me in on his most private political plannings, conferences, hesitations, and decisions," Steffens noted, probably with some exaggeration, in his autobiography.

At the time, Steffens conceded, he was observing the political process only from the point of view of a newspaperman and an "ordinary reformer" without trying to nudge Roosevelt in any particular direction.

But the vicious political wars that played out daily before Steffens would not leave him passive for long: The battleground of New York politics, featuring numerous attacks and pressures on Roosevelt from all sides, was an ideal setting for a future muckraker. Steffens observed that the bosses and businessmen were willing to "use up" Roosevelt in the same way that they influenced any other politician for their own purposes. According to Steffens, Roosevelt used to tell him how they approached his office with demands for privileges, making offers of contributions and backing for Congress and even the White House. And while he sometimes satisfied their needs, Roosevelt, Steffens felt, was a practical politician who governed first. He was no easy mark for the lobbyists.

"They want the earth," Roosevelt once remarked to Steffens, "and they would destroy me and themselves and the earth itself to get it." Republican reformers and good government types, derisively known as *goo-goos*, had become anathema as well to Roosevelt. Reflecting on his victory in the gubernatorial campaign, he rattled off a bipartisan list of enemies on all sides in a letter to a friend: "I was delighted to overthrow Croker and Carl Schurz, Dr. Parkhurst and Chief Devery, Godkin, Ottendorfer, Pulitzer and Hearst: the most corrupt politicians within the Republican ranks, the silly 'Goo-Goos' and the extraordinarily powerful machine of Tammany Hall." While Steffens remained on good terms with Parkhurst, the minister, whose obsession for reform exasperated the more practical Roosevelt, came in for particularly withering criticism from the new governor. "Of course," he wrote to a friend in January 1899, "it is not worth while discussing it [police reform] with Dr. Parkhurst or other men who take irrational views, especially when they themselves are the men who have been most responsible for turning the city over to Tammany." A year later, Roosevelt dismissed Parkhurst and his allies as "dishonest lunatics."

Steffens kept up the pretense of writing the Roosevelt biography for a few years, admitting, "It was a good excuse to be near him when he was a source of news, as governor and as president. Many a good story came out thus." All of which contributed to his article for *McClure's*. "Theodore Roosevelt, Governor," appeared in the May 1899 issue and was a "jim-dandy," McClure thought. "I could read a whole magazine of this kind of material," he declared, possibly envisioning the far more influential work Steffens would soon be producing for his magazine. In the meantime, the name *Steffens* was becoming associated in the public mind with access to power.

As the *Commercial Advertiser* gained momentum in the new year, Steffens took no vacation in 1899, having only Saturdays and Mondays free, and his staff was equally busy. But there were no complaints. "We all feel that now when we have reached our first goal and have got the paper on a paying basis, we should not relax, but should work the harder in order next fall to be well on the way to prosperity and power," he told his father, adding proudly, "It is a happy crowd I am working with at present. Success has elated us."

Unfortunately, for Josephine, who had waited long for literary success, the situation was markedly different. Steffens tried to breathe life into her writing career by publishing her work, often focused on feminist themes, in the newspaper, assistance that Josephine almost surely accepted with great reluctance. She finally became a published author when her novel, *Letitia Berkeley, A.M.*, was brought out by a Boston publisher in 1899, four years and many revisions after she thought she had completed it. The few reviews that appeared were mixed. A critic in the *New York Times* praised it as a "noteworthy new book, . . . the voice of a clear-sighted consciousness." Others, though, attacked it for immorality. In Steffens's hometown, the *Sacramento Bee* called it "lecherous," a book "absolutely unfit for any youthful reader," and one that "should prove altogether uninteresting to any healthy-minded man or woman." (Josephine thought the review was written by a "prig," but Steffens disagreed, feeling that it had to have been a minister. "It takes a clergyman to be salacious and to see corruption where there is none.") Of most importance, sales of the book were minimal.

Josephine's health, still fragile, grew worse with the discouraging news, but her failure as a novelist was hardly the chief reason. The book itself, the story of a couple similar to Steffens and Josephine, mirrored the troubles that beset them, hurts and slights that Josephine could see far more easily than her distracted husband could. The list was lengthy and in plain view. Their failure to have children after years of trying; her own mother's illness; Steffens's long hours spent editing, writing, and socializing both in and out of the house; Josephine's quiet, growing understanding that Steffens's first love was the hectic, fascinating New York world of politics, culture, and money, not merely the company of an increasingly frail but devoted wife—all were the silent burden Josephine carried with increasing difficulty. Steffens and Josephine no doubt cared deeply for one another, which was sufficient for Steffens, whose daily plate of activity was rarely less than full. Sharing the crowded plate, Josephine had sadly come to realize, was the price she paid for her marriage.

Away from the newspaper, Steffens's literary career was progressing, if sporadically. In his scarce free time, he again attempted a novel, this one based on the notorious Schmittberger case. "I am trying to write my novel evenings, Saturday afternoon, and Sunday," he informed his father at the start of 1900. "It is a bigger job than I thought, but it goes." A year and a half later, Steffens was even less encouraging, stating that he had finished sixty thousand words and "the tale isn't half told yet." (The novel would stretch to one hundred thousand words, but never be published.) Despite several tries, Steffens would find that the form of a novel, with its demands for stylistic complexity and reflection, simply was not the literary style that suited his talent, and he never published one. His skill lay in immersing himself in the lives around him, coaxing revealing stories from normally reticent sources, gathering essential facts, and reporting them in a compelling, humanistic style that put the breath of life into the news. Readers were eager to have their news filtered through the lens of Steffens's observations, which is what made him an exceptional journalist—but not a novelist. Regardless of what he wrote, he now felt that his full name was "too long and unlovely," he told his father, for literary purposes, so his first name—Joseph, that of his father—was dropped.

Maintaining his conservative political leanings, Steffens joined a Republican district club in New York, taking some pleasure in noting to his father, "They were a bit frightened lest with my 'pull' with Roosevelt and other big leaders I was going into it to get something, but I told them I wanted nothing . . . and I was welcome." But Steffens was no party cheerleader and left the club three years later. "It is all fraud and buncombe, lying and thieving, disloyalty and selfishness," he commented even at the start. "The Republicans are worse than the Democrats,—but they are not fools; they are intelligent rascals, so I prefer them." Still, the 1900 presidential election, keeping McKinley in the White House, this time with Roosevelt as vice president, met only with Steffens's very cynical approval. "The hypocrites have beaten the fools," he told his father, labeling McKinley "the arch-American hypocrite."

Steffens, though, acknowledged that he had good reason to savor the victory. "Stocks are booming," he declared, and he himself was one of the profitable bulls. Better yet, with Roosevelt on the winning ticket (Boss Platt, livid over Roosevelt's dominance of New York politics—"I want to get rid of the bastard. I don't want him raising hell in my state any longer"—helped engineer Roosevelt's elevation to the national scene), Steffens again had ready access to power. He had already written several magazine articles on Roosevelt over the past two years and, at thirty-four, seemed to have a future that even most seasoned journalists could only envy.

Through all of Josephine's recurring illnesses, his work at the paper, and his laborious efforts on a novel that he hoped would establish him as an author and not merely a reporter, however, Steffens's own health declined. "I was emptied of energy—done, for once," he admitted, telling his father that he been suffering from nervous prostration symptoms for some time. Hutchins Hapgood noticed the change, describing Steffens as "strangely tired . . . tired physically and mentally, his esthetic agility impaired." The paper itself, while turning a profit after earlier predictions of disaster, had lost much of its originality, which had been its main appeal to Steffens. For the owners now, profit had regained its accustomed primacy.

The moment seemed opportune, Steffens believed, for a dramatic change: He would leave the *Commercial Advertiser*. He felt himself growing stale and wished for an extended break to complete his novel. "The move contemplated," he wrote to his father, "is to give myself a chance at the kind of success I always have hankered for, that of an author." Financially secure himself as a result of his stock investments over the years, Steffens could afford such a leave, and he evidently was not the only one at the paper who thought he needed one. Steffens one day overheard an employee in the business department telling Wright, "We've got out of that man just about all there ever was in him." Hutchins Hapgood thought that particularly as his boss's editorial responsibilities increased, Steffens simply grew tired of the job.

The final push came in early May 1901 from the popular monthly *McClure's Magazine*. Sam McClure was already favorably impressed by Steffens's previous work, which had appeared in the magazine as recently as the March issue. At the prompting of August Jaccaci, who was both Steffens's friend and *McClure's* art director, Steffens was offered a salary of five thousand dollars to be the managing editor. General Manager John S. Phillips had urged Steffens to consider starting within a week, but Steffens insisted first on a free summer. Josephine was skeptical of the *McClure's* arrangement, feeling that her husband was "too artistic in temperament" to handle such daily stress. The final agreement was that Steffens would take a reasonable break before joining the magazine. He parted on friendly terms with the *Advertiser*'s staff on June 1, looking forward to a restful summer with Josephine "far from a town."

First, though, Steffens returned alone to California, his first visit home in nearly thirteen years. Although he had recently seen his parents and two sisters, Lou and Dot, in New York on their way back from studying abroad in Europe, Steffens was gratified to be with his family again. He took particular satisfaction in his trip down to Santa Barbara, where he stayed with his recently married sister, Dot, and her husband, John James Hollister, at their memorable Hollister Ranch, which was set among thirty-nine thousand magnificent acres of family property commanding a stunning expanse of the Pacific Coast. The ranch became a kind of West Coast anchor for Steffens and would remain so for the rest of his life. Hollister's father, the fortune-seeking William Welles Hollister, had established the family name on the West Coast after driving five thousand sheep from Ohio to California and purchasing land that at its peak covered more than two hundred thousand acres from Monterey County to Santa Barbara. Dot had met her husband in the first class at Stanford. A strong but solitary man with a gentleman's ways, Jim had inherited the vast but somewhat untamed territory and, through patient determination, would transform it into a profitable cattle ranch. Dot and Jim Hollister were opposites—she was firm in her convictions and not afraid to express them, while he maintained a reserved but overarching presence on the ranch, known to ride for hours checking on fences and workers without uttering a word. "What he does," Steffens told his father, "he does without a strain, and I noticed in him that calm sense of reserve power which I have found in the big men of Wall Street. He has repose, because he has strength, maybe even power, and if a crisis ever comes in their lives she [Dot] will find James Hollister a big, brave man."

Of almost equal importance to Steffens during his California stay was his emotional return to the Neely ranch, where Steffens had passed so many pleasurable hours as a boy on horseback. This American boyhood experience would be central to his story of unlearning in his landmark autobiography and would capture the imaginations of so many readers. He later sent a warm letter of gratitude to the elderly Mr. Neely, explaining that it did him good, morally, to find the same man he knew as a boy. Sometimes, children are fooled into idolizing undeserving adults, Steffens acknowledged, but in the case of Mr. Neely, he had been on the mark. "I must have put away in my heart many a little note of sharp observation," he wrote, for he increasingly admired and loved the Neelys, "the friends of my childhood."

Back in New York, Steffens stole away with Josephine in July 1901 to pass the rest of the summer in a fifty-dollar-a-month cabin in the Adirondacks town of Old Forge, where he had no difficulty at all relaxing. He slept twenty hours the first day and nineteen the next before settling into a pleasant daily routine of walking and writing. Steffens told his father that he was working diligently on his Schmittberger novel, with Josephine moving similarly along on a new novel. He also was working on a political article, "Great Types of Modern Business— Politics," that would appear in the October issue of *Ainslee's* and signaled his growing fixation on how business was corroding democracy, pointing out that J. P. Morgan in the private sector and Croker in the public were bosses of a similar stripe, and reform was no more than a strictly controlled form of voter appeasement. "It had better not circulate much in Sacramento if you are running for Mayor," he warned his father, "since it is against the business men in politics."

Otherwise, the vacation was as leisurely as Steffens had hoped. By August, Josephine stopped cooking, and housekeeping was ignored. "Either of us could write $50 or $100 worth of stuff in the time and with less trouble than it takes to cook and clean up in a week," he boasted. Josephine's father came up for several weeks and regaled Steffens with tales of his Amazon explorations as a young Smithsonian scientist. Beyond that, there were few visitors, nothing but "dreamless nights and dreamy days" with Josephine. "Don't you think it all very fine?" he asked his mother.

6

THE WHITE HOUSE BECKONS

MORE THAN TWO months of dreaming and writing fiction in the Adirondacks apparently was sufficient for Steffens, especially after President McKinley, not far away in Buffalo, was shot twice in the chest by a young anarchist on September 6. Barely a week later, the president was dead, sending Vice President Roosevelt, also vacationing in the Adirondacks, careening down muddy, unlit mountain roads in true Rough Rider style to reach Buffalo for the momentous oath of office.

For Republican power broker Marcus "Dollar Mark" Hanna, who almost single-handedly had installed McKinley, a safe Republican for business, in the Oval Office, the astonishing turn of events seemed an utter disaster. Under Hanna, the Republican Party had shed any lingering effects of Lincoln's idealism while shamelessly promoting the unholy alliance of business and politics, heavily dependent, as Steffens would soon begin to see, on massive amounts of graft. Having held the White House almost without interruption since the Civil War, the party had increasingly placed its faith in the capitalist hands of Andrew Carnegie, John D. Rockefeller, Jay Gould, Philip Armour, Leland Stanford, Collis Huntington, Cornelius Vanderbilt, and others—men who had no use for headstrong, reform-minded politicians like Roosevelt. The poet Orrick Johns, later a friend of Steffens's, recalled that the trust giants had been lampooned for years in "every conceivable symbol" suggesting bloat and duplicity, including "the fat man, the octopus, the boa constrictor, mastodon, Mammon and Mark Hanna covered with dollar marks." The death of McKinley and the ascension of Roosevelt was, to Hanna, a calamity. "Now look," he cried. "That damn cowboy is president of the United States!" Even Steffens conceded before McKinley's death that "Roosevelt as President would cause almost a panic" on Wall Street. When it became reality, the news, to Steffens, was genuinely electrifying.

Having spent the entire summer writing and lounging but with his friend Roosevelt now suddenly on his way to the White House, Steffens contacted *McClure's* about resuming his work at once. The magazine hastily agreed. "It was like springing up from a bed," Steffens wrote, "and diving into the lake— and life. The water was cold."

In Steffens's view, the best and most realistic hope for improvement in the American political landscape was the rise of Roosevelt. No machine bosses or corporate captains were likely to intimidate the Rough Rider, who relished a tough skirmish over power. "The gift of the gods to [Roosevelt] was joy, joy, joy in life," Steffens wrote, and reformers clearly shared his joy once Roosevelt had attained the presidency in 1901. Along with Steffens, they flocked to Washington that year, filling Roosevelt's offices for days at a time, triumphant and secure in their faith that government service would no longer mean blatant giveaways of public money or laws shaped to promote an even greater flow of wealth into the accounts of the nation's most privileged citizens.

And Roosevelt did little to discourage such thinking. Once in the White House, he seized the reins of power with such enthusiasm that, as Steffens observed, he seemed to want not only a spirited political debate but also liter- ally a fight for his life. Steffens recalled one evening when William Allen White and he had joined Roosevelt in the White House. After dusk, Roosevelt grabbed both of his guests and pulled them out to the street where, for over an hour, he "allowed his gladness to explode." Exercising his feet, his fists, his face, and free words, he laughed at the unfortunate luck of Boss Platt and Mark Hanna, both of whom had sought to bury Roosevelt in the vice presidency, only to see him rise to the very top of the political ladder. With McKinley's assassination in mind, he acted out his own response should any assassin come near him. Checking the shadows of trees where any such attacker might be hiding, the president showed with vigor how he would pummel anyone foolish enough to challenge him. "It may have filled Bill White with terror," Steffens conceded. "What I sensed was the passionate thrill the president was actually finding in the assassination of his assassin."

Roosevelt certainly had the enormous energy that would be necessary to reform the system, but, Steffens wondered, did he have the will? Steffens watched the Senate, "a chamber of traitors," as he saw it, drone on in its daily support of corruption and knew that even Roosevelt would be hard-pressed to rehabilitate such compulsive grafters.

One day, Steffens pressed Roosevelt on the matter. The Senate solidly opposed the president on reform—what could he do about it? Hopeful that the vigorous Roosevelt would declare war on graft, Steffens instead was disappointed to hear that Roosevelt, in fact, was already prepared for compromise. If the Senate bosses would approve Roosevelt's measures "to the hilt," he would not unduly harass them on other issues, and he had already informed them as much. Roosevelt apparently was not troubled by the machine if it was his own machine: He "was a politician much more than he was a reformer," Steffens concluded, unfairly ignoring the likelihood that Roosevelt would get no reforms at all if he spoke only to reformers. Moreover, in those first months, Roosevelt had every intention of becoming an elected president in 1904 and was not eager to lose votes right out of the gate. Steffens assumed that at the very least, Roosevelt would not relent completely to Rhode Island's Nelson Aldrich—the acknowledged boss of the Senate for the past decade—or to Morgan or any other power broker. Listening to both sides, Roosevelt ultimately followed his own instincts, which left neither the reformers nor the conservatives taking his support for granted.

Having spent considerable time with Roosevelt, Steffens undoubtedly believed that his own words carried added weight with the president. In an article on Roosevelt published in the *New York Mail and Express* the following year, Steffens might have been projecting his own optimistic view of his personal ties to the president: "He takes counsel and ponders it well. There isn't an effective man in American politics who listens so eagerly to advice as he; I doubt if any man has taken so much of it from others. He fairly seizes, devours, and, truly, he digests and makes his own the food for thought thrown to him. Few think of him in this phase, because few have seen him in doubt." Steffens, as in the past, would continue to have an impressive amount of contact with Roosevelt, but the implication that the president was especially partial to Steffens's words was mostly wishful thinking, although both enjoyed the exchange.

The move to *McClure's* marked a key turn in Steffens's career. At the *Commercial Advertiser*, he had established important connections and polished his journalistic style, but the job would have remained that of a city editor and reporter, hardly enough for Steffens, who, once he recovered his energy, was poised for a grander stage. The surging growth of American magazines at the start of the century was an obvious attraction to someone with Steffens's ambitions. More than five thousand magazines were in publication, with *McClure's* among the most profitable and respected, attracting the largest amount of paid advertising of any magazine in the world. Inexpensive, popular—nearly four hundred thousand readers subscribed—and highly regarded by critics, *McClure's* offered an excellent opportunity for Steffens to impress both the public and the newsmakers.

Behind the magazine's success was the eccentric, restless, and indomitable S. S. "Sam" McClure. Born in Ireland and raised in a poor immigrant family in Indiana, McClure was, above all, a survivor. With "a Napoleonic belief in his own star," as noted *Atlantic* editor and former *McClure's* staffer Ellery Sedgwick observed, McClure established himself in publishing as a young man. Unfortunately, the first issue of his magazine came out in May 1893, the moment the stock market took its worst plunge in nearly sixty years. Of the twenty thousand copies printed, more than half were returned, and the magazine was losing a thousand dollars a month.

But McClure, reflecting his frontier upbringing, persisted. Maintaining an inexpensive price and publishing high-quality writing, he had the magazine turning a profit within a year and becoming highly competitive. He was constantly seeking out the next story, the next talent, the next shift in the public consciousness—to get it first was Sam McClure's principal aim. His mind "embraced everything an editor needs to store there—and nothing more," Sedgwick wrote. "Of the past he knew nothing, but every contemporary idea seethed promiscuously in his brain." And with impressive results. Earlier in his publishing career, he had already introduced many exceptional writers, including Robert Louis Stevenson, Rudyard Kipling, Joseph Conrad, and Arthur Conan Doyle, to the American reading public. McClure sought more talent of that caliber to boost his magazine, and he found it first in the graceful, compelling writing of Ida Tarbell.

It was Tarbell, in fact, who thrust *McClure's* into the public spotlight, a moment for which she had been well prepared. Highly intelligent, firm, but always decorous, Tarbell graduated as the only woman in her class at Allegheny College before becoming a journalist. After she embarked on a somewhat fledgling start in Paris, McClure offered the young writer a full-time position in 1892, a decade before Steffens arrived. Her *McClure's* articles on Napoléon during the centennial celebration of the French Revolution and her later, exhaustive articles on the life of Abraham Lincoln sent subscriptions of *McClure's* soaring by more than one hundred thousand. In Tarbell, McClure had secured one of the great reporters of the era, one whose name would soon be synonymous with muckraking.

With Tarbell a stunning success, McClure searched for other writers who might offer a similar journalistic style. His efforts produced, among others, three men who had little in common except a remarkable ability to entertain and inform the public. First, McClure brought in William Allen White, a jovial, pot-bellied, fearless Kansan already well known as the owner and opinionated editor of the *Emporia Gazette* and the author of the anti-populist editorial "What's the Matter with Kansas?" This partisan shot by White met with such approval from Republicans that they reprinted a million copies of it. White had first caught McClure's attention in 1896 with a collection of short stories on Kansas life that McClure bought for publication. A lifelong Republican who saw no saints in either party, White made his mark at *McClure's* with his witty sketches, some-times bordering on libel, of public figures spanning the political spectrum, nota-bly William Jennings Bryan, Grover Cleveland, Boss Platt, and Mark Hanna.

Next was Ray Stannard Baker, an idealistic, introspective journalist from Chicago. Baker, in sharp contrast to White, took a very sober, rather uncritical look at American prosperity in a series of articles before turning his attention to Cuba. An article by Baker on corruption in the military, as well as a later por-trait of Roosevelt as he was about to leave New York with the Rough Riders, ensured Baker's place with the magazine. A novelist and a romantic at heart, Baker dreamed of writing the Great American Novel. "If only I could have a small steady income, and a little time to myself," he told his father, "I could do the kind of work best suited to my tastes and my talent." But McClure did send Baker out into the world he yearned to see, where his curiosity and keen eye for detail gave McClure—and readers—well-crafted stories that met with public acclaim. He was hardly an enthusiastic muckraker, though, in the early days at *McClure's*. "I did not want to reform the world," he wrote, "what I wanted was to understand it."

Then came Steffens, "the most brilliant addition" to *McClure's* staff, in Tarbell's view. While Tarbell had a markedly different personality from Steffens and often felt uncomfortable with his incessant candor and mischievous wit in the office, she readily acknowledged that Steffens's voice added something unique and vital to the reform struggle. Steffens, she observed, was "incredibly outspoken, taking rascality for granted, apparently never shocked or angry or violent, never doubtful of himself, only coolly determined to demonstrate to men and women of good will and honest purpose what they were up against and warn them that the only way they could hope to grapple with a close corpora-tion devoted to what there was in it was by an equally solid corporation devoted to decent and honest government."

Steffens admired Tarbell's own work, as well as her peacemaking talents in what was an acrimonious workplace, particularly with McClure present. And he knew that she alone could be counted on to produce work. Steffens never met a deadline he could not miss, a trait evidently widely shared at *McClure's*.

"There was never any doubt of her copy," he wrote. "It was so reliable, always on time, the rest of us were all unreliable."

White and Baker were a better fit with Steffens. White considered Steffens a warm friend and often saw him over the next two decades, including visits to his Emporia home. Baker, having spent years with both the powerful and the destitute, shared with Steffens a sense that only an honest, deliberate study and understanding of each side would lead to genuine social improvement. While more reserved than Steffens, Baker later recalled their time together in the fondest terms:

> He comes back to me as I write with astonishing vividness, turn of speech, glance of eye, feel of hand, many little incidents of no consequence but of the essence of our intimacy. The common likings, familiar divergencies, chance meetings, confidences given and withheld, letters written and received—all that make up the texture of a long friendship.
>
> I think we might never have been irresistibly drawn together, never have instinctively sought each other out, if we had not become associates in the same enterprise, eagerly engaged in similar tasks, meeting familiarly every day, discussing ideas and projects that we considered GREAT. I soon came to like and admire him.

Around the time that he joined *McClure's*, Steffens started spending summers along the shore of Cos Cob in Greenwich, Connecticut, where Baker would visit on Sundays, passing the day on Steffens's sailboat or merely relaxing in conversation. After spending a significant amount of time with Steffens, Baker came to see him, as many did, as a "Socratic skeptic," a man who constantly asked "deceptively simple questions." For each of them, uncovering the truth was the essence of their work.

Inevitably, a man of Steffens's quirky character could not garner sympathy from all. Even journalist Will Irwin, who had a long-lasting friendship with Steffens, noted, like Baker, the Socratic resemblance, but not favorably, commenting that Steffens "displayed all the impudence of Socrates." A young hire named Mark Sullivan, who spent less than a year at the magazine as a fact-checker before moving on to establish his own distinguished writing career, had only scorn for Steffens. While finding Tarbell and Baker "kindly, tolerant, modest, gently humorous," Sullivan viewed Steffens as a self-serving, arrogant, and overrated fraud. In the office, Steffens was rude to McClure, Sullivan felt, and acted like a "frustrated dictator."

Exactly why Sullivan had such spite for Steffens is unclear. Their personalities certainly differed, and it is possible that Steffens, in jest or otherwise,
may have provoked Sullivan with a sharp comment in the office. Sullivan also
may have found absurd Steffens's later transformation from celebrity journalist to wealthy radical. Nevertheless, Sullivan's disdain for Steffens was simply
not widely shared. As opinionated as Steffens was, most of his contemporaries
respected him, some becoming close friends for years. A typical example is
Upton Sinclair's reference to him as "a devoted friend." Perhaps a comment
Steffens made years later applied to Sullivan and others along the way: "Nobody
will remain long a friend of mine who doesn't perceive that I say lots of whimsical things that are to be rejected and forgotten as meaningless or the opposite
of what I mean."

McClure himself had no doubt regarding Steffens's literary talent. At the
moment, however, McClure needed someone to handle the editorial desk, where
Tarbell and Baker, both too valuable to be confined to the office, had taken
turns temporarily and reluctantly. The magazine owner assumed that Steffens
would effectively complement the staff, so Steffens was hired to work—and
sit—in the office.

But McClure was not naive, and he soon understood that Steffens as a desk
editor was a mistake. Dealing with copyright issues, negotiating with authors,
scheduling meetings, and enforcing deadlines necessitated a level of patience and
attention to detail that eluded Steffens. And the writers themselves were rarely
in the office, leaving Steffens somewhat adrift. McClure oversaw the work of
Tarbell and Baker, leaving the management of the other writers to Steffens, who
usually sided with them in any disagreement with McClure. Simply working
with McClure himself was a challenge for Steffens. Tarbell recalled that Steffens,
despite making a "brave effort" to cope with the boss's "meteoric goings and
comings," seemed "bewildered by what went on in the excited staff meetings
held whenever Mr. McClure came in from a foraging expedition."

Certainly no one questioned McClure's effort to uncover news. Whether
in America or overseas, he sent back letters crammed with articles or even bare
headlines, ripped in haste from newspapers, trumpeting the next grand scheme
for a brilliant story. He loved to set sail on one of his extended journeys and
return in a whirlwind of excitement, his voice breathless to enlighten the staff
on all he had learned. White claimed he talked like a pair of scissors, clipping his
own sentences in midstream. Baker likened him to a live volcano. Steffens concurred with both. "He was a flower that did not sit and wait for the bees to come
and take his honey and leave their seeds. He flew forth to find and rob the bees."

Steffens as an editor was hardly alone, however, in his impatience with McClure. To the chagrin of the entire staff, McClure had one particularly exasperating fault: In his search for news, too often he could barely distinguish the significant from the trivial. Steffens recalled, "We had to unite and fight against, say, five out of seven of his new, world-thrilling, history-making schemes." McClure often vociferously dismissed their objections until Tarbell, the tactful one in the group, restored peace. The real antidote to McClure in the office was his old friend and business partner, John S. Phillips, a Harvard man who oversaw much of the magazine's daily operations and whose exceptional diplomatic skills kept McClure in check, the writers producing, and the office functioning tolerably. McClure's role, however, was not insignificant. Sedgwick recalled the paradox: "A week in the McClure office was the precise reversal of the six busy days described in the first chapter of Genesis. It seemed to end in a world without form and void. From Order came forth Chaos. . . . Yet with all his pokings and proddings the fires he kindled were brighter than any flames his staff could produce without him."

Steffens's patience at *McClure's* was growing short. Although an article of his, titled "The Overworked President" (yet again on Roosevelt—just "hackwork," Steffens called it), appeared in the April 1902 issue, Steffens in the same month pointedly acknowledged the temptation to look elsewhere for employment. He told his father that he was considering buying "a little weekly paper" in Greenwich. "It attracts me because I'd like to own a paper, make it count, and then I want to have it behind me in the town I'm to live in." Moreover, at *McClure's*, he had lost any opportunity for his own fiction, concerned that his novel would remain unfinished. He considered getting out of journalism for a year or two, living on his savings, and trying to bring the book to closure. "It takes nerve to give up $100 a week to try to live on nothing a year, but a heart's desire that has survived so long a siege of routine labor should be satisfied or killed. Which?" he asked.

In an effort to give himself a place to relax and write when the time presented itself, Steffens sought summer refuge in the picturesque fishing village and artists' colony of Greenwich's Cos Cob, where an accomplished group of impressionist painters, including Childe Hassam, spent some of their most productive years. Steffens stayed at the Holley House—"a great, rambling, beautiful old accident"—very near the dock, along with an eclectic cast of other creative types who worked undisturbed among the blue-collar villagers. "I went there whenever I became so loaded with facts that I had to run away to 'think it out' and put it down," he wrote. "Cos Cob was a good place to think."

In affluent Greenwich, wealth—and the property it could purchase—was a fact of life among many visitors, Steffens included, and he and some friends took a sporting pleasure in checking local land values, passing many hours "real estating" by visiting "good old New England houses," plots, or farms. While the goal was to look but not buy, Steffens failed by purchasing seventy acres of "lovely wilderness" just outside Greenwich; he later sold the property for twice the price.

But a magazine office in New York was far less inspiring. Steffens needed to get out, McClure knew, and do—something. "Meet people, find out what's on, and write yourself," were McClure's instructions at the close of 1901. "So," Steffens told his father, "I may turn up in Sacramento on my way to China some day." As events unfolded, he was correct about living out of a suitcase: By mid-May 1902, Steffens had visited Kansas City, Topeka, Chicago, St. Paul, Minneapolis, Duluth, St. Louis, Louisville, Cincinnati, and Cleveland.

7

MUCKRAKING SENSATION

AFTER STEFFENS'S TRIP to Washington for the Roosevelt article and his weeks in the office as an editorial "false alarm," McClure dispatched him on assignment to Chicago, where he was supposed to cast about for writers, editors, leading citizens—anyone of interest he thought could contribute a worthwhile manuscript to the magazine. Steffens at first was not enthused by his vague instructions and, once in Chicago, was hardly encouraged by what greeted him. In New York, he seemed to have known everyone, from the governor down to the East Side immigrants, but in Chicago, he was merely one among the city's teeming millions. Inauspicious as his debut was, Steffens did not remain anonymous for long. Power brokers and political bosses across the country would soon easily recognize Steffens's name, as in city after city, he stunned the nation with muckraking stories revealing the demise of its own democracy.

Sam McClure did not send out Steffens for mean-spirited purposes, however, and the magazine's decided tilt toward muckraking came about largely without intent. History and biography, in fact, dominated its early issues and proved popular with readers. For much of the 1890s, *McClure's*, led by Ida Tarbell's lavish articles on Lincoln that were praised by Woodrow Wilson and countless other critics of note, could have been mistaken for a Civil War reader aimed at those still celebrating the victory of the Union army. Even Tarbell's stunning work on John Rockefeller and his Standard Oil trust would contain muted praise for one of America's great corporations.

It was *McClure's* fiction that proved the breeding ground for the later muckraking focus of the magazine. Hamlin Garland provided a striking endorsement of the working man in his vivid articles on the bleak, dangerous conditions that thousands of steelworkers endured in the Homestead mills of Pittsburgh.

Stephen Crane followed in a similar vein with his first article for *McClure's*, "In the Depths of a Coal Mine." Such riveting fiction—moralistic stories of hard-scrabble, working lives or of political scandal—from Garland, Crane, Jack London, Brand Whitlock, and a host of other writers is largely what inspired both *McClure's* editors and its readers to demand precisely what Steffens was prepared to give them.

As more and more Americans examined their own society, they saw an appalling view of how overwhelming success had been attained by a privileged few. Huge trusts, with a generous assist from government at all levels, seemed to have gained control of the country with no fear of dissent or even the law. "Do you think I can carry on business according to New York law?" Cornelius Vanderbilt once asked with righteous indignation. The sheer size of the companies seemed to leave them accountable to no one. In Boston, one railroad alone employed eighteen thousand people, more than three times the size of the entire state government of Massachusetts.

And as the new century dawned, corporate consolidation was rampant. Copper, sugar, steel, oil, banking, tobacco, beef, and the railroads all were dominated by a few unimaginably wealthy industrialists. The transformation, to the delight of Hanna-minded profiteers, had come even more swiftly of late: Three-quarters of the trusts, including giants such as United States Steel, Bethlehem Steel, the American Tobacco Company, and American Portland Cement, were organized in a mere six-year period (1898–1904). It was a "trustification of money," as a later commission labeled it, leaving increasing numbers of citizens irate over the blatant pillaging of the American economic system and its underpinnings of fair competition.

In a pre-muckraking climate twenty years earlier, when great American fortunes were made and multiplied without much pause, conscience, or comment, Henry Demarest Lloyd had been a lonely voice against the trusts. On the pages of the *Atlantic Monthly* and the *North American Review*, he exposed the rapacious methods of Rockefeller and his fellow monopolists. In his memoir, William Allen White recalled that as late as 1890, America resembled a sleeping colossus: "Obviously, the distribution of wealth which nature and nature's God had written in tablets of stone would be undisturbed through all future ages. Revolt, reform, progress, change—all were unthinkable."

Now, Americans wondered how a limited government could rein in such powerful interests or resist generous corporate "contributions" to legislators for the purpose of ignoring the law while granting enormous economic privileges to the trusts. In fact, *trusts* became such a term of derision among the American public that magazines, with increased circulation in mind, featured an array of articles under the inflammatory headline of "Trusts." With a rabid nationwide public clamoring for every scandalous detail, magazines paid muckrakers handsomely to examine the business dealings of the hated trusts. The muckraking was so exhaustive that Sam McClure ran not single articles but whole, comprehensive series on specific trusts or lines of corruption in what Steffens called "the System," while insisting that his writers produce carefully researched, accurate stories. He had no wish to risk a libel suit.

The magazines, with their increasing national circulations and heavily detailed articles, were the key to the spread of muckraking and reform. The *Arena*, under the evangelical leadership of editor Benjamin Orange Flower, had started early down the muckraking road in the 1890s, and over the next decade, influential magazines followed with explosive results. Samuel Hopkins Adams rocked American medicine manufacturers in 1905 with his impressively documented series of *Collier's* articles titled "The Great American Fraud." The following year, *Cosmopolitan* published David Graham Phillips's scathing piece "The Treason of the Senate" just before *Everybody's*, in the probing articles by Charles Edward Russell, exposed the unseemly profits accumulated by the wealthy Trinity Church in the slum housing market. (When the church attempted to tarnish Russell by branding him a muckraker, he replied, "I am glad to be called 'a muck-raker.' The only thing I object to is living in a world full of needless horrors and suffering without uttering one word of protest, however feeble and unheard.")

Politicians added their own pleas for fairness and democracy. William Jennings Bryan, Eugene Debs, Henry George, and other public figures railed against the wayward path of the entrepreneurial elite, with the loudest voice of all, at least for a time, being that of Roosevelt himself, who carried the fight against the trusts from Albany to the White House. Ultimately, it would be *McClure's*—and particularly Steffens—at the forefront of the muckraking charge.

As Steffens cast about for his own angle on reform, he resurrected his fascination with power—how men attained it, how they used it, and how it changed, or failed to change, their thinking. On Wall Street, Steffens had observed the workings of capitalism and free enterprise with great interest. Now, he wanted to study it on a closer level, to understand how certain men in business and politics are drawn toward temptations, legal and otherwise, that result in vast personal fortunes while possibly ruining others or even themselves.

At the start, Steffens, still largely a Republican sympathizer, was driven by curiosity and even admiration toward those at the top. Novelist Brand Whitlock recalled the humble beginnings of Steffens's quest. One afternoon at *McClure's*, Steffens announced to Whitlock, who had stopped by for a visit, "I'm going to do a series of articles for the magazine on municipal government." When Whitlock wondered aloud what Steffens actually knew about municipal government, Steffens replied, "Nothing. That's why I'm going to write about it."

So Steffens landed in Chicago, seeking a story that would meet McClure's expectations. Steffens's contact there was William Boyden, a prominent lawyer who advised Steffens to investigate "a very quiet little old German gentleman," the timber titan Frederick Weyerhaeuser, in St. Paul. As Boyden explained, Weyerhaeuser had bought up large tracts of forest in the west and northwest and now was doing the same in the south. When Steffens wondered exactly where the story was, Boyden replied that Weyerhaeuser had made himself one of the richest men in the country, yet most of the public had no idea who he was.

Steffens's ignorance was no less than that of the public, so he ventured to St. Paul for a closer inspection. He discovered that Weyerhaeuser did not grant interviews, and the magnate waved away Steffens as well. But evading Steffens was no simple task, as Louis Filler observed: "His courtesy was more than deference or form: it was a tribute to the essential humanity and importance he saw in everyone. Trying to understand people, he made them feel important."

Weyerhaeuser evidently was not immune to Steffens's persuasive powers. After his initial rebuff of Steffens, he went on to spend the entire morning with the reporter, discussing not the tedious details of his timber business but the ethics behind amassing a great fortune. After some prodding from Steffens, Weyerhaeuser admitted that he had often reflected on his decision to pursue vast wealth and had wished to talk it over with someone. But he could not bring himself to do it—not with a pastor, not with a business partner, not with anyone. Yet, he now found himself speaking confidentially to a magazine reporter.

According to Steffens, Weyerhaeuser revealed how he achieved power and used it politically, as well as how he justified his actions, almost challenging Steffens to question what he was hearing. Steffens, though, expressed understanding, and Weyerhaeuser continued on at length. "We were shut in there all the forenoon, three or four hours," Steffens recalled. "I did not try to help or hurt him, just listened, and he talked himself out."

Unfortunately for Steffens, he had a compelling story that he could not publish. The larger point, however, was that men of power were willing to confide in Steffens, and he had no hesitation in encouraging them to do so. Steffens left Weyerhaeuser, determined to know more.

From Chicago, Boyden pointed Steffens toward St. Louis, a city where rampant bribery among government officials and businessmen had outraged a conscientious Southerner, Joseph "Holy Joe" Folk, who had the unenviable challenge of being the circuit attorney. Brought up in a strict, conservative family environment that emphasized the virtues of the Bible and the rule of law, Folk, somewhat like a virgin in a brothel, was stunned to see how the bosses and their sycophants controlled the system in St. Louis, from elections to appointments. As Folk provided the sordid details to Steffens, the reporter could see the prosecutor's world "being all slashed to pieces." But the meeting was essential for both: Steffens was eager for a municipal story of genuine, indisputable graft, and Folk needed someone to publicize his cause. Steffens supported Folk's work to the point that he not only stunned the nation with his exposé on St. Louis, but also later went as far as to write some of Folk's campaign speeches in the 1904 governor's race in Missouri.

A publicly genial but rather detached man who had little use for local cronies or even close friends, Folk had been installed by bosses assuming he would be easily manipulated. But he refused to play the political game by the standard rules, even to protect his fellow Democrats in St. Louis, including the city's notorious Democratic boss, Ed Butler. Instead, Folk pushed his prosecutions to the full extent of the law, eventually bringing charges against the chief culprit, Butler himself. Orrick Johns, whose father, George Sibley Johns, the reform editor of the *St. Louis Post-Dispatch*, was all too familiar with Butler's chicanery, described the boss as a man who "straddled the town like an invisible Colossus, drawing booty from every utility, city contract and almost every legislative act. For twenty years or more, he was a dictator immune to all appeal, and not above having his persistent enemies put out of the way for good," a fact not lost on Folk.

One bribery case exploded in January 1902, revealing an unholy alliance of government officials and businessmen, including councilmen, state legislators, bank presidents, and company directors. With the editorial backing of the *Post-Dispatch*, Folk pursued all of them (even as the police commissioner defended the accused) and eventually obtained confessions of sweetheart deals that had businessmen obtaining franchises, grants, licenses, exemptions, and public properties from the government.

The extent of the corruption astonished Folk. The government, he told Steffens, "represents bribery and business, not the people—in St. Louis." When he added that graft made the government responsive only to the worst of the people, Steffens replied, "Or—the best." Indeed, as both of them could see, it had been some of the best minds in St. Louis that had kept the illicit system functioning so efficiently for years.

Steffens, with significant help from Folk and George Sibley Johns, now had the story he sought. In his editorial capacity for *McClure's*, he asked the former city editor of the *Post-Dispatch* and local muckraker in his own right, Claude Wetmore, to write an article based largely on Steffens's research. Steffens added his own name to the byline when he inserted some specific details in the *McClure's* style, particularly on the role of Boss Butler, which made Wetmore somewhat skittish. Steffens initially titled the article "St. Louis Upside Down," later changing it to "Tweed Days in St. Louis," reflecting his growing sense that urban corruption had a certain uniformity. The story appeared in the October 1902 issue of *McClure's*, one month ahead of Tarbell's first Rockefeller installment, and launched *McClure's* as the leader among the muckraking magazines, with Steffens's work a prominent reason why. Expedited the same year by President Roosevelt's shot across the business community's bow—government prosecution of Morgan's Northern Securities Company for antitrust violations, the start of Roosevelt's trust-busting campaign—serious, overdue reform was becoming the watchword of the American political landscape. Steffens's timing was perfect.

Reaction to the *McClure's* story was immediate and heated. Nearly every reader apparently had an explanation as to why St. Louis, the nation's fourth-largest city, was essentially a fiefdom of Boss Butler. Steffens noted that the Republicans blamed the Democrats, Easterners looked down upon St. Louis as a "Western" outpost, New Englanders saw too many Germans in the city, businessmen ignored their own complicity and asserted that more business and less politics was the solution, and seasoned Europeans simply dismissed the entire outcry as the growing pains of a young country. Steffens acknowledged that he had shared some of these same beliefs and, just like most Americans, never questioned the moral assumption "that political evils were due to bad men of some sort and curable by the substitution of good men."

His education in graft illustrated to Steffens that even respected men, maybe *especially* respected men, could act with duplicity and thrive in the process while apparently feeling no shame. Indeed, many were pillars of their communities. Did that make them "bad" men? And, Steffens wondered, did American capitalism rest on a basic truth: that any man, reputable or otherwise, could act deceptively and largely with impunity from the authorities while both reaping windfall profits and maintaining his public honor?

Still, the moral weaknesses of ordinary people were dwarfed in scale by those of their leaders. Steffens was fully aware that he had stumbled upon a vital flaw in American democracy. In St. Louis and elsewhere, people were being governed and indeed often had their working lives determined by an invisible alliance of government and business leaders whose deeds were unmentioned in any school textbooks and unsanctioned by any legal document. Had the visionary founding fathers imagined an autocrat like Ed Butler in every city across the land? As William Allen White asked, "Where in the constitution are the functions of the boss described? Where in the constitution may one find how the thing we call capital gets into government at all?" Steffens was no constitutional scholar, but he had every intention of examining these American bosses and understanding the system that supported them so lavishly. Simultaneously, his political mindset was evolving. Previously a nominal Republican when he leaned politically at all, Steffens now was seeing clearly that both a conservative, stand-pat approach was no solution and party distinctions were irrelevant when the issue was graft.

Steffens's fixation on the power brokers and his determination to trace the circuitous routes of the graft, however, immediately put him at odds with McClure. While the magazine owner was generally pleased with his reporter's efforts, calling the St. Louis story "a corker," he urged Steffens to take aim not at the criminals but at the civic pride of the unwitting victims, namely, most of the public citizenry. If the people could be awakened to the lawbreaking that surrounded them, McClure felt, democracy might yet be restored. "I hope the people will rouse themselves," he wrote to Richard Gilder at *Century*. "It is up to magazines to rouse public opinion."

And McClure was definitely not interested in Steffens's hypothesizing or blanket condemnation of capitalism. The facts were what mattered to McClure. Steffens's writing would have to reflect McClure's stance: Not every businessman was a criminal, and St. Louis, at some point, would need to be reexamined with an unbiased eye. Steffens was hardly keen on adopting such an approach, particularly since he was fully aware that Tarbell's articles met less editorial resistance and that McClure had much greater faith in her judgment. For the moment, Steffens and McClure carried on with their business, each watching the other with a wary eye.

Having reported on such a blatant example of a corrupt political machine, Steffens was eager to find out how pervasive the American addiction to graft might be. Folk and Steffens both saw the strong likelihood that if St. Louis was so morally tainted, other cities were as well. In each case, Steffens hoped to find the source of the corruption and, ultimately, a way back to democracy.

McClure agreed that Steffens needed to examine additional cities. Tarbell was already well into her exposé of Rockefeller and Standard Oil; adding a series by Steffens on the municipal "boodlers" (government officials steeped in bribery), McClure expected, would be an explosive combination. The notion of muckraking cities struck such a chord with McClure that he was pressing Steffens to get overseas as well, specifically, to Birmingham, England. Caught up in the spirit of the mission, Steffens also saw Naples as a city worth his attention.

McClure, however, had already settled on the immediate target: Minneapolis, where a trickle of small news items over the past year had surged to a flood involving a citywide scandal. McClure had become so fixated on the theme of systemic corruption that he had devised his own explanation of the problem. The trouble, he claimed, lay with democracy, or the lack of it. Citizens were not exercising their obligation to oversee their own civic affairs, leaving at every level of government a dangerously large vacuum that had obviously been filled by men such as those that Joseph Folk was trying to incarcerate in St. Louis. The answer, in McClure's view, was to assign power to a strong, effective leader—a man not unlike McClure himself, Steffens, somewhat indelicately, pointed out—and allow him to govern the city. Steffens broke with McClure on this point, preferring a different approach. He hoped to examine a number of cities where the political system was rigged and to understand exactly how the corruption had begun. "We had a pretty hot fight," Steffens recalled, "and McClure won." Steffens was dispatched to Minneapolis to write, as Steffens interpreted it, that "democracy was a failure and that a good dictator was what is needed."

Steffens need not have worried: Minneapolis, like St. Louis, was abundantly corrupt. The main grafter was the mayor himself, A. A. Ames, a doctor-turned-politician who pacified the police force by appointing his equally felonious brother, Fred, as chief and generously spreading the money among the officers. For years, the Ames brothers controlled nearly every illicit activity in the city.

In his autobiography, Steffens gave a fascinating account of the Minneapolis police department's version of law enforcement. The goal of the Minneapolis police, Steffens wrote, was not to prevent crime but to "protect, share with, and direct the criminals." Mayor Ames and the police force, after gathering advice from professional criminals, made a schedule of prices "for the privilege of breaking the laws," as Steffens saw it. Saloons and houses of prostitution made monthly payments to the police to look the other way while business flourished. Ames actually set up robbery "games" to increase the police take. Criminals of all stripes were not only allowed to work their trade but also encouraged to bring in their fellow lawbreakers if these part-time bounty hunters were willing to share the spoils with police.

Like so many of their ilk, the Ames brothers made not only sizable profits but also bitter enemies, and two of them, Billy Edwards and Charlie Howard, both swindlers, were seething in jail after being out-swindled by the Ameses themselves. As in St. Louis, Steffens learned about the system from an inside source, this time a man named Hovey Clarke, the foreman of the grand jury and the driving force behind the Minneapolis investigation. Edwards and Howard provided Clarke with the most damning piece of evidence in the case, the Big Mitt Ledger, a week-by-week accounting of the names, dates, dollar amounts, and other specifics. Steffens's reportage stunned the citizens of Minneapolis by proving that their own public servants had been defrauding them for years.

One glaring common denominator that Steffens noted in Minneapolis and New York was that both police departments were thoroughly corrupt. And from Edwards and Howard, Steffens learned that the officers in Minneapolis were amateurs compared with the police in San Francisco, Seattle, Chicago, and New York; these larger city forces conducted far more sophisticated operations. Yet Steffens could see that polished or otherwise, the involvement of police was essential in city after city. Corruption could not flourish without their support.

The aftermath of the Minneapolis scandal provided Steffens with another lesson. The Ames regime was finished, allowing Clarke the opportunity to install a well-educated idealist, Percy Jones, as the new mayor. Jones must have seemed the perfect successor to the scheming Ames, one who would see that government officials served the people rather than themselves. "He was one of a group of the sons of successful citizens," Steffens wrote, "who had heard that bad men made our good American municipal government bad and, therefore, decided that they, good men, would go into politics and make the bad government good."

Minneapolis's problems did not disappear with the Ames brothers, however. There remained the matter of the police force. How, Steffens wondered, could police control crime if they were honest, and, rather than negotiating with criminals, arrested them? Edwards and Howard had already assured him that the situation was the same or worse everywhere. Why would Minneapolis be any different?

Steffens decided to approach the new mayor. Jones had been doing what the public expected—appointing sincere people to power, particularly in the police department, and attempting to form a responsible government. But honesty, he admitted to Steffens, had its limitations, and it came in many forms. When Jones tried to limit prostitution, for example, landlords denounced him for removing some of their high-paying tenants, while the clergy and good citizens were outraged that the city's leader was allowing if not actually promoting sinful behavior. Soon, further reforms had brewers, saloon keepers, and other businessmen united in protest. Minneapolis clearly was not ready for honest government.

It was apparent now to Steffens that graft-infested municipal government in New York and in Minneapolis. His thoughts returned to St. Louis. Steffens was eager to learn if a scientific theory could be formed on the basis of the assumption that corruption everywhere was not only endemic but identical, and he could easily test it in St. Louis with Folk's assistance. McClure had no patience with scientific theories of graft, but was thrilled with Steffens's work in Minneapolis. The story, he said, was exceptional. "You have made a marvelous success," McClure gushed in a November 7 letter to Steffens. "I think [your article] will probably arouse more attention than any article we have published for a long time." Three days later, McClure heaped further praise on his star reporter: "Your articles have been more important than anything appearing in any other magazine. I am planning the magazine for the next few months, and especially wish to keep the great boom on that we have got on account of your stuff."

Steffens, though, was impatient to know whether the same pattern would be found in St. Louis. He hurried down to press Folk, who confirmed that the police there had employed a similar system to what Steffens had seen elsewhere.

As Steffens's muckraking exposed an astonishing level of urban graft, not only Steffens but an increasing number of Americans understood that corruption was endemic in public life, funded by private profiteers. *McClure's* confirmed the sorry plight of the country in spectacular fashion. With a simultaneous assault on industry, labor, and government, McClure ran Tarbell's third chapter on Standard Oil, Baker's account of the nonstriking miners caught up in the United Mine Workers' coal strikes in Pennsylvania, and Steffens's exposure of Minneapolis ("The Shame of Minneapolis: The Rescue and Redemption of a City That was Sold Out") all in the explosive January 1903 issue.

McClure found the plundering of American freedom, the lapse in morality, and the cynical disrespect of the law so egregious that he inserted a special editorial focusing on the dire situation. He appealed to the good sense of the public and for the return of personal responsibility at all levels of society:

Capitalists, workingmen, politicians, citizens—all breaking the law, or letting it be broken. Who is left to uphold it? The lawyers? Some of the best lawyers in this country are hired, not to go into court to defend cases, but to advise corporations and business firms how they can get around the law without too great a risk of punishment. The judges? Too many of them so respect the laws that for some "error" or quibble they restore to office and liberty men convicted on evidence overwhelmingly convincing to common sense. The churches? We know of one, an ancient and wealthy establishment [Trinity Church in Manhattan], which had to be compelled by a Tammany hold-over health officer to put its tenements in sanitary condition. The colleges? They do not understand. There is no one left; none but all of us. . . . We have to pay in the end, every one of us. And in the end the sum total of the debt will be our liberty.

In a *McClure's* article two years earlier, Theodore Roosevelt had been slightly more succinct: "No hard-and-fast rule can be laid down as to the way in which such work must be done; but most certainly every man, whatever his position, should strive to do it in some way and to some degree." After seeing the January issue, he invited McClure to the White House.

The seminal muckraking issue sold out at newsstands, and in a scene reminiscent of Reverend Parkhurst's glorious reform campaign a decade earlier in New York, letters poured in from readers who were certain that an examination of their own local affairs would provide abundant grist for the muckraking mill. "Evidently," Steffens said to an editor, "you could shoot me out of a gun fired at random and, wherever I lighted, there would be a story, the same way." Other magazines, notably *Collier's*, *Leslie's*, and *Everybody's*, quickly grasped what the public was demanding: articles that not only entertained and informed but also exposed. Americans were captivated by the muckrakers and their ability to provide names, dollar amounts, and other titillating specifics.

Eager to capitalize on the magazine's success, McClure directed Steffens to turn to Chicago, a city where, common wisdom held, the corruption would dwarf that of Minneapolis and further startle the reading public. Magazine sales would spiral ever higher in the muckraking frenzy.

Steffens, though, wanted to focus on a smaller city, where the existence of graft was less likely, to test his theory that corruption was widespread and identical. Again, Ida Tarbell intervened, the result being a compromise that sent Steffens back to finish reporting on Folk's struggles in St. Louis. Privately, Steffens intended to gather all the facts that McClure demanded and then use them to prove his own ideas.

The issue in St. Louis became not merely one of corruption but one of a more insidious nature: Was American democracy a myth? After Steffens had taken Folk's findings and fashioned them into a readable, damning account, the people in St. Louis would have been hard-pressed to detect any hint of democracy around them. Steffens later recalled that he had shown how the majority of citizens were herded into parties and duped into transferring their loyalty from support of a democratic process to the party machines, which then used their power to "sell out franchises, permissions, and other valuable grants and public properties to the highest bidders, sometimes 'good' local business men, sometimes 'bad' New York and other 'foreign' financiers." Folk had learned of, and Steffens reported on, several specific cases of shameless corruption, one involving the sale of the city's water supply for $15 million.

It was an astonishing indictment that ultimately resulted in Folk's political demise in St. Louis. In court, he dutifully pursued Boss Butler (who shrewdly brought along his wife, his three sons, a daughter-in-law, and a grandson for the occasion) and the other bosses, winning convictions in every case except one. Yet, as he consistently "won" in the legal sense, he found that increasing numbers of citizens in St. Louis felt that their lives were being hindered rather than helped. The removal of the bosses hurt businesses, profits, and stock values, leading to cries of protest. The plain truth uncovered by Folk was that large numbers of "good" people benefited more, directly or indirectly, from corruption than from strict enforcement of the law. The Missouri Supreme Court, where any mention of reform garnered little sympathy, agreed, overturning most of Folk's convictions. "The machinery of justice," Steffens wrote, "broke down under the strain of boodle pull. And the political machinery did not break down." Indeed, the city's Democratic political machine was livid at Folk for pursuing fellow Democrats as vigorously as Republicans. Steffens's March 1903 article, "The Shamelessness of St. Louis," laid the crisis bare but hardly reformed the city.

Steffens no longer had to seek out examples of municipal graft—stories poured in unsolicited. The most intriguing was an invitation from the Gould railroad interests, now managed by the children of financier Jay Gould, who had died a decade earlier after earning, amid stiff competition, the reputation of being one of the great economic predators of the nineteenth century. The Goulds asked Steffens to muckrake Pittsburgh, where the city and state bosses, they claimed, had combined to block them from the railway competition, and the Goulds had abundant proof to offer. Steffens understood that in this case, there seemed little difference between the accuser and the accused. "It might be that the Goulds' plan was to talk business diplomatically to the faces of the Pittsburgh bosses while I was kicking them from behind," he conceded, "but I didn't care."

His real concern was that he would be working alone, with no inside help, in Pittsburgh. For Steffens, Pittsburgh was uncharted territory. And his source was the Goulds, who would not be mistaken for Holy Joe Folk. "I was afraid," Steffens wrote, "that a lone-handed attack upon a city might expose me more than it would the grafters." McClure himself grumbled about Pittsburgh, preferring to see Steffens look into what was undoubtedly a more sensational story in old Philadelphia.

Yet, Pittsburgh suited Steffens's purposes in important ways. Unlike New York and Chicago, it was new and would be seen as such by readers. Of most importance to Steffens, he wished to test a development in his theory of corruption: that a state's system of graft must mirror that of its cities. Steffens hoped to investigate Pittsburgh and Philadelphia before heading to Harrisburg to muckrake the state of Pennsylvania.

Steffens's initial impressions of Pittsburgh were not encouraging. The city, with its blast furnaces spewing a dense plume of smoke that blanketed the rivers and darkened the skies, "looked like hell." Having lured Steffens to Pittsburgh, the Goulds promptly ignored him, leading Steffens to conclude that their ability to secure sizable amounts of graft had improved considerably of late, rendering his services unnecessary. Newspapers reported his presence; detectives, he believed, were following him; and even the hotel clerks shunned him. He was truly alone until he met Oliver McClintock, a burly businessman with a flowing white beard who had been a political outcast in Pittsburgh for years. Even his own family tried to silence him. But, for Steffens, McClintock proved to be Pittsburgh's version of Joe Folk, a man with the heart of an idealist and the head of a reformer. Over many years, McClintock had pieced together the picture of graft in Pittsburgh, but until Steffens arrived, no one had listened. McClintock was preaching to a deaf—and bought—city.

Armed with McClintock's plentiful facts, Steffens forged ahead with his article. He learned that the city had not one but two bosses, Christopher Magee and William Flinn, who worked as a team for their own separate ends. "Magee wanted power, Flinn wanted wealth. Each got both these things; but Magee spent his wealth for more power, and Flinn spent his power for more wealth. Magee was the sower, Flinn the reaper," Steffens explained.

"Pittsburg: A City Ashamed" ran in the May 1903 issue, confirming that Pittsburgh differed little from the previous cities except that it had two bosses who worked in unison. What most intrigued Steffens was his discovery that the graft led directly to Harrisburg. Less thrilled was McClure, who had instructed John Phillips to take an editorial knife to the article, which he did. With each passing article, McClure saw Steffens, unlike Tarbell and Baker, as something of a renegade. He wrote to Phillips in March 1903, "I have been thinking seriously of the attitude Steffens always takes in regard to the people, and I not only feel that he is wrong in his attitude, but that such an attitude is discouraging and calculated to lessen the value of an article." He was particularly uncomfortable with Steffens's ongoing approach to businessmen. "Steffens has a notion that the business man is a coward," McClure wrote, "and that the business man is to blame for political corruption, and he makes every fact bend to this notion."

Behind McClure's angst was a libel suit that had been filed after Steffens's Minneapolis article. The complaint ultimately dissolved, and Steffens, in fact, would never pay any damages related to his work, in spite of the powerful names he tarnished. Thirty years after Steffens had reported on New Jersey's progressive political leaders, a historian took up the task of looking into Steffens's credibility only to learn that "after painstaking research I was coming up with essentially the same picture of New Jersey politics that Lincoln Steffens had drawn." Moreover, the public had a voracious appetite for his stories. While McClure may have been uncomfortable with their editorial slant, his readers felt decidedly otherwise.

Before Steffens approached Harrisburg, he established himself in Philadelphia, where he expected to come upon another Folk or McClintock eager to explain how democracy worked in the City of Brotherly Love. Unlike his experience in Pittsburgh, Steffens was certain of what he would find in Philadelphia, a city as unknown to him as Pittsburgh had been. His theory of corruption was holding up well and emboldening him even as it was infuriating McClure. "Your theory is getting you," he barked at Steffens. "You think you know so much that you won't be able to see and report the news." McClure saw graft as exceptional, criminal, and obviously newsworthy; Steffens, on the other hand, was more and more certain that it was, in fact, unexceptional and natural, meaning that it could possibly be "repaired" or at least dealt with more effectively than by simply incarcerating the old bosses and creating employment opportunities for their successors. The conflict gave McClure the distinct impression that Steffens was freelancing rather too much. As matters developed, Philadelphia would not help Steffens's cause.

Steffens quickly ascertained that Philadelphia had the same basic machine as did the other cities. And not only was its graft familiar to most citizens, but the details of the operation had been publicized for years by a fearless editor at the *North American*, E. A Von Valkenburg, who ignored death threats in his zeal to inform his readers.

So there were few secrets in Philadelphia, but when Steffens examined the system closely, he found that while the results were the same—the business of the government was often whatever activity the businessmen would subsidize—the grafters did not use the same maneuvers that he had seen before and expected to see again. There was, for example, the state boss, Senator Matthew Quay, who handpicked the new city boss, a ward politician named Israel Durham. Steffens had not seen a system where a state boss could simply choose a city boss with no resistance. And the grafters took their arrogance to new heights. During elections, they would stuff ballot boxes with votes for George Washington, Benjamin Franklin, and other founding fathers, and even mocked the reformers by writing in the reformers' names on ballots.

One day, Steffens went "in desperation" to see Durham for at least a hint of an explanation. Durham agreed to see him, and the two, according to Steffens, had a long, sober discussion on graft. Steffens was particularly interested in a "volcanic eruption" of blatant giveaways and other deals that all passed intact—how did they dare attempt such open thievery? Because, Durham explained, graft on a grand scale was guaranteed to overwhelm the political system. A single crime can be solved; a half dozen simultaneously have much better odds of success. The magnitude of the corruption had stifled dissent in Philadephia.

As an amused Durham smiled, Steffens sat stunned. Where, now, was his theory of corruption? He tried to reconsider, taking into account this latest obstacle. The conclusion that seemed most sensible was that age mattered. Philadelphia differed from St. Louis because its system of graft was older and more entrenched. According to this theory, St. Louis, even after Folk enacted whatever reforms he could, would also come to accept a higher level of graft, as Philadelphia did. Moreover, Steffens believed, all of it was a natural process that, as it played out in front of him, would eventually sink a democracy into a plutocracy.

Like Weyerhaeuser before him and many others later, Durham was an excellent example of a powerful man who willingly participated in corruption, yet who was what Steffens would come to call—in admiration—an "honest crook." In city after city, Steffens spent hours huddled with such men, often speaking confidentially to uncover the facts. Initially, he expected these influential figures—the enemies of high-minded reformers—to be the source of the problem. Instead, just as his theories of corruption evolved, his assessment of the bosses also changed. In the legal sense, there was no doubt that they were criminals. To obtain their ends, they skirted the law whenever necessary, and they did not deny it except, as Steffens noted, under oath.

As Steffens got to know them better, however, he understood that they often were intelligent, educated, and industrious men who, for reasons Steffens was eager to explore, devoted much of their talent to amassing personal power, usually at the expense of the public. The unsettling point to Steffens was that these bosses, men like Durham, were also among the few people truly interested in and capable of making the system function, for better or worse.

Steffens pondered this point at length in his autobiography, noting that "big, bad men" simply had not been expected to do good and so followed the well-worn path of graft, where, Steffens acknowledged, the rewards and applause lay. He conceded that "Iz" Durham, despised in Philadelphia by reformers, was "the best man I met in that town, the best for mental grasp, for the knowledge of life and facts in his line, and—he had one other advantage which is something akin to honesty but must be described in other terms. The New Testament puts it the most clearly and briefly. Jesus said that He could save sinners; the righteous He could not save."

The righteous, of course, were the reformers, who certainly were sincere in their desire for change but largely in the abstract sense. Steffens vividly recalled St. Louis: "The petty honest men who do not know . . . when or how they sin, they will not face and so they cannot deal with things as they are. In St. Louis they thought they were for reform, and discovering that they had stock or friends in the graft, turned cowards and persecutors of Joe Folk just as their kind forced the Romans to crucify the Jewish Messiah." Sinners, by contrast, did not feel any need to justify their behavior or make excuses. "That is why it is such a comfort to sit down and talk with them," Steffens observed. "They accept, and you can start with, the facts, as you can in a conversation with scientists. . . . Some day, when they are asked to, they may help us to save society."

Steffens, though, was not about to switch his allegiance from reform to graft and in fact was eager to look at other cities, but the Philadelphia story had a curious conclusion that gave him a glimpse of the challenges that lay ahead. His article, "Philadelphia: Corrupt and Contented," appeared in the July 1903 issue. Sometime later, when Steffens was visiting at the White House, Roosevelt grabbed him by the arm and pulled him aside, upset at Steffens's treatment of Senator Quay, the old state boss from Pennsylvania who was now gravely ill in a Washington hospital. Steffens protested, not quite accurately, that he was denouncing only crimes, not criminals. Roosevelt brushed aside Steffens's plea and lambasted him.

The main point of the episode, Steffens understood from his long experience with Roosevelt, was that the president frequently found it necessary to bloviate on a particular matter before settling on a position of compromise. Roosevelt had never been entirely comfortable with the news-gathering methods and views of muckrakers, including Steffens, but he respected their work. The real issue was that even a trust buster such as Roosevelt occasionally wanted to hear an admiring comment on his own privileged class. Steffens, however, was more interested in the truth about government, and he no longer expected to find much to admire in the political system.

Eager to muckrake another city and test his latest notions, Steffens planned to focus on older cities, believing, or at least guessing, that corruption was a process that occurred in phases and was therefore predictable. Old Philadelphia, for example, was the future for St. Louis. New York and Boston, older still, may be Philadelphia's road ahead. Steffens wanted a city that fostered worse corruption than Philadelphia—Boston seemed a good bet—but McClure repeated his preference for Chicago, and Steffens ultimately agreed. He was sure that he would find a "sensationally wicked story" in the "wild, young western city." Again, he had miscalculated.

Steffens arrived in Chicago as a celebrated muckraker expecting to locate sources, including the bosses, who would explain all the graft in minute detail. His informants, however, told him stories that were neither sensational nor wicked. In Chicago, Steffens found that the bosses did not control all the power or money. No one owned the mayor. The reformers, of all people, actually controlled the city council. The machine, he understood, did not rule Chicago. What had happened?

Steffens appealed to a tall, imposing defense attorney in the city who had been making a local name for himself and undoubtedly understood the system. After keeping Steffens waiting outside his office, Clarence Darrow finally appeared, studying Steffens's card while moving slowly toward him. When the lawyer was nearly upon Steffens, Darrow erupted in tearful, uncontrollable laughter. "You are the man that believes in honesty!" he bellowed as they shook hands. Stunned, Steffens could hardly respond before Darrow laughed even harder at the crusading journalist from New York. Humiliated, Steffens retreated from the office, unable to imagine that Darrow, remarkably, would later become one of his closest, most reliable confidants.

Steffens recovered quickly from Darrow's outburst. He went directly to the Republican boss, U.S. Representative William Lorimer, who spoke almost respectfully of the reformers and the voters in Chicago while making little effort to hide his scorn for Steffens and his mission in the city. Steffens, who had expected to find embattled reformers struggling for recognition and hardened bosses in control of the city, was taken aback. What kind of boss was Lorimer? His theories of corruption proving pitifully unwarranted, Steffens turned to Chicago's leading reformer, Walter Fisher, whose explanations required Steffens to be, for the first time, a muckraker of good news.

Chicago was not a city with a halo. Gambling, prostitution, liquor deals, and police graft were commonplace, entrenched activities. "The New York Tenderloin," Steffens wrote, "was a model of order and virtue compared with the badly regulated, police-paid criminal lawlessness of the Chicago Loop and its spokes." But reformers, by narrowing their objectives, pursuing attainable goals, and having endless perseverance, slowly made headway, particularly in gaining control of the city council, which had been dominated for years by railway magnate Charles T. Yerkes until his own rapacity reached such appalling levels that he departed Chicago in 1899 as a social and political outcast. The reformers' refusal to be intimidated ultimately gained them a seat on the council. George Cole, a five-foot-tall rock of indignation nicknamed Old King Cole, ignored the wails of the city's elite as he named names, publicly and delightfully, outlining the indiscretions of each rogue on the council and overseeing a political rehabilitation of the city, ward by ward. When Cole's health failed, other reformers carried on his work with the same determination—and success.

Steffens acknowledged that the reformers had not failed, and wrote accordingly in his article "Chicago, Half Free and Fighting On," in the October 1903 *McClure's*. This startling piece of good news inspired other cities to examine more carefully the municipal efforts of, most ironically, Chicago.

The interest in Steffens's article on Chicago illustrated that readers, however cynical muckraking may have left them, still cared to hear as much about reform and the way forward as they did the ancient tale of graft. There was a market for stories on good government, so Steffens was instructed to seek out another.

He next settled on a city few would have looked to for ethical guidance: New York. Steffens, though, understood the political stage and actors in New York intimately—he had witnessed reformers get elected and conditions improve. His old friend Max Schmittberger, back on the police force, could point to the incessant complaints from the underworld as proof of the department's reformation. The new mayor, Seth Low, son of a wealthy China trader and former president of Columbia University, surrounded himself with government and business experts, not Tammany grafters, and these experts chose not to dismantle the whole system but to tinker with it so that public and private interests would be fairly served.

Or so they thought. It did not take Steffens long to understand two things: New York did have good government, and it was going down to defeat in the fall elections. A big problem was that Low, "pecuniarily honest," "conscientious and experienced and personally efficient," and whose administration had been "not only honest, but able, undeniably one of the best in the whole country," had, according to Steffens, a fatal personality flaw. "Mr. Low's is not a lovable character," he explained.

What Steffens observed was simply that people wanted a humane, personal, quid pro quo type of government, not good government. When the laws were fair and applied to all, everyone complained. The Tammany heelers resented their waning influence among judges and politicians wary of being targeted by the muckrakers or the authorities, while the poor were stung by an unyielding government no longer sympathetic to their hardship. Even some reformers, for reasons that left Steffens baffled, were lukewarm toward Low. People apparently preferred good government in the abstract, but bad government—the kind to which they were accustomed—in their real lives.

Steffens's November 1903 article was titled "New York: Good Government in Danger," and the fall elections went as he expected: Tammany ousted the reformers. The New York voters had brought back the good old days, scoundrels included.

8

THE SHAME OF THE CITIES

FINDING HIMSELF "ALL up in the air," his theories on corruption in tatters, Steffens retreated to Cos Cob to reshape his muckraking articles into a book, *The Shame of the Cities*, to be published by the McClure, Phillips Company. At one point convinced that he could provide a scientific explanation of corruption and maybe even a cure, Steffens now offered little analysis except to urge the public to compare leaders like Roosevelt and Folk to the grafters they had been returning to city halls for years. He struggled to find a new explanation for all he had observed. One conclusion he reached was that he had spent sufficient time with municipal governments. He would now turn his attention to the states, where the graft was more extensive and, maybe, he would yet discover the science in corruption.

Experienced at analyzing the moral failings of others, Steffens inevitably began to look inward and question his own ethics. How did he compare to those who either could not resist the temptation of evil or could not imagine themselves as deficient in any significant way? In the fall of 1903, a humiliating but minor incident involving an unintended slight by Ray Stannard Baker gave him pause. What struck Steffens was the realization that he was incapable of accusing himself. "With all my growing contempt for good people," he admitted, "I was one of them." He saw that reformers—"those law-abiding backbones of society"—supported change until it affected them personally, especially in their wallet. Then, suddenly, the change was "going too far." But Steffens had seen that no reform could get anywhere without going too far, without hurting the very people, including himself, who supported it until it actually took effect. "I was preferring the conscious crooks; and yet I was one of the righteous," he conceded. His painful confession, ironically, lifted a heavy burden from Steffens, for now he could be free to be "good" without the righteousness. He wrote with a certain pride, "I was never again mistaken for an honest man by a crook." Explaining their own misdeeds, political bosses and business leaders felt comfortable confiding in Steffens, he believed, because they saw him essentially as one of their own.

As 1903 closed, Steffens, still a young man at thirty-seven, had achieved fame that few journalists ever experience. *McClure's* subscriptions hovered in the gaudy four hundred thousand range. To readers impatient to learn who Steffens would "do" next, his name was synonymous with muckraking. Success bred success for him in other ways as well: National magazines such as *Collier's Weekly* (where Norman Hapgood was now the editor) and *Bookman* were publishing his work. *The Shame of the Cities*, including his articles on St. Louis, Minneapolis, Pittsburgh, Philadelphia, Chicago, and New York, had a ready audience. A London editor told him of the mark he had made in England and assured him of a prominent position if he wished to move. Even a cigar company joined the rush to praise Steffens by naming a cigar after him and featuring his face on the box. And Steffens was already looking beyond America to reporting on Mexico, China, Russia, and Europe, while a deal that would make him part owner and editor of a new muckraking magazine was under discussion. "Everything, everything goes well with me, so much so that somehow it scares me," he told his father. "If I wished money, I could turn from what I am doing and make it in piles. Offers of amazing rates are made to me for articles on any subject."

As Steffens's—and *McClure's*—success continued unabated, he clearly relished his "little triumphs," as he called them. "I enjoy them," he admitted to his father, "and I don't see why I shouldn't. The curses come, too, and I take them heartily. Why not the praise?"

He reveled in the success of his colleagues as well. "Of course you know what a crash your article [in *McClure's*] made among the lies and the self-righteousness of the hypocrites," he wrote to Baker. "The triumph was the greatest a man can have with the pen: you made both sides see themselves as they are. . . . I verily believe we all will accomplish something yet." He confided in his father, "If I am to have so much influence, I want to make it a power for the possible and worth while."

President Roosevelt had "come around," as Steffens termed it, obviously aware of the potential benefit Steffens might provide in Roosevelt's upcoming campaign. Steffens and McClure had visited Roosevelt in mid-October to discuss publishing a series of hagiographic articles highlighting his fight with capital and labor on behalf of the public. "He has asked me to write the most important things that are to be said next year. . . . It will make a sensation," he told his father. Against Steffens's wishes, McClure later squelched the idea of promoting Roosevelt, preferring to have Steffens focus on muckraking.

In December, Steffens informed his father that he would soon be back in Washington "for a short confab with the President" before starting a new assignment for *McClure's*. "The general title for the whole series [on the states] is 'Enemies of the Republic,' and I think they will make trouble for some damned big rascals who think they are above the danger mark. Roosevelt may be beaten, but he will not be beaten without some pretty stiff fighting, and, not personally for him, but for what he stands for, I expect to deal some of the heaviest blows."

In fact, presidential politics was a complex issue between McClure and Steffens. As circulation numbers remained strong, McClure began to fancy himself a king maker, announcing to a surprised Steffens before the start of the "Enemies of the Republic," "I believe we can do more toward making a President of the United States than any other twenty organs." Steffens wondered about the wisdom of such an effort and whether it might, in fact, serve to weaken the magazine at the height of its glory, but McClure was unfazed. "You can trust me absolutely," he replied. "I feel the utmost confidence in my editorial judgment and instincts. I do not believe that I will go wrong." He grew even bolder in a later conversation with Steffens, declaring that *McClure's* had "entered upon the greatest campaign that any periodical has ever undertaken. I think it will develop into both a political and business field that we hardly now suspect."

Yet, the man McClure truly wanted to see in the White House was not Roosevelt as much as Missouri's Joe Folk, and he gave Steffens clear instructions on his return to St. Louis: "Tell Folk from me that he is the candidate of McClure's Magazine at the present moment for President in 1908." The initial step in the process was installing Folk in the governor's office.

But Steffens, whose contradictory findings in the cities left him puzzled over the political process from city halls up to the White House, was less certain of the situation. He wrote to his father in January 1904, "Maybe I can do some campaigning this year for somebody, Folk (Dem.) and Roosevelt (Rep.). I'm pretty mixed on parties, but that's my point: that parties are damned frauds. 'Vote for the United States,' is my cry; 'neither for the better party nor for the best man.'" A couple of weeks later, referring to an upcoming visit with Roosevelt, he told his father, "I am not for individual men. I should take care to characterize Mr. Roosevelt exactly, as I know him, and he will not like that. No, if I can't get well up on top of my subject, I'll drop it."

Steffens's visit to Missouri in late 1903 intrigued him, largely because it allowed him the opportunity to test his latest notion: Cities would not change until states did. "The State was the unit of action for good or for evil," he now believed, and he did not suffer from a lack of choices regarding disreputable statehouses. His father offered California as a state "governed by a railroad," but Steffens viewed Missouri as the best place to test his latest hypothesis. Folk, running for governor, was eager for *McClure's* to expose the lawbreakers at the state level and offered to assist Steffens by again sharing his compelling evidence.

Steffens's own outline appeared in April 1904 as "Folk's Fight for Missouri," detailing the pervasiveness of graft that reflected the same political deal-making he had seen earlier in St. Louis. The corruption ran wide and deep: Railroad interests, trusts, and businesses paid state officials lavishly to assure the desired legal outcome. It was an operation of admirable efficiency, marred only by its all being illegal. Steffens portrayed it as a body ravaged by cancer:

> The stream of pollution branched off in the most unexpected directions and spread out in a network of veins and arteries so complex that hardly any part of the body politic seemed clear of it. It flowed out of the majority party into the minority; out of politics into vice and crime; out of business into politics, and back into business; from the boss, down through the police to the prostitute, and up through the practice of law into the courts; and the big throbbing arteries ran out through the country over the State to the Nation—and back.

To identify the source of the graft, Steffens approached legislators and "big boodlers" themselves, including William Ziegler. A baking-powder tycoon indicted for bribery in Missouri (and a heavy advertiser in *McClure's*), Ziegler nevertheless impressed Steffens as an "ideal citizen" in some aspects and did not scorn the aim of the muckrakers. Steffens saw Ziegler as "a generous, able, courageous, and rather humble-minded man" who was eager to tell Steffens his story, which turned out to be more damning than even Folk would have imagined. Ziegler had paid off everyone, from legislators and governors to chemical experts and newspapers, to promote his agenda. The strange thing about Ziegler, Steffens noted, was that once the tycoon had detailed his own corrupt behavior, he had the imagination, like Iz Durham, to be shocked. "I didn't want to do that," he said repeatedly. "I simply did not see it so. I fought each fight as it came up. . . . I certainly did not mean to change the government."

The shame spread as high as former presidents. Grover Cleveland, then living in retirement in Princeton, asked to see Steffens, who assumed that the former president was disturbed to read of the ongoing corruption emanating from deep within his own Democratic Party. But Cleveland said nothing of Democrats and did not even question Steffens's findings. He merely spoke of the stain left on democracy and on America, as well as his inability to imagine the extent of the greed. "I suppose," he told Steffens, "I'll never be able to see that bribery and corruption can be done by good men and that it is a process changing the very nature of our government. No, I cannot see that."

Steffens, too, wondered how such talent and intellect could tolerate what was an orgy of public looting. These men, Steffens believed, genuinely viewed America as a great country and themselves as its rightful leaders, but they were blind, willfully or otherwise, to their own collective sabotage of the democratic system. Steffens wrote, perhaps with Ziegler and Cleveland in mind, that it was "the inability of the minds of powerful men who knew the facts, who make the facts, to form them into a picture."

But in his article, Steffens was less charitable, describing in detail what was clearly a well-oiled machine and calling it "the System," a term of derision meant to place blame for the powerlessness of the individual in society. The affliction, he saw, was "a system, a regularly established custom of the country, by which our political leaders are hired, by bribery, by the license to loot, and by quiet moral support, to conduct the government of city, state, and nation, not for the common good, but for the special interests of private business." He concluded, simply enough, that "the highway of corruption is the 'road to success.'"

Others agreed. Even lifelong Republican William Allen White, from the distance of his memoir in the 1940s, had no difficulty recalling and describing almost blandly the seamless, insidious connection between money and power that Hanna-minded Republicans facilitated with such ease four decades earlier: "Interstate corporations, chiefly the railroads, were controlling legislatures which elected United States Senators who, in turn, had the appointment of federal judges, so that reforms in the legislature, the governor's chair, the Congress, or the White House, had a hard time of it. The courts took care of that." Jacob Riis wrote of the system in New York: "The world must be weary of it to the point of disgust. We fought it then; we fight it now. We shall have to fight it no one can tell how often or how long."

Regarding the Missouri election, Folk had told Steffens, "Nobody can realize the infinite ramifications of this thing." But one immediate result of Steffens's investigative work was that the people of Missouri made up their minds to act. Following a bruising campaign, with opposition newspapers ridiculing him as "Fungus Folk," "Holy Joe Joke," and "the Missouri Messiah," Folk and

McClure achieved their aim—Folk was elected governor in 1904, after which Folk sent a letter of gratitude to Steffens. But once he actually initiated reforms, necessarily upsetting some delicate egos in the process, Folk found the citizens turning on him. Still, Folk's efforts, in conjunction with Steffens's writing, alerted the Missouri public to the decay of their own government. Folk himself, seemingly a role model for Jimmy Stewart's Mr. Smith, later took the fight to Washington as an idealistic reform candidate for president in 1912 before losing badly and dropping off the political map.

By early 1904, Steffens's celebrity status as a muckraker was unrivaled. White compared Steffens's political investigative work to that of de Tocqueville, William Randolph Hearst had invited Steffens to dinner in New York, and Brand Whitlock later declared that Steffens's work had never been equaled. *Bookman* ran a very praiseworthy article by Riis on Steffens's influence. E. L. Godkin's son, Lawrence, told Steffens, "I am sorry that [my father] did not know you, for I am sure that there is no writing in the cause of political reform being done to-day which would have received from him as much commendation as yours." *The Shame of the Cities*, while selling only three thousand copies, nonetheless was "being reviewed everywhere" and made "quite a stir," as Steffens proudly noted. Charles Edward Russell, in the *Chicago Examiner*, called it the most important book of the year. Thrilled by the book but hopeful that Steffens would look upon socialism as the cure for graft, Upton Sinclair wrote such a persuasive—and lengthy—letter to him that Steffens tried to have it published as an article in *McClure's*.

In his introduction to the book, Steffens stated that his articles were written and published "with a purpose," that is, "to sound for the civic pride of an apparently shameless citizenship." Steffens wrote at length about the people's abandonment of their own civic responsibility—"the misgovernment of the American people is misgovernment by the American people"—and even dedicated the book to these citizens, "to the accused." He was unsparing in his collective critique of American hypocrisy. "The corruption that shocks us in public affairs we practice ourselves in our private concerns," he observed, adding that "there is no essential difference between the pull that gets your wife into society or for your book a favorable review, and that which gets a heeler into office, a thief out of jail, and a rich man's son on the board of directors of a corporation." Yet Steffens, having found graft entrenched in city after city, still saw a beacon of hope in his countrymen. "We Americans may have failed," he acknowledged. "We may be mercenary and selfish. Democracy with us may be impossible and corruption inevitable, but these articles, if they have proved nothing else, have demonstrated beyond doubt that we can stand the truth; that there is pride in the character of American citizenship; and that this pride may be a power in the land." He wrote of setting fire to the American pride, a pride that "may save us yet."

Steffens's gathering fame also gained him entrance to New York's Collectivist Society, also known as the "X" Club. Meeting once or twice a month in a private room at a midtown Italian restaurant, Steffens joined other liberals, including Norman Hapgood, Charles Edward Russell, and John Dewey, in lively discussions of politics, religion, literature, and science. It was a setting ideally suited for Steffens's personality—heated, intellectual debates with men at the height of their profession—and one that he would enthusiastically return to in various clubs and salons throughout his life.

For much of February and March, Steffens spent considerable time in New York and Washington, where he spoke at length with Roosevelt and Grover Cleveland about the president's ongoing debate with Wall Street. Steffens hoped to write "a big thing" on the dispute, but took pains to assure his father—and himself—that he would not be a puppet of the president. Still, Roosevelt trusted Steffens sufficiently to ask him about reliable local contacts throughout the states, and Steffens offered his father's name for California. Should the article not materialize, Steffens planned to spend the year covering the campaign or muckraking additional states, keeping a sharp eye on the privileged in either case.

Following Missouri, Steffens looked to the powerful men of Illinois to view their version of democracy. As he expected, the art of graft in Illinois was practiced on both sides of the aisle. And the corruption, as he knew from his previous investigation of Chicago, was another community effort: Merchants, contractors, health inspectors, police, and lawmakers all participated in the plunder. The gallant reformer in Illinois was the state's attorney for Cook County, Charles Deneen, a politician, Steffens noted, who was responsible for so many convictions of business grafters that there was a Bankers' Row of jail cells in Chicago. And the identical political process manifested itself in both states: Folk and Deneen, having cracked the reform whip in the big cities, carried their message statewide and went on to win governor's seats. Reformers, Steffens saw, actually could defeat the political machines, at least until the reforms touched the lives of the voters. Steffens's exposé of Illinois, "Chicago's Appeal to Illinois," appeared in the August 1904 issue.

More intriguing to Steffens was a challenge presented to him by an Illinois railroad president, himself an experienced grafter, to investigate the reformers with equal zeal. Not surprisingly, the president had a candidate in mind:

progressive Governor Robert La Follette of neighboring Wisconsin, a railroad adversary who spoke so strongly of democracy, his faith in the people, and his disgust of bosses that Wall Street "was drained dry," it was later said, in its effort to silence the relentless reformer. The railroad titan offered to generously assist Steffens in his attempt to muckrake La Follette.

The governor duly qualified as a unique and controversial figure: a Republican resented by Wall Street and Roosevelt together. Big business cursed him as a demagogue, a socialist, and a hypocrite, while many reformers themselves kept their distance from him. In fact, the *New York Times* published a growing rumor that Steffens had been sent on an investigative mission by Roosevelt himself to "get a true insight into the situation as regards Gov. La Follette and the Republican Party." And Steffens, in fact, was ready to be convinced that La Follette was the self-righteous fraud that his opponents portrayed him to be.

But the critics' proof, Steffens found, did not support their assault on La Follette. They hated the governor—there was no doubt of that. But their arguments against him only convinced Steffens that La Follette must have some sense about him. To Steffens, La Follette's moves "seemed fair, . . . his methods democratic, his purposes right but moderate, and his fighting strength and spirit hopeful and heroic." Not only had their tactics failed, but the wailing businessmen spurred Steffens on: He was eager to report "the story of a straight, able, fearless individual who was trying to achieve not merely good but representative government." The next step for Steffens was to meet the "little giant" of Wisconsin.

Steffens reached La Follette in Madison in late June. La Follette was pleased to see him, assuming that the muckraker was firmly on his side in the struggle for reform. Steffens, in fact, had supported the reformers in every article, but he nevertheless had no intention of being viewed as a strict partisan. An awkward family dinner ensued at the La Follette's home, where Steffens foolishly insulted La Follette's wife, Belle, to establish a lack of bias. (Belle later diplomatically described Steffens as "polite but reserved.") Steffens and La Follette nevertheless agreed to meet again, with the governor recounting the details, complimentary or otherwise, of his career, and Steffens assessing the information and writing the article unedited. The meeting was the start of a devoted friendship: In time, Steffens became nearly a beloved member of the La Follette family. Belle La Follette would write to Louis Brandeis in 1910, "The other day Robert [Jr.] said, 'Mother, I believe I like Mr. Brandeis the best of any one we know.' Then he qualified it—'Of course not better than Mr. Steffens but better than almost any one else.' And that is the way we all feel."

Steffens found La Follette a fascinating figure. Determined, idealistic, and filled with the patriotic faith of a midwesterner, La Follette was appalled when he encountered the scheming world of American democracy. In 1880, he began a public career in Wisconsin as a district attorney eager to confront the machine bosses and establish fairness in government, and he had the personality to do so. A short, solidly built man who used the perfect blend of persuasion, intimidation, and humility in his speeches to attract voters, La Follette was, as Steffens put it, "a dictator dictating democracy." La Follette acknowledged the demanding challenge of achieving economic democracy, but in an uplifting, encouraging way that drew people toward him. And the people themselves were always the focus of La Follette. Late in his life, he could still write, "I had then, and have had ever since, absolute confidence in the people." La Follette's "sincerity, his integrity, his complete devotion to his ideal, were indubitable," Steffens wrote. To many Americans yearning for reform, La Follette was the most compelling voice of the progressive movement at the turn of the century.

While Steffens's hopes for a scientific breakthrough remained decidedly unfulfilled, he sensed that the system would benefit significantly from radical reform advocates like La Follette. And as with Folk in Missouri, Steffens's muckraking in Wisconsin helped sway the voters. His article on La Follette's efforts, "Wisconsin: Representative Government Restored," appeared in the October 1904 issue of McClure's, and La Follette retained his governor's seat the following month. A grateful La Follette wrote to Steffens: "No one will ever measure up the full value of your share in this immediate result. It is very great," while Belle called it "a veritable bomb."

Far less impressed by the Wisconsin piece, however, was Roosevelt, sensing that the preponderance of national muckraking, not unlike Parkhurst's earlier evangelical efforts in New York, was beginning to have corrosive rather than cleansing effects. In his article, Steffens had spotlighted the role of Henry Payne, Roosevelt's controversial postmaster general and former chairman of the Republican State Central Committee in Wisconsin, in a Milwaukee public railway scam. Roosevelt, while not denying Payne's checkered past, was incensed nonetheless. "Poor Payne is sick either unto death or nigh unto death," he bristled in an October 2 letter to Lodge. "This attack on him in McClure's Magazine by Steffens was, I think, the immediate cause of breaking him down; and I am convinced that it is an infamously false attack." Payne, who had been in poor health for months, died that same month.

The rest of the nation did not share Roosevelt's indignation, and the October issue sold out quickly, helping McClure's remain competitive in the increasingly frantic world of muckraking. Still, sales of *McClure's*, while remaining steady at close to four hundred thousand, had fallen behind *Everybody's*, which had been riding a wave of popularity on the strength of Thomas Lawson's stunning "Frenzied Finance" series, an insider's revelations of financial malfeasance and ethical wrongdoing, most particularly among insurance companies and Standard Oil. Even with the masterful work of Steffens, Baker, and Tarbell, *McClure's* was challenged to satisfy the public demand during muckraking's peak years.

9

THE SHAME OF THE STATES

ROOSEVELT WAS ELECTED in his own right in 1904, handily defeating the respected but comparatively tame figure of Alton Parker. Taking no chances, Roosevelt had sought the support of conservatives by naming three of them— Elihu Root, Joseph Cannon, and Henry Cabot Lodge—to run the Republican Convention that year, assuring crucial votes from big business in November. The appointments were a less-than-encouraging sign for reformers, including Steffens, keeping a watchful eye on the president. In fact, Steffens's next exposé would strongly illustrate the ongoing need for reform but would find little favor with Roosevelt.

In the summer and fall, Steffens had been working on the story of Rhode Island, where revelations of statewide corruption, already common knowledge among the local population, were becoming a national story. Steffens had been in the state only briefly when he came upon "the best-established, most accepted, most shameless system" in his wide experience.

Each level of government played a key role in maintaining the illicit system. For example, Governor Lucius F. C. Garvin, a "fine old New England gentleman, the kind of man most New England gentlemen think they are," not only wielded no power but openly admitted it. Then there was General Charles Brayton, a blind veteran of the Civil War, who provided all necessary governance by controlling the state's affairs through his domination of the legislature and ensuring that the lawmaking body acted in the best interests of the businessmen who routinely came before him to plead their cases ("he had had himself admitted to the bar so that he could take fees instead of bribes," Steffens quipped). Finally, Nelson Aldrich, the Senate boss known for his staunch support of Standard Oil and Wall Street, was the overseer of the whole Rhode Island operation, a man whose artful skills as a political manipulator were admired—and feared—as much in the Senate as they were in Providence. It seemed perhaps fitting that Aldrich, a multimillionaire himself, was also the father-in-law of John D. Rockefeller Jr.

The Rhode Island graft was so extensive—and accepted—that Governor Garvin was moved to write a remarkable letter on the dilemma to the state's own general assembly in 1903, two years before Steffens arrived. After noting that bribery was a matter of "common knowledge" in the state, he pointed out the uncomfortable fact that "many Assemblymen occupy the seats they do by means of purchased votes" and that their denials "should not deceive any adult citizen of ordinary intelligence." Even General Brayton acknowledged the graft, but thought little of it: "The Democrats are just as bad, or would be if they had the money."

Steffens saw that approving Rhode Islanders, upholding their proud tradition of bribery, made effective use of the ballot box to sustain the practice. Their votes came quite inexpensively, as the governor openly conceded, and the money was well invested. One year in Little Compton, all seventy-eight voters studied the ballot and settled on the same candidate for state senate. A Democratic leader admitted to Steffens that as long as he paid the money, reelection was guaranteed. "My town is all right," he told Steffens. "The Republicans can come in there with more money than I have, and I still can hold it. Suppose they have enough to pay ten dollars a vote and I can give but three; I tell my fellows to go over and get the ten, then come to me and get my three; that makes thirteen, but I tell them to vote my way. And they do." The obvious conclusion Steffens reached was that the "good old American stock," the common man, had relinquished any civic responsibility in Rhode Island, and the men they elected were weaned on graft from the start of their careers, confirming Steffens's belief that older states had more, not less, corruption.

The larger point, Steffens perceived, was that the reassuring notion that men of means were immoral and stole elections but ordinary men were just and voted honestly (women, of course, were not yet even eligible to be bribed for votes) was a myth. "Wherever the farmers, wherever the common people are tempted to sell out," Steffens wrote in his autobiography, "they are found to be as corruptible as the better people, whether politicians, business men, aristocrats or church men." He observed that political corruption was not a matter of individual character but of pressure, and that most people would succumb if money, even modest amounts, appeared in their pockets. And it was pointless to blame only the flagrant profiteers. "There is no reform but reform," Steffens, concluded, "and reform begins at home—with all of us."

Relations between McClure and Steffens remained somewhat tense. After seeing a draft of Steffens's Rhode Island story, McClure, traveling once more in Europe, grew impatient: "Aldrich article is wrongly constructed & poorly worked out. It has so many faults that I cannot take them up," he wrote in another complaint to Phillips. "Steffens' articles must never be rushed," McClure went on. "I was amazed and frightened that after our experience with [the articles on Illinois and Wisconsin], it was proposed to rush this in. I don't want any of his articles printed until I am perfectly satisfied. His articles are far & away the most terrible stuff we can handle." McClure calmed down sufficiently to concede that Steffens's work was "necessarily full of dynamite," but he concluded that only Phillips, Tarbell, McClure himself, or "a few outsiders of great experience & wisdom" should be allowed to edit such inflammatory copy. Phillips carried out McClure's wishes and revised the story, titled "Rhode Island: A Corrupted People," which ran in the February 1905 issue.

The attack on Aldrich proved too much for Roosevelt as well, who told Steffens of his displeasure, which he later repeated in a pointed letter. While claiming to "know nothing" of the Rhode Island situation, the president, sensitive to any challenge of his personal power, declared that it was an "absurdity" to call Aldrich the "boss" of the country. Closer to the situation was a Rhode Island reformer, James Higgins, who wrote to Steffens the following year, "I believe the present reform and anti-boss sentiment of our state owes a great deal of its strength to your famous article in *McClure's*," a private expression of gratitude often displayed toward Steffens after one of his muckraking sweeps through a city or state. Indeed, Governor Garvin himself had sent Steffens letters of support.

Steffens still wondered if he could uncover a fraudulent reformer. Such a story would not only attract interest from readers but establish a sense of balance in his muckraking. La Follette had been a very false lead in that direction, but the resolutely ethical mayor of Cleveland, Tom Johnson, seemed a more likely candidate because, unlike many reformers, he had no financial worries. Steffens had passed through Ohio in the spring of 1902 for a closer look at the politics of the state and was thus well aware of Johnson's reputation. A controversial, unapologetic reformer, one worshipped by supporters and reviled by opponents, the Ohio man had made a fortune in street railways before entering politics on the outspoken side of the citizens. Johnson was high on a moral pedestal and, Steffens speculated, possibly poised for a crash. Also of interest to him in Ohio was the city of Cincinnati, where graft had been an integral part of the political system for years. In what would be his final article in the series on states, Steffens looked to Ohio to investigate leaders in both cities.

In truth, Steffens had hoped to be finished with cities. Other states and the federal government itself, he saw, had extensive corruption that could yield even more explosive revelations than the public had yet heard. But Cleveland's Mayor Johnson was a tempting target, so he launched his probe of the state along the shores of Lake Erie. The obvious assumption Steffens had to start with in Ohio was that one of the most proficient grafters in history, Mark Hanna, was the guiding force behind the state's entrenched system of fraud, and in fact Steffens was planning to highlight the power broker in the piece. But Hanna's death in February 1904, in the midst of Steffens's work on Ohio, caused McClure, already skittish over the reporter's aggressive style, to delay publication of the Ohio story indefinitely. In the article, Steffens addressed the matter directly. "We must begin with Marcus A. Hanna. He is dead. I don't believe in 'nothing but good of the dead'; I believe that true obituaries of our great men would do the living good. But I hoped to be able to tell about Ohio without saying much about Mr. Hanna. That is impossible."

Tom Johnson's life, unlike Hanna's, was an American rags-to-riches story until, Steffens noted, he "read a book." As a young boy in a poor family, his Southern parents ruined after the Civil War, Johnson went to work selling newspapers. With the aid of a sympathetic railroad conductor who provided the child with a monopoly on the papers delivered by train to his town, Johnson learned early the tremendous advantage to be gained by cornering a market. He remembered that lesson well on his remarkable path to becoming a millionaire. Johnson controlled the street railway business in several cities, including Cleveland, where his chief competitor was Hanna, who denounced Johnson as a "socialist-anarchist-nihilist."

Then came the turning point in Johnson's life—the influential book. Johnson was riding one day on a train between Cleveland and Indianapolis when a train boy offered him a copy of Henry George's *Social Problems*, a socialist view on how the wealthy easily improved their means while the poor found it difficult to maintain even their hardscrabble lives. Having more interest in profit making than in social inequity, Johnson waved the boy away. But a conductor urged him to reconsider, so Johnson, his faith in conductors still strong, agreed to read it, and he found himself so engrossed that he read almost without stopping. Eager to hear more of George's views, he went on to read *Progress and Poverty*.

Johnson found that he could not rebut the charges put forth by George. From his personal experience, he knew that a man determined to protect his millions could evade or safely violate any law. "I continued in my business with as much zest as ever," Johnson wrote, "but my point of view was no longer that of a man whose chief object in life is to get rich." George and Johnson went on to become great friends, and at George's urging, Johnson became a politician, entering the House of Representatives as an Ohio Democrat in 1892. Finding the House replete with state bosses, Johnson retreated to Cleveland in the hope that as mayor, his political vision could be implemented on a more manageable scale. In 1901, at the age of forty-six, Johnson became mayor.

Thus, Johnson was not to be the disingenuous reformer Steffens had imagined. Instead, the reporter saw Johnson just as he had seen Folk, La Follette, and, at times, Roosevelt: as an advocate for the average person—Johnson spoke out strongly, for example, in favor of women's suffrage—devoted to removing the bosses from the public's business. As Steffens pointed out, Johnson "was not merely a good rich man, like Seth Low, out to 'give' us good government." He was a convert "from plutocracy to democracy." Where the people were concerned, Johnson cared.

What dawned on Johnson as mayor was that *privilege* was the key that Steffens had sought for uncovering the source of corruption. All forms of privilege—special legislation, creative legal interpretations from judges, police willing to accept a bribe and demanding that their brethren follow suit—were necessary for the illicit system to function effectively. "It is privilege," he told Steffens, "that causes evil in the world, not wickedness, and not men." And focusing on the role of privilege did indeed guide much of Steffens's future muckraking.

Johnson tirelessly promoted his popular reform agenda in Cleveland while being accused of having "gone back on his class" by Hanna and other outraged opponents. "This was said," Steffens wrote, "by men who almost in the same breath would declare that reform was not a class struggle, that there was no such thing as class consciousness, no classes in America." City councilor Fred Howe, a Johnson reformer who was an expert on municipal government and later became one of Steffens's closest friends, recalled that Cleveland at the time "was an armed camp. . . . If any kind of cruelty, any kind of coercion, any kind of social, political, or financial power was left untried in those years to break the heart of Mr. Johnson, I do not know what or when it was."

Meanwhile, the people of Cleveland clearly appreciated what they saw in their devoted crusader against privilege, returning him to the mayor's office for four terms. Steffens would find no hint of scandal associated with Johnson. Instead, Steffens became a lifelong friend and often took advantage of Johnson's open house to enjoy many entertaining evenings of unlearning.

During his time in Cleveland, Steffens stopped by the city council office, where he first met Howe. Some who knew Steffens only from his sensational investigative articles undoubtedly imagined him to be a loud, unscrupulous, self-righteous publicity seeker. They were far off the mark, as, initially, was Howe himself:

> I pictured him big, blond, and fierce, a militant reformer, hating corruption. The man who appeared had soft eyes and a quiet voice. Something unusual in the cut of his clothes, a pointed beard, and flowing tie suggested an artist. He seemed not to be hating any one or anything. I thought there must be some mistake—my visitor must be someone else. But he brought a letter from Ida M. Tarbell, whom I had known since my boyhood days in Meadville. And acquaintance furnished me the astonishing discovery that Lincoln Steffens was an artist rather than a reformer.

And even though Steffens's muckraking of Johnson yielded nothing, Howe, who admired Johnson greatly, was impressed. "My estimate of muck-raking rose greatly from seeing him [Steffens] at work," he wrote. "He was exact, painstaking, unflinchingly accurate."

Steffens respected Howe's zeal for reform as well. A deeply thoughtful and well-educated lawyer—he had a PhD from Johns Hopkins—who found the practice of law too dull and restrictive for someone wanting to dramatically alter society, Howe entered politics on the side of the progressives and became a natural ally of Steffens, who later wrote of Howe, "I think he and I see things more alike than any other two human beings that I know of." Howe's activist wife, Marie, a former Unitarian minister, also earned Steffens's respect. The Howes and Steffens, not surprisingly, would remain close friends for the next thirty years.

From Cleveland, Steffens moved on to a strikingly different city, Cincinnati, which was ruled by Republican boss George Cox, a former saloon-keeper and councilman known for his honesty in apportioning the graft most equitably among both parties. A large, gruff man who ran the city from a small room above his saloon, Cox did not attempt to mask his grip on the city. He ordered his men to openly spy on Steffens, who found that everyone he approached suddenly suffered memory loss concerning matters of local government. Largely through a newspaper editor with copious files, Steffens was able to piece together the tale of corruption and to do it accurately, as Cox himself proudly admitted during conversations in which Steffens shrewdly encouraged his vanity.

With publication of the Ohio article postponed, Steffens considered the problem of privilege and formed a view that he later included in his autobiography. His words, despite his impressive credibility as a muckraker, could hardly have been embraced by any but the most cynical Americans: "The ideals of America are antiquated, dried up, contradictory; honesty and wealth, morality and success, individual achievement and respectability, privileges and democracy—these won't take us very far." Yet Steffens remained encouraged by the efforts of men like Tom Johnson and Bob La Follette, choosing to study the affliction of privilege and, always with science in mind, to search for a cure. A severe case was the state government in New Jersey, where Steffens planned to go next.

Steffens understood that the economic plundering of New Jersey had begun long before the twentieth century, tracing it all the way back to a land grab by Alexander Hamilton. By 1904, nearly two hundred of the nation's biggest trusts were chartered in New Jersey. Steffens concluded the first half of his stinging, minutely detailed exposure of New Jersey with a blanket admonishment: "Jersey shows, plainer than any other State or city, how we are all betraying one another, and that what we Americans lack is . . . representative government; not good government, not reforms, not privileges, not advantages over one another, but fair play all around, and, before the law, equality." His article "New Jersey: A Traitor State," appeared in the April and May 1905 issues of *McClure's*.

In the early days of his research in Ohio, Steffens had made the surprising discovery that he had a talent for public speaking, and there was a demand to hear him. His low voice, barely audible at times, and his inexperience had discouraged him from participating in public platforms, but as readers across the country devoured his articles and as *The Shame of the Cities* was about to appear in bookstores, Steffens was swamped by speaking invitations. A man rarely at a loss for words in private, Steffens performed well ("the evening seems to have made a sensation," he wrote to his father after one of his first talks in January 1904), and offers to speak, including a lectureship at the University of California–Berkeley, continued to arrive from across the country.

Steffens's article "Ohio: A Tale of Two Cities," finally appeared in the July 1905 issue of *McClure's*, creating a political firestorm. In late June, Roosevelt sent off a letter of more than one thousand words questioning conclusions Steffens reached on the basis of possibly untrue, or misrepresented, events. The president began, however, by noting that he was "especially interested" in Steffens's fawning portrayal of Tom Johnson, as Roosevelt had heard "the direct reverse" from Secretary of War Taft. He then stated his main objection: "I do wish that you would not repeat as true unfounded gossip of a malicious or semi-malicious character. When you do so you naturally impair the whole value of your article." He offered the example of a train conversation between Mark Hanna and Roosevelt that he found to be "a pure invention," aimed at putting the president "in an unattractive light." Steffens's assertion that Hanna had "created" McKinley and manipulated matters in his favor was equally misguided. "It is perfectly true that Hanna did an enormous amount in helping to secure McKinley's nomination," he wrote, "but it is absurd to speak as if this were the only, or even the chief, factor in McKinley's nomination. . . . I was the most powerful independent Republican in the district; yet the machine and I put together were beaten in the convention to nominate delegates, and we were beaten because, to my great astonishment, I found that there was a real popular sentiment for McKinley as against [Thomas] Reed—a sentiment neither bribed nor bought nor engendered in any fictitious fashion." Indicating his growing annoyance with the consequences of muckraking, he declared, "In my judgment, we suffer quite as much from exaggerated, hysterical, and untruthful or slanderous statements in the press as from any wrongdoing by businessmen or politicians." The president politely closed the letter with the offer that should Steffens care to continue the discussion, "I shall of course be glad to see you."

From Steffens's point of view, however, Roosevelt was at the moment the one who was unaware of the facts in Ohio, particularly in Cincinnati. The reporter feared that Roosevelt might unwittingly help Boss Cox by supporting the reelection of Governor Myron Herrick, a product of the Ohio Republican machine that had already sent McKinley to the White House and would do so again with Taft and Harding. Steffens alerted Roosevelt to the immediate plight of the Ohio voters. Cincinnati was ruled "absolutely" by Cox. "I never saw anything like it," was Steffens's assessment, stiff criticism indeed from a man who had seen powerful bosses. The voters of Ohio were "good Republicans," Steffens saw, who would be swayed by Roosevelt's words if he threw his support behind Herrick, the Republican machine's choice. Steffens's take on Herrick was that he was "not a bad man," meaning that he could do "dishonest things honestly." Of most importance, though, to Steffens was that Herrick was a machine pawn.

Not only did Herrick lose his reelection bid, but Cincinnati's reformers, who could scarcely imagine that the end of the Cox reign was possible, apparently were ill prepared to replace the old boss. After defeating the machine in Cincinnati, they gave back the mayor's office in the very next election. Boss Cox resumed power, and almost like an addict, Cincinnati returned to its old habit of graft. And Cox, who had challenged Steffens to name a better machine in the whole country, was a great example, Steffens saw, of the power of privilege.

No stranger himself to privilege, Roosevelt in 1905 was mired in a controversy over sizable campaign contributions given by insurance companies to the Republican Party the previous year. Hopeful that the president might set an example in purifying the political process, Steffens wrote to him on September 24, asking him to consider returning donations to corporations involved in national legislation and to encourage small, individual contributions instead: "Mr. President, if you did what I suggest, you would make the millions feel that it was their Government, as it is, and that you and your administration were beholden to the many, not to the few."

Steffens must have struck a nerve, as four days later, Roosevelt protested vigorously in a letter even lengthier than his previous correspondence regarding Ohio. Indignant, chiding Steffens for his superficial and unfair analysis, he insisted, "Most emphatically at the present time I feel beholden to the many more than to the few; and I feel beholden both to the many and to the few only in the sense that it is my duty to do my level best both for the many and for the few." Regarding the motives of those who bestowed large amounts of cash on his campaign—$150,000 came in from J. P. Morgan, the same amount from insurance companies, $125,000 from Standard Oil, $100,000 from steel magnate Henry Clay Frick, and more, for a grand total of $2.2 million—Roosevelt, apparently with a straight face, declared, "I do not know of a single corporation which contributed last year which now desires legislation. . . . But if they contributed under the impression that thereby they would secure any improper favor, or immunity for wrongdoing, all I can say is that they entirely misread me. . . . I think that an immense proportion of whatever was given, was given simply with the idea that I and the forces I represented stood for the good of the country." He added with characteristic bluster, "It is nonsense for me to express any regret, for the fault is purely theirs and not mine." He allowed that only four contributors, to his knowledge, had requested favors, and three of those were for signed photographs. "In short, my dear Steffens," he wrote assuredly, "I think that if you will reflect a little you will come to the conclusion that in the first place your premises are wrong, and that in the next place for me to follow such a line as you indicate would be simply silly."

Steffens was particularly well informed on the scandalous behavior of the life insurance firms, as he had been spending considerable time that summer investigating the operations of the increasingly notorious Equitable Life

Assurance Society. "It's hard and long and forever turning up new phases," he wrote to his father on August 5 from Cos Cob. "But I stick to it." And for good reason—among some giant insurance looters, Equitable stood as one of the worst offenders, having accumulated billions in assets and established ties with the biggest tycoons in that age of excess while gouging customers with high premiums and low dividends.

More titillating was the brutal struggle for control of the company, about to pass into the hands of the founder's son, James Hazen Hyde, who in his twenties was making $100,000 a year serving as vice president and on the boards of forty-eight other companies tied to Equitable while apparently doing little other than enjoying his wealth. In January 1905, he gained a measure of well-earned notoriety by hosting a French-themed party at the Sherry Hotel in New York, where guests attended in Louis XIV attire, the interior of the hotel featured live trees to resemble a French orchard, and the whole affair cost $200,000. It was with Hyde in mind that Steffens wrote, "Business with them is almost holy, holier than religion which it has hurt; holier than education which it is hurting, holier than the Government of the United States which they regard as a mere instrument of business, holier than even the character of the American nation." Indeed, George Perkins, an Equitable executive, went beyond even Steffens's appraisal, declaring from on high that "our profession requires the same zeal, the same enthusiasm, the same earnest purpose that must be born in a man if he succeeds as a minister of the Gospel."

Upon examining the insurance corruption, Steffens was fascinated by "the likeness of the business graft in a business to the so-called political graft in our cities and States." Regarding the life insurance companies, he observed that they presented themselves as the "sacred trusts of widows and orphans," not unlike the benevolent hand extended by bosses and machines when soliciting votes, all of it corrupt. Steffens then asked the next logical question: "If a public, non-profit, trust business is as bad as the life insurance, what must be the condition of some of the private businesses that are run only for profits?"

Yet, *McClure's* grinding assault on corruption and seemingly on the American way of life inevitably began to exhaust readers. *McClure's* received letters inquiring why its writers were not capable of producing any complimentary articles on the American system. The dissenters were hardly a majority, but Sam McClure acknowledged their objections by telling Steffens to accentuate the positive in his next story. In his earlier article on Ohio, Steffens had observed, "Cheerful idiots who think themselves optimists often ask me why I don't find something good now and then, somebody to praise. . . . I notice, however, that while my evil reports seldom cause resentment, the moment I begin to speak well either of men or of conditions, my mail roars with rage and burns with sarcasm or sorrow. Then I am a fool or a liar." Steffens nevertheless chose to cooperate with McClure for the moment, dropping the life insurance story in favor of a few light pieces on Greenwich, Connecticut—articles that McClure recognized were only wasting Steffens's talent.

Promising to maintain a positive spin while still muckraking, Steffens received McClure's reluctant blessing to continue focusing on the democratic debacle of New Jersey. Two individuals in this populous state—Jersey City mayor Mark Fagan and state legislator Everett Colby—intrigued him by their efforts in resisting the plentiful graft.

An idealistic, devout Irish Catholic undertaker, Mark Fagan—"first in my heart," Steffens declared—rose to be the "New Idea" Republican mayor of Jersey City. In his article on Fagan, "A Servant of God and the People" (published in January 1906), Steffens, using his human-interest style that readers found so compelling, highlighted Fagan's impoverished childhood, during which he learned to battle by defending his sidewalk turf while selling newspapers. As a progressive Republican mayor, mild-mannered but persistent, Fagan found himself confronting the machines that oversaw the railroad terminal, the docks, and the trolleys. Fagan pressed the issue vigorously in Trenton, ultimately losing but not before exposing the ugly workings of the system. Fagan served the people of Jersey City as mayor for five years before election losses in 1907 and 1909 ended his political reign. Sometime later, Steffens met him at the Metropolitan Museum of Art, where Steffens asked about his disappearance. "The church," Fagan replied, explaining that the bosses had instructed church leaders to undermine his popularity because Fagan, a Catholic himself, had supported a strong public school system. He quietly finished his career back in the funeral business.

Of an entirely different lineage was Everett Colby. This son of a railroad baron followed his father's example and money to become a force not in railroads but in statewide Republican politics. Steffens again focused on his upbringing, wryly noting the handicap of a wealthy start: "There is a constantly growing class of rich men's sons who can throw as much strength, nerve and concentrated intelligence into sport as their fathers put into the game of life; but, having been brought up only to play, they can't work—'can't,' not 'won't.' They don't know how; they don't know anything but games, and they cannot learn. Everett Colby was headed straight for this fate."

Colby did, in fact, end up on the playground at Brown, where he continued to compete athletically as captain of the football team. But he opened his mind as well by focusing on debate, and he graduated with a dream of a political career. Recognizing the value of his handsome face and hefty wallet, the Republican state machine envisioned him as an effective public speaker who could cast the party in a respectable light and invigorate fund-raising efforts. After initially serving the machine dutifully, Colby grew appalled by the extent of the graft and left to join the reform efforts of Mayor Fagan, a fight Steffens vividly portrayed in his article "The Gentleman from Essex" in the February 1906 issue. Representing Essex County in the state assembly and state senate for a decade, Colby readily acknowledged Steffens's role in his political success, thanking him in a letter for "stirring up the people of the whole country and especially in stinging the people of New Jersey."

Steffens's muckraking efforts had been richly rewarded in the 1905 elections. In cities, including New York, Philadelphia, and Cleveland, and states throughout the East, grafters were turned out of office by angry voters. La Follette himself moved up to the U.S. Senate. Few doubted that Steffens played an instrumental role in the shift. "Ohio recognizes your message, Cincinnati responds to it, Cleveland vindicates it, we all appreciate it" was the cable from Ohio, signed by Tom Johnson, Fred Howe, and city solicitor Newton Baker (later mayor of Cleveland and secretary of war for President Wilson). Another note arrived from Harlan Stone, then a young law professor at Columbia University: "I think you more than any other one man may take credit for the result of the elections wherever 'boss or no boss rule' was the issue." Clearly, muckraking, with Steffens in the lead, was the impetus for much of the public outrage.

Of the sweeping electoral changes, among the most satisfying to Steffens was the rise of an old friend, novelist Brand Whitlock, to the mayor's office in Toledo. Entering the political realm several years earlier, Whitlock had served as secretary to Toledo's legendary mayor, Sam "Golden Rule" Jones, who had infuriated the businessmen responsible for his election in 1897 by deciding that Christianity, not the Republican boss, would be his political guide. A successful businessman himself, Jones noted that he gained his nickname because while most employers pocketed eight of every ten dollars of profit produced by their workers, Jones kept only seven. Quietly quoting Jesus and Walt Whitman at every turn, Mayor Jones listened patiently to vagrants in his office, visited jails to hear out the prisoners, and forgave prostitutes while chastising American society for preying on the poor and the helpless. Newspapers ridiculed him, churches denounced him, and the Chamber of Commerce repudiated him. Even Steffens once complained to Whitlock, "Why, that man's program will take a thousand years!" But the citizens of Toledo were more than satisfied with their mayor's unorthodox style: Golden Rule Jones was reelected twice—"Everyone is against me but the people"—and died in office.

Whitlock, encouraged by Tom Johnson and Steffens, agreed to enter the mayoral race. With the memory of Jones as his political guide, Whitlock, a Republican, embraced reform with a human face beyond even what Steffens thought possible, inspiring him to call Whitlock "the most advanced leader in American politics today." Steffens perhaps also felt a kinship with Whitlock because, as Howe observed, Whitlock was "primarily an artist, like Steffens. His political life was an accident." It was also successful, as Whitlock emerged victorious in the mayoral race.

Growing stronger was Steffens's belief that reform was not a road to permanent change but a limitation, a guarantee that any adjustment would be short-lived and would only delay genuine progress. His understanding of this fatal flaw of reform laid the foundation of what later became a veritable axiom for Steffens: that total rebellion against government may be the sole mechanism to achieving true democracy. Indeed, in a January 1906 talk at the Majestic Theatre to the West Side YMCA, he asserted, "Graft is not sporadic, but in the strictest truth the organization of graft is the Government." It was a belief that would later bring Steffens infamy he could not have imagined.

Despite Roosevelt's growing irritability toward muckraking in 1905, Steffens was of no mind to lose complete faith in the president as an arbiter of change, and Roosevelt still sought his company. After appeals from Steffens, Roosevelt, never one to squander time, agreed to meet him during his midday shave, a habit that Roosevelt apparently preferred, meeting Ray Stannard Baker and others in the same way. The ebullient Roosevelt (one journalist compared his monologues to Niagara Falls) would shower him with opinions once a subject was broached, leaving Steffens little chance to respond, so the reporter prepared carefully for each talk.

What Steffens remained most eager to attempt was an exposé of the federal government, an idea that he could hardly expect the nation's chief executive to support unconditionally. With a face full of shaving cream, the president one day heard Steffens plead his case for an investigation into the honesty of the government and whether the politicians in Washington reserved their sincerity for the public or for Wall Street and the railroads. Steffens proposed to go through the White House and Congress in search of honest government, but he felt that he needed Roosevelt's backing to confer sufficient legitimacy on the effort.

As he finished up his shave and hurried out the door, Roosevelt characteristically gave Steffens a verbal thrashing for being entirely too narrow-minded about what constituted effective political leadership and expecting a level of honesty that was beyond the reach of mortal men, especially politicians. Yet, Steffens was encouraged, for he understood that Roosevelt did much of his thinking through his vocal chords—shouting, preaching, laughing, ridiculing, lecturing, explaining, and producing additional utterances until he had formed an opinion he could live with. "He was not," Steffens wrote, "an intellectual; he was a man of action. He read everything, he knew a lot, and he had what he knew always handy. He could talk well on many subjects. But he often did not know why he did what he did, gave reasons instead of his actual motives for conduct." And his barrage against Steffens confirmed to the muckraker that his idea of examining the nation's government was at least gaining consideration in the president's mind.

Steffens maintained his pressure on the president, often reporting to Roosevelt on his findings of how difficult it was for democracy to flourish anywhere. Roosevelt "reacted like a democrat and like an historian," Steffens wrote, "but he was slow to move himself." On one occasion, Roosevelt insisted that he was doing his part by supporting a bill regulating railroads. Steffens begged to differ, pointing out that Roosevelt would compromise because that was his preferred method of governing. And after Roosevelt showed him a letter from the president of the Pennsylvania Railroad asking for the bill to be softened a bit, Roosevelt admitted that he probably would accede to some of the changes.

Finally, in January 1906, after the McClure Newspaper Syndicate commissioned Steffens to write a series of articles examining the national government, Roosevelt relented. Addressing a note to "any officer or employee of the government," Roosevelt wrote, "Please tell Mr. Lincoln Steffens anything whatever about the running of the government that you know (not incompatible with the public interests) and provided only that you tell him the truth—no matter what it may be—I will see that you are not hurt."

The, result, however, was not vintage Steffens. Newspaper editors, including those at the *Boston Globe*, the *Washington Post*, and the *New York Times*, found his stories unilluminating, lacking the gripping style of exposure they associated with Steffens's best work. John Phillips complained as well, upset that Steffens had substituted his own generic critique of corruption for that of the specific details anticipated by readers.

Roosevelt himself had strong doubts regarding Steffens's investigations. In comments on congressional behavior that could not have surprised the experienced Steffens, Roosevelt asserted, "In Congress there is more harm to be apprehended from the narrow, rancorous partisan, from the uncouth, unlicked demagogue, and from the mere puzzle-minded obstructionist, than from the man who is improperly sensitive to the influence of great corporations. The latter exists, too, and I have had to fight him; but I have had more often to fight the three former." Defending his own legislative approach while taking a shot at a rival Republican with whom his relations would further deteriorate, Roosevelt bragged, "I have come a great deal nearer getting what I wanted than, for instance, Governor La Follette in Wisconsin came to getting what he wanted in the matter of legislation and appointments."

Following the successful example of *The Shame of the Cities*, Steffens collected his stories on state graft in a book titled *The Struggle for Self-Government*, giving readers another look at the theft of democracy in Missouri, Illinois, Wisconsin, Rhode Island, Ohio, and New Jersey. Publication of the book was delayed by McClure for a year, to 1906, following the death of Mark Hanna, whose nefarious schemes were detailed by Steffens in the Ohio piece. The public was by then well aware of the corruption in nearly every corner of public and private business, and many people had already read Steffens's pieces in magazine form. Consequently, people did not rush to purchase the book, which sold under a thousand copies. Nor did the book receive more than the damnation of faint praise from the *New York Times*. While Steffens was acknowledged to be "among the first of the muckrakers," he was also labeled the "Comstock of politics" whose book "is a dramatic narration of facts which should cause Americans to blush with shame and disgust, but it is nothing more."

10

GOODBYE TO ALL THAT

BY 1906, *McCLURE's*—AND muckraking—was at the height of its popularity. Subscriptions and advertising remained strong, and *McClure's* staff of journalist-superstars was unrivalled. Ida Tarbell had been pursuing the story of John D. Rockefeller and his oil, Ray Stannard Baker was reporting on labor, and Steffens had muckraked numerous city and state governments, while the mail remained largely supportive. And the writers themselves, each publicly celebrated, displayed remarkable restraint and mutual admiration. Baker, for example, found the works of Tarbell and Steffens a "constant inspiration" during those triumphant days. "Never shall I forget the memorable editorial discussions and conferences we had," he recalled.

Yet, muckraking increasingly was gaining notoriety, particularly among power brokers, as a threat to the well-being of America, and was about to suffer a blistering attack from the president himself. The change of heart from President Roosevelt toward muckrakers, whose tedious fact-finding and explosive revelations had helped promote his own assault on the monopolies and trusts, displayed both his swagger and his hypocrisy—or, some suggested, his political wisdom.

While muckraking had its benefits, the tumult was not all to the good, Roosevelt felt, and he acted accordingly. On October 4, 1905, less than two weeks after scolding Steffens on his simplistic notion of returning campaign contributions, Roosevelt met with Steffens and McClure to address the rationale of muckraking. In a letter written later the same day to McClure, Roosevelt lamented, "It is an unfortunate thing to encourage people to believe that all crimes are connected with business, and that the crime of graft is the only crime. I wish very much that you could have articles showing up the hideous iniquity of which mobs are guilty, the wrongs of the violence by the poor as well as the wrongs of corruption by the rich." More specifically, he noted, "I think Steffens ought to put more sky in his landscape."

Others, while decidedly a minority, agreed regarding Steffens. The *Sacramento Record Union*, for example, was quite harsh in its condemnation: "The kind of work that Mr. Steffens has been doing appears to have the inevitable effect of destroying that fair spirit of human good will and optimism which is the surest and best inspiration of every sound and wholesome mind." The mayor of Chicago dismissed Steffens's whirlwind investigative approach by commenting that the impressions the reporter gleaned were no different from those of someone looking out the window of a fast-moving train.

In the March 1906 issue of *Cosmopolitan*, William Randolph Hearst, labeled "the most potent single influence for evil we have in our life" by Roosevelt, increased the president's ire toward the new journalism by publishing David Graham Phillips's stunning first installment of "Treason of the Senate," as muckrakers, including Steffens, increasingly set their sights on the biggest target of all, Washington, D.C. (John Chamberlain observed that Phillips, despite hitting a raw nerve in America, "was not the best man in the world for the job— Steffens . . . would have turned out far more reliable stuff.")

In a private speech before the Gridiron Club in Washington, Roosevelt, while failing to specify any names, was sharply critical of the attacks upon men in public life. In a meeting with Roosevelt the next day, Steffens quipped, "Well, you have put an end to all these journalistic investigations that have made you." Roosevelt, already backtracking, assured Steffens that he did not mean the reporter, insisting that the objection was mainly to Phillips's attack on "poor old Chauncey Depew." The president was referring to the New York senator who had campaigned for Abraham Lincoln, been general counsel for Vanderbilt's railroad holdings, and survived Phillips's criticism to live another twenty-two years before passing away at the age of ninety-three. Three days after the speech, in a letter to New York attorney George William Alger, Roosevelt was more forthcoming, expressing his "indignation" over "the indiscriminate and untruthful abuse gathered in magazines like the *Cosmopolitan* and aimed at every prominent man in politics or industry, whether he does well or ill." The president, as Steffens noted, also undoubtedly felt "the satiety of the public with muckraking."

The following month, Roosevelt expanded on his previous remarks at the Gridiron Club, delivering a much-anticipated public broadside that erased any doubt as to his assessment of muckraking. At the ceremony marking the laying of the cornerstone of the House of Representatives office building on April

14, 1906, Roosevelt, appearing before senators, congressmen, cabinet members, Supreme Court justices, and foreign dignitaries, denounced muckrakers for finding all of the dirt and none of the gold, mindful of the man with the rake in Bunyan's *Pilgrim's Progress*. The president warned that the man "who never thinks or speaks or writes save of his feats with the muckrake, speedily becomes, not a help to society, not an incitement to good, but one of the most potent forces of evil." The president did not mince words:

> The liar is no whit better than the thief, and if his mendacity takes the form of slander, he may be worse than most thieves. . . . The wild preachers of unrest and discontent, the wild agitators against the existing order, the men who act crookedly, whether because of sinister design or from mere puzzle-headedness, the men who preach destruction without proposing any substitute for what they intend to destroy, or who propose a substitute which would be far worse than the existing evils—all these men are the most dangerous opponents of real reform.

Like any astute politician, Roosevelt made sure to plant his feet on both sides of the issue. He questioned the "amassing of enormous fortunes" while declaring, "No amount of charity in spending such fortunes in any way compensates for misconduct in making them," an ambiguous stance that he would maintain for the rest of his presidency.

Tarbell noted that Roosevelt should have aimed his barb at the robber barons, who were the true muckrakers of great wealth. Still, by demonizing the nameless writers (he probably had foremost in mind Upton Sinclair—*The Jungle* had been serialized and published in book form in 1906—and Phillips) as radicals who create a "morbid and vicious public sentiment," Roosevelt used his bully pulpit to cast *muckraker* as a pejorative term. Journalist George Creel recalled that Roosevelt, "in speech after speech, shaming those that he once praised," repeatedly sounded the alarm against reform run amok.

McClure, who had at times found Steffens ready to believe the worst in anyone, tended to agree with the president, not that McClure, as his staffers knew too well, worried about consistency in his reasoning any more than Roosevelt did. Earlier he had insisted to Baker that "all of our stories have been stories of achievement—as of how Folk achieved in St. Louis—and the result has been enormous encouragement for right minded people in other cities."

Steffens, in Roosevelt's view, was not the only objectionable reporter at *McClure's*. After Tarbell explained to the president that they were only following the facts, Roosevelt exploded, "I don't object to the facts, but you and Baker are not *practical*." Quite upset himself by Roosevelt's abrupt change of heart toward the muckrakers, Baker wrote to Roosevelt of the importance of presenting the truth to the American people, "the letting in of light and air." Roosevelt replied bluntly, "I want to 'let in light and air,' but I do not want to let in sewer gas."

Steffens, in Cleveland, assured a reporter that Roosevelt was not aiming at him. The president's message had been misunderstood, said Steffens, adding that the only point he himself disagreed with was Roosevelt's refusal to acknowledge that the essence of the problem was the system itself, which "rewards an honest man with a mere living and a crook with all the magnificence of our magnificent modern life." Still, if he took Roosevelt at his word, Steffens was being as disingenuous as the president.

Regardless, Steffens, like Tarbell and Baker, had lost some respect for Roosevelt as a bulwark against the corrupt elite. Steffens, however, did maintain his contact and friendship with the president without shying away from their differences. In a lengthy letter to Roosevelt the following year, Steffens asserted, "This is a point on which you, Mr. President, and I have never agreed. You seem to me always to have been looking down for the muck, I am looking upward to—an American Democracy. You ask men in office to be honest, I ask them to serve the public." Roosevelt, in the meantime, maintained his balancing act by publicly criticizing the radical reformers while continuing to tweak the system with modest proposals such as an inheritance tax.

Coinciding with Roosevelt's swelling impatience over muckraking, rumblings of discontent rattled the offices of *McClure's*. Beneath a veneer of profitability and loyalty, an inner turmoil had been festering for years at the magazine. "It was miraculous," staffer Ellery Sedgwick recalled, "how in that incandescent office the forces of attraction and repulsion were kept so nearly in balance; that with all the subterranean rumblings and occasional little spurts of flame, the explosion was so long postponed." The situation grew increasingly untenable until McClure ultimately faced a full-scale revolt. "Nothing fails like success," was the flippant explanation offered by Steffens for what became a momentous mass defection of editors from *McClure's* in 1906.

To a casual observer, matters at the magazine had not appeared so volatile. McClure was a very generous man who took an active interest in the work of his writers and truly wished to satisfy them. A formal, buttoned-down approach in the office was never his style, and he was well known for the generous salaries he paid (two thousand dollars per article, for Steffens) and the time—years, if necessary—he allowed his writers to pursue and report a story well.

McClure's, however, was disintegrating on several fronts. Roosevelt's outrage was just one of several serious challenges the magazine faced. The early muckraking years had been rewarding, but never quite as profitable as McClure might have expected, and the magazine, despite solid circulation numbers, actually was losing money by 1906. While people were buying the magazine, the cost of providing such in-depth, national stories grew prohibitive.

Tarbell, Baker, and Steffens were sufficiently involved in their reporting that the work alone had been a strong reason for remaining, not that the accompanying prestige and money were less important factors. Inevitably, though, McClure's irascible nature in the office often made management-staff relations more volcanic than collegial. In fairness to McClure, his untamed energy had done much to establish the success of the magazine. But his relations with his staff, never idyllic, started unraveling at an early stage. Brimming with praise for an idea or an article one moment, McClure would quickly disparage it in favor of something else. He was absent from the office for long periods, often abroad in Europe. At times he seemed oblivious to the perspectives of the highly talented writers he himself had assembled. He frequently edited articles, especially those of Steffens, to the point of frayed nerves on all sides. And McClure's blatant extramarital affairs, including a heated romance with a tall, young, dark-haired woman named Florence Wilkinson, whose own pathetic writing McClure allowed to be published in the magazine, were a serious distraction. Tarbell was particularly incensed, calling McClure "a Mormon." Even to Steffens, who was on assignment much of the time, the growing chaos was obvious: "I realized that those who had to live and work every day with [McClure] were learning to hate him."

Steffens never grew to hate his boss, but McClure's latest grandiose business venture, which involved starting a book publishing company, a life insurance firm, and even his own bank seemed ludicrous to Steffens and the other staffers who had endured his odd ways for years. McClure envisioned such vast profits that he would establish private charities, including settlement houses for street people. His writers foresaw bankruptcy.

The ultimate blow for Steffens occurred when McClure proceeded with what Steffens saw as a foolhardy, hypocritical scheme of starting a new magazine, to be called *McClure's Journal*, with millions of dollars that McClure had secured from the same big banks and insurance companies that Steffens and his colleagues had been exposing as threats to democracy. In fact, at McClure's insistence, Steffens had spent months working on the Equitable insurance story only to be told by McClure that it would be handled by a younger writer. But the incident involved more than life insurance. After meeting with the family of one of the insurance executives, McClure chastised Steffens for tormenting the man nearly to the point of death with his investigations. "Political influence right in my own office!" Steffens recalled. "I resisted. I would not be pulled off like a heeler by my boss." When the executive did, in fact, die, Steffens felt chagrined. Still, he stood by his views. "No man and no employer buys my mind, when he hires my pen, and I shall not sell my liberty for any price," he told his father.

As the situation at the magazine deteriorated, McClure sensed collapse and began training new editors, including Willa Cather, whose collection of stories, *The Troll Garden*, had been published the previous year by McClure. The young writer would go on to become the new managing editor at the muckraking magazine even though she saw social reform articles as the antithesis of literature. *McClure's* was a house divided, and it would not stand much longer.

By March 24, a total rupture was imminent. Phillips and Tarbell confronted McClure in his office, demanding that McClure give up ownership of the magazine. On the other side of the door, Steffens and others, listening intently, could hear the shouts of accusations and denials until McClure, defeated for the moment, departed the room in tears.

The fight was essentially over financial control of the magazine. One night, John Phillips, who had been McClure's business partner for twenty-five years, visited Steffens and proposed that they team up with Tarbell, Baker, and others to buy out McClure. The plan called for several members, including Tarbell and Steffens, to each contribute fifty thousand dollars toward the acquisition. Although Steffens himself had been offered a salary of twenty thousand by William Randolph Hearst and half the profits to start a magazine, and the other *McClure's* writers were earning exceptional salaries, they were not nearly secure enough financially to take on such responsibility without worry. Still, the option of remaining as they were at *McClure's* had lost all appeal.

But the magazine had been the driving force in McClure's life, and he was not going to submit voluntarily to such a draconian proposal, so confusion reigned for several more weeks. After bitter wrangling and recriminations, with rumors of the chaos abounding throughout the publishing world, the final split came in early May 1906. Phillips, Tarbell, managing editor Albert Boyden, and others, unable to convince McClure to sell, simply resigned, with Steffens and Baker, away on assignment, in agreement. No doubt Baker summed up the basic feeling of everyone when he wrote to his father about the situation: "I feel that I should remain with my associates, who are not only my friends, but who have contributed largely to whatever success I have obtained." McClure, livid, announced that he would remain editor for as long as he lived and denied that the exodus of his staff had any connection to Roosevelt's recent shots at muckraking.

In an awkward predicament was Steffens, who had agreed to write a series of articles for *McClure's* on a dynamic reformer, Judge Ben Lindsey of Denver. It was an obligation he honored under strained circumstances, traveling to Denver in the spring of 1906 at the height of the dispute. (McClure referred to Steffens in those final days as "our friend, the enemy.") Relations were so acrimonious that some of the departing writers believed—and may have hoped—that McClure would not survive such a devastating loss. Steffens, while no avid admirer of McClure, did not doubt that he would nevertheless rise again. "He has lost his staff," Steffens wrote to his father, "but he is organizing a new one, and he will succeed with it." And with Cather managing a group of eager new writers, McClure did precisely that. Even Steffens did not leave entirely, contributing articles to *McClure's* as late as 1916.

In June 1906, the former *McClure's* writers collectively purchased the *American Illustrated Magazine*, formerly *Leslie's*, bringing with them journalist William Allen White, who by then had transformed himself into a "bleeding reformer," and satirist Finley Peter Dunne. Phillips served as president, and Steffens vice president, and the group recast the magazine with a focus on arts, science, education, and politics. It was what *McClure's*, minus McClure, probably would have become. Securing money for the transaction, however, was a challenge. The group agreed to pay $460,000 for the magazine, with more than a third of it needed almost immediately. So Steffens and the others, imbued with the spirit of their new adventure, ambitiously turned their attention to fundraising, Steffens contributing $10,000 of his own money.

The transition was not seamless. Skirmishes with McClure continued, as did the need for money. Finding adequate time to actually research and write the articles for the first few issues of the *American* was a challenge for everyone, most notably Steffens. With some urgency, Boyden asked Baker for a submission that he could publish, reminding him that all they had at the moment was whatever Steffens would send, "and he is not the surest proposition in the world as you know," Boyden added.

An early publicity announcement showed that the writers remained idealistic, however busy they were, and were determined not to be miscast by Roosevelt or anyone else as vengeful, narrow-minded cynics: "We shall not only make this new *American Magazine* interesting and important in a public way, but we shall

make it the most stirring and delightful monthly book of fiction, humor, sentiment, and joyous reading that is anywhere published."

The high-minded aims of the magazine were genuinely felt by its staff. "We
really believed in human beings: we really believed in democratic relationships,"
Baker insisted, having been personally unsettled by the wave of criticism, particularly Roosevelt's, that swept over the ugly facts uncovered by the reformers.
"We 'muckraked' not because we hated our world but because we loved it.
We were not hopeless, we were not cynical, we were not bitter." Steffens concurred: "Every man in this whole country who is for better things is with us,"
he wrote to his father, "and it is hoped that we can make a publication which
will strengthen the hands of all such men and all good movements." Throughout
Steffens's life, his father's words held special significance for him, despite the
distance between their personal philosophies. Steffens sought his advice and
imagined the pride his father would take in watching the birth and growth of a
magazine that "in a way, is a grandchild of yours," he wrote.

The new child at first was "a feast of fun" for Steffens as he worked alongside like-minded reformers toward a common goal. Under the name of David
Grayson, Baker was submitting a series of warm country sketches based on his
own childhood in rural Wisconsin and his present family life amid a small, close-
knit New York town that he cherished. Steffens loved the pieces, sending Baker
a long note admitting his own guilt mixed with deep respect for Baker's new
tack. "I was ashamed because I never had realized that there was in you such
a sense of beauty, so much fine, philosophic wisdom and, most wonderful of
all,—serenity," he wrote, adding that Baker's view was "an extraordinary thing.
It did me good; it reminded me of art and right living and the love of man for
man." Steffens's words moved Baker so deeply that he carried the letter in his
coat pocket. "It was certainly one of the finest appreciations that ever I received
in my life," he later admitted.

Another fellow staffer who intrigued Steffens was Dunne, already a national
literary institution and a close friend of Roosevelt, Mark Twain, and Norman
Hapgood. His wickedly pointed humor found its best expression in the satiric,
astute remarks of Irish barkeeper Martin J. Dooley, whose cutting dialect was
practically the voice of Chicago, if not America, at the turn of the century. From
behind the bar at the Archey Road saloon, Mr. Dooley served up drinks and
endless commentary on whatever event of the day in Chicago, Washington, or
elsewhere had defied all logic or legality, often both. His loyal customer, Mr.
Hennessy, faithfully lent him the only ear he needed. Dunne was a wealthy man
by the time Steffens met him.

But as much as the words of Mr. Dooley captivated America, what Steffens and others at the *American* found most curious about Dunne was that he made every possible effort to avoid actually having to write. "He could not make himself write," Steffens observed. "I never knew a writer who made such a labor of writing; he seemed to hate it; he certainly ran away from it whenever he could." When Dunne was thinking out a Dooley story, progress seemed a miracle. "He would talk about it from this view and the other and still another angle for days, at dinner, at lunch; and you could hardly stand it or stop him," Steffens recalled. But Dunne's keen eye for hypocrisy established him as a mainstay among the talented group.

Much of Steffens's own time was taken up by a controversial profile he was writing on the nation's foremost "man of mystery," William Randolph Hearst. Hearst did seem an appropriate subject for a muckraker, especially since he was a congressman in the process of frightening New York's political establishment by considering a run for governor as the candidate of his own party. "Hearst's nomination drives all decent-thinking men to our side," Roosevelt commented to Henry Cabot Lodge, "but he has an enormous popularity among ignorant and unthinking people." (Roosevelt's fears proved unfounded with the election of Charles Evan Hughes, the only Republican to win a statewide office in that year of intense muckraking.) An immensely wealthy publisher who competed with Joseph Pulitzer in promoting scandal, and one whose own private behavior seemed to embrace immorality, Hearst made certain that his newspapers—"yellow rags," critics called them—featured the sensational and the shocking, in words and pictures, that no decent person would dare look upon, his detractors charged.

But after some research, Steffens saw that his article on Hearst would disappoint other *American* staffers. By now he had met enough intelligent grafters and simple-minded reformers that he treaded cautiously with Hearst, an approach that nearly caused a *McClure's*-like rupture at the magazine. Dunne, in particular, was quite familiar with Arthur Brisbane, Hearst's notorious public relations operative, and wanted to see Steffens expose the controversial publisher as Steffens had done for so many previous bosses. The satirist considered the self-absorbed Hearst largely a creation of Brisbane and was therefore disgusted when Steffens refused to reveal the truth. Ironically, Dunne himself had never jumped on the muckraking bandwagon. Mr. Dooley once observed, "We come home at night an' find that th' dure has been left open an' a few mosquitoes or life-insurance prisidints have got in, an' we say: 'This is turr'ble. We must get rid iv these here pests.' An' we take an axe to thim."

The article became a paragraph-by-paragraph struggle among the editors, notably Phillips, and led to an office fracas bearing out Tarbell's admission to Dunne that "we are pretty brutal and skeptical with one another." Even Steffens's friends were at a loss over his motivation for such work, suspecting that Hearst's minions, notably Brisbane, had led him astray. In the end, only Tarbell's moderate voice quieted the noise and allowed Steffens to get on with his writing.

Steffens, however, maintained his cautious style. He spoke to Hearst at length, over five interviews, including a train ride from Chicago to New York, using the same patient, probing, almost empathetic approach that had become his trademark. Hearst called him the most effective interviewer he had faced. What he said convinced Steffens that Hearst had a more perceptive and agile mind than others were willing to concede. In fact, he wrote later, Hearst "is so far ahead of his staffs that they can hardly see him." Steffens addressed the stereotype of Hearst and found it somewhat wanting: "Some people who do not know him call him cruel; they see the ruthlessness of an absolute egotism in his eyes. There is egotism, and it is ruthless; indeed, there is something of the insolence of his class in it. But it isn't mere self-assertion. His is the unconscious egotism of an absolute self-sufficiency."

And while Steffens's article did acknowledge the shadowy side of Hearst's intensely private life, years later, in his autobiography, he revisited his portrait almost apologetically. Steffens remembered the enigmatic publisher as "a great man, able, self-dependent, self-educated (though he had been to Harvard) and clear-headed; he had no moral illusions; he saw straight as far as he saw, and he saw pretty far, further than I did." Moreover, Steffens pointed out, Hearst's own revulsion toward the domination of insiders in the present political system led him to advocate positions that would severely curtail the benefits of privilege. Hearst's chief fault, Steffens felt, was that he paid too little attention to morality, although he understood that to Hearst, only hard, economic morality could permanently and effectively change society.

Steffens's article, "Hearst, the Man of Mystery," appeared in the November 1906 issue of the *American*. Roosevelt summed up the sentiments of disappointed Hearst detractors in a letter to Taft: "[Steffens] has recently written an article on Hearst which, tho faintly condemning him, is in reality an endorsement of him."

Over the summer, Steffens, enjoying a lifestyle befitting one of the country's leading journalists, moved with Josephine and her mother into an eighteenth-century farmhouse on the waterfront of well-to-do Riverside, Connecticut, just across the harbor from Cos Cob. The new home, named Little Point, became a refuge for Steffens over the next few years, where he could sail, write, and entertain at his leisure. For Josephine, whose time was increasingly spent caring for her aging mother, Little Point was a pleasant environment but another reminder of the unforeseen marital compact in which she acquiesced, featuring a part-time husband and a comfortable home financed by his personal success and, for her part, only a generous inheritance of twenty-five thousand dollars from her father.

Apart from his work on the *American*, Steffens was involved in a high-minded effort to fight special interest lobbies preying on Congress. A magazine, *Success*, already having published a number of influential muckraking articles, lent its support to the People's Lobby, a group of prominent men whose aim was to give the public a voice and oversight role in the actions of Congress. On September 18, 1906, the *New York Times* headlined the news:

a people's lobby to watch congress
Twain, Steffens, Mitchell, and Others in a New Plan.
WILL SHOW UP ALL SECRETS
And Keep the Records of Good and Bad Legislators—President
Roosevelt's Friends Behind It All.

The lobby's governing board featured not only Steffens, Twain, and United Mine Workers president John Mitchell but also the noted attorney Frank Heney, soon to be a close friend of Steffens's, and William Allen White, among others. The group pledged to be nonpartisan and beyond taint. "We can guarantee to the citizens of this country," *Success* declared in an editorial, "that there will not be a man on the Governing Committee who would for an instant consider a proposition to sell out the People's Lobby." And while the board members had already made a financial contribution to the cause, it was duly noted that additional donations of "more than a dollar" would be welcome.

Ironically, Mark Sullivan, who so recently at *McClure's* had found little to admire in Steffens, was elected president of the lobby. With a newsletter for subscribers and regular space in the pages of *Success*, the group showed it would be anything but a docile watchdog of Congress. The government's two most powerful bosses, House Speaker Joseph "Uncle Joe" Cannon and Rhode Island's Senator Aldrich, were prime targets and for good reason, as Steffens had pointed out in an article earlier that year: "The Congress stands, like a common council, for business. The Congress represents honestly what the State legislatures represent corruptly—business. Speaker Cannon is proud of it; Senator Aldrich admits it; nobody denies it." The pair came under such public and internal pressure that by 1911, Cannon, a staunch conservative known as "the czar," had been stripped of his leadership role and Aldrich had resigned altogether, leading to significant reforms in the selection process for House committee members and the direct elections of U.S. senators.

With the Hearst episode and a fall lecture series behind him, Steffens prepared for a special journey to California. The trip would offer Steffens an unusual opportunity to move beyond the machine politics of the East and examine a government run by workers. San Francisco was a rough-and-tumble labor city far removed from the polished sophistication of East Coast graft. Steffens wanted to learn if a young labor government would be free of the entrenched corruption that plagued the older states.

More importantly, California, with all of its natural splendor, was home to Steffens, the place where he had privately longed to retire one day with Josephine. Unfortunately for Steffens, the subject was of no interest to Josephine, who was comfortably settled in Little Point and loathed the Golden State. She had heard Westerners rave about its stunning beauty and—to an Easterner—almost unimaginable weather, yet she had not the slightest desire to be any closer to the Pacific. California was no vision of paradise for Josephine.

The only possibility of convincing her, Steffens foresaw, was to present the journey as a kind of business trip—round trip, of course—and hope that nature would fare better than Steffens's entreaties. No amount of enthusiasm from him would persuade her as quickly as a few hours of California sunshine. At least, that was Steffens's "California theory."

The plan began well enough when Josephine grudgingly agreed to go along on the Western tour, which was largely aimed at locating the colorful attorney Frank Heney, a reformer and a fighter out West "against every evil he saw," Steffens wrote. With markedly differing outlooks, Steffens and Josephine departed Little Point in January 1907.

The first stop was Denver, where Steffens caught up with several old friends, including Ben Lindsey, who had been the subject of Steffens's article "Ben B. Lindsey, the Just Judge," which had appeared in the October–December issues of *McClure's*. As judge of the Juvenile Court of Denver, Lindsey had been an influential voice of change, largely responsible for establishing a more humane system of handling juvenile offenders. His approach received national attention while inflaming his opponents, particularly those supporting child labor, to the point that Lindsey received not just vitriolic attacks but also death threats.

Journalist George Creel, working in Denver and a friend of Lindsey and Steffens, recounted the viciousness aimed at the judge. "All of the 'reformers' of that earlier day—Folk of Missouri, Tom Johnson and Brand Whitlock of Ohio, Francis Heney of California, La Follette of Wisconsin—were made to run a gantlet of abuse and defamation, but not one was ever called upon to undergo greater persecution than Ben Lindsey," Creel wrote. "As if grinding poverty were not enough—he lived in a half basement that a small salary might be poured back into his work—enemies pursued him until the end with tireless malignity. Not even Francis of Assisi was more pure of life, and yet they accused him of vilest immoralities."

Steffens admired Lindsey to such an extent that their relationship became another example of the blurred line Steffens drew between his personal preferences and professional responsibilities. Ten thousand copies of his *McClure's* article were ordered by Lindsey for promotional use in his ill-advised independent run for governor in Colorado, which split the state's progressive vote. Although Lindsey lost badly, his friendship with Steffens remained strong.

After their stay in Colorado, Steffens and Josephine next journeyed to Arizona. There, Josephine found herself enraptured by the exotic landscapes and wide horizons that spread across the desert. But Arizona was just a prelude to the astonishing vistas of New Mexico. "I saw my wife gasp at its purple mountains," Steffens recalled, pleased that the Southwest was casting its spell. Day after day of endless sunshine, with not even a hint of rain, had to leave a deep impression on any Easterner, he assumed. And they had not even reached the California border yet.

Steffens's "California theory" worked perfectly until Josephine and he actually entered the state, staying at the Scripps ranch, when Steffens's faith in nature failed him. Clouds rolled in almost immediately before a drizzle became a downpour, leading to widespread flooding. Torrential rains followed them from Southern California to San Francisco, where Steffens fell ill. Josephine, her old doubts of the West revived, demanded to leave, so they caught a train to Portland, where they found—more rain. Then Josephine herself became sick before the final, genuinely tragic blow came in April: a telegram warning Josephine to come home immediately. Her father was dying.

She departed as quickly as possible, to no avail. Her father passed away the day after she left Oregon, and with him died Steffens's California theory. Weeks passed before Steffens and Josephine spoke of the West again, almost as if the trip had not happened. "Nobody could tell us about sunny California," Steffens lamented.

Again, Steffens and Josephine were apart, another bitter reminder to Josephine of her entrapment in a flawed relationship. She remained devoted to Steffens, serving as his secretary and helping to write some of his speeches, and may have even still loved him in a sentimental way, but her outrage over the diminution of her own life both professionally and, increasingly, personally, simmered. In a December letter to the lawyer in charge of their German affairs, she did not try to hide her discontent: "My husband has become famous, but at a high price. He is practically never at home. He is constantly traveling and then writing. . . . I expect him for Christmas. A few days at home, and then away he goes again."

With Josephine in Connecticut, Steffens remained in Portland to pursue a new scandal. Timber speculators, upholding a long tradition of land fraud in the West, had seized hundreds of thousands of acres across the Northwest, causing Roosevelt to assign Heney to the investigation. Steffens, in Oregon to do a series of articles for the *American* on Heney's work, arrived after the fact, and the two became fast friends. Heney had already prosecuted the case, exposing lumber companies, railroads, and government officials, including a U.S. senator. For his own purposes, Steffens methodically pressed Heney, witnesses, and other parties to assemble the facts of the case.

One of his chief informants was Charles J. "C. J." Reed, a former jury commissioner and the father of a rambunctious boy, John. The younger Reed would later befriend Steffens and bedevil the American government. Reed had been brought in by Heney as a U.S. marshall to replace his uncooperative predecessor and provided Steffens with an inside view of the scandal. Some years later at a Portland club, he reminisced with Steffens of "the crowd that got the timber and tried to get me." Reed pointed to a table and said, "There, at the head of the table, that's my place. That's where I sat. That's where I stood them off, for fun for years, and then for months in deadly earnest." While Reed somewhat overstated the opposition he faced, Steffens himself met local hostility when, the following year, the *Portland Oregonian* expressed the need "to get rid of literary buzzards like Steffens."

The facts that Reed and others supplied to Steffens came as no surprise. The main culprits were the timber companies and state and federal officials who for years had rigged timber grants and public land sales on a vast scale. When noted investigator William Burns entered the fray, an array of power brokers attempted to derail the work of Heney and Burns. As the scandal reached into Congress and federal courts and other authorities, President Roosevelt was compelled to transfer judges, remove U.S. attorneys, and appoint marshalls before a fair trial could be held. A Republican senator, Charles Fulton, who complained to Roosevelt that Heney seemed intent not merely on investigating the crimes but on destroying the party, received a pointed response from the president: "Mr. Heney has uncovered such a dreadful state of affairs in Oregon that I would not be justified in refusing to back him in his efforts to bring the offenders to justice. Mr. Heney cannot hurt the Republican party, and your wrath should be reserved not for him but for those Republicans who have betrayed the party by betraying the public service and the cause of decent government." Dozens of the chief betrayers were indicted, including most of the state's congressmen.

At the same time, more graft was being uncovered in San Francisco, bringing Steffens, Heney, and Burns to California. San Francisco had its own boss, Abe Ruef, who bore little resemblance to the city bosses on the East Coast. A well-educated Jew, fluent in several languages, Ruef rose to power by gaining control of a labor party of union workers on his way to dominating city hall. Relentlessly stalking him was a crusading reformer, a self-made, firmly idealistic newspaper editor named Fremont Older, ten years older than Steffens and the man who "started it all," Steffens believed. A tall, strong Wisconsin farm boy, Older moved to California on his own as a teenager and survived by working as a printer across the state. After he settled into the newspaper business in San Francisco, he publicly denounced the grafters and aimed to help establish an ethical city government.

But Boss Ruef's new labor administration, unlike its Eastern counterparts, was not accustomed to "the license and the easy money" of politics. "They had more power and more money," Steffens wrote, "than they had ever dreamed of having, and the effect was not to give them that 'sense of responsibility' which is supposed to turn radicals into conservatives. . . . This Labor government, went off, like a lot of college students, on a joy ride, a grafting drunk." San Francisco was a fascinating story that Steffens was eager to pursue.

Tensions had always been high between Older, the managing editor of the *San Francisco Bulletin*, and Ruef, but the friction heated up considerably after the 1901 mayoral election, in which Eugene Schmitz, with a strong boost from Ruef, emerged victorious. Older sent Schmitz a note urging him to treat the office with respect, meaning, to avoid Ruef. Schmitz replied that he and Ruef were friends and would remain so. "This was the beginning," Older wrote, "of the struggle that led into every cross-section of San Francisco life; into the depths of the underworld; to attempted murder; to dynamiting and assassination—the struggle that involved some of the biggest men in the business world, and wrecked them." Steffens observed that "nobody was ever secure" in San Francisco politics: "Ruef the boss cheated Schmitz, Schmitz cheated Ruef; and they both cheated the supervisors, who cheated them."

Following Schmitz's election, graft throughout the city intensified, not all at once, but, as Older observed, "the times were ripening for it." Although Older relentlessly targeted the mayor and Ruef up to the next election in 1905, voters overwhelmingly chose another four years of graft. Incensed, Older headed to Washington, D.C.: He wanted Heney to come to San Francisco to prosecute the mayor. Older met with Roosevelt and explained the situation, only to be told that while he sympathized, Roosevelt himself needed the services of Heney at the moment, a predictable response, given the Oregon debacle and Roosevelt's unstinting admiration for Heney, "a close and intimate advisor."

Back in San Francisco, Older later turned for help to Rudolph Spreckels, the young president of the First National Bank and son of the notorious sugar magnate, Claus Spreckels, who, as Steffens delicately termed it, headed "a family of individuals." Rudolph Spreckels agreed to help finance the effort to oust Schmitz. Idealistic, scrupulously honest, but a supremely liberal and opinionated millionaire, Spreckels "had not learned any illusions to lose," Steffens wrote, and he shared Older's obsession to rid the city of graft, contributing $100,000 to the cause. Working together, they enjoyed initial success in 1906, when Heney, looking at his hometown, which had been devastated by the recent earthquake and tragic fires and which was riddled more than ever by graft, decided to return and investigate Ruef's illicit operation—for free. Burns agreed to join him. And Steffens, preparing some articles on San Francisco for the *American*, participated in their strategic discussions, his observations often making a difficult case even more complex. He pointed out, for example, that while Ruef undoubtedly was involved in bribery and other illegal activities, he was not the sole or possibly even the main instigator. Certainly, he was willingly accepting payoffs while offering bribes across the city, but not with his own money; others, probably local businessmen otherwise looked upon as community benefactors, were providing the necessary funds to facilitate the corruption.

The plot thickened on a daily basis. To ruin Older, Ruef had saloon keepers pull their ads from the *Bulletin* and went as far as to smash the windows of the offices and break the arms of the paper carriers. It was not long before a grand jury, beyond the reach of Ruef, was convened, and in the fall of 1906, Ruef was indicted for extortion. But as Older knew, they had barely begun to comprehend the extent of the corruption.

The diligent work of Heney and Burns, along with Older's zealous reporting in the *Bulletin*, effectively curtailed Ruef's ability to run the city. Ruef loyalists, threatened with jail and personal ruin, began confessing. As Steffens had suggested, the network of graft was vast. Ruef, Schmitz, and the intimidating figure of Patrick Calhoun—president of the powerful United Railroads, grandson of John C. Calhoun, and a local hero to rich and poor alike—were in charge of the fraud.

Bribery played its natural role in the scandal. Ruef had accepted a $200,000 bribe from Calhoun in return for a lucrative trolley franchise. Calhoun had tried to buy off Spreckels as well, only to be refused in an attempt that Steffens characterized with his trademark humor. "Patrick Calhoun offered Rudolph Spreckels a bribe," Steffens wrote. "Let me hasten to add that business men may not call it bribery; such as Mr. Calhoun would call his proposition to Mr. Spreckels 'business'; and it was 'business.' But one of the evidences that have gone to persuade me that the ethics of American politics is higher than the ethics of business, is that this typical piece of 'business' would be called bribery and corruption in politics, even by the low-down politicians themselves. They might take the bribe, but they would take it knowing that it was a bribe."

The trials, however, plainly showed the challenge Older faced, one that Steffens could have predicted. Half the city cheered him for his pursuit of the criminals, while the other half, particularly the well-off who had benefited so extensively from the old system, shunned him, calling him a hack for Spreckels and a persecutor of the city's leaders. And Older was not alone. When the members of the exclusive Pacific Union Club, including influential and graft-laden civic leaders, understood that Heney intended to push the investigation as hard as possible, they turned their backs on Heney after pointedly telling him not to bring Steffens to the club anymore. Older, Heney, and the prosecution nevertheless persisted in their work. Mayor Schmitz was dragged back from a European trip, tried, and found guilty of bribery. Ruef confessed his part in May 1907 and would go to trial. Older reveled in the victory. "Ruef Squeals Like a Cornered Rat," screamed a headline in the *Bulletin*.

But as Steffens had pointed out, Older knew that Ruef and Schmitz were just highly paid front men doing someone else's bidding, in this case, Calhoun's. The ruthless railroad tycoon paid some thugs to kidnap and kill Older, a plot that almost succeeded. The situation grew even more bizarre during the retrial of Ruef, when a hired gun of Calhoun's walked up behind Heney in the courtroom on November 13, 1908, and shot him in the head, nearly killing him. Heney's replacement was the dynamic Hiram Johnson, whose courtroom theatrics finally helped clinch the case and sent him on his progressive way to the California governor's office and, later, the U.S. Senate.

Steffens came in for some praise from Chester Rowell, the reform editor of the *Fresno Morning Republican*, who applauded him for his insight and influence on Heney. Yet, in pursuing a scandal that made national headlines, the graft prosecution in San Francisco produced little change. Schmitz was convicted and later released on a technicality, while Calhoun was exonerated by a jury—and a city—weary of rebuilding itself from the ashes and hearing disgraceful revelations, day after day, of how far the city had sunk politically. Only Ruef, whose long run of good fortune had ended, was punished. After breaking down in tears on the witness stand, he ended up in San Quentin, with a sentence of fourteen years. It was this legal but blatantly unjust resolution to a scandal involving scores of guilty individuals that sent Older along with Steffens on a remarkable path to forgiveness.

Steffens had seen such outcomes before. None of the truly powerful suffered much more than a bit of nervousness during the case. Steffens, though, remained far less interested in the names of the guilty parties than in the *what*—what was it about the system that produced such contempt for democracy and fairness, and how could it be cured? After many talks with Steffens during the case, Older himself, who had put his own life in danger only to see the flow of graft barely interrupted, began to question the validity of the present legal system and his own fiery views as well. He was particularly disturbed over why a bright, talented college man like Ruef, who had graduated from the University of California with high honors at the age of eighteen, would enter the system and choose to focus all his intellect and energy on cheating the public. Was Ruef, Older asked himself, worse than or even as bad as the respectable men of wealth, Calhoun being a prime example, who benefitted so handsomely through replaceable pawns such as Ruef, but who never themselves feared passing an hour in prison?

Soon, Older's mind had changed completely. "I was fifty years old," he later wrote, "when Steffens woke me up to the realities of life, and it was by his guidance that I finally dragged myself out of the 'make-believe' world that I had lived in all my life. Steffens made me face life as it is."

Older had to reconsider his own long-held moral certainties. His diligent pursuit of Ruef, he saw, had missed the mark. Reflecting Steffens's influence, Older wrote in his memoir, "Ruef did not make those conditions. It was we, the people, who had made them. . . . Other men, equally guilty, were walking abroad in the light of day, enjoying friends, success, popularity. We had not altered the conditions in the least. . . . It came to me that I should not have directed my rage against one man, human like myself, but that I should have directed it against the forces that made him what he was."

Deciding that mercy was his best recourse, Older went often to see Ruef in prison and fought for his parole, which did not come until Ruef had been imprisoned for ten years and which cost Older many of his friends, although not Steffens. Steffens's own growing belief in the Golden Rule, and forgiveness, would get an even louder rebuke several years later in the political furnace of Los Angeles during the notorious McNamara murder trial.

For Steffens, one of the most enlightening parts of the case involved a conversation with William F. Herrin, the chief attorney for the powerful Southern Pacific Railroad (known simply as SP to Californians, who understood that the railroad essentially controlled their government) and the state boss of both parties. More influential than Ruef or Calhoun, Herrin easily could have been a target in San Francisco's prosecution of graft, but the investigation exhausted itself before reaching the upper echelons of power.

During the trial, however, Herrin surprised Steffens with an invitation to talk. Herrin did not choose to speak of San Francisco, though. He started with Oregon and his own role in the timber affair before the topic changed to Steffens's growing area of expertise—how, from the grafters' side, the system actually functioned.

Herrin explained to Steffens the illicit operations in detail—how he, the railroad boss, became de facto overseer of all political deals in California. He started with a fund, sought contributions from other businesses hoping to benefit from legislative decisions, and paid for party conventions, delegates' expenses, and campaign funds. It was a costly machine to operate and one, Steffens was surprised to learn, that often struggled for sufficient cash in spite of the millions of dollars passing through: "That moment was the first time I realized the effort required to make the world go wrong."

Older and his team, Steffens saw, had temporarily staggered the political machine in San Francisco, but more than that would have required a much deeper probe. The result was no fundamental reform in the city. When Steffens put forth the idea that punishment might actually be part of the problem—that the criminals, who after all had taken money but not lives, should be spared prison and allowed to bare the system from top to bottom so that genuine, lasting reform could actually occur—even liberals and progressives wondered if Steffens were suffering from muckraking fatigue. Of more practical concern to the *American*, however, was that Steffens did produce a series of articles based on his West Coast investigations, including admiring profiles of Burns, Spreckels, and Oregon reformer William S. U'Ren, that were published in 1907–1908.

At the height of the San Francisco scandal, Steffens was working both coasts in his investigations, but had given up hope in his efforts at muckraking the federal government back in Washington. Having a friend in the White House was not the advantage Steffens had anticipated: The permission granted by Roosevelt the previous year for federal employees to confide in Steffens had proved to be of little value. But given Roosevelt's open antipathy toward the sweeping, accusatory nature of muckraking and his admonition to federal employees to refrain from spreading gossip, Steffens could hardly have been surprised that those serving under the president would resist his overtures.

His lengthy March 7 letter to Roosevelt was a somewhat rambling mix of congratulatory, humble, and gently scolding remarks. He noted his inability to obtain more than perfunctory responses: "It seems to me that too many of your Federal officials are like [Senator Gilbert] Hitchcock. They think their information is for the President and not for the press and the people. They want to conduct in private their investigations and report the result in their dull, unreadable reports, or develop them in the slow course of criminal procedure."

He challenged Roosevelt to confront the crisis of corruption at the federal level: "What I am after is the cause and the purpose and the methods by which our government, city, state, and federal, is made to represent not the common, but the special interests; the reason why it is so hard to do right in the United States; the secret of the power which makes it necessary for you, Mr. President, to *fight* to give us a 'square deal'. . . . And I am going to find out."

Responding sternly to Roosevelt's request that Steffens turn over any information he found on government malfeasance, Steffens asserted, "I cannot do that. There is a principle involved there: the freedom of the press. I think I am a careful, conscientious, responsible reporter. Certainly I work hard to get my statements not only correct, but just. But I must report to my readers, the public, and not anyone else." Careful then to repair any damage, he nevertheless almost mischievously inserted Roosevelt's own derisive term for Steffens and his ilk: "Fighting dishonesty as you are, you are doing more than all the rest of us so-called muckrakers put together." He concluded by apologizing for the length of the letter and hoping that the president would take it "in the spirit in which I write it."

His spirit undoubtedly was sincere, but the changes Steffens was by then seeking bordered on socialism and would have been politically unacceptable for any president, even a reformer like Roosevelt. Indeed, in his response, the president further reined in Steffens by amending his own initial note of permission, limiting Steffens's search to officials in the executive branch. "It is not my business to be the means of circulating stories about members of the Senate and House," he declared. "If any Senator or Congressman does anything crooked and it comes within my power or duty to get at him, I certainly will get at him . . . but this is an entirely different matter from circulating stories on the truth or falsity of which I have no power to pass." He closed the letter by asking Steffens to see him when the reporter returned home.

Not that Roosevelt, increasingly impatient with what he viewed as the merciless probing of public figures, regretted Steffens's difficulties. When the president read of some critical comments directed at Supreme Court Justice William Moody, a Roosevelt appointee, he was unsure as to whether Steffens was responsible, but pointedly wrote to Steffens in November:

> You and I do not agree—and I suppose from our standpoints cannot agree—about writing on matters like this. You recollect writing me last year that what I called 'gossip' you regarded as particularly valuable for your purposes. I think that the difficulty is that writing on your method you often make a most admirable impressionist picture, which expresses in a general way needed truths; but that the details of your picture, when worked out in accordance with such an impressionist scheme, are apt to be seriously in error.

Along with Roosevelt's presidency, more years of muckraking would pass before Steffens would have the opportunity to return to Washington to investigate the political maneuverings of the most powerful bosses in the nation.

After passing through Los Angeles, Steffens returned East and enjoyed a leisurely summer at Little Point. After his tiring cross-country trip, he wrote to his father of his refreshing dips in the "cool harbor water" after which he relaxed in "ducks and short-sleeved shirts." Josephine, he reported rather naively, was "well *content*" and had the place "in perfect shape." It was an idyllic summer for Steffens, as he passed each day by writing in the morning and using the afternoons for "play," most often on his sailboat.

In late August, Steffens and Josephine took a boat across Long Island Sound to Oyster Bay. After a stroll through the town, Steffens, along with several admirals and federal officials, joined Roosevelt and his family for lunch in the leisure and privacy of his Sagamore Hill home. Roosevelt had lived there for years with no phone; as governor, he had a drugstore in Oyster Bay take his calls and deliver the messages by courier. The president greeted Steffens with "Hello, old man," before launching into a discussion of Heney ("I wish I had some more Heneys"), the reforms coming out of San Francisco (which did not impress

Steffens), and the resistance his own reforms met from big business. When
Steffens wryly commented that Roosevelt could easily institute his reforms until
they actually touched the major companies, the president, according to Steffens,
replied, "I tell you, if it should come to a choice between the business good and
the enforcement of law against lawlessness, I will let the prosperity go."

With Steffens seated next to the tireless president, the conversation moved
through Roosevelt's next speech, the history of the Mongols, Steffens's magazine work, and the situations in Puerto Rico and Japan. "It was a simple lunch,"
Steffens recalled. "The President eats very fast, faster even than I, and he talks
all the time." Josephine, tellingly, spent the day alone, walking six miles through
Oyster Bay—"seen the whole place," Steffens wrote—before meeting Steffens at
the dock late in the afternoon.

As Steffens may well have told Roosevelt, his own work at the *American*,
in fact, was at a crossroads. Steffens had given his editors an ultimatum: If his
work continued to be heavily edited, he would leave. By late summer, both sides
had agreed to a cease-fire of sorts while management considered his demand.
But at forty-two, he felt a growing urge to abandon magazine work and try
writing on his own, hardly a foolish notion. He was, after all, a genuine literary
star, and for legitimate reasons.

There were two sides to the disagreement, of course. Phillips had fumed in
New York over Steffens's high-handed manner, the tardiness of his pieces, and
his refusal to document clearly—at least clearly enough for Phillips—his sources.
Steffens undoubtedly felt that his brilliant reporting at *McClure's* had earned
him some immunity in that regard, but Phillips realized that the *American*,
unlike *McClure's*, was not strongly positioned to fight a lawsuit. The fact that
Steffens was billing the magazine for the personal expenses of Josephine and her
mother only further annoyed Phillips.

Most of the staff tended to side with Phillips, feeling that Steffens had taken
on too much the sense of a freelancer. Even August Jaccaci, the former art director at *McClure's* and a friend of Steffens's, saw Phillips's point. "His view of the
Steffens matter *is perfectly just*," he wrote to Tarbell. "I am so glad this single
disturbing element is going to be eliminated—it's too unjust to all the rest and
above all to John. What a lunatic that Stef is! Because he has been my friend I
trust he is going to get such rough experience as may do him good and save him."

But Steffens was not interested in being saved, ultimately choosing to leave
the magazine. Tarbell, with years of experience working alongside Steffens, had
a unique perspective on his departure. Besides his obvious resentment toward
the limits of journalism, particularly when his own work was being edited, she

felt that the notion of the Golden Rule had seized his imagination after his experience with Older in San Francisco. He did not see the Golden Rule as a practical antidote that powerful politicians would eagerly apply to social problems, but Steffens, Tarbell believed, wanted the freedom to sound out power brokers on its merits. She recalled that Steffens's impatience boiled over one day in the office after he learned that Charles Edward Russell, angered that muckraking had pointed out many social ills while doing little to remedy them, had joined the Socialist Party. "Is that not what we should all be doing?" Steffens had demanded to know.

While not actually inclined to join the socialists or any other party, Steffens by then had clearly shed his old, conservative political leanings. In a May 1 letter to La Follette's wife, Belle, he extended his "love to all,—Tories, Socialists, Anarchists, even the Republicans." Regarding the *American*, he was less interested in keeping up the politically impartial image of the magazine than in breaking free to see far more of the world and what might bring people, especially grafters, closer to the Golden Rule.

In addition, Steffens noted a disturbing trend: As the magazine's success grew, he found himself relaxing in his articles, sliding toward a stance of gentle criticism that caused no serious discomfort for anyone but still caught the eye of the public—and sold magazines. "All by myself, without any outside influence, I was being bought off by my own money, by the prospect of earning money," he admitted. So, in February 1908, he quit. "I promised myself," he wrote, "never again to work where my money was."

Despite the rancor on both sides, the parting must have been reasonably amicable, as the *American* continued to publish Steffens's articles for several years. In fact, when White and his family returned to New York from a summer vacation in Europe two years later, it was Steffens along with Baker, Tarbell, and Phillips who gathered at the dock to greet the family.

Underlying the decision for Steffens was his waning interest in muckraking. By his own account, he had never even foreseen such a career for himself. "I did not intend to be a muckraker. I did not know that I was one till President Roosevelt picked the name out of Bunyan's *Pilgrim's Progress* and pinned it on us." He later observed "how little" muckrakers had actually learned, noting somewhat harshly that when he suggested that economic democracy was a possible cure for the corrupt system, they "would look blank. . . . Comfortable mental peace was their form of death."

Of course, there were exceptions, those who had flamed out on muckraking but sought other avenues in their pursuit of economic justice. For Steffens,

Charles Edward Russell, "one of the most earnest, emotional, and gifted of the muckrakers," stood out. Steffens recalled that after meeting Russell one day and asking him what all of their efforts had been about, Russell's face "looked as if he had suffered from the facts he saw and reported." Full of passion, Russell lamented, "I couldn't keep it up. It was too fierce, the conditions, the facts. . . . I couldn't stand it." The state of affairs led him to the Socialist Party. "I had to have something to believe," he told Steffens. Steffens admired Russell's remaining active in the cause, while Steffens himself, sharing Russell's frustration but not his dedication, temporarily withdrew from the muckraking scene. Two years would pass before he would again undertake any serious investigative work.

Muckraking itself was approaching its nadir, after considerable success. Steffens, Baker, Tarbell, Russell, Sinclair, Phillips, and Hopkins were household names; reform came to housing, insurance, elections, prisons, taxes, child labor, and food processing; and industry goliaths, notably Standard Oil and Southern Pacific Railroad, were broken up. But the public appetite for scandal, so voracious at the turn of the century, had evidently been satisfied, if not overwhelmed. Still, interest in serious political reform, particularly among the growing ranks of the progressives, did remain strong up to the bitter end of Woodrow Wilson's presidency, when it was abandoned until the Wall Street crash and the Depression reminded people of why muckraking had mattered thirty years before. By then, Steffens would be in his final act on the public stage.

11

"IF YOU ARE NOT A SOCIALIST"

STEFFENS WAS NOT idle after leaving the *American*. In June, *Everybody's* published his article "Roosevelt – Taft – La Follette—What the Matter Is in America and What to Do About It," an analysis of the 1908 presidential race. Steffens, with encouragement and hope, confided to La Follette in a May 28 letter that much of his mail over the article expressed "gratification that I 'appreciate' you and your 'lonely fight' in the Senate. You are deeper rooted in the heart of this nation than you think."

After some uncomfortable speculation over Roosevelt's involvement in the article, the president responded with a long letter to Steffens on June 5. Perhaps owing to Steffens's recent departure from the *American* and his shift from muckraking to more mainstream political affairs, Roosevelt wrote with enthusiasm, but, in this particular case, chided Steffens on his political naïveté. Roosevelt expressed his innocence concerning his personal involvement in the article as well as ample comment on other matters, including opinions on Steffens's own work:

> I am often interested in what you say; I sometimes agree with it and sometimes not; but I am always a hundred times more interested in some idea that you develop in the course of what you say about me than I am in what you thus say about me. . . . Indeed, often I have been so wholly uninterested in your view of me, and so genuinely interested in your view of something else which you have developed in connection with the former, that I have simply forgot that you were expressing any view of me, and concentrated my attention on the other matter.

Steffens had hit a nerve with Roosevelt. The journalist's assessment of La Follette as a fighter of "fundamental" evil while Roosevelt, lumped together with Taft, aimed his attacks at merely "specific" evils, was a contrast the president termed "childish." "I am fighting evil in the mass," Roosevelt wrote, "in the only way in which it is possible to fight it, when I fight different evils in the concrete." Referring to La Follette and his followers, Roosevelt observed icily, "I believe in the men who take the next step; not those who theorize about the 200th step." Eager, though, to engage Steffens further on the topic, Roosevelt insisted, "If you will come down to see me I will go over all this more at length with you, and for once, instead of passing by or brushing aside what you say about me or anyone else with which I disagree, I will tell you just what I *do* disagree with."

Steffens responded at equal length several days later. Assuring Roosevelt that the president had had no undue influence on the story, Steffens launched into a detailed discussion of what ailed America, namely, the refusal of politicians, particularly in Congress, to reform the system while instead obstructing Roosevelt's own efforts at improvement: "I want to see our public men required to announce their remedies for our evils, and by these and, afterwards, by their records, judged, defeated, or reelected." Steffens went on to question the practices of his old nemesis, Senator Aldrich, still one of the stalwarts of the Senate, before going on to the "better example" of Senator John Kean of New Jersey, who, he felt, was an excellent case study of the problem:

> I don't know that he is dishonest at all; but whether he is or is not, I believe he honestly believes that the government should continue to represent what it represents now; railroads and great corporate business. As for the people, to him we are probably nothing but "passenger traffic"; "consumers," "wage earners," and, sometimes, a "troublesome vote. . . ." Is it "childish" to observe that if the Senate were once made truly representative, a President like you could put through, not a few compromised, amended bills, but all the legislation we all so much need?

Steffens then focused on the root cause of the government affliction that Roosevelt had fought largely in vain, one that Tom Johnson had already identified. "'The evil,' which so irritates you, is something which is neither new nor unobserved. It is privilege. Trace every case of corruption you know to its source, and you will see, I believe, that somebody was trying to get out of Government some special right; to keep a saloon open after hours; a protective tariff; a ship subsidy; a public-service franchise." The solution, Steffens believed ever more strongly, was public ownership in certain areas, and on that point he offered Roosevelt his own plank for the upcoming Republican platform: "We believe in the public ownership of any business that shall continue to find it necessary to its success to corrupt politics, government, and the people of the United States."

Steffens closed on a personal note, offering gratitude for Roosevelt's attention and his understanding of their complex relationship: "I think we see things differently, fight them differently; express ourselves differently, and that your patience with me has been founded, like my very great respect and my very quiet but very genuine affection for you, upon the sense that, at bottom, I in my humble way and you in your whole splendid career are working toward the same end."

Roosevelt replied on June 12 to the "nice letter" from "friend Steffens." The president agreed with Steffens's views on the problems arising from privilege: "I am heartily with you in the campaign for the abolition of privilege." But he had little patience with Steffens's push for public ownership, fearing that it would lead to socialism and in any case would change little. In his experience, Roosevelt observed, corruption flourished in public hands as easily as in private; he cited the postal service and Tammany Hall as notorious examples. What was needed, he believed, was a *"fundamental fight for morality."* He offered to discuss the topic further with Steffens either at Oyster Bay or at the White House.

Steffens, after attending the Republican Convention in Chicago in mid-June (and seeing Taft's organization make the Republicans "again the conservative party of America"), was hardly in a patient mood, however, and on June 20, he fired off another letter to Roosevelt from Cleveland. Socialism was fine with him, he wrote, if it came to that, but he did not see why it should. He thought that the "greater privileges," those that had led to the most serious transgressions, could be removed largely by taking out the profit motive that the government itself was providing by participating so enthusiastically in the graft. He noted that Johnson was trying to do precisely that in Cleveland, adding that if such an effort were successful, all the talent and intelligence that for years had kept the graft flowing could then be utilized to help run the system properly and root out the remaining, smaller forms of corruption. He naturally agreed with Roosevelt on the fight for morality, at least economic morality, with the ultimate goal, as he saw it, being "to level all privileges and, *thus*, equalize opportunities." As Roosevelt had suggested, the two did get together again at Oyster Bay on June 27.

Steffens next turned to the political left and interviewed Socialist Party presidential nominee Eugene Debs and prominent socialist Victor Berger at Berger's home in Milwaukee, for an *Everybody's* article. Debs captivated Steffens. For all of the socialist's unswerving allegiance to the working class and the underprivileged and his bold defiance of the law to the point of being regularly imprisoned, Debs was hardly a typical agitator for change. What many recalled instead was his soft, almost unassuming side that deflected attention always back on the plight of the individual workers themselves. A young Ray Stannard Baker met Debs during the bloody 1894 Pullman strikes in Chicago and found him "a sensitive, warm-hearted man" devoted not merely to unionism but to "the human problems of the workingman." Clarence Darrow, who also met Debs during the strike and somewhat reluctantly took up his case, wrote in his memoir, "There may have lived some time, some where, a kindlier, gentler, more generous man than Eugene V. Debs, but I have never known him. Nor have I ever read or heard of another. . . . He was the bravest man I ever knew."

Now, more than a decade later, Steffens saw the same firmly idealistic, nearly prophetic man. In a letter to Brand Whitlock, who worried that he might be squandering his vote by supporting Debs in the 1908 presidential election, Steffens did not deny the challenge facing Debs but implored him, "Don't choose between the two evils. Vote for that sweet, good, passionate lover of mankind who offers hope and service. . . . Why, your whole political career is a demonstration that we should vote for what and whom we want and that that's the way to beat the Republicans and Democrats and so elect,—well, Sam Jones, Brand Whitlock, 'Gene Debs."

The article, "Eugene V. Debs on What the Matter Is in America and What to Do About It," appeared in the October 1908 issue of *Everybody's*. Debs himself loved Steffens's work and gave him a hearty endorsement: "You have written from and been inspired by a social brain, a social heart and a social conscience and if you are not a socialist I do not know one," he wrote to Steffens. Other socialists saw Steffens as a new compatriot and wrote to him in hopes of enlisting his aid. For his part, Steffens simply told his sister Laura, "I certainly am socialistic, but I'm not yet a Socialist."

Steffens had attended the Democratic Convention in July as a syndicated columnist and found presidential nominee William Jennings Bryan to be sufficiently progressive, if still uncomfortably close to the established order. His own views on the best political way forward remained in flux. "I simply don't know where I'm at," he conceded to Laura. "My articles are telling the truth. I'm trying to find out. I have some facts. I know things are all wrong somehow;

and fundamentally; but *I* don't know what the matter is and I don't know *what* to do about it. So I'm listening to all but the ignorant. . . . I'm playing a long, patient game, but before I die, I believe I can help to bring about an essential change in the American mind." When he compared the parties themselves in a newspaper column, though, he could not help venting a frustration that would long outlast Steffens himself: "Both the old party organizations are corrupt. They have served and they are devoted to the interests which have corrupted and are still corrupting them."

Yet, as the election approached, he was feeling flush with enthusiasm. "The world is moving very fast," he told Laura, "but in the right direction, and that's all we optimists can ask." He was inspired to the point of encouraging Upton Sinclair, still savoring the success of *The Jungle* and considering a visit to Sacramento, to "call on my good old father and mother; Tories, but my sister, Laura, will understand you." Laura diplomatically squelched the idea. Ironically, Sinclair did not visit Sacramento until he ran unsuccessfully for governor a quarter century later, when the Steffens family home had become the governor's mansion. Sinclair later recalled, "I climbed . . . four tall flights of stairs, and I said: 'God save me from having to live here.' My request was kindly granted."

Conceding to Laura, "I couldn't vote for either of the other parties; their candidates are good men, but blind," Steffens cast his "protest" vote for Debs, whose 420,000 votes—nearly identical to his 1904 total—showed that his supporters were unwavering but pitifully outnumbered. Taft, with Roosevelt's very public but ultimately misguided blessing, easily defeated Bryan, ushering in four more years of Republican rule that began harmoniously but would end in one of the most bitter, divisive splits in American political history.

As Roosevelt's presidency wound down in late December, Steffens, at the urging of Fremont Older and other California progressives, gently but directly suggested Heney's name as attorney general to Roosevelt for President-elect Taft's consideration. Steffens was well aware that Roosevelt admired Heney and viewed Taft as his obedient successor. By that point, however, Roosevelt, about to be absent from political power for the first time in more than a decade and, moreover, indignant with what he saw as the unsubstantiated charges brought by muckrakers against public figures, claimed in a private letter to have "given up reading Steffens." An additional obstacle was Taft himself, whose political pedigree had been publicly questioned by Steffens. The president-elect sent Steffens a polite note of consideration and nothing more, effectively scuttling Heney's prospects.

Steffens, who had already acknowledged the growing political schism between Roosevelt and himself, chose to maintain a gracious tone: Three months after Roosevelt departed the White House, Steffens sent him a warm letter of congratulations on his accomplishments and wished him good luck on his upcoming African hunting trip. Steffens also continued his good-natured habit of teasing Roosevelt to highlight a legitimate point, in this case possibly anticipating the bitter feud between Taft and Roosevelt that lay ahead. "I can see you coming back stronger even than you are now," Steffens told him, "and not only physically but in all other ways, both good and bad." Roosevelt himself may have felt a similar foreboding, having told William Allen White the previous August, "Down at the bottom my main reason for wishing to go to Africa for a year is so that I can get where no one can accuse me of running, nor do Taft the injustice of accusing him of permitting me to run, the job." As events later unfolded, Taft would undoubtedly wish Roosevelt a very extended African stay.

12

BOSTON

STEFFENS HAD LONG expected to investigate Boston, where much of the American-style graft had been born and nurtured and where, Steffens was sure, it still thrived. Across the country, many reformers had attempted—unsuccessfully, for the most part—to enlist Steffens to muckrake and publicize their cause, but in the spring of 1908, Edward A. Filene had convinced him that Boston was now worth his time.

Filene, once described as "a cross between a Jewish pack peddler and the prophet Isaiah," fascinated Steffens. A highly successful department store owner in Boston whose personal wealth totaled upward of ten million dollars, Filene nevertheless was as keen as Steffens to find out why American business and government paid more attention to flouting the law than following it. Like Steffens, he chose to look scientifically at the problem in an effort to devise a solution that did not merely expose but also eliminate the cause. Nine-tenths of the problems in society, he insisted, were the result of men who would not look at facts honestly and respond accordingly.

Steffens was encouraged to find that Filene was not just a thinker: He acted. With his five-floor department store thriving in downtown Boston, Filene became one of the city's influential men, but hardly typical of the breed. A life-long bachelor, he lived comfortably but not ostentatiously (he never owned a car), gave away millions but could not abide the waste of a nickel, and, strangest of all for a wealthy American man at the turn of the twentieth century, was an outspoken and unrepentant liberal. He firmly believed that any profit-minded businessman had to be a liberal to protect his own interests. To be a conservative—a preserver of the past, closed to the burgeoning creativity of a country whose collective mind was forever fixated on a more prosperous future—was an illogical approach for an ambitious individual.

At the moment, Filene was particularly concerned about the fate of his own city. One gnawing problem was that each business owner, he observed, was operating in a vacuum, too often unaware of what enterprises lay across the street. So Filene worked to merge various and often recalcitrant groups of merchants, who at times found his obsession for democracy insufferable, into the first unified, local Chamber of Commerce before going on to establish additional Chambers of Commerce throughout American cities and abroad. He was also a strong voice in Boston's Good Government Association, which was founded in 1903 by business and legal interests and predictably mocked by its detractors as yet another misled, idealistic crowd of goo-goos.

A strong local supporter of Filene was his good friend, Louis Brandeis, "the people's attorney" and the growing bane of corporate America. Against strong opposition, Brandeis had helped Filene himself to successfully establish public ownership of Boston's subways a decade earlier, and his reputation was that of a sharp, fearless attorney with an intense focus on justice that served the common good. He voiced support for the minimum wage, the rights of trade unions and women, and strict limits on trusts, and developed the "Brandeis Brief," arguing cases not only along legal lines but with a broad outlook on the long-term social and economic consequences of any judicial decision. It was Brandeis who wrote this condemnation of lawyers in 1905: "Instead of holding a position of independence, between the wealthy and the people, prepared to curb the excesses of either, able lawyers have, to a large extent, allowed themselves to become adjuncts of great corporations and have neglected the obligation to use their power for the protection of the people." Not surprisingly, Brandeis was a favorite of the progressives in general and Steffens in particular. Filene and Steffens, in fact, had discussed the prospect of promoting Brandeis's name to Roosevelt for an appointment. "He would make a corking Cabinet officer," Steffens told Filene. Steffens had accurately assessed Brandeis's potential contribution as a public servant, but events would make Brandeis wait somewhat longer before taking his distinguished place in the nation's history.

Brandeis, for his part, had been sizing up Steffens as well. On March 16, the lawyer wrote to Henry Beach Needham, a former *McClure's* editor now involved in fund-raising for the financially strapped People's Lobby. Having previously advised Needham to approach Filene for a contribution, Brandeis now recommended Steffens: "I am glad you sent Lincoln Steffens Filene's letter. Mr. Steffens is in very close relations with him, and I think he can do more with Filene than anyone else." Several weeks later, Brandeis described a family dinner, with Steffens as a guest, at which Steffens "sat up till near midnight talking eternal verities. It was interesting to hear him talk on Folk—and Charlie Nagel—as well as other things galore." Brandeis and Steffens must have seen a good deal of one another over the next two years, as Brandeis, hoping to coax a supportive article from Steffens, began a December 1910 letter to him, "Having borne so patiently on many occasions my talk on savings bank insurance, you will, I am sure, be glad to see what we really have accomplished." Steffens and Brandeis would remain close for more than a decade.

Despite Filene's effectiveness as a businessman, he called his life "the failure of a successful millionaire." He saw, as Steffens had, that people simply were not prepared for democracy and the responsibility that accompanied it. In his own highly profitable department store, he had tried to bestow power on his eight hundred employees by letting them establish workplace policies and govern themselves, only to be met with requests for shorter hours and a holiday but nothing more. Actual exercise of power held little appeal for them or, Filene saw, for the citizens of Boston in general. So Filene summoned Steffens to Boston. The Athens of America needed to be modernized and freed of graft, and a muckraker might energize the process.

Steffens had agreed in February 1908 to assist Filene, and was intrigued by the undertaking. "I really expect to enjoy my Boston work," he wrote to Filene in mid-July, "and to have the personal satisfaction for once of going to the bottom of a city and of writing not merely a limited number of words but all that I can find out."

The agreement was that Steffens, for the enticing sum of ten thousand dollars, would devote a year of his time to investigating conditions in Boston and producing a report for Filene and prominent local leaders selected from the Boston City Club, a civic improvement group. Proceeds from sales of the report would help fund Steffens's generous salary. "I expect to give my entire time to Boston," he told Filene, "to go more completely into the condition there than I ever have done in any other city, and to write a report which will be the best thing that I have ever done." It also gave Steffens an opportunity to directly shape public policy, at least in an advisory role, rather than merely reporting on it.

The assignment, as Steffens saw it, was very nearly a personal crusade. He told Filene that it would be "profoundly interesting" for him to state his findings as a direct appeal to Bostonians. He anticipated that his efforts would reveal how much a city could improve itself if its own citizens were made to see the problem and agree to undergo the sacrifices necessary to make things right. And he would not be alone in his efforts. The secretary of the Good Government Association, Edmund Billings, pledged to do "everything in my power" to aid Steffens, while the city planned to diligently promote the project, with signs appearing on store windows, mail packages, and public transportation.

With Josephine, her mother, three servants, a canary, a dog, a cat, and thirteen suitcases, Steffens left Riverside in late September 1908 and settled in a house on fashionable Beacon Hill. Steffens met with Filene's committee of "earnest, representative men," which included Brandeis, to determine how to reform Boston without causing, as the committee feared, another revolution. The problem, in Steffens's view, was that the people of Boston were completely accustomed to graft and would need a new "vision" of the future, a plan that would inspire them to make changes themselves. All agreed that "visionary" was the operative word for their effort. They wanted to examine every aspect of Boston life—political, religious, business, and social—and formulate a unified plan that laid out a bright, appealing, and starkly different future of Boston.

Steffens floated the idea that the plan for a new Boston would be completed by 1922, but the members of the committee, probably hoping to live to see the day, forged a compromise of 1915. Accordingly, Steffens's work became known as the Boston—1915 plan. The project was highly ambitious, with failure an obvious possibility, as Steffens admitted in a letter to Upton Sinclair: "I don't expect it to succeed; that is to say, I can't let myself think it can." Boston itself had somewhat stronger expectations. The *Boston Post* declared, "We have always wanted Steffens ever since he climbed up on the pole of distinction as the one great and sublime municipal reformer of the age," while another paper began its story, "The most interesting immigrant in Boston is Lincoln J. Steffens."

Steffens agreed to do the research, expose the graft, and promote the plan as much as possible. The committee, as Steffens expected, wanted to install some reputable, good men in control, only to hear Steffens pointedly rebut their plan. If any city ever had been run by good men, he declared, it was Boston. Aristocrats, businessmen, and even the clergy had controlled the city for more than two centuries, with such undemocratic results that Filene had felt compelled to gather his committee in a desperate search for an alternative way of governing. No, Steffens said, Boston did not need any more good men; it needed strong men, men who may be reviled by many but who have the intellect, the determination, and the shrewdness to make a democratic system function—fairly.

Steffens's proposal left the committee wondering if he were a visionary or a fool, so Steffens initiated the reform process himself by asking the committee to identify the worst grafter in the city. The response was unanimous: Martin

Lomasney, the notorious Ward 8 boss and staunch opponent of the goo-goos. The following day, Steffens visited the "bad" ward and found Lomasney in a large second-floor pool hall. The writer understood the skepticism of the committee when he looked into Lomasney's "heavy jaw and hard face" and wilted a bit, seeing no hint of cooperation in Lomasney's calculating eyes.

After Steffens introduced himself, Lomasney immediately tested him. "You did not come here for your health," Lomasney declared. "Now be frank about it. Lay your cards on the table. I want to know what your graft is." As best he could, Steffens quickly explained his goal of muckraking and reforming Boston. Lomasney stood there in the spacious pool room, eyeing Steffens and saying nothing. He certainly did look "bad, cold, hard" to Steffens. And Lomasney, whose favorite expression was "Never write if you can speak; never speak if you can nod; never nod if you can wink," was not afraid of silence. Steffens must have stood his ground well, as Lomasney noted that Steffens appeared amused and lost his composure only momentarily.

The awkward conversation staggered along until Steffens, as he had so often done, manipulated the conversation to a point where personal views, however reluctantly, were being exchanged. Steffens told Lomasney that the problem with leaders was that they often gained the faith of the people but used it only to make careers for themselves. The result was the "failure of democracy." Instead, he told Lomasney, leaders had to get away from the individual selfishness of success and pursue a "social ideal." His goal in Boston, he said, was to develop such leaders among political men like Lomasney, "who seem to me to be the first and worst traitors."

And Lomasney, rather than repudiating Steffens, invited him into his warm office, where he pointed to a safe that contained papers documenting graft across the city, valuable information that might serve as Lomasney's legal defense, should the unlikely need ever arise. To Steffens, Lomasney would speak only about his own dealings, which, over the course of many nights, were more than adequate in giving Steffens a clear view of the political underworld of Boston. "I gave it to him straight," Lomasney recalled.

The result was that Steffens judged Lomasney, the feared ward boss and an eighth-grade dropout, to be one of the most able men in the city. "He was honest," Steffens wrote. "He had intellectual integrity. He saw things straight and talked straight about them." Lomasney, in Steffens's view, might be very useful after all.

With Lomasney's words in mind, Steffens carried on his work with optimism, finding the people of Boston "pleasant" and only the biting northeast wind a nuisance. "It's going to be a severe winter for my California blood," he admitted to his mother.

Soon Steffens was giving speeches nearly every night in Boston, and in early December he reported to his mother that people continued to treat him "beautifully," but added, "I am always well received till I write my articles. After that they speed the parting guest, and I go, grinning, amused, and instructed." To Laura he sent Christmas greetings, adding with some regret, "How little that day means to us that have no children! J. and I and her mother hardly keep it at all."

Meanwhile, Steffens was pleased to receive a letter of support for his muckraking work from the publishing magnate E. W. Scripps, a man Steffens greatly admired. Founder of the United Press two years earlier, Scripps oversaw an empire of more than thirty newspapers read by millions and was the kind of iconoclastic, larger-than-life figure that often intrigued Steffens. Radical journalist Max Eastman was certain that "nothing like Scripps could have come to pass outside of America, and yet nothing is more un-American . . . than the way he piled up a fortune without working."

A humorless bear of a man with a rather fierce countenance matched by his abrasive personality, Scripps lived absolutely as he pleased. He had a great fondness for whiskey and a weakness for adventurous women in his younger days, never any religious beliefs, and always a distinctly low opinion of humanity, not excluding himself. "Whatever is, is wrong," he told Eastman. Still, after false starts as a teacher, a druggist, and a window-blind stenciler, he had built his wealth from a single newspaper in Cleveland using a very basic approach—a clear-eyed vision of what could bring him genuine satisfaction: enough power to let him live freely; a keenly practical view of what succeeded in business; and an exceptional, intuitive grasp of which individuals could help him attain his goals. He was a private man who, Steffens noted, preferred to spend his time alone studying "life in all forms." He did so by reading, thinking, and talking—to individuals like Steffens. And much of his thought had gone toward analyzing the same crisis of democracy that Steffens was confronting in Boston.

Steffens took the liberty of showing the Scripps letter to William James over dinner at his Cambridge home and came close, he noted, to changing James's skeptical mind on the matter. After his talk with James, Steffens sent a lengthy response to Scripps, acknowledging the challenge facing him but also his belief that progress was possible. With typical optimism, he told Scripps, "We are seeking the biggest and often the most selfish men in the community." The city's leaders were interested in hearing more, Steffens wrote, despite the obstacles. "If they start, I don't see how they will have the face to quit," he observed.

For the moment, Lomasney remained a key figure in Steffens's effort to save Boston from itself. During one of their talks, Steffens asked about police graft, wondering especially about Lomasney's remarkable method of sparing petty criminals jail time in case after case. Why did he do it? Steffens asked. Steffens did not really expect an answer, but Lomasney surprised him. "I think," Steffens recalled him saying, "that there's got to be in every ward somebody that any bloke can come to—no matter what he's done—and get help. Help, you understand; none of your law and your justice, but help." Small wonder the wards were so loyal to the machines, Steffens thought.

He presented his findings to Filene, who agreed that their plan would have to extend to everyone, including bosses like Lomasney, if Boston were to get genuine reform. Others agreed, and Steffens suggested a committee of professionals to be present in a ward, providing the public aid that was obviously needed. Brandeis volunteered on the legal side, while Filene had the names of others in business and among the clergy willing to donate their time. However, they also needed an individual to represent the corrupt, a man who preferably, as Steffens wrote, "had done wrong enough himself to understand guilt." Someone, in other words, the neighborhood could trust. Steffens nominated Lomasney for the task.

When Steffens approached Lomasney with his plan that would essentially put Lomasney himself out of business, the ward boss accepted the challenge of working with the reformers. The problem, though, lay with Lomasney's crew, who undoubtedly would see Lomasney, a man already benefiting handsomely from the rigged system, as a traitor, which was precisely what transpired. They were livid, "kicking like steers," Lomasney told Steffens. At times they refused to speak with him. Steffens, ever positive, offered to help relieve some of the pressure facing Lomasney by addressing the men himself. Guardedly hopeful, Lomasney agreed and arranged the meeting.

Steffens's efforts with Lomasney's crowd began inauspiciously, as they glared at him in silence. However, as Steffens diplomatically reminded them of the obvious—how corrupt the system had become in Boston—and offered a fairer alternative, faces slowly relaxed and questions, doubting but sincere, were asked. While nothing was resolved, the discussion continued well into the night before Lomasney called an end to it. It was not a victory by any means for Steffens, but progress had been made.

The Boston—1915 plan was officially announced to the public following a March 30, 1909, meeting at the Boston City Club, with Steffens present. With some bemusement, social commentator and *Survey* editor Paul Kellogg noted the extent of the "'hurrah, boys' element" in the businessmen's approach and likened their enthusiasm to the "zest of a group of school boys turned loose in an apple orchard." Steffens saw no apple orchards, however, telling Laura a month later that the corruption in Boston was the worst he had seen anywhere. Gaining agreement on any hint of change was a grinding effort. "It is like reforming drunkards," he told her. "These men are drunk with power and greed and selfishness, so habitually drunk that, as I say, some of them are hopeless. . . . It's a hard nut to crack, this city, and I sometimes doubt that I'll ever get it right." Cynical opponents of the plan confirmed Steffens's fears, labeling the effort "Filenethropy" and pledging to pay not a nickel in new taxes.

Regarding Lomasney, Steffens found that getting it "right" may have been futile from the start. Lomasney and his men held no grudge against Steffens, but they lacked confidence that the Boston—1915 plan would succeed, partly because of their experience with the candidates for office. "We know them, and as a practical matter they are no good," Lomasney declared. Ultimately, Filene's committee and Lomasney's group could not find enough common ground on which to build the new democracy envisioned by Steffens, and for that failure, Steffens accepted some of the blame. Lomasney and Steffens, though, never forgot one another. When Steffens later passed through Boston in 1912, he found that Lomasney "has sworn by me so much around town that everybody knows that I am his one weakness." Nearly two decades later, Lomasney eagerly offered to help Steffens with the Boston portion of his autobiography, and when the ward boss died in 1933, Steffens wrote an admiring obituary:

> Once named to me as the worst, Martin Lomasney proved to be one of the best men in Boston.
>
> He had strength, rough kindness, tribal loyalty and rarest of all— intellectual integrity. He could think straight in whatever he did. He put his kind of people on the map.
>
> He lifted the Boston Irish from agents to partners in the game and they played it as Martin saw it played by his betters. And he learned it in Boston, you know, not in Cambridge; as the one way of life without hypocrisy and without cynicism.

Steffens did find a measure of happiness in the summer of 1909, as a collection of his previously published, effusive articles on his personal heroes of democracy—Mark Fagan, Everett Colby, Ben Lindsey, Rudolph Spreckels, and William S. U'Ren—came out in book form under the appropriate title of

Upbuilders. Steffens, who viewed the articles as his best work, dedicated the book to his father, and his first words in the foreword display the enthusiastic nature Steffens had shown since his childhood days in California: "Is it hope that is wanted? Wide-eyed optimism? Here it is, in this book. And faith? Faith in democracy? It is here. And a hint as to what one man can do? Here it is. Here are faith in the many men; hope for all; and, for the few who think they would like to lead, encouragement, the inspiration of humble examples, and some notion of how to proceed." It was hope, faith, and individual action that had brought Steffens his own success, and he was eager to show that muckrakers and intelligent reformers could do more than bemoan the status quo.

He also wanted to illustrate two other observations: that there was no social mold that produced intelligent leaders, and that the voters possessed a mass sense of where they wanted to be led. "*Wherever the people have found a leader who was loyal to them; brave; and not too far ahead, there they have followed him and there has begun the solution of our common problems.* It has not mattered much who the leader was, or what. His religion has made no difference, nor his social status; not his financial conditon, nor his party. . . . Certainly the first rule for the political reformer is: Go to the voters. . . . They can afford, they are free to be fair." *Upbuilders,* however, never found a wide audience and had sold only 684 copies nearly a year after publication.

Ready for a distraction from Boston and having come nowhere near completing his Boston—1915 manuscript, Steffens looked elsewhere for signs of change. Another entrepreneur who shared his desire for reform and had the money to wield significant influence was the American soap manufacturer Joseph Fels, another of Steffens's "inspired millionaires." Not unlike Filene and other successful men Steffens had met, Fels made his fortune as a capitalist before choosing to invest a substantial amount of it in an effort to overhaul the very economic system that had rewarded him so handsomely. From Fels's own words, it is clear why Steffens felt a kinship with the wealthy reformer. "I believe," Fels once wrote, "that the fortunes acquired by many people, are largely due to unjust economic conditions, and from the moral point of view, these conditions are responsible for what is practically a system of robbery." More to the point, he told a dean at a theology school, "I am using all the money I have as best I know how to abolish the Hell of civilisation, which is want and fear of want." Judging that the necessary changes could come only from the Left, Fels saw great promise in the Fabian socialist movement that attracted George Bernard Shaw, H. G. Wells, and other liberal British intellectuals, and tirelessly promoted the single-tax ideas of Henry George.

Fels visited Steffens at Little Point in 1909 to discuss his reform ventures, telling Steffens that he had $250,000 to put toward an unspecified cause. Fels's heart, like Henry George's before him, was set on the single tax, based on the belief that property was the main source of wealth and should therefore provide the bulk of the tax collections, and it was in that direction that much of the money went. The Fels Fund Commission was established to promote the single tax and other economic reforms; Steffens, Fred Howe, and Daniel Kiefer, Steffens's booking agent for lectures, were among the commissioners.

The goal was to distribute $50,000 a year over five years not to large philanthropic institutions, which too often proved to be financial black holes, but to experienced individuals in the field who could best identify the areas of genuine need. The policy, according to Steffens, was to seek out such workers and provide the necessary money, no strings attached. Much of the attention went to the progressive movement in Oregon, led by U'Ren, a fervent single taxer.

Although Steffens, according to progressive journalist Louis F. Post, a Fels Advisory Committee member, was "as convinced a Single Taxer as you will find anywhere in this country," the efforts of the Fels commissioners, while sincere, proved futile. Reflecting on the disappointing experience, Steffens saw that showering money on the most avid single taxers only hindered the movement. Disagreements broke out over policies, personal animosities grew raw, and outside events, particularly the gathering political storm in Europe, distracted many. Most problematic, Steffens observed, was that money softened up the workers. What had been to campaigners a grassroots effort fought daily on a tight budget now was a well-funded operation that required meetings and elaborate plans. "With money to use as a force, they did not depend so much on persuasion. Even the fanatics," Steffens conceded, "slackened their propaganda."

Money, at least an excessive amount of it, was not the solution, Steffens saw, although he had no better ideas: "My conclusion from my experience in philanthropy was that it is a failure." Fels himself had the same reaction. Steffens recalled the time Fels was asked to intervene in an effort to save the starving children in London. The millionaire replied that charity could not save the poor children but that he would be willing to pay for the removal of their corpses, to be displayed in front of the Houses of Parliament. Even Fels, though, could not restrain himself from parting with much of his fortune in the elusive search for progress.

The desire for change was evident elsewhere as well. During the summer of 1909, Steffens and Scripps settled on a plan to gather a number of local and national reformers, mainly progressive Republicans, at Scripps's two-thousand-acre ranch near La Jolla over the Christmas holidays. As Steffens explained to Tom Johnson, the plan was to "think about and perhaps to agree upon an issue, or a slogan, which would crystallize the sentiment of the American people today and give a common point to all the now separate fights that are being waged." Steffens hoped to gather Johnson, Frank Heney, Robert La Follette, Louis Brandeis, forestry expert Gifford Pinchot, and about a dozen others in his effort to unify the movement. By September, Steffens, spending his own summer on the Marblehead seacoast in Massachusetts, had received enough confirmations to feel that the meeting would occur as planned.

But Steffens had miscalculated. Traveling to California over the holidays was already an unappealing prospect to many, and Scripps, in one of his frequent mood swings, abruptly withdrew the invitation altogether in the fall. Steffens must have taken the cancellation in stride, as George Boke of the San Francisco Citizens League of Justice, who had frequently corresponded with Steffens regarding the meeting, offered his gratitude for Steffens's patience with Scripps's "lack of courtesy."

In late summer came Steffens's first extensive contact with John Reed, then a student at Harvard. Reed asked Steffens for assistance in putting together the *Harvard Monthly* (Reed was on the editorial board), but Steffens reluctantly declined for the moment, being "in the midst of my book" and about to leave for Riverside. He offered to help later, however, and on October 8 sent a lengthy letter to Reed, outlining his views on the topic. Steffens pointed out that editors often try to "make" a magazine by first finding a topic of interest and then finding a writer for the story. Such a method had its merits, he conceded, but stressed, "We all hate it." He explained, "We all do our best work when we are permitted to write that which is in our minds and hearts to tell. And as an editor I found that that was the way to work." He closed the warm letter by telling Reed, "I'd like to have a whole evening with your crowd."

The November 1909 elections were far less satisfying to Steffens, bringing stunning losses that dealt a severe setback to the reform movement itself and would have turned the Scripps meeting into a wake. Tom Johnson, to Steffens's shock, lost in Cleveland. "I have felt the defeat of Mayor Tom deeper than I care to say," Steffens admitted to Brand Whitlock. "It is not a catastrophe; I can pick out the good in it, but I feel afraid that he feels it deeper than he cares to say." Indeed, Johnson, exhausted and with little left of his personal fortune, withdrew from public life and was dead within two years, to be buried next to his political mentor, Henry George, in Brooklyn. Frank Heney in San Francisco (tainted by his pursuit of the local elite in the Ruef case), Mark Fagan in New

Jersey, and reform candidates in Philadelphia all went down to defeat as well—only Whitlock in Toledo survived Election Night as a reformer. Just back from California, Brandeis wrote sympathetically to Steffens, "I saw both Heney and Spreckels, and grieve with you and others as to the result there and in Cleveland. I hope to see you soon."

Steffens, who had left Boston fairly certain that reform nationwide had acquired the necessary momentum for success, was discouraged but tried his best to maintain the long view. "I feel these things very deeply," he admitted to his father, yet to Whitlock he summoned enough hope to write, "I know the cause moves on." How to prevent the cause from moving on to irrelevancy was the challenge facing Steffens. In January 1910, he wrote optimistically to Laura, "It looks as if my candidate for mayor might win in Boston. . . . He is James J. Storrow, the leading banker of the city, and a little like Spreckels; a little; about as little as Boston is like S.F. But he has seen some light, and,—we'll see." A week later, Storrow, a civic-minded Brahmin with a distinct inability to speak before a crowd, went down to defeat to the legendary populist John "Honey Fitz" Fitzgerald, who repeatedly spelled his opponent's name as "$torrow" and successfully framed the election as a struggle of "Manhood Against Money." While Steffens retained hope that elections over the next several years in Boston would yield competent leaders, he wrote impatiently to Older in February 1910, "Reform has got to come with crooks in office. This pursuit of good individuals to perform for democracy the work of democracy is delaying and hurting democracy."

It was a difficult winter in other, more important ways, as well. In November, while Steffens was away in Boston, the family dog had been killed by a car, a loss that was particularly harsh for Josephine, under growing nervous strain, to bear. "My dear Lincoln," she wrote, "I mourn him and I miss him so cruelly, that I cannot keep the tears back from my eyes or keep my voice steady." Then, on the last day of the year, a house fire at Little Point, awakening Steffens and Josephine at four in the morning, destroyed a bedroom and the living room. Such disruption weighed heavily on an increasingly fragile Josephine, whose vulnerability remained undetected by her distracted husband.

Steffens never retreated far from the cause of reform, particularly the removal of privilege. His support for blacks at this time is a case in point. Steffens moved largely in white, upscale circles throughout his career, particularly after his years as a young reporter on the Lower East Side. With the black community, he had had no extensive contact. But after the mid-August 1908 race riots in Abraham Lincoln's home town of Springfield, Illinois, where two days of mayhem saw roaming white mobs burn black homes and drag an eighty-four-year-old black man, married to a white woman, from his residence and hang him from a tree, white and black liberals responded. Oswald Garrison Villard, editor of Steffens's old paper, the *Evening Post*, promoted the "Lincoln Birthday Call" on February 12, 1909, for a conference and public discussion of the dire conditions facing blacks. Among the prominent signatories to the call were Steffens, Jane Addams, William Dean Howells, W. E. B. Du Bois, Ida Wells Barnett, Charles Edward Russell, Brand Whitlock, and Charles Parkhurst, and it was this initial effort to raise the national consciousness toward the racial dilemma that led directly to the formation of the National Association for the Advancement of Colored People (NAACP).

By the spring of 1910, understanding the motivation of both the grafters and the reformers became nearly an obsession with Steffens, leading him into a careful study of Christianity, a topic he had pondered at times ever since the days of Mrs. Neely's stern lectures. Steffens had considered how the morality of Christianity had been applied or ignored by Americans in their daily lives, and the recent political turbulence in the city of Milwaukee sparked his investigation of Christianity in America.

Corruption had flourished under Mayor David Rose, leading to a backlash among voters, many of whom turned to socialism in hopes of improving basic city services. The result ushered in Milwaukee's era of "sewer socialism." In a graft investigation, a Milwaukee ward boss complained that certain areas of the city were not even worth attempting to bribe, because they were all socialists. Milwaukee, in fact, embraced socialism to the point of electing the nation's first socialist mayor, Emil Seidel, and congressman, Victor Berger, in 1910, although the intensity of the struggle was reflected in Berger's comment to Steffens: "Your letters cannot come any too soon nor too often. . . . However, I am by this time accustomed to get bouquets from one side and rocks from the other."

Like many on the Left, Steffens closely followed the situation in Milwaukee and made several visits to observe the miracle. How, he wondered, could the socialists there resist the allure of graft that was so easily available? He did not believe that they were any more honest than others, but concluded that a strong, collective sense was driving them, almost missionary-like, toward their goal: a sincere vision of hope for a better world. "And suddenly it occurred to me," he wrote, "that Christianity conveyed such a faith, hope, and—vision. And the good people that went so wrong, in politics, had that belief." Taking a break from the Boston—1915 report ("I haven't finished 'Boston' yet. . . . Maybe Boston will finish me," he told his father in May), Steffens had ample time and motivation to read the New Testament and "see what the good, church-going Christians believed." His aim, he had told his mother in a December 21, 1909, letter, was to take on "the biggest thing I ever tackled. . . . I want to tell Christians what their Christ said they should do. . . . I cannot expect to convert the Christian Church to Christianity, but I can show what would happen if they would but believe."

In the comfort of Little Point, with his feet up on his desk and a pipe in his mouth, Steffens, slowly, absorbed the New Testament. The experience jolted him. It was "an adventure so startling," he wrote, "that I wanted everyone else to have it." Jesus, Steffens found, was not merely a reformer but a radical. "The doctrine of Jesus," he observed, "is the most revolutionary propaganda that I have ever encountered. He was against all the evils my reformers were against, and others besides. Jesus denounced interest on money; He opposed the state; He was an anarchist, and His followers practiced Communism."

Did the Christians know this? Did the churches preach it? Eager to explore Christian America to find the answers, Steffens took his muckraking eyes into church pews across the nation over a period of several years. Wherever he happened to be on a Sunday, he attended a Protestant or Catholic church service. He watched carefully and listened intently, learning a great deal in the process—but not about Christianity. "I never heard a Christian sermon preached in a church," he declared. He did not even hear love and understanding being offered to anyone but the "good" people in the audience. It was not only a religious catastrophe, but a human one as well, Steffens felt. "If the Christians and Christian churches could be converted to Christianity," he imagined, "the world could be reformed and the Christians saved, they and all men; wars would cease, peace would be permanent, business would be a service instead of a graft or a gamble, and evolution would proceed without revolution." Instead, as Steffens later wrote, "every real reform movement I ever saw in the United States, and I saw them all, revealed the truth, that the churches—all of them were against democracy."

Although the series on Christ never materialized, Steffens's discovery of the New Testament rekindled his view of a democratic society that lived by its own ideals. And he would soon attempt—disastrously—to personally apply the Golden Rule of Christianity in a legal passion play of life and death.

13

A DEATH IN THE FAMILY

STEFFENS PASSED SUCH a relaxing spring in 1910 that others grew concerned. "I appreciate your reflections on my disappearance from print," he wrote to Laura on April 9, but assured her that it was a temporary lull. According to Steffens, it was precisely his settling into such a life of leisure rather than work that resulted in his return to the magazine world. Josephine had remarked to her husband that his new, carefree pace was like dying, and Steffens could not disagree: "I thought—I would not have dared say it—that dying was not so bad. It was the pleasantest and perhaps the most serviceable thing I had ever done. I could go mow the lawn, sail out in my boat to talk to the oystermen, walk over to Cos Cob, and loaf."

Steffens enjoyed various forms of loafing. Frank Heney, living with his wife across the water in Cos Cob, visited every day. Away from home, Steffens gathered with other progressives, including Louis Brandeis, *Collier's* editor Norman Hapgood, and Ray Stannard Baker in New York to talk politics. At other times he stopped by the *American* to see Finley Peter Dunne and the rest of the staff, or the newspaper rooms "where they really work." Steffens was also the president of the Liberal Club, which met regularly near Gramercy Park and whose members included Charles Edward Russell and Charlotte Perkins Gilman. "A bourgeois uptown organization of mossbacked liberals" in the unabashed view of poet and club member Clement Wood, the club encouraged genteel, intellectual discussions on topics such as labor legislation and censorship restrictions. The discussions reflected the comfortable social standing of its members and distinctly separated the club from its more famous bohemian successor that, in 1913, would meet above Polly's Restaurant in the Village.

Perhaps his favorite place to relax, however, was in the offices of *Everybody's*. Unable to resist the chance to chat with editors, Steffens visited the offices so frequently and offered so much advice that they insisted on making him a part-time member of the editorial board at the gaudy salary of ten thousand dollars. Steffens settled for less—"I did not want to feel that I had to earn that much"—before joining the magazine on a regular basis in the spring of 1910.

While Steffens had been futilely promoting democracy in Boston, *Everybody's* had continued to amass profits from Thomas Lawson's series of stunning exposés on the business scandals, including the life insurance graft that Steffens had previously investigated for McClure, in "Frenzied Finance." "The result," Steffens wrote, "was such an exposure of high finance that the management of my cities looked like good government." To build on the success of Lawson's work, *Everybody's* viewed Wall Street as a prime muckraking target for Steffens, who eagerly agreed.

What he found in Lower Manhattan were some cosmetic changes from the previous decade but a system that remained largely intact, businessmen still no different from politicians. He observed that men he had known years ago as stockbrokers and underlings were now "swelling around" as presidents of banks and trusts. Steffens saw their pride and congratulated them on their achievements, but he also understood that they were still subordinates, "only fronts for the old president or some owner of the bank who had retired to the quiet seclusion of boss . . . exactly as in politics."

So Steffens reacquainted himself with Wall Street, the goal being to produce a series of articles on big business that would parallel his earlier muckraking efforts. He wanted, he told Laura, "to turn attention to Business as the source of corruption and as models of bad government."

One of the people assisting Steffens in his research was a cub reporter who had arrived at *Everybody's* through Steffens's own attempt to shake up the stodgy management of "long and well-trained newspapermen," including himself, who were far too rigid in their ways to even recognize graft or, if they did, to care. Steffens sought a fresher approach that undoubtedly would benefit from the work of younger minds than his. New talent was needed, Steffens asserted repeatedly, finally exhausting the patience of editor E. J. Ridgway, who told Steffens to go out and hire the young recruits he insisted were necessary. To find them, Steffens returned to Harvard, where he had already spent considerable time during his Boston research, seeking "the ablest mind that could express itself in writing." Among the impressive Class of 1910 graduates that included

John Reed, T. S. Eliot, Heywood Broun, and Stuart Chase, Steffens learned that one stood above all others: Walter Lippmann.

The only child of affluent, second-generation German-Jewish parents, Lippmann seemed destined for success from an early age. As a boy, he shook hands with President McKinley, met Admiral George Dewey, and was familiar with the capitals and culture of Europe from his family's annual summer excursions. Lippmann graduated from Harvard after four years that had prepared him almost perfectly for his work with Steffens. His life had not veered significantly from the typical path of a child of wealth until Lippmann, as a volunteer, witnessed the squalor of the tenement rows destroyed by a devastating 1908 fire that left many homeless in the nearby industrial city of Chelsea. Seeking a way toward a better world, Lippmann helped form the university's Socialist Club, where fierce debate and stimulating guest speakers, including Steffens, who spoke on the reform efforts of Tom Johnson, fired the idealistic imaginations of the young students. Lippmann went on to contribute articles to several campus publications, most notably the *Harvard Monthly*.

The energetic, intellectually curious Lippmann had a mind for politics and a talent for writing that caught Steffens's eye. He quickly observed that Lippmann was no practical careerist but a young man devoted to educating himself and learning how the capitalist system, behind the public facade of fairness, actually worked—an approach not unlike that of the young Steffens twenty years earlier. Lippmann, who had already assisted George Santayana at Harvard, asked Steffens intelligent, thoughtful questions that convinced Steffens of Lippmann's perceptive nature.

Steffens did not have to coax Lippmann to join him: The young man, in fact, saw Steffens as his savior. After an unsatisfying stint at a Boston newspaper, Lippmann approached Steffens directly about his aim to write. "What I have dreamed of doing is to work under you," he admitted. "Can you use me in your work? There is no position I should go at with more eagerness, because there is no kind of work that appeals to me as much as yours does." And money was not an issue for Lippmann, who had an allowance from his parents and lived quite simply. "Opportunity to work and learn" he wrote earnestly, "is the thing I am looking for."

Steffens responded quickly, explaining candidly that the job would involve many hours of typing and menial labor and paid only fifteen dollars a week. But the subject of their work—"doing" Wall Street—was the attraction. Moreover, Steffens was determined to have Lippmann by his side: "I'll try to be square with you, but I want you very, very much."

Lippmann readily agreed to leave Cambridge and assist Steffens. While Steffens stayed behind at Little Point to write the articles, Lippmann, who had taken a small room near Steffens's house, was dispatched not only to New York but also across the country, from Washington to Kansas City, Chicago, and other cities, to dig for facts. "Keen, quiet, industrious," Lippmann was a quick study, Steffens saw, who understood what he learned and repeatedly questioned not only the stockbrokers and messenger boys on Wall Street but also the experienced men, such as Older, Whitlock, Spreckels, and Steffens himself.

At first skeptical of Steffens's theory that the system of political and business graft was largely similar at all levels, Lippmann soon saw that his own research led him to the same conclusion: "We found that the anatomy of Big Business was strikingly like that of Tammany Hall: the same pyramiding of influence, the same tendency of power to center on individuals who did not necessarily sit in the official seats, the same effort of human organization to grow independently of human arrangements." Their discovery, Lippmann acknowledged, seemed "to be typical of the whole economic life of this country. It is controlled by groups of men whose influence extends like a web to smaller, tributary groups, cutting across all official boundaries and designations, making short work of all legal formulae, and exercising sovereignty regardless of the little fences we erect to keep it in bounds."

Starting in September 1910, *Everybody's* published their work over the next eight months as a series of articles under the heading "It: An Exposition of the Sovereign Political Power of Organized Business." And "It" did not go unnoticed. The articles led to the formation of the Pujo Committee in the House of Representatives, where an investigation of the big-money trusts ultimately resulted in the Federal Reserve Act of 1913, which dictated more-effective supervision of American banks.

Recognizing that the young Harvard man was a unique talent, Steffens pressed him hard to develop and later recalled his own insistence on getting Lippmann to sum up a thought in one clear sentence: "When Lippmann showed me a paragraph, I'd say, 'Good, but just what did you want to say?' He said he meant to say what the paragraph said, but I'd shake my head and wonder, till in a rage he would plunk it all out in one good clean sentence. Then I'd say, let's put that sentence into the paragraph, and,—well, he learned to do it."

By chance, the affluent town of Greenwich, Connecticut, next to Riverside, became a prime muckraking target of Steffens and Lippmann's. During one of Steffens's lectures, another pillar of the community—a banker—had told

Steffens that while the muckraker's work across the country was very impressive, Greenwich itself was a model of honest, local government where reporters like him would be wasting their time. Naturally, Steffens begged to differ. When he did so publicly in a talk given in New Britain, Norman Talcott, a Greenwich newspaper editor, challenged Steffens to back up his claim. Steffens agreed to investigate the local system and present his findings at a later town meeting, the goal being not necessarily to point a finger of blame but to inspire town leaders to "think what they themselves could do to make it a better place to live in." More devilish was Erwin Edwards, editor of the *Greenwich Graphic*, who informed Steffens that he had "been fighting the ring here alone" for years and hoped to see Steffens "sweep this town clean."

Steffens sent Lippmann and the Steffenses' gardener, a man named George, to observe the goings-on in Greenwich, catch the gossip, and find out who controlled the town and how they did it. The pair were more than up to the task, enabling Steffens to piece together a picture of Greenwich that confirmed his suspicions.

On December 30, 1910, at a packed town meeting that was even attended by New York reporters, Steffens asked for permission to show that Greenwich was as corrupt as any place he had examined. When he started his presentation by asserting that at the last election, some voters were paid $2.50 a vote but Italians received $2.75, the crowd, all except the bosses in the back of the room, was stunned. With Lippmann diagramming on a blackboard, Steffens then went on for an hour, explaining the corrupt nature of American government and business, focusing on how connections and privilege tied the whole system together, the foundation being the voters who endorsed the undemocratic enterprise at each election. Steffens never mentioned Greenwich by name. It was only after some prodding from Steffens that the silent crowd realized that Lippmann had been drawing up the government of their beloved town. Their mixture of applause and embarrassed laughter signaled that Steffens had achieved his aim, and soon the crowd itself was shouting out the names of the local bosses for Lippmann to plug into the appropriate slots on his diagram of a corrupt government.

Steffens finished by asking if, now, everyone agreed that Greenwich had lost its halo. The majority of the crowd noisily approved over the howls of protest from the "typical leading citizens, property-holders, [and] taxpayers (as they call themselves)." The remedy, Steffens suggested, was Christianity: When leaders represented not their own wallets but the people, as Jesus had, democracy would flourish.

By the end of the eventful evening, Lippmann had enjoyed himself, George was bored, and Steffens had passed "two hours of as exciting sport as I have ever had." To his own amazement as much as anyone else's, he had muckraked his own town.

Local reaction to the evening was mixed. Some claimed with relief that Steffens had failed to meet the challenge of proving corruption. But in an editorial, the *Greenwich Press* saw otherwise: "Of course, no well-informed, fair-minded person believes the story. . . . It is quite true that Mr. Steffens . . . said nothing that could ruin any man's private character or furnish a neighborhood with malodorous gossip. But he . . . showed that we are, today, living under a system where the people are not represented, where government by the people is a howling farce."

Lippmann and Steffens soon headed in different directions. Lippmann was well on his way to a career that would make him one of the legendary American journalists of the century, while Steffens, who had already achieved such fame, continued his search for democracy. Although an older Lippmann would observe that Steffens was "too whimsical for a permanent diet," he was most grateful, in those early days of his career, for the training. He once responded to Steffens's inquiry as to whether Lippmann had benefited from their time together:

> Lord, if I could tell you and make you believe it. You'd know then why "Everybody who knows you loves you." You gave me yourself and then you ask me whether it has been worthwhile. For that I can't write down my thanks. I shall have to live them. Whenever I understand a man and like him, instead of hating him or ignoring him, it'll be your work. You've got into my blood, I think, and there'll be a little less bile in the world as a result. . . . You gave me a chance to start—you know what that means to a fellow who has an indifferent world staring him in the face.

Steffens thoroughly enjoyed their time together as well, although he understood that Lippmann's exceptional analytical skills someday might be used to upstage the muckrakers themselves. "We have been the blind leading the blind," Steffens admitted to Heney in December 1910. "But we have led, and not so very far astray, and we are beginning to see the light. I suppose some young fellow like Lippmann will expose us some day, and I say, let 'em expose us. No one can throw more dirt on some of us than we have eaten in our private humility."

Throughout 1910, Steffens continued to support socialist and liberal movements nationwide, spending significant time with Heney, Ben Lindsey, and

Rudolph Spreckels. Steffens was hopeful but hardly confident concerning the electorate in general. "They really deserve to hear such stuff for all eternity," he wrote to Whitlock about one of the mayor's speeches, "but I notice that they cannot read, not anything that is longer than a meal. They can't fix their attention on a bit of paper that long (unless it is covered with figures). So my fear is that they may miss something in it."

In August, Steffens's mother fell ill, sending Steffens hurriedly back to California. Unconscious, she passed away before Steffens could have a final word with her, although he later took comfort in the belief, he told his father, that she "could have wished for nothing." After returning to Little Point, he urged his father to correspond frequently—"it is the regularity that I am after."

At the same time, Steffens was forced to confront another matter that competed awkwardly with his work and too often reflected poorly on Steffens himself: his marriage. In the letter to his father, he noted that Josephine felt "much nearer to all of us than she did before mother died," a revealing comment in that Steffens, who had lived with Josephine for nearly twenty years, remained oblivious to Josephine's own long-standing need for companionship and her searing loneliness within her own marriage. His ignorance, though, would soon be removed all too tragically.

Through the summer and fall of 1910, Josephine's health failed again. Often bedridden, she suffered from depression and numbness in her arms and legs. Steffens wrote to his father in October, "Josephine is still very sick. Her nerves are better, but her stomach is all out of condition, and she suffers a good deal, not only from the sick spells but from headaches. She lies abed, with her nurse at hand, and hardly speaks at all." Days of apparent improvement were followed by cruel relapses. By Christmas, Steffens feared the worst. "Hope is still held out to us," he reported to Laura on the bleak holiday, "and we hang on to it, as J. does, but, like her also, we wonder how long it can last. I sometimes wonder how long it should last, for the suffering is intense and pathetic."

Three days later, a team of doctors gave Steffens the dreaded news: Josephine had Bright's disease, a failure of the kidneys. She might linger for months, but she would not recover. What pained Steffens most through the anxious months of waiting was to see Josephine's strong-willed struggle for life, her insistent focus on the future, even while on her deathbed, as Steffens could only tell her encouraging lies. She yearned for life, unable to accept the cold reality that she had been cheated by fate. For Josephine, the end to all of her pain came on January 7, 1911. Josephine's distraught mother, two days before her eighty-third birthday, recorded the tragedy in her diary: "My poor girl died last night at midnight and left me desolate. She went just after midnight. Lincoln and I were called in just before midnight. I kissed her. She said goodbye to each servant and said you have been faithful to me. Then I kissed and her husband kissed, and she went."

Letters of condolences poured in to Steffens, but nothing could shield him from a crushing truth: Josephine had died tormented by resentment, and Steffens was no innocent bystander. In his eight-hundred-page autobiography, he devotes barely a page to the passing of his wife of nearly two decades; his words, however, describe clearly a piece of the tragedy that was Josephine's life and death:

> My wife, who had, as she thought, given up her life to her mother, stayed home when she might have traveled with me, regulated her whole being in the belief that her mother, so much older than she was, would die first, and then she, the daughter, could venture forth and— live. When Josephine Bontecou took to her bed, knowing she was to die first, she was so enraged that she refused for days to see her mother, and then when she did she reproached her—tragically. For the mother, too, had given up her life, as she thought, to her daughter; she had lived with her, gone with her to Germany when Josephine wanted to study, traveled with her when we traveled and married and traveled— where we wanted to, not always where the mother preferred to go.

Seeing Josephine's terrible fight against what so certainly lay ahead, her fury at having her future cut off, affected Steffens at least as much as her actual death. He simply had never imagined such feelings simmering inside his own spouse, and he commented upon it repeatedly at the time. To Ray Stannard Baker, "The whole thing is beyond words. . . . The end knocked me down"; to Belle Case La Follette, "The pathos lies in this, that Mrs. Steffens did not want to go; not yet. . . . You understand? She wanted to live, and she died"; to Harlow Gale, "It was not alone [the] loss that hurt, it was the knowledge I had that Josephine was not willing to die. She had not finished her job; she hadn't done her best, and she wept sadly, oh, very sadly over that."

Steffens then was confronted with his own selfish contribution to Josephine's pitiful end, and he should not have been surprised by what he learned. Josephine had left behind a carefully written diary that gave unsparing judgments of those around her, most particularly Steffens. His personally satisfying life had come at a steep price, he discovered. The diary provided "such a portrait of a husband as I have never seen in literature," he wrote. "The fact that I was the husband did not hinder me from seeing what an ass a 'good husband' is in the eyes of an intelligent wife who is thinking of him, who is thinking always of graft or business or—something else; who is always at hand but never at home." (Indeed, Steffens conducted his Greenwich town meeting at the height of Josephine's illness.) Two years later, in a letter to his young niece Jane, he offered a wry but honest comment on what husbands like Steffens contribute to the domestic side of a family: "I don't count husbands much; I never did; not even when I was one myself."

The truth, far too late, hit Steffens straight on. Although he had lived with Josephine for years, he had hardly known her most strongly held thoughts. She was the backbone of his life, the person he talked to so readily about the issues in *his* life, and she had almost always listened and tried to advise and encourage him. The roles, however, were seldom reversed—Josephine's issues were not often Steffens's. She had her mother to confide in, which was as far as Steffens saw the matter. Now, from the grave, Josephine's message was all too apparent to Steffens.

Intensifying the tragedy was the sorry plight of Mrs. Bontecou, who had been with Steffens for the past two decades and dearly wished to remain at Little Point, but her son insisted that she join him at his home in Troy, New York, in the spring. In the weeks prior to her departure, she repeatedly expressed in her diary her devotion to Steffens and her reluctance to leave. "Only Lincoln here. He is kindness itself to me"; "I grieve at parting from Lincoln, who has been always lovely to me"; "Oh how I hate to leave dear Lincoln"; and "My heart is broken at leaving Lincoln. I shall perhaps never see him again," were entries from early 1911. In late March, having moved in with her son, she wrote of her loneliness in her diary: "Now always alone." In early April, she made two entries on separate pages, noting Steffens's upcoming birthday on April 6. After receiving a letter from Steffens, she replied to "Dearest Lincoln," thanking him "a thousand times" for his love and support: "I shall always hold close in my heart the memory of the happy years passed with you and with her in your home and when we were left alone together how you comforted me and were as a son to me."

Despite Mrs. Bontecou's fondness for Steffens, it was no secret that Steffens, while a brilliant journalist who seemingly could not bring himself to hate anyone, hoarded his time, carefully protecting his freedom to roam as he chose and avoiding any limitations on his freedom that might have distracted him from himself. And it was usually done with a smile on his face. Hutchins Hapgood, who knew Steffens for nearly forty years, saw the conflict within Steffens perhaps better than his friend and tactfully addressed it: "He was, I think, to the end a lover of the pure social truth, wherever and however it could be found. For this reason, he avoided all personal commitments and shunned by a kind of instinct emotional entanglements. He once said to me, 'You bare your bosom to the knife, and I run around the corner.'"

And while Steffens felt undeniable and painful guilt for the role he played in his wife's unhappiness and dearly missed her, he could not grieve for a lost love, because he had not felt love in his marriage for many years. The hardships he recorded in his autobiography were that without Josephine, he did not know the addresses of his friends, how to pay his taxes, or where to buy his underwear. "I was lost," he admitted, perhaps more than he even knew. In fairness to Steffens, though, he probably shared this trait with most successful men of his time.

Now, at forty-five, with Josephine gone, he sensed, correctly, that only a return to his work would distract him from such miserable feelings. He admitted as much to his old friend Gale a month after Josephine's death: "I hardly know what to do. I have my work, of course, and I keep plugging away at that. . . . But the joy of it is gone. It's duty now. . . . It isn't real and natural. Being bound to do it, however, I guess I'll not only go on, but maybe will pick up some lead of pleasure again. I don't know." Two weeks after Josephine passed away, he had an inkling to investigate death itself, telling Whitlock, "I'd like to see if death cannot in some way be made as beautiful as life. Why has no one ever studied that? We must not let it remain as it is, a wreck, a sudden disaster."

Two aspects of Steffens's work that always entertained him were politics and travel, and he predictably returned to them in the spring of 1911. A revolt was brewing among Republican progressives toward the increasingly intransigent Taft, who time after time sided with the most conservative members of Congress. Having lost hope that Taft would support any reform, a group of influential party members, including La Follette, Brandeis, Heney, Howe, Ray Stannard Baker, and Amos and Gifford Pinchot organized the National Progressive Republican League in January, with the unstated goal of unseating the great traitor, Taft. And their candidate to replace him was obvious: the fiery La Follette. Offshoots of the league quickly formed, one being the Progressive Federation of Publicists and Editors, with Steffens, eager to push reform, among its more prominent members. The unwillingness of Roosevelt, however, to offer the progressive revolt anything more than tepid support—he had been working diligently, in fact, on a compromise to heal the intraparty wounds—momentarily restrained the league's influence.

With more freedom now than he had anticipated or desired, Steffens again headed west in April, along with Lippmann and Steffens's pet bulldog, which

Thomas Lawson had given him and which Steffens had appropriately named Frenzy—"I love the little bruiser as I love some of my bad politicians," he told his sister Dot. Following the family visit, Steffens, having rented out Little Point, returned briefly to New York before setting off in June on a journey across the Atlantic with a Boston Chamber of Commerce party. His stay in New York, though, would prove not quite brief enough.

One of the more interesting people in Steffens's life at that time was a woman of intrigue even by New York's colorful standards. Two years younger than Steffens, Mary Austin—mystical, intense, opinionated, a vivid chronicler of desert and Native American life—had made her literary name in 1903 with *The Land of Little Rain*, a widely praised collection of essays on the truth and beauty of desert life in Southern California. She was writing, Steffens said, "what had never been written." She was also living what had rarely been lived. Equally at ease in the fashionable literary settings in Manhattan and with tribal life in the Mojave Desert, she raised eyebrows with her knee-length hair and sartorial creativity, often preferring flowing Greek robes, the beads and leather dress of an Indian princess, or, as William Allen White observed, "the most God-awful hats that made her look like a battleship." At the National Arts Club in New York, she was affectionately referred to as "Old Sitting Bull." She wrote prolifically, often sitting high up in a tree in a wickiup—an Indian lodge made of brush and poles—in Carmel, and had meditated in a convent in Italy. Whether talking to the powerful (she was friendly with Theodore Roosevelt and Herbert Hoover) or to ordinary souls, she offered unsolicited, and unapologetic, opinions. In fact, she saw herself as a prophet. Others saw her as a gifted, insightful writer with an unimaginable range of eccentricities and, ultimately, a great loneliness that she could never shake.

In her autobiography, Austin wrote that she saw Steffens in Carmel after the earthquake that devastated San Francisco in April 1906. It was probably their initial meeting. They evidently did not see one another again until 1910, when Austin arrived in New York to help produce her play, *The Arrow Maker*. They may have met through Emma Goldman, a mutual friend. With Josephine's health in tragic decline, the timing of the encounter was bound to produce complications—and did.

The relationship that developed between Steffens and Austin was complex and much more heartfelt on Austin's side than Steffens's. As a successful, intelligent woman unafraid to speak her mind, Austin, not surprisingly, caught Steffens's attention. In the same Christmas letter to Laura in which he spoke of the imminent death of Josephine, Steffens noted that he had "been seeing" Austin and called her an "odd but interesting woman." He convinced her to keep a diary of her impressions on New York, apparently challenging her to write a book on the city that would rival *The Land of Little Rain*. In the opening passages, she confides that "Steffy" has shown a good amount of interest in her. He went on to lavishly praise her latest book, *Lost Borders* ("her prose is . . . conscious, beautiful poetry"), in a June 1911 review in the *American*.

No doubt both were ready for a significant other in their lives, but for sharply different reasons. As 1910 closed, Josephine was nearing the end of a slow death that forced Steffens to take a painful look at his personal failings. The chance to unburden a lot of his doubts and regrets on a patient and sympathetic woman must have been highly therapeutic to Steffens, and he evidently took advantage of it far more than was wise or fair to Austin. To encourage their mutual interests, he urged her to embrace the city. She wrote in her diary of Steffens's wish for her to know and love New York as he did: "Steffy is saturated with the city . . . and he can't understand that it will take me more years to learn my way about in it than were necessary to know the trails from Mojave to Lone Pine."

She, in turn, made no secret of her wish to find a strong man she could truly admire and love. In her short story "Frustrate," she had written, "I thought if I could get to know a man who was big enough so I couldn't walk around him . . . somebody that I could reach and reach and not find the end of,—I shouldn't feel so frustrated." In her frustration, she had already left behind a mismatched husband and placed her mentally ill daughter in an institution; with Steffens, a man at ease with presidents, she had reason to assume that she had finally found her savior. While Steffens in fact looked rather physically fragile, he had a ready supply of charm that he used unsparingly. This, along with his impeccable taste for clothes, neatly trimmed goatee, and curious eyes that peered out from behind his round spectacles, gave him what to many was at least a slightly intimidating but compelling air of intellect. Steffens, recalled socialite and arts patron Mabel Dodge, captured her completely.

Before leaving New York on his family trip to California in April, Steffens, through a miscommunication, did not see Austin before leaving, and she wrote to him the following day, "You cannot imagine how sorry I was to have missed you last evening," concluding with encouragement, "I shall keep a candle burning for the success of your journey and quick return." Apparently responding to a later letter, Steffens assured her in May that he would not grieve over Josephine forever, while at the same time pushing her to write to him: "If you wish to put yourself down on paper you may do so with me and be sure, oh, absolutely sure, that you will be read as I would be read—with the wish only to understand."

Probably unknown to Austin (or, if she knew, she repressed the thought), the style of the letter is quite common to many Steffens wrote to both men and women throughout his life. His sincerity is obvious and deliberately so— Steffens undoubtedly felt it as he sat and penned the words. At times, the sincerity remained firm, his correspondence and relationship with Laura being an example. More frequently, though, the sincerity was fleeting, particularly when it involved women and required Steffens to make a commitment of his valued personal time. Josephine and his former fiancée, Gussie Burgess, knew this side of Steffens well, and Mary Austin soon would as well.

The notion of a commitment was interpreted very differently in this case by Steffens and Austin. Steffens was back in New York where whatever had existed between Steffens and Austin came to a crashing and, to Austin, stunning finish. On June 6, checking on a double apartment that she thought would be suitable for them, Austin came upon Steffens and another woman looking at the same rental. Gussie was in New York as well, working as a music teacher at Hunter College, and, following an unhappy marriage, had reunited with Steffens after being separated for over twenty years.

Austin was livid, even feeling suicidal at times. She fumed in her diary that the episode would "bear bitter fruit in my own life." In her semiautobiographical novel, *A Woman of Genius*, published in 1912, the heroine, Olivia Lattimore, reflected on the disastrous end to her hopes with a man resembling Steffens, and her fierce will to survive:

> I suffered incredibly. I had given all I had . . . and all at once, without my knowledge or consent he had dropped me into the class of women who may be taken or dropped for the mere liking or disliking. He wouldn't have taken a newspaper from a street stand and not left the customary penny. But he had taken me . . . and my price had been great love and lasting. How often we had said that to one another . . . such love as ours . . . *such love as ours!*

Austin was not a woman about to be trifled with and abandoned. After spending some time in Carmel before moving back to New York more than a year later, in the fall of 1912, she defiantly took an apartment across the street from The Players, where Steffens was staying. Apparently obsessed with Steffens, she stalked him, his friends claimed, in every corner of New York, from

Dodge's apartment into Carnegie Hall. "It appeared," Dodge wrote, "to be not so much a wound to the heart as to her sense of power." Still, her heart clearly felt the blow as well. For more than a year after the incident, Austin deluged Steffens with dozens of pages of letters, at times condemning, lecturing, cajoling, pleading, and generally making every attempt to maintain a presence in his life. Her points were not subtle: "This is the second time in the last few months that I have taken the greatest pains to make concessions, and in both cases you deliberately turn your back on me"; "Now don't call me hysterical; I am no more hysterical than you are when you take men to task for misusing public office"; "I know that you do not see that I am trying sincerely and simply to save you from yourself, not just turning aside and giving you up"; "I am glad to get a human letter from you"; "You betray me, lie to me, cheat me"; and "You break my heart, damage my work, destroy my health, wound and insult me by putting my most sacred feelings at the mercy of a woman not my equal" were typical comments in Austin's torrent of analysis, ultimately an exercise in futility.

Steffens withstood it all. He apparently saw Austin as a friend, even a very good friend, and was gentle in his responses to her ongoing outrage. But he would not consent to the conditions she was demanding. He had a satisfying relationship with Gussie and certainly did not need Austin as she clearly needed him. Austin, though, would have nothing to do with a "friendship" truce, obviously what Steffens preferred. Her letters indicate her belief that theirs was a true romance. Steffens did not view Austin in that light, showing interest in her writing and intellect more than anything else. Austin herself was known to friends as a highly fragile personality with enough vanity to have taken a close relationship and, in a flight of fancy, imagined a love that did not exist. Of course, Steffens could have informed Austin of Gussie's presence before the apartment-hunting incident, but given Austin's reaction when she did finally learn the truth, it is not hard to understand why Steffens, not the most decisive man in any personal relationship, chose not to.

In an interview conducted more than fifty years after the incident, Elsie Martinez, wife of artist Xavier Martinez and a Carmel friend of Steffens's, recalled that Steffens told her that he had planned to marry Austin and even pressured her to do so. Steffens was capable of saying nearly anything to a woman, so it is not impossible that he discussed marriage with Austin. But the timing of their relationship makes that scenario unlikely. Not until December 1910 was it clear that Josephine was going to die, and Gussie appeared on the scene shortly thereafter. That he would have brought up marriage with Austin in such circumstances is unlikely, even for Steffens. Known as a raconteur, he may have been embellishing the telling of the tale with Martinez. Also, Martinez herself, an irreverent woman, was fond of a good story and may have created some of her own details, or she may have simply not remembered events correctly from such a distance. According to her account, Steffens asked Austin to marry him in Carmel (four years before Josephine died); Austin and Steffens, at Austin's urging, went back to New York together after meeting in Carmel; Austin was often reluctant to see Steffens in New York; Ella Winter, later to become Steffens's second wife, was with Steffens when Austin encountered them at the apartment; and Ella wanted the apartment immediately so that she and Steffens could marry and live there—all falsehoods.

Strangely, though, Steffens and Austin remained on civil terms for years. They continued to get together at least on occasion, and they certainly did see each other at Mabel Dodge's salon—Steffens probably introduced Austin to Dodge, and the two women became rather close. It was through the bittersweet words of Austin, in fact, that Dodge learned much of the bizarre history between Steffens and Austin. In December 1912, as she prepared to leave for California, Austin told Steffens that she hoped to see him from time to time and wished him luck with his work on Christianity. She was still writing to him as late as 1920, referring to him as "Steffy." In 1932, long after their falling out, Austin sent a letter to Dodge with yet more analysis of their relationship.

Their autobiographies, though, reflected an ultimate coolness between them. Austin mentioned Steffens only once in passing, and Steffens ignored her altogether. Austin's simmering revenge toward Steffens came in her novel, *No. 26 Jayne Street*, not published until 1920, in which a man resembling Steffens is rejected by two women. When Austin had finished unleashing her anger in writing the book during a stay with Mabel Dodge, she came out of her room and told Dodge, "I killed a man this morning." Only in fiction, though: Steffens never bore any scars from the assault.

Although he would have preferred to stay in New York and write, the extremely awkward situation with Austin and encouragement from Fred Howe, a municipal expert, persuaded him to head to Europe in mid-June with a Chamber of Commerce party to observe the progressive governments running many of Europe's cities. Not surprisingly, given the events of the past year, Steffens spent the trip "savage with irritability," contemplating another change of direction in his life. Just before his departure from America, the *New York Globe*, formerly Steffens's old paper the *Commercial Advertiser*, had contacted him. Henry Wright, still in charge, asked him to return and reorganize the news departments, and with his following of young protégés eager to assist him,

Steffens was very tempted to take another plunge into investigative journalism. He considered the matter at length during his European tour, returning to New York on August 22.

But the summer trip had exhausted him, so, after a brief stop in New York, he stole away to a cottage on Martha's Vineyard in late August, informing Lippmann and John Reed but almost no one else of his whereabouts. He also told Reed, who lived in Greenwich Village and had encouraged Steffens to rent an apartment in Reed's building, that he would be taking two rooms there. For the moment, alone, he spent his days swimming, walking, reading, writing, and, most of all, resting.

Evidently the break more than refreshed Steffens. In late September, he wrote full of vigor to his sister Lou and her husband, Allen Suggett, a liberal-leaning dentist to whom Steffens had grown close. ("I count you a discovery," he had written to Allen the previous year.) He was taking the *Globe* position, he told them, regardless of the consequences. He knew it would "wreck" him again, but he did not care. There was a big job ahead, and he meant to tackle it. His aim was to reform news reporting in a way that would be "copied everywhere." It was a challenge, but Steffens felt he was ready. "I am myself again," he assured them.

Steffens took over his duties on October 2, 1911, and once more eagerly pursued the news. Single again, he moved into the rather unkempt but bustling apartment building in Greenwich Village, where, as he observed, "youth lived and Reds gathered." His timing was most opportune, as the Village was just entering its bohemian heyday, about to be overrun by a fascinating, chaotic mix of young poets, painters, actors, socialists, writers, feminists, and labor leaders who embraced personal freedom and, often, the comparatively wizened Steffens himself, his meticulous, formal clothing notwithstanding. Among the impressive throng arriving on the scene were Lippmann, Theodore Dreiser, Hutchins Hapgood, Bill Haywood, Max Eastman, Djuna Barnes, Edna St. Vincent Millay, Emma Goldman, Eugene O'Neill, Margaret Sanger, and perhaps the most recognizable Villager of all, Hippolyte Havel. With his unruly mass of hair and a fiery red moustache, the volcanic anarchist's favorite expression, "bourgeois pigs!" succinctly captured the Village ambience, as did his rebuke to a police officer after being arrested for urinating in a gutter: "You mean I don't even have the rights of an ordinary horse?" The zest for experiment and free thinking helped rejuvenate Steffens.

At 42 Washington Square, Steffens lived one floor below an apartment full of recent Harvard graduates, including the irrepressible John Reed. Steffens remembered his young friend well from his Boston days when Reed, a member of the Socialist Club along with Lippmann, had attended Steffens's speeches on campus. Although intimidated by the older muckraker ("I was afraid of him then—afraid of his wisdom, his seriousness") Reed approached Steffens afterward, inviting him to address the staff of the *Harvard Monthly*. Steffens's suggestion that they carefully examine—muckrake, really—the inner workings of Harvard itself was just the type of investigative catalyst Reed was seeking, and he soon paid homage to Steffens by praising the older man's new work, *Upbuilders*, in the *Monthly*.

When Reed graduated from Harvard, he had a reputation among some as a self-centered, publicity-seeking rake. Steffens, while immensely fond of Reed, understood the sentiment, recalling that when Reed arrived in New York in March, the young man was "nothing but a bundle of fine nerves, bulging energy, overweening vanity, and trembling curiosity." And happiness—"No ray of sunshine," Steffens wrote, "no drop of foam, no young animal, bird or fish, and no star, was as happy as that boy was."

Reed gave no end of worry to his parents, who missed him dearly back in Portland. "I think and talk of you every day, and love you and am proud of you every hour," his father, C. J. Reed, wrote to him. For some practical help, however, the senior Reed asked Steffens, his old friend, to keep an eye on the impulsive young man. "Get him a job, let him see everything, but don't let him be anything for a while," Steffens recalled him saying. "Don't let him get a conviction right away or a business or a career. . . . Let him play." Steffens happily complied, getting Reed a part-time position at *American Magazine*, where Steffens and the other *McClure's* refugees had landed several years earlier, and offering a word of advice: "Do well what you have to do, but keep the job in its second place."

John Reed could not have found himself in a place more suited to his boundless energy and inquisitive nature than the Village. His own chaotic apartment became a frequent shelter for artists, radicals, and countless lost souls. After a full day spent chasing a story, reading manuscripts of reputable writers or bad poets and joyfully rejecting them, or indulging in a long lunch filled with wine and intense conversation, Reed would return to 42 Washington Square for a night of heated banter and pleasure with any number of guests, some of whom simply camped out on the floor.

Reed wanted the full Village experience, and Steffens assisted by introducing him to not only Theodore Roosevelt but an array of socialists, anarchists, labor leaders, and others. But Reed, like Steffens many years earlier, wanted to see the city at street level as well. A poet at heart, Reed roamed about New York seeking the full range of human adventure stretching before him, from the tramps in the Bowery to the swells of Fifth Avenue, from the restaurants of Little Italy to baseball games at the Polo Grounds, striking up conversations with panhandlers, streetwalkers, and longshoremen while spending money freely (mostly his father's or Steffens's) at Broadway shows, the Metropolitan Opera, or fashionable uptown restaurants. He slept under bridges and with prostitutes. His New York life would influence him for the rest of his days. "I couldn't help but observe," he wrote, "the ugliness of poverty and all its train of evil, the cruel inequality between rich people who had too many motor-cars and poor people who didn't have enough to eat. It didn't come to me from books that the workers produced all the wealth of the world, which went to those who did not earn it."

Although Reed seemed intent on meeting the entire Village, his mentor above all was Steffens. "More than any other man, Lincoln Steffens has influenced my mind," he wrote several years later. "Being with Steffens is to me like flashes of clear light; it is as if I see him, and myself, and the world, with new eyes." Steffens treated Reed along with Lippmann as his protégés. Reed sought his advice and opinion on matters from politics to art, money to love ("When you really fall in love, you'll know it, and,—then, Jack—I'll be for you, no matter who she is. For I *believe* in love. . . . And in you, Jack. Wait for the real thing. It's worth waiting for"), and Reed's breathless outbursts provided just the companionship that Steffens, reborn in New York, savored. Steffens recalled vividly how Reed would often barge into his room and wake him up to blurt out his stories about whatever had just passed before his eyes:

> Girls, plays, bums, I.W.W.'s, strikers—each experience was vivid in him, a story, which he often wrote; every person, every idea; Bill Haywood, some prostitute down and out on a park bench, a vaudeville dancer; socialism; the I.W.W. program—all were on a live level with him. Everything was the most wonderful thing in the world. Jack and his crazy young friends were indeed the most wonderful thing in the world.

Reed gushed on to such an extent that Steffens, no doubt sleepless and seeing the young poet's talent slipping away, felt obliged to give him a word of advice: "Write it down."

His own thoughts, influenced by the unexpected setbacks in the 1909 elections, were somewhat less wonderful. He saw that his earlier ideas, including those he was putting forth in his Boston—1915 plan, were doomed to fail. Only a much stronger jolt, he believed, would purge the rotten system of centuries of graft. Evolution, his earlier hope, was out. "Nothing but revolution could change the system," he now believed.

To that end, Steffens became increasingly active in the Free Speech League. Founded in 1902, after the assassination of President McKinley led to a series of repressive laws aimed at anarchists, the league was spearheaded by the tireless writer and lawyer Theodore Schroeder, whose radical views on speech and obscenity laws made him a highly controversial figure. In April 1911, Steffens and Whitlock were among those named as league officers. Schroeder evidently exercised his own freedom of speech to no end, causing Steffens to quip, "I believe in Free Speech for everyone except Schroeder." While Steffens was never as active as Schroeder, he was vocal in his support of labor, particularly the anarchists, often in tandem with league president Leonard Abbott. The league's persistent and aggressive efforts ultimately led to the formation of the American Civil Liberties Union in 1920.

One incident that left Steffens indignant was an editorial in the October 1911 issue of *Everybody's* advocating strong censorship of sexually explicit plays. Steffens replied immediately. "Any censorship by authority is unsatisfactory," he asserted, conceding that while most Americans assumed they had freedom of speech, they did not—"not by a long shot." Noting his connection to the Free Speech League, he explained that he had no love of obscenity but had love of liberty. And regarding obscenity, repression was not the solution. "The cause of obscenity is ignorance and mystery. Why not cure ignorance with knowledge and so dissipate the mystery?" he suggested. But the people themselves, he acknowledged, were guilty of letting others deprive them of their own free will to make such changes. "It is a constant source of dull amazement to me," Steffens observed, "with a tongue in my mouth and a pen in my hand, to hear preachers, teachers, and editors forever appealing to force. . . . Have we no faith in God and natural laws? . . . No hope in Man, who is . . . so very, very willing to be led?" Yet, when Steffens's own free will led him back to California, a potent mix of Christianity, socialism, and dynamite nearly destroyed his career.

14

DYNAMITE

THE GRIPPING NEWS story of the time was the controversial McNamara case in Los Angeles, which mushroomed into a historical event so full of intrigue, rumors, charges, countercharges, secret deals, partisan recollections, and absolute hatred on both sides that even now, the facts of the case—and Steffens's role in it—remain somewhat unclear.

A deadly explosion was the catalyst. In the midst of a bitter labor quarrel involving a union of iron workers, the headquarters of the *Los Angeles Times* had blown up just past midnight on October 1, 1910. Twenty-one workmen were killed in what *Times* owner Harrison Gray Otis, the city's self-appointed strongman, called "the crime of the century."

The prosecution contended that the blast was caused by the explosion of a suitcase packed with dynamite that ignited several tons of stored ink and turned the building into an inferno. Who would inflict such damage was no mystery to Otis. Organized labor, so influential in San Francisco, was far less prevalent in Los Angeles, and for years the combative Otis and the *Times* had been outspoken in their efforts to stifle any union activity, to the point that Los Angeles had come to be known as "Otistown" to angry workers. Just the previous summer, Otis had strongly promoted the enforcement of antipicketing laws; his influence resulted in the arrests of hundreds of strikers. Now, Otis saw the violent hand of labor striking back, and he had no intention of wasting time by waiting for police reports or the collection of evidence. "Unionist Bombs Wreck the 'Times'" blared the next *Times* headline, printed at a separate plant. In his editorial, Otis chastised the enemy with poetic zeal: "O you anarchic scum, you cowardly murderers, you leeches upon honest labor, you midnight assassins." Adding more drama to the scene, Job Harriman, the socialist candidate for mayor and Otis's chief nemesis, was poised to win the upcoming runoff election against the more moderate and "good government" incumbent, Mayor George Alexander.

To investigate the bombing, Alexander brought in William Burns, by then the nation's leading private detective—with the ego to match—who had been working on a number of cases involving bombings of construction sites. Burns, although respected by Steffens for his cleverness and tenacity at uncovering the truth in his previous investigations in Oregon and San Francisco, was not in good favor with either labor or Otis. The *Times* owner had objected strenuously to his pursuit of railway owners in San Francisco in the case that Steffens had covered in 1907. Burns's sleuthing took him to the Midwest, where he rounded up two brothers allegedly involved in the deaths. In Detroit, James McNamara, the younger of the brothers and the man rumored to be behind numerous other bombings of buildings put up by nonunion workers, was arrested first, on April 12. Barely a week later, John McNamara, the secretary of the Bridge and Structural Iron Workers Union and possibly the mastermind of several previous industrial explosions, was taken into custody and whisked—kidnapped, labor charged—to California for trial. Both men ended up in a Los Angeles jail, where they became immediate martyrs to labor leaders. While John impressed even the prosecution with his solid bearing and grace under pressure, Burns felt that "there was no such thing as conscience" concerning James. What's more, it was James who was accused of the actual crime. Both brothers, Burns claimed, were "deep in the dregs of immoral living" while spending one thousand dollars a month of union money "to finance murder and destruction." The McNamara brothers became known as the "dynamiters," among the most famous prisoners in the country.

On his summer trip abroad, Steffens had discussed the McNamara case with Burns in Paris and British labor leader Kier Hardie in London, as well as with the labor crowd in New York, and he knew the trial was sure to be front-page news. His interest in it lay not so much in the innocence or guilt of the accused—he acknowledged "an undoubting belief that labor, if not the McNamaras, was guilty" (not surprising, given his time spent with Burns)—but in "the cause, consequences, and the significance thereof." And he saw himself as uniquely poised to take on the assignment. "It's a delicate job, somewhat like handling dynamite," he acknowledged, "but somebody has to tackle it hard; why shouldn't I be the McNamara of my profession?"

Vengeance was keen on both sides, and the case was developing into a pure class struggle. Capitalists, none more than Otis, wanted the union violence that had been escalating across the country crushed and the McNamaras hanged as cold-blooded killers. Labor leaders, while insisting that the McNamaras were innocent, countered that they were being forced to take drastic measures in defending themselves because they were targeted for extinction by Otis and other anti-union, open-shop capitalists. Others said that gas leaks, which workers in the aging building had been complaining about for months, had caused the blast. Public opinion in Los Angeles, already leaning toward the Left politically, was inclined for the moment to believe in the McNamaras.

Otis, still robust in his seventies, was a key figure in the proceedings. Descended from an old-stock New England family and named after his more notable relative, Massachusetts Senator Harrison Gray Otis, "General" Otis had enlisted in the Civil War and was twice wounded, which led to his proud preference for his military moniker. Later he had gone west, bought the struggling *Times*, and rescued it from near oblivion. Almost single-handedly, he turned it into a paper of influence, especially in the war on organized workers, who were known as sluggers, rowdies, trouble-breeders, ruffians, industrial vampires, and other epithets to *Times* readers. The *Los Angeles Times* building itself had the design of a fortress, and Otis's own mansion was called "The Bivouac." Ever prepared to show labor where he stood, the General kept a case of loaded shotguns near the managing editor's desk and fifty rifles in a tower room. If Los Angeles, a city whose robust expansion, most agreed, had resulted from the dictates—and money—of Otis, was to be the battleground of the fight against labor, Otis had no plans to take prisoners.

Steffens hoped it could be a war without prisoners at all. He saw the McNamara story as the latest, and perhaps most significant, clash in the epic struggle that had been intensifying between the workers and owners for years. In his muckraking days, he had often observed how power was used not for democratic purposes but for maintaining the spoils system of profit and privilege, which, Steffens suspected, would play itself out again in Los Angeles. His goal was to give readers a panoramic view of the story. The daily details of the trial mattered less to him than what he saw as the brutal David and Goliath class battle being fought in the background, a fight he was sure would be reported from the moneyed side, if at all.

Steffens aimed to gather support from a consortium of newspapers that would allow him to provide an in-depth look at the trial, which would have a wide readership. Wright assisted by calling other major dailies and eventually persuading more than twenty papers to carry Steffens's reports. In early November 1911, Steffens went to Los Angeles feeling "well-backed." More than sixty other journalists had preceded him.

After some aggressive coaxing from American Federation of Labor (AFL) president Samuel Gompers, Clarence Darrow ("the attorney for the damned, the orator of the minority," as Steffens described him) had agreed to defend the McNamaras in what was shaping up as a life-and-death case not only for the defendants but for labor itself. Even as vicious as the tactics between both labor and capital had become, the movement could hardly expect public sympathy for murder by dynamite. So labor, almost in a panic, made a nationwide appeal for money (which immediately flowed in) and paid Darrow whatever price was necessary to ensure victory. Burns claimed the figure ran into the millions; it was at least six figures. Darrow himself estimated that $350,000 would be needed to meet the challenge. With his sizable ego and dexterity at influencing others, legally or otherwise, Darrow, labor hoped, would be well worth the expense.

Although Darrow had made much of his money representing corporate interests, his history was one of solid support for the workers' cause, particularly his staunch defense of the Pullman strikers and Debs more than a decade earlier. More recently, in a sensational murder trial in Idaho, Darrow had gained an acquittal of the brawny, hard-drinking, one-eyed William "Big Bill" Haywood, then the secretary-treasurer of the Western Federation of Miners. Darrow, who once described society as "organized injustice," was seen as a leftist sympathizer if not a closet radical himself, well suited to defend the working class.

Now, the cause of labor had arisen again with the McNamaras. Steffens, who had known Darrow for years, understood the strengths and weaknesses of the high-profile lawyer who once more carried the hopes of labor. While Darrow could be a courageous man with nerves of steel even in the tensest moments, he also had a tendency toward deep cynicism and at times quickly descended into obvious worry and doubt. In the McNamara case, Darrow did waver between a vocal but risky defense of the brothers and a safer, out-of-court settlement. At all costs, Darrow wanted to avoid the death penalty for the brothers. Steffens was concerned, seeing Darrow as "more of a poet" than a fighter. Not that the attorney had no power; Steffens simply saw his power and his weakness in the same trait: his "highly sensitive, emotional nature which sets his seeing mind in motion in that loafing body."

Nevertheless, Steffens was pleased to be working with Darrow, who had been eager to persuade Brand Whitlock, a mutual friend, to come out from Ohio and help with the defense. Whitlock, however, was in the middle of a mayoral race in Toledo and declined the invitation. Had Whitlock come, Steffens's role in the case almost certainly would have been even more pronounced than it was. Darrow set up an elaborate defense team led by the unlikely duo of Lecompte

Davis, an experienced, pro-union Kentucky lawyer and Joseph Scott, the city's leading Catholic attorney and a member of the Chamber of Commerce. Completing the quixotic defense team were Indiana judge Cyrus McNutt and Job Harriman himself.

On the morning of his arrival on November 6, Steffens went to the courtroom, where lawyers were still jockeying over jury selection. Steffens had been sitting there for only a few minutes when Judge Walter Bordwell summoned him to come to his chambers at the next recess. After a pleasant greeting, the judge asked Steffens what his purpose was for attending. With a slight laugh, Steffens told him that he was there "to try this case." Bordwell smiled, replying that he thought trying the case was the job of the judge.

Steffens hardly agreed, pointing out to Bordwell that the judge could not try the case fairly. Then the reporter launched into his theory of the class-war nature of the whole affair and his belief that the only concern of the judge was who blew up the building rather than the much larger matter of what deplorable working and living conditions would cause people to act so desperately in the first place.

Bordwell, of course, responded that Steffens was going far beyond the scope of the case, which, Steffens said, proved his own point. "That is why we radicals say that one cannot get justice in the courts," Steffens insisted. Soon Bordwell, a Taft Republican, had heard enough and ended the conversation. In his autobiography, Steffens noted, with some exaggeration, that everyone at the time was calling him a red, but he took it in stride: "People who call such names are only trying to say that, somehow, you are not in the herd; you are different; and that is a compliment, however clumsy." By the end of the trial, Steffens would be the recipient of many such compliments.

Darrow gave Steffens the investigative freedom he sought, starting with permission to talk to the McNamaras. Although the trial was expected to be lengthy, Steffens had told Bordwell that he could elicit the truth from the McNamaras in an afternoon, because he would not "put on an air of righteousness, climb up on a raised dais, and [act] as if I had not and could not ever commit a crime." As for Bordwell's approach—and the approach of most courts—Steffens later wrote to Dot, "Oh, the fraud of it all. And the hypocrisy. And the injustice. If we would only come out and face the facts, we'd soon get it right. But no; that's impossible."

When Steffens met the McNamaras on November 17, he found them to be very close brothers determined to support the labor movement, regardless of the personal cost to themselves. Steffens largely assumed their guilt from the start, practically wanting to skip past the trial in order to address the much broader issue of social justice. "I don't have to wait for the verdict to know the truth about the McNamara case. . . . The real case is outside of that [murder], in economics and psychology, and only the press can try it." He half-jokingly referred to the crime as "justifiable dynamiting."

In fact, as Steffens explained to Laura in mid-November, guilt was a key component of his strategy. "I want to assume that organized labor has committed the dynamiting and other crimes charged against it, and raise the question: Why? Why should human beings, as they are, feel so hateful that they want to kill?" he asked. "Their explanation; their view of it all, I propose to get, understand, and so state that anybody, even an employer of labor, can comprehend it. . . . You see, I'm willing to state anybody's position in anything, even dynamiting, even bribery, but I don't want to lie, too."

Steffens explained to the defense lawyers and the McNamaras that he was there not merely to cover the trial and report on guilt or innocence but to, in effect, publicize the complex reasons behind labor's anger and expose the root causes of the simmering class struggle while warning that the defendants' lives could be placed in jeopardy. James, even facing death, was eager to cooperate, according to Steffens, if Steffens could get out labor's story in full detail to a mass audience. For the moment, though, Darrow kept his distance from such an audacious plan.

On November 19, Darrow and Steffens went down to "Miramar," E. W. Scripps's sprawling forty-room, single-floor home, located near La Jolla, to sound out Scripps on the dilemma and, from Steffens's point of view, to give Darrow some relief from the tense atmosphere in Los Angeles. Scripps, smoking one Key West cigar after another and flicking the ashes on his trademark woolen vest, spent considerable time discussing the McNamaras and other issues with his guests. He was sympathetic to labor, pointing out that capital had all the tools of power at its disposal and often used them, leaving labor little choice but to retaliate. In fact, in an essay supporting the McNamaras, Scripps had gone even further than Steffens toward a radical consideration of the case: "These men that were killed should be considered what they really were—soldiers enlisted under a capitalist employer whose main purpose in life was warfare against the union." For the moment, Scripps agreed with his guests that an out-of-court settlement was the best of the unpleasant choices. Fremont Older, later brought down from San Francisco by Darrow, also agreed. But the AFL, publicly opposed to violence, was paying Darrow's substantial defense bills, and it was doing so for one reason: a verdict of innocence.

It was on the train ride back to Los Angeles that Steffens contemplated the use of Christianity to resolve a murder case. Christianity, particularly its emphasis on forgiveness and humility, had weighed heavily on his mind for some time. He expressed his fervor in a letter to editor E. J. Ridgway, who published the letter in the November–December 1911 issue of *Everybody's*: "I have come up out of the muck believing that Christianity will work; that we can trust mankind; that liberty and reason, education and patience and kindness; in brief, that faith, hope, and charity would save the world. And I mean now. I mean right here in the United States in this year of our Lord, 1911." Yet Christians themselves, Steffens had seen, could marvel at the teachings of Christ but feel quite shocked and threatened when expected to adopt them.

Of most interest to Steffens was the radical Christian act of forgiveness. He believed in it, largely because he had tried it so often when seeking help from sinners—"political bosses and business bosses, out-and-out crooks, hard-boiled editors, rough-neck rascals"—who frequently responded with lengthy confessions. And having seen the effects of a system that routinely favored punishment over forgiveness, Steffens was eager to try an experiment in justice using Christianity's power of forgiveness.

His idea was fairly straightforward if stunningly idealistic: to reach an agreement sparing the lives of the guilty sinners—the McNamaras—so that labor and capital could move beyond the obstacle of a single murder trial and sit down for an open, comprehensive talk over their grievances. The goal was to settle Los Angeles's ugly labor situation at the negotiating table, rather than convict and hang the McNamaras and guarantee more violence on both sides. What Steffens really wanted was an amnesty, not just for the McNamaras but for all jailed labor agitators. The obvious difficulty was in convincing powerful individuals in Los Angeles, most leaning hard to the right, as well as the public, to accept such a controversial scheme.

Steffens's version of the ensuing events undoubtedly inflates his own role in the murky affair, but he was nonetheless a notable player. Steffens informed Darrow of his plan to gain freedom for John McNamara and something less than capital punishment for James. Darrow, of course, was skeptical and hesitant to go along with anything that might jeopardize the lives of his clients. Still, he did not prohibit Steffens from trying on his own, removed from the media glare. Darrow could always deny any involvement if Steffens stumbled.

Starting out on the path of least resistance, Steffens first approached the influential Republican Meyer Lissner, whom the muckraker had met on a visit to Los Angeles the previous year. Progressive but not radical in his thinking,

Lissner supported Mayor Alexander and was a powerful ally of Governor Hiram Johnson. Lissner took some time to come around but, eager to see the demise of the socialist Harriman, eventually agreed and gave Steffens a list of the more difficult "big, bad men" whose consent would be needed for any amnesty to work. At the top of the list was General Otis. Called "a creature who is vile, infamous, degraded, and putrescent . . . with gangrened heart and rotting brain" by Governor Johnson (the personal hatred was mutual), Otis seemed an immovable mountain. Even Fremont Older's wife, a generous spirit, could only offer the backhanded compliment of Otis being "an honest man who believes in the sacredness of property above all else."

A prominent lawyer and friend of Lissner, Thomas Gibbon, helped to arrange a meeting with Otis's son-in-law, Harry Chandler, the Los Angeles Times president who, as Steffens observed, was "a hard-headed, materialistic money-maker without a sentiment in all his make-up." Most improbably, Chandler agreed to cooperate but, according to Steffens, insisted that Otis be informed only at a later time. When Steffens eventually did brief Otis on the plan, he—stunningly—went along as well. The obvious question was, Why? Circumstances, as the cunning Otis knew well, were favorable. What he would stand to gain from a guilty verdict was significant: the certainty that Harriman's bid for mayor would be ruined and, along with it, the future of socialism and any hint of unionized, open shops in Los Angeles. Of course, the deal had to be reached before Election Day on December 6.

The plan continued its path up to the hard-nosed district attorney of Los Angeles County. John Fredericks, a former commander in the Spanish-American War, now looked upon not only the McNamaras but Darrow himself as the reviled enemy. Fredericks was intrigued by the prospect of guilty pleas but insisted on stern punishment for the McNamaras before further talks were held. The detailed statement given by Ortie McManigal, who had been arrested along with the McNamaras, provided Fredericks all the leverage he needed for a conviction. McManigal clearly implicated the McNamaras in the Times bombing and others, revealing that a paper trail of evidence was sitting in a union vault in Indianapolis. Once the prosecution secured the documents, the guilt of the McNamaras was a foregone conclusion. "My God, you left a trail behind you a mile wide!" Darrow had moaned to James after seeing the incriminating papers. Scott recalled hearing James's own, earlier confession: "I intended to do some damage," James said, "to scare them. That's all. How could I know ink was in those barrels? How could I know that there was a gas main underneath that particular spot?" So punishment was inevitable, and Fredericks wanted life in prison for James and ten years for his older brother, which would satisfy Darrow's insistence on keeping the young men alive. Of course, like the others, Fredericks also wanted the plan in place prior to the election to seal Harriman's fate. Still, Steffens felt his own plan had a chance. At least it was not dead.

But when Fredericks saw Darrow in court on November 23, the annoyed district attorney asked, "What is this gink Steffens trying to do?" Darrow claimed to know little more than Fredericks about the deal—only that James would plead guilty if John could be set free. Fredericks, insisting on punishment for both, was not impressed.

At a certain point, the biggest player of all, Judge Bordwell, had to be informed of the plea-bargain possibility, if not the amnesty. According to Steffens, he gave the details to Bordwell before both agreed that it might be better if the judge "didn't know" then (and Bordwell later claimed just that). In fact, as the extremely delicate negotiations dragged on while potential jurors, more than five hundred of them, were processed, it was critical that no one outside the circle of confidants be aware of the scheming. Any public rumor of a guilty plea for the prisoners would have infuriated organized labor, which was completely behind the McNamaras. The reason, depending upon one's level of cynicism, was either that labor believed in their innocence and the justice of its cause or that labor realized they were guilty and absolutely could not afford such an outrageous truth to be revealed. An admission of guilt would cripple the labor movement, and any hint of an actual amnesty would shock the whole nation. "Publicity would have meant certain death," Darrow wrote.

Cracks, though, inevitably began to appear. In a front-page scandal, papers blared the news that one of Darrow's assistants, Bert Franklin, had been arrested on November 28 for offering a bribe to a juror on a Los Angeles street and had to be bailed out by Darrow and others. Darrow, naturally, was immediately under suspicion as well, although the newspapers did not mention that Darrow, inexplicably, was present at the scene of the arrest. According to Steffens, Darrow himself, while insisting on his innocence, offered to be prosecuted for bribery if the McNamaras were set free, which would have been a significant coup for Fredericks in his personal war with Darrow. And the ambitious Fredericks, an Otis supporter with his eyes on the governor's seat, was more than eager to pursue Darrow and settle with the McNamaras out of court on their way to jail. Steffens learned of the arrest in the afternoon and, that night, was the guest of honor at a newspaper banquet, where he urged the members of the press to consider its role in improving labor-capital relations. Titled "Our Job," the speech, Steffens claimed, was a hit. "They took it all in, with eyes, mouth, and ears," he told Laura. "Afterward they came up and wanted more. I gave them more."

As Steffens's plan staggered forward, it was agreed that another group of about twenty influential Los Angeles politicians and businessmen, including the president of the Los Angeles Chamber of Commerce and former mayors and congressmen—none "idealists and reformers," Steffens noted—should be brought in on the negotiations to ensure that any plan of compromise have ample support citywide. At a November 29 meeting, Steffens warned the gathering that only a comprehensive settlement would begin to dissuade labor from future acts of aggression. The result was that even this conservative group agreed that it would abide by whatever result the talks between the two sides yielded, and it would consider the labor-capital conference that Steffens so dearly sought.

On November 30, Thanksgiving Day, the McNamaras met with Darrow, Steffens, and other lawyers to discuss their increasingly bleak situation. Darrow made it clear that both men would need to plead guilty or James, at least, would face the death penalty. James strenuously objected to the two guilty pleas, offering to hang if it would set John free and provide some cover for organized labor, which would suffer grievously enough from even one guilty plea, but Darrow wanted above all to avoid a verdict of capital punishment, believing that murder had not been the intention of the brothers and that their lives should be spared. Scott recalled that the brothers would not hear of a guilty plea for both until the prison chaplain, Father Edward Brady, using an old Bible from the boys' childhood, convinced them to accept the deal. In any event, Darrow was well aware that James was too passionate, particularly in his desire to spare his brother a guilty plea, to safely take the stand, and any jury that saw the overwhelming evidence against the McNamaras was not going to acquit, leaving the noose a likely outcome for at least one of the brothers. A pre-trial deal with the prosecution was Darrow's only hope.

The arrangement was finally set, the result largely of negotiations between Darrow's assistant, Lecompte Davis, and Fredericks, who of course could not guarantee that Judge Bordwell would concur in his final sentencing. Both McNamaras would plead guilty, James would get life, John a shorter sentence, and no other suspects would be charged. The bribery case against Darrow, so important to Fredericks, would be dealt with later. Steffens also pushed for the labor-capital conference to be included as well. A general amnesty was certainly gone from consideration, although the amnesty may never have been taken seriously by anyone other than Steffens.

The press and the public had been oblivious to all of the maneuvering behind the scenes. The next morning in court, as huddled discussions between Fredericks, Darrow, the defendants, Steffens, and others took place, the crowd of more than sixty reporters, European as well as American, sensed a backroom deal. Their interest was aroused even further when Fredericks asked the judge for a continuance until two o'clock, which Fredericks used to demand fifteen years in jail, not ten, for John. All eyes were on defense lawyer Lecompte Davis that afternoon, when he stood up and announced that the McNamaras were changing their plea from not guilty to guilty.

"That court seemed to fly apart," Steffens recalled. Reporters raced to the telephones, and the public, seemingly in a flash, learned of the outcome and the murky details surrounding the case. On his way out of the court, Steffens heard the cries of the mobs, misled until the end, lambasting the court. In disgust, angry men threw their McNamara and "Harriman for Mayor" buttons on the ground. Samuel Gompers, who had believed in the McNamaras' innocence, tearfully told the press, "I am astounded. . . . It is lightning out of a clear sky." Gompers's role was so controversial that on December 3, Steffens felt compelled to send a telegram to the *New York Times*, declaring that he had had no contact with Gompers throughout the trial. The AFL, with the public in an uproar, issued a clear statement distancing itself as far as possible from the McNamaras and asserting that it "joins in the satisfaction that the majesty of the law and justice has been maintained and the culprits commensurately punished for their crime. . . . It is cruelly unjust to hold the men of the labor movement either legally or morally responsible for the crime of an individual member." Labor, in fact, felt so betrayed and deceived that Gompers urged the dynamite investigation to proceed as vigorously as necessary, while other labor leaders declared that a hanging was not cruel enough for the McNamaras. Otis and the relentless Burns, by then already pursuing other labor agitators under orders from President Taft, became instant heroes to conservatives across the country, as socialism in Los Angeles was dead and the national labor movement crippled.

As Steffens's connection to the McNamaras was hardly a secret—all of the major California newspapers covered his involvement, vague as it was to the public—people in his own hotel let him pass by only in a "hostile fashion." Back at Hutchins Hapgood's apartment in New York, trade union activist Anton Johannsen, who was originally thought to be one of the dynamiters as well and had been appointed by the AFL to the McNamara Defense Committee, bitterly burst into tears, cursing Steffens for leading labor astray. Eastman recalled Steffens being ridiculed as "an old-maidish fuss-budget who ought to be teaching a Sunday-school class." It was a labor disaster from coast to coast and, many agreed, set back the labor cause at least a decade.

As part of his arrangement with Fredericks, Steffens had agreed to withhold his own report for the following day's papers and to explain the case to other reporters. They gathered in his hotel room, where Steffens dutifully informed them of what had been negotiated over the past days. Steffens saw that the reporters listened but did not comprehend. It was not the details, confusing as they were, that baffled them. It was the notion itself—forgiveness instead of punishment, especially in a murder case—that left them stunned. They reported the story but did not grasp it, Steffens knew.

His own story, published the following afternoon and continued two days later, noted that both sides essentially had pleaded guilty by agreeing, however reluctantly, to the conference, although Steffens could not hide his deep disappointment over the cries for revenge and justice that swept the country. He did not mention Christianity. Other reporters, though, had heard rumors and asked him about it, wondering if he had been trying to apply the Golden Rule. Steffens avoided answering the question directly, but to no avail. Papers across the country ran stories about "Golden Rule" Steffens, some of them mocking his interpretation of Christianity.

Not everyone castigated Steffens, however. He received congratulations from some on the Far Left and substantial financial offers for statements, as much as one thousand dollars for two hundred words. (He refused them.) The sudden attention reminded Steffens, he wrote to Dot, "of the olden days when I began to expose cities. I'm famous again. I'll use it to make people think. They'll listen again now." Steffens, seemingly in denial, refused to acknowledge that much of the public had already heard quite enough from him for the moment.

Still, Steffens understood the opposition and what likely lay ahead. With uncharacteristic bitterness, he told Laura, "I see and I've written about how the Christian world leaps on these men when they are down. They all want blood. We meant to have them forgiven and everything wiped out, a new deal and an attempt to stop the war. But the public is too fiendish. It will probably spoil it all. It makes me sick."

What remained in the case was the commentary and the sentencing from Judge Bordwell. Darrow and the defendants had serious concerns over his leniency, as Bordwell, starting with jury selection, had done little to hide his leanings toward the prosecution. James had warned Steffens, "Watch out for that judge. He'll bust your whole plan." So Steffens paid the judge a visit at Bordwell's club. The two focused on the challenge of a judge, a law-abiding citizen, to truly understand the nature of a crime and to issue a fair sentence. The judge heard Steffens out and, according to Steffens, agreed that he would address the crime with a reasonably open mind.

When clergymen spoke from church pulpits the following Sunday, at least a loud minority wanted to see justice. "The sermons of that black Sunday turned the tide against us," Steffens wrote. "They came like the cries of a lynching mob and frightened all the timid men who had worked with us—and the judge." Steffens, though, overstated the extent of the clerical outrage, as members who were more liberal did express degrees of sympathy with the labor cause. In a piece in the *Los Angeles Tribune*, the Reverend Reynold Blight cited the support of other clergy: "There is no denying that the application of this [golden] rule would tend to make marvelous changes in the attitude of employer and employee toward each other." He concluded by asking, "Is it not time?" But Steffens's vocal critics obviously had struck a very sensitive public nerve.

Bordwell could see what was perfectly obvious: Some churches had turned on Steffens, capitalists hated him because he coddled criminals—labor criminals, at that—and labor shunned him for his deception. Bordwell himself undoubtedly despised inquiring journalists such as Steffens, who often made the news as much as reported it. When the judge rose from his chair in the small courtroom to conclude the case on December 6, Steffens watched him retreat to the standard forms of justice. Bordwell excoriated the McNamaras as murderers, and their future would be a jail cell: James received a sentence of life imprisonment, while John was given fifteen years. And the men, indeed, were guilty as charged. James had planted the bomb at the *Times* building, as he had done at numerous other anti-union work sites in recent years. But he was stunned to hear of the deaths—there had been none from the other explosions—and was nearly suicidal for weeks afterward before recovering and resuming his dirty work with dynamite at other locations in the East and the Midwest. John, the mastermind, had planned the bombings from Indianapolis. When Bordwell finished his sentencing, James looked at Steffens as he was led out and said, "You were wrong, and I was right. The whole damn world believes in dynamite."

The fog of controversy that had been growing regarding Steffens's actual role in the case continued as well. Some key figures, in fact, had seen reason for hope in his strategy. On December 2, former Los Angeles mayor Meredith Snyder, one of the businessmen consulted during the negotiations, wrote that he had cooperated with Steffens's effort because "it would result in bringing about the better understanding between capital and labor, employers and organized labor, throughout the country." Harbor Commission lawyer Thomas Gibbon concurred: "We hope that employers of labor throughout our Nation may take this opportunity to readjust their relations with labor on a basis of greater fairness and mutual consideration of each other's interests."

The same day, however, Fredericks had called Steffens merely a "go-between" in the negotiations before virtually erasing his part entirely, asserting, "I have had nothing to do with Lincoln Steffens, nor do I personally know that he had any connection to the case. I have never talked with him." He repeated the point the following day: "I never knew him except just as a newpaper man among the rest of them, and did not know that he had undertaken to help the defense to get me to turn J.J. McNamara loose." Bordwell, in a statement to the press, went even further, singling out Steffens and making clear that "the court was not swayed by the hypothetical policy favored by Steffens (who, by the way, is a professed anarchist) that the judgement of the court should be directed to the promotion of compromise in the controversy between capital and labor." Adding a final blow and echoing Fredericks, he insisted that Steffens had had no influence at any point, implying that the case had been cut short only in the interest of saving money.

In his reply, Steffens denied that he had taken credit—or blame—for the change in plea but noted that Harry Chandler, in the *Times*, had acknowledged Steffens's role in the settlement efforts. He closed with a passionate criticism of both judge and district attorney: "I would rather go to the penitentiary with the McNamara 'heroes' [Bordwell had scoffed at any heroism on the part of the McNamaras] than be classed with Judge Bordwell and District Attorney Fredericks, admitting that the action taken to-day was prompted not by mercy but by wisdom and the desire to save the county money."

Burns, the victorious private investigator, got into the act in March 1912 in a talk at the Liberal Club in New York, where he called Steffens "a friend of mine" but believed that Steffens had been hoodwinked by Darrow. "I'll tell you about Steffens," he confided to his rapt audience, most of whom were close to Steffens, who had only recently stepped down as president of the club. "With the best of motives in the world he was simply taken in by the clever Darrow," Burns explained. "Darrow led him to believe that his proposition was being given weighty consideration. What he did not know was the pressure we had on Darrow that made the saving of Darrow a thing of prime importance." Given such conflicting accounts, Steffens's actual role in the case, as well as his influence on the key players, is difficult to say with precision. That his role was significant, for better or worse, is certain.

The same day of sentencing, December 5, saw the inevitable electoral outcome for Job Harriman, who had been kept in the dark by Darrow and Steffens
about the McNamaras' guilt, apparently because neither had the heart to give
him the crushing news that his political career in Los Angeles would soon be
finished. He was trounced by Alexander in the mayoral race, losing by more
than thirty thousand votes. The role of Otis in all the negotiations is unclear, but
the result was that the McNamaras went to jail, Harriman was out of politics,
organized labor was disgraced, and Steffens's Golden Rule was a mockery, giving Otis the equivalent of victory on a silver platter.

Had no one died in the blast, Steffens might have retained a small hope for
public sympathy, particularly considering the growing support in Los Angeles
for Harriman and the Left through the autumn of 1911. But with Steffens
focused on the Golden Rule while the public, in disbelief, had to accept that
twenty-one innocent men were dead because of dynamite, he had no persuasive
argument.

Not only was socialism denounced in Los Angeles, but the McNamara
case fractured the Left nationwide. The Socialist Party sought to distance itself
from violent methods, leading to its expulsion of Haywood amid protests from
within its own ranks, including Lippmann, and unwittingly sending Haywood
on to his greatest labor success in the Bread and Roses strike the following
year in Lawrence, Massachusetts. Many other influential voices weighed in as
well, using Steffens as a prime target. In an article titled "Murder Is Murder,"
Theodore Roosevelt all but named Steffens in his indictment of the McNamara
defense in Los Angeles:

> Since the startling outcome of the McNamara trial certain apologists
> of these men have made themselves conspicuous by asserting that these
> depraved criminals, who have on their seared souls the murder of so
> many innocent persons—*all of them laboring people, by the way*—
> are "victims," or at worst "fanatics," who should receive sympathy
> because they were acting in what they regarded as a "war" on behalf
> of their class! The plea is monstrous in its folly and its wickedness. . . .
> Murder is murder, and the foolish sentimentalists or sinister wrong-
> doers who try to apologize for it as an "incident of labor warfare"
> are not only morally culpable but are enemies of the American people,
> and, above all, are enemies of American wage-workers.

From the opposite end of the political spectrum, Emma Goldman, while not
supporting the McNamaras' use of violence, ridiculed Steffens for his timidity

and naïveté in trusting the side of capital: "Such people never seem to learn from experience. No matter how often they had seen the lion devour the lamb, they continued to cling to the hope that the nature of the beast might change. If only the lion could get to know the lamb better, they argued, or talk matters over, he would surely learn to appreciate his gentle brother and thereby grow gentle himself. . . . And those infants believed. They accepted the promise of the sly and cunning beasts."

More moderate voices, including Louis Brandeis, condemned the crime but had no interest in joining an aroused public determined to see a hanging. Speaking before a Senate committee, Brandeis chose his words perhaps more carefully than Steffens had:

> In the midst of our indignation over the unpardonable crimes of trade union leaders, disclosed at Los Angeles, should not our statesmen and thinkers seek to ascertain the underlying cause of this wide-spread, deliberate outburst of crimes of violence? What was it that led men like the McNamaras to really believe that the only recourse they had for improving the condition of the wage-earner was to use dynamite against property and life? Certainly it was not individual depravity . . .
> Is there not a causal connection between the development of these huge, indomitable trusts and the horrible crimes now under investigation?

Reflecting on Steffens's tarnished name, Darrow himself, admittedly biased, tried to present Steffens as he knew him, a man of substance who genuinely wanted justice to be more than a reflex of revenge: "He understood the industrial question as well as any man I ever knew. He did not believe in violence any more than I believed in it, but he was in full sympathy with the workman's cause," Darrow wrote. "In fact, it was due to his intelligence and tact, and his acquaintance with people on both sides, that the settlement was brought about. Mr. Steffens knew all the strong men back of the prosecution, and was busy urging a general amnesty and a better feeling in all sections between capital and labor, with which many of them were in full accord."

John McNamara, according to a socialist reporter, later regretted his guilty plea, suggesting that in jail, he had been misled as to the amount of support the brothers had on the outside, with his information coming mainly from Darrow and Steffens. He would, he said, rather have given his life than fracture the labor movement so grievously. He would be released from prison in 1921 for good conduct. His brother James, ever defiant, remained at San Quentin until his death in 1941 at the age of fifty-nine.

Reporter Sara Bard Field, later a close friend of Steffens's, had a particularly intriguing role in the case—her radical sister, Mary Field, was Darrow's mistress and was also covering the trial as a journalist. Darrow had made sexual advances toward Sara as well, while she was having her own own affair in Los Angeles with Charles Erskine Scott Wood, a good friend of Steffens's from his Oregon timber investigation. Before the jury selection had even taken place, a frustrated Darrow had told both women that the McNamaras were "guilty as hell." Sara later observed in an interview that Steffens "took very great cognizance of [the McNamaras' fate] in this case, because it would have been much worse if these men had been proven guilty. . . . I think that he felt that, weighing everything, it was not only morally or ethically right to do this, but it was also the sounder thing to do politically. He had no illusions about it. I think that the persistent statement that one hears of Steffie [that he] was a dreamer was a very poor sizing-up of his mentality and his character."

In New York, Steffens reunited with his circle of young writers, ready to return to his old life. John Reed was particularly welcoming. Supporting Steffens's efforts in Los Angeles even though Reed was "staggered" by his former mentor's ill-considered attempt to use Christianity as a tactical maneuver, Reed had doggedly promoted the disgraced muckraker. Following a Christmas Eve dinner with Reed, Steffens relayed Reed's words to Laura: "Sure enough when I went to the club, they all jumped on me, and I fought, back to wall, and they'd do me up." But, Reed admitted sadly, "I couldn't down them." Only Lippmann, Reed said, was able to do it. Still, Reed composed an ambitious poem, "Sangar," as a tribute to Steffens. The poem, later published by Harriet Monroe in *Poetry*, mixed mythology and politics, describing how Sangar, an aging medieval knight, leaps into battle to stop the carnage only to be killed by his warrior son, an eerie, if not literal, foreshadowing of things to come between the two radicals. Steffens appreciated the poem, although he unfortunately later misinterpreted it as a personal denunciation. On Christmas, Steffens took his new family—"all the homeless young poets, painters, and sculptors here in my neighborhood"—to dinner.

Meanwhile, as letters of outrage from clergymen arrived at his door, Steffens saw "no end of it all," and his experiences in Boston and Los Angeles, while bold in their intentions, were undeniable failures. "For years after when we'd speak of this trial," Sara Bard Field recalled, "he would say how far it pushed him into an examination of the whole evil system in which we were caught." But his optimism, as usual, ultimately prevailed. "It doesn't matter. I can laugh, so all is well," he told Laura.

15

THE WHITE HOUSE AGAIN

IN JANUARY 1912, on the heels of the McNamara disaster, Joseph Steffens passed away. Lincoln Steffens could look back upon a satisfying life with his father. Their respect had been mutual, and their love sincere. "For myself," Steffens wrote to Laura after hearing the news, "I feel, as I did about Mamma, that life had been good to Dad; that he had lived it as he wished; that he had enjoyed his children and his grandchildren; that there had been no great sorrows and not much pain. It was over. . . . So I shall not grieve." In March 1909, he had written to his father, who was ill at the time, "I like to think of you as at peace with all your neighbors and yourself, and not busy; not bothering about business and such things. Let them go. You have been a good man, a good citizen and a good father; you know it, your fellow-townsmen know it and, certainly, your children know it." Soon after, he dedicated *Upbuilders* to his father.

Steffens once more was in the mix of presidential politics that now involved several personal friends. While a dominant personality had yet to emerge among a field of Democrats that included Woodrow Wilson, the Republicans had just the opposite problem: too many strong men all eyeing the prize. La Follette, the relentless standard-bearer of Republican progressives for two decades, was already running hard for the nomination, but more as an insurgent among the ranks, making a lot of noise but finding it difficult to make much headway. On January 22, Steffens showed his political preference by being among a group of prominent progressives who greeted La Follette at the train station upon his arrival in New York for a Carnegie Hall speech. That night, in front of a packed hall, Steffens sat on the stage with other members of the progressive Insurgents' Club and heard La Follette give a spirited defense of the cause that was received, the *New York Times* reported, "with wild acclaim."

At the same time, Theodore Roosevelt, although publicly insisting that he would not oppose the incumbent Taft, privately fumed. The problem was that the president, essentially handpicked by Roosevelt as his successor at a time when Roosevelt almost certainly could have earned a third term had he not voluntarily removed himself from the race, had settled in far too comfortably with the conservative wing of the party and betrayed many of the progressive values established by Roosevelt. Indeed, a number of Republican progressives, believing La Follette too polarizing a candidate to win a national election, had been clamoring for a return of Roosevelt to the White House ever since the early days of the Taft administration. Roosevelt heard ample vitriol from them, including a letter from an Indianapolis publisher who berated Taft as "a damn, pig-headed blunderer."

Not that there was any love lost between Roosevelt and La Follette, either. La Follette still saw Roosevelt as far too willing to cut deals with the entrenched interests, while Roosevelt looked upon La Follette as a brave but uncompromising, narrow-minded demagogue. Behind the scenes, Roosevelt was quietly using his estimable influence in lining up Republican support to "pull" himself into the race while slowly stifling support for La Follette by refusing to endorse his fellow progressive. Brand Whitlock, on La Follette's side, wrote to a friend abroad, "You would laugh if you were in this country now and were to see how the standpatters are trying to bring [Roosevelt] out as a candidate for president again, in order to head off La Follette, who is a very dangerous antagonist to Taft." Some of the "standpatters," though, included old Steffens friends Frank Heney and Ben Lindsey, highlighting the political delicacy of the situation. Steffens was not endorsing any candidate—the man who would support democracy was the one he wanted, and he expected that it would be a Republican and undoubtedly hoped for La Follette. But among Republicans, an obstacle for both La Follette and Roosevelt in the nominating process, of course, was beleaguered President Taft himself.

Steffens met with both Roosevelt and La Follette in New York and looked forward to a visit soon from Hiram Johnson, who was now being talked about as a vice presidential mate for Roosevelt. La Follette was "bully," Steffens told Allen: "He is for the cause, not himself, and wants to act, at once, and in the best interest of ultimate results." Steffens took a far different view, however, toward the reluctant Roosevelt, who was "mussing up the whole Progressive movement with his 'To be or not to be.' And he won't make a statement. He talks to us privately, but not convincingly; at least not to all of us. He simply isn't clear himself. He's undecided, wabbles and, of course, the Taft side makes the most of it." Wilson himself referred to Roosevelt's "insane distemper of egotism."

Roosevelt, in turn, had little sympathy for the impatience of Steffens and others. When one of Roosevelt's advisors declared that he would like "to kill Lincoln Steffens" and "bottle up" Gifford Pinchot, Roosevelt replied that he agreed with at least the first suggestion.

Steffens's doubts, though, had merit. With a determined Taft aiming for renomination, the Republican Party was careening toward a damaging split, the best of all worlds for the desperate Democrats, who had not occupied the Oval Office since the last days of Grover Cleveland.

Through the spring of 1912, Steffens followed a meandering path. A series of sketches in *Everybody's* on the presidential candidates failed to excite Steffens, who was less interested in the campaign than in the labor protests and strikes that were springing up across the country. Labor groups, upset by the McNamara trial but aware that Steffens remained one of their strongest advocates, asked him to speak at numerous rallies to explain, as an insider, what actually had happened and why labor had been found guilty.

Workers in New England were exceptionally vocal in their dissent, which came as no surprise to Steffens. Recalling the entrenched graft that he had observed there in his muckraking days, he commented acidly to Laura, "New England is ready to blow up. I wish it would. It deserves all it can get." Circumstances came close to granting Steffens's wish during the bloody 1912 Bread and Roses strike, which involved thousands of mill workers, most Italian, Polish, Russian, Syrian, and Lithuanian immigrants, against textile manufacturers in Lawrence, Massachusetts. When Steffens arrived in March to cover the conclusion of the two-month conflict, Bill Haywood, then leader of the radical Industrial Workers of the World—the IWW's Wobblies—greeted him with, "There's none of your Golden Rule in this, is there?" Following Steffens's reassurance, Haywood agreed to update him on the situation. Steffens described the meeting for Laura: "He spent the whole day taking me around, telling me his plans, his philosophy, his hates and his love. He is a loyal labor leader; crude, rough, violent, but true. So of course labor won." Later, in a letter to Dot, Steffens noted the paradox in his close relations with the radicals, who sought him out to discuss their plans even though Steffens insisted that he did not "approve of force, violence, and revenge." He described the "sadness in their eyes" when they told him that his way of thinking was sound but would never materialize, because "the higher-ups won't see it."

Steffens's love life, following his debacle with Mary Austin the previous year, had settled into a more stable routine with Gussie. How to inform others, particularly his sisters, of his private life was a familiar problem for Steffens.

Evidently, he never did more than mention Austin to them, and he would not even identify Gussie by name at first, before finally opening up in a letter to Laura written more than a year after Josephine's death, giving her a detailed account of the complex situation. After the deaths of her parents, Gussie faced some financial hardships, and a "courteous" young man helped her out and eventually proposed. She accepted, almost out of duty, but found no love in the marriage and faced great inner conflict herself—"a free soul with a Puritan mind," Steffens described her. Her husband, now rather poor, would not agree to a divorce. Legal obstacles stood in the way as well.

Then Steffens reemerged in her life. He readily acknowledged that the situation between them was less than ideal, noting that Gussie still saw him as "the college boy" and could not "put him and the muckraker together." Almost certainly with Mary Austin in mind, he admitted, "I know abler, handsomer women, with whom I can talk to greater heights and depths; just the sort of women I'd have thought I'd prefer. But I don't." He concluded, "Remember, Laura, when you think of G. and when you see her, that she is and must be alone in the worst, the hardest part of this; that she wonders at herself and does not approve of her conduct; that she is on delicate, difficult grounds; and that she has to confide in so far only me, a man, an interested man, her lover." Their relationship, however unorthodox, was back in place.

In May, after a short stopover in New York, Steffens returned to California, where much of his summer was spent defending Darrow against the old charge of bribery. When Steffens first arrived in Los Angeles, his immediate interest was drawn more toward the acrimonious free-speech fight being waged down in San Diego, where local ordinances prevented the Wobblies from making their familiar soapbox addresses to the public. As Steffens heard details of the spreading labor protest from Johannsen and Emma Goldman, he yearned to know more. "I wish I could go and get and write that story," he told Laura. "I shouldn't. . . . But San Diego is certainly a ripe, rich story, which everybody seems to be afraid to write." The fear, evidently, did not affect the *San Diego Tribune*. Its March 4, 1912, editorial attack on the Wobblies left nothing to the imagination: "Hanging is none too good for them, and they would be much better dead; for they are absolutely useless in the human economy; they are the waste matter of creation and should be drained off into the sewer of oblivion, there to rot in cold obstruction like any other excrement."

But the trial of Darrow had an urgency of its own. Bert Franklin, Darrow's assistant who had been accused of bribing a juror, was at the root of the problem. Franklin's basic job had been to gather information on the potential jurors, as both the prosecution and the defense were seeking any advantage in the heated competition. Private telegrams were read, listening devices were planted, witnesses were intimidated, personal items were confiscated, and collaborators were paid. Without exaggeration, Steffens called it a "dirty business."

But just two days before the McNamaras' guilty plea, Franklin had been arrested and charged with offering a four-thousand-dollar bribe to a juror. Franklin did not deny it and later pleaded guilty himself, giving a full confession to Fredericks, who, with some enthusiastic help from Burns, pursued Darrow relentlessly. And Burns, Steffens thought, was even more determined in his efforts against Darrow and labor. The detective, Steffens wrote to Dot, "is here to make sure of getting Darrow. Maybe he will. Fredericks can't, but Burns is a genius; more like T.R. than any other man I know." Many felt that Burns was hoping that Darrow could lead him to a bigger prize: the implication of Gompers in the McNamara bombing.

Besides Fredericks and Burns, Darrow had other sizable problems. Labor had angrily withdrawn its support—both Gompers and Debs scorned Darrow, while Johannsen accused him of having personally profited by more than two hundred thousand dollars from the trial. Darrow now faced a well-financed prosecution team with only limited means to defend himself. And few of his personal friends other than Steffens and Fremont Older came to his side. In late December, with the McNamara debacle still being cursed nationwide and Darrow about to be indicted, the attorney had descended to thoughts of suicide. Seeing that Darrow—angry, dispirited, drinking heavily, and alone—was vulnerable, Steffens wanted to rescue an old friend, guilty or otherwise. He told Laura that this was an occasion "not for an umpire, but a friend." Steffens felt his place was with the besieged attorney: "If it's any comfort, I'll show him my soul, as black as his; not so naked, but—Sometimes all we humans have is a friend."

From Steffens's point of view, it was a perfect setting for him not only to support Darrow but also to have some fun as well. He knew that both sides despised each other and that Fredericks, who resented Eastern celebrities like Darrow and Steffens—"Stinken Leffens," to Fredericks—was eager to grill Steffens, the radical, in court. After all, Steffens knew that the governorship of California might be the prize for a successful prosecution by Fredericks, a swiftly rising political star who had just returned from a visit with President Taft in Washington. But there was opportunity for Steffens as well. After the public humiliation of the McNamara case, it was a splendid chance for him to publicly redeem himself. "I was eager for the fray," Steffens wrote, and events left no doubt that he was.

Darrow's trial began in mid-May. The early case against him, which included allegations of bribing jurors, paying witnesses to leave the country or testify falsely, and attempts to destroy physical evidence, was even stronger than Darrow and his colorful—and usually victorious—lawyer, Earl Rogers, had anticipated. Fredericks opened with a withering, vengeful address to the jury, lambasting the character of Darrow in the bluntest terms possible. The prosecution then launched into an attack on labor, dragging in other notable figures, most especially Gompers.

Observing the growing animosity in the early weeks of the trial, Steffens himself remained a very public figure in Los Angeles, giving talks at various clubs and gatherings around the city, including a noteworthy and heated debate with a large group of radicals still angry at Steffens over the fate of the McNamaras. Seeing Steffens in the local spotlight no doubt annoyed Fredericks even more, and in mid-July, he finally called the reporter to the witness stand. Steffens initially believed that in the long term, good would come of the whole affair if issues were aired completely, but not without "a terrible, useless cost of suffering, bad feeling, and long-enduring class-hate." Fredericks intended to have Steffens himself experience some of the suffering.

Typically dressed for the occasion, sporting a tight vest and an orange tie, Steffens was first questioned by Rogers (Steffens in his autobiography mistakenly recalled being questioned by Darrow) before facing off against Fredericks. The attorney rose and approached the stand. Pointing his finger in Steffens's face, Fredericks demanded to know if he was an "avowed anarchist," as Judge Bordwell had charged.

Fredericks's antics only amused Steffens. "There was the typical lawyer," he later wrote, "the conceited, unfair prosecutor whom I had seen abusing his power over weak witnesses all my life." With a smile, Steffens responded to the question.

"Oh, I'm worse than that. I believe in Christianity."

Taken aback, Fredericks found that all he could do was ask Steffens to explain such a random remark. Waving his hand across the audience, Steffens replied, "Well, you see, Captain Fredericks, those people out there, they are anarchists, socialists, labor men, and they believe, like you, in justice; but I'm a muckraker, and I tell you that things are so bad in this world that justice won't fix them. It's too late for that. I believe that nothing but love will do the job. That's Christianity. That's the teaching that we must love our neighbors."

How that was worse than anarchy escaped Fredericks, who continued to interrogate Steffens for several hours, all of the questioning wasted. With each new question from Fredericks, Steffens found an opening to give "elaborate, philosophic addresses" to the jury on the plight of labor, going far beyond the scope of Darrow's guilt or innocence. Steffens provided Fredericks with little of the testimony—or satisfaction—he had keenly anticipated. Far from being an object of derision, Steffens had overmatched Fredericks and perhaps turned the minds of the jury. Speaking not just to those assembled in the courtroom but to a national audience fascinated by the moral paradox of Darrow's career and by his own compelling resurrection, Steffens seemingly astonished everyone. A "gasp . . . ran around the room as the intense little man warmed up to his subject," one newspaper reported from the scene, while front-page headlines blared, "Steffens pleads for use of golden rule in solving problems of labor, holds courtroom spellbound" and "Steffens Outwits District Attorney."

In fact, Fredericks had recovered sufficiently from Steffens's initial responses to put on an impressive display of cross-examination, pressuring Steffens to admit to some flaws in his own presentation of the facts, but it was too little, too late. Even the judge, who felt obliged to offer Steffens a fan during his testimony in the sweltering heat, conceded that Steffens had been the most interesting witness he had ever heard. Steffens told Laura that when he had asked Fredericks if he were free to go after his testimony, the district attorney replied, "I wish you had gone two or three days ago." In a typically upbeat assessment of his own performance, Steffens wrote, "Everybody thinks that, if it isn't denied (and I don't see how it can be) . . . my testimony will have freed Darrow," adding, "I roasted Judge Bordwell so hard that he may come back. But I have more for him if he does."

His prognosis concerning Darrow ultimately proved accurate, with significant help from Darrow himself. As thousands of curious onlookers attempted to jam their way into the building at the close of the trial, eager to see if the aging, downcast lawyer could summon up his old magic, Darrow, seemingly rising from the dead, delivered his own brilliant closing argument to the jury, a two-day speech described contritely by an opponent as "one of the great all-time performances ever seen and heard in any courtroom since Cicero." Full of passion, he insisted to the jury members, some in tears as they listened, "I am not on trial for having sought to bribe a man. . . . I am on trial because I have been a lover of the poor, a friend of the oppressed, because I have stood by Labor for all these years." He further asserted, "Steffens was right in saying that [the *Times* bombing] was a social crime."

While the evidence against Darrow was close to overwhelming, to the point that many observers and even close friends—including Steffens—assumed his guilt, Darrow's display of oratorical and intellectual brilliance, combined with the obvious physical and emotional toll the ordeal had taken on him, left most hoping for an acquittal. The jury apparently felt no differently—the members met for barely a half hour before granting Darrow his freedom, with Steffens's riveting testimony also a strong reason why.

News that summer of another friend, however, saddened Steffens. C. J. Reed—John's father—passed away on July 1 in Portland. It was a tough blow to the son. His mother had hoped that he would meet the "proper" types of people in New York, respectable people who would have an appropriate influence on him, but Reed had admired his indulgent father largely because he had courageously defied the power brokers in the timber case, which left him few friends in Portland but a deeply impressed son. Steffens, hoping to see young Reed develop his abundant talent, had encouraged him in a direction in which he was already headed—bucking the system—one that Reed's father had trod himself. Now, grieving in Portland, Reed looked back nostalgically on the city he missed so deeply and composed one of his best pieces of writing, the comic, tender poem, "The Day in Bohemia, or Life Among the Artists."

The poem combined satire and humor in celebrating one day of bohemian joy, Greenwich Village–style, in the lives of the carefree radicals—Reed and his friends—of 42 Washington Square. Filled with all that excited Reed about his New York experience, the poem was dedicated to Steffens, "one of us; the only man who understands my arguments." His affection for Steffens could not have been clearer:

> *Steffens, I hope I am doing no wrong to you*
> *By dedicating this doggerel song to you;*
> *P'raps you'll resent*
> *The implied compliment,*
> *But light-hearted Liberty seems to belong to you*
>
>   . . . .
>
> *Well, if these numbers recall a good year to you,*
> *And, as to me, certain things that are dear to you,*
> *Take them, you're welcome,*
> *I'm with you till Hell come,*
> *Friend Steffens, consider me quaffing a beer to you!*

One stanza captures a dream precious to both Reed and Steffens:

Yet we are free who live in Washington Square,
We dare to think as Uptown wouldn't dare,
Blazing our nights with argument uproarious;
What care we for a dull old world censorious
When each is sure he'll fashion something glorious?

The bond between the two would grow even stronger when they later reunited in New York.

In August, Steffens went up the coast from Los Angeles to San Francisco, Oregon, and Washington, where he made a string of speeches at business clubs, colleges, and even high schools. His words were so eagerly received that Steffens wrote a letter to all of his sisters announcing he had "come back." "People are ready to hear me again," he declared, giving details of crowds of a thousand or more cramming into halls, lining the sides, urging him to "go on" in his labor talks, most of which, sooner or later, got around to the fairness of the McNamara case. His only weak performance, Steffens felt, came before a packed church in Seattle; the crowd got the speech well enough, but he noted "how out of place Christianity sounds in a church."

After returning to New York in mid-September, Steffens clearly felt he was home again. He reported with pleasure to Laura that the magazines were pursuing him once more, with *Metropolitan*, the *American*, and *Everybody's* eager for articles on labor. Through his crowd of young, intellectual friends, he kept up with the contemporary art and drama scenes, and noted with pride that Lippmann, once his understudy, had just completed a book, *A Preface to Politics*. "He dined with me last night, and he is in a bully state of mind," Steffens observed. And his letters at the time give a running commentary on the presidential campaign. "Wise" politicians were surprised by Roosevelt's staying power in the race, Taft was dead, and Wilson was favored by insiders and the machines, he told Laura.

Steffens had always been careful to keep in touch with his family in California, especially Laura, but his trip there for the Darrow trial and the chance to visit with them again sparked a wish for greater involvement on his part. He had been away—studying in Europe, muckraking America, living a married life back East—for years, and now, as best he could, he wanted to strengthen the family ties. He confided as usual in Laura: "I want to be in the family from now on. I don't want to be kept out again, as I have been for the last fifteen years or so. I'll make all the sacrifices I can to get in and keep in." Given his initially furtive relationship with Josephine and his nearly unconscionable insensitivity toward Gussie over decades, Steffens, if he had been "kept out" to some extent by his family, could hardly wonder why. Undoubtedly, the deaths of his parents, the passing of Josephine, his renewed romance with Gussie, and, maybe most significant of all, his quickening descent into middle age, all combined for his change of heart.

Steffens maintained a vigorous, detailed correspondence with his sisters and showed a particularly sincere interest in the progress of Dot's four children, the twins (Jane and Clinton) and John Jr. and Joseph. Steffens had been an absentee uncle, but now strove to be more of an active presence in their lives. To Jane and Clinton he sent several long, witty letters of affection, one thanking them for a photograph of the twins—"love illustrated," Steffens called it. He also had Joseph stay with him for a few days in the fall of 1912, seeing the sights of New York that included a harbor cruise out to Ellis Island, courtesy of Fred Howe, Steffens's old friend and now the U.S. commissioner of immigration for the port of New York. "He is a dear boy, simple, direct, and an unusually keen observer," Steffens told Dot.

Steffens, of course, had long had an active interest—perhaps too active for the more conservative Dot—in the education of young people. (One of his later articles in *Harper's Weekly* was titled "How to Get an Education Even in College.") He offered to gather information for her on the elite private high schools in the East. His report was vintage Steffens: He listed the best schools along with anecdotal comments collected from some well-placed friends before addressing the nub of the problem: "But I find it hard to form a judgment because all the men who know these schools are fellows whose judgment I'd not take on anything else. They have no sense of education. It's all 'character' (in their sense) and social connections. What I want to know is whether a school has any good teachers in it. . . . It's no easy job to find out what I want to know."

One school he was certain was useless: the Taft, a Yale school headed by William Taft's brother. "Cut out the Taft school," he warned Dot. "It produces Tafts: good, healthy, honest boys. . . . Yale is the worst of the great colleges. You can save a boy who has been to any other college, except Yale. Yale makes Yale men. You may say that Harvard makes Harvard men, and it does, but I know several Harvard men who have got over that and become men."

Through the last months of 1912, Steffens went on another successful lecture tour through the eastern states. The November elections, though, had been a personal disappointment to him, as local reform efforts went down to defeat in a number of states; U'Ren's effort in Oregon was one of the defeated. The

Republican nomination crisis had played out as many party faithful had feared. Roosevelt, after seeing the limited but genuine momentum that La Follette had built up among progressives, yet convinced that La Follette could not defeat Taft, came out from the shadows and did indeed jump into the race on February 24. Vastly outspending others in the primaries, Roosevelt headed toward his own showdown with Taft, once a good family friend but now a bitter rival, at the convention.

With ethical principles forgotten, votes being secured in any way possible, and charges and countercharges thick in the air, the campaign descended into a brutal tug-of-war between Roosevelt and Taft. A local Republican convention in Missouri was referred to as the "ball bat convention," an indication of the personal weapon of choice among attendees. After being labeled "a dangerous egotist" by Taft, Roosevelt returned fire by calling the president "a fathead" with an intellect not quite equivalent to that of a guinea pig. La Follette, meanwhile, in front of Steffens's eyes, suffered a political calamity in Philadelphia in February. On a night that he felt sick to the point of nausea, La Follette stumbled badly in a banquet speech, berating the press in such a rambling manner that observers wondered if he had suffered a nervous breakdown. Losing key supporters to the magnetic and less radical Roosevelt, he fell out of the running altogether.

Although initially shaken by the Roosevelt surge, Taft leaned on the party's well-established patronage system to easily secure the Republican nomination, prompting an enraged Roosevelt to reorganize his forces into the Bull Moose Party. Taft had no hope of defeating his former friend and patron, and remained in the race apparently out of both spite for Roosevelt and hope that he could preserve the conservative wing of the party from Roosevelt's onslaught. Predictably, Roosevelt and Taft split the Republican vote in November and sent many progressives (including La Follette) and liberals over to Wilson or even to Debs, who was running on the Socialist ticket. One message was clear: With both the liberal Wilson and the "progressive" Roosevelt finishing ahead of Taft, who received a paltry eight electoral votes, and nearly a million Americans voting for Debs despite the McNamara debacle, the country wanted reform on a national scale. It was the last time it would happen for a generation.

Steffens was disturbed but not surprised by what had befallen the divided Republicans. The increasing vitriol of Roosevelt, who seemed to be speaking out even more forcefully in his later years, and the relief felt by a weary Taft upon being turned out of office were clear indications that neither warranted the honor of election. Perhaps Roosevelt's warning to Taft just before the 1908 election—"I hope your people will do everything they can to prevent one word being sent out about either your fishing or your playing golf. The American people regard the campaign as a very serious business"—signaled that any election of Taft would be one time too many. Steffens was no enthusiast of the new president, either, as Wilson had only recently shifted from near conservative to progressive, hardly an encouraging sign to Steffens.

Nevertheless, Steffens held out some hope for Wilson, who as New Jersey governor had faced down party bosses and signaled more of the same as president. As more than fifteen thousand letters regarding office seekers landed on Wilson's desk, there was talk that Norman Hapgood, Steffens's friend and editor at *Collier's*, might end up in the cabinet. More interestingly, Louis Brandeis's name was floated as attorney general, although Brandeis had supported La Follette's candidacy earlier in the year and Taft in 1908. "If he does some fur will fly," Steffens predicted of the Brandeis appointment. (Wilson reluctantly passed over Brandeis for the moment after hearing strong doubts expressed by wealthy Boston Brahmins, although Brandeis became a trusted private advisor to the president.) Overall, Steffens saw little to get excited about in Wilson, who at best, he judged, would be a progressive not fully detached from his more reserved past.

Another sour note came in late November with the news that Darrow would be dragged through the courts again in January on charges of having bribed an additional juror in the McNamara case. Once more, he asked for Steffens's aid. Desperately trying to finish up the endless task of writing his Boston manuscript and not earning any money at the moment, Steffens was in no mood to cross the country. Understanding, however, that Darrow was in jeopardy, Steffens had no intention of abandoning him. In mid-February 1913, he was again on the way to California.

Two weeks before leaving, Steffens informed Fremont Older that he had spoken to President Wilson about two labor proposals that were more shocking than the McNamara case. Wilson, according to Steffens, agreed to assist on one of his points—intervening in the trial of a suspected dynamiter, Anton Johannsen—and promised to consider the other, an issue that remains unclear. The whole episode underscored Steffens's sharp turn toward labor and, for the moment, away from political reform.

Steffens's testimony for Darrow in late February was not nearly as dramatic as that of the previous summer. With the theatrics of the first trial in mind, the judge and the prosecuting attorney, both new to the case, agreed that there would be no more lengthy discourses of propaganda disguised as testimony from Steffens. Still, under careful questioning from Darrow and through clever responses to the outwitted prosecutor, Steffens managed to present enough of his points so that the judge, in good humor, later told Steffens he should be admitted to the bar. "It may be exciting and it is risky business in a way," Steffens admitted to his sister Lou, "but it certainly is fun." The trial itself proved more problematic than Darrow, Steffens, or most observers expected, ultimately ending in a hung jury. The charges were dismissed, leaving Darrow free once more. Some time later, Steffens met with Fredericks, who had failed to conquer Darrow in the first trial. "Anyhow, it was a good fight," Steffens recalled the attorney saying. "And that's all it was," Steffens wrote, "that's what our whole Christian civilization is—a good fight."

Back in New York by summer, staying at The Players hotel, Steffens dutifully if somewhat reluctantly pushed ahead with his ill-fated Boston—1915 book. The previous year, he had written to Dot, "I've been in Boston. . . . I hate it. I don't know why. The people there are awfully good to me. . . . But the general spirit is so far, far, far back that it gets on my nerves." Steffens had been getting on the nerves of the Boston reformers as well. Since late 1910, they had been pleading for something of substance from Steffens, who gave them only meaningless dates that came and went. "You must be surely aware of the feeling on the part of my Committee that there has been a great deal of procrastination in the matter of producing copy of the forth-coming book about Boston," Edmund Billings, echoing Steffens's exasperated editors at *McClure's* and the *American*, wrote sternly to Steffens. "You will remember that since last November a year ago we have had promises from you of copy at certain times which so far have never materialized. . . . You have signally failed to fulfill [your obligation] and apparently do not appreciate that fact. . . . Can't I have something definite from you as to an actual date which you will keep?" Finally and mercifully for Steffens, he completed the book on July 6, 1913, in New York. "I know you'll be glad," he wrote to Lou. "The Boston Committee won't." He told her that if the Boston reformers wanted to publish it, his work was finished. Otherwise, he would give it to his literary agent to shop around. "And I'll not care what the result is. I really don't," he insisted. "I've fulfilled my contract. I have made myself do what I didn't want to do. I've won—a victory over myself. And I'm free. That's the point. I'm free now to do the things I do want to do. I'll never start a long thing again."

His Boston work gave him no reason to change his mind. His report to the committee was met with silence, while his book *Boston—1915* excited no one in the publishing world. What had gone wrong? Steffens looked over the wreckage and came up with some possible reasons. The book, four years in the making, was unconscionably late. Yet, there may have been a feeling among the committee that Steffens had done his job too well, if tardily. The entrenched system that was Boston had been uncovered—it was a portrayal about which the committee members could only squirm and quietly agree to bury. Another reason, he conceded, was that it simply may not have been his best work.

Still, other factors undoubtedly contributed to the failure. The impractical Steffens and the impatient Filene, bold and optimistic as they were, hardly possessed the skills necessary for such a delicate task of persuasion. Moreover, the public, busy as always pursuing its own interests, was never taken aside and clearly informed of what this rather mysterious scheme called Boston—1915 involved. A group of city power-brokers pontificating on ways to salvage an unethical system in which they themselves had been active participants was unlikely to turn many heads and, in the end, did not.

Another possibility was more complex: that Steffens was examining and presenting the problem in ways that must have struck some as uncomfortably close to treasonous. He believed that the founding ideals of America, established in New England—"darkest America"—and still taken for granted by most citizens as the prime virtues of the country, were actually the principal cause of the present evil.

Steffens noted that serious ethical lapses were present almost from the start. The Puritans and their descendents had learned well how to preach the ideals of Christianity, which they sincerely believed in, while conducting their business affairs in a rather different, un-Christian fashion. The new American economic system required "thrift, cunning, and possessions," which eventually enabled certain privileged people "to live without the necessity to do work, which they said they believed in and gradually learned to avoid." In all events, Steffens wrote, they kept their religion safely out of their business and politics so that they could be simultaneously righteous and profitable: "They formed, as we all do, watertight compartments of the mind, learned from the start to think one way and do another."

And, Steffens saw, little had changed over the centuries. His cure for Boston, a city that had "carried the practice of hypocrisy to the nth degree of refinement," was not a solution but merely a hope: to stop the charade of grafters, often the most revered of citizens, from believing in their own honesty, and for all to put social welfare above self-interest. A final observation from Steffens concerned bosses, who possessed the necessary fortitude and ego to be decisive, and their bureaucratic sycophants, or "heelers," to Steffens. "The Boston—1915 Plan fell into the hands of the heelers," Steffens conceded, ensuring a quiet death for his work. "*Only* principals will give life to—anything."

16

Fun on Fifth Avenue

New York itself, however, invariably gave new inspiration to Steffens, much of it recently coming in the larger-than-life form of socialite Mabel Dodge. An aristocratic, intelligent, spirited woman with a passion for culture and those who made it, Dodge had, as Steffens sized her up, "taste and grace, the courage of inexperience, and a radiating personality." And opinions that were often blunt. Enthralled by Italy and three years in Florence, where, in a fifteenth-century Medici villa, she hosted a salon frequented by Gertrude Stein, Eleonora Duse, and André Gide, and, to cope with a bored (and boring) second husband, dabbled in affairs with her chauffeur and her son's tutor, she sobbed to her son upon returning to New York, "We have left everything worthwhile behind us. America is all machinery and money-making and factories—it is ugly, ugly, ugly!"

Dodge, who arrived in New York in November 1912, had the good fortune to live across the street from the renowned Brevoort Hotel, a high-end haven for creative types. Her husband, Edwin, empathetic but often distracted (by football games in particular), tried to encourage his wife if not their marriage by occasionally bringing home an artist, well known or otherwise, to entertain her and relieve the utter hopelessness she sometimes felt. One night, he returned with the sculptor and bon vivant Jo Davidson, which led them to Hutchins Hapgood and on to many others. Each visitor had a circle of friends to add to the eclectic mix, although Hapgood—"one of the most attractive and lovable human beings I ever knew," Dodge, a romantic at heart but a radical in spirit, wrote in her memoir—brought in more characters than anyone. They bonded quickly, sharing a deep frustration that they were mere "spectators" of life, existing "between" worlds. Soon enough, Dodge knew not only Steffens but Lippmann, Emma Goldman, Margaret Sanger, and Max Eastman. Being

Hapgood's close friend, Steffens frequently saw Dodge, who was struck by his "rapier-keen mind" and "sudden, lovely smile."

One evening over tea in Dodge's palatial and uniquely stylish apartment at 23 Fifth Avenue (the walls, the curtains, the chairs, a chandelier, a bearskin rug, and a marble chimney front were all white, "a refuge from the street," as Dodge initially saw it), Steffens proposed an idea that would transform her life and energize his own. He told her that she had an extraordinary ability to "attract, stimulate, and soothe" people to the point that they spoke to her unabashedly. "Why not organize all this accidental, unplanned activity around you, this coming and going of visitors, and see these people at certain hours," he asked. "Have Evenings!"

The paradoxical Dodge, who would eagerly throw open her home to hordes of festive guests but barely utter more than a greeting to them—"I never talked myself except to one or two people at a time, and preferably to *one*"—resisted the idea at first, seeing it as altogether too formal for her taste, until Steffens squashed the notion of organizing anything. "Let everybody come!" he insisted. "All these different kinds of people that you know, together here, without being managed or herded in any way! Why, something wonderful might come of it! You might even revive General Conversation!" The result was the inimitable "Evenings" at the Dodge salon.

Hutchins Hapgood and arts critic Carl Van Vechten, in addition to Steffens, were enthusiastic early promoters of the salon, and Dodge, having experienced salon life in Europe and determined to produce her own version of intellectual evenings in her home, showed that she was more than up for the task. Starting in late January 1913, her salon for free speech opened one or two nights a week, usually Wednesdays or Thursdays, with nearly everyone welcome. And seemingly everyone, including Steffens, appeared. "Poor and rich, labor skates, scabs, strikers and unemployed, painters, musicians, reporters, editors, [and] swells" all came by, Steffens recalled, some just hungry for the lavish midnight buffet that awaited all but most eager for radical debate.

They were rarely disappointed. Dodge skillfully brought together speakers, often luminaries in their fields, with opposing views, producing animated exchanges covering a wide spectrum of topics. "I wanted, in particular, to know the Heads of things," Dodge wrote. "Heads of movements, Heads of Newspapers, Heads of all kinds of groups of people. I became a Species of Head Hunter, in fact." Her personal hope was that all the rhetoric of these leaders would somehow lead to a new consciousness, clearer, more liberating causes for humanity to pursue, and, ideally, a new world order.

Evening speakers included an elite array of radicals and thinkers: Bill Haywood, with his black eye-patch more intimidating than his actual words, gave a spirited defense of the strikers in Paterson, New Jersey; Emma Goldman scolded those who could not see the merits of anarchism; Lippmann, barely in his midtwenties (he was brought there by Steffens and once used as a doorman to keep out the press), explained soberly and persuasively the new theories of Freud and Jung—the salon was an intellectual inferno. The topic of Freud in particular generated heated discussions not only in Dodge's salon but also across Greenwich Village. The discussion did not spare Steffens, who now looked back on his own analysis as a muckraker as rather simplistic. Listening to Lippmann and A. A. Brill, Freud's American translator, explain the new psychology, Steffens was shocked to hear "that the minds of men were distorted by unconscious suppressions, often quite irresponsible and incapable of reasoning or learning. . . . I remember thinking how absurd had been my muckraker's descriptions of bad men and good men and the assumption that showing people facts and conditions would persuade them to alter them or their own conduct. . . . There were no warmer, quieter, more intensely thoughtful conversations at Mabel Dodge's than those on Freud and his implications."

A fitting topic for Dodge's salon was sex—her dog was named Climax—and she naturally selected Hutchins Hapgood to engage her audience on the matter. As he often did, Steffens chaired the Evening, which that night was titled "Sex Antagonism," and he watched while Hapgood, fashionably drunk throughout his address, offered his listeners such insightful pearls as "men are the victims," declaring that their unfortunate challenge was "how to get the heat without the lie," prompting Steffens's quip "Quite Steinesque."

It was the Evenings at her home that brought Steffens, and so many others, in close contact with Dodge and helped to establish her reputation as an essential figure in the Village. Her ability to facilitate the boundless energy that marked her Evenings was impressive. "No one felt that they were managed," Steffens observed. "Practiced hostesses in society could not keep even a small table of guests together; Mabel Dodge did this better with a crowd of one hundred or more people of all classes."

But while she was quite successful in attracting stars to her salon, she did not always show a keen interest in their actual words. When it was complimentarily suggested to her that her home must be filled with fascinating debate, she replied, "Oh, I never listened to what they said, I only watched the interplay of personality." Such candid comments from Dodge, highlighting her enthusiasm for the events themselves over the theories and viewpoints that flew around her

Evenings, led some to see largely pretense in all of it, judging the gatherings—and Dodge herself—to be more theatrical than substantive. "A rich woman amusing herself in meeting celebrities of different kinds" was feminist writer Mary Heaton Vorse's unabashed view. And Dodge's mystical air did little to quiet those who doubted her intellect. Even Hapgood, in the midst of praising Dodge, observed, "She does not create anything. She only promotes. . . . This woman acts entirely on instinct. She knows and thinks of nothing except the thing that possesses her at the moment. . . . She believes she is controlled by God."

Dodge, though, did have an admirable passion and talent for promoting art and culture, as well as a genuine sensibility for leftist politics, which became apparent within weeks of her arrival in America. Not only were her Evenings a remarkable success, but Dodge threw herself into other challenging work as well. She took a leading role in funding and publicizing the noteworthy post-impressionist art exhibition at the Armory Show in New York, served on the advisory board of the revolutionary new magazine, *The Masses*, and helped organize the Paterson Strike Pageant at Madison Square Garden in support of the silk strikers.

Ultimately, the salon, Steffens noted, helped change the public perception of Greenwich Village, although hardly in the manner Dodge had hoped. What had been a neighborhood better known for cheap rents and no shortage of decrepit apartments was becoming almost chic, a kind of Latin Quarter in Manhattan. Small theaters and art galleries sprang up, and midtown shoppers and tourists took the time to cruise through the Village for a look at the new trendsetters. Steffens did not recall it as being exceptionally fashionable back in 1911, judging his own lifestyle to be "Bohemian, but not the fake sort." If it was not fake, it was hardly genuine, either. Steffens was not about to starve in Greenwich Village.

When Dodge inevitably met the golden boy of the Village, John Reed, the affair that sprang up between them was comfortably bohemian: The passion was sincere but brief, and Dodge, for good measure, was eight years older than Reed. Individuals, Dodge recalled, were "flowing in and out of the apartment" at the time, and one of those who necessarily flowed out was her woefully misplaced husband, Edwin.

Envisioning and inventing the future was an emotionally charged topic of conversation in the cafés and salons of the Village, but living for the moment was the joie de vivre for most, and Reed and Dodge embraced the spirit. Their romance was real, yet they were an odd couple by any measure. When Reed, for example, wanted to explore the seedy Lower East Side, Dodge would insist on going by limousine. If he spent too much time with his radical friends at

The Masses, she would threaten to take poison, and one time did. He read newspapers voraciously, with an endless appetite for international news in particular, while Dodge's taste ran toward culture and personal beliefs. Reed had an irrepressible need for other women, Dodge a desire only for Reed. After they returned from a European trip and found Steffens, Hapgood, and others eager to resume the Evenings at her apartment, she tried to make the salons even more stimulating in hopes of satisfying Reed's insatiable need to be at the center of any intellectual commotion, and the desire of so many other Villagers to see him there. But her lover only soared to new levels of energy and independence, leaving her exhausted and despondent. When he came home one night full of a story about how he had discovered the beauty and mystery of life during a long, intimate talk with a prostitute on the street, Dodge, desperate for a monogamous relationship with Reed, threw herself on the floor and tried to faint.

By November 1913, their relationship strained to the limit, Reed fled Dodge and went to Boston, telling only Steffens of his plans. Reed's note to Dodge was a melodramatic lament of passion and self-indulgence that could have been written by many others in the Village and, in various forms, probably was: "Good-by, my darling. I cannot live with you. You smother me. You crush me. You want to kill my spirit. I love you better than life but I do not want to die in my spirit. I am going away to save myself. Forgive me. I love you—I love you." Within a week, Steffens sent on a couple of letters to put Reed's mind at ease concerning Dodge, who had been talking of suicide. He told Reed that she was with the family of Hutchins Hapgood and would be traveling with them for a few days. "You stay put and,—don't worry," he advised the distraught Reed, who of course returned to New York and, in good bohemian form, joined Dodge in bed.

The domestic bliss between them lasted about two weeks before *Metropolitan* editor Carl Hovey, seeking a war reporter, called Reed on Steffens's recommendation and dispatched him to cover the Mexican Revolution. Dodge pursued, catching up with Reed in Chicago and eventually landing with him in a shabby hotel on the border in El Paso. Confused and desperate, knowing that Reed would soon be shadowing Pancho Villa, Dodge confided her misgivings in long letters to Steffens and Hapgood. On Christmas Eve, 1913, Steffens wrote back, assuring her that Reed would make his mark in Mexico and that the best thing for Dodge to do was return to New York and devote herself once more to the Evenings. Dejected and alone, Dodge was soon back on Fifth Avenue.

While he enjoyed his time at the salon, Steffens had not actually published much in the previous year, although one of his articles, "A King for a Queen," appeared in the April 1913 issue of *The Masses*. Max Eastman, fresh out of

Columbia University, had taken over the relatively genteel socialist magazine in late 1912 and transformed it into a voice of the Far Left. The editorial statement of purpose he soon adopted came directly to the point: "It has no dividends to pay, and nobody is trying to make money out of it," the statement read. "Frank, arrogant, impertinent, searching for the true causes; a magazine directed against rigidity and dogma wherever it is found; printing what is too naked or true for a money-making press; a magazine whose final policy is to do as it pleases and conciliate nobody, not even its readers."

Featuring blunt commentary on birth control, free love, the single tax, labor strikes, and other topics vital to the Left, *The Masses* under Eastman garnered international attention. Its circulation reached forty thousand, and owing to its decidedly New York flavor, the magazine became a cause célè-bre in Greenwich Village. A cast of luminary Leftists joined Steffens in the pages of *The Masses* over the next few years, including John Dos Passos, Edna St. Vincent Millay, Bertrand Russell, George Bernard Shaw, Upton Sinclair, and, naturally, Reed and Dodge. Steffens himself preferred to publish in the more mainstream magazines—they paid real money—but while he was living in Greenwich Village and engulfed by the mad, youthful energy of change that surrounded him, his heart was not far from the ideals guiding *The Masses*.

Eastman got on well enough with Steffens, especially when the magazine, as was often the case, needed a cash infusion. With his myriad connections, Steffens was, in Eastman's words, "a sort of cherishing godfather to all revolutionary enter-prises." More compelling than money to Eastman, though, was social justice, and in that regard, Steffens and others, including Fremont Older, Clarence Darrow, and Hutchins Hapgood, disappointed *The Masses* editor. He viewed them as "sentimental rebels," men who lacked sincerity and "were as purely American a phenomenon as the red Indians." Eastman at times took particular exception to the "pertly optimistic" Steffens. What vexed Eastman was his sense that Steffens, an intelligent man, was not inclined to use his intellect, relying instead on clever remarks and pithy anecdotes to captivate listeners, including Eastman. "Steffens learned to be happy without hard thinking by developing a kittenish delight in paradox," Eastman observed, noting how Steffens "would sit back and watch it 'sink in' with a complacence which I, with my damnable paternal inheritance of soft-soap, always played up to instead of saying as my soul wanted to: 'Steff, let's lay aside our cleverness for once and try to think things through.'"

The radical thinking of *The Masses* spread to the Liberal Club, where Steffens had served as president. Younger and more vocal free thinkers—many of them associated with Greenwich Village—gained control of the club in mid-September 1913 and moved it to an old brownstone at 137 MacDougal Street, southwest of Washington Square. It was there that the Liberal Club associated with Reed, radical writer Floyd Dell, Theodore Dreiser, Susan Glaspell, and many other Villagers found its fame and helped make Greenwich Village a magnet for bohemians and artists of all types.

Steffens, although in his mid-forties, had always felt at home with Reed and the new generation of Villagers, so he followed them down to the Village, maintaining his captivating wit even with the youthful audience. Ardent communist and poet Orrick Johns recalled how exciting it was "to hear Steffens talk of his encounters with important people in the Socratic idiom of paradox peculiar to him. His system and his charm lay in finally leading you to make his point for him," Johns wrote, describing the aspect of Steffens's character that so often fascinated—or exasperated—his audience.

The Liberal Club was located one floor above the legendary gathering spot in the Village, Polly's Restaurant. Polly herself, Paula Holladay, was a quiet but dedicated anarchist who had moved from Middle America (Evanston, Illinois) to the heart of the Village, where she and Hippolyte Havel became lovers. The decor of the restaurant reflected the two sides of Polly's character: It was a modest, single room on street level with a kitchen in the back, but its yellow walls were covered with an eclectic array of paintings in cubist, pointillist, futurist, and other experimental styles. Dell, a highly skilled practitioner of Village life himself, exercised his sexual freedom with Edna St. Vincent Millay and countless other women. He recalled that Havel served as "cook, waiter, dishwasher and chief conversationalist," while she, as the waitress, served tasty, inexpensive lunches and dinners to "the wildest and noisiest horde of young folk in America." It seemed that everyone in the Village, including Steffens, frequented Polly's Restaurant and the Liberal Club. The MacDougal renaissance peaked in the fall of 1916, when performances of the Provincetown Players, highlighted by several plays of Eugene O'Neill's, began next door to the Liberal Club at 139 MacDougal.

Returning to New York in November after crossing the country on his "most successful" lecture tour to date—the lectures had focused on the McNamaras and the Golden Rule ("I showed them that there was more dynamite in it than in nitroglycerine," he told Laura)—Steffens retained his momentum. *Metropolitan Magazine* offered to serialize Boston—1915 and wanted Steffens to report on the business angle of the unfolding revolution in Mexico. He had no interest in writing the business story, but hoped to sound out President Wilson or Secretary of State William Jennings Bryan on the Mexican situation.

Of more immediate importance was a five-hundred-dollar prize Steffens won in a literary contest, against two thousand entrants, sponsored by the *Metropolitan*. His article, "The Case for Inequality," appeared in the February 1914 issue. "I need this triumph to help me get back some of the prestige I had lost," he admitted to Laura. He told Lou that he hoped the Boston—1915 article and the contest publicity would "set me up again," conceding, "You were right, all of you, in saying that my long silence had hurt me. I can see now that it did." Inquiries had come in from *Everybody's*, *Harper's Weekly*, *McClure's*, and Henry Wright at the *Globe*, all signs, he hoped, that he was "coming back," which was clearly the case. *Metropolitan* made good on its offer regarding Boston—1915, publishing portions of it in the February, March, April, and May issues in 1914. Three of Steffens's articles appeared in *Harper's Weekly* in April and May, and two others were published by *McClure's* and *Bookman* that spring.

In mid-January, he spoke again with President Wilson about the labor situation involving pardons for some of the accused lawbreakers. And through the winter, he met with IWW committees, radicals, and the unemployed, as the plight of the poor became headline news in frigid New York.

Much of the uproar resulted from the arrest of a young man named Frank Tannenbaum, who had been spending a good deal of his free time in the office of Emma Goldman, reading and helping her publish the anarchist magazine *Mother Earth*. But the evening classes that Tannenbaum attended at New York's Ferrer Modern School, which had ties to the recently transformed Liberal Club, are what truly fired his sense of indignation. With anarchism heavy in the air, an array of intellectuals and radicals at the school (including Steffens, who lectured on the McNamara case; Darrow; Goldman; Hutchins Hapgood; Jack London; O'Neill; Dreiser; Sanger; Elizabeth Gurley Flynn; and many others) filled the students' heads with social theories and utopian visions. In this environment, Tannenbaum was inspired to take up the cause of the neglected underclass in a dramatic way.

Impatient with the empty words of sympathy typically directed at the poor, Tannenbaum—an "inspired and inspiring" young man, according to anarchist leader Carlo Tresca—decided to act. On several snowy nights in late February and early March, he led hundreds of homeless men from church to church, seeking food and shelter. The roving crowd met with mixed success until the night of March 4, when they tried to enter a Catholic church during mass. Words were exchanged, the police were summoned, and Tannenbaum was taken into custody. Steffens, along with Haywood and Tresca, attended a meeting of the International Workingmen's Defense Conference to raise money for Tannenbaum, who on March 5 appeared in court, where many voiced support for the young agitator. "What are these men to do?" Steffens asked. "It is against the law to beg and to tramp the streets without a home. They are out of work, with nothing to eat and no homes in which to sleep. What are they to do?"

Pushing their right to protest, the unemployed quickly appealed to the Free Speech League, inspiring Steffens to approach his old friend, Max Schmittberger, who, in a remarkable ascension, had been named chief police inspector of New York in 1909. Steffens sounded out Schmittberger as to what he and Leonard Abbott would be allowed to say publicly amid the growing turmoil without risking a night in jail. In a letter to Laura, Steffens reported that he told his audience that Schmittberger had given him at least some flexibility in speaking out, a freedom the people themselves had as well. But Steffens insisted that they should have still more liberty to say "anything whatsoever," adding that it was a shame that unemployed immigrants and poor had to "fight alone" for American ideals. As the Wobblies in particular were prohibited from organizing public meetings, the Liberal Club and the Free Speech League took up Tannenbaum's cause, holding outdoor rallies, with Steffens one of the principal speakers.

Several of the rallies went beyond heated rhetoric. Goldman and her fellow anarchist and lover, Alexander Berkman, organized a protest on March 21, 1914, starting with speeches at Union Square before leading a belligerent crowd up Fifth Avenue all the way from Fourteenth Street to the Ferrer School on 107th Street. Sensing trouble, Steffens spoke beforehand to both the new police commissioner, Arthur Woods, and Schmittberger, urging them to show restraint. "Police Will Be Lenient. Lincoln Steffens Promises the Meeting Will Be Orderly," blared one New York headline.

While the actual parade of demonstrators, including Steffens, was boisterous and confrontational but hardly a destructive rampage, the newspapers sensationalized the protest, especially after hearing Goldman's fiery rhetoric in Union Square: "Your toil made the wealth of the nation. It belongs to you. The rich are keeping it from you. The officials do nothing to help you. . . . Go to the churches, go to the hotels and restaurants, go to the bakeshops, and tell them they must give you something to keep you from starving." A *New York Times* front page headline declared, "Anarchists Spread Alarm in 5th Ave." Similarly, *New York American* readers must have feared for their lives when they read of "a human boiling pot in Union Square," "a seething stream of excited men and women," and "one of the most riotous class demonstrations that New York had ever known." As for Steffens, the paper reported that he was unsuccessful at persuading the police to cooperate, although the next day, he told Allen, "I got the cops to stand by." The truth lay somewhere in the midst of the confusion.

In a March 23 editorial, the *Times* singled out Emma Goldman, "a professional lawbreaker," as one of the main culprits responsible for "inciting an ignorant assemblage to violence," insisting that "that incendiary woman should be placed under lock and key and left there." In a letter to the paper, Steffens immediately defended Goldman's freedom to speak out, stating that just as the *Times* had the right to lambaste her, "so should Emma Goldman be permitted to incite the mob to action." Given the paper's animosity toward the protesters, the letter, not surprisingly, went unpublished.

Two weeks later, however, at another mass rally in Union Square, the police had little intention of standing by. As the *Times* gleefully reported, the police left "many broken heads among agitators." Steffens witnessed the clashes and wrote to Laura the next day, "I've seen such things for 20 years now, but I can't get used to it. It lifts my stomach every time I see a policeman take his night stick in both his hands and bring it down with all his might on a human being's skull!" In the end, none of the turmoil aided Tannenbaum, who landed in jail for a year, passing his time absorbed in books by Nietzsche, Marx, and Tolstoy—books that Steffens delivered to him from Mabel Dodge.

As he became more active in labor affairs, Steffens gravitated toward the militant Industrial Workers of the World, whose often violent opposition to capitalism excited the comfortable radicals in Steffens's Village crowd while infuriating corporate and political bosses and even organized labor leaders themselves. Entire cities, San Diego being a prime example, felt threatened as well, taking aim at the Wobblies by passing ordinances banning street meetings even though the Wobblies, at their strongest, never amounted to more than five thousand members. But to the Far Left, there was a certain romantic air about the Wobblies in their relentless if chaotic push for class conflict, their efforts to support and empower the most exploited of all—the unskilled, unemployed, and poor—and their rejection of capitalists and politicians as a unified group of profiteers.

The second large IWW strike in Paterson had drawn many of the Left's more notable figures, including Steffens, Reed, Lippmann, Eastman, and Sanger. Steffens's growing connections to the IWW and other radical groups caused some of his own friends to wonder aloud if he was not jeopardizing his career by associating with such an unruly crowd. Certainly, his rhetoric had heated up of late. At a January 1914 meeting of a women's suffragette group at Cooper Union, Steffens, uncharacteristically, echoed the spirit of those turbulent days in words as radical as any Wobbly's. "Let [women] destroy buildings, let them destroy anything they want to destroy," he declared. "Labor may have to kill someone to get what it wants, and the women must try and understand. Forms of force are all wrong, but all are necessary."

The flame of protest, ignited by anarchists and bohemians, burned brightly, but not for long in the Village. Mabel Dodge's salon had run its course after several years, and Polly relocated her restaurant in 1917, the same year that *The Masses* folded under government pressure and Emma Goldman and Bill Haywood were imprisoned. The Liberal Club, the last to fall, went under in July 1918, split apart by the war and empty coffers. Steffens was in California at that time, soon to return to New York before sailing for postwar Europe. Formerly a satisfied Republican, he had moved firmly to the left during the Village years, later becoming one of the most outspoken left-wingers of his generation.

In the spring of 1914, with his article on college appearing in the April 11 issue of *Harper's Weekly*, Steffens gave additional thought to the education of Dot's children. Visiting the Morristown School in New Jersey with the briefly reunited John Reed and Mabel Dodge (Reed was an alumnus, while Dodge's son was a current student), Steffens introduced Reed, who had been invited to give a speech on Mexico. Both praised the school profusely, and even Steffens found no grounds for dissent, although he felt that Dot, whose heart was set on Groton for Jack, had no reason to change her mind. When Jack later attended Groton and found himself at the bottom of his class, Steffens reassured Dot, "That's where he belongs. I was always near the bottom. I think I graduated at the bottom from Berkeley. . . . I don't care to see a nephew of mine lead in scholarship. No, I didn't tell Jack that. All I said to Jack was to 'beat the game, Jack. It isn't much of a game, but beat it.'" After Dot questioned Laura on the wisdom of Steffens's words to an impressionable young student, Steffens explained to Laura, "I had been 'educated' up to about 24 years of age, and had had to work hard for another 24 years, not to learn the truth, but to get the cultured lies out of my head."

Steffens genuinely had high hopes for Jack as he entered his high school years, but not, he told Dot, for the American system of education, asserting that schools and colleges were in no better shape than government or business. Education was "dead," he said, because teaching had become "routine" and learning "drudgery." He blamed it on an education system that was immune to change and made courses, especially in math and science, utterly boring. "There is a fascination, there is something akin to poetry in the way mathematics works," Steffens pointed out, and he could imagine the pleasure a student would take from the subject under an "inspired" teacher. But Jack was not likely to find such a teacher, so Steffens advised his sister to ask him questions about everything, and if he gave standard answers, she should "kick the ground out from under him." It was her duty to "chuck his mind full of big questions and disrespect for the little we know." Steffens himself wanted to tell the boy what "poppycock" most of the books on politics, sociology, and other important topics were. "It's all to be done all over by some boy, like Jack," Steffens wrote with hope.

Laura was single and rather sympathetic to Steffens's increasingly radical views, Allen and Lou were childless and at least as agreeable as Laura, but Jim and Dot were conservative and affluent and raised their children accordingly. While Steffens never actively interfered with their efforts, he tweaked Dot occasionally for her traditional approach. Steffens wondered how children, after years of strict parental influence and schools that encouraged learning but not thinking, could ever view life honestly, on their own. And he surmised that the process would be far more difficult for children burdened by money and expectation. With his pointed wit, he had raised the issue directly with his sister two years earlier:

> Your poor children are likely to be rich. You are working for them, others are saving for them. . . . It will take a lot of seeing, feeling, and thinking to save them. It can be done, but,—that's what their Uncle Lincoln would worry over them for. I wouldn't introduce them to people who could help them; I'd show them the people they could help. I'd show them the outlines of cities. I'd show them the beauty of smoke and din and dirt. . . . And I wouldn't hurt your children, Dot. I wouldn't tell them a thing. I'd only ask them to look and see,—what they see, not what I see. I'd not give them words; I like to avoid words, to clear the view.

17

REVOLUTIONARY ROAD

IN EARLY JUNE 1914, Steffens was briefly in Washington, where he tried—unsuccessfully—to see Woodrow Wilson. Steffens's old dream of muckraking Europe returned with the approach of summer; contrary to the promising start of the new year, he found himself without any work. In Europe, he hoped to uncover, like an archaeologist, the origins of the plague of corruption that had crippled democracy in Europe's child, America. He also expected to see the future of his country, the next stages of political growth or, more likely, the deterioration that lay ahead. With the freedom to undertake his largest muckraking challenge to date, Steffens sailed for England in mid-June, where he would find that graft was the least of the problems across the Atlantic.

From London, he wrote to Laura of his early efforts to contact British government officials for discussions on political conditions there. He was delighted to have arrived in London "at the height of the season for everything," but he may as well have joined the theater goers and shoppers, for his inquiries met with little but silence. The British government ignored him. As he reported to Laura, it was nearly impossible to arrange a meeting with any official, and when he finally did so, they professed ignorance as to his line of questioning. Graft, they insisted, was not repulsive but necessary and indeed admirable. "They may be grafters," he wrote, "but they not only don't know it, they don't know what graft is. . . . Graft here is a vested interest; a reward of merit, and, sought by all, is highly respectable." Worse, the owners of the newspapers themselves, Steffens saw, were not seeking "to protest evils, but to get in on them." Even H. G. Wells and the Chesterton brothers, G. K. and Cecil, did not understand. "Only an Englishman" he concluded, "can muckrake England for the English; and he'll have a tougher job than I had in 'the States.'"

So Steffens abandoned England and in late June moved on to France and then to Germany and Italy. His timing for such travels, however, was disastrous. Archduke Francis Ferdinand of Austria-Hungary had been assassinated on June 28 in Sarajevo. Within six weeks, Germany, Austria-Hungary, Russia, France, and England would be engulfed in war. In Italy, which had not yet entered the fighting, Steffens briefly settled in the countryside outside Rome to write a couple of short stories—"down to the last period"—before meeting Gussie in Florence. They managed to catch a Greek ship filled with fleeing Americans as well as "cockroaches, rats, and bedbugs" out of Venice for America, where they arrived in mid-September, ending what would be Steffens's last attempt to do a thorough and fair analysis of a European system that was on the precipice of collapse, for in Europe, Steffens had glimpsed "the long-expected, well-prepared-for, sudden war."

As Steffens pondered his European experience, frustration set in. What he wanted to explain to Americans was a lengthy story that he feared would require patience and serious thought of a population accustomed to neither. He recognized the challenge, asking, "How would one make a young, vigorous, optimistic people on a virgin, rich part of the earth's surface look ahead to those old peoples on old ground and see that the road we were on would lead up over the hill and down to Rome, Egypt, or China?" He wondered how he could show them that the same political corruption in their country was what had led Europe to the pursuit of trade routes, empires, and wars that would eventually lead to the revolution "which alone could change our course and our minds and save us."

After spending two weeks catching up on all his correspondence in New York, Steffens again looked to the future. Having been in Italy at the outbreak of the war, he might have been expected to stay on in Europe and report the major news story of the times. But what he wanted most of all was to witness a revolution. He thought he already understood the causes and purposes of the European war—"the financiers of London, Paris, Berlin, and New York were dividing the world into spheres of influence and disagreeing over the disposition of some regions"—and that such a war would eventually bring on his desired revolution. But Steffens initially favored no army, agreeing with George Bernard Shaw that soldiers on both sides should turn and shoot their commanding officers, and was not interested in waiting for the undetermined day of rebellion to arrive. So in Italy, he had "looked around" for a genuine revolution and found Mexico.

In the midst of a chaotic revolution that lurched between inspiring and pathetic, Mexico beckoned the increasingly radicalized Steffens, who, back in

America, offered his reporting services to several editors. And for Steffens, work in itself had become imperative. As Laura and Lou both pointed out to him, his production in recent years, despite intermittent periods of interest among publishers, had been inconsistent at best. His sisters speculated that he might have simply become lazy, particularly since Gussie had returned to his life. Steffens denied that she was the culprit, but agreed that something had certainly changed. He could not identify the cause. He only knew, he told Laura, it was true: "Something happened to me about the time I was half-way along in my Boston book. It lasted till Josephine died, and then for a year; so that some people thought it was her death that did it. I know better."

Across the ocean, Jack Reed's vigor had again resulted in a scandal that ensnared Steffens. Reed was in France to cover the war but managed to find himself in love as well. This time, it was an affair with the wife of a sculptor who was a friend of both Reed's and Mabel Dodge's. Dodge, who had shown Steffens the cables from Reed explaining the awkward situation, wrote back sympathetically, while Steffens informed Reed that Dodge had spoken with him at length and remained supportive. "I can tell you she is either very noble or very much in love with you," Steffens wrote, adding with his usual encouragement, "It's beautiful to be in love. . . . All I wish is that it will be good, all good, forever." Forever it was not, however, for either Dodge or the new lover, as Reed had already met a radical beauty, Louise Bryant, back in Portland, who was as adventurous and free-loving as Reed. Even Dodge later admitted that she was attractive, while Catholic activist Dorothy Day, who met Bryant at the *The Masses'* offices, was more to the point: "She had no right to have brains and be so pretty." Bryant would soon be the new love in Reed's life and a presence in Steffens's as well.

With a nervous eye on the growing fight across the ocean, voters in the fall elections gave Steffens little cause for cheer, retreating from the progressives, particularly candidates in Roosevelt's fledgling Bull Moose Party (including Frank Heney) to the "old gangs," most notorious among them the rehabilitated, arch-conservative Joe Cannon. But the struggle, unpredictable and across a wide spectrum, remained. Steffens's disappointment was, he said, only personal for his defeated friends. "In the bigger sense," he wrote to his brother-in-law Allen, "I can't lose any more; not I, myself. I'm not sure enough of what is right to put my heart into any political contest to be stabbed and stepped on. Taking the long range view I can see progress everywhere."

Eager to view the situation south of the border, he booked passage for Vera Cruz in mid-November. Sailing from New York through the Caribbean to the

Gulf of Mexico, Steffens recalled the beauty of the "slow, peaceful voyage in the backward world, with nothing to disturb one but the war news from the civilized front." In a letter to Dodge, Lippmann noted in good humor that the revolutionary conditions in Mexico were perfect for Steffens. "When does Stef go?" he asked. "Isn't he wonderful? Nothing can disillusionize him."

He arrived in Vera Cruz on December 4 in the camp of rebel leader Venustiano Carranza. The armies of the audacious but self-destructive Pancho Villa and Carranza had competed in toppling Mexican dictator Victoriano Huerta, as well as each other. From his distant view in New York, Steffens had not been quite sure of the situation in Mexico or whom to support, so he paid a visit to Wall Street to research the story before leaving. When he asked one Wall Street insider about Mexico, part of the Mexican puzzle quickly made itself clear. "It's barbarism, savagery," the investor complained. "Why it's war, war, and you know what war is. There are five or six armies marching up and down that country, destroying property, and taking towns, looting them, murdering people wholesale and retail, and—" Steffens merely replied, "Are you speaking of Europe?" When he understood that Wall Street—"so steadily wrong on social questions"—was betting on Villa, Steffens headed straight for Carranza.

Steffens hoped to speak to Carranza first before going to Mexico City to hear the stories of Villa and another rebel faction leader, the dashing, fiery Emiliano Zapata, although the rail link between the cities had been cut. What interested Steffens most was not any battle news or territorial gains or losses but the politics and economics of the war. Earlier, he had told Reed, "It's no use for me to see battles. I must try to grasp the war; as you must some day, when you get eye-blind as I am." Steffens believed that the Mexican Revolution could provide a kind of peace-making template that could be applied elsewhere, Europe being the most significant possibility.

Beyond the guns and uncounted casualties in Mexico were, Steffens saw, the "tremendous power of the quiet hope of the people." He conceded that their yearning for a better life, no different from that of their ancestors stretching back centuries, was likely to be lost in the shrill voices and inevitable cynicism that always accompanies war coverage. Yet, he had no doubt that he would ultimately report the truth. "It's the old story," he wrote to Laura, "of the true and the beautiful being so covered with dirt that one can hardly see it. Fortunately I have been a miner so long that I can see gold in the rock. I am not discouraged by quartz."

In Vera Cruz, Steffens also saw the predictable friction between the occupiers and the occupied. In an almost absurd diplomatic row that began with the

failure of Mexicans to salute the American flag, President Wilson had reluctantly dispatched troops to Vera Cruz in the spring of 1914 to try to halt arms
shipments from Germany and, in his missionary-like determination to spread
freedom, to save Mexico from its own tyrannical government. Some saw it as a
blatant, imperialistic grab of markets and power by the Americans, but Steffens
looked for the best in Wilson's decision, believing that he did have the noble
hope of bringing a hint of democracy and freedom to a land ignorant of both.
Reed, who had made a name for himself as a war correspondent with some
sensational dispatches covering his adventures with Villa ("If all history had
been reported as you are doing this, Lord!" Lippmann declared), differed with
Steffens. The younger man insisting on the need to spare Mexicans "our grand
democratic institutions—trust government, unemployment, and wage slavery."

Reed had a point insofar as the American presence was not welcomed by
much of Mexico. The situation on the ground there bore small resemblance to
Wilson's high-minded ideals. The American soldiers, Steffens saw, were con-
temptuous of the Mexicans, who repaid them "with hate." Other influential
Americans present were politicians and businessmen who wanted to Americanize
the country as quickly as possible. Wilson later asked Steffens why Mexicans
inconveniently resisted American assistance. Steffens replied that when it came
to foreign adventures, the Americans were naive—you cannot commit rape a
little, he told the president. Wilson's reaction can only be imagined.

In Vera Cruz, Steffens approached Carranza, who, suspicious of America,
rebuffed him and did not speak openly with him until months later in Mexico City.
Steffens decided to cut short his stay in Mexico and return to New York in early
1915. By late March, he had settled on another cross-country trip to California,
stopping briefly in Chicago to consult with Darrow on the McNamaras. When
he reached Los Angeles, Steffens found that the McNamara affair, more than
three years after the fact, continued to unfold. The district attorney's promise
not to pursue others connected to the dynamiters had been broken. Steffens,
already harshly ridiculed for his earlier role in the trial, attempted futilely to
hold the prosecutors to their word. While he never withdrew his support of the
McNamaras, the authorities no longer cared to hear any more from Steffens,
who returned to New York by early summer.

Mexico continued its hold on Steffens. He saw that Wilson was focused on
the upheaval, yet had been receiving advice that Steffens, with an eye on recent
Mexican history, feared was misguided. To provide a better understanding of
the reality in Mexico, he produced two articles: "The Sunny Side of Mexico"
was published in *Metropolitan* in May 1915 and illustrated the hypocrisy and

duplicity of his own countrymen, partly by the use of an imagined dialogue between the somewhat naive Steffens and a Wall Street veteran anxious to exploit and Americanize the backward Mexicans. His "Making Friends with Mexico," published in *Collier's* on November 25, 1916, explained the background on the political intrigue and bloodshed that led up to the current conflict.

Mexico, Steffens observed, was the old, sad story of money, power, and poverty that cursed weak nations everywhere. For more than a quarter of a century, Mexicans had lived in the firm grip of President Porfirio Diaz. After seizing power in 1876, Diaz wasted no time in thrusting Mexico into the modern world, taking over a country that was in political shambles and barely touched by the industrial revolution. The only way out, Diaz believed, was to attract capital, and capital did not flow to places like Mexico. Ruthlessly silencing the newspapers and crushing any dissent ("he took those murderous brigands," Steffens's Wall Street insider raved, "he stood 'em up along a wall, and he shot 'em. No judges, no juries, no—poppycock. Just a word and a volley"), Diaz convinced outside investors that Mexico was open for business. And predictably, from Spain, France, England, Germany, and the United States, money did flow in to the resource-rich and completely corrupt nation. From an investor's point of view, Mexico was a spectacular success.

And, in Steffens's eyes, it was a political blueprint taken from his own country, the only difference, he noted, being that Diaz "had to import his own financiers." He observed that Diaz was "president and boss (McKinley and Hanna) in one, with his corrupt but able political ring, and the powerful business and clerical ring back of it, which cast and counted the votes of the people, and used their power and their pitiful faith to get and sell or give away concessions, lands, mines, oil claims—privileges for 'the friends of Diaz,' as they were actually titled."

By 1910, Diaz's orgy had fractured the country. With rebel leaders Pancho Villa in the north and Emiliano Zapata in the south leading peasant revolts, Diaz resigned. One of his successors would be military leader Victoriano Huerta, a brutal dictator and, in Steffens's estimation, "a drunken crook." President Wilson, having barely settled into the White House, quickly made his position on Huerta and Mexico clear: "I will not recognize a government of butchers." In April 1914, he put his words into action, sending the U.S. Marines to seize Vera Cruz, leaving seventeen Americans and over one hundred Mexicans dead in the assault. Over some harsh criticism at home and in Mexico, the deed was done, Huerta was soon gone, Mexico was leaderless, and the bloodshed continued unabated.

Steffens entered the conflict later in the year by joining Carranza's forces in Vera Cruz. When Steffens arrived, Zapata and Villa not only opposed Carranza but threatened to join forces against him. The new year brought little change as civil war ravaged the country from north to south. After Villa's army was defeated by Carranza's forces at Celaya in April 1915, however, the balance of power began to clearly shift over to Carranza.

Steffens had gone to Mexico to study the process of revolution, and the example before him—an impoverished nation dominated by shifting alliances and power grabs as thousands of peasant soldiers slaughtered each other while the aristocracy remained firmly entrenched—was not, Steffens wrote, "going according to Marx." He did not feel any more encouraged after reading an account in the *New York Times* hinting that Wilson now planned to push for a provisional government that would include not only Carranza but the weakened Villa.

Consequently, Steffens fired off a pointed letter on July 31, 1915, to "Colonel" Edward M. House in Washington. This top confidant of Wilson's could, Steffens knew, be reliably counted on to approach the president on the Mexican debacle. House's political rise was an intriguing American story. Raised in a wealthy and rambunctious Texas family—in prep school he kept a knife and a gun—House became a power broker in his native state, where a governor had bestowed on him his nickname. In one of the more curious relationships in American political history, House was now Wilson's most trusted advisor, a man who operated as the power behind the throne, even though he held no formal appointive or elective office and had quite a different personality—much more sociable and less bookish—than the president. Noting House's particular interest in foreign policy, Norman Hapgood referred to him as "the actual though not the nominal Secretary of State." Wilson himself did not deny House's access. "Mr. House is my second personality," he once claimed. And to the benefit of Steffens, House was keenly aware of the valuable role performed by newspapers, maintaining good relations with young journalists, including Lippmann, William C. Bullitt, Herbert Bayard Swope, and Lincoln Colcard. Steffens and House shared a mutual interest in Mexico, so Steffens put forward his suspicions that a plan to marginalize Carranza had been forced on Wilson in the interests not of the Mexican people but of Wall Street. "If I were a Mexican," he assured House, "I would fight this to the death." House quickly sent a reassuring letter to Steffens, although the matter remained far from settled.

The next week, Steffens traveled to Washington to attend an international conference of South American countries gathered to determine a course of action regarding Mexico. Steffens was appalled by what transpired, viewing the whole affair as an effort by vested interests, particularly foreign speculators and the Catholic Church, to prematurely snuff out the Mexican Revolution and, above all, to remove Carranza from power. "I cannot understand why our Administration does not recognize the Carranza government," he wrote to House, insisting that Carranza's movement was "sincere, earnest, radical."

House replied that it had become impossible to reason with Carranza, who would not even discuss the prospect of sharing power in Mexico. Wilson's wish for a representative democracy to emerge from the political turf battles that had paralyzed Mexico since the days of Diaz was a nonstarter to Carranza, who had no intention of watching Mexico be torn apart again. Steffens, seeing Carranza as another of the "good" bad men who dominated the machines in America, rejected immediate democracy in favor of Carranza's slower, practical, trickle-down approach. He pushed his view with House, reminding him that the Mexicans had never had a free and fair election, and that Carranza's caution was justified, because the Mexicans "don't know how to vote," adding that the Carranza was "mainly permissive" in his decrees.

Carranza, who later dealt with Zapata's challenge to his leadership by assassinating him and used federal troops to brutally settle labor disputes, was never the democratic figure imagined by Steffens. But Steffens had been won over by Carranza's statesmanship and his economic goal, paramount to the deprived Mexican masses but never fully implemented, of returning the land to the people. So in October, the same month when Wilson formally recognized Carranza as the Mexican leader, Steffens headed south for a better look at the new regime.

Steffens not only supported the revolution but hoped to participate as an advisor. "The Mexicans know my interest, and they favor me unanimously," he informed Laura in early November. A month later, he told Lou and Allen, "I'm putting ideas into the heads of Mexican leaders and they like them, and me. In fact, I'm pretty well in on the inside of the Mexican revolution, and I've attended meetings of the Guatemalan revolutionary junta." Steffens got himself invited to accompany Carranza, who was now warming up to Steffens, on a long train journey through Mexico, with stops in major cities.

One point that Steffens pushed vigorously with Carranza was ownership of Mexico's oil. American and European oil interests looked upon Mexican oil as rightfully their own, while Steffens reminded Carranza that the oil, unfortunately for the investors, was under Mexican soil and should benefit Mexicans. Steffens's name became anathema to the oil men in America when the drafters of Mexico's new constitution used Article 27—practically a declaration of war to foreign oil interests—to preserve Mexican control of the oil. The article was passed, despite the best efforts of influential American congressmen and oil interests to block the law. Carranza, however, was not nearly as concerned about oil as were many of the younger, more radical politicians involved in writing the constitution, so Steffens's influence was probably not what he or American oilmen thought it was.

Steffens's view of Mexico's future fluctuated with changing events. Just before departing for Mexico in October, he wrote to Upton Sinclair that he was looking forward to staying there until "that beautiful revolution with its wonderful hopes is over and busted. For I have no doubt that American and British capital will buy it up and out and set up civilized law and order." On Christmas, though, he was pleased to report to Allen and Lou that "the revolution is running over the foreign and Mexican capitalists like a clean roller. . . . It's a joy to hear them holler."

Steffens returned in 1916 to a cold, wet spring in New York—"what I needed after the winter in Mexico," he admitted to Allen. Meanwhile, in Washington, Wilson had to contend not only with unending crises in Mexico but also the intractable war in Europe, which he was desperately trying to keep an ocean away, as well as his own reelection. With six thousand American troops under General John Pershing already pursuing Pancho Villa's elusive army deep into Mexican territory to avenge his murderous raid over the border into Columbus, New Mexico, and oil interests and Wall Street advocating an all-out invasion, Wilson was hard-pressed to keep the fragile Mexican peace. Steffens, who had seen Carranza being pressured by the United States, went to Washington and saw that Wilson did not possess the truth on Mexico. "I never found President Wilson informed on anything that I knew about in Mexico," Steffens asserted. Wilson had some details but "none of the color, no background, no such interpretive facts as an executive has to have to act upon." Steffens blamed the State Department, which, he believed, harbored its own prejudices in Mexico.

In a number of lectures, Steffens had pointed out that Americans belonged in Mexico as much as Germans belonged in Belgium, and that American oil and mining developers looked at Mexico and envisioned the day when America's southern border would touch Guatemala. If necessary, a brief border skirmish to secure such a lucrative prize was well worth it. He noted the delight that Mexico bashers took in Villa's attack in New Mexico, seeing it as a guarantee of an invasion. Wilson, though, "had no love for the oil men," Steffens wrote. "He despised them and their methods. He used to say that all business men who went into foreign countries should go at their own risk, not at the risk of the nation, not at the risk of war." And not only were the oil companies praying for war, but the Germans, desperate to keep America out of their own grinding slaughterhouse in Europe, were urging both Villa and Carranza to take up arms against the bully neighbor.

Increasingly, Steffens sought to position himself in a mediating role concerning the Mexico-U.S. quandary. In March, just before departing Mexico for New York, he had written to Dot of discussions he had had with other Americans; the discussions led him to believe he might be able to "pull off some sort of colonial policy." Now, in Washington, Steffens directly addressed the crisis. With senators and members of Wilson's cabinet, particularly Secretary of War Newton Baker, Steffens talked up Mexico and the importance of viewing the revolution as an obviously chaotic but legitimate attempt by Mexicans to reclaim their own country. Deploying the army, he stressed, would be seen as a blatant thrust for power, proving only that profit and prejudice, not the spread of democracy, guided America's foreign policy. Steffens believed in Wilson's intention to ensure that Mexico would not be sold to the highest bidder. Overall, Steffens felt, Wilson had a "marvelous record" during his first term. The time for peace in Mexico, though, was short.

When the hysteria reached a point where armed conflict seemed imminent, Steffens went to the White House. Unable to see the president, he dictated a "silly note" to Wilson: "A war due to irresistible causes is bad enough, but a war made by misinformation is unforgivable, and I, for one, will never forgive it." Apparently, his note struck a chord, as the White House called Steffens's hotel and left messages that he return the following morning, July 5. Meeting with Wilson in the White House library, Steffens stated his case—that Wilson's advisors had convinced the president of Carranza's intent on war, while Carranza feared that Wilson himself did, in fact, want war. Steffens informed the president that he had seen numerous cables from Carranza, shown to him by Carranza's Washington lawyer, plainly stating his reluctance to fight. According to Steffens, Wilson heard him out, took his word on Carranza's intentions, and expressed his gratitude for Steffens's "very valuable information," stating that there would be no war for the moment—only more negotiation.

Steffens soon was portraying himself as a central figure in the unfolding drama. The next night, he visited the La Follettes and gave them the details of what he felt had been a very successful meeting. La Follette, who had vigorously supported Wilson in his noninterventionist policy, wrote to a friend two days later, "No one knows—that is but few know—the real inside of the Mexican affair but it was a close shave." Over the next few weeks, Steffens was even more enthusiastic. He told Lou and Allen, "My plan for the settlement of all the [Mexican] row is working out exactly," and informed Laura, "It's going my way beautifully on the Mexican issue. [State Department Counselor Frank] Polk showed me today his last note to Carranza, and it goes far to yield all the Mexicans demand. And that's what I keep pleading for,—from both sides: to yield; not to be proud and punctilious, but to get together. Well, they both trust me now, so I'm ambassador for both sides, as they both know."

His later claim to have "stopped a war" in Mexico was a sizable dose of hyperbole, even by Steffens's inflated standard. Numerous factors entered Wilson's thinking, including his awareness of America's past mistreatment of Mexico, his distaste for any war of conquest, his desire to avoid getting bogged down in Mexico with the European crisis in full fury, and, probably, Steffens's modest contribution at the White House and in the journalist's ceaseless talks with the power brokers around Wilson.

Ultimately, the Joint American-Mexican Commission of 1916 was unable to resolve the crisis, American troops were withdrawn the following January, Carranza himself was assassinated in 1920, and Mexican-American relations remained sour for years afterward. Even Steffens conceded that it would now take "a generation or two" to get the Mexicans' trust, only adding in a letter to House in 1916, "We have started." For any president, the problem of Mexico may have been impossibly complex from the start, but as Norman Hapgood, a loyal friend and trusted advisor to Wilson, noted, it was one of the few issues that Wilson had trouble getting his agile mind around. When Hapgood once asked the president early in his term if the crush of great matters kept him awake at night, Wilson replied, "Only Mexico, because that is a situation I do not understand." Steffens could well believe it.

Seeking an education on revolution, Steffens observed in Mexico mainly the impossibility of the task confronting Carranza and the Americans' "gleeful, malicious rejoicing in all the Mexicans' blunders and inefficiencies." Still, Steffens saw it as a "rich experience" that taught him that revolutions on the ground have little in common with those in the textbooks. And his conclusions reinforced what he had learned years earlier as a muckraker. "The social problem," he told Dot, "will not be solved by good men and intellectuals, but by intellectuals, practical men, and many, many rascals; in a word, by all sorts and conditions of men." He also observed that revolutions are not started by the gunfire of revolutionaries. Long before the bullets dominate the landscape, the seeds of revolution are planted by rapacious, corrupt, and inept governments that refuse to change.

1 8

To Russia

STEFFENS'S EFFORTS IN Mexico found enough of a receptive audience among Democrats that he was asked, with Wilson's approval, to write the Mexican chapter of the Democratic Campaign Book for the 1916 election. Although Wilson had won election easily four years earlier, the heavy pressure on him to avoid entanglement in Europe and Mexico made 1916 a legitimate race between Wilson and the Republican candidate, Supreme Court Justice Charles Evan Hughes, a "churchman" in the "Taft class," Steffens observed, unless Hughes had "learned something in the Supreme Court; which is not commonly done." Hughes secured the nomination only after Roosevelt had tried his utmost to do so himself at another divisive Republican convention. "Wall Street is for TR," Steffens had written during the campaign, an indication of Roosevelt's stunning and thorough conversion from a proud, Republican progressive to a reactionary conservative. Steffens believed that Roosevelt, in fact, had lost any ability for reflection. After a brief conversation with Roosevelt at *Metropolitan Magazine* the previous year, Steffens commented to Allen that the former president's mind "goes on about its business, regardless of what you throw into it."

For both parties, the war in Europe, not the chaos in Mexico, was becoming the issue of the day. Steffens understood that maintaining Wilson in office was paramount, so along with Hutchins Hapgood, Fred Howe, Ida Tarbell, Ray Stannard Baker, and a host of other progressive writers organized by George Creel, the former muckraking journalist and ardent Wilson backer, Steffens participated in a series of syndicated articles supporting the president.

The urgency of Steffens's Mexican message inevitably faded with time. In early September, he was informed by the Democrats that his version of Mexican-American affairs would not be adopted, possibly because his aggressive portrayal of Wilson's interest in resolving the Mexican quagmire had the president, in the minds of his advisors, looking a bit too desperately in the direction of peace. In July, Hughes also had given Steffens a half hour to plead his case for Mexico, but Steffens felt he was speaking to a mind already closed on the matter.

Steffens bounced between New York, Boston, and Washington throughout the spring and summer of 1916 before heading out on a fall lecture tour sponsored by the Fels Fund. Through Pennsylvania, Ohio, Illinois, Missouri, Wisconsin, the Dakotas, Texas, Nebraska, Colorado, and the West Coast, Steffens spread his version of the truth on Fels's favorite, the single tax, and, of course, Mexico. Headlines in city after city blared Steffens's message: "America can learn much from Mexico, says Lincoln Steffens"; "Mexico is entitled to change, Lincoln Steffens says United States should keep hands off"; "Lincoln Steffens brings the truth out of Mexico"; "Mexican raid plot Wall Street plan, Steffens charges" were typical.

And the message evidently found its mark. Among many letters of praise, a local editor from Lincoln wrote to Steffens's booking agent Daniel Kiefer, "None of your other labors for justice and democracy has given such result in these parts as your service in giving us an opportunity to have Lincoln Steffens for an evening. Steffens drew a capacity audience . . . and he trapped that crowd in entertaining and sympathizing with revolutionary ideas in a way I have never seen surpassed. The impression which he made was simply tremendous." Similar words came from Kansas City, where Steffens addressed a packed City Club luncheon and, later, a full temple gathering of fifteen hundred people. "Our meetings yesterday were by far the most successful we have ever had," a correspondent wrote. "One man, whom I had always regarded as an ultra conservative, told me he had never been so moved with enthusiasm for ideals of democracy in his life. . . . [Steffens] stirred his audience to the depths. . . . When he talked of the old ideals of liberty, I saw eyes grow moist and when he delivered that message of his of hope and faith and confidence in our fellows, a basic brotherliness, he seemed to fairly weld the audience together."

The November elections were a triumph for Wilson and the Democrats, who, despite reduced majorities in both houses of Congress, had seized victory as Republican progressives defected en masse. The president had handily defeated Hughes, whose campaign, ironically, was weakened throughout by the increasingly shrill and divisive voice of Roosevelt, bellowing for a war the country was eager to avoid and ridiculing Wilson as a buffoon and worse. "He enjoyed his hate of Wilson," Steffens observed. The president could hardly have discerned at that point if Roosevelt or Henry Cabot Lodge, his ceaseless antagonist, hated him more.

But victory for those on the left was sweet. From Sioux City, Steffens wrote to House on November 18, "I feel,—I have felt for just about eight days now, like writing a mile to you, mostly rejoicing." He did not doubt Wall Street's thirst for oil, however, so he urged House to encourage Wilson in his "yield" policy toward Mexico and in "any kind of a peace move in Europe."

In early January 1917, Steffens complained mildly to Reed, "I'm off to Washington for a week. . . . Not China, not even Frisco." But barely a week later, Steffens had solved the travel problem, sailing once more to the Caribbean—to Cuba, Haiti, the Dominican Republic, and Puerto Rico, to see, as he termed it, what would happen to Mexico after the American invasion. Wilson, determined to avoid a full-scale war in Mexico, nevertheless had done little better than many of his predecessors at pacifying America's southern neighbors, having already sent in soldiers to establish order in Nicaragua, Haiti, and the Dominican Republic during his first term. Steffens had fading confidence that Wilson could stave off establishing an even larger American presence in Mexico.

While he enjoyed the "cool and fresh and rich" climate, as well as the easy hours ("just the thing for an ex-reporter," he admitted to Reed), Steffens observed the intrusive hand of American profiteering at work. From Puerto Rico, he reported to House, "There are eager business men here and . . . at Santo Domingo all ready to gobble up the bargains in land over there; sugar and coffee lands, especially." He told House that someone like Fred Howe was needed as a civil governor to establish a system that would "avoid the evils at home and here in Porto Rico." In the end, the Caribbean was little more than a pleasant break for Steffens before his return to New York and the ominous sounds coming from the Atlantic and beyond.

The approach of spring in 1917 brought no sense of hope or renewal to Wilson. The news from all sides seemed dark and was getting worse. Pershing's pursuit of Pancho Villa across much of Mexico had ended in futility (at a cost of $130 million), but the mayhem and atrocities of Mexico's civil war continued, encouraging the American voices supporting an actual invasion. Chaos had erupted in Russia as well, where bread riots in Petrograd had, with stunning speed, toppled the unsuspecting Nicholas II from power and set in motion changes that were far beyond Wilson's control.

At the moment, however, Mexico and Russia seemed mere footnotes to the catastrophe that had been unfolding in Europe for the past three years and now threatened to engulf the United States as well. Finding little virtue in the trenches of either side, Wilson asked in obvious exasperation, "Is the present war a struggle for a just and secure peace, or only for a new balance of power?" Barely a week after the beleagured president had delivered his noble but clearly futile call on January 22 to all sides for "peace without victory," the Germans stunned the administration by disclosing their intention to immediately resume unrestricted submarine warfare, leaving Wilson, with memories of the 128 dead Americans on the ill-fated *Lusitania* still fresh two years on, no choice but to cut diplomatic relations with Germany. In a letter to Allen, Steffens cryptically informed him, "It seems that just before the German U-boat order was published, private arrangements for the beginning of peace negotiations had proceeded so far with Germany that I was about to be sent for." As to precisely who would send for him in such a crucial moment, and why, Steffens did not elaborate.

More astonishing news came in late February, when Wilson was informed of a decoded cable from Germany to Mexico. Known as the Zimmermann telegram, having been sent by German foreign minister Arthur Zimmermann to the German minister in Mexico City, it revealed Germany's intention of persuading Mexico, a country where peasant armies were killing their own fellow citizens by the thousands, to form an alliance against the United States, with Mexico retrieving the American Southwest as a prize. Americans were now stunned to realize that Germany was a clear and present danger—to themselves. And Wilson, the peace and neutrality president, increasingly found himself operating as a war president. As the war fever grew, Steffens left New York for Washington in mid-March, expecting he would soon return to Mexico and eager to do so. "I've been told," he wrote to Allen, "that my plan to go on to Mexico may take me into the hottest place of all if war is declared; and most useful, since I am regarded by the Mexicans as a friend of Mexico."

In Washington, he spent several days moving easily among power brokers to get an inside slant on the situation. On his first day in the capital, Steffens met with Secretary of War Baker at 9:00, Secretary of the Navy Josephus Daniels at 11:00, former State Department Counselor Frank Polk at 11:30, Wilson's private secretary, Joseph Tumulty, at 12:00, Mexican Ambassador de Negri at 3:30, and Frank Heney at dinner. He gave Laura an intimate glimpse of power when he described how Secretary Baker sat with one foot up on his desk, jerked his pipe out of his mouth, and said, "Well, I guess this king business is pretty near over" before praising the Russian Revolution. He reported to Allen that all of the men expected a declaration of war on Germany soon. "But they don't know. Only the President knows," he admitted, adding that the State Department encouraged his trip to Mexico, with Polk advising that he avoid Vera Cruz for personal safety.

The Steffens's home in Sacramento, purchased from Albert Gallatin in 1887 (when Steffens was twenty-one), later to become the governor's mansion

Joseph and Louisa Steffens, the parents of Lincoln Steffens

Steffens at twenty-eight, in his early days as a New York reporter

Josephine Bontecou Steffens

Theodore Roosevelt as governor of New York, 1899. The photo accompanied a Steffens article that S.S. McClure called a "jim-dandy"

Charles Parkhurst, New York's crusading minister who looked upon the city's leadership as a group of "polluted harpies"

Steffens in an undated photo

S.S. McClure, "a flower that did not sit and wait for the bees to come and take his honey and leave their seeds," in Steffens's view. "He flew forth to find and rob the bees."

Ida Tarbell, who called Steffens the "most brilliant addition" to the *McClure's* staff
COURTESY OF PELLETIER LIBRARY, ALLEGHENY COLLEGE

The San Francisco graft prosecutors: Francis Heney, William Burns, Fremont Older, and Rudolph Spreckels
COURTESY OF BANCROFT LIBRARY, UNIVERSITY OF CALIFORNIA, BERKELEY

Edward Filene, who called his life the "failure of a successful millionaire"

Louis Brandeis: "He would make a corking Cabinet officer," Steffens believed

Walter Lippmann, Steffens's cub reporter

Mary Austin, an "odd but interesting woman" to Steffens

John Reed: "Everything was the most wonderful thing in the world," Steffens observed of his protégé

Steffens, *circa* 1915, with the "little giant" of Wisconsin, Robert La Follette (center) and Andrew Furuseth

The dynamiters, James and John McNamara

Woodrow Wilson, following his election in 1912

Jo Davidson working on his "Buddha" sculpture of Gertrude Stein in his Paris studio

Steffens and his son, Pete.
COURTESY OF PETE STEFFENS

Steffens with Jane
Hollister, his niece
with "no bunk at all."
COURTESY OF RARE BOOKS
AND MANUSCRIPT LIBRARY,
COLUMBIA UNIVERSITY

Steffens and Ella with friends Charles Erskine, Scott Wood and
Sara Bard Field, "beautiful works of art"
COURTESY OF THE HUNTINGTON LIBRARY

Art Young's view of Steffens, in *New Masses*

Steffens, Ella (seated, center), arts patron Albert Bender (with hat), and Robinson Jeffers (standing, far right)

Two events in late March, however, diverted all of Steffens's attention away from Mexico and Germany: an unexpected chance to see the revolution on Russian soil, and the failing health of Lou. The opportunity to get inside of Russia caught Steffens completely by surprise but excited him more than anything had in years. For the Bolshevik revolution, he expected, would bring the genuine, radical reforms so many on the left had longed for. "It was," Theodore Draper observed, "as if some Left Wing Socialists had gone to sleep and awakened as Communists." Sidney Hook recalled a "gifted journalist who, having converted to Communism almost overnight, insisted that his wife redo their apartment in red, including the window curtains." Steffens was neither a socialist nor a communist, but the dream of revolutionary upheaval on the road to a genuinely democratic future burned as brightly in his soul as any party member could have wished.

The key to Steffens's journey was the wealthy plumbing manufacturer and great American friend of Russia, Charles C. Crane, who had already traveled to Russia on six occasions, welcomed many Russian notables, including Paul Miliukoff, the new minister of foreign affairs in Russia's Provisional Government, into his home and given substantial aid to the revolutionaries. Steffens encountered Crane by chance on March 22, when Crane quietly told Steffens that he was headed to the State Department for a passport to Russia, on a mission for the Wilson administration, which had formally recognized the nascent government. Crane hoped to get to Petrograd. It would be a groundbreaking opportunity for Steffens, who, naturally, leaped at the offer.

Both the actual purpose of the trip, and who had set it in motion, were unclear. Nearly a month after the group had already departed America, the *New York Times* published two articles showing the confusion then surrounding relations with Russia. The paper reported that Wilson was putting together a team, probably to be led by Elihu Root, to go to Russia with the aim of promoting democracy and assisting Russia in its war with Germany. On the same day—April 21—another *Times* article claimed that Steffens, in Russia on a mission planned by La Follette, was to act as an advisor to the Russian government in writing its constitution, following his limited role in the same capacity in Mexico. The story noted that Crane had supported Wilson in the election, but that the Wilson administration insisted Crane was traveling only in an unofficial role that the government could not specify, and that it had been unaware of Steffens's presence on the trip. One unidentified source told the *Times* that Crane had gone to determine what material assistance America could provide to the fledgling Russian government.

Whether even Steffens himself knew the true nature of the mission is unclear, but that was hardly cause for concern on his part. Speaking no Russian and with no intimate knowledge of the culture, Steffens saw the impromptu trip to Russia as "the very thing to do." Along with Crane, he obtained his passport and hastily prepared for what he fully anticipated would be the grandest adventure of his already eventful life.

A family crisis, however, distracted him even in the midst of his exhilaration: His sister Lou had suffered a stroke and was gravely ill in California. The news hit Steffens hard. He had known of her worsening condition since January, when he may have already feared the outcome. "We are not an expressive family," he wrote tenderly to Lou. "We don't tell one another what we feel; not often. But I want to tell you now, Lou, that I love you." Nearly twenty-five years earlier from New York, when Lou was a student in Rome, Steffens had expressed quite clearly to his father his feelings for Lou: "She is the most absolutely feminine character I ever saw, lovely, pure, good, and dangerously affectionate." Now, a letter from Laura that Steffens received on March 20, two days before his conversation with Crane, detailed Lou's decline and left Steffens "deeply shocked." "It gives me a sense of paralysis myself," he wrote in reply to Laura. "For I can picture her lying there as you describe her: silent, still, and yet with her beautiful spirit smiling out."

The emotion of the moment gave Steffens an existential pause; he reflected on death, on how the timing of it—not the actual passing of life—made all the difference. Pondering the death of an older friend, he observed, "He had his life as he wished to have it, and that's good. I don't grieve over his death. It's like Dad's; Mother's; Mrs. Bontecou's. . . . But,—I don't like these unfinished lives. There's something violent, even criminal about them, and they wound, like a bomb, others near the principal. I can't help thinking and feeling for Allen and you when I ache for Lou. And I can't help seeing how she enjoyed living."

Lou and Russia, however, were pulling Steffens in opposite directions. His letters to Laura, indicative of his inner turmoil, explain why he chose Russia. On the day that he met Crane and was seized by the prospect of witnessing a revolution that almost certainly would change history, he sent Laura a letter that was a strikingly insensitive but, in fact, perfectly honest account of his torn loyalties. "One thought," he confessed, "holds me hard: Lou. If I go, ask her to wait for me; till I get back anyhow. I might return ahead of Crane; as soon as I get the story I want. And it's my story. There's no American in Petrograd now, Crane says; only two English writers, and none that understands the fundamentals."

Two days later, he wired a telegram to Laura that closed, "Sorry to go now but opportunity too great to miss. Best hope for Lou."

Within three days, Steffens was preparing to board a Norwegian liner in New York, headed across the Atlantic. At that point, Steffens composed the letter that Laura and the rest of his family might have expected earlier. They knew from hundreds of previous letters and from the course of his entire adult life that while Steffens treasured his family, his heart had always been with "the cause": a fundamental, seismic shift in the nature of governance—the place hardly mattered—that would extinguish the advantages of the privileged while restoring democracy for all. But Steffens rarely paused long for the benefit of a single person, and his painful awareness, bordering on shame, of his inward focus runs uncomfortably through his words:

> I soon leave to go to the ship, and I go heavy-hearted. I was hoping for a telegram for you. I had hoped to have it a good one with good news. For my mind is full of self-accusing and self-defense. Your last letter, with Allen's, called me home, and if I'd been on my way to Cuba I'd have gone. But I can't do both now. It's now or never for Russia.

After listing the compelling reasons for his need to go—largely to gain access to the inner circles of the new Russian government and witness the story as it unfolded—he conceded,

> They may not appeal to you. But I have seen the Mexican Revolution. I want to understand revolutions. There are not many. I cannot miss any of them if I am to know what they are really like. . . . It seems to me I must be there. It seems to me that Lou would want me to be there. And I guess now after five days of doubt and suffering, I guess I shall be. I'll be there with a great sorrow in my heart and many doubts and hours of self-accusation, but I can't help thinking that I am doing what I ought to do. Love to Lou and Allen and a word to Dot; I haven't written her, and, Laura, if I have done what you wouldn't have done, forgive me and help me to forgive myself; you and Allen.

On April 2, news of Lou's death reached Steffens in Nova Scotia, where his ship had been held for inspection. He had braced himself for the inevitable, but the pain was deep. Trying to reassure himself as much as the rest of the family, he added, "It's a wound. I know that, too. It seems that it will never heal, but it will. It is a wound, and wounds do heal. I wish I could make you sure of that. I wish I could make myself sure of it." Contrasting him with Hutchins Hapgood,

Mabel Dodge understood that Steffens, emotionally, was a man alone: "He was very kind and amused and patient, and he was without the tragic sense of life that Hutch had, so, one felt, tragedy would never really touch him. He would know how to dodge it and flit away. Well—he was safe all those years."

As Steffens expected, the tumult over Russia helped his wound to heal quickly. The Atlantic crossing itself was like a scene from a spy thriller. Traveling with Crane and Steffens was a war correspondent, William Shepherd, of United Press, who had made his name reporting the first zeppelin raid on London. Other fellow passengers included exile Leon Trotsky, a group of fellow Russian revolutionaries, a Japanese radical who shared Steffens's cabin, a collection of war messengers, spies, smugglers, and arms dealers, and "no tourists." The ship was stalled for days in Nova Scotia while British soldiers searched it repeatedly before removing Trotsky from the ship altogether, but not before Steffens, naturally, had seized the moment to huddle with him and the other Russians. Once freed, the ship journeyed far north past Iceland and through the war zone of the North Atlantic before docking safely in Norway. Steffens, Crane, and Shepherd then headed for Sweden, where they caught an all-night train up the east coast. On sleds part of the way, they went through Finland and, finally, trailing Lenin but ahead of Trotsky, across the frozen Russian frontier to the revolution.

Steffens, a veteran of Mexico, was not surprised to see the inefficiency and confusion that greeted him in Petrograd. He could live in chaos. Trying to understand it and record it, though, was a different matter. In his autobiography, he recalled the challenge:

> History? How can you get history in the making, on the spot, as it happens? There were several histories all going on together, unconnected, often contradictory narratives that met and crossed, and—they were all "history." We heard aplenty of them; we must have missed many more. Nobody could, nobody will, ever hear them all. History is impossible. Putting together the stories I heard, the stories of the old government, of the new government, of odd witnesses, of soldiers, sailors, workers, of the Soviets, I lay, not the history, but my history, straight like this. It is not the truth; it is my compact version of some truth and some lies that counted like facts.

For the battered Russian people, already traumatized by the slaughter and unimaginable sacrifices of World War I, when soldiers were sent to the front unarmed and told to rely on the weapons of the dead soldiers lying all around them, when shortages of basic necessities went on day after endless day, the distinction between lies and facts must have seemed irrelevant in the final years under Nicholas II. Taking control of the Russian military himself in 1915 while largely leaving the rest of the country in the hands of his overwhelmed wife, Alexandra, and her personal guru, Rasputin, Nicholas practically invited a palace coup. And the outraged populace, surprising much of the outside world, including Lenin in Switzerland and Trotsky in America, finally did just that and took matters into their own hands in early 1917.

Steffens and his party arrived in Petrograd in late April or early May, not long after the bread riots and widespread strikes there had set in motion events that would quickly doom the czar. Royal authority in the city had collapsed on February 28 (by the old Julian calendar) as the parliamentary Duma seized power and, in the chaotic confines of the Tauride Palace, created the Provisional Committee. Acknowledging his plight, the fatalistic Nicholas, writing privately in his diary, "All around me I see treason, cowardice and deceit," quietly abdicated on March 2.

The Provisional Government received almost immediate recognition from the United States, which was eager to be out from under its embarrassing and hypocritical alliance with the brutal imperialists. As Steffens soon understood, however, with the aid of an interpreter, the new government was tied up in its own power struggle with the Petrograd Soviet, a "stinking mob of delegates" whose members were "milling around in confusion" in the Tauride Palace that both groups shared. Confused or not, the Petrograd Soviet was serious in its opposition, had the support of the Petrograd soldiers themselves, and was moving ahead with its own plans for reforming the destitute country. The Petrograd mob functioned in the crudest of conditions, swept up in endless, emotional speeches given in the increasingly rancid hall where they cooked, ate, and slept, a setting that left an indelible impression on Steffens: "I was halted, as by a blow, by the stink of the mob inside, and I could see the steam rising, as from a herd of cattle, over those sweating, debating delegates." Comparing the Provisional Government with the Petrograd Soviet, one observer noted that "responsibility without power confronted power without responsibility."

At the same time, other soviets, in what seemed a blooming of democracy to many on the left, appeared across Russia, all of this occurring while the real war for the West—World War I—raged on. The irony of the growing influence of the Bolsheviks was that the actual revolution and sacking of the czar, after months of rampant rumors promoting uprisings from every direction, had caught them by surprise. Lenin and Trotsky were not even in the country at the time. Making sense of the Russian chaos and finding a way to explain it back home became Steffens's challenge.

"We hated it." These simple words described the frigid March weather, loathed by Steffens and Shepherd, that left them huddled in their apartment each evening in front of a fire that they had gotten only with a bribe. (Crane had the better fortune to be staying in the private home of a friend.) But surrounding events began to take on a certain order and meaning. Night after night, they heard a rumbling noise, like herds of cattle, passing just outside their door. "There they go again," Shepherd would groan as the mob stumbled blindly across town, pursuing the latest rumor or being out merely because the revolutionary air seemed to coax people from their homes in the depths of a Russian winter, for no immediate purpose. "That was democracy," Steffens wrote, "simple, stupid, literal, but conscientious. That was government by the people in Russia."

To determine as best they could what had happened in Petrograd, Steffens, Shepherd, and Crane ventured out each day, going along the "menacing, empty, apparently frightened streets" to call on anyone who could shed some light on the turmoil. They met Miliukoff, Crane's old friend and now the foreign minister and nominal leader of the Provisional Government, and reformer friends of Miliukoff's. The latter group was certainly more entertaining, filling their visitors' heads with stories of the bizarre Rasputin, street fighting, and the sweet taste of freedom after the czar.

They also met the American ambassador to Russia, David Francis, a man with distinctly stylish taste. The former Missouri governor and secretary of the interior, now in his sixties, had arrived in Petrograd in 1916 with a black valet, a portable cuspidor (into which he could reportedly spit accurately from eight feet away), a Ford touring car, a team of horses with American flags stuck in their bridles, and a penchant for poker. Referring to the colorful horses, one diplomat noted that riding with Francis left the impression of being on a merry-go-round. John Reed, hardly an admirer, called the ambassador "the Stuffed Shirt." Still, Francis initially abided the revolution and encouraged Washington to do the same, an approach that resulted in American loans of more than $300 million to Russia.

But as they began to grasp the power transformation across the city, Steffens and Shepherd tried to help Ambassador Francis understand that the important action was happening among the decrepit Petrograd Soviet, not the Provisional Government. Ambassador Francis, however, hopeful that some form of democracy would emerge from the chaos, held firm to the official American line of recognizing only the new government. Unlike the soviets, the Provisional

Government agreed to keep up its Allied war effort and abide by the secret territorial treaties, previously agreed to by the czar, that were hardly a secret anymore.

Back in Washington, Russia was just one part of the ominous European challenge facing Wilson. In fact, as Steffens well knew, President Wilson had become totally preoccupied with what was now his war as well. On the evening of April 2, following the startling Zimmermann telegram and the torpedo sinkings of three American ships, Wilson, who once declared that it would be a "crime against civilization" for America to enter the fighting, had gone before a special session of the House and Senate to ask for a declaration of war against Germany in order to make the world "safe for democracy." His declaration, "We have no selfish ends to serve. We desire no conquest, no dominion. We seek no indemnities for ourselves, no material compensation for the sacrifices we shall freely make. We are but one of the champions of the rights of mankind," expressed Wilson's beliefs at their core. Still, Wilson, who had been reelected on a peace platform, must have been deeply troubled to find himself joining the European slaughter and stepping into the quicksand of Russian politics.

Steffens had had enough contact with Wilson and experience in Washington to assess the man and the moment. In his autobiography, he reflected on that most difficult spring: "President Wilson, who believed in the right of regulation and despised corrupting, compromising business men, protected Mexico from us as he protected us from Europe—for a while." He felt that Wilson was "a liberal of the old school of Jefferson" and was the strongest liberal America could have chosen. However, when Wilson failed, liberalism, too, failed—"and it did fail." In Steffens's view, the president did not understand Mexico or its revolution and weakened further when England sent British Foreign Secretary Arthur Balfour with his liberal "bunk" to talk up American intervention in Europe. "Then we went in with our leader," Steffens wrote. Clearly, there was little time in Washington to comprehend all the tumult from Petrograd.

But the noise from the Russian capital and elsewhere in the country grew louder throughout the spring. Unorganized public crowds continued to gather, eager for news but largely bewildered by the endless gossip. Rumors were everywhere. Complicating matters was the fact that Lenin had slipped back into the country from Switzerland on April 3, helped through by Germans hoping to disrupt the already dysfunctional Russian war effort and greeted by thousands of cheering Bolsheviks waving red banners.

A typical revolutionary scene unfolded just before Miliukoff inevitably fell from power in early May. Amid the confusion, the mob marched once more, to Miliukoff's headquarters, anticipating an explanation of where matters stood politically. In particular, they were angered by persistent rumors that Miliukoff had intentionally evaded the Provisional Government's agreement that Russia would give up claims to land grabs after the war. (In fact, Miliukoff had clearly confirmed such rumors in an interview conducted by the intrepid and pro-Bolshevik British journalist Morgan Philips Price and published by the *Manchester Guardian* on April 26.) The crowd waited, Steffens among them, until after midnight. Miliukoff never appeared.

The following night, they returned, and Miliukoff, who was viewed as a scholarly and decent, if rather conservative, man among the Russians, appeared on his balcony. With the silent crowd listening intently, Miliukoff acknowledged that yes, the Russians did seek Constantinople as a warm-water port and year-round outlet for trade. The agreements with the Allies remained. Russia, in the midst of its revolution, stood with the capitalists.

The crowd, including Steffens, left quietly, and Miliukoff soon was gone from power. The new leader ultimately was thirty-six-year-old Alexander Kerensky, a man who had ties to both the Provisional Government and the Petrograd Soviet. In his dashing between the two camps and addressing the massive public throngs desperate for reliable news, Kerensky seemed only slightly less than mercurial in those early months of the revolution. For the moment, his official title was minister of war. And more war was what the Russians would get.

Looking at Russia as Steffens did in those early, heady days of cataclysmic change, Miliukoff, Kerensky, Lenin, the soviets, the roaming mobs, and the widespread exhaustion and suffering, his genuine enthusiasm for the upheaval is not remarkable. Many others jumped on the Bolshevik bandwagon as well. Steffens was looking keenly, nearly desperately, for signals that the Russian people truly had endured enough misery and were poised to shake free from their historical straitjacket to seize power, finally, for themselves. Only an incurable romantic, however, could have sincerely believed that a democratic order would evolve from the massive, crippled, dysfunctional state that was Russia in 1917. Steffens believed.

Kerensky's immediate problem was the war, which had never captured the hearts of the Russian people. To average Russians—poor, hungry, with no future—the world of their allies in Paris and London was utterly foreign. How many Russians could explain why their sons, brothers, fathers, were dying for the British? Or for Constantinople? The Russian people were exhausted by the fiasco of the war and wanted out. But Kerensky, facing heavy pressure from the West to actually step up the war effort in an attempt to keep the Germans engaged along the Eastern Front, found that for the moment, making war against the Germans, or at least pretending to, was easier than making political peace with his own countrymen, particularly the outraged Bolsheviks, now led by Lenin and the recently arrived Trotsky. So Kerensky's official line remained that Russia was in the war, along with the Allies. Peace was not an option. At the same time, Germany continued its own desperate efforts to support the Bolsheviks and to remove Russia from the war.

A flash point to many Russians, Steffens saw, was their own country's designs on the territorial spoils to be divided at the conclusion of the war. If the war could be cleansed of its moral impurities, Steffens insisted in a June letter to House, Russians would fight. What they wanted to hear as an incentive was talk of a permanent peace with no conditions such as land grabs, punishments, or other acts of imperialism. Only then would they pursue the fight. Yet there was little inclination in America to visit the subject of war spoils.

Even a strong leader in Russia would have been severely tested under such circumstances, and Kerensky, Steffens said, was not that leader: "It was a comic and also a tragic show, that provisional government's efforts, at our behest, to force a people who, newborn to freedom, as they thought, interested in a revolution full of possibilities—land, liberty, justice, and permanent peace with all the world—to carry on a war that they were through with."

When Steffens, along with Shepherd and Crane, met Kerensky, the Russian leader complained that he was powerless. "He could but follow; he could not lead; and he was astonished," Steffens observed. "The throne was nothing but a chair. I had never heard a man express with such searching frustration as Kerensky did his distress at the emptiness of 'the palace of the Czars.'"

Steffens felt that the real embryo of democracy—at least democracy as the exhausted and brutalized Russian people, who had never known freedom, might have imagined it—was in the growth of the soviets. The Petrograd Soviet, for example, publicly favored shared wealth, eight-hour workdays, and the abolition of the dreaded police tactics of violence. The exact nature of the soviets, however, was somewhat unclear back home, as Steffens would later see. American liberals looked on them as beacons of democratic hope, relatively free of Bolshevik influence, that would eventually have a moderating effect on the worst abuses of the revolution. Radicals, conversely, rejoiced in the soviets, precisely because of what the radicals viewed as the soviets' Bolshevik identity. John Reed said that it was "an absurdity" for anyone to support the soviets and oppose Bolshevism.

Then there was Lenin. In the midst of the countless speeches emanating from the government, the soviets, and hordes of street proselytizers, Steffens saw that curious crowds gathered to hear Lenin's undeviating, relentless Bolshevik voice speak with certainty and determination of the future. Lenin had no mass appeal at the moment. In fact, his impatience to throw out the Provisional Government, marginalize the Mensheviks, and essentially start a second revolution astonished even some fellow Bolsheviks. But he also was building a loyal following.

Steffens one day went to hear Lenin's "firm, short, quiet message" to the people in that early stage of the revolt. The future dictator's almost mesmerizing words, recalled by Steffens in his autobiography, intensified the muckraker's embrace of Bolshevism:

> Comrades, the revolution is on. The workers' revolution is on, and you are not working. The workers' and peasants' revolution means work, comrades; it does not mean idleness and leisure. That is a bourgeois ideal. . . . But some day, soon, you—we all—must go to work and do things, act, produce results—food and socialism. And I can understand how you like and trust and put your hope in Kerenski. You want to give him time, a chance, to act. He means well, you say. He means socialism. But I warn you he will not make socialism. He may think socialism, he may mean socialism. But comrades . . . I tell you Kerenski is an intellectual; he *cannot* act; he can talk; he cannot *act*. But . . . you will not believe this yet. You will take time to give him time, and meanwhile, like Kerenski, you will not work. Very well, take your time. But when the hour strikes, when you are ready to go back yourselves to work and you want a government that will go to work and not only think socialism and talk socialism and mean socialism—when you want a government that will do socialism, then—come to the Bolsheviki.

Indeed, the Bolshevik message grew more appealing as Kerensky's own situation, Steffens observed in two meetings, became increasingly untenable. The Bolsheviks demanded an immediate end to the war, while Wilson and other Western leaders implored Kerensky to stand and fight Germany. Crane and Francis, alarmed at the distance between the demands from Washington and the reality in Russia, cabled back that the old Russia was gone: Kerensky had no alternative but to heed public opinion, and the public had no more stomach for the war.

Still, Kerensky told Steffens, President Wilson might succeed where he could not. The secret treaties formed among the Allies remained the problem: The

Russian people wanted no part of the brazen imperial agreements designed to carve up Europe and Arab lands among the victors. If, Kerensky proposed, Wilson could publicly renounce the reviled treaties, the Russian leader might be able to convince the soldiers to persevere. It was a most unlikely possibility among the Allies, most of which were intent on salvaging at least a territorial gain from the horrific slaughter. Still, Kerensky thought it worth the effort, so he teamed with Crane and Francis in urging Steffens to return to America and deliver the message to the president.

In late spring, Steffens set out from Petrograd, traveling in style with the new Russian ambassador to the United States, Boris Bakhmeteff, and his entourage. Crane and Francis had assured the ambassador that Steffens was close to President Wilson, gaining him the unexpected privilege, although Steffens found little in common with the more conservative Bakhmeteff.

After leaving the vast expanse of Russia behind and crossing into Japan, Steffens thought he had landed in heaven. "Japan," he marveled, "is a thing of beauty. I had never imagined that any civilized country, any civilization, could be so lovely as Japan." The colorless steppes he had stared at day after day gave way to rice fields stretching seamlessly out to the stunning mountains across the horizon. And everything appeared to be neat, clean, and, above all, orderly, from the columns of uniformed Japanese women who carried luggage to the elegant palaces, shops, and teahouses of Tokyo. "I sailed away from Japan," he wrote, "with such a sense of graceful perfection as no poem, no works of art, no city, state, or nation had ever given me before. . . ." He added (twenty-four years prior to Pearl Harbor), "If there should be a war between Japan and the United States, I would secretly pray that it might be a war without victory. Japan may be socially and economically all wrong, . . . but [it] proves that right and wrong are not the only tests of excellence."

Steffens arrived in Washington on June 25, giving La Follette the details of his Russian adventure over dinner that night. The following afternoon, Steffens, carrying his letters of appeal from Crane and Francis, called on President Wilson, who was expecting him. Delivering the message from Kerensky to "a silent, thoughtful man," Steffens received the only diplomatic answer Wilson could offer: He did not know what Steffens was talking about. "I know nothing of those secret treaties," Steffens recalled him saying before the president went on to clarify his point:

That makes it difficult for me to do what Kerenski and Governor Francis ask. If we had such a treaty ourselves, if we were a party to their making, then I could say to our allies, "Let us abrogate our treaties." That would be easy, human, diplomatic, polite. But having no such treaty and having no knowledge of those treaties, I would have to say, "Here, gentlemen, do you meet openly before the world and tear up those secret treaties of yours!" No, that is hard. That I cannot very well do.

"But the way he said it and what he meant was clearly understandable to me," Steffens wrote. "He evidently knew what I was talking about. He knew of those secret treaties, not as an ally, not officially as a party to the making of those treaties, but only as I and the public knew of their existence." In fact, in late April, British Foreign Secretary Balfour had shown copies of the treaties to House, and the two subsequently discussed the postwar division of Europe in a meeting with Wilson at the White House, although the president, as House was keenly aware, had little taste for the brazen diplomatic practice of land seizures. On May 18, Balfour sent the treaties directly to Wilson, who apparently continued to pay them little heed, which may explain his measured approach to Steffens's report.

Wilson, however, did not treat Steffens as an innocent. His response to Steffens suggests the more important point that he was searching for a solution, nonpartisan to the extent possible, to a war that had exhausted a continent and now had dragged American soldiers across the ocean. The president heard Steffens out and asked many questions about the situation in Russia, at times obviously disturbed by what he heard, pausing to reflect for long moments, gazing out the window. He closed by asking Steffens about his personal plans before saying good-bye.

Steffens himself needed far less reflection on the topic—he had already formed an opinion that he would hold for his remaining days. "The revolution is very inconvenient," he wrote to Upton Sinclair on June 29, just after returning from Russia. "But also it is very, very beautiful."

19

SELLING PEACE

"DONE ALL I promised and more for the Russians," he informed Laura. What Steffens wanted next was a trip to California to see his family, although, as he told Allen on June 30 after returning to New York, he had a lot of unfinished business right there that seemed to grow with each passing day. "Every unpopular cause, everybody in any trouble, wants me to do this or that," he wrote. Colonel House, waylaid in Massachusetts by hay fever, urged Steffens to come up and talk Russian politics. The editor at *Everybody's* wished to see him (and later agreed to publish several of Steffens's Russian articles). And Emma Goldman, who was facing prison for giving speeches opposing the draft, asked Steffens to be a witness at her trial. On July 3, he testified that he had covered Goldman's first speech in America twenty-five years ago and had never heard her urge violence. It was the conviction and imprisonment of Goldman and Alexander Berkman in June 1917 that led to the formation of the League for the Amnesty of Political Prisoners, yet another protest group counting Steffens, as well as Margaret Sanger, Helen Keller, and Roger Baldwin, among its members.

Steffens did get to California for two months at the end of summer, visiting Allen, Laura, and Dot's family. From there, he observed the mood of the country. Having finally been drawn into World War I, Wilson was now working tirelessly to get the American people, who had reelected him to maintain neutrality, enthusiastic about sacrifice in support of the war effort with "Wheatless Mondays" and "Meatless Tuesdays" and the need to send American soldiers across the Atlantic to save Europe.

And the war fever, Steffens saw, did take hold. In mid-August, he wrote to La Follette, who strongly opposed American involvement: "Rage is developing, the war rage. . . . It is as dangerous as madness and as unapproachable to reason."

Still, he urged La Follette to tone down his objections to Wilson's policies, to no avail. Ray Stannard Baker heard the same shrill voices at a Harvard Club dinner, when the mayor of New York demanded that the widely reported German atrocities in Belgium be duplicated by the Allies on German soil, a remark that drew enthusiastic applause. But Steffens was already looking beyond the battlefields to the postwar future. With an opportunity for lasting peace and genuine democracy to emerge from the war in Europe and particularly the revolution in Russia, Steffens did not plan to sit idly in California for long.

His published writing at the moment was focused on Russia. His articles varied in quality and accuracy, all marked by Steffens's devotion to the revolution and his strong desire to educate Americans on it. In "What Free Russia Asks of Her Allies," published in the August 1917 issue of *Everybody's*, Steffens found little difference between the justice and freedom that American liberals and Russian revolutionaries sought, and he challenged the two governments to fight the war on the side of "ideals" rather than merely for the old prize of territory.

In its September and October issues, *Everybody's* ran a two-part series by Steffens, "Rasputin—the Real Story," apparently aimed at both informing and shocking the public. Establishing himself as an authority on Russia and presenting an inside slant on the bizarre life and death of the mystic, Steffens used the story to explain the overthrow of the czar and to illustrate that Nicholas was no more difficult to understand than any American machine boss. When Rasputin ran afoul of the monarchy, or the "system," his removal was necessary but in the process hastened the downfall of the crown itself. Two later pieces on Russia, "Midnight in Russia" (*McClure's*) and "The Rumor in Russia" (*The Nation*), are romantic portrayals of the Bolshevik throngs as harbingers of freedom and Russia's Christian-like rendezvous with a "Kingdom of Heaven," far removed from the capitalistic grip of corruption, privilege, and poverty that stifled democracy in America. As the self-anointed interpreter of Russian life to Americans, Steffens was long on sentiment but short on reality in his efforts at persuasion.

To further spread word of Russia, Steffens and his agent, Kiefer, set up a series of fall lectures that would take him from California through the Midwest on his return to New York. In a long explanation to Colonel House, marked by some embellishment, Steffens set out his purpose in hitting the lecture trail. He wanted to discuss the terms of a permanent peace with a public that was understandably "all war" at the moment. Steffens hoped to turn public attention to a consideration of how the inevitable peace should be handled and what sacrifices Americans would be willing to make in order to establish a lasting peace. He acknowledged that public opinion was "very intolerant" of any peace overtures, but with his patient, gentle offering of his Russian story, he reported that even "very difficult" audiences "let their minds reach a bit" on the topic. He reminded Kiefer that the Russians themselves were against any peace that was temporary: "They see that an armistice would be like planting another war," he wrote, adding that Russian leaders aimed to settle any differences that "might ever lead to war."

Steffens began his talks in late September, financed largely by local organizations. One of his first talks, to the Women's City Club in Los Angeles, almost never happened after he received a wire from the club's president. Fearing that Steffens's talk would be pro-German and anti-American, she declared that the club would allow "absolutely no criticism of our Government." As his tour unfolded, he warmed to his topic while rumors and accusation swirled around him. In Milwaukee, his appearance was nearly canceled because he was "pro-war," but a throng of a thousand curious citizens appeared and "were more than relieved by what I said," Steffens informed Laura. More than two hundred people were turned away at the door of a packed theater in Chicago, where Clarence Darrow presided over an audience of "pacifists, pro-Germans, and pro-war folk," among others, who listened to Steffens with "not one kick." The early jingoism that confronted him, in fact, was an inspiration. "As soon as I get to shooting from one town and state to another," he told Allen, "I'll be living in the present again."

Even those who did not share his view of Russia could not deny his effectiveness behind the podium. He undeniably had the gift of persuasion. Helen M. Wayne, no admirer of Steffens's, attended one of his talks in New York later in the year and vividly described his well-practiced method:

> I heard Lincoln Steffens give a most eloquent talk to some two hundred and fifty clubwomen, presumably on "Russia," holding them spellbound for nearly two hours, and all the while subtly preaching revolutionary socialism between the lines. . . . Mr. Steffens, who has that magnetic quality of voice which is so musical and sympathetic that people are often swayed by it regardless of logic, was steadily inserting here and there some powerful (if specious) arguments for straight revolutionary Socialism. Here we arrive at the crux of the matter: It is through their very idealism, their desire to do the right thing toward people, that the shrewd propagandist can often influence high-minded American men and women actually away from common sense.

Steffens continued to give his controversial brand of propaganda through Grand Rapids, Peoria, Louisville, Pittsburgh, Baltimore, and other cities, where the political heat only amused Steffens. "Just a line to say I'm not arrested yet," he wrote to Allen from Peoria. "Everybody else is, and some of them are wondering how I get by. There have been sheriffs present, and Federal stenographers have taken down my lectures for some official reading. . . . But when I come and speak, they all take it, both the pro-war and the anti-war folk." And as in the previous fall, newspaper headlines—"Russ democracy to be model—Steffens," "Socialist state aim of Russians, Steffens avers," "Russian masses rule, says Lincoln Steffens"—tracked his progress.

From Baltimore in early October, Steffens sent a long, pensive letter to La Follette reflecting on the state of the union. People were polarized, with the pacifists and the warmongers shouting past one another. "I feel that it is almost insanity," he wrote. Both sides, Steffens believed, had "lost their moorings. The war had swept away their religion or their philosophy, rolled flat all the grooves on which all their thinking [had] been done." But he felt that neither side was beyond compromise if voices, including his own, remained calm and respectful ("I've never been more gentle"), trying to steer the conversation back to the goal of a lasting peace. Steffens obviously was referring in part to La Follette's own aggressive opposition to Wilson's war policies. He admitted that the senator, a longtime friend, had every right to his approach, but reminded him that the country needed the legislator's leadership more than ever "in tone and temper, as well as in thought and action." The upheaval in Mexico and across Europe was inevitably going to be resolved, and Steffens wanted as much support as possible for a peace that went beyond merely revenge and spoils.

Although he got two or three requests a day for an appearance as he traveled from city to city, Steffens looked to Colonel House and Washington for a greater say in the national discussion of war and peace. On October 18, he sent to House a "big scheme" to nudge Wilson further along in the right direction. His proposal, however, was hardly one that Wall Street or Wilson could embrace in the heated atmosphere of 1917. Aware that the war had divided the country basically along class lines—the rich supporting it and the poor and working people more lukewarm—Steffens suggested that Wilson, above all, should "practice mercy, as Lincoln did," particularly toward dissenters.

Wilson, Steffens knew, had not entered the war with the full support of the country. The Socialist Party had split over the war, the opposition to the conflict having swept out such respected voices as Upton Sinclair and Charles Edward Russell. The Wilson administration, in turn, aggressively exercised its prosecutorial power by arresting socialists nationwide, including Debs, for speaking out or otherwise opposing the fighting. The leading socialist paper, the *New York Call*, itself prosecuted under the Espionage Act, reported that "hundreds of socialists were beaten and forced to kiss the flag on their knees." The government prohibited mailings of *The Masses*, charging the magazine with violating the Sedition Act.

Even more vexing to the government was the extremist IWW members, hundreds of whom, including Bill Haywood, were rounded up and jailed. Steffens advocated a halt to all such prosecutions, particularly those aimed at the Wobblies, whom Steffens vigorously defended. He also supported a pardon of labor prisoners, including the McNamaras, in "an act of clemency so big, so loud, so unmistakable, that all men will get it and feel it," and an agreement among the pacifists and the prowar camp to stop their relentless personal attacks. Steffens for years had believed that the distrust between labor and money was a major reason for so much of the strife not only in America but also across much of the world. Indeed, with the anguish of the McNamara case still fresh in his mind, Steffens, joined by Older, Reed, Carl Sandburg, and others, had organized the National Labor Defense Counsel to, in Steffens's words, "substitute real defence for bribery, perjury and,—all that." In a promotional letter, counsel organizer Ida Rauh (Max Eastman's wife) was more blunt: "Help us to crush the forces that are trying to crush labor."

Still, Steffens knew well that his ideas, so closely linked to labor, remained far from those of the increasingly angry population or the growing autocracy of the Wilson administration. He closed his proclamation to House, "Please don't scorn my faith. It is good. I got it in the muck." To Allen, he simply acknowledged, "I may be a fool, but I'll be a big fool, at least." At the end of the year, news came from House that he had delivered Steffens's proposal to Wilson. Despite the busy holidays, Wilson did consider Steffens's thoughts to the extent of asking him to write a brief explaining why he felt the Russian situation was being mishandled, while dismissing a truce with the IWW as "impracticable."

Steffens's blanket approval of the revolution was separating him even farther from the American mainstream as events in Russia dramatically moved beyond any influence from the West. To the shock of European and American leaders, the government under the indecisive efforts and authority of Kerensky, who had been named prime minister in mid-July, fell on October 24 "like a pack of cards," Morgan Philips Price observed. Only four days after Kerensky himself had conceded in an interview that Russia was "worn out," the Bolsheviks seized control of the Winter Palace, the czar's former Petrograd home, against pitifully little opposition. Kerensky, who in the early, heady days of the revolution had called it "a moment when every man came into touch with what is universal and eternally human," was now confronted by the starkly unsentimental side of revolution and fled to England. The Provisional Government was gone, and the second Russian Revolution within the year was complete, with the Bolsheviks now ruling from a makeshift barracks in the Smolny Institute, a Petrograd girls' school. How Steffens must have envied Arthur Ransome of London's *Daily News*, Price of the *Manchester Guardian*, Rhys Williams of the *New York Evening Post*, Bessie Beatty of the *San Francisco Bulletin*, and Reed, some of the only Western journalists to witness the overthrow.

The new government policy in Russia was "War Communism," involving the confiscation of private property, the nationalization of banks and large industries, and the dismissal of any obligation to pay off the nation's debts. How had the prospects for at least limited democracy in Russia been lost so abruptly to Lenin and Trotsky and their revolutionary following of Bolsheviks?

Steffens had last seen Russia in May, but he had observed enough to grasp the basis for the most recent upheaval. In the spring, the Bolsheviks had not garnered anything approaching majority support. Lenin himself had just returned to the country from years in exile. Yet, no other group had a majority, either, and the political factions seemed to be splintering even more as time passed. In such an environment, Steffens saw, no one could get a majority until one of the countless minorities stepped up and *acted*. Speaking to such a confused crowd desperate to be shown direction, the voice of action would prevail, and Lenin and the Bolsheviks, more than others, embodied action.

Steffens had seen evidence of this firsthand when he crossed the vast eastern expanse of Russia on his return to America. All along the way, crowds shouted support for the Bolsheviks, in some cases firing on Bakhmeteff's train to make certain the ambassador got the message. Individual soviets, local political groups of dedicated Bolsheviks, in fact, had sprung up across the land. Bolsheviks had triumphed in Russia, Steffens concluded, for the reason that they "had a plan and that everywhere they had trained leaders to act together on the instant the wired instructions came to them. The Bolshevik preparation for the revolution, the discipline, program, and propaganda, was perfect." In fact, the Bolshevik "preparation" was not nearly as flawless as Steffens portrayed—there was confusion on all sides for much of 1917—and Lenin's iron-fisted vision of the Russian future ultimately produced yet another nightmarish existence for millions. Moreover, Lenin's "trained leaders" were, above all, devoted revolutionaries. Steffens saw it all as necessary steps toward democracy.

The idealist in Steffens had hopes that the revolution would bury the old system of graft and power alliances, ushering in democracy in Russia and beyond, although he acknowledged that America was far from ready to be counseled from abroad. "We are so cocksure of the rightness of our own false ideas," he told Dot, "that we are likely, now that we are getting into world politics,—we are pretty sure to misunderstand every people and every crisis that rises."

Actually, at the highest levels of the American government, much thought was being given to finding some good in the Russian chaos and avoiding the misunderstanding that Steffens feared. House, always a moderate toward the Bolsheviks, urged Wilson to give them "the broadest and friendliest expressions of sympathy and a promise of more substantial help." Wilson was no less hopeful. Trying to take a historical view of the political earthquake in Russia but instead displaying a dangerous underestimation of Lenin's contempt for the West, Wilson expressed his hope to Congressman Frank Clark: "I have not lost faith in the Russian outcome by any means. Russia, like France in a past century, will no doubt have to go through deep waters but she will come out upon firm land on the other side and her great people, for they are a great people, will in my opinion take their proper place in the world." At about the same time, Trotsky, head of foreign affairs under Lenin, was writing with a bit less diplomacy: "If the peoples of Europe do not arise and crush imperialism, we shall be crushed—this is beyond doubt." It was a sign of Steffens's infatuation with the revolution when he wrote the introduction to Trotsky's *Bolsheviki and World Peace*, published the following year.

Yet nothing would be in its proper place, Wilson knew, until the war had been settled. And peace had to be won at home as well as overseas. It was the delicate selling of the peace to the American people that saw Steffens play a curious and risky role.

By late 1917, the war had exhausted Europe, and rumblings of peace could be heard across the continent. In his annual message to Congress in December, Wilson himself asked, "When shall we consider the war won?" In fact, there were so many conflicting reports coming in regarding the actual conditions in Europe that the State Department sent Ray Stannard Baker, an ardent Wilson supporter, abroad to find out exactly which way the political winds were blowing. In private, Wilson and House already had secretly put together a group of specialists—historians, geographers, political scientists, and others in a group whose work came to be known as the Inquiry (later to become the Council on Foreign Relations)—to map out the road to a just peace that was essential, in Wilson's view, to preventing a repeat of the past three years.

The group's work led to Wilson's climactic Fourteen Points speech to Congress on January 8, 1918, when he outlined the terms for peace in Europe, with several of the points, including the ban on secret treaties, the establishment of free trade, and the evacuation of German troops from Russia and other countries, aimed clearly at reassuring Russia of Western intentions, as well as building a lasting peace in Europe. And for that to happen, he would need the backing of the American people when he headed to Europe for peace talks.

As Steffens was keenly aware from his previous lecture tour, however, Wilson had a sizable problem. The country in 1918 was well prepared for war, not peace. Waging the war abroad was what people expected of Wilson; coaxing them to look ahead to the peace was the obvious challenge for the president. In late 1917 or early 1918, House met with Steffens, who earlier had refused to promote the war, to discuss a possible role for him in talking up the peace.

The administration's plan was overseen by House and Creel. Having been named by Wilson in April 1917 as chairman of the Committee on Public Information (CPI), Creel set out to promote nationalism and Wilson's war aims while effectively suppressing domestic dissent. Bitter opposition from both Republicans and radicals like Max Eastman did little to slow the flood of government propaganda washing over the populace at home and overseas. House and Creel had compiled a list of prominent peaceniks, headed by Jane Addams, who had been chosen to persuade Americans of the necessity of a just peace. The speakers, though, would be on their own—the hand of the administration could not be seen as guiding their efforts.

Fine—why not send them out? Steffens asked. "We're afraid to," House replied. "In the present state of the popular mind they might be lynched." Ironically, just as Creel and others had used progressive rhetoric about Wilson's peacekeeping ability to to ensure his reelection in 1916, they supported Wilson's call to war just a year later. And now, many of the same faithful were gathered to resell peace. Attempting to sort through the competing political messages was the challenge facing a skeptical American public.

Steffens's role was to help clarify Wilson's position. House wanted Steffens to be among the first speakers to go out, canary-like, to test the national mood. His reasoning was that if Steffens could lecture successfully on peace in Europe, with an emphasis on the situation in Russia, then the administration had some hopes of whetting the public appetite for judicious, and not vengeful, settlement terms for the war. Steffens, of course, could not reveal that he was speaking on behalf of Wilson. It was purely a patriotic service, House conceded, but one that

Steffens, who had labored for years in support of genuine reform, might find attractive as a participant in the effort to rebuild Europe.

Interestingly, House's sympathetic view of Steffens's insistence that the administration show patience with the Bolsheviks had serious diplomatic consequences for his traveling companion from Russia, Ambassador Bakhmeteff. House had initially seen a great deal of the representative of the Provisional Government in the summer and fall of 1917 and acknowledged that his conversations with Bakhmeteff had influenced Wilson's peaceful overtures to Russia in his Fourteen Points. But once the Bolsheviks were in power, Bakhmeteff, no sympathizer, saw less and and less of House, and his pleas to oppose the revolutionary government went nowhere. The blame, Bakhmeteff felt, was with the Bolshevik supporters, most particularly Steffens, who had gained House's ear on the Russian crisis.

"Very gingerly," Steffens accepted House's offer, aware that a flag-waving lecture tour was hardly consistent with his increasingly radical views. His decision revealed the depth of his faith in Wilson, who acknowledged his gratitude with a note to Steffens on January 25, 1918:

My dear Mr. Steffens:

I am heartily glad you liked the message and you evidently approve of the parts for which I hoped the most by way of influencing a complicated situation.

Cordially and sincerely yours,
Woodrow Wilson

As Steffens talked his way across the country, however, international events grew more complex. A "clog in your peace machinery," Steffens wrote to House on February 1, was that Trotsky and other Russian officials seriously questioned Wilson's sincerity or political ability to implement his own proposals. Steffens felt strongly enough to recruit Lippmann to prod House as well, particularly on the vital matter of approaching Trotsky with a representative trustworthy to the Bolshevik. Lippmann told House, "Steffens believes, quite shrewdly I think, that the only way to reach Trotzky is to give him the assurance needed on the authority of somebody in whom he has complete confidence. That is to say, if somebody who is a friend of Trotzky could say to him that the President means what he says, it would make a great difference in Trotzky's behavior."

At that critical historical juncture, Steffens's point was hardly irrelevant. In the Polish town of Brest-Litovsk, site of German headquarters for the Eastern

Front, Trotsky, representing a collapsing Russia, was in the unenviable position of trying to negotiate a peace treaty with Germany. The harsh terms initially dictated by Germany led Trotsky to attempt to stall the talks until the German people, exasperated by the endless war, might rise up and join the Bolsheviks in revolt. At least, that was the desperate Russian hope. Germany's military, though, responded by charging across the Russian front on its way to Petrograd. Time and military strength were not on the Russians' side.

In his own letter to House, Steffens urgently offered to work through John Reed, who was then in Russia and supporting the revolution so intensely that there was talk of making him the soviet consul to New York. Stressing the need to "use any means open to us to get the right result," Steffens told House that he had already written a note to Reed, yet to be delivered, instructing him to go to Trotsky and the rest "to clear up their minds" on Wilson. But time was of the essence, so Steffens urged House to allow him to cable a message to Reed, clearly stating America's honest intentions.

International relations, though, rarely work with such dispatch, and Steffens's plan was no exception. Reed himself, who wanted to follow his wife, Louise Bryant, home to America, found himself stranded indefinitely in Norway when the State Department refused to recognize his passport. Steffens and Bryant reacted with a pointed cable to Reed on February 25: "Don't return. Await instructions." Shortly after, Steffens again cabled Reed, "Trotzky making epochal blunder doubting Wilson literal sincerity. I am certain President will do whatever he asks other nations to do. If you can and will change Trotzky's and Lenin's attitudes you can render historical international service." Reed thought the effort useless, but passed the note along to some local Bolshevik officials. (The *New York Post*'s Williams characterized Steffens's effort urging Reed to nudge Bolshevik leadership toward a more sympathetic American view as "idiocy," adding that "Steff himself would not have done [so] later.")

Steffens harbored his own doubts concerning the viability of the present Russian government, as well as the success of his own speaking tour, but remained characteristically upbeat. On February 17, at a meeting of the National Radical Conference in New York, he joined a crowd of more than two thousand Bolshevik supporters advocating an immediate peace and alliance with Russia. A week later, he wrote to Allen, "The news from Russia, the march of the Germans toward Petrograd and their fierce imperialist demands as the price of peace with Russia, may knock out the interest in my subject." Steffens, though, took some comfort in his ongoing belief that revolt in Germany was still possible, in spite of the increased war effort.

Exactly how Steffens hoped Trotsky would act in such a delicate situation, even had the Russian trusted Wilson's intentions toward Russia, is unclear, and on March 3, 1918, time ran out altogether for the Russians. Desperate to relieve German military pressure, they signed the humiliating Brest-Litovsk Treaty, giving up claims to Ukraine, Finland, the Baltic provinces, the Caucasus, and Poland. Their acquiescence pushed them east all the way to their mid-seventeenth-century border. The agreement stunned the West but probably should not have. With or without American aid, Lenin was eager to get the agreement with Germany, but the punitive treaty did remind the Bolsheviks that they had left themselves defenseless by gutting the Russian military (Trotsky would consequently have to rebuild what became the Red Army). The treaty also alerted Wilson to the harsh reality that Germany was not about to negotiate from weakness.

For the moment, Steffens persisted in his own clearly futile efforts to bridge the understanding gap between Russia and the United States at the highest levels, sending a cable—also signed by Louise Bryant—directly to Lenin and Trotsky on March 4: "Important you designate unofficial representative here who can survey situation, weigh facts and cable conclusions you might accept and act upon. Will undertake secure means of communication between such man and yourself."

But as the political situation in Russia deteriorated, particularly between the government and the anti-Bolsheviks, relations between the Russian and American heads of state were no better. Wilson often vacillated on the Russia problem and sincerely wished that Bolshevism would yield, in some convenient way, to a form of democracy. Still, when he sent a conciliatory cable to the recently assembled Soviet Congress on March 11—"The whole heart of the people of the United States is with the people of Russia in the attempt to free themselves forever from the autocratic government and become the masters of their own life"—the Russian reaction was hardly encouraging. Three days later, Moscow replied to Washington:

> The Russian Socialist Federative Republic of Soviets takes advantage of President Wilson's communication to express to all peoples perishing and suffering from the horrors of imperialistic war its warm sympathy and firm belief that the happy time is not far distant when the laboring masses of all countries will throw off the yoke of Capitalism and will establish a socialistic state of society which alone is capable of securing just and lasting peace, as well as the culture and well-being of all laboring people.

Steffens took a reserved approach to the strained relations. "Wilson's message to the Russian Soviets is a credit to him," he wrote to Allen the following day, "but it isn't exactly what the Russians need to hear. He could have gone much farther. I'll bet he wanted to, and that some of his advisors held him back. And then, too, of course he can't pledge his allies. He can't say that we won't stand for the robbery of Russia." In fact, Wilson would have gladly stood for the robbery of Russia—and the removal of the great obstacle of Bolshevism—if a functioning democracy would emerge in its place.

The American people themselves, Steffens observed, remained unenthusiastic about their government's peace efforts. As Steffens spoke to one audience after another, he saw "pain on the faces" before him. They were not ready to hear that a permanent peace meant no victory and no punishment and that Americans would have to talk with the enemy and settle the causes of the war in a fair way, leaving "no rancor and wrongs to bring on another war." In Chicago, some of his audience stood up and left. One woman told him that she could not bear the idea of making peace with "the Huns." As he traveled west, he saw that particularly parents with sons at the front "could not—literally it was impossible for them to—think of the president treating fairly with the Germans as human beings and with Germany as a civilized country."

The lectures inevitably wore thin on Steffens. "This speaking is all very well for in between, but it isn't my job," he told Allen in mid-March. Still, Steffens lectured from coast to coast. By the time he reached California, he had given, by his count, seventy-five talks, and they were not going unnoticed. Twice, he told House, federal authorities took down his words, causing Steffens to seek Creel's help. Creel offered to assist Steffens by showing him a secret service report on the matter. But when Steffens asked Creel if he should cease his work, Creel said no, that the president still looked hopefully to the Russians as potential allies, and anything that helped Americans to understand them was beneficial.

So Steffens continued along the West Coast, through Palo Alto, Santa Barbara, and Los Angeles, before the peace train stalled, not surprisingly, in San Diego. After a reporter labeled his speech one of Bolshevism, the chief of police and federal authorities confronted him and asked if he were criticizing the government. Without missing a beat, Steffens told them that he had been criticizing the United States government for twenty-five years, but he was not against Wilson's peace. "As a matter of fact," he wrote House, "I believe that the ideas I meant to utter that night . . . were those of the Administration, and unless I had misunderstood you and the others in the Administration with whom I had talked, it is a lecture which would be highly approved by the President."

Public opinion in San Diego absolutely favored the police, who prohibited Steffens from making any more speeches. Letters of praise for their action poured into the department, a local minister compared Steffens's words to "poison gas," and newspaper headlines such as "Muckraker Artist Is Stopped," "Steffens Tells All About 'Big, Beautiful Russian Mobs' in Dangerous Talk," and "Squelched Lecturer Leaves Town" fanned the flames of discontent. "I think I should cancel future dates," he cabled House, "unless you can wire me some advice to proceed to show officials privately." On May 8, Steffens received a letter from House agreeing that he temporarily cease. A week later, House wrote that he was "distressed" to hear of Steffens's reception. "Unless you have undergone a radical change since we talked, I cannot believe your speech justified the criticism which seemed to have been heaped upon it."

Steffens's tour on behalf of President Wilson, however, did not survive the San Diego debacle. He nevertheless took the liberty of aiming a parting shot at W. H. Porterfield, the editor of the *San Diego Sun*. In a long letter to the paper, Steffens chided him for accusing Steffens of giving a "sinister" talk and being a public danger: "I'm not dangerous. I'd like to be. I used to try to be dangerous, but only as you want to be: to the grafters, crooks, and traitors who undermine our American Government, corrupt our churches, schools, press, and business; and debase our American ideals of democracy, liberty, and independence." San Diego, Steffens charged, was one of the three "most timid" cities in the country, and the problem lay not with Steffens, the messenger, but with Porterfield and his city.

20

THE PARIS POWER GAME

HIS PEACE TALKS over, Steffens stayed on in California visiting family through the summer of 1918. Allen Suggett had married Laura in May, and Steffens took time to visit the newlyweds and his sister Dot and the rest of the Hollisters. He kept up with Russian events partly through his correspondence with John Reed and Louise Bryant. Reed by then had thrown all his support to the revolution. Steffens easily understood the motives of his young friend, having spent his own career exposing the myth of American democracy. Still, he repeatedly expressed his faith in Wilson and his frustration with those on both the left and the right who cynically dismissed the president's view of greater freedom and self-determination across Europe and beyond.

Not having contacted Reed for several months, Steffens wrote to him on June 1, explaining that he had been "off over the hills and out in the valleys," but was eager to be informed on the latest developments in Russia. "Tell me about it, Jack," Steffens urged. "I know you have the story of a lifetime and that you are writing it." After complaining that it was nearly impossible in California to get news of Russia, including articles Bryant had written, Steffens wrote hopefully, "I wish you would write me the rest. And, if there is anything you need that I have, tell me that, too."

As the State Department had seized Reed's personal papers, what Steffens had that Reed needed were well-placed connections. Whether they would be willing to rescue Reed, a well-known pariah, was questionable. When Steffens's offer of assistance reached Reed a week later, he replied immediately, saying he had wanted to write "many times" but did not know where to reach Steffens, and wished they could have "a good talk." He explained he had been making many speeches and written some articles, but the newspapers "were afraid to touch them," and his notes had been confiscated. "I am therefore unable to write a word of the greatest story of my life, and one of the greatest in the world," he complained. "I am blocked. . . . If they don't come pretty soon it will be too late for my book—Macmillan's won't take it." He added that his mother, Margaret Reed, wrote "daily," threatening to commit suicide if he did not stop embarrassing the family.

Steffens promised to do what he could about Reed's papers, adding, "I haven't much hope of accomplishing any result, but I'll try." He suggested that Reed try Lippmann, who, as an assistant to Secretary of War Baker, did have influence, but the idea was a nonstarter. For Lippmann, the Harvard days of flirting with socialism and radical thinking were long past. Now a liberal solidly behind Wilson—he helped the president draft the Fourteen Points—Lippmann had little sympathy for Reed's enthusiastic embrace of Russia and indeed had had a falling-out with Reed that severely strained their friendship.

A greater obstacle was that Steffens himself gently disagreed with Reed's eagerness to act. In a letter, Steffens pointed out that they shared a deep distrust of the old order, of egotistical, acquisitive men whose success grew from the status quo and who would not be deterred, no matter how many millions lay dead on battlefields. "They are showing what they care about law and order, constitutions and precedents. Talk about scraps of paper!" he wrote to Reed. At the same time, he urged Reed to think carefully at such a delicate historical moment: "You do wrong to buck this thing." Steffens pointed out that the war had been inevitable and the results "typical," but he knew well from the reaction to his own lectures it was too soon to expect the public to grasp it all. "You must wait," he stressed. "I know it's hard, but you can't carry conviction. You can't plant ideas. Only feelings exist, and the feelings are bewildered. I think it is undemocratic to try to do much now." He went on to admit that he, too, was at a crossroads: His lectures produced little income, and the magazines at the moment were silent. He simply planned to write what he could and hope that his own literary landscape would change after the war. His final remark in the letter, concerning Bryant, could have applied to Steffens himself twenty years earlier: "She said among other things [in a letter] that she didn't believe people wanted what they said they wanted! I'm afraid Louise is seeing the world."

Reed, though, having not only recently lived in Russia but also marched in the Petrograd streets with the Bolsheviks, was full of revolutionary fever and would not be dissuaded by Steffens or anyone else. Writing respectfully but firmly, knowing that Allied soldiers were already fighting on Russian soil against the Bolsheviks, he challenged Steffens's advice in almost prophetic terms: "I am not of your opinion that it is undemocratic to buck this thing. If there were not the ghost of a chance, if everybody were utterly for it, even then I don't see why it shouldn't be bucked. All movements have had somebody to start them, and, if necessary, go under for them. Not that I want particularly to go under—but—"

Reed at the moment was hardly about to wilt, and some of his strongest words of dissent could have come from Steffens himself. Discussing Bolshevism in America, he offered up a vintage Steffens outlook with only a slightly sharper edge. "The American working class is politically and economically the most uneducated working class in the world," he wrote. "It believes what it reads in the capitalist press. It believes that the wage-system is ordained by God. It believes that Charley Schwab is a great man, because he can make money. It believes that Samuel Gompers and the American Federation of Labor will protect it as much as it can be protected. . . . When the Democrats are in power, it believes the promises of the Republicans, and vice versa. It believes that Labor laws mean what they say."

With some help from Steffens, Reed was set to leave his own indelible mark on history. True to his word, in September Steffens reached out to Colonel House concerning Reed's confiscated papers. By November, the papers were back in Reed's hands, and the story of revolutionary Russia that obsessed him was about to be told.

Squirreled away in an apartment above a Greenwich Village restaurant, buried in his own stacks of newspapers, notes, and other materials, and smoking incessantly, Reed hunched over his typewriter for days on end, pouring out his sometimes biased and inaccurate but emotionally truthful epic, revealing his grand view of the movement that had seized his soul. Emerging one morning for a cup of coffee, he ran into Max Eastman, who was shocked by what he saw. With a "gaunt, unshaven, greasy-skinned, a stark sleepless half crazy look on his slightly potato like face," Reed nevertheless flashed "concentrated joy in his mad eyes" as he assaulted the unsuspecting Eastman with the details of his work. He was, Eastman understood, "doing what he was made to do."

When *Ten Days That Shook the World* was published the following March, the reviews reflected the passion that had produced it, and the book sold five thousand copies in three months. The Wobblies looked on it as a bible of sorts, distributing it in prisons (Bill Haywood read it in Leavenworth Penitentiary, and Emma Goldman in a Missouri prison), while radicals across the country shared copies to spread the words of Reed. In the confusing swirl of facts mixed with spin and misinformation that dominated American discussions of Russia, Reed undoubtedly was most pleased that he—finally—was able to put in front of people's eyes the genuine inspiration and vision that constituted the Bolshevik revolution as Reed saw it. Steffens's protégé had made good.

Steffens viewed the war's end with trepidation, seeing Europe's leaders as "imperialists" in any peace conference. Their vision of the war's aftermath bore little resemblance to Wilson's more idealistic future hopes. Ray Stannard Baker, taking the pulse of France and England in particular, saw up close what Steffens had perceived from a distance: The next fight would be among the Allies themselves. Baker bluntly told the State Department, "The men who are in control both in France and England today are men who . . . have for the most part little or no sympathy for our war aims as expressed by Mr. Wilson. . . . What they really want is a new world domination with themselves and ourselves dominating; what they decidedly do not want is a democratic peace."

As rumors spread about peace terms in Europe, Steffens remained as engaged as possible in the political arena. On October 10, back in New York, he wrote to House of his cross-country trip and the mood of the masses. They had fallen in step with the war effort, but the "sudden idea of peace" had left them stunned, particularly the complicated turn away from the clearly defined "winner/loser" outcome they absolutely expected. Steffens, however, believed in Wilson's terms. "If a way could be found," he told House, "to say pretty soon that what the President is driving at is not an armistice; not even peace, but permanent peace, the present state of the public mind would be cleared."

One essential point that remained unclear to Steffens and even Wilson himself was the exact situation on the ground in Russia. The civil war that had broken out in early 1918 between the Bolsheviks (Reds) and the anticommunists (Whites) brought on still more chaos, terror, and distrust on all sides. In one of the more controversial—and confused—scenarios of the war, the Allies and U.S. Ambassador Francis, a strident hawk toward Bolshevism, pressured a reluctant Wilson to support the Whites militarily and to divert German forces from their penetrating spring offensive on the Western Front by deploying soldiers to the strategic northern Russian ports of Murmansk and Archangel. A significant amount of Allied war matériel, intended for Russian use against the Germans, had been stored (the bulk of it in Archangel) but was not sufficiently secured. In fact, the local Bolshevik Soviet in Archangel had already begun hauling the supplies inland without consulting the Allies.

Wilson, who had advocated the removal of foreign troops from Russia in his Fourteen Points, resisted until the summer, when five thousand Americans joined Allied forces in September, against the wishes of Wilson's own consul in Archangel, Felix Cole, who argued that America "could make more friends in Russia by the proper use of sugar, boots, fishnets, and machinery than by 200,000 or 500,000 troops." (Francis replied that the Bolshevik government was a corpse "so putrid that it should be removed in the interest of public health.") Heightening the disarray, a unit of Czech-Slovak soldiers, deserters from the Austro-Hungarian army, were trying to make their way across Siberia and engaged in extensive clashes with the Bolsheviks, actually overthrowing the soviet in Vladivostok. When the Czechs appealed to the West for assistance, another seven thousand Americans landed at Vladivostok, escalating pressure on the Bolsheviks.

By the fall of 1918, the bewildering situation in Russia, particularly with American soldiers now engaging the Bolsheviks in Archangel, left Wilson's hopes of a cooperative Bolshevik government and a Russian population receptive to his supportive words in tatters. His comment to House in July—"I have been sweating blood over the question of what it is right and feasible (*possible*) to do in Russia. It goes to pieces like quicksilver under my touch"—only grew in truth as the year wore on. Lenin felt increasingly besieged in Moscow and acted accordingly, setting up an emergency government, strengthening the Red Army, and allowing the dreaded Cheka, the secret police, to accelerate their brutality in the Red Terror against suspected traitors and other opponents. The atrocities committed by both Reds and Whites as the war raged on made any serious diplomacy nearly impossible in such carnage.

With the hope of hearing some details on Russia, Steffens went out to Reed's home in Croton-on-Hudson in mid-October to visit Reed, Fred Howe, and Rhys Williams. One of the first Western journalists in revolutionary Russia, Williams, like Reed and Robert Minor, had supported Bolshevism by writing for the Bureau of International Revolutionary Propaganda under the direction of Karl Radek. Williams now was promoting the Bolsheviks in frequent lectures. The group informed Steffens as best they could with their own bits of news. From Brandeis, now on the U.S. Supreme Court, and House, Williams had learned that the severe pressure from England and France, not merely the threatening path of the revolution, had pushed American soldiers into Russia. Reed insisted that Lenin did not "bargain his way" out of Switzerland back to Russia but had traveled unnoticed with two trainloads of other Russians. The Sisson documents (journalist Edgar Sisson's papers allegedly exposing the Bolsheviks as German agents) had been a media sensation upon their publishing in September 1918, but Steffens dismissed them as fraudulent, which, in fact, they were. Despite the documents' acceptance by Ambassador Francis, Creel, and even Wilson himself, Steffens reported to Allen that the documents "were knocked out here by the

Evening Post. . . . It is the Red Terror,—the reports of killing and looting,—which has stuck in the mind out East, not the Creel stuff."

Steffens, of course, hoped that the revolution would be allowed to run its course, confident that its ultimate outcome would benefit not only Russians but everyone else. But events in Russia remained hard to gauge. After informing Allen of what he had learned lately of Russia, Steffens added, "Again I warn you that I am giving you the gossip, not the news. I hope soon to have news." Steffens's difficulty in determining the truth inside Russia was not remarkable. All manner of unfounded stories in American newspapers—the death of Lenin, constant collapses of the Bolshevik government (between 1917 and 1919, the *New York Times* alone published nearly one hundred reports of the demise of the Russian government, an open editorial wish of the paper), the decimation of the Red Army, the unfettered promotion of free love, and the Sisson affair, among others—further clouded the already murky view of Russia.

By early fall, with the Hindenburg Line breached and German forces retreating, the American rush to peace—and to Europe—was on. House, now at the height of his power as Wilson's most trusted aide, told Steffens on October 16 that he was headed for Europe the following morning, for Washington had learned "from all quarters" that Germany had agreed to surrender. When Steffens immediately reminded House of an earlier promise to include Steffens at the peace talks, House, according to Steffens, replied, "I'd rather have you there than any man I know." House advised him to see Creel and Polk and, if necessary, the president, with House's blessing. Steffens feared that his "radicalism" would scare off Wilson, and House acknowledged that he had received many complaints over Steffens's work, but that Steffens should not worry. He also confirmed Steffens's story on Wilson's reluctantly entering Siberia only to avert divisions among the Allies at a critical moment, inspiring Steffens to tell Laura, "H. thinks better than most on the Bolsheviki."

Over the next three weeks, Steffens sent anxious letters to Allen and Laura with the latest word on his passage to Paris and on the Washington politics of peace, now churning out facts and rumors by the minute. On October 18, Steffens informed Allen that *Everybody's*, which had published his work for over a decade, had withdrawn its offer to Steffens of reporting from Paris, stating that his radical views hampered their advertising efforts. "They wanted my ability, my connections, my experience—everything but my name," he told Allen with amusement. Steffens then called the magazine's bluff, unsuccessfully, by offering to write anonymously. More hopeful was news from House, who, true to his word, had pushed Steffens's name with Polk.

Two days later, Steffens, almost giddy with excitement, again showered Allen with a detailed account of the latest developments. Creel agreed to back Steffens on the trip. Peace was anticipated within two weeks. Opposition from England and France to permanent peace was "fierce, but impotent." The big stumbling block, surprisingly, was Italy, which had expected to share the spoils of victory, especially after sacrificing six hundred thousand dead to the Allied cause, yet now found itself marginalized. Overall, Steffens was well pleased with Wilson's firm plan for peace. "That is hard reading for all empires and all imperialists," he wrote with pride.

In Washington, Steffens connected again with Brandeis, spending an evening with his old friend. "Practical, meaty, but full of spiritual vision," Brandeis urged Steffens to look ahead, to imagine the great adventure of the future that lay before the world. So much was yet to be determined in Paris, and Brandeis, like everyone else in Washington, speculated on the outcome. Long a friend of labor and a pariah to industry captains, Brandeis certainly caught Steffens's attention when the jurist asserted that the Bolsheviks' own violence had guaranteed that Bolshevism would have no appeal to the West. Steffens fervently hoped otherwise, but remained open to whatever change was coming. "It's a view. Not mine," he told Allen and Laura, "but it's a view to get. I suppose I'll lie awake and think of it. For I find my mind is groping for the future just ahead, into which I'm going and into which I want to go prepared, with my old ideas loosened at the roots ready to chuck."

On October 28, Steffens reported to Laura that the trip was all set. Creel promised him passage, along with Fred Howe. Wilson's own plans were somewhat less apparent, as not everyone in Washington wished him well abroad. Senate Republicans, who had no interest in Wilson's permanent peace, formally protested his departure, and from his sickbed, Theodore Roosevelt weighed in, asserting that victorious England should take whatever spoils it chose. Steffens confided to Laura, however, that the president would indeed be going—no great shock, given Wilson's personal investment in shaping the international political scene. Optimistic as ever, Steffens foresaw Wilson's crowning achievement resulting from the talks: president of the League of Nations. He closed his letter succinctly: "Peace vs. punishment (of Germany): This is the issue."

By November 1, however, Steffens was again uneasy. No passport had come; Howe's had arrived, but not his. Four days later, nothing had changed. "I am worried of course," he told Allen. "My assurances from Creel, House and Polk, with the President's agreement, are good, but . . . there is nothing sure."

What most annoyed him was the "sudden change of front" among the
Allied leaders. He saw signs of the dreaded "Imperial Peace" being developed
by the "thrones" and their "foot-stools," all trying to protect themselves from
the specter of Bolshevism, not to mention the loss of their own power. It was
the kind of spark that ignited Steffens's radical side. "They may save so much
[Imperialism] that the revolution will break everywhere," he wrote. "The world
will roll on and over them."

Hyperbole aside, what he really believed and deeply regretted was the
strong possibility that the "imperialists" had squandered their opportunity for
peace, however fragile, in Russia and were well on their way to doing the same
in Germany. "This is the lesson of Russia," he explained. "If the tories there had
been able to unite behind Kerensky and grant the people a little, they might have
saved their system. But they couldn't. They drove the Russians, hungry for land
and food, to the Bolsheviki. Watch the same thing happen in Germany."

Finally, on November 7, Steffens—impressively—had good news for Allen
and Laura: His precious passport had been issued, although not without difficulty. The French and the English both resisted granting him a visa. Naval
and other U.S. military authorities had brought up his past "speeches in San
Francisco and elsewhere; Socialist, Pacifist, and pro-German." But Steffens had
been prepared. "I said, 'House knew,' and it all faded," he wrote with obvious
relief.

His only remaining problem was the unfortunate fact that he was a passenger without portfolio. Once sought out by editors and read by millions,
Steffens now found himself with no employer or audience. Only his friend Max
Eastman, editor of the ill-fated *Masses* successor, *The Liberator*, had offered
him any work in Paris, and Steffens was not quite ready for such a limited role.
"I may have to publish in the radical publications," he told Allen, "but I'll not
do it till I'm excluded from the middle-class magazines." Even though his political leanings made many uncomfortable, few questioned his skills. Frank Polk at
the State Department, hardly a haven for radical thinkers, conceded that while
he did not agree with Steffens's perspective, Steffens "is the greatest reporter we
have ever had. And when he reports a thing, it is true." Still, the mainstream
media were not eager to hear the truth according to Steffens.

For Wilson, as Steffens was about to see, trouble that had been brewing for
over a year would continue to plague the president at home and in Paris. With
America at the height of its war hysteria yet bitterly divided on Wilson himself,
and the Germans being portrayed and hated as baby killers, the president sought
not only peace but a peace that many considered soft on the belligerents. Having

spent his childhood in a defeated South, Wilson knew the ruinous effects of a vengeful peace and had no interest in repeating the mistake on his presidential watch. When the armistice ending the war was signed on November 11, Wilson urged Congress to resist the impulse for retribution: "To conquer with arms is to make only a temporary conquest; to conquer the world by earning its esteem is to make a permanent conquest." Not all, however, agreed. Led by Massachusetts Senator Henry Cabot Lodge, a conservative fixture in Washington who utterly despised Wilson, the Republicans had heard more than enough lofty rhetoric, and they ridiculed Wilson for his boondoggle notion of a League of Nations and a "new" world. Just weeks before his death, Theodore Roosevelt continued to berate the president, declaring that "Mr. Wilson has no authority whatever to speak for the American people at this time."

European leaders, no less wary of Wilson, as he appeared to be dictating the terms of surrender to the Germans while taking the entire peace process on his own shoulders, waited across the ocean for their turn at the righteous president. Stunningly, all of this was happening during what historians have judged to be his greatest period of statesmanship, when he skillfully used steely resolve and moral persuasion to offer whole nations the hope of a brighter day rising from the wreckage of Europe.

Within a few days of the armistice signing, Steffens was standing on a crowded New York pier, waiting to board the French ship *Lorraine*. Already on edge and eager to depart before any more passport problems developed, Steffens received a jolt when, as he stood on the dock, he was suddenly slapped on the back. Steffens whirled around to hear a hearty "Hello" from an old acquaintance (through Mabel Dodge), the sculptor Jo Davidson. "If you do that again, I'll kill you," Steffens growled to an astonished Davidson before walking away.

After boarding, Davidson went down to check his cabin and bumped into Steffens again. The two, as chance would have it, were cabin mates. Steffens's humor had hardly returned, leaving Davidson wondering if he could find another cabin on the packed ship. A short time later, Steffens finally approached Davidson to make amends, explaining the reasons behind his uneasiness.

The two friends thoroughly enjoyed each other's company on the trip. While Steffens had his own trove of entertaining stories, Davidson could match him and break into song or humorous imitations of practically anyone, explaining why Davidson was such a welcome guest in so many venues. Nearly twenty years younger than Steffens, Davidson had traveled far since the days of his poor childhood among the Russian Jews on the Lower East Side that Steffens had known so well. Having already sculpted busts of President Wilson, George Bernard Shaw, and Joseph Conrad, among other notables, he now was heading to Paris to take advantage of the historic occasion by making busts of the Allied leaders gathered there. Armed with letters of introduction to French Marshal Ferdinand Foch and Prime Minister Georges Clemenceau, Davidson had high hopes.

In Paris, Davidson soon had his bust of Marshal Foch. Pressing his friend for any news or gossip, Steffens asked him what the general had said during all that time. "I don't know. I was busy working," was Davidson's only response. Steffens fumed in his usual good humor: "Here is a man who spent the whole day with the Marshall of France and he doesn't know what he said!" Davidson, in fact, became a fixture on the Paris scene, going on to do busts of Clemenceau, General Pershing, Lord Balfour, Colonel House, Bernard Baruch, and many others. Filene alone bought ten of the bronze busts. Among Davidson's later work was a bust of Steffens as well.

In addition to what he could glean from Davidson, Steffens quickly sought news from other friends. He called on House, dined with Lippmann, who was traveling as House's assistant, and relied most heavily on good friend Will Irwin, a former magazine reporter and now chief of the Foreign Department of the CPI. He also mixed with the old *McClure's* staff. Ida Tarbell, in Paris writing for the Red Cross magazine (edited by John Phillips), organized a lunch at which Steffens, Baker, White, and Howe shared memories of the days when America was less weary and certainly more innocent. Muckrakers had hammered away at the innocence, and now the war had ended it altogether.

With no public forum but a mind bursting with news to report, Steffens frequently wrote long, detailed letters to Gussie and his family. The letters provide a fascinating account of the "moving, ever-changing play" that was the Paris peace conference. Steffens may have considered himself lucky to be in Paris, though, and not New York, as the harassment of the American Left reached its peak with the hysteria of the Red Scare of 1919–1920. During the Bolshevik propaganda hearings in February–March 1919, the U.S. Senate would hear such enthusiastic support for the Bolsheviks in the testimony of John Reed, Louise Bryant, Rhys Williams, and others that fear of homegrown communists spread. Under the orders of newly appointed Attorney General Mitchell Palmer— "young, militant, progressive, and fearless," in the words of Joseph Tumulty, and a man with his own presidential ambitions—five thousand agitators, ranging from anarchists to pacifists, were arrested in raids, more than two hundred of them deported to Russia.

But such dissent was heard nowhere near the arrival of the American president. The expectations of millions of Europeans were inflated to a point that could be explained by one simple, unbearable truth: the deaths of millions upon millions that had decimated a generation of young men across a continent. While European leaders resented Wilson's astonishing popularity among their own people, he was arriving as a prophet of peace to the war-weary masses.

The reception that Wilson received in Europe was one of those rare historical occasions that can hardly be exaggerated, no matter how often the story is told. Sailing out of New York on December 4 on the *George Washington* and joined by an escort of several destroyers, Wilson became the first sitting American president to leave the country. His entourage reached the shores of Brest on December 13, and at that point, Wilson could have had no doubt that Europeans welcomed him as a messiah. As he was taken by car to the train station, Wilson could see the whole town crowded along the street, throwing blossoms and hoping to catch a glimpse of their American savior. Steffens heard stories that many French knelt and prayed along the train tracks as Wilson passed through the Brittany countryside that night.

His arrival in Paris the next morning was greeted by a massive outpouring of over a million people. At a station brilliantly decked out with flowers and flags of every color, Wilson was welcomed to France by French President Raymond Poincaré and Prime Minister Georges Clemenceau. Overflow crowds, waving American flags and shouting "Vive Wilson" and "Vive l'Amerique" crowded along the Champs-Élysées for a glimpse of Wilson's carriage as it passed on the way to Hotel Murat, where Wilson would be staying, while a hundred thousand jammed into the Place de la Concorde. Wilson unquestionably had immense political skills, an ego befitting a president, and an intellect that surpassed the vast majority of his predecessors, yet he was essentially a reserved, reflective man by nature. The public outpouring of affection and hope showered on him in Paris and soon thereafter in London, Rome, and Milan, must have not only strengthened his idealistic vision of peace but also deepened his concern over whether he could meet the awesome, perhaps impossible, task he had set himself.

As Steffens asserted, Wilson had returned to Paris as the "spokesman of public opinion." But the other leaders had not been idle. Clemenceau and British Prime Minister David Lloyd George in particular had improved their own standing among their citizens, knowing full well that passing days—and passing optimism—would inevitably be the scourge of Wilson's popularity.

Shortly after Wilson's arrival in Paris, Steffens did manage to catch the president's attention and exchange "a few words." With House, he had already had "several good talks," and the two had spent a day taking a long drive together through the Bois de Boulogne outside Paris. Like most others, Steffens was not immune to the historical thrill of the moment. "I feel that I am seeing all this wonderful thing as it happens," he wrote to Gussie.

Unfortunately, the "wonderful thing" was happening at a snail's pace. Even though Russia had collapsed into civil war, Germans were starving, and people across the vast, leaderless Austrian Empire were busy establishing their own new borders out of the power vacuum, the sole news out of Paris was the endless serenading of Wilson by the French, which continued for days. House, apparently also caught up in the frenzy, labeled one reception at the Hotel de Ville "beyond anything in the history of Paris." Steffens was no less starry-eyed, remarking after spotting the king of Italy, "But then, kings are getting to be commonplace here."

Steffens bided much of his time at the Hotel Crillon, the American head-quarters where House and the rest of the American mission stayed. On a quiet Christmas Eve, Steffens wrote to Laura of his hope to go on to London with Wilson on his goodwill tour. He commented again on the complete trust the people placed in Wilson as the president prepared for the certain fight that loomed ahead with the European leaders. Steffens remained optimistic, believing that Wilson had been handling the partisan posturing well. He noted by example that Wilson understood how the French felt about the Germans and was "careful to show them that he does." Steffens predicted that Wilson would show similar concern for the Italians' point of view because "the people there also want the finer, higher thing: peace."

Amid a crowd of journalists, Steffens did join the presidential party in crossing the channel to London on Christmas Day, where more adulation awaited Wilson, and the same a few days later in Italy before the return trip to Paris. There, on January 18—the same date, tellingly, that France had signed its treaty of defeat with Germany in 1871—peace talks, at long last, got under way, quickly dominated by the Council of Four: the United States, Britain, France, and Italy. The missing giant was Russia, and while there was some sentiment, particularly from Wilson and Lloyd George, to have a Russian presence at the talks, Clemenceau, displaying his well-earned reputation as a domineering personality with a fierce nationalistic pride, made it clear that no Bolshevik would ever set foot on French soil.

Steffens clung to his faith in the president, who was "hanging to his points," he told Allen, but the signs of trouble were increasingly apparent to him as well. He noted that England and France "seem to have got together" against Wilson, and the Italians were still insistent on more land. The French, in Steffens's view, were the main obstacle facing Wilson. Clemenceau, though nearly eighty years old, was the real rival, "the man who broke Wilson," Steffens observed, seeing the conflict as a cultural and philosophical gap that could not be bridged: "It was a struggle of American idealism and good will against French realism, of the American reformer, the Anglo-Saxon liberal, against the intelligent French radical." Referring to France with a keen eye, Steffens commented, "We are setting up a nation with a declining population in control of great natural resources next door to a growing nation, Germany, in reach of but dispossessed of mines which her growth will need." Overall, the atmosphere in Paris suited Steffens nicely. "I never have seen together so many people I know. It is like a review of my whole life on the personal side. I am enjoying it immensely."

The first few weeks of the peace talks were a long, slow, secret process to Steffens and the other journalists. Steffens might have expected better, as Wilson had assigned Baker to handle press relations. But pressure, particularly from the French and the Italians, to keep a lid on the negotiations made Baker's job trying at best. Not that any of the reporters should have been surprised. Two years earlier, Norman Hapgood had already called on Clemenceau to register, on behalf of journalists, a complaint that the French leader had eliminated nearly all war news from the government. Clemenceau simply replied, "Certainly. Why not?" before sending Hapgood away.

21

"I Have Seen the Future"

Early on in Paris, Steffens heard that a commission might be sent to Russia to determine the actual conditions there and perhaps to make some diplomatic headway with the Bolsheviks in particular. At the peace conference, only Wilson and Lloyd George seemed interested in broaching the issue of Russia, but if a fact-finding group were to go, Steffens was ready to join. "How I would like to be upon that commission," he told Allen. "Some people are arguing me for it, but I doubt that they can put me on."

Western leaders, regardless of their sentiments, could hardly ignore Russia. The Bolshevik government had not conveniently collapsed, as the Allies had hoped. Allied troops, frozen in, continued their miserable fight in the northern Russian ports. If and when to bring them home was a heated question in the political corridors of Paris, London, and Washington. Some, notably Winston Churchill, then British minister of war, preferred a final military solution to rid the world of Bolshevism. U.S. Senator Hiram Johnson took a different tack in a blistering speech on December 12, questioning Wilson's Russia policy, demanding to know when American soldiers would be coming home. He reminded the country of possible missed opportunities with the Bolsheviks, noting that Lenin and Trotsky were desperate for American aid at the time of Brest-Litovsk, a request that died in layers of bureaucracy and indecision.

Moreover, with a civil war raging, Bolshevists openly advocating world revolution, and Lenin coyly prosecuting the war while signaling an intention of peace with the Allies, the overall situation was a blatant obstacle to any comprehensive end to the fighting or the formation of a League of Nations. A new diplomatic approach was an obvious if politically delicate next step, and the clumsy Allied failure over the proposed Prinkipo talks would help Steffens reach Moscow.

Feeling compelled to make at least a vague overture to Russia to discuss their differences, Wilson and Lloyd George, with the grudging cooperation of Clemenceau—"sometimes in politics it is necessary to hold conversations with criminals," he conceded—worked to set up a mid-February 1919 conference with the Russians on the remote islands of Prinkipo, off the coast of Turkey. Neither Wilson nor Lloyd George was optimistic of conclusive results—no surprise, given that the actual objectives of the meeting were never clarified and no official invitation was ever sent to the Russian government. In fact, the Allies had not yet lifted their blockade of Russia after the armistice with Germany.

In January, Ray Stannard Baker asked Steffens's old friend, William Allen White, along with George D. Herron, a Wilson loyalist, to be the American representatives at Prinkipo. But further planning ground to a halt in the ensuing weeks, and when Clemenceau was shot and wounded on February 19, any hope of securing his approval was lost, and the issue of Russia temporarily receded from the highest levels of discussion at Versailles.

Amid the ongoing confusion of the preparations for Prinkipo, a commission, as Steffens had hoped, was formed to visit Moscow directly. The responsibility was ultimately given to William C. Bullitt, a young, ambitious State Department bureaucrat then serving as chief of the Division of Current Intelligence Summaries at the Versailles Conference. Each day, in his official duties, Bullitt had briefed high-level members on the American side, including Wilson, House, and Secretary of State Robert Lansing, on military and political intelligence, and he had grown increasingly concerned over the great question of Russia. Frustrated watching Russia descend from an ally to an enemy, Bullitt, despite being only twenty-eight, was outspoken in his opposition to military intervention in Russia—intervention supported so vigorously by Churchill and somewhat less so by the French and the Italians. Wilson, who once said, "To arrest revolutionary movement by means of deployed armies is like trying to use a broom to sweep back a high tide," felt that he was operating blindly. The civil war was not going well, when he knew how it was going at all. Reports from the Whites, eager for support, were highly unreliable, while mixed signals were coming from the Bolshevik government. More-accurate information on Russia was essential.

On January 19, 1919, Bullitt sent a memo to House urging that an American group be sent to Russia for a firsthand look at the actual conditions there, going as far as to suggest specific names—Judge Learned Hand, Rhys Williams,

William Allen White, and Raymond Fosdick (an aide to General Pershing)—for the assignment. Around the same time, Steffens put forward a similar idea to House, who had discussed Russia with Steffens a number of times.

Sensing the urgency of the crisis in Russia, Wilson, although preoccupied with the League of Nations draft and his imminent departure for America, met with House on the morning of February 14. The president agreed with the gist of Bullitt's proposals and accepted that a mission was appropriate, but with a somewhat less conspicuous group. Wilson had no interest in being caught "recognizing" the Bolshevik government in any way, but did support informal contacts as a reasonable way forward.

On February 17, House, who shared Bullitt's basic ideas on engaging the Bolsheviks, asked him to undertake the delicate assignment. It seems likely that Bullitt was chosen partly because, should things go awry, it would be easier for the United States to distance itself from any official link with a junior operative like Bullitt. His stated assignment in Russia was given to him several days later by Secretary Lansing. (Lansing did not even support the mission, once remarking that Bullitt was being sent to cure him of Bolshevism.) Bullitt was to study "conditions, political and economic, therein, for the benefit of the American commissioners plenipotentiary to negotiate peace," with an apparent understanding, at least on House's part, that a face-to-face meeting with Lenin to find a resolution to the war was the key objective. House recorded this note in his date book on February 17: "Talk of methods and reviving idea of negotiating with the Soviet government."

Bullitt also received specific instructions from House concerning conditions for a cease-fire, food, and other relief aid after an armistice, and withdrawal of foreign troops from Russian soil. With additional directives in writing from Lloyd George's personal secretary, Philip Kerr, Bullitt assumed that he could negotiate with some authority, as the trip had been unofficially sanctioned by both the American and the British governments. That assumption would soon prove dramatically false.

Bullitt eagerly went about selecting his own team. Along with Captain Walter W. Pettit, an army intelligence officer fluent in Russian, and Robert Lynch, a naval secretary, Bullitt chose Steffens. Bullitt had been a journalist before the war and admired his older, experienced colleagues, particularly Steffens, White, and Baker. Obviously, Steffens's knowledge of Russia and prior experience there influenced Bullitt's decision as well—Steffens's presence could help assure Russian leaders of the legitimacy of the mission. Steffens's role on the mission was to be a political observer and sort of liaison, or, in Steffens's hopeful eyes, a mediator if necessary. None of the members were anti-Bolsheviks, and only Bullitt, who had limited diplomatic experience, would be negotiating with the Russians.

Steffens, of course, was desperate to go in any capacity, for at the moment, revolutionary Russia had become a romantic, almost mythic, ideal to many on the American Left. While some, notably Upton Sinclair, were distressed by the endless brutality, others looked on the mere survival of Lenin and the communist cause through the difficult days of 1917 as a sign that the Russian struggle deserved admiration and support. Steffens was equally certain that a special fire was burning within the Russians, one that the world had to know of.

On February 20, the day after the attempted assassination of Clemenceau, House told Bullitt to leave for Russia as quickly as possible, amid the paralysis of Allied talks on a course of action toward Russia. Two days later, the "semi-official" Bullitt group, as Steffens called it, was off to England. During a brief stay at the Carlton Hotel in London, Steffens wrote to Gussie, bursting to tell her all the details but unable to say much of anything. He settled on an obvious hint: "I am here only in transit: going somewhere else. I can't say where. . . . You may guess my destination. It's a place I want to go." And he had the highest hopes for success. "I am full of our project," he gushed, "expecting something good to come of it, something decisive and climactic." The West was at a crossroads, he saw, and he would have some influence—more than a little, he hoped—in the direction it took. It was a moment he had waited a lifetime for.

Steffens recalled the journey as "a pretty noisy secret mission," with Bullitt and Lynch "tumbling like a couple of bear cubs all along the Arctic Circle," apparently to mislead anyone who might be suspicious of their plans. Evidently their cover was tighter than Steffens imagined. The *New York Times* did not even report on the trip at all until a month later, on March 22, and the very brief story incorrectly noted that the third member was journalist Walter Weyl, with no mention of Lynch or Pettit.

All except Bullitt got seasick on the stormy North Sea, but from Stockholm on March 3, Steffens wrote confidently that the trip was going well and "there will be no hitch at this end." Sure of what had to be done, he expected to stay only for a few days before hurrying back to Paris to report to House.

After some official difficulties involving their Swedish guide Karl Kilborn, a communist on good terms with Lenin, the party, upon entering Finland, crossed into Russia and on to Petrograd, with Kilborn going ahead to make the necessary connections. Their nighttime arrival on March 8, though, could not have inspired much optimism in the group. Petrograd, they found, was a deserted city, the Russians by then having moved their capital to Moscow. Even the train station was empty, and Steffens saw "nobody in the dark, cold, broken streets."

While the rest of the exhausted party went straight to bed in a run-down hotel with unheated rooms in the dead of winter, Steffens and Kilborn spent the first night roaming from hotel to hotel in search of any Russian official who would speak with them. When they finally located Grigory Zinoviev, the controversial head of the Petrograd Soviet, he abruptly turned them away. Kilborn, embarrassed, had been led to believe that Lenin would direct Foreign Secretary Georgy Chicherin, Trotsky's successor, to greet them, which is eventually what happened. In a number of meetings with Chicherin, Bullitt asserted that Bolshevik compromises would be supported by America and could lead to a peace agreement. Encouraged, Lenin agreed to see the party in Moscow. "I am certain from conversation already held that the Soviet government is disposed to be reasonable," Bullitt wired House.

Lynch had remained in Finland and Pettit in Petrograd, leaving Bullitt and Steffens to go on to Moscow on March 10, where their accommodations improved dramatically. The two stayed in a heated palace with servants. Food was scarce for most Russians, but Bullitt and Steffens dined night after night on caviar. With so much food on the table, they were eagerly joined at mealtimes by high-level Russian officials, including Chicherin. They spent evenings attending operas, on one occasion sitting in the czar's box. During the day, Bullitt and Chicherin met regularly, while Steffens, in his daily jaunts, scrutinized the city, trying to understand the revolution he had hoped to see in his own country but was now viewing in a vastly different setting.

What he observed was the widespread privation and endless struggles of nearly everyone. Starvation was common, with corpses lying in the streets. But Steffens expected such misery in the midst of a historic revolution. What intrigued him more was what the people thought. Were they genuinely behind the revolution? Did they support the radical changes that would require a complete restructuring of their lives? Steffens's own mind was not exactly open on the matter: He wanted the revolution to succeed, just as he wanted to find Russians who agreed with him, which he did. Not that he "got" all of what he was seeing, he conceded, but it was enough for a start. He observed that "Soviet Russia was a revolutionary government with an evolutionary plan." The Bolsheviks' plan, he wrote, was to "seek out and remove the causes of" poverty, graft, privilege, tyranny, and war. He acknowledged that they had set up a dictatorship while "laying a basis" for a true political democracy. "It was a new culture, an economic, scientific, not a moral, culture. . . . No wonder it was confusing and difficult," he wrote.

Bullitt, determined to put a shine on his reports, was nearly ecstatic in parts of his assessment. He declared the red terror over and blamed the American blockade for the atrocious food shortages throughout the country. Lenin, he said, was regarded as a prophet, far above even Trotsky. Elsewhere in his description, however, Bullitt was more honest: The Russians were starving. Of more importance to the mission, Bullitt and Steffens would soon be sitting across from the great leader.

With conditions in Russia, in fact, deteriorating to the extreme, Lenin needed a way out of the civil war, at least temporarily, and clearly an agreement with the West could provide such an escape. In that sense, Bullitt could be useful. "There was no doubt," Kilborn wrote, "that Lenin was happy about the delegation."

Lenin and Bullitt met on March 14, with Lenin accepting most of the terms without change. He gave a document to Bullitt, essentially Lenin's view of an acceptable Allied proposal, which offered to lift the Allied blockade and remove Allied troops. In exchange, Russia would agree to consider repaying some of its debt, reestablishing trade, granting a general amnesty for prisoners, and giving up claims to huge tracts of land. The caveat: Russia's offer was good only until April 10, less than a month away. Bullitt would have to work swiftly, and he cabled House accordingly on March 17: "You must do your utmost for it," he urged. House complied, offering congratulations on the mission and sending Bullitt's cables along to Lloyd George. Lenin's own view, later expressed in a memoir, was that the agreement would severely punish Russia and would last only as long as the Whites could actually hold the wide swaths of Russian territory they now had, which he doubted would be long at all. Still, as the harsh living conditions worsened in Russia, Lenin needed an agreement, however temporary.

Bullitt also set up Steffens's interview with Lenin, which took place later the same day. Steffens had met numerous presidents and industry titans over the years, but the meeting with Lenin, coming as it did just past the start of the greatest revolution of his lifetime, was obviously exceptional. At first glance, the Russian dictator, the "Red" most feared by the West, seemed hardly a menacing figure at all. Dressed in old clothes and seated calmly behind his desk at the far end of his large yet modestly furnished office, Lenin rose as Steffens entered the room, greeting him with a nod and a handshake, his "open, inquiring face" looking directly at Steffens. The two men sat down before Steffens, earnest and respectful, raised the essential points. Would Russia restrain itself from fueling unrest throughout Europe and beyond? No, Lenin replied.

He then leaned back and, with a smile toward Steffens, stated the obvious: Russians would aggressively promote their agenda abroad just as Lenin knew the Europeans had every intention of doing in Russia. Propagandists on both sides had their roles to play. Would the frightening killings of the Red Terror cease? Steffens continued. Who wanted to know? Lenin asked. When he heard the answer—Paris—he rose and with "hot eyes" came straight to the point:

> Do you mean to tell me that those men who have just generaled the slaughter of seventeen millions of men in a purposeless war are concerned over the few thousands who have been killed in a revolution with a conscious aim—to get out of the necessity of war and—and armed peace? But never mind, don't deny the terror. Don't minimize any of the evils of a revolution. They occur. They must be counted upon. If we have to have a revolution, we have to pay the price of revolution.

Composing himself, he told Steffens to ignore his outburst. In the end, Lenin noted, progress would not come without a price, a tragic one, regardless of who led the revolution. But the revolution must go forward—history demanded it.

Lenin disingenuously went on to tell Steffens that the terror actually hurt the revolution, that the revolution could have gone ahead without the killings by simply threatening violence and letting the rich and other intellectuals escape with their lives. But in the end, he acknowledged his long-standing belief—"however it is done, it has to be done"—which was exactly the rationale that prevailed in the bloody years that followed.

Steffens felt that the key to Lenin, unlike the besieged Wilson, was that he had a plan: He knew where he wanted to go and the way of getting there. He could see beyond the violence. "Lenin was a navigator, the other a mere sailor," he observed rather unfairly in his autobiography, given that Wilson, who had his own visionary plan, could hardly destroy his opponents in implementing it. Steffens had seen firsthand the misery and exhaustion of the Russian people. He had no illusions about the daily hardships faced by a typical Russian. Yet, he was satisfied. Pettit's comment, "Petrograd is a temporary condition of evil, which is made tolerable by hope and a plan," echoed Steffens's own feeling.

Expecting that Western leaders were waiting anxiously for news out of Russia, the Bullitt members, back in Paris on March 25, were eager to report their success. The previous day, Steffens had written to his family from London with the utmost confidence: "We were very successful at our end. . . . We saw everybody in power, of course; had long talks with them; saw the conditions of the country and people; and we got a proposition which seemed to us more than fair and not to be rejected."

His letters following the Bullitt mission confirm Steffens's fervent belief that the trip had gone well and should strongly influence the peace talkers. He reported that he had met Lenin, Trotsky, and other leading figures in Russia. "We heard all their story, the struggles of it, the costs, the faults and all the hopes," he told Marie Howe. Truly inspired, he wrote to Laura, "There is more vision, there is more idealism and also more realism at Moscow than there is at Paris." Three days after returning, Steffens spoke of Russia at a dinner with a small group of historians, including James Shotwell, who noted in his journal, "Of all evenings in Paris, this was as interesting as any I have spent."

Steffens's official report to Bullitt, "Report on the Bullitt Mission to Russia," was intended as a private document, but in his determination to promote Russia, Steffens must have hoped that it would ultimately reach a wider audience. The assignment certainly was a matter of urgency to him. He explained to Marie Howe, "I was asked to write a report upon the political situation of Russia and I most awfully wanted to do that. And I have done it now. It is short, but I took a lot of time to write it. I wanted to make it easy to read and effective. Whether I have done that or not, the thing is done and has gone to the top."

His report was upbeat concerning Russia's future. The destructive phase of the revolution, he felt, was over, and order was taking hold: Crime was down, prohibition established (Steffens blamed the violence partly on vodka), and work required. Opposition to the government was dwindling. Pride in Mother Russia was up.

Steffens nevertheless did not gloss over the horrific aspects of the new Russia. The communists, he wrote, had established "the most autocratic" government he had ever seen. Lenin himself called it a dictatorship and said that another year of starvation would be necessary. Everywhere, there were shortages of food and fuel. As far as Steffens could tell, everyone, including Lenin, ate one decent meal a day. Most of the wealthy had left the country, and those few who remained saw their businesses smashed and all interest, rent, and other profits confiscated. Money itself, Steffens noted, was due to be phased out over time. He conceded that "hunger, cold, misery, anguish, disease" had resulted in "death to millions." Still, he concluded that the new Russian leaders were "idealists sobered by the responsibility of power" and men who preferred "to compromise and make peace" with the West, if possible. He urged Bullitt to impress upon the Allies the sincerity of the Russians and the critical nature of what they had said.

Bullitt's own, more detailed, official report did not attempt to hide the misery, either—"Russia to-day is in a condition of acute economic distress"; "Mortality is particularly high among new-born children"; "Every man, woman, and child in Moscow and Petrograd is suffering from slow starvation." But his overall emphasis, like that of Steffens, expressed optimism toward the Russian dilemma, with comments such as "The terror has ceased" and "Good order has been established." One of his conclusions demonstrated the urgency he felt the situation warranted: "No real peace can be established in Europe or the world until peace is made with the revolution. This proposal of the Soviet Government presents an opportunity to make peace with the revolution on a just and reasonable basis—perhaps a unique opportunity."

In the meantime, Steffens was interviewed by British intelligence officers and by House, while Bullitt gave a lengthy report to House on the night of his arrival, asking for a meeting with Wilson, now back in Paris. The president, though, begged off, complaining of a headache. Concerned that Wilson hear firsthand of the Russian proposals, Steffens, recalling a promise that Wilson had made years earlier about hearing him out in a legitimate crisis, tried intervening, sending a note—"It's an emergency"—to the president. Still, Wilson remained silent. Bullitt instead reported the next day to a group that included Secretary of State Lansing. The meeting went well, Bullitt felt, but Wilson remained either ill or too preoccupied with the peace treaty to see him. So House, who was initially buoyed by Bullitt's enthusiasm ("at last I can see a way out of the vexatious [Russian] problem," he wrote in his diary on March 25) contacted Lloyd George, where matters for Bullitt would grow complicated and, ultimately, truly ugly.

The British prime minister met with Bullitt on March 27 and understood that the young emissary had a compelling argument, but, waving a copy of Lord Northcliffe's conservative *Daily Mail* at Bullitt, pointed out that the British press and the House of Commons were excoriating him over any hint of weakness toward Russia as rumors of Bullitt's mission began to swirl. The *Daily Mail* editorial that particularly upset Lloyd George, "The Intrigue That May Be Revived," written by Henry Wickham Steed, was an assault based on the possibility that a Prinkipo-type advance toward the Russians was being seriously considered. Another anti-Bolshevik article from Steed followed a day later. A well-known historian and an influential conservative who embraced controversy, Steed not only rejected any negotiations with the Bolsheviks, but was one of the loudest of the voices claiming that the Bolsheviks had been funded by international Jewish bankers. Steed cited in particular Jacob Schiff and Paul Warburg, who, he later wrote in a memoir, "wished above all to bolster up the Jewish Bolshevists in order to secure a field for German and Jewish exploitation of Russia." In this environment, Lloyd George had to tread very carefully with Bullitt, wondering if perhaps another visit to Russia, preferably by a conservative senior diplomat, might silence some of the critics.

Meanwhile, House, who had been very nearly setting American policy toward Russia in the absence of any specific directives from Wilson, had his own change of heart concerning the whole matter after a private meeting with the president on March 27 and a meeting with Steed diminished his previous hopes. Bullitt made one more desperate appeal to Wilson in early April, but he was ignored, possibly because the president was receiving reports from Washington as news of the Bullitt mission leaked and opinions on both sides sharpened. In late March, the State Department informed Wilson that a member of the Russian-American Chamber of Commerce asserted that American Bolsheviks were counting on an upbeat report from Bullitt and Steffens regarding the Soviet government. Newspapers back home also were taking Wilson to task for his "weakness" on Russia. A headline in the March 24 *New York Tribune* read, "Wilson Sees Russia by Steffens' Eyes," virtually portraying Steffens as a policy maker. On March 25, the day the Bullitt members returned from Russia, Herbert Bayard Swope met with Bullitt and Steffens and cabled a report of the mission—"[Bullitt] and Lincoln Steffens found conditions in Moscow under far better control than had been pictured"—to the *New York World*, reflecting the immediate interest in the story.

Wilson, in fact, had not even brought up the mission's report at the Paris talks, apparently maintaining complete silence on the subject of Bullitt. Unknown to Bullitt, Steffens, and others, Wilson at that point had a dangerously high fever and other health complications that would make his final, exhausting efforts at peace all the more trying.

Moreover, Clemenceau himself had not yet been approached on the topic— junior French officials had been earlier briefed by Lansing—when the British papers began running sensational stories of a secret Allied deal, perpetrated by an American envoy named "Bulet" or "Bullit," which would recognize the Lenin-Trotsky leadership. For his part, Steffens was eager to reveal what he knew and resented being unable to talk. "The other reporters are angry about it," he told Marie Howe on April 3. "They want to hear our news, and we are willing to tell it all. I have promised not to write it myself till I have given them a shot at it. And I have no doubt that we shall be released before long. We must be. The correspondents are digging out the facts of our business and from our report with uncanny shrewdness. Several officials have read it. . . . It is just like gossip. Each one of these tells others and,—so the matter leaks. . . . Comedy."

Speculation regarding Steffens intensified to such an extent that Wilson, Steffens claimed, interceded on his behalf. In a letter to Brand Whitlock several years later, Steffens recalled the episode: "After the Bullitt incident, when all the secret services were pestering me in Paris and the papers were hot after me, Wilson stepped out of the group of premiers at the Crillon and, with a crowd looking on in astonishment, put his arm over my shoulder and whispered in my ear,—nothing. He meant to rebuke the detectives and reporters, and he certainly did it."

The outrage, however, went on unabated. Churchill, still advocating war and well aware of the rumors concerning a Russian deal, stoked the fires by demanding a public accounting of Russian barbarism to enlighten the British public and quash any notion of bargaining with the Bolsheviks. On April 5, the government accordingly provided the House of Commons with an incendiary pamphlet, *White Paper on Bolshevik Atrocities*, which, among many graphic accusations, said that Bolshevik prisons could only be found in "the darkest annals of Indian or Chinese history." The report sent both the voters and the Parliament into an anti-Red tirade. Lloyd George was compelled to backpedal furiously and lie to Commons on April 16 by denying that there had been any approaches to Russia, but, deftly shifting the onus to Wilson, added that if an American had been to Moscow on such a mission, it was up to the president to inform the conference. Years later, *Nation* editor Oswald Garrison Villard recalled, "Of all the many falsehoods of statesmen I have chronicled in forty years, none was more unblushing and flagrant than Lloyd George's evasion in the House of Commons on April 16 of the fact that he had full knowledge of the Bullitt mission into Russia."

Wilson, who had not even been present in Paris when the Bullitt mission was given final instructions and sent out, was also in a difficult position due to his own ignorance of the details of the case. In July 1919, referring to a *Nation* article that was critical of the Allied handling of Russia and that focused on the Bullitt mission, he wrote a memo to Joseph Tumulty: "This is an amazing article. I know of no such 'Allied terms' as are here quoted, and do not for a moment believe that it is true . . . to state . . . that Messrs. Bullitt and Steffens did take a memorandum into Russia and that memorandum was in the handwriting of Philip Kerr, Private Secretary to Mr. Lloyd George." Of course, Bullitt possessed precisely such a document.

In an effort to pursue another direction while possibly salvaging the Bullitt opening with Moscow, House, after his March 27 meeting with Wilson, came to favor a much simpler plan of food for peace, supporting the efforts of Herbert Hoover, head of the American Relief Administration, to feed the Russians in exchange for an end to the fighting and, of course, the hope of undercutting the appeal of Bolshevism. Steffens himself had had a conversation with Norwegian explorer and humanitarian Fridtjof Nansen, encouraging Nansen's interest in providing food to Russians. Resorting to such a minimal offer was a far cry from the comprehensive agreement that Bullitt had envisioned, but, at such a late hour, there seemed no other alternatives. On April 7, Steffens joined his friend George Barr Baker, a former editor of *Everybody's* now doing relief work in Europe, and Hoover for lunch to discuss feeding the Russians. It was the first time Steffens had met Hoover.

Hoover wanted to hear more about conditions in Russia. His fellow Republicans had little interest in feeding Russians, particularly Bolsheviks, and earlier had tried to prosecute Hoover for working in a private capacity to feed the Belgians. But Hoover, who sympathized with the Russian people, had nevertheless approached House about getting food into Russia. The Bolshevik government, though, was another matter to the future president. While Bullitt was pleading for Wilson's attention on Russia, Hoover was insisting to Wilson that he have nothing to do with the "murderous tyranny." Steffens, for his part, was not seeking handouts but was seeking peace for Russia. "The invitation to lunch with Hoover," he wrote to Laura, "was a chance for me to prepare his mind to give up his charity and come to business." Although Hoover's interest in aiding the Bolsheviks involved only food, Steffens felt that food was at least an opening with the influential Hoover.

The meeting got off badly when Hoover, in an objectionable mood, blistered Steffens with angry questions about the Bolsheviks. Steffens was not sure if Hoover despised the Russians or him or both, but he restrained himself until Hoover demanded to know if the Russians could actually "make a go" of their "fool system." "Suppose that after two or three hundred years of the communistic system," Steffens replied, echoing Lenin, "the world should break out into a world war, kill off twelve millions of men and then come to a peace conference as incompetent, sordid, and warlike as this, would you say that Bolshevism was a go?" Hoover "seemed to get that, completely," and the rest of the lunch passed reasonably well. For the moment, Hoover seemed immune to any serious thought of aiding Bolsheviks, although the food scheme remained alive. Lenin, open to American economic agreements and humanitarian aid, wanted the food and urged his negotiators to tell the Americans, "Just start shipping!"

And it was in this atmosphere of political disarray, with rumors competing against more rumors and Steffens ever eager to divulge his story, that he made the infamous remark, or variations of it, so attached to his name: "I have seen the future, and it works." The comment obviously reflected his faith in the revolution to succeed and his contrasting pessimism toward American democracy, not merely the appalling facts on the ground in Russia.

But his often-expressed, idealized vision of Russia, given with such enthusiasm, was an easy target for critics and even friends. William Allen White was biding his time in Paris watching the Prinkipo plan die of neglect when the Bullitt members returned to Paris, Steffens arriving "bug-eyed with wonder," White recalled. The two friends spent "many a long hour" going over Steffens's adventure, even though news of the trip was officially confidential.

And Steffens, it seemed, wanted to inform everyone in Paris about the news from Russia, particularly as more of it leaked and his own role emerged. "Like the ancient mariner," White wrote, "Steffens was always stopping the wedding guests and telling his Russian story until they beat their breasts in despair." With each telling, the story had the same insistent, optimistic clinching line that later was remarkable only for its apparent absurdity. To White, to Bernard Baruch (sitting for Jo Davidson at the time), to Marie Howe (in a letter), to anyone who would listen, Steffens repeated his optimistic assessment. He may have borrowed the infamous phrase from Bullitt in Moscow, when the mission leader was so enamored with the prospects of success that he could not resist making similar comments himself. But Steffens said it so often, and with such conviction, that posterity has firmly attached it to his own legacy.

White recalled one day at the Crillon when a group of journalists, who respected Steffens but may have heard quite enough about Russia, goaded him on the Russian miracle to the point that Steffens exclaimed, "Gentlemen, I tell you they have abolished prostitution!" Feigning shock, one of the reporters held up his hands and cried, "My God, Stef! What did you do?" Amid all the laughter, Steffens "blushed like a beet," White remembered, and then ran off, eager to spring his tale again on anyone who would listen.

In the meantime, Bullitt had not given up hope. With the April 10 deadline looming, Bullitt sent a desperate telegram to the Russians on April 6 seeking a ten-day extension. Inevitably, however, the April 10 deadline passed. The belated Allied offer of food to the Russians, ignoring the far more thorny but essential political questions raised during the Bullitt mission, was put forward to the Russians on April 17 and ultimately died in a fog of counterproposals and political posturing on both sides. Feeling betrayed by Lloyd George and abandoned by Wilson while recognizing that he had been played as a dupe and that the entire Paris peace process had become largely an Allied power play, Bullitt fumed for several weeks before resigning on May 17. In a letter full of accusation, he told the president, "I was one of the millions who trusted confidently and implicitly in your leadership and believed that you would take nothing less than 'a permanent peace' based upon 'unselfish and unbiased justice.' But our Government has consented now to deliver the suffering peoples of the world to new oppressions, subjections, and dismemberments—a new century of war. . . . It is my conviction that the present league of nations will be powerless to prevent these wars, and that the United States will be involved in them."

Steffens, twenty-five years older than Bullitt, watched his frustration and understood that Bullitt was unlearning in the most painful of circumstances. All of the young man's flailing and venting, he saw, was futile, as was his own previous belief in the power of reform and the effectiveness of the ballot box. Such liberal thinking, from Bullitt, Steffens, or anyone else, was delusional, as he saw in the reaction of Bullitt, who "was not to be mollified." Bullitt joined a group of other young liberals (Adam Berle Jr., Christian Herter, and Samuel Eliot Morison) who were so outraged by the treaty that they met to plan a protest, including resignation. Steffens attended their meeting, where he was asked for his advice. He acknowledged that in the muckraking days, he would have shared their anger and quit, but his thinking had changed since the Russian Revolution. "I was sure that it was useless—it was almost wrong—to fight for the right under our system; petty reforms in politics, wars without victories, just peace, were impossible, unintelligent, heroic but immoral," he wrote. "Either they and we all should labor to change the foundation of society, as the Russians were doing, or go along with the resultant civilization we were part of, taking care only to save our minds by seeing it all straight."

What had gone wrong? The situation across Europe and America at the moment the Bullitt members returned to Paris probably was too complex and delicate for any leader to show the boldness, for better or worse, that would have been required to address the Bolsheviks as near equals. With Communism spreading dangerously outside Russia, particularly in Eastern Europe, and striking workers on the streets in Allied countries, no Western leader wanted to encourage the revolutionary fervor by recognizing that the Bolsheviks had formed a functioning government. Wilson himself was ill, heavily involved in straining talks with France over Germany, and did not wish to be distracted by Russia. By mid-May, he was exasperated enough to concede that "the proper policy" was to "clear out of Russia and leave it to the Russians to fight it out among themselves."

For his part, Lloyd George had shown initial concern toward Bullitt before an outraged press and Parliament forced him into a hasty retreat to quell the political firestorm. Clemenceau undoubtedly would have wished Bullitt banished from the country had he been officially approached at any point. Adding to the hysteria were erroneous reports, highlighted by the Paris press in late March and April, that the White forces, led by the notoriously unreliable Alexander Kolchak, had marched to the doorstep of Moscow, giving oxygen to the delusional hopes of Allied leaders for a military victory in Russia. But Kolchak's forces were routed by the Red Army, and he would be shot dead by the Bolsheviks within a year.

Adding to all the political and military pressures, the Allied politicians ultimately had to answer to the people, and in America and Europe, the public had little desire for supporting the Bolsheviks, for more negotiations, or for more politics at all. Americans wanted to enjoy life again and forget about politics for a while, and they left no doubt on this point by soon replacing Wilson with President Warren Harding and enthusiastically ushering in the Jazz Age, while Europeans were intent on rebuilding their battered cities and towns. A peace resolution had to be reached in some way at Versailles, and the results of a hastily arranged meeting involving an obscure, inexperienced bureaucrat, an old muckraker, and Lenin were viewed very skeptically. The *New York Times*, for example, minced no words on the matter. In an April 6 editorial, the paper ridiculed the prospects of democracy in Russia as "an astonishing delusion." Pointing to the Bolsheviks' methods of "blind destruction," the *Times* asked, "Why, then, was it thought to be necessary to send personal, unofficial envoys to Russia to confer with the authors of this devastation? Why, in particular, was it thought expedient to choose for this mission men disqualified for impartial service by their extreme radicalism, their known and avowed sympathy with the aims of the Bolsheviki, men of no competence for a task demanding close observation and sound, unbiased judgment?"

So the Bullitt mission ended in dismal failure. Bullitt never forgave Wilson and, in a curious political twist, accepted an invitation by Republicans to address the Senate Foreign Relations Committee regarding both the Versailles Treaty and the president's cherished dream of a League of Nations at a September hearing. Bullitt spoke bluntly—he produced the infamous memo of instructions from

Kerr—infuriating some in the administration but drawing no reaction, yet again, from Wilson. Bullitt's venomous words helped cripple Wilson's effort to sell the league to the American public, but in his diary, House conceded, "Candor compels me to record that in my opinion Bullitt told the truth." Steffens largely agreed with House, but added, "I don't see why [Bullitt] had to blame Lansing and the rest. He knows better. We came to an understanding of all such things on that trip in many a good talk. Well, no matter. That is Bullitt's story, and no man shall say I butted in on it."

Steffens took the failure of the mission largely in stride, seeing it mainly as another piece of evidence proving that the West was too intent on derailing peace to look objectively at Russia. His own report to Bullitt was read before the Senate Foreign Relations Committee in September 1919 and published in full in the October 4 issue of *The Nation*, finally reaching the public audience Steffens wished so dearly to influence.

In fairness to Steffens, he was not alone among informed observers in his high expectations for revolutionary Russia. In 1919, White, then fifty-one and still a Republican, wrote to a friend, "Russia is coming along all right in spite of the stupidity which seems to be inspiring the world in dealing with Russia, but Russia is only suffering the martyrdom of birth which every new idea must suffer in the world." Colonel House himself commented, rather too flippantly, that he did not care what form of government Russia adopted as long as it left the rest of the world in peace. Perhaps the most ardent believer of all was Bullitt himself. Fifteen years later, after being named by President Franklin D. Roosevelt as the first U.S. ambassador to the Soviet Union, he wrote to Steffens of "how beautifully things are working out" under Communism, encouraging the aging and infirm Steffens to return for the view. "You have been so right about everything that has happened in the United States and the rest of the world for so many years," Bullitt gushed, "that it is just time for you to blossom as a prophet in your own country and many others." Within a disillusioning two years of observing Stalin up close, however, Bullitt would resign, exasperated again as a diplomat in Russia.

Wilson's own frustration with Russia peaked in June 1919, when he finally recalled American troops from the chaotic Allied campaign in Archangel. The futility of the fight was captured by John Cudahy, an American ambassador: "When the last battalion set sail from Archangel, not a soldier knew, not even vaguely, why he had fought or why he was going now, and why his comrades were left behind, so many of them beneath wooden crosses." In all, nearly five hundred Allied soldiers lost their lives in the ill-fated campaign. When Bolshevik forces took control of Archangel and Murmansk in early 1920, anywhere from ten to thirty thousand Russians—Allied collaborators—met the same fate.

Steffens stayed on in Paris to watch the final days of the peace talks as they came to a staggering close in the spring of 1919. The fate of the League of Nations, sacred to Wilson but to few others, was precarious. Already, unrest was brewing in Hungary, Egypt, Turkey, the Istrian Peninsula, and elsewhere. Republicans at home vilified the league, and the war-battered countries of Europe had more interest in the immediate, practical matter of rebuilding their lives as best they could than in embracing a complex, Wilsonian future. The visionary American president had become the obstacle, many asserted, not that he withheld any of his abundant resourcefulness from the effort. Even Lloyd George admitted, "The rest of us found time for golf and we took Sundays off, but Wilson, in his zeal, worked incessantly."

What Wilson hoped to avoid above all was a "mean peace." In the end, that was precisely what he was handed. With his health declining along with his international prestige, Wilson could not protect his Fourteen Points or the League of Nations from the assault they faced in Paris and in Washington. Compromises, amendments, giveaways, and harsh terms for the Germans marked the final, tragically flawed agreement of June 28, 1919. Germany was punished, Russia was ignored, and the league was on life support. It was a credit to his statesmanship and his diplomatic skills that Wilson was able at all to insert some of his idealistic views in the final agreement, particularly considering that he was the only Allied leader who went to the talks with no intention of adding territory under his own flag. His fate, though, was to be scorned by Republicans for entangling America internationally and by liberals for missing the opportunity to set the world on the path toward peace and genuine freedom. Even Wilson's close relationship with Colonel House did not survive the bruising Paris talks.

Steffens's comments reflect the frayed nerves of the moment, felt by many. "We are going to have a League of Nations, weak, wrong, capable of great abuse; and we shall get a peace also, full of dynamite which will burst into war," he predicted to Allen. The vengeance of the West, he asserted, would unintentionally bring in a new age "and newer men, with a fresher culture" and with minds that were "clear of all the trash which blinds these Paris Conferees." But the transition would be harsh, leading Steffens to conclude, "I think now that the stupid class war is inevitable all over Europe."

Steffens did not blame Wilson for the fiasco but felt frustration with him nonetheless. He admitted to Laura, "The failure here is complete, but that does not matter. What matters is that the President does not see it so. He is going to join in the fight over the treaty and the League, and so will not help, as he could and should, to direct the attention of the public mind to the cause of the failure. He is righteous. If only he were intelligent, scientific!"

His impatience with Wilson grew out of his heightened, and undoubtedly unrealistic, expectations of a man he deeply respected. Wilson had backed down, true, but events over the past few weeks had conspired against the president. Clemenceau in particular, holding fast to his views grounded in realpolitik, steadfastly resisted Wilson's proposal of a just peace and any leniency toward Germany throughout the spring, while Lloyd George, a liberal prime minister confronted by a hostile Parliament in London, vacillated between the two leaders. Steffens aimed his more deeply felt barbs at Clemenceau and Lloyd George, seeing their purposes as "devilish." "They know just what they have done. It was what they meant to do," he wrote accusingly. "It is more satanic than anything I have believed the good will of humanity was capable of. They have prepared for the next war, which they believed inevitable, and they did it under the camouflage of Wilson's ideal of permanent peace." Indeed, Count Ulrich von Brockdorff-Rantzau, the head of the German delegation at Versailles, had hardly accepted the peace treaty before declaring "We are Germans. We will not forget. We will rise from this shame."

A group of liberals, including Steffens, Felix Frankfurter, Norman Hapgood, Henry Morganthau, and others, hoping to salvage at least some hint of repudiation of the old political order, pleaded with Ray Stannard Baker: Tell the president to stand firm and insert some of his bold ideals back into the treaty, and liberals worldwide would stand by him. Baker presented their thoughts to Wilson, who of course agreed that the treaty was flawed, but it was far too late in the process. Nothing changed.

Before leaving Paris, Wilson, who had rarely addressed reporters directly during the negotiations, gave a mass interview to a group of fifty. Steffens found the president, after enduring grueling weeks of often-exasperating talks, humble, matter-of-fact, positive, "and, of course, informed." His reply to a question from Steffens implied that for all his pride and his determination to push through a just peace in the face of withering criticism, he understood that the goals he had set were noble but unreachable. Steffens asked him whether he was satisfied with the peace terms. "Yes," Wilson replied. Steffens, who still admired the president, offered him another opportunity at honesty and repeated his question. After a pause, Wilson faced Steffens and said, "I think we have made a better peace than I should have expected when I came here to Paris."

On the evening of June 28, following the signing of the treaty and what must have seemed to Wilson little more than a bittersweet farewell at the Élysée Palace, the president left France's shores to return home and fight to preserve what remained of the League of Nations. Steffens, too, was tempted to leave, but chose to stay behind to study the aftermath of the Versailles peace on a continent desperate for stability. Two days before Wilson's departure, House, recognizing Steffens's awkward situation, wished the journalist well: "I do not know of a more accurate student of revolutionary movements or one who has a sounder method of meeting them. I am sorry that the public generally have a misconception of your ideas and purposes. If I can help you in any way to visit such countries as you may think advisable, please give me that pleasure." When Steffens did return to New York the following year, he told cartoonist Art Young, then drawing for the socialist magazine *Good Morning*, "There's nothing to do now but laugh—laugh like Hell!"

22

PETER

FOR STEFFENS PERSONALLY, the most important consequence of Paris was his chance encounter in April with a young Australian student from the London School of Economics. Exceptionally bright, energetic, as eager to change the world as Steffens was, and, at twenty-one, less than half his age, Ella Winter managed the impressive feat of distracting Steffens's attention from the political heavyweights at the peace talks. She was so full of life, so set on thinking and acting like a radical, that Steffens could not help but smile at her youthful zest to grab the future and make it good. "She was as joyous," he wrote in his autobiography, "as Jack Reed was when he came out of Harvard to see and sing life. He only sang. This girl danced. Her eyes danced, her mind, her hands, her feet danced as she ran—she literally trotted about on her errands. . . . She was not for me, of course. Too young. But I felt something. . . ." Both apparently felt something, and Ella would bring him unimagined joy, a genuine fulfillment that he had never before known with a woman, for the rest of his life.

Born in 1898 and a self-described "avid tomboy" as a child, Ella had grown up near Melbourne, the daughter of a transplanted German businessman, Adolphe, and a strict mother, Frieda, both former Jews who had themselves and their three children baptized as Lutherans to escape the anti-Semitism they faced in Germany and suspected they would meet elsewhere as well. While Ella loved both parents, she adored her father, a gifted pianist who regaled the family with songs from Schumann and Schubert in the evening, yet also a man marked, in Ella's words, by an "indefinable sadness." But she looked upon him as "the God-being of my life" and conceded in her autobiography, "I was certain I could never marry anyone but my father."

When Ella was eleven, her parents decided to return to Europe, settling the family in London. As she passed through adolescence, Ella, despite her love for her family, devoured the words of Oscar Wilde, yearning for the time when she herself could break free of home and its restrictive chains to see all that had been forbidden her. The onset of the war, however, nearly brought financial ruin to her alien family in England when her father was left jobless, and they survived only through the generosity of an Australian friend. Her college dreams of Oxford or Cambridge dashed, Ella instead settled for the London School of Economics, a "dull, red-brick building right on the street," she noted ruefully, "with no fields or river, not a flower, not a spire."

Her disappointment was short-lived. Filling her time with intellectual pursuits, Ella joined a radical student club, became secretary of the student union, tutored with Harold Laski, and frequented Fabian lectures of Shaw and Wells. Yet, she remained eager to see what lay beyond her college world. It was Ella's enthusiasm for learning that earned her the chance when one of her professors, a friend of Harvard law professor Felix Frankfurter and obviously impressed by Ella's acumen, asked her if she would like to assist Frankfurter, who was in London on behalf of the American government to study England's experience in the war. Ella had landed a job "such as I could have imagined only in my dearest dreams." And when Frankfurter, out of government, later went off to Paris to promote Zionism at the peace conference, Ella, against the wishes of her anxious mother, dashed off to join him.

As many of the world's most prominent statesmen passed through Frankfurter's office, Ella had numerous chances to heed Frankfurter's advice: "Use every opportunity to meet people in person. . . . You with your zip and energy belong to the United States; you ought to go there, but take my counsel now, use every chance to make personal contacts. They are what count in life."

A dinner that Frankfurter was giving for a group of journalists offered Ella a chance to mingle with influential men, as Frankfurter instructed Ella to make the arrangements. "Have you ever heard of Lincoln Steffens?" Frankfurter asked Ella, who acknowledged that she knew nothing of either Steffens or muckraking. "He's a great wit, Stef is, fond of saying things differently," Frankfurter went on. "You can learn from him, he'll give you a different picture than you got at the London School of Economics."

In search of Steffens, Ella went to the Hotel Chatham, where Steffens, feeling slightly ill, surprised the young messenger by greeting her at the door in his bathrobe. The encounter left an indelible impression on Ella. "The man was not tall," she recalled, "but he had a striking face, narrow, with a fringe of blond hair, a small goatee, and very blue eyes, and he stood there smiling. The face had wonderful lines. . . . There was something devilish—or was it impish?—in the way this figure stood grinning at me. 'Hullo, nice girl,' the voice said, and melted all my anxiety." When she informed him that she carried a letter, Steffens chuckled, "A love letter?" This was the American wit—light, teasing, often too direct and personal for European taste—that she had heard of.

Having an impulse to politely leave but intrigued by her new acquaintance, Ella handed him the letter and paused while Steffens read it. "Felix giving another of his parties? To meet the most important people who'll very importantly tell him what's unimportant?" Steffens went on in the same vein, captivating Ella until she realized that she had spent her entire lunch with the peculiar American journalist.

Soon thereafter, Ella came upon Steffens on a less auspicious occasion, one that was most uncomfortable for her and, for Steffens, was part of a much larger historical moment. On a spring day along the Bois du Boulogne, Ella was enjoying what she hoped would develop into a romantic outdoor dinner with a handsome Rhodes scholar who was in Paris on League of Nations work. As they were relaxing under a tree, Ella was stunned to notice a boatful of chattering people pull up to the bank, where Frankfurter, Bullitt, Steffens, and others disembarked, throwing her friend into a near panic at being "discovered" in a delicate moment by such luminaries. He quickly finished their dinner together, anxious to join the others and conclude the socially awkward separation.

In fact, Bullitt and Steffens had recently returned from their secretive Russian mission, still hopeful of persuading Allied leaders to act on the opening with Lenin. At that moment, they were listening to Kerensky discuss the ongoing violence in his homeland, just the type of political atmosphere that left Ella livid, as she was acutely aware of being no more than a bystander—and a woman, at that—in the gathering and that her special evening was dashed. Excusing herself, she asked how long it would take to walk to the end of the Bois. In a "maddening, mellifluous voice," Steffens quipped in reply, "That depends on whom you're walking with." Amid the laughter and snickers of the male audience and the bitter realization of a stillborn romance, Ella stalked away, certain that she would have nothing more to do with Steffens and his American wit.

As the peace conference concluded, disheartened idealists like Ella saw only more darkness ahead. One night soon before her departure for London, Ella came upon Steffens, whose mind may have understood the conference's outcome long ago but whose heart was hardly different from Ella's. They agreed to

walk together, a stroll that took them through the better part of the night, with
Steffens speaking of Jo Davidson's work among the power brokers in Paris and
the plight of the McNamaras back in California while Ella poured out her frustration at seeing the world reject a new future for more misery, Steffens lending
a sympathetic ear. The following night, a similar scene played out between the
two, and then another. As they walked along the Seine, with Ella distraught over
the political gloom of the moment, Steffens said in his quizzical way, "Look at
the river, little girl. Don't you have any room for beauty? Don't you ever just
look and enjoy? What is the river doing? Look at those lights—where are they
going, what is *their* heavy purpose?"

"A dancing Seine-light night," Ella answered.

"Ah," Steffens replied. "That's what an artist would see. So you *do* have it
in you. I was afraid for a moment you were all brain, all set to see things wrong."
And when Steffens pondered what to call his special, dreamful friend, knowing
that what the rest of the world called her would hardly suffice, he thought of
perpetual youth, and Peter Pan. "Peter! That's your name," he exclaimed, perhaps making a proper fit for a tomboy who placed herself in circles dominated
by powerful men.

After Ella's return to London, they continued to exchange letters through
the summer. Ella, who was the first to write, later explained, "What fascinated
me was that Steffens was not only observer and reporter but always and very
deeply teacher and friend. . . . He particularly loved students and young people,
to whom he wanted to explain what he thought caused the 'evils' he had found,
what made men act as they did, and how things might be better." For the time
being, Steffens had to offer his explanations through the mail.

Steffens remained in Paris for most of the summer. Still largely ignored by
the magazines, Steffens continued to write detailed accounts to his family and
to Gussie. He squawked about the pullout of most of the American delegation
before many of the negotiations had been finished. "We are all here for the
spectacular, the interesting part of the work, but the dull routine of the long
finish,—not for us. . . . Austria, Hungary, Russia, Turkey, and all Asia Minor
do not regard the remaining as negligible," he griped to Laura. And while he
opposed the "policy of infinite compromise" offered by House, who had stayed
behind to prop up the league, Steffens had no patience with the closed minds of
the flag wavers, either: "Patriotism is bunk; superstition; prejudice."

Steffens, meanwhile, was having his own personal adventures in Paris. He
told Gussie that he was being followed "a good deal" by detectives and had seen
copies of their reports on him. "It is idiotic," he complained. "I never do a thing

along the line of my work that I don't tell some of my official friends. . . . I have never concealed anything."

In fact, he spoke with just about anyone who had knowledge of events in or out of Paris. In midsummer, he discussed the matter of European Jews over lunch with Brandeis, who was just back from a visit to Palestine, and Frankfurter, who was returning from Poland. Steffens found Brandeis, a strong supporter of the Balfour Declaration, so moved by his experience that he looked as if "he had seen a vision." The Supreme Court justice said he now understood why Jews wanted the old country, and that their plans there would include room for Christians as well. "Somehow he made me feel that it was going to be done," Steffens admitted to Laura and Allen. Frankfurter had seen a rather different situation with the Jews in Poland. He told of pogroms, the Jewish curse, still haunting their lives, but he spoke, Steffens noted, with a touch of sympathy for Poles as well. Filled with the fresh air of power and dreams for the future of their abused country, young Poles in particular were understandably eager to act. Their enthusiasm for change, however, did not embrace the Jews. For Steffens, it was a lively, fascinating exchange of ideas over yet another pressing European issue that had been given short shrift in Paris.

In late August 1919, Steffens moved on to Berlin for a few weeks. There, as in Paris, events often rudely reminded him that his old ideas were no more enlightened than anyone else's. He was not writing much, he told Dot—he was mostly thinking about the world, trying to see the way forward. "One conclusion after another of mine is dying the death," he admitted, "and I suppose I ought to say that I have been unthinking a lot. I am unlearning, first, the things they are teaching your boys at school and now, the things they will learn for themselves. . . . You have no idea how much my thinking centres around your children: the lies they are learning and how to save them from the errors I have made; and am still making."

What Steffens saw in Germany was a broken system that required change but that also feared the prospect of Bolshevism. In letters to Filene (who, like Steffens, supported Russia's right to succeed or fail in its experiment with Communism), the Howes, and Allen, Steffens wrote at length about the struggles of labor and maintained his view that only Lenin had seen it straight—the system had to be dismantled and rebuilt. Still, his unlearning continually gave him pause. In one of his many mood swings during the postwar confusion, Steffens announced to Allen, "Now I am a pacifist against the class war. It is too fierce, too expensive, too atrocious. It is not scientific. . . . The diagnosis is false, and evolution IS POSSIBLE. Only, doggone it, the evolutionists won't evolve,—not while they have their precious privileges to protect." But his doubts, as often as they arose, never truly shook his faith in Russia. Even when Emma Goldman, who as a teenager had left an oppressive home in Russia for New York and in 1918 had hailed the revolution as a miracle, was later deported to Russia as a result of the Palmer raids and found herself, she lamented, in hell, Steffens was unfazed. "It isn't important whether Emma and I get liberty. The important thing," he maintained, "is that Bolshevik Russia shall go through its tyranny patiently and arrive at liberty for the whole Russian people and perhaps for the whole world; not me and Emma."

Of all the aspects of the new Russia that concerned Westerners, the terror loomed largest, and Steffens's words clearly suggest that he understood that the terror, in some way, had to be explained. Steffens saw Lenin as a liberal at heart who, as he had insisted to Steffens in Moscow, did not want the terror but saw no way around it. The sincerity of Lenin concerning a peaceful alternative to terror was dubious, but Steffens took him at his word and largely agreed. "My theory," Steffens explained, "is that the righteous can be saved, that they do not have to be killed. It is only a matter of propaganda. . . . A Red Terror should be possible of control." But Lenin himself had been an ardent revolutionary from a young age, and he did not stray from that path. Under his dictatorship, the average Russian could more easily envision the grave than democracy. Steffens, however, was determined to see a revolution succeed, leaving his vision perilously selective and himself too reliant on Lenin's words rather than his own common sense, particularly for a man who had actually been to Russia and viewed the misery.

From Berlin, Steffens returned to Paris in the fall and then to London, where Ella arranged for him to address editorial groups on the Russians. The conservative *Times* continued its assault on Bolshevism, quoting Steffens and Bullitt to bolster its case. "I've been tempted to answer," he told Laura, "but I restrain the impulse," mainly out of fear of losing his passport. He did not see the British situation as hopeless, though. Calmly and methodically, he explained to his audience, including Steed of the *Times*, that after the nearly suicidal debacle of the war, they had either to accept Bolshevism or "find and show the people another way." Going backward, he believed, was not a solution. Even Steed, Steffens claimed, complimented him on his presentation—"my report was the best document he had seen." An editor at the *Herald* talked of giving Steffens some assignments, while various labor editors had met with him to consider forming an international labor news service to compete with the Associated Press. "So it goes better here," he acknowledged.

The fall passed pleasantly for Steffens mainly because he was "meeting everybody" in London. Everybody, of course, featured Ella, whom he introduced to his family in a November 4 letter to Laura and Allen. "She's a child, a girl of twenty-one, a student," he explained a bit timidly for obvious reasons. "She 'took to' me somehow, and when I arrived here, she took me, managed me, told people they ought to see me and they believed her. They have taken me up, and I'm a go. She's a brilliant girl."

Their relationship headed toward love, if not already there, Steffens and Ella met every day for lunch or dinner, with Ella eagerly bringing him to Fabian lectures where they could talk with Bertrand Russell, Wells, and others. She also brought together her father and Steffens, who gave his moving version of the injustice of the McNamara case, drawing a sympathetic nod of agreement. Otherwise, Steffens and Ella talked incessantly—of his boyhood spent on a pony, the muckraking days at *McClure's*, the joyous character of John Reed, and Ella's own reminiscences. "All the time," Ella wrote, "feeling was growing between Stef and me."

But the true nature of the relationship remained as mysterious to others as it did to them. Ella's friends warned her against getting involved with a father figure, while her mother was nearly frantic with worry over Steffens's intentions. Remarkably, Ella herself still knew nothing of Steffens's personal past. So one afternoon, she raised the matter and listened intently as Steffens revealed the details of his untidy relationships. There were no children involved, he told her, but he had been married to the tragically unfortunate Josephine and now remained unattached, with the notable and difficult exception of Gussie, whom he could not even bring himself to name in front of Ella. He spoke of how he had jilted her for Josephine, had unexpectedly taken up with her once more, a result partly of her own unhappy marriage, and could not contemplate hurting her again. Steffens assured Ella that he would somehow manage the situation with Gussie, and Ella accepted his words with a heavy but hopeful heart.

When Steffens's month in London ended, he closed his letter to Ella on his final night not with a farewell but with a look, full of optimism, to the future: "No goodbye is goodbye, not when we so want to say Hello. So—as I said before—hello, Peter, dear, dear Peter."

After returning to Paris on December 9, Steffens wrote obsessively to Ella, sending lengthy letters at least once a day. In painstaking, expressive detail, they exchanged views on the exact nature of their "friendship" and the direction it should take, each clearly hoping it would blossom into full love even as they expressed caution over how rapidly the bloom should develop. Ella's first letter came swiftly and with "a kiss and the tears"; Steffens replied that he was surprised and pleased by how quickly she wrote, adding, "And tears. I wish I had seen you cry. I love joy." Ella envisioned their romance as a Shakespearean scene, with her death right on the heels of Steffens's. He viewed the matter a bit more clearly: "I don't want to tell it you as I see it, Peter. It hurts me too much."

Still, the delicate matter of appearances tugged at them. On December 11, Steffens confided to Ella, "Maybe I could be your friend . . . but—Let's not rush it. It's like going to work after all these months of play. I hate to. I will, yes, but,—not yet. Now is so,—so sweet. God, Peter. It's some job we have cut out for ourselves: to be friends! But, then, maybe we'll fail."

That week, Ella spoke truthfully to her mother about Steffens, which Steffens saw as the proper move even though his own feelings about a future with Ella remained hazy. On the twelfth, he wrote to her as "a friend," explaining what he wished for, or did not:

> It's not important what you do. All I care about is that you find out soon which sort of thing you do best; more happily. That's all. That's all I want or ever shall want of you: that you have all the chances a man has to find yourself and grow, bearing flowers or fruit; joyously. Is that love? Is that friendship? Bah! Categories . . . I love flowers, Peter, and birds, and horses; animals, and men, bad men and good men; and I love you.

Yet, he closed the letter by stating in a somewhat equivocal way: "This is not a love-letter, Peter. This is the letter of a friend."

It was obviously unfair of Steffens to expect any woman, particularly one who had already imagined dying with her lover, to parse such language. In reality, each had fallen completely for the other, and all of the posturing and questioning and sentiment that dominated their letters was simply the language of love. Three days before Christmas, Steffens offered the confession that Ella so wanted to read: "And you, Peter,—I don't know why, but I feel like apologizing for saying it so—you are the one. I love you. I love you with all my heart and mind, with my body, bones—and all my imagination." The mutual agonizing over their relationship did not end, though, most likely because of the age difference and the increasingly sorrowful presence of Gussie, but it was all to ease their consciences. There was no doubt that Steffens and Ella wanted to be together.

Happily fixated on Ella, Steffens still maintained his brisk correspondence with others. Four days before Christmas, he sent a long, affectionate letter to

Hutchins Hapgood, his first contact with his old friend in years. *The Story of a Lover*, Hapgood's controversial novel that had to be published anonymously and then was prosecuted on charges of pornography, had just been published. But Steffens, who had read a previous draft years earlier, now felt a bit of nostalgiac guilt over some changes he had suggested. "I was sorry for what I felt," he wrote. "For the outstanding character of the thing to me is, as it was, beauty. One doesn't cut and stick inserts into a thing of beauty. It reminds me of what Neith [a co-worker and, later, Hapgood's wife] and I used to do to the things you wrote in the olden days on the old *Commercial*." He went on to say that he had bought a gift for Neith in Berlin and thought often of both of them, perhaps having never quite forgiven himself for the cutting remarks that both he and Josephine had directed at them years ago. "I neglect the art of personal friendship," he admitted in closing, "but I do really love the friends I neglect," urging Hapgood to keep in touch. Sadly, Steffens would be hearing from Hutchins and Neith within two short months, following the untimely death of their seventeen-year-old son, Boyce, from the Spanish flu.

Neglect, though, was not an issue between Steffens and Ella. When they were not obsessed over how much they missed each other, Steffens and Ella wrote prodigiously on another subject close to their hearts: labor. They examined the declining labor conditions around the world, criticized governments for their blindness toward the value of their ill-treated workers, and generally tried to retain their faith in the labor cause, even as it was under attack seemingly everywhere.

Steffens himself was routinely chastized in America as a stooge for the Reds and the Wobblies, but he was stunned to find out that Fred Howe, caught up in the Red hysteria and antilabor wave that had struck America, had resigned as commissioner of immigration after refusing to accept orders to conduct secret deportations. In his memoir, Howe recalled that one of the final blows was talk of sending a boatload of immigrants back to Russia: "Many of them I had personally examined and found held on the most trivial charges." Acknowledging his fate, he quit with only the regret of having witnessed the brutal unfairness of the system. "I had seen the government at close range, with its mask off; it existed for itself and for hidden men behind it, as the realists in Paris had said. It was as dangerous to the innocent as to the guilty. It was frankly doing the bidding of business," he concluded. The government, though, had seen it quite differently, claiming that letters of appeal to Howe from Emma Goldman, Elizabeth Gurley Flynn, and others on behalf of labor protesters, many of them Russians, had resulted in the release of hundreds of prisoners on Howe's watch.

His own assistant commissioner stated that under Howe, the island had become "a forum for the preaching of Bolshevism." Ever faithful to his friends, Steffens took the view that Howe had been guilty only of "humanity, sanity, and mercy, but those are great crimes nowadays."

For all of his support of Russia and of the labor struggles in his own country, Steffens nevertheless understood that none of the parties in the labor fight were untainted. All of them used—and abused—power for their own ends. In an interesting exchange with Ella, Steffens pointed out the major limitation that all sides shared: They were run by . . . people:

> Labor unions, even industrial labor organizations, are monopolies, privileged evil interests, developed out of the need to fight capitalistic monopolies; weapons in the class war of class interests, and as unscientific as a machine gun or a trust. Of course. Labor is capitalistic in its objective, its methods and its ethics. . . . Our job is to point out the interests that corrupt, suggest their removal and understand why men will prefer to smash the whole thing and build anew. Lenin is not right. Nobody is right. That is the opportunity for Peter. And God! it would be glorious to have a woman seize it.

Indeed, while Steffens had spent his own energies tirelessly promoting the cause of labor and exposing the grafters and imperialists, he encouraged Ella, perhaps respecting her youth and her female perspective, to move differently, to hear all arguments, to reflect deeply, to educate herself. "You are not a friend of Labor; you are not an enemy of Capital," he observed. "Please don't take that position. You are not a Socialist, not that I could ever discover or wanted to discover. You are a young scientist. A poet too and, I hope, an advocate of whatever you find upon examination to seem true."

As the year closed, Steffens pondered his next move. He considered returning to the United States, but that option "seems too horrible," he told Marie Howe. "There is nothing to do there," he explained, "except to fight for the impossible, Liberalism. The Government, the American Legion, the investigating committees and the good people generally are doing all that can be done for the revolution. And it's a good job they are doing." By contrast, he acknowledged that the work that had brought him fame had been well-intentioned but wrongheaded: "We Americans made a great mistake having that brief period of muckraking. It set back our death more years than we devoted to it. It protracted the age of folly; did harm, and no good. . . . What I really think is that, since our muckrakers did not know and therefore did not tell us what actually was the matter, but only taught us morality, they stretched out the age of honest bunk and held us back."

Steffens chose to remain on the European continent, unemployed but hardly without means. Since 1915, he had been renting Little Point to Owen Young, who had recently founded the Radio Corporation of America (RCA) and would soon be chairman of General Electric. Young agreed to buy the property for thirty-five thousand dollars, yielding Steffens a steady stream of income that, along with other investments, totaled roughly five thousand dollars a year, more than enough to subsidize the genteel lifestyle of fashionable clothes, cafés, seaside resorts, and trains across Europe that would mark his leisurely expatriate years.

One immediate reason why a return to the United States for Steffens was out of the question was that the ill-fated Gussie had arrived in Paris from New York. Sensing both her uneasy acceptance of his lengthy stay in Europe and her loneliness, Steffens had suggested she come to France for a change of scenery despite her being unaware of Ella. For the moment, Steffens faced the prospect of lifting Gussie's spirits in some way while being perfectly aware that their future had already come unglued. He now faced the uncomfortable choice of having to hide his relationship with Ella or confess. He had already raised the matter with Ella, his logic portraying the vexing indecision and illusion that so often marked Steffens's relations with women:

> Our love doesn't want its fate decided by some other relationship. And it shan't be. . . . Each should be worked out by itself. . . . I think, as you say, that I should meet the ship and flow on with her a while, giving that old relationship a chance to find itself, and then form itself, all by itself. It may be more than I think it is. It was always fine; incomplete, but smooth, quiet, comfortable. . . . I believe, that if you were not there at all, she and I would pass on into a friendship that would last for life; and be good, very, very good; affectionate, but without love.

Steffens could see the entire disaster approaching but simply chose to let it happen, assuming that it would somehow resolve itself over time. When Gussie most needed a reliable partner, Steffens could only offer her the same uncertainty to which she had become distressingly accustomed. In his personal relations, he had little skill in being subtle. He was even worse at lying, and Gussie soon grasped, intuitively, that she had a competitor.

In his letters, his inconsistent versions of events and his innocence over the nature of his relationships with both Ella and Gussie, and their own feelings, are remarkable. To Ella, he wrote,

> She knows about Us. I didn't tell her at first; she was too ill. But, Lord, I can't conceal anything like that, and she's a woman. There was something the matter. She felt it, of course; said nothing for a few days, and then asked. I told her the story. She took it as you said she would and as I knew she would. And now she wants to be my friend. Like you. So I'm going to be a lover completely surrounded by friends!. . . . You see, I can laugh yet; even at so serious a subject as myself. But I don't mean to pretend that there has not been some anguish,— all around. There has been nothing ugly in it, however; not from any angle. Some day we must all three meet, we good friends of Stef.

Laura got her version of the story as well from Steffens:

> It was, it is, hard on G. She is really not well. . . . She suspected and I had to tell her all about that little, passing fancy of mine for the young girl here. She counts it as more important than I do, now. . . . But I also want early to say to you that I did, and I do, like E.W. very much, but it is her young genius that attracts me, and that's all. . . . I should not have told G anything about it, but I can't conceal much and, of course, once having mentioned it, I couldn't keep it in perspective. G. wanted to release me at once, and go home, but I objected to that. It is right that I go away myself. But I'll go back to G. and I'll return with a fresh sense of the true nobility that is in her. I hope you will write to her and, when you do, show her some affection. She not only loves me, she is a very true friend of mine.

But Steffens, amazingly, could function perfectly well in the midst of such personal chaos, and with the dawn of 1920, his mind was focused, as usual, on the future. Eager to see and understand the postwar changes that dominated Europe, Russia, and beyond, Steffens continued to fill his letters home with breaking news across a wide spectrum. He told his family of a possible trip to Kiev to observe the tension between the Ukrainians and Bolsheviks, expecting a mediating role for himself after an encouraging talk with former Labor MP George Lansbury; the fears of England over both the stability of Persia, India, and the rest of its eastern empire and the rise of labor at home; the hopes of the Italians to have, unlike Russia, a bloodless revolution; and the unrest in the Baltic states. Within a week, with Gussie remaining in Paris, he was off to England and then Denmark and Germany. In Copenhagen, he met with Maxim Litvinov, the Russian ambassador negotiating the end of the British blockade of his country, and Lansbury, now a newspaper editor. "We talked blockade-lifting, and the consequences; Third International; conditions inside; and,—everything," Steffens reported to Ella.

He was less enthusiastic, however, back in Berlin, although the ongoing misery there, he told Allen, could only strengthen the Russian hand. "Germany is depressing. It is worse than it was when I was here last fall," he wrote. "Bankers and business men are saying to the reporters that confessed bankruptcy is the only way out. . . . But as usual on our side, it is late. We should have tackled the peace itself from the start as a world problem, and as such settled it; not as a punitive or graft thing. I wish our statesmen could grasp the fact that their folly is the best card counted upon by the Bolsheviks."

By early February, Steffens was back in Paris. Gussie, he learned, had left for Monte Carlo, shaming Steffens into writing a letter to Allen in which he took a rare, honest look inward. "It was a terrible thing I did to her: bringing her over here to be made well, then putting her up against a half-explained situation which hit her fluttering heart and,—leaving her to think, to feel it almost alone," he admitted. "Am I a blankety-blank? I don't know. But certainly I can do fierce things to those that love me. . . . I am really puzzled to understand myself. But I guess that is because I don't want to see myself so straight as, for example, you may be able to do."

The same letter, however, reveals the essence of Steffens's problem. His heart, in truth, lay not with Ella or Gussie but, as ever, with his incessant pursuit of revolution. His eagerness to be a witness to the future, wherever it might be, took precedence over any unfinished business in his personal life. Feeling both homesick and guilty, Steffens nonetheless told Allen that the geopolitical game in postwar Europe was too compelling to ignore. "I mustn't quit this yet," he insisted. "It is opening a clear vision of the future. . . . I can see that it is to be a Socialist state, better, much better than ours. . . . It is the next stage after Socialism which would interest me. For, of course, I am not a Socialist and I am,—something else." For the moment—an interlude that would stretch another three years—Steffens kept up appearances with Gussie, adored Ella, and looked ahead.

From Monte Carlo, Steffens pondered his next move while analyzing the shifting political situation in Europe. To his nephew Jack, he wrote that Lenin was not trying to be "good" but "wise," adding, "The stuff you read in the papers about him and about Soviet Russia is mostly lies." He told Allen of the political chaos in Germany, yet he found the turmoil far more intriguing in Italy, where devastating strikes, mainly by socialists but from a generally united labor front, threatened to bring down the government and cripple the already weak economy. So Steffens headed to Rome with Gussie, who was "better, much better" in the spring.

Taking in old Rome was "a rich and suggestive" experience for Steffens, reminding him that the past was a guide, if imperfect, to what lay ahead. "I wonder what men would do if they could visualize the future, as one has to do here," he wrote Allen. "For when I say that Rome makes me think of the past I really mean that it reminds me of the future." Aside from long days of sightseeing, however, Steffens also saw that the radical Italian socialists, unlike the Reds, were not radical at all in their approach to the future. He found that they had no plan of action. Instead, they gave countless speeches, dutifully stayed home from work, looked wistfully up at the Russians, and ultimately did little but paralyze the country and enable the rise of Mussolini. Still, Steffens admired their patience in trying to remake their own country. And their willingness to consult Moscow was not lost on Steffens: "I have got a deep respect for the movement in Italy and the wisdom of its leaders."

23

EXPATRIATE

FOR STEFFENS PERSONALLY, the most significant development during his time in Rome was his decision, after years of consideration, to begin work on *Moses in Red*, his story of revolution told as a biblical parable of Moses trying to deliver a doubting people to the Promised Land. The book would take years to write and, other than his immensely successful autobiography, would be Steffens's last major work. The idea had come to Steffens during his muckraking days, when he had decided to give the New Testament a serious reading. With fresh eyes, he examined the life of Jesus and was struck by how the dreamers of his own time, men such as Tom Johnson and Edward Filene, had struggled in their quest to establish new, more progressive ways of organizing human affairs only to be ultimately overwhelmed by the entrenched powers, not that he equated them with the Messiah.

Part of the problem, Steffens believed, was that the Christian church and its people did not wish to find the hand of God in science. Every natural phenomenon under God, from a chemical reaction to a revolution, had a cause, and the cause had to be understood scientifically for the result to be altered or prevented. "Arresting revolutionists does not arrest the revolution any more than prohibition stops drinking," he observed. Prayers, piety, belief in good and evil—all were fine but useless without an understanding of the natural laws. A scientific understanding and even peaceful management of revolution, Steffens was convinced, was possible if it was studied and evaluated properly. Lenin had said as much to Steffens. And the story of Moses was *the* revolution for Steffens to study. He shaped the tale as a justification of the Russian experiment itself, although the liberties Steffens took in doing so somewhat weakened his message.

Steffens found much that was instructive—the labor struggle, the dictator, the terror, and the endless unlearning—in the story of Moses. He explained to Gilbert Roe, a good friend and former law partner of La Follette, that in his own work on Moses, "Jehovah symbolizes Nature; Moses, the reformer, and leader; Pharaoh the King or the employer-capitalist; Aaron the orator and the Jews as the people. The parallel with the Russian or any other revolution is striking." Through the burning bush, God commanded Moses to organize the Jews and deliver them out of Egypt to the Promised Land. But arousing the slaves, who were "tired out, spiritless, and accustomed to the routine of bondage," to break free, was the challenge, Steffens wrote. God saw the dilemma and used a slight by the king—the boss—against the slaves to push them toward Moses' view, and more dramatic scenes, such as turning dust into lice and slaughtering cattle, among other acts, were required to implement God's plan.

The final plague was, as Steffens saw it, the Red Terror. The firstborn in all Egyptian families were killed, and only then did the Egyptians push out their own slaves and did the slaves themselves feel compelled to go. Moses, leading his people to the Promised Land, was now the dictator. And God cared for them. But the people were not satisfied with freedom. They wanted more. So they danced and sang and ate well, all of which brought on the White Terror. God was angered. Moses pleaded for mercy, but he was now the leader of the Jews, and justice would be dispensed by him. Moses' version of the terror left three thousand men dead. Still, the Jews were not ready for the Promised Land. They complained more, and God vowed punishment. Except for Caleb and Joshua, who had followed God's word, everyone over the age of twenty would die, for only the children, innocent and untainted, were qualified to enter the Promised Land.

Moses himself, like many reformers, was too old to finish the task. He would see the Promised Land only from a hilltop across the Jordan River before his death, for there was too much unlearning necessary for those old enough to remember Egypt. "They must learn new ideals, statutes, customs, and a little higher religion. That is what a people in progress have to do. And they could not do it; they cannot, not the older generation, neither of the people of Israel, nor of the Russians, nor—of any other people," Steffens observed, including himself.

Despite such enormous sacrifices, the Promised Land did not prove to be heaven, either, to the Jews. It was a harsh place filled with enemies and required continous toil. "It had to be fought for, conquered, cleared, plowed, planted, watered—created," Steffens wrote. Moses, Steffens believed, would have been disappointed, as were many Russians. But God understood otherwise: "He knew that heaven is not paved with gold, and that it should not be. He knew and He knows that lands of promise are nothing but lands of opportunity, where men, by their labor, by their growing strength and by their dawning intelligence, may make, if they will, not only a good, but a beautiful living; and not only a beautiful life but a beautiful race of men."

Not that Steffens was unaware of why much of the public mind begged to differ. Evolution was slower, easier, and less painful; revolution, he conceded, was a horror. Such influential thinkers as Bertrand Russell and H. G. Wells had already rejected the violence. "They believe in evolution, not revolution," Steffens wrote. "Well, they are getting evolution. . . . They shall wander around in the wilderness of peace conferences, politics, constitutional liberty, strikes, debate, and race poverty till they die." Fascism and the Ku Klux Klan were evolutionary and brutal but not as brutal as the road to the Promised Land, so people preferred them, even in the aftermath of an evolutionary world war that killed millions. "That is the point," Steffens asserted. "The evils of revolution happen in a revolution. They have to be studied, therefore; not merely shied at, but examined and then, perhaps, when they are understood scientifically, they can be avoided or used." And, he pointed out, the majority in the West accepted the biblical terror as well as trench warfare, Mussolini, the White Terror, and the KKK, while at the same time condemning the Reds, often in the name of God. With his sympathetic nod toward the shock treatment administered by dictators and his condemnation of the righteous reformers, Steffens, in *Moses in Red*, had abandoned any pretense of hope that even the liberalism of American progressives could lead to a democratic future.

After their return to Paris in June, Steffens and Gussie again parted—Gussie returned to New York, while Steffens, along with Ella and Filene, headed to Vienna, where the "long lines of thin, desperate women" waiting for food appalled Ella. Steffens agreed. "We saw Wien, and it is hell," Steffens wrote to his family.

It was during the postwar period that any common cause between Steffens and the mainstream political spectrum in America was lost. In a note to the Italian ambassador, Secretary of State Bainbridge Colby, with the Red Terror clearly in mind, expressed the American position: "It is not possible for the Government of the United States to recognize the present rulers of Russia as a government with which the relations common to friendly governments can be maintained." Steffens, though, grew more and more impressed by Lenin's handling of the revolution. In his letters, he repeatedly defended or praised him, observing that Lenin, for example, "thinks straight," has a "cool, scientific mind," and "taught" the British "something."

Steffens, who had always prided himself on his own curious, open mind and scientific approach, believing that every problem had a cause that could be identified and altered for the better, now had permanently changed course. Whether it was his advancing age (fifty-three), impatience borne of thirty years of muckraking and unlearning, his highly romantic notion of Russia, or other reasons, Steffens had settled his mind. Capitalism was the illness. Revolution was the cure, terror included. Steffens believed from long experience that capitalists had no desire to change their undemocratic system, however slowly. Without evolution, the only solution was to overthrow the profiteers, endure a hellish transformation, and emerge with a system of genuine liberty and justice for all. Such was the future Steffens anticipated. Wilson had fought the war to make the world safe for democracy; Steffens looked around from the victors' circle and did not see democracy anywhere. The only path left to him was chasing revolutions.

By October, Steffens had returned to the United States, for the first time in nearly two years, to be with Gussie and to see his family in California. Gussie apparently had come to accept, if grudgingly, the presence of Ella, and showed her forgiving nature over the next few months. At least that was how Steffens interpreted her behavior. "She is used to me now," he told Laura, "and I can settle down and feel at home more with her than with anybody I know. . . . She knows me and she accepts me as I am."

Publishers, however, had little interest at the moment in Steffens. Despite all that Steffens had seen in Europe, the demand for his work was nil. The managing editor at *Collier's* was a longtime friend of Steffens's who promised to do all he could to promote a story on the Armenians, but even he "was up against the System in his own office," Steffens observed. A vague offer of help came from John Phillips, the former *McClure's* editor, now at the *Evening Post* in New York, and another from *Everybody's*. None of the plans, though, reached fruition. Not that Steffens was unnerved. "I'm not a bit discouraged or depressed," he insisted to Laura. "I have some news, real news, and I'll put it over somehow. You'll see. And the prepossession against me is nothing but the price I have to pay for my independence and straight reporting."

And Steffens was keen to share his perspective. He sent letters to both President Wilson, who by then was too ill to see almost anyone other than his wife and physician, and Colonel House. In November, Steffens took a short trip to Washington, where he met with Attorney General Palmer and Secretary of State Colby. He naturally urged Palmer—a most unlikely ally of any political prisoner, having put many of them behind bars himself—to grant amnesty to Eugene Debs and release him from jail. Palmer pointed out to Steffens the difficulty in the Debs case, as the socialist leader continued to defy the government and in fact had not even requested a pardon. They went on to discuss Mexico and Russia, topics that "scared" Palmer, Steffens thought. Steffens himself was hardly in a position at the moment to threaten anyone, but the attorney general did remark to Steffens, apparently in good humor, "You're dangerous. You are all soft-spoken, you radicals, but you go out and you—you're a menace."

The 1920 election of Warren Harding, a Republican who offered the country unswerving support for big business, an intellect dwarfed by Wilson's ("he has nothing to think with," Wilson once told Ida Tarbell), and a handsome face matched with an amorous appetite that evidently charmed women successfully and often, signaled the country's desire for a caretaker president and its rejection of grand political schemes on an international scale. William Allen White, who as a Kansas delegate at the Republican National Convention had warned fellow delegates, "If you nominate Harding, you will disgrace the Republican Party," later conceded, "It was not in the stars to elect anyone in 1920 who advocated anything seriously."

In the face of such willful complacency, Steffens persisted in his efforts to explain Bolshevism to his countrymen. In late November, Steffens took his soft-spoken radicalism on a lecture tour through the East, telling of what he had seen over the past two years, particularly in Russia. Steffens stunned some audiences and bored none. Before a crowd of nearly two thousand in a Toronto hall, Steffens was cheered to the point of embarrassment. Journeying from city to city, though, his talks met more resistance as they grew "clearer, firmer, [and] redder." In Johnstown, Pennsylvania, he guessed that one-third of his audience was "visibly shocked." "Apparently I am to talk every night," he told Laura, "until I land in San Francisco or jail."

Steffens managed to avoid jail and was back in New York on New Year's Day 1921, stopping only momentarily before embarking on another lecture trip west, sponsored by a new radical organization called the Red Star League. Motivated by the engaging crowds of Americans eager to learn about "the future" or to lambaste Steffens as a traitor, Steffens spoke across the country, always in demand, proud that two mayors along the way had found him dangerous enough to be prohibited from addressing the local citizenry. By early February, Steffens reached California.

A talk in Seattle had introduced Steffens to a young woman who yearned for the promise of Russia as much as Steffens himself. Anna Louise Strong, a minister's daughter who finished high school at fourteen and had a doctorate at twenty-three from the University of Chicago, was a brilliant, determined, but rather aimless woman when Steffens met her. Her experiences as a free-lance reporter for the *New York Evening Post* had convinced her to take up the cause of labor. She publicized the persecution of the Wobblies, read voraciously on Lenin and the revolution, grilled radicals such as Louise Bryant and Rhys Williams when they were passing through Seattle, and loudly opposed the American entry in the European war. Still, she yearned for a role on a grander stage.

Sitting in a small, poorly lit booth at Blanc's, the café popular among Seattle dissidents, Strong poured out her frustrations to Steffens after his talk. She was especially troubled by the growing squabbles among her radical "comrades" themselves, with the more demonstrative turning on the moderates. When Strong voiced her wish to achieve a compromise, Steffens replied, "Never! The gulf will grow wider! It is growing all over the world." Dismayed, Strong spoke dreamily of Moscow. She would give anything, she said, to go. Steffens, who had left behind his dying sister to make the journey four years earlier, calmly asked, "Why don't you then?"

"By a lightning flash," Strong recalled, "four words of Steffens revealed that everything which held me in Seattle was completed; only inertia kept me now." She asked how she could enter Russia. Working with a charity group, possibly the Quakers, was her best chance, Steffens explained. Strong did eventually get to Russia, as well as Communist China, and remained in touch with Steffens until his last days, going on to become one of the most renowned—and partisan—reporters of her time.

Following a February stay with his family in California, Steffens headed south for his third and final visit to Mexico, arriving on March 9. To Steffens, little had changed. He saw some friends to catch up on the political gossip, watched the oil men keep their distance from him as they went about their business, and understood that the mass of Mexicans distrusted the United States as much as ever. "It's Paris all over again," he wrote to Allen. "Much talk of peace, all thought upon oil and gold and lands; and preparedness for war." Steffens spent considerable time explaining the Russians to Mexican labor leaders, certain that they understood.

Reminding himself that the more favorable revolution remained in Russia and eager to return there in the spring, Steffens and his traveling companion, Jo Davidson, found themselves unable to gain permission to enter the country, never getting past Stockholm. So they went to Paris via Berlin before Steffens again sailed for America in June. He would continue crisscrossing the Atlantic for the next six years, pursuing revolutions and, more successfully, love.

After another summer visit to California, where he split his time between San Francisco and Lake Tahoe, Steffens, still jobless, was back in New York in September. A call came from Herbert Hoover, now secretary of commerce. He needed Steffens's help in convincing the Reds in America, largely distrustful of Hoover and the entire Harding administration, to support his relief efforts in Russia. "It makes me laugh," Steffens told Laura. "These people who so often denounce me for my connections with the Left are glad I am there sometimes and reach out to use my relationship with the Reds. Well, I am willing to be used." The Reds, too, supported Steffens's involvement, so he once more entered the labor fray.

The basic conflict was that while Hoover was insisting that his sole purpose in Russia was to feed the people, the Reds strongly suspected that the government—through Hoover—was subtly using food supplies as an anti-Bolshevik propaganda tool. An article written a few months earlier by a member of the American Relief Administration in Hungary had flatly stated that the efforts of Hoover were aimed at weakening the Bolsheviks, and Max Eastman and others demanded that he deny it. Hoover merely ignored the charge. In the unusual role of compromiser, Steffens stated the obvious—that the administration opposed the Bolsheviks—but suggested that the relief efforts go forward in any event, as they would provide crucial assistance to the Russians while possibly thawing relations between the government and the Left at home. For the moment, the plan went ahead.

Steffens remained visible on the national scene with another series of lectures through the Midwest and a lengthy public letter appealing for amnesty of jailed labor leaders, most notably Debs. Although Steffens was not always able to sway his audiences, he clearly relished the podium. He advised Allen, who had given a local talk of his own, on his style: He never wrote his speeches, bringing only a few notes to the platform that he sometimes did not even use, and largely relied on a chronological narrative. And he gauged his listeners carefully. "As I look over an audience, I get their status, mood, etc. Unconsciously I feel that," he wrote. "As I go on, I see the audience laugh, frown, smile, shake their heads, applaud: signs of how they like it, how they feel, and I literally rise on that. I extend a statement to clear off a frown, I shorten a statement, when I see they have got it. I feel my way."

Meanwhile, Steffens received encouraging news from Washington: Postmaster General Will Hays had agreed to discuss the labor amnesty with

Steffens. Hays, having served as Harding's campaign manager, seemed a sensible conduit to the president. Steffens noted with cautious optimism in his lengthy November 1 letter to Hays, "I have heard you say things which indicate that you understand that politics is the doing of public business with some sense that public opinion, the mute longings and the suppressed spirit of the masses, are elements in the job."

Steffens explained the justice of an amnesty, not only for Debs but for all the war and labor prisoners, and recounted the spirit of hope and then the bitter disappointment left behind by Wilson: "We had [the spirit] when we went into the war. We had it when we went into the peace, too. But Mr. Wilson, in his disappointment or his sickness, was hard. He yielded nothing. . . . No soft word came from him, no peace. The American People have gone back to work (and to fight) at home, without ever anybody speaking a single kindly word from the heart. And that's not true to us, Mr. Hays; that does not represent us. We, the American People, have a soul." He ended with a simple plea: "Make peace, Mr. Postmaster General, give us peace."

As Steffens hoped, the letter captured the attention of Hays, who agreed to meet him in Washington. The entire effort to gain amnesty, even simply for Debs, faced long odds, Steffens acknowledged. He had heard that the American Legion "raised the deuce" with President Harding himself when a pardon of Debs had previously been mentioned. But Steffens was prepared, if Harding wished, to meet any opponents and plead his case. Of course, the notion of Steffens, now known not as a muckraker promoting democracy but as an enthusiastic Red, influencing the American Legion was dubious. Steffens, however, remembered his old promises to the McNamaras. "Of course it's an awful lot to get actually done, this amnesty," he wrote Allen and Laura, "but won't it be great if it is done!"

Steffens did not meet Hays until December 4 in Chicago, where Hays explained the situation. Steffens's letter had substance, Hays felt, so he had taken the liberty of reading it to the full cabinet. No one, including the president, who kept referring to it as "that letter," voiced strong objections at first. Once the discussion progressed to the details, though, the insurmountable hurdle was plain: They would have to release not only the political prisoners—the least controversial group—but the dynamiters and other serious offenders as well. A full pardon—"the magnificent Thing," Steffens called it—clearly was not an option. So, Hays told Steffens, a compromise was reached. Debs and others who had merely spoken out against the government would be released, while the rest would stay imprisoned.

Steffens replied that such a limited pardon would merely extend the problem and not "break the hate." Hays said that he appreciated Steffens's point but could do no more. Steffens would have to address the president directly if he wanted further action taken, a challenge that Steffens readily accepted if Hays could make the arrangements. The eventual plan involved Steffens meeting with Harding and appealing to Debs to cease any public protest upon his prison release and instead limit his pronouncements to appeals for food aid to Russia. In the meantime, Debs remained in jail. "So here I am," Steffens joked with Allen, "keeping 'Gene Debs in jail."

Within a week, Steffens was in Washington, where the initial signs were mixed. After some trouble gaining permission to see Debs, who was in an Atlanta prison, Steffens was able to arrange a meeting. Hays, unfortunately, was sick and had left Washington. President Harding would meet Steffens, but with Hays gone, Steffens still needed someone to advocate his cause within the White House, aware that Harding would most likely adhere to the advice from his inner circle. Steffens looked hopefully to Hoover, who listened impatiently to Steffens's proposal before deciding that he could have nothing to do with giving freedom to murderers. Alone, Steffens decided that if Harding showed any sign of agreement, he would persist. Otherwise, he would accept defeat for the moment and return to New York. One positive development was that Steffens did visit Debs, who "saw it all," accepting the terms of the amnesty.

Soon, however, "the magnificent Thing" seemed finished. Harding, in his December 17 meeting with Steffens, was most cordial and "had the impulse," Steffens saw, but could not accept a general amnesty. Steffens noted that Attorney General Harry Daugherty, part of the "Ohio gang" of grafters who enjoyed late nights of poker and whiskey with the president, wanted pledges of allegiance and apologies from all the prisoners but Debs, which Steffens rejected as merely a business deal, not an amnesty. Steffens had pushed the president hard to no avail. "So,—I fell down once more," he conceded.

In fact, Steffens did not fail in his efforts for Debs. Harding asked Daugherty to speak personally to Debs with the intention, Daugherty later told Clarence Darrow, of determining if there was a politically acceptable way of releasing Debs. After spending a day with Debs, Daugherty brought Harding's wish to fruition. "I never met a man I liked better," Daugherty admitted to Darrow, and on Christmas Day, barely a week after Steffens had pleaded his case with the president, Debs was set free. Steffens was elated, both for Debs and for Bolshevism. "I am glad, very glad, and I know now that he is clear on Russia,"

Steffens reported to Laura. Darrow noted ironically that he had admired Wilson and distrusted Harding even though Wilson had put Debs in jail and Harding granted his freedom. Undoubtedly echoing Steffens's sentiments, Darrow acknowledged that he never again thought of Harding and Daugherty without reminding himself, "Well, they pardoned Debs!"

Steffens did not dwell on his unsuccessful efforts for a general amnesty. Within a week of speaking to Harding, he informed Laura and Allen that he was on his way to California hoping to go on to India to "see and talk with Gandhi." The other type of revolution—nonviolent—might be of interest, he conceded, although his main hope still lay in Russia and Mexico. He also envisioned a return to Russia for the summer of 1922 and finally a trip back through Europe before returning to New York in the fall. After all of it, he conceded, "I might even have some wisdom at last."

Steffens, in fact, did not get back to Russia that summer, but he indirectly became caught up again in a controversy involving the American relief efforts on behalf of Russians. In a report to President Harding in February, Hoover stated that among the groups purporting to aid Russia were two hundred "frankly communistic organizations," many of which were under the umbrella of the American Federated Russian Famine Relief Committee, headed by Steffens. Although a committee spokesman stated that neither the committee nor Steffens had any official connections to Russia, the organization was said to have collected $260,000 in donations that were ultimately distributed by Soviet authorities themselves. The ensuing spat between Hoover and the committee's secretary went back and forth for several days before George Barr Baker, head of the American Relief Administration under Harding, scolded the radicals for maligning the admirable work of Hoover, noting that the Russians themselves must be thinking, "Heaven save us from our friends!"

Steffens, a friend of Baker, did not comment publicly on the dispute but could hardly have said that the charges were baseless. The day before he met with Harding, Steffens had told Allen and Laura that Debs had agreed "that the thing for him to do was to go out with or after me to plead for bread for Russia,—to be sent to the Soviet government direct." Several weeks later in California, he wrote to Dot, "I have to watch the Reds tackle the whole social problem, which, I think, will have to be done before the farmers can do theirs. I don't know; I only think this. It seems to me that in a capitalist system the capitalist is bound to win. I dunno. I am guessing." The episode was minor by the standards of the leftists caught up in the earlier Palmer raids, but it served to further connect Steffens with the Far Left—and Russia—in the public mind.

From California, there would be no passage to India for Steffens. The problem lay with the British government, which mysteriously refused to issue him a visa, placing not only India but the entire British Empire—and Ella—off limits to him. While he had heard from a friend that someone at the State Department sabotaged his application, Steffens really had no idea as to the source of his troubles. So, after his winter stay in California, he headed back east to investigate. But in New York, Steffens's inquiries of several former foreign officers of Britain, Frank Polk, and Leland Harrison at the State Department led nowhere, spurring him to ask House for help in early April.

In the meantime, Steffens was free to travel to continental Europe, where additional postwar talks were being held, this time at an international conference in Genoa. In truth, the gathering was a recognition that Versailles was not working, with nearly every affected country questioning the treaty for a seemingly endless list of reasons, leading the prime ministers of England and France, Lloyd George and Aristide Briand, to call the conference in hopes of at least stopping the bleeding. It was the first opportunity since the end of the war for Germany and Russia to meet on equal terms with other European nations (America declined to attend) and was Russia's first formal attempt to enter European diplomatic circles after the revolution, so Steffens had every intention of attending.

To entice Jo Davidson to come along, Steffens informed him that statesmen from thirty-four nations would be in Genoa, guaranteeing another mass production of sculptures at what Lloyd George called "the greatest gathering of European nations which has ever been assembled on this continent." Steffens himself was so taken by the idea that he promoted it with Glenn Frank, the editor of *The Century*, who agreed to pay Davidson for an illustrated story on the conference.

So Steffens and Gussie, along with Davidson, traveled together, initially passing several weeks in Paris and Berlin before joining the Genoa meeting in early May, nearly a month after the start. The Italian port was certainly prepared for the occasion. Colorful flags of Europe flew from countless buildings; horses pulled foreign dignitaries in open carriages along the narrow, stone-paved streets; and celebrities packed cafés and hotels. And everyone, it seemed, expressed opinions and spread gossip. "There were sensational rumours every night, and denials every morning," journalist George Slocombe recalled.

The journalists crammed into a new hotel overlooking the harbor, where rooms were cheap at $1.50 a night. Davidson noted that the throngs of foreign journalists, including Slocombe, Guy Hickok, Max Eastman, and George

Seldes, seemed to outnumber the delegates, who came in droves themselves. In a letter to his wife, Yvonne, he wrote that politics was hardly the only motivation that brought so many, certainly including Steffens, to Italy in the spring: "The sun, shining, the Mediterranean, is all that has been written about it, a gradation of deep lustrous blue to bottle-green, beautiful hills dotted with trees and Italian villas."

The main news at the start of the conference was that the Russians were coming, and they arrived with a bloated delegation of more than eighty. With Mussolini poised to take power in Italy, the presence of the Russians was acknowledged by tight security across the city. But running street clashes between young Italian communists and Mussolini's Fascisti, determined to shut out the Red menace, reminded the diplomats that peace was merely a veneer in Italy and in much of postwar Europe as well. Slocombe, after viewing the Genoa slums, observed that such misery may have given birth to the whole communist movement in Italy.

Surprisingly, Steffens found himself working as a paid reporter in Genoa, having been "loafing along" in the city until he received an offer from Hearst's Universal Service to assist its correspondent there. The setting was ideal. "It is just like old times at Paris," Steffens told Laura. Davidson was so busy again with his work, as Steffens had expected, that the president of Ukraine, while sitting for his own bust, joked, "It seems that posing for one's bust is part of the business of the Genoa Conference."

Steffens invited Seldes, Davidson, and others to join him at a trattoria in a working-class area—a wall bore the graffiti *Viva Lenin*—for nightly gatherings of enthusiastic drinking and conversation. Ernest Hemingway, who covered the conference for the *Toronto Star* but left Genoa before Steffens's arrival, had earlier regaled the journalists with his Italian war stories, yet, Seldes noted, "mostly we listened to Steffens."

The first shock of the conference came on April 16, when the unwanted and unexpected—at least by the Western allies—Treaty of Rapallo was signed by the two problem children, Germany and Russia. By establishing diplomatic relations—the first significant recognition the Bolsheviks had received in Europe—the treaty ended the political isolation of each country. Negotiated by foreign ministers Walter Rathenau and Georgy Chicherin, the agreement promised economic cooperation and signified that neither country intended to remain at the mercy of the West.

Next, on May 2, came an eruption that, given the number of oilmen and reporters crowded into the conference, was nearly inevitable. The Genoa "oil scandal," as it came to be known, involved an explosive rumor of a deal allowing a British oil group a monopoly on Russian petroleum. The story, reported in numerous versions in papers around the world, caused a momentary uproar among oil companies and diplomats. In fact, there had been talks between the two sides but no signed agreement or even any discussion of ownership of the Russian oil fields. In his autobiography, Steffens's compelling portrait of the scandal offered more imagination than fact, focusing on a young journalist, Sam Spewack, who sniffed out the oil deal, broke the story singlehandedly, and faced down Lloyd George at a news conference. Spewack, then a young journalist for *The World*, did go on to fame as a Tony-award-winning Broadway playwright, but Steffens gave him something of the Broadway treatment himself in his own version of the Genoa oil business. Still, Steffens's larger point—that oil drove much of the Genoa agenda—was right on target.

Slocombe reported that Steffens made a rather inept but unsurprising attempt to insert himself into the political maneuverings of the conference. In Slocombe's presence at the Hôtel de Gênes, Steffens again met with Russian Foreign Minister Chicherin, who, according to Slocombe, had only a vague memory of either Steffens or Bullitt from their clandestine visit to Russia. Regardless, Steffens, recalling America's aggressive designs on Mexican oil, suggested to Chicherin that Russia not sell but lease certain lands to the West, possibly placating both sides. But Mexican history held little interest for the proud Russian intellectual, abruptly ending any role Steffens had hoped to play in high-stakes oil negotiations.

The Genoa conference broke up in mid-May, having strained British-French relations, ridiculed the League of Nations, infuriated Germany and Russia, largely ignored the Italy-Yugoslavia dispute over Fiume, avoided other festering border skirmishes, and exasperated, to some extent, nearly every country attending. The blame, many believed, fell on the shoulders of Lloyd George, who had arrived in Genoa with such high hopes, but due to impatience, hubris, and the immense challenge of the task itself, had fallen far short of success. Viewing the diplomatic carnage, Steffens gave his own summary of the proceedings: "What a farce!"

Steffens headed from Genoa directly to Germany and from there, he hoped, to Russia. Although he found Germany, more than three years removed from the war's end, still a dependent and defeated country, Steffens himself enjoyed an inexpensive and pleasant stay. He worked on *Moses in Red* ("I can't finish it because I have no English Bible here, but I can't let it alone either," he told Laura and Allen), debated the Russian situation with Emma Goldman ("she still denounces the Communists"), and passed leisurely days of morning and after-noon walks, early evening naps, a public concert, and finally "bed; study Italian; sleep." The trip to Russia, however, did not materialize.

By the summer, Steffens had left Germany for France, where he spent the rest of the year, mainly in Paris. He naturally kept abreast of the ongoing peace negotiations in Paris and reported much of it back to Laura and Allen. As he watched the European powers attempt to produce order from the geograph-ical chaos left by the war and Versailles, he noted to Laura and Allen with some humor that justice concerning territorial borders and the independence of nations had been upstaged by the old three-letter word that had so recently fascinated the conferees in Genoa:

> The trouble down there in Asia Minor is oil. The British jumped in while the war was on and nobody looking, and they copped off all the good things they could see. . . . The French woke up late to what had happened; they were awfully busy, you remember, fighting Germany. The war was over before they realized that their friend and ally had gone in behind their back and gobbled up a lot of good things from among the weaker nations and so extended the Empire during the war against empire. The French were told to go on down there and get what was left. . . . But all the while the French were at it, the British were having the French accused of imperialism and militarism! And the French were denying the charge! Talk about comedy!

As a place to call home in 1922, Paris, the moveable feast for a lost genera-tion, served Steffens exceedingly well. He already knew, or would soon meet, many of the great writers who had flocked to the city, including Ford Madox Ford, Ezra Pound, and John Dos Passos. One of the true revolutionary art-ists, Steffens agreed, was Gertrude Stein. When young worshippers descended on her apartment at 27 rue de Fleurus, "she gave them all they would take," Steffens recalled in his autobiography. Jo Davidson completed a large, marble statue of her, a "massive, serene Buddha," as Steffens saw it, one that befit her abundant physical and intellectual presence. He remembered her "perfect little dinners," where "you felt there her self contentment and shared her com-posure," catching "glimpses of what a Buddha can see by sitting and quietly looking."

Another "good revolutionary influence" was Pound, who, Steffens observed, "incited the younger men to jump the barriers." At the time, Pound evidently was impressed by how far Steffens himself had gone on the Russians. He attended a talk Steffens gave on October 29 and, as Mary Colum noted rather ruefully in her memoir, was utterly captivated:

> Ezra insisted on taking us to a lecture by Lincoln Steffens on Soviet Russia. . . . The lecture seemed to me of an appalling dreariness, and I hated being dragged to it, with all the interesting things in Paris one could go to. But Ezra listened to it with rapt attention, his eyes glued to the speaker's face, the very type of a young man in search of an ideology, except that he was not so very young. He seemed to have an intense interest in new political and economic ideas.

Pound's political intensity, however, would eventually lead him not to Bolshevik Russia but to Fascist Italy, where both Steffens and he would share a fascination for the dictatorship of Mussolini.

Steffens's favorite, though, was Hemingway. When they first met is not exactly clear. By July, Steffens had become part of the stream of illustrious visitors to Gertrude Stein's apartment, where he may well have met Hemingway at least briefly. The same could have been true at the welcoming apartment of William and Sally Bird, founders of Three Mountains Press, who provided a place "for the rebels to conspire and play in," Steffens noted. Although the Birds's apartment was small, the couple "gathered in the workers, writers, painters, musicians. That's where I observed the best of them," he recalled fondly. The two did meet at the Lausanne conference that November.

To Steffens, not only did Hemingway have a writer's imagination, but his personality—Hemingway the dynamo—was striking: "Walking along the street with him, he would go boxing in the air, fishing, bull-baiting—all the motions. In Paris, where they approve all eccentricities, nobody noticed except to smile with this big, handsome boy, squaring off to phantom-fight you. He was gay, he was sentimental, but he was always at work. . . . He was forever playing he was what he was writing. And he was straight, hard-boiled honest, too."

Some years later, in a Chinese restaurant in Paris, Hemingway and Dos Passos tried to convince Ella that she could be a writer. Steffens recalled that Hemingway, making a left jab at her jaw, told her, "You can. It's hell. It takes it all out of you; it really kills you; but you can do it. Anybody can," adding, "Even you can, Stef." After he had listened to a number of Steffens's worldly stories, Hemingway considered writing his biography.

Steffens admired Hemingway for his devotion to his craft. After reading *1919* years later, he felt the same about Dos Passos. "He does it," Steffens observed. Dos Passos "is one of the three of four kids in literature who are breaking away from the old schools and seeking, and in this case finding, a new way to get nearer to the art of showing things as they are, beautifully." Hemingway himself believed that the craft of writing demanded honesty and persistence. Steffens conceded that it might be a matter of "utter honesty and hard labor," but added, "my association with writers like Hemingway has persuaded me that it is a mere matter of genius, not any moral or intellectual gifts; authors are seldom even intelligent; art is evidently the effect of some fairy's wand waved over the wrong infant before even the fairy could judge."

The fairy, Steffens observed, had touched another exile in Paris. The novel that would cause the greatest literary stir of the century inspired him to write a lengthy letter to Allen in October in praise of the work: "I have been reading a book which I recommend, certainly to all writers and with reserves to all wishers to know and understand men. *Ulysses*, by James Joyce." While Joyce in his psychological analysis may have gone "wrong on some people," Steffens noted, the book, just published in Paris, impressed him immensely. "Joyce has said the first, not the last word, in the artistic handling of the subconscious. He makes a lot of old writing look void," Steffens wrote, not afraid to add, "He thinks a lot like me."

Two months later, Steffens and Jo Davidson, who did two busts of Joyce, were invited to an afternoon tea to meet the literary lion. Steffens's letter to Laura shows that Joyce's reputation for ill health certainly preceded him: "I hear that Joyce is an empty man. He put all he had into that book, spent ten years on it and now talks only of his ills: he is almost blind, has other troubles and they so interest him that he talks of nothing else. As somebody said, Nature used him up and has cast him aside empty. But we'll see. Everybody isn't a very good reporter." Steffens evidently found that "everybody" was correct about Joyce on that occasion, but he was happy to report to Allen the following summer that the situation for the afflicted Irishman had markedly improved. Steffens had stopped in a restaurant to chat with Joyce, his partner Nora, his daughter Lucia, and Pound and found Joyce looking "very much better than when I saw him last winter; he talked with some life."

24

<hr>

THE FUTURE REVISITED

IN THE EARLY 1920s, Steffens witnessed on the European political scene a bold, new face who had every intention of breaking ranks: Italy's Benito Mussolini. Steffens had seen the severe unrest in Italy and expected dramatic changes, maybe even rivaling those in Russia, from the Italians. But the changes in Italy ultimately would come from the opposite end of the political spectrum and in a relatively milder form, with Mussolini's stamp of Fascism dominating his country for years after Lenin's death brought on the even more brutal reign of Stalin.

If the war had left millions of Russians destitute and angry, Italians, who were on the victorious Allied side, felt hardly less aggrieved. Postwar Italy was a land of devastation. Businesses failed, workers could not earn a living, strikes and shortages abounded, millions of returning soldiers found little assistance, inflation was rampant, the lira was almost worthless, and even the spoils of territory the victorious Italians had been promised proved an illusion. The huge popularity of the socialists in 1919–1920 resulted merely in ongoing deprivation for the average Italian. After watching their battered country be pushed by the Left to the brink of chaos, middle-class, conservative Italians, who had supported the war only to feel betrayed in its aftermath, reacted by pinning their hopes on the compelling figure of Mussolini. Skillfully consolidating his own power, Mussolini, following his dramatic march—unopposed—on Rome, had installed himself as the leader of Italy by the end of October 1922.

The Lausanne conference was held a month later, convened among diplomats largely from England, France, Italy, Greece, and Turkey to settle the territorial dispute between the Turks and the Allies, particularly the Greeks, that had outlasted the war. Steffens and another Genoa-sized crowd of journalists at the conference looked forward to gauging what the brash Italian leader had in mind for his country. When the reporters gathered in a hotel suite with Mussolini, Steffens recounted, the Italian leader made certain that they would understand the disdain he felt toward his interrogators: Mussolini pointedly read silently from a French-English dictionary that he was holding upside down. The reporters quietly seethed, although Steffens thought it was great theater.

Once he was certain that his message had been received, Mussolini threw down the book and demanded questions, meeting only more silence. In French, Mussolini again challenged them to speak. The first victim was a writer for *Le Temps*, which had been highly critical of Il Duce. In a wavering voice, the French writer managed to utter an inquiry as to the chances of peace being achieved at Lausanne, before the thunder struck. "*Le Temps*! *Le Temps*!" Mussolini sneered, leaning forward to confront the poor man. Then he turned to the other journalists with equal disrespect, giving brief, curt answers signaling his utter boredom.

Steffens's fate was no different. When he asked Mussolini how he had seized power so precipitously in an enlightened country such as Italy, Mussolini's "fierce face expressed his contempt for me and my kind and our dead logic," Steffens recalled in his autobiography. Mocking him, Mussolini asked, "You're a correspondent? Yes. You saw the war? Yes. And the peace? Yes. And the revolution in Russia? Yes. Well, did you learn anything?" In the face of the onslaught, Steffens muttered that, yes, he had learned some things. "Some things!" Mussolini boomed. "Do you think now any of the things you thought before you saw the war, the peace, and the revolution?" The exchange evidently was most memorable. In a letter to Upton Sinclair in 1935, Ezra Pound pointedly recalled the uncomfortable moment: "I hear Steff has at last decided to play in. Hell, thass a ten years delay. However, the Muss. once asked HIM (Steff) hadn't he LEARNED anything."

What a question to ask Steffens, the disciple of unlearning. Had he unlearned anything over the previous decade? Not enough, Steffens conceded to himself. The whole episode later reminded him of his encounter with Einstein in Berlin. Steffens had asked Einstein how he had been able to see what other brilliant scientists could not. "How did you ever do it?" Steffens inquired. Einstein simply answered, "By challenging an axiom."

And that was the key, Steffens felt, to Mussolini. While he had an overwhelming personality and an insatiable lust for power, he also could think and learn—and adapt. He had been a vocal socialist calling for reform, had seen the success as well as the struggles of Lenin in Russia, and then had chosen for Italy not a move to the left but in the opposite direction. "Was that what the divine Dictator meant us to see—that there was a method, good either way?" Steffens wondered.

The Lausanne peace talks themselves, Steffens saw, mocked democracy with countless speeches and promises, and had sunk, exhausted, to a comic level. He described the scene to Allen:

> They are doing little about peace, so little that [British Foreign Secretary] Lord Curzon, who presides, cautioned the delegates yesterday to speak more of peace. He advised that they mention at least the word in every speech they make. Of course the reason Curzon said that is that he is just now under the influence of [Emile] Coué, the mental curist, who makes all his patients say twenty times each day: "I am better today in every way than I was yesterday," but the advice really shows the state of affairs at this conference.

The West, as Steffens saw at Lausanne, had no plan except to return to the old ways of governance. England and France were back in charge of Europe and still bickering over which of them owned the oil in the Middle East. Mussolini had become the latest strongman in Europe to seize his country's imagination. America, again on the diplomatic sidelines (except to insist on its own oil grab in Iraq), sent only observers to the conference. But with Wilson out of office and nearly out of life itself, replaced by a president who, it was widely understood, was a figurehead, America was no longer the player it had been in Paris. After eleven weeks of political entertainment, the conference dissolved in February 1923, not to reconvene for five months.

Lausanne had attracted many of the same reporters from Genoa, including Hemingway, who, with Steffens by his side, received some jarring news in early December. Hemingway had shown Steffens his horse racing story, "My Old Man," which Steffens liked so well that he insisted on submitting it with a personal note to an editorial friend at *Cosmopolitan*. (The story, despite Steffens's help, was rejected.) Steffens, also impressed by a dispatch Hemingway had written while covering the agonizing return of a million destitute Greeks trudging home across Asia Minor ahead of the conquering Turks, remarked that the scene depicted by Hemingway was vivid in his mind.

"No," Hemingway corrected him. "Read the cabelese, only the cabelese. Isn't it a great language?"

Steffens agreed, seeing Hemingway as the young writer with the "surest future." He sent a complimentary note to Hemingway's wife, Hadley, on her husband's talent, and asked Hemingway if he could see more of his work. Steffens's attention obviously excited Hemingway, as he instructed Hadley, who had been ill and remained in Paris, to send him the rest of his work. Hadley told a Hemingway biographer that she was eager to get the manuscripts to her husband "because of Ernest's letters singing high praises of Lincoln Steffens, his new friend, to whom I felt certain he would want to show these chapters."

Afraid of losing the manuscripts in the mail, Hadley decided to carry them herself, so she packed everything except the story "Up in Michigan" in her suitcase and prepared to join her husband by train. At the Gare de Lyon in Paris, however, disaster struck. After finding a seat on the train and placing the suitcase on a luggage rack, Hadley left the train and passed about half an hour strolling along the platform. When she returned to her seat, the suitcase was gone. Much of what Hemingway had written—an unfinished novel, around a dozen stories, and some poems, including handwritten originals, typescripts, and carbon copies—all packed neatly in manila folders, was lost.

Steffens accompanied Hemingway to the train station on December 3, where Hadley, petrified, broke the news. "I had never seen anyone hurt by a thing other than death or unbearable suffering except Hadley when she told me about the things being gone," Hemingway recalled. "She . . . cried and cried and could not tell me." How Hemingway himself felt about the mishap, which became a legendary part of his life story, remains unclear. Hadley told Hemingway's sister, Marcelline, that the episode nearly killed him, and Hemingway certainly made efforts to maintain the drama at Hadley's expense: "3 years on the damn stuff," he complained to Pound, and later went much further in *The Garden of Eden*, where Catherine Bourne steals her husband's stories and burns them.

Steffens, however, thought that Hemingway took the news bravely. And apparently without panic, as it was Steffens and Guy Hickok, not Hemingway (as he claimed in *A Moveable Feast*), who soon returned to Paris and checked the station's lost-and-found office for the missing works. But on December 9, Steffens reported to Hemingway that nothing had turned up and that a reward of 150 francs, which Hemingway had suggested to publisher William Bird, would need to be significantly higher. After hearing the disheartening news, Hemingway, in fact, spent Christmas skiing with Hadley and friends and did not return to Paris until mid-January.

In *A Moveable Feast*, Hemingway wrote that Hadley had planned to surprise him in Lausanne with the manuscripts. While she certainly did surprise him, Hemingway's memory must have betrayed him, as both Hadley, who even in old age could not recall the incident without crying, and their son, Jack, connected Steffens, innocently, to the calamity. Hadley said that she packed the manuscripts only because of Hemingway's excitement over Steffens's enthusiasm for his work, which she had heard from both, while Jack was certain that his mother brought the manuscripts on specific instructions from Hemingway, recalling many conversations in which both parents indicated that Hemingway, in fact, had requested the manuscripts. "He specifically wanted to show the things to Lincoln Steffens," Jack said.

And ultimately, as literary critic Malcolm Cowley noted, it may not have been the literary disaster it seemed: "With his work destroyed as if by fire, he could start from the beginning and build another structure on new lines. . . . I have known many apprentice writers, but no other who was willing, at twenty-three, to put aside everything he thought he had learned and start again with the simplest things." Steffens encouraged him with blunt but necessary advice: "I am afraid the stuff is lost, Hem. . . . I am sorry, but I guess you will have to rewrite your 'early works' or do better things hereafter to make up for them."

Steffens, through with Lausanne, intended to relax over the winter holidays in Paris. But the curious phenomenon of the French psychotherapist Emile Coué, whose mantra of positive thinking Steffens had mocked at Lausanne, changed his plans. With Davidson, who wanted to do a bust of Coué, Steffens visited Coué's office in Nancy, where they waited among a crowd of "halt, lame and nerve shattered people who came from all over, hoping for miracles," Davidson recalled. Steffens did not need a miracle, but he took the treatment anyway, failing the test of keeping his hands clasped because, as he recounted the moment, "I did not think I could not open. I thought: 'This is interesting. I will see if I can open,' and of course I could and did." He did have some fun one night at Davidson's expense by repeating, "It will pass, it will pass," when he wished for a bowel movement and subsequently hurried to the bathroom. "Jo nearly died," he told Gussie. In the end, Davidson got his bust and Steffens grudgingly acknowledged that Coué was admired by a considerable number of satisfied patients.

On January 31, 1923, Steffens sailed for New York. His sisters, Allen, and Gussie had all chided him for his whirlwind lifestyle that was producing, as far as they could see, very little writing. Steffens himself acknowledged to Laura, "My conscience talks about it all the time. I must do something."

What he did, however, was merely more of the same, traveling on to California to pursue his favorite hobbies of listening and talking. From San Francisco, he complained to Davidson that the sculptor was "a darned stinker" for not sending Steffens enough gossip from Paris but was delighted to be back in his California circle again. "A great crowd. As warm and good as our gang in Paris," he glowed. Laura, Allen, Fremont Older, and an assorted collection of labor leaders, writers, and an occasional "poet or an ex-convict, an editorial writer or crooked lawyer—anybody that is 'wise'" all congregated regularly with Steffens. Not that everyone in California was pleased to see the native son. The editor of *The Sacramento Bee* leveled a blistering attack on him, calling Steffens "a Radical and a Red of the deepest dye. . . . The proper place for Lincoln Steffens is in jail." Steffens remained unpeturbed. An indignant newspaper editor could not faze a man who had been banned from the British Empire.

Steffens was in New York for the spring and again in Paris with Gussie by summer. They idled away several weeks in Italy, including "bully excursions" by boat to Capri and Ravello. "Boating is the way," he raved to Laura. "I would be glad to do the Greek Isles on a yacht." His deceptive ways with Gussie, though, continued, as Steffens was quick to grab the mail each day in their Sorrento hotel, eager to remove any letters from Ella that surely added to his delight in the Italian sun.

On instructions from Glenn Frank, who wanted Steffens to write a series of articles on Italy, France, Germany, and Russia for *Century*, he tried for another interview with Mussolini but was turned down. Interestingly, others from the former *McClure's* group were equally fascinated by the Italian strongman. Several years later, Mussolini evidently enthralled Ida Tarbell in a thirty-minute interview that he closed by kissing her hand, leading the witty Viola Roseboro, a manuscript reader at *McClure's*, to observe, "Mussolini certainly did put the comehither on the statesman lady." Tarbell's three-part series for *McCall's* on Mussolini, "The Greatest Story in the World Today," proclaimed that Mussolini was Italy's Moses. Sam McClure also fell under the spell of Il Duce, reporting to his wife that he found him "full of force & Charm and kindliness" and adding for emphasis that his own heart "beat hard for a long time after I met him." Possibly after years of documenting the theft of American democracy, the former muckrakers were eager to observe how an intelligent, patriotic leader would cleanse such an infested system.

In late August 1923, Gussie returned to America, having given Steffens her blessing to remain in Europe. "She wants me to do whatever I feel like doing so long as it is work, and I love her for that," Steffens wrote to Laura, perhaps intentionally ignoring Gussie's obvious contrast between work and Ella. Free again to roam, Steffens made what would be his final trip to "the future" (now known as the Union of Soviet Socialist Republics, but always "Russia" to Steffens), leaving from Berlin on August 31. With a small group that included

Robert La Follette and Jo Davidson, who hoped to get a bust of Lenin (but did not—Lenin was too ill), Steffens experienced a veritable homecoming.

After a rough trip crossing the Baltic, the party stayed briefly in Petrograd before arriving in Moscow "on a perfect train of Pullmans, with every comfort," and was settled in the "best guest-house," Steffens reported. But Steffens opted for a less costly hotel with more colorful gossip while meeting with friends "a-plenty." Max Eastman, Rhys Williams, and Anna Louise Strong all greeted him, as did Bill Haywood, having fled the United States to escape a jail sentence. The future had not been kind, however, to Haywood, "the loneliest soul in Asia," Steffens judged. After receiving a personal welcome from Lenin, Haywood fell into disfavor with the Soviet government, and in 1928, alone in Russia, the once fiery revolutionary would meet a broken, pathetic death.

Various government officials, sitting for Davidson, spoke frankly with Steffens on Russian life. Night after night, Steffens and his friends took in concerts, operas, and ballets. Davidson observed that entertainment was booming in the city, theaters in particular buzzing with patrons. Steffens even received an invitation to a sunny Crimean resort, which he declined only to avoid a return across northern Europe in winter. All in all, Steffens saw "a city come to life."

The government encouraged him to speak with opposition parties. If Steffens took up the offer, however, whatever criticism he heard had little effect. While La Follette came away from the trip appalled by the brutal Bolshevik approach to governance, Steffens found that the future of Russia looked brighter than ever. In his letters, Steffens could hardly heap enough praise on the communist state. It was as if he had waited a lifetime to witness a successful revolution, and Russia, no matter how untidy, was it. He also rarely hesitated to remind others—and himself, undoubtedly—that in the face of international ridicule, he had been right. He proudly told Gussie, "The big points are that the Bolsheviki have yielded nothing. They are on their course, proceeding as they began and they intend to see it through ruthlessly. . . . Conditions are amazingly improved and their state machine of federated industries is pulling out of the hole of war, famine and corruption. All that I said about this is true, still true. I had begun to doubt myself, but I needn't have doubted."

On September 30, Steffens returned to Paris, exhausted from "six weeks on the go" and a "slow, nervous, wearing journey" home. Several days after returning, he had tea with Pound and Ford Madox Ford, who discussed progress on Ford's new magazine, *The Transatlantic Review*, and saw Hutchins Hapgood as well. Meanwhile, Steffens poured out his Russian euphoria in letters across the ocean. To Laura, he echoed his words to Gussie three weeks earlier: "Russia is strong. All I have ever said about it is true, and more also. The Bolsheviki have not retreated, they have not yielded, they don't mean to surrender." His greatest words of praise for Russia and the inevitable future that he saw came in a long, effusive letter aimed at lifting the spirits of Fremont Older, weary but unrepentant in his fight to reform San Francisco: "The brave new Thing is here. They may have to fight, but . . . the New will win. You can go up on the ranch and watch the sun rise tomorrow morning, and you can make a face at it. For I tell you that the human sunrise I have been seeing is beautiful, colorful, sure as that of the daily Light." Steffens would not return to Russia, but he never again doubted its legitimacy.

By the fall of 1923, Steffens had outlasted the will of the British government and, three years after his request, was issued a visa. In late October, he was in London, which meant Ella Winter. Steffens initially planned to return to Paris after a couple of weeks in London, spending some of his time researching the Bible for *Moses in Red* and much of the rest with Ella, who was doing her own research at Cambridge. In Steffens's absence, Ella had not spent her time idly. Believing that Steffens would be a close friend but nothing more, she had been seeking a love of her own, only to find that while there was no shortage of men willing to date her, most had no interest in commitment. Two did propose marriage, including the widowed father of a close friend. Still, she had missed Steffens deeply, and watching her father suffer a slow, painful death from cancer had increased her emotional isolation. For Ella, the return of Steffens was a blessing.

The two weeks, not surprisingly, stretched into three months, during which Steffens confessed to the dilemma he had created—again—with Gussie by refusing to make a necessary choice. As was often the case, Steffens acknowledged that his own behavior mystified him. "Logic doesn't work in human relations, I guess," he told Ella. "I try to understand myself as I tried to understand the bosses in my muckraking days. I 'got' them, but not myself. I don't know anything about myself. I'm as much a dub as any man can be about personal relations." Ella felt some sympathy for Gussie, but, in all likelihood, probably not much more than Steffens, who, Mabel Dodge observed, always had "a small devil in him that liked to play with dynamite in human souls." Back again with Steffens, Ella wrote, "we were illicit, illegal, and deliriously happy."

Steffens was next on the move to Paris at the invitation of Louise Bryant, to discuss the ill-fated Reed, who had suffered what was seen by some as a tragic but glorious revolutionary death from typhus in Russia three years earlier. In a curious twist, Bryant had gone on to marry William Bullitt, whose own mission in Russia, as well as his previous marriage, had ended rather differently. With a laugh, Steffens remarked to Ella, "Louise is going to have Billy's baby, and she wants to talk about her first husband, Jack." Bryant also insisted that Steffens be present for the birth, apparently still viewing him as both a good friend and a parental figure. Ella, telling her mother that she would be doing some translation work (a technical truth—she was translating a German book on the intelligence of apes), crossed the channel with Steffens in February 1924.

Steffens continued to write, with minimal success. He worked doggedly on his Moses story, while Ford included a Steffens piece on Russia, titled "N.E.P.'s," in the February issue of *The Transatlantic Review*. Ford, however, quickly regretted his involvement with a Bolshevik sympathizer. Although he considered himself an old Tory, Ford found that he was in the slightly ridiculous position of having to fend off charges of promoting Reds. Chastened, Ford never again used a politically charged article in *The Transatlantic Review*.

Although they stayed in different apartments in a weak attempt at propriety, Steffens and Ella were inseparable, with Steffens proudly introducing her to his own Paris circles. In addition to socializing with Bryant and Bullitt, they became close friends with Jo and Yvonne Davidson, attending the theater (Steffens at times in an evening cape and silk hat) and dining together to the point that Ella and Yvonne developed a particular mutual fondness. Through Steffens, Ella entered the vital world of Sylvia Beach's bookshop, Shakespeare and Company, where she met Margaret Anderson and Jane Heap, publishers of the journal *Little Review*, which had caused such controversy by printing excerpts from Joyce's *Ulysses*. One night, when Bullitt heard Steffens reading aloud from *Ulysses*, Bullitt shouted at him, "Think of the baby, our child—what will it turn out to be if it hears language like that?" In Guy Hickok's Paris office of the *Brooklyn Daily Eagle*, Ella saw a great deal of Hemingway, who often sat slumped in a chair, mumbling about boxing, shooting, skiing, or bicycle races before jumping up in great excitement and sparring alone. Ella was closer to Hadley, a "somewhat bewildered" wife, Ella thought, who tried her best to accommodate Hemingway's demanding lifestyle while caring for their infant son, Bumby. At Gertrude Stein's apartment, Ella befriended Alice B. Toklas while Stein directed her attention to her more renowned guests, Jo Davidson being a favorite. Ella felt both the keen embarrassment of her own inexperience and Stein's haughty nature when Steffens once asked Stein for advice on how Ella should pursue a writing career. The full response from the Buddha was, "Write." Like Stein, the indefatigable Ezra Pound possessed "undaunted assurance" but had given up hope on Hemingway, he told Steffens, because the ambitious young writer had produced a story with "a clear meaning."

By spring, Steffens desired some sun and a place to write, so they headed south to the small Italian village of Ospedaletti, just over the French border along the Riviera, leaving behind an astonished Hemingway and undoubtedly others as well. In a letter giving Pound "the dirt as it appears" and a typical dose of his anti-Semitism, Hemingway reported, "Abe Linc Steffens gone off to Italy with objectionable 22 year old Bloomsbury Jewine who treats him like Gauguin treated Van Gogh." Hemingway apparently reveled in the delicious scandal. Two months later, again writing to Pound, he turned Ella into a teenager: "You heard of course of Steffens marriage to a 19 year old Bloomsbury Kike intellectual. The last chapter in the book of Revolution."

Events could only have increased Hemingway's fascination. In the spring warmth of Ospedaletti, the titillating love story reached fruition: Ella was pregnant. The news stunned Steffens. He had lived more than fifty years without "a conscious wish" for a child and had expected to pass many more in the same manner. He thought he might even be sterile, given his experience with Josephine. Now, an Italian doctor was telling him that in seven or eight months, fatherhood would be upon him. "I stared at the man a dizzy moment," Steffens wrote, "then picked up my fallen jaw and went to a window overlooking the sea, the Mediterranean—the road to China—where I was going next, to Siam and the South Seas, to liberty and learning. I saw, blocking the course of every ship that sailed, a baby—a muling, puling, bawling tyrant."

Hours of bewilderment passed before it occurred to Steffens that subconsciously, he had always wished for a child but had been too preoccupied to acknowledge it. Ella, unwed and supposedly in Europe working on a translation, had been equally stunned by the revelation from the doctor. She had expected to be a career woman, active in the politics and culture of her time—not cloistered in a house as the mother of an illegitimate child. Her mother, appalled, initially warned her that she would not have the child in her home. Sick day after day, Ella unleashed her frustration not on Steffens or the baby but, of all things, the Italian Riviera. "I hate this place," she complained, possibly echoing the sentiments of some other expectant mothers there but assuredly no one else. By the end of April, they were on the move again, settling in a beach hotel in nearby Alassio.

All that separated Steffens from complete bliss during this time was the realization that he had betrayed Gussie, not for the first time and not when she was healthy enough to withstand such a blow. Over the next few months,

Steffens relied heavily on Laura, as did Ella and Gussie herself, for understanding. Steffens called his sister "the Supreme Court of Final Appeal for us all." Laura's patience in reading and responding to all of Steffens's lengthy, confused letters filled with guilt, doubt, denial, and, most of all, hope was a great comfort, although even Laura's understanding had its limits. In a moment of aggravation, undoubtedly intensified by Gussie's suffering, she told Steffens, "You used to be a genius and unique, now you're going to be a father and there are millions of those." Allen later explained to Ella that Laura fretted ceaselessly over her brother's well-being. "In fact," he told her, "she doesn't think you give him a break."

Steffens's first cry to Laura, among several, went out on April 16. After a detailed explanation of how he initially got mixed up with "that London girl," as Laura called her, Steffens focused on the obvious dilemma, admitting, "It's the second time I have done this to her!. . . . One of the deepest secret desires of my life is about to be fulfilled. If it were not for G., I'd be inexpressibly happy. As it is, I am,—all mixed up."

It was late May before Steffens received Laura's answer expressing her understanding of the plight of both Steffens and Gussie, if not her approval of her brother's handling of the predicament. Steffens was relieved by her tempered reply, although a solution eluded him still. "I don't seem to care how miserable I am or may be; what hurts so is that I am hurting other people: you and G. and our friends, who never will understand. How can they, when I don't?" he asked. He reported that he had received "a long, firm, kind and yet very proud letter" from Gussie, asking for one month together with Steffens that summer, which he quickly agreed to. He closed by repeating his own confusion: "I love them both; in different ways, but both truly, genuinely. How can this be? I don't know."

In her grief, Gussie was firing off long, nearly daily letters to Laura as well, clearly struggling to accept her unfortunate fate. Her words were heavy with emotion: "L has let me go out of his life without one word of respect"; "L himself does not think the union will be permanent"; "How could he hurt me so often!"; "I am surprised at myself but can't help feeling that I have had all the suffering"; "L repudiated everything he had ever written me and so I gave up trying to understand what had happened."

At the same time that he agonized over Gussie, Steffens, in typical fashion, thoroughly enjoyed Ella's company and the beauty of Italy. Spending most of his time with Ella along the warm Italian Riviera that he often proudly compared to California, Steffens at fifty-eight found life gratifying. He brought Ella to Florence to show her off and perhaps lift her spirits by introducing her to Charles Erskine Scott Wood and Sara Bard Field, surprising them at breakfast one morning in their hotel. "I think that you and Sara have to learn to practice my theory: that there is a time in life when we should cease to carry the burdens of this world, withdraw from the fighting and working, and become spectators," Steffens had written to Wood, prompting the California couple to embark on their leisurely tour of Europe.

Unmarried and with a wide difference in ages, like Steffens and Ella, they did not lack for eccentricities. Wood, with his flowing white hair, scraggly beard, and outspoken radical views, was another of Steffens's colorful friends—they had met in Oregon when Steffens was reporting on the land fraud case—with an improbable past. At various times a soldier, a lawyer, and a poet, and always a savant with a zest for life, "the Colonel" had graduated from West Point, fought in the Nez Perce War, become close to Chief Joseph, defended Emma Goldman, written for *The Masses*, and befriended Twain, Steinbeck, Darrow, and Ansel Adams, among others. "He's a remarkable proof that a human can survive the system," Steffens observed. Sara, married to a minister at the time, had initially met Wood through Darrow in 1910 and encountered Steffens the following year at the McNamara trial while working as a novice reporter from Oregon. In 1914, she divorced, transforming herself into a crusading suffragette.

Ella took to the new couple immediately, and they spent memorable days exploring the small, scenic towns dotting Tuscany, San Gimignano being a favorite. All four would remain lifelong friends. Twenty years later, Ella wrote to Sara, "You two practically ushered in my whole adult life, our marriage, our baby—the greatest thing in Stef's life, his greatest joy and certainly now mine. From those days in Florence on you always meant more to us, in a deeper and more personal way, than any other element we came in contact with."

In his restless way, Steffens contemplated a return to New York, telling Filene that he had no interest in campaigning for Calvin Coolidge, but "if the Democrats should put up a man I would like to see get into the White House, I am sure I could help such a man by making a stump tour for the President, with the true reasons for reelecting him." In the meantime, Steffens and Ella took a leisurely and idyllic summer trip down the coastline and across the scenic, green hills of the Italian countryside, from Genoa to Rapallo, Portofino, and Milan before reaching their final destination, Lake Como ("about like Tahoe") and Bellagio, where they spent most of July.

Pondering his literary future, he settled on an idea that perfectly suited a muckraker who had cajoled and chided presidents, promoted revolutions, met newsmakers on both sides of the Atlantic, fallen in love with a woman nearly young enough to be his granddaughter, and entered on fatherhood in his fifties: "This winter I intend to write my own Life," he told Filene, warning him, "You business men might buy me off from this dire purpose; it would be worth a good deal to you to stop it."

The prospect of writing a memoir was hardly new to Steffens. Two years earlier, *Century*'s Glenn Frank, who published a number of Steffens's stories, had offered him $750 per chapter for a serial version of his life, which Steffens found a "very good proposition." "It didn't hit me at the time Glenn Frank asked me for it, and I didn't know I had been chewing it over," he wrote in a May 1922 letter to Laura and Allen. "But evidently I have been considering it, for I find myself actually organizing the thing and it is so uppermost in my under-mind that I am guessing that when I do sit me down to write, that is what I shall find myself doing. No telling, however; not for sure."

Steffens had promised Gussie some time together in August, so he and Ella headed back to Paris. With Ella's pregnancy, the question of marriage loomed over them. Bullitt had informed them that traveling together to America would be difficult if they remained unmarried, a kind of "moral turpitude," reminding them that Maxim Gorky had been rejected for a similar personal dilemma. So Steffens and Ella agreed to marry in a public registry in Paris, with Steffens asserting that the procedure was just to get "that document." Later, he suggested, they should secretly divorce. The wedding ceremony itself, "cold and judicial," Sara Bard Field recalled, filled with bureaucratic belligerence from the French officials, took place on August 19 in Paris. Afterward, the couple were joined at a more cheerful breakfast celebration by the Davidsons, the Bullitts, and Colonel Wood and Sara Bard Field. Jo Davidson entertained the group by making quick sketches on one tablecloth after another, keeping the unfortunate waiter busy replacing them.

Ella was soon off to Bavaria for translation work, leaving Steffens to keep his promise to Gussie. Their first encounter came on August 4, when they walked together in the Tuileries gardens, Gussie unburdening herself. "She had it all pretty much as it is," Steffens wrote to Ella. "Her accusations are true; I admitted them, and it really did her good. The truth is healing. Of course it was distressing; it is, but she was fine. I certainly do respect G.; her mind and her character."

The two spent the next week together, with Gussie doing most of the talking ("she had her indictments all drawn and she presented them one by one") and Steffens making no effort to defend himself. When Gussie revealed that she could not help feeling guilty herself over the situation, Steffens gave a sympathetic ear, aware that the talking itself, in some way, comforted her. "She was relieved," he confided in Laura. "She said so several times, and I could see her face clear gradually and feel her nerves quiet down."

For Steffens, it was a problem without a solution. He blamed Gussie for nothing and deeply regretted that he had to make such choices in life at all, for, as he told Laura, he harbored no animosity toward anyone. "I love G. I love E.W. I love Dr. I love you. I love Older. I love Yvonne Davidson and Jo. I love lots of people and I mean *love*," he wrote. "There are differences, of course, but the biggest is not sex; not with me; and this is no sex adventure, this with E.W. She is a charming, sensitive, understanding person."

Gussie herself understood, finally; there would be no more false hopes, although her earlier illusions about Steffens had provided much of the meaning in her sad life. Steffens, attached to Ella, had made his choice. How he could love two such very different women—one for more than three decades—must have been a mystifying heartache that Gussie carried to her grave.

Hemingway, naturally, commented on Steffens's return to Paris, refusing to feign any sympathy for his troubles. In a letter to Gertrude Stein, he reported, "Steffens is in town with his Old Girl. His wife is with child in Germany. He has got the old one over to show her the new one. Its just like in the monkey house at the Zoo. If this one is a boy he wants to have a girl. His Friends all rally round him. Not me."

Hemingway's evident spite for Ella and his mocking of Steffens's love life, however, may well have been a typical case of Hemingway's glib nature masking a gentleness and generosity of spirit that his friends knew well. In his memoir, Hutchins Hapgood recalled that several years after Steffens's death, when Hemingway and his second wife, Pauline, were living in Key West, Hutchins and Neith saw them on occasion. Over dinner one evening, Hemingway railed against Steffens for his foolish marriage to such a young woman. Hapgood, perfectly aware that both Hemingway and he had been close to Steffens, objected loudly to Hemingway's attack on their old friend. As Neith and Hutchins got into their car and were about to leave, Hemingway, repentant, chased them down. "Hutch," he said, "you know I didn't mean anything against Stef. You know I have always loved him and have really no criticism of him." Hapgood wrote that such an example of Hemingway's "youthful spontaneity" was what appealed to him, and no doubt it had attracted Steffens as well.

By the end of the summer, Ella, now six months pregnant, and Steffens were back in Italy. Ella wanted a warm, clean house with plenty of hot water, while

Steffens preferred a place full of flowers and views of hills and the sea for the
big event. Both found what they were looking for in a villetta in San Remo, just
east of Ospedaletti along the Riviera. When he was not busy inviting the Howes,
the Davidsons, and other friends over for a visit to his "little paradise," Steffens
spent most of his time "swinging along with Satan" (no publisher yet in sight
for *Moses*), reading, and napping. He was thrilled about becoming a parent and
shaping the new life, telling Filene, "It is to be the greatest baby on earth and
is to be brought up dead onto business and statesmen. . . . And it is not to be a
muckraker either."

The statesmen who concerned Steffens that summer were the American presidential candidates. La Follette was putting up a "courageous, hopeless" progressive campaign against President Coolidge and his other challenger, Democrat
John Davis, a campaign that Steffens encouraged Filene to support. "Nobody
likes to pay for dead dogs," Steffens conceded, "but that is the noblest sort
of campaign contribution I know of." Still, Steffens believed that La Follette's
effort was no more relevant to the future than those of the major parties. After
La Follette's respectable but ultimately disappointing showing in the November
election, attracting nearly five million votes (16.6 percent), Steffens told Fred
Howe, himself lamenting the death of liberalism in America, that La Follette and
the progressives made him tired but he would love to give La Follette America
"to play with" even though it was beyond repair.

Howe respected both Steffens and La Follette but held a different perspective. In his view, La Follette alone had carried on the fight for the people. The
prewar radicals, lamentably, had "laid down their arms." Looking around for
the old voices of change, Howe observed, "Steffens spends most of his time in
Europe. . . . Brand Whitlock has gone back to literature, Newton Baker to the
law. Fremont Older edits the San Francisco *Call*. Joseph W. Folk is dead. . . .
Was the fight too hard?" He might have added that Ida Tarbell herself was trumpeting the virtues of big business. Only the lonely crusade of La Follette endured,
as he fought trusts and big money and often his fellow senators to represent the
people. To the end, La Follette "never compromised with a conviction," Howe
wrote.

But, as he explained to Marie Howe, Steffens saw La Follette's vision of
progress as a mirage: "I think his religion has been blown up. It was mine too.
. . . But there has been a war, a revolution, many peacemakings and they were
sad and costly failures. . . . I don't see how any mind could have sat by and seen
all these things happen and not learned,—enough to change our conception
of political conduct. And they were La Follette's methods and creed that were

blown up, not only Lloyd George's." And looking ever faithfully to Russia, he added, "Democracy cannot be achieved by democratic methods."

But in Italy, Steffens's thoughts generally were with Ella and their own future. To others he raved about her, trying to persuade the doubters while assuring those who liked her of their wisdom. He told Laura that Ella was not at all the intellectual, calculating radical that she imagined, although that description was not totally untrue. (Steffens noted that for his taste, Ella was not radical enough.) Conversely, he was delighted by Marie Howe's acceptance of Ella and urged Fred and her to come by as soon as possible. Steffens made no secret of their wish for a girl—they bought only girls' clothes and had stacks of them—who would "have every chance that boys get now; and then some." Ella's mother wanted her to return and have the baby in an English hospital; Steffens insisted the birth would take place in the Italian sunshine and at home, where he could start the child's unlearning. "All the books tell you it's the first weeks that count," he declared. Against the loud protests of their Italian servant, a woman named Giulia who claimed to have given birth to eleven children and lost another nine, Steffens and Ella hired an English maternity nurse who had previously cared for Scott and Zelda Fitzgerald's daughter, Scottie. The wait finally ended on November 21, 1924, and the girls' clothes were unnecessary.

25

FINALLY, A FATHER

PETE STANLEY STEFFENS came into the world at 6½ pounds, lots of space between his eyes, and, as his father proudly noted, no long upper lip—"He will not be righteous," Steffens asserted to Allen. Throughout Ella's labor, Steffens dealt with his own stress by rambling on with the doctor about possible birth defects before retreating to the kitchen, where he swatted forty-three flies before Pete, mercifully, made his appearance.

Never at a loss for words, Steffens spared few in rejoicing over the new family member. Enthusiastically thrusting himself into the time-honored tradition of comparing babies, Steffens, with Pete less than a week old, declared to Jo Davidson, "No doubt other men will be thinking themselves in my class because they have a boy. I mean to put a stop to it. Hemingway, for example,—I got a letter from him today, in many respects a very good letter (considering that he is a young writer not yet respectably published), but he has a boy and he spoke of his boy in the same breath with mine. I am going to call him down too." Steffens, in fact, had sent Hemingway a letter on the very day of the birth: "I can hear him crying up there now. He's sorry he's not a girl, I guess."

The child's name, predictably, also did not escape controversy. Allen felt that "Peter" or even "Stanley" was the proper way to address the boy, but "Pete" seemed to be the one that was taking hold. Steffens assumed that Pete would choose any name he wanted when he grew up, but explained to Allen his initial strategy in the naming game: "I gave him the two names, so different, in order that, if he becomes (as he may) a roughneck, he can be Pete; if he turns up a high-brow he can drop Pete and be Mr. Stanley Stef." By the following summer, when the family was living in Switzerland, Steffens reported, "He is known as Pete, and we, his mother and father, are spoken of as 'the Petes.'"

The birth gave even Steffens a fresh outlook on life at the very ripe age of fifty-eight. With tongue only partly in cheek, he insisted to Jo Davidson that the "old, frivolous days" of exposing grafters were finished. The child, "quiet, dignified, absorbed in whatever he is doing," had set Steffens straight, and he happily admitted that the boy, not the father, would be the teacher. Often it would turn out that neither was doing the teaching, but Steffens, with a flesh-and-blood investment in the future, always showered the boy with affection, encouragement, and, of course, questions. "He was devoted to no person," Hutchins Hapgood commented in an understatement, "except perhaps to the child of his old age." Mabel Dodge went further, saying that Steffens never learned how to love until Pete was born.

And Steffens, halfway around the world from his own birthplace, was exactly where he preferred to be. "Italy is the best place in the world for a father to have his children in. The Italians adore children," he wrote. "I advise any man about to become a father to go to Italy (bringing his wife along, of course)." As his own son grew, Steffens claimed that it was the warmth of the Italian people that taught the boy cheerfulness and politeness.

But Steffens could not avoid reality even in idyllic Italy. One day, a priest came to the house and offered to christen the boy, starting, as Steffens saw it, "the process of mind-fixing and standardization." Giving the unsuspecting priest a gentle but firm reply, Steffens sent him away. The child had no need for the church. "Babies are born all right," he asserted. "They are not born with, they do not know any of the bunk that makes us grown-ups make war and money, constitutions and best-sellers. . . . They have no convictions, no principles to blind them. Anyhow my baby hasn't, and I am going to try to save him from all such sure things."

Steffens felt he had to save him most of all from "Their" education; if he could accomplish that, the boy would have an opportunity to grow up and "play the game and win, without believing in it or in his own lies: a humorous man of the world, a true prophet of the beautiful life to come on this earth and, perhaps, if he is good, the father of a girl baby." In other words, nearly the man Steffens had hoped to be. And when Dot predicted that parenthood would push her brother toward conservatism, he replied to Laura, "I find that it does not work that way. I am more radical than ever and precisely because I have a child. . . . I certainly can prevent a child from getting or holding long the unscientific bunk that now passes for knowledge."

Steffens, nearly past middle age, sat back and enjoyed fatherhood while Ella exhausted herself to the point where she decided temporarily to give up her writing to focus solely on caring for Pete (her occasional maternal clumsiness drew a rebuke from the English nurse: "What *did* they teach you at that London School of Economics?"). Age and gender being obvious factors, much of the authority in the family was assumed by Steffens. Their later residence in California was clearly the choice of Steffens, who also continued to look on Ella not only as his wife but as a pupil, with Steffens paying particular attention to her "education" on radicalism and the Russians.

Lengthy letters continued to flow out of San Remo through the winter. Political news went to Laura and Allen and friends, particularly Brand Whitlock and the Howes. A favorite topic, of course, was Mussolini. Steffens vacillated on the effectiveness of the Italian leader's governing style, calling him a "political genius" but one without the pure vision of Lenin, acknowledging, "anything may happen in Italy this next year,—anything." Other letters about Pete went to California and to "Grandma," Ella's widowed mother in London, who, over time, had developed a warm friendship with her son-in-law while, to the benefit of Ella, she refrained from trying to raise Pete from afar. Steffens eagerly wrote the letters to Grandma from the point of view of Pete, giving the boy an early literary start of sorts. Both types of letters motivated Steffens, but the infant world of Pete, so new to Steffens, captivated him most. He studied the behavior of his son with the same scientific approach he had tried for years to apply to the world of grafters. "I am intensely interested," he told Laura, "more than as if I were a young careerist, in the mind of the child."

In clinical detail and at great length, he described the boy's habits, moods, likes, and dislikes. A typical example was a letter to Laura several months after Pete's birth: "He never sucks his thumb or fingers. He does like a mouthful of cotton-wool. . . . He seems to be comforted by something to chew on or suck for half an hour; I imagine it keeps the saliva going to help his digestion, which is not perfect. The nurse gave him a doubled strip of cloth about an inch with a little water soaked in it. He mouths it a while, then drops it and stares around till he goes to sleep. He is what they call a good baby, crying very little and always for cause."

With wit and sometimes wisdom, Steffens included many of his own philosophical musings in the letters "from" Pete to Grandma. He once described a game of pirates between father and son, the son complaining because he always had to walk the plank blindfolded: "My papa says no grown-up ever knows where he is going and that I got to get used to being blindfolded, that I will make a good soldier and a better voter if I am brought up that way."

Steffens was no ordinary father. Admitting to Filene, a lifelong bachelor who loved children, that Ella raised Pete while he spoiled him, Steffens was nevertheless proud of one parental achievement on his part: He had taught Pete to urinate in a pot. He did it by telling the boy that he would go to Harvard if he learned, but otherwise would have to settle for Oxford or Cambridge. No matter where the boy went, Steffens told Filene, he was free to be anything he wanted except a businessman.

Those reading Steffens's reports from Italy were virtually his only audience. In the spring of 1925, he had finished writing *Moses in Red*, yet had no publisher in mind, despite Glenn Frank's inclusion ("my one and only last editor") of an article-length prequel, "Moses: A Miracle of Mercy," in the December 1923 issue of *Century*. A Steffens article titled "Radiant Fatherhood" was requested by *Cosmopolitan* and then rejected, never appearing until after his death. By contrast, his autobiography, which publishers actually had inquired about, was forming, chapter by chapter—but as yet only in his mind.

With no significant income from his writing, Steffens turned again to Wall Street, capitalizing on Coolidge prosperity an ocean away. "I put some money into the stock market," he teased Allen, "when your friend Cal was elected on the theory that the crooks had really been scared by La Follette and would rejoice and go dotty when the sure result was announced of the election. I did not risk much. . . . I have had some good profits, some of which I have taken and the rest of which I shall soon call in. . . . I wanted to pay for the baby, and that I have already done several times over." In his autobiography, he noted with pleasure, "It was all romance, and Wall Street paid." By late spring, the Steffens family prepared to leave behind "two years of such happiness" in San Remo for a summer stay in the Swiss mountain village of St. Cergue-sur Nyon.

The 1924 election had been La Follette's last hurrah as a public figure. He died just after Steffens arrived in Switzerland, where Steffens read the news in a local French paper. His condolences to Belle La Follette expressed not only his grief but his unshakable optimism and faith in those who demanded change. "It hit me hard," he acknowledged. "But the feeling I had was not so much sorrow as triumph. Bob is a victor, one of the very few. His life is a success." True, he conceded, La Follette had not been willing to go as far as Steffens for change, "but we did not differ in the faith that the war must and will be carried on."

Steffens at the moment was not fighting any wars of his own. He did gently chide Max Eastman after the publication of Eastman's book *Since Lenin Died*, which bitterly chastized the inner struggles of Russian leadership that resulted in Stalin's rise and the severe criticism of Trotsky. Steffens took issue not with Eastman's assessment of the tumultuous situation in Moscow—he agreed that the revolution was in a hellish phase—but with the fact that he reported the power struggle at all, fearing that it would retard the still-maturing revolutionary cause in the public mind. "The fight must be fought out within the party—the machine, as we used to call it—has to be supported, even as against Trotsky," he wrote Eastman. He added, in a cautionary note reflecting a belief in which he never wavered, "Nothing must jar our perfect loyalty to the party and its leaders."

Interestingly, Eastman assigned the blame for Steffens's rigid support of the Russian regime to Ella, whose earnest belief in the revolution had transformed Steffens "from a sentimental rebel preaching Jesus to both sides of the class struggle to a hard-cut propagandist of the party line," Eastman argued. A much more realistic scenario, though, was that Steffens, who for years had been seeking a successful revolution that would discard privilege and tradition and usher in a new age of genuine democracy and freedom, encouraged Ella on a journey she was already most eager to undertake.

After a pleasant summer at St. Cergue with Dot's daughter, Jane Hollister, as their guest ("She is so intelligent, and so quiet and natural about it. No bunk at all," Steffens told Laura), the Steffenses moved on to Paris for a few months, where Steffens later stayed with Jane while Ella and Pete went on to London for a visit with Grandma. In late September, Steffens received his first "letter" from Pete, who told him of the radiant sunshine in England. Steffens quickly educated the boy on the weather and its far-reaching implications:

> Sunshine in England! I know, my son, that you will have to learn some day to lie. You may go into business, you may be a politician, a diplomat, a lawyer; you may even become a gentleman and have to have good manners. But . . . you must not acquire the habits of success and polite society until we have given up all hope of your entering the arts or science. . . . The sun does not shine in England. It is against the law. It would be indecent to pour light upon the English. They are a respectable people. . . . You, an Italian, born and brought up in sunshine, should not be fooled ever,—not on that subject.

Pete would not be fooled for long; by early October, the family was once more in the warmth of Alassio, settled at Casa Montagu, high above the Riviera, where Pete and his parents could reacquaint themselves with "the sun all day," Steffens was pleased to note. Pete certainly was given plenty of latitude by his parents. Both Ella and Steffens doted on the boy at times, with Steffens preaching the truth of life, always with humor, to his "piccolo Pietro." But Steffens was also determined that Pete have ample freedom. The result was that Pete wandered nearly at will and sported a steady stream of bumps and bruises as evidence. In those early days in Italy, Pete was often given four or five hours a day to explore while Ella composed her novel and Steffens worked, at times being returned to the house by the gardener after taking a precipitous plunge off a ledge into the bushes. One day after Pete had climbed two flights of stairs alone ("Pete *solo*" he would say with pride) to look for his father, Steffens asked their Italian cook to keep a better eye on him. She quickly put Steffens in his place by telling him that Pete had been climbing—and falling—for months and knew perfectly well how to handle himself. Amazed and impressed, Steffens replied, "I've never heard him crash or cry." "Cry!" the cook shouted. "The signorino does not cry. He's an Italian."

The only cloud in Steffens's beach life was the disquieting memory of Gussie, who had caused him some guilt by refusing to communicate any longer with him. "What is the use of taking a course in such a matter as this of ours?" he asked Laura. "It may be all right with a child, like Pete, but among grown-ups sentiment can be trusted a little. . . . I can help G., I could ease any pain she suffers alone and we shall always be friends. Why behave like strangers?" Yet, to a sad extent, they had always been strangers.

Steffens looked forward to what he expected to be a full winter of work, which now meant the *Life*, although its beginnings were not auspicious. Acutely aware of the enormity of the creative task that lay ahead, he put off writing until Ella interceded. She had always enjoyed hearing his witty anecdotes and observing their effect on other listeners, so she took to writing down a number of Steffens's musings offered to their steady stream of guests. Soon she had fifty pages of his life on paper, and Steffens understood the message. Working steadily in the top floor studio that had been set aside for his work, Steffens had finished the first four chapters by the end of November. In fact, he had composed so much of the story in his mind that he could hardly put down the words fast enough in his book "full of indiscretions."

Steffens contacted family members and friends throughout the winter for help recalling events, as well as comments on the manuscript. A flurry of letters in particular went out between the Howes and Steffens. Fred himself, partly out of frustration that the country had descended from Wilson all the way to Coolidge, wrote his own memoir, *Confessions of a Reformer*, which was selling respectably. Steffens pledged to imitate his style of exposing the world, particularly the "ignoramuses that are so sure that THEY know." "Gimme the crooks or the honest men who are honest up to their brows, like Fred,"

Steffens told Marie. "And me, the sweet little boy that did get his hair cut finally and so went forth and took the world as he found it; not as it seems, but as it is."

Two particular challenges faced Steffens: what to title the book and how to address his personal life. The first was infinitely easier to resolve. His instinct was to name it *A Life of Unlearning*, but he conceded to Howe that a similar title to his, such as *The Confessions of a Muck-Raker* or *A Muck-Raker's Apology*, would be acceptable as well. The title itself was not of particular interest to Steffens—whatever would help sell the book was the best title.

Steffens's personal life was a different matter. His comments to Fred Howe show that he had not unlearned as much about his life as he thought:

> One question I'd like to ask you: Shall I say anything about my wives? I can see that if one does bring them in, truly, one cannot be a hero, unless one lies a little. That is bad enough when a fellow has but one wife to confess. But I have three to own up to the mistreatment of. I don't see how I can ever mention them. Do you? My wives had no part in the development of my discovery of the world. They are not essential to the story. It's all a mere matter of courtesy. You got out of it by dedicating your book to Marie. I can't dedicate it to any one wife.

He later explained to Marie that the remark about leaving out his wives "was a subconscious expression of my sense that mine is not an inside but an outside story," but, in fact, Steffens ultimately did dedicate the book to Ella. Still, the minimal attention given to Josephine and Ella in the book shows the discomfort Steffens felt in addressing his most personal side, absolutely preferring to focus on his public life. An additional comment of his to Fred Howe— "I'm indifferent just now to anything but the fun of writing this story"—is not hard to believe. For her part, Gussie had had enough of Steffens's apologies and explanations, demanding that he not mention her name anywhere in the entire book. Howe, on the other hand, probably saw nothing amiss; after he had finished the manuscript of his own autobiography, Marie asked him, "But Fred, weren't you ever married?"

The *Life* progressed quickly, partly because of the daily prodding from Ella, who had no patience with Steffens's constant revisions in search of the perfect text. By early February 1926, Steffens, writing by hand on small notepads, had finished nine chapters on his boyhood—recollections that Marie Howe found compelling enough to advise him to bring them out as a separate book on childhood. He conceded to Hutchins Hapgood, who had been helping Steffens attract a publisher, that the book was "not muckraking, philosophy or even fact knowledge" but "a series of short stories." It was merely a start, however, to a compelling succession of stories. Steffens explained, "I mean to tell how the fool boy hero of it discovers the world bit by bit; he was looking for the 'good' and found nothing but the beautiful." To a fellow radical such as Hapgood, Steffens felt the need to add, "The optimism of it may affront you; it certainly will astonish my old readers." Steffens's admiration of the growth of his own son as he wrote his *Life* only made the words flow more easily. "He is a bully boy, Hutch, healthy, happy, bold," he declared, adding self-consciously but with pride, "On this theme, Pete, I could write pages; and I find I do, even to people who don't care a damn." Yet, as he relived his childhood, he acknowledged to Marie Howe, "I was always naïve; I am yet in some things."

The interest of Steffens's friends in his work was matched, finally, by publishers. Both Macmillan and Liveright sent offers for the *Life*, although *Moses in Red*, his "bully story," would be published by Dorrance, a vanity press. He also enclosed some guilt money for Sinclair's run for governor in California: "It is money made in Wall Street, so keep it mum." Visits from friends, including Eastman, Whitlock, and Jane Hollister (who often took care of Pete) gave Steffens welcome reprieves from his daily writing in Alassio.

One constant was the family's roaming lifestyle. In late May 1926, Ella, Pete, and Jane were off to London to spend the summer with Ella's mother while Steffens headed for Paris. Meeting old friends there, including Eastman, Jo Davidson (hard at work on a memorial statue of La Follette), the Birds, and William Bullitt and Louise Bryant, Steffens resumed his bachelor habits of "art, music, literary revolt, and the money politics of the French." He remained in Paris just long enough to be among the witnesses to one of the genuine cultural spectacles of the decade: the riotous June 19 performance of George Antheil's compositions *Symphony in F* and *Ballet Mécanique*.

The score for the ballet, depending on the listener's taste, was either inspirational or appalling. Antheil, the American *enfant terrible* who was adored by Pound and his cult of Futurists for his unconventional performances across Europe, had aimed at producing a work featuring more discordance and tension than Stravinsky's *Le Sacre du Printemps*. And he wanted to ensure that the people who heard it first never forgot the experience. He succeeded.

Antheil reserved the largest and, of course, the most chic theater in Paris, the Théâtre des Champs-Élysées, for the debut. On the evening of the nineteenth, crowds streamed through the doors. "It was a sight as well as a sound," Steffens wrote Ella, providing the colorful details: "I stood outside and saw, I think, all the queer people in Paris, French and foreign, men and women. Wild hair, flannel shirts, sticks, no hats and big hats for both men and women, and, note well, many intelligent faces. 'Everybody,' in brief, that is anybody; all the correspondents and their wives, all the painters, poets and, of course, musicians, with Rolls-Royce and Hispano loads, too."

Faces in the crowd included Douglas Fairbanks, Mary Pickford, T. S. Eliot, Joyce (with Nora and the children), Constantin Brancusi, Serge Koussevitsky, Sylvia Beach, and, most noticeably of all, Pound and his boisterous gang of Antheil enthusiasts. What they witnessed was nothing less than stunning. After the relatively sedate opening of *Symphony in F*, Antheil's version of classical music's future came crashing through. An orchestra of eighty-five musicians wielding instruments such as saws, hammers, electric bells, fans, xylophones, two airplane propellers (courtesy of a local flea market), and sixteen mechanical pianos gave the audience all that they loved or feared.

As the ballet churned along, the crowd split apart, some booing and hissing at the outrageous noise, only to be countered by Pound and his balcony ruffians in some well-chosen French. Fights erupted in the aisles and even among the orchestra as the ballet boomed on. Pound could not resist entering the fray, banging heads and calling everyone imbeciles. The climax of the rowdy evening undoubtedly was the propellers: Once they started whirring, William Shirer reported, people opened umbrellas in self defense and periwigs flew off men's heads, landing softly against the back wall. Steffens, who had "promenaded a bit" with Pickford, found Antheil's future "a beautiful thing." He told Ella, "I don't see why the kicks. It's new; it was 'discord,' true, but beautifully. . . . And the crowd rose to it. Antheil had a triumph."

In a complete turnaround, Steffens was in the quiet hot springs of Carlsbad in Czechoslovakia the next day. He had been enjoying himself too much in Paris, just as in the days of Versailles, he told Allen: "I decided to cut it all out and run." He relaxed by taking the cure at the springs and listening to Beethoven and Schubert morning to night. His intention in Carlsbad was to work in silence, but within a week, the silence was unbearable. "I am alone, as I wished, and I am getting so that I can hardly stand it," he wrote to Laura.

Watching vacationing Germans around him enjoying their tennis, their beer, and their Beethoven while many of their countrymen remained impoverished from the war made Steffens wonder if he or anyone else had learned anything. Greatly missing Ella and Pete, he sent off one of his long, philosophical letters to

Pete that looked ahead with hope. Adults "have a game called tennis which they work at hard rather than do anything useful," he wrote, adding,

> But work, real work, for what we call duty or the truth, that is more fun than tennis. . . . Your mother or your Cousin Jane will explain this to you, if I am gone. . . . You are to have the straight of it, my boy; and the straightest of the straight is that we don't know anything; not any of us; not Jane, not Peter, not I. . . . But I have a funny old faith that, if a little fellow like you is shown everything and allowed to look at everything and not lied to by anybody or anything, he, even Pete, might do better even than Joyce did what *Ulysses* was meant to do; he might see and show that there is exquisite beauty everywhere except in an educated mind.

With Pete, Steffens was adamant on the point that grown-ups, especially himself, had no more insight than did children, and that no one was ever finished learning anything except those who thought they were finished. The lesson proved useful one night several years later, when Steffens brought Pete along to hear one of his lectures. On the way home, Pete whispered to his father, "Daddy, why do people listen to you and ask you questions? Don't they know you don't know anything?" "No," Steffens whispered back. "You and I are the only ones who know that and, more, we are about the only people on earth who really know that we don't really know anything."

What Steffens did know about was Russia, and on July 20, he wrote to Matthew Schmidt, the anarchist who had been convicted of helping James McNamara in the *Times* bombing and who remained in prison. Steffens made certain that Schmidt, hopeful of parole and a chance to get to Russia, would not go unprepared, as many had, and flee in shock. "You will like it if you are prepared for the worst, and I can tell you the worst better than any Tory spy, I who am for it," he wrote. Yet, Steffens acknowledged that he preferred to remain in the past, in Europe and America. And for good reason. "I don't want to live there," he wrote to Schmidt. "It is too much like serving in an army at war with no mercy for the weak and no time for the wounded. Youth can stand it." In any case, he noted, he was "not credited" in Russia anymore. Lenin had never forgiven him for the failure of the Bullitt mission. "I was the Red, the others mere Whites, and Lenin had no time to be just," he explained. The result, Steffens admitted, was that the Russians "are harder on me than on Emma Goldman."

By August, Ella, Pete, Jane, and a visiting Filene had joined him and moved down to Salzburg for the next month. For Pete, not yet two years old, German became the third language he was immersed in beyond the English of his parents. Ella and Jane, only eight years apart in age, had formed a bond in London and shared some of their time by joining striking miners in protest. They apparently also shared Steffens's curiosity in the future but chose to visit a German peasant family with notorious psychic powers for insight. Steffens, who gently mocked their efforts, had once given them a flurry of excitement at a table-tipping in Alassio by giving the table a well-disguised nudge of encouragement.

Particularly keen to experience a séance was Jane, later to become a renowned Jungian analyst (she herself was analyzed by Jung in the 1930s), and Steffens over time developed a deep respect for his inquisitive and sincere niece. Jane, after some youthful resistance to an opinionated mother and a conservative father, found herself drawn toward her rebellious and admiring uncle. She remembered him as "positive and generous," always trying to "find the best in one." Jane had grown up much like Steffens himself. Born in the Steffens's home in Sacramento, she spent many days alone with her brother, Clinton, riding and exploring the vast canyons, beaches, and grazing lands of the family property, developing a lifelong passion for the preservation of nature, while her parents tended to their ranch business. Predictably unsuited, as Steffens had been, for the classroom, she dropped out of Bryn Mawr after one year to join Steffens in Europe.

For the Steffens family and Jane, the summer passed pleasantly. Ella reported that the mornings were "all Mozart, Bach, Bartok," the afternoons a walk in the hills, and the evenings often "a new exhilarating entertainment." They attended performances of *Turandot* and Goldoni comedies followed by lavish, celebrity-laden banquets given by theater legend Max Reinhardt at Schloss Leopoldskron, where Steffens and Ella joined actors, writers, composers, poets, and dancers in scenes, Ella recalled, that resembled the Arabian Nights. The guests dined on "whole lambs, boars' heads, suckling pigs, game of all varieties, and feasts of talk, too." Politics on his mind as well, Steffens passed a Sunday afternoon in August deep in a discussion of Mussolini with Theodore Dreiser.

From Salzburg, the Steffenses went on briefly to Paris. When Davidson was away in America working for the oil magnate Ernest W. Marland, the Steffens family relocated to Bécheron, France, to spend the winter at the Davidsons' home. Twelve miles from the nearest city and four hours from Paris, the temporary home was hardly ideal for Steffens. Ella, though, was working on her novel and wanted a reprieve from their hectic life. Steffens could work in his head, he told Laura, and was less bothered by their constant travels. Still, he needed to write as well, and their new home had ample privacy. Steffens, again writing for

Pete, was happy to tell Pete's grandmother that Davidson had immortalized the boy. "I have been made permanent," he wrote, "by my Uncle Jo Davidson, the mud man. He has made a monument in infancy out of me and is going to show it all over, he says. Me and Rockefeller or maybe it is more polite to say Mr. Rockefeller and Ella Winter's baby."

In Bécheron, Steffens pressed on with his autobiography. The fate of *Moses in Red*, unfortunately, was not offering him any encouragement. After he had worked periodically for nine years on the text, it was finally published by Dorrance in 1926. Viewing the results, Steffens may have wished he had spared the effort. While friends such as Charles Erskine Scott Wood and Fremont Older gave it friendly reviews, and Filene personally sent out fifty copies to luminaries that included Jane Addams, Newton Baker, and Brandeis, the book seemed doomed from the start. A fire in the publisher's warehouse burned all but four hundred copies of the book, and given the mood of the country, even that number was unnecessary. Americans indulging in the carefree ambience of the Jazz Age were not about to be distracted by a book preaching the virtues of a bloody revolution based on a biblical figure. Libraries bought a few copies. With the public, Steffens conceded to Jo Davidson, it made "no stir."

By mid-December, Steffens was making plans to return home to California. Davidson's time with Marland was partly the cause. Reading Davidson's glowing reports of the energy and imagination of big business in America, Steffens was eager to view the economic changes there. He had also heard from Fremont Older, who still wrote often to Steffens on the McNamaras, that Steffens might be of some use in gaining freedom for the dynamiters if he could return. Ella herself had been corresponding with James McNamara, who took an active interest in Steffens's new family and sent enlarged photos of Pete that he had done in the prison workshop. Steffens was more than willing to try again to assist. So following a late winter stay in Paris, Steffens and family left Europe behind. Now past sixty, Steffens hoped he would at last find a permanent home.

After a stormy overseas voyage, Steffens, Ella, and Pete arrived in New York, where they stayed in Greenwich Village and spent three weeks in a whirlwind rush to catch up with old friends of Steffens's. Ella became close to Marie Howe and, through Howe, gave her first American talk to an audience at Heterodoxy, a feminist organization. The *New Masses* staff welcomed Steffens back with a festive lunch, where Eastman, Floyd Dell, Michael Gold, and cartoonist Art Young relived the memories of their lively Washington Square days. More time was spent with Anna Louise Strong, Robert Minor, and Clarence

Darrow, who teased Ella over Steffens's unflagging belief that "you can improve man." Darrow took them briefly to Baltimore to meet H. L. Mencken, a hero to Darrow but whom Steffens found unimpressive.

By early May 1927, twenty years after his disastrous trip west with Josephine, Steffens, brimming with pride, could show off his home state to Ella and Pete. As the train passed through the Sacramento Valley, Steffens, moved by the sight of the vast playground of his youth, could scarcely speak. It was not just California, however, that had drawn him back. As Davidson had insisted, and Steffens now saw, America itself was a new nation. The country had entered the war "a conceited but secretly rather humble second-rate country," Steffens recalled, only to emerge "self-assured," giddy with a new swagger encouraged by the "hate and envy" other countries now aimed its way.

Steffens, still seeking the path to democracy, became uncharacteristally swept up in the capitalist euphoria. He conceded that Russia could not help but feel jealous of one aspect of the new international juggernaut: its efficiency. "They coveted not our reformers and good men," Steffens wrote, "but our big, bad captains of industry; and they envied and planned to imitate our mass production, not our Constitution, laws, and customs, not our justice, liberty, and democracy." He saw both countries headed for the same prosperity, only in America, the new businessmen were thinking creatively and leading the way to lasting reform. Eight short months before Wall Street crashed, he would tell Davidson, "Big business in America is producing what the Socialists held up as their goal: food, shelter, and clothing for all. You will see it during the Hoover administration, which proposes to deal with the problem of unemployment profitably. . . . It is a great country, this; as great as Rome. What it needs is a bit of Greece." Steffens went as far as to send an approving letter to Eastman concerning his recent book, *Marx and Lenin: The Science of Revolution*, which argued that Russia's revolutionary leaders had lost touch with the public. "A cleaning out of the Bunk will help, not hurt the Socialist state to get on to Communism without a state," Steffens wrote to Eastman.

Ella, too, with her fresh eyes, helped Steffens to see the change. "I wonder if that is not the vital point about America, that this is an experimental country," he recalled Ella saying. "Anybody can see anybody. Everybody is willing 'to try anything once,' as they say. Nothing is final or fixed. Everything, from high buildings to automobiles, from railroad coaches to cooking stoves and factory machinery—all but your Constitution—is tentative, temporary, to be scrapped some day for the next good thing."

While uncertain as to exactly where the new road would take America, Steffens was sure that he would rather gamble the future of his country on the side of Henry Ford ("a reformer without politics—a radical"), Filene, Marland, and other business "scientists" than with well-intentioned liberals. Steffens noted that Filene, who had come up with his own idea of the highly lucrative "Automatic Bargain Basement," known to Boston shoppers simply as Filene's Basement, actually was pleased when he realized that mail-order houses and chain stores—his new competitors—had hit on even more progressive ideas for the economical distribution of goods.

Happy to be home, Steffens stopped briefly in San Francisco to see Allen and Laura, and met with Older for news on the dynamiters. Darrow, who still wanted to press the point that the men believed they were blowing up an empty building and had not intended to kill anyone, hoped to help as well and was keeping in touch. Conditions, though, were hardly ideal for much optimism over the case. By 1927, with peace and prosperity well entrenched across the American landscape, labor agitators were a vocal but marginalized force. Organized labor had moved so far toward capital that it was urging workers not to strike but to work harder to maintain the high wages. Socialists and organized labor leaders, along with Washington, denounced the Bolsheviks. The late 1920s seemed hardly a time for Steffens to expect a sympathetic hearing on labor radicals. Yet, he felt a glimmer of hope. The visceral hatred of labor a decade ago had diminished, coinciding with the economic surge. And the progressives had taken control of government in California. For Steffens, it was worth the effort.

In Los Angeles, Steffens first went to see District Attorney Asa Keyes, who agreed to help if the *Los Angeles Times*, which had been the victim of the deadly blast, could be persuaded as well. That meant involving *Times* general manager Harry Chandler, who had continued to attack labor as harshly as his father-in-law had. Yet, according to Steffens, Chandler now assured him "quickly, easily, without any objection" of their release, although he claimed to have no pull with Sacramento. It was up to Steffens to change political minds.

Next was the governor, Clement Young, a liberal Republican Steffens knew little about but was eager to engage. In a letter to Young, he suggested that the governor join the governor of Massachusetts, who was reconsidering the Sacco-Vanzetti case, in a similar gesture toward the McNamaras. Ironically, when the two met, Young began by taking Steffens on a tour of the governor's mansion. The nostalgiac viewing, however, did little to soften the challenge facing Steffens. Young agreed only that he would abide by whatever recommendation came out of the parole board. To further the cause, Steffens also had a successful meeting with William Randolph Hearst to gain his editorial support, and wrote a long letter to the editor of *The Sacramento Bee* detailing the flaws in the original case; the letter was published on July 27.

On August 23, Steffens and Ella accompanied Older on a visit to San Quentin to see James McNamara and Schmidt, John McNamara having already been released several years earlier. The news was not encouraging. Thinking of Ferdinando Sacco and Bartolomeo Vanzetti, who had been executed earlier that day, a resolute McNamara told them, "No quarter, that is the message of the day. Let Labor get it, and all will be well." Steffens conceded to Darrow the next day in a letter, "If you feel very bad about this, think how I am getting it, I, with my idiot optimism and a square meal of dirt to eat." Later, in his autobiography, Steffens pledged, "If the reformers are defeated and men with imagination ever get back into power, I shall try again." Jail was where the dynamiters remained.

In the meantime, Steffens and Ella had met in Los Angeles with the improbable Jack Black, a convicted burglar who had been "reformed" by Older and wrote a remarkable autobiography, *You Can't Win*, which Steffens had vigorously promoted—"It is a fascinating narrative and an amazing revelation"—in a lengthy letter to publisher Horace Liveright. The family then went up the coast to the Hollister ranch, a perfect setting for a travel-weary family. In such comfort, Steffens forged ahead with his book while Ella, having abandoned her novel for the moment, worked on a number of newspaper and magazine articles.

Ella's exuberance and intelligence had "conquered everybody here," Steffens assured her mother, adding that the same had been true "everywhere along our long road." For Ella's part, she found Dot, unlike Laura, to be a chatterer, eager to point out that they were conservatives, that Ella and Steffens were left-wing intellectuals, and that not everyone agreed with Steffens. Jim Hollister, a state senator, was quite a different type—a strong man who spoke slowly, with great deliberation given to each thought. Regardless, they were well matched, and both Dot and Jim, Ella was surprised to see, worked rigorously and equally on the upkeep of the ranch. Jim rode daily on the range with his cowhands, while Dot managed the cultivation of the vast fruit orchards. Ella herself was thrilled, finally, to be included in Steffens's family.

To Steffens's delight, the Hollister ranch proved a paradise for Pete, who was smothered with attention by Dot, Steffens, or Ella in the early morning before one of the maids took him down to the beach for "a bully long morning in the everlasting sun, sand, and water." He played with his new cousins in an outdoor setting not so different from that of Steffens's own childhood, going horseback riding and watching cattle roundups. One afternoon, when Jim and

Jane had returned from a day's work on the ranch, they presented Pete with a Shetland pony that had belonged to the Hollister children, undoubtedly reminding Steffens of his own special pony that would play such a prominent role in his autobiography.

Altogether, the ranch days spent surrounded by his family left Steffens as optimistic and high-spirited as he had been for years. "Life gets better and better as I live it," he wrote in a June letter. "Every chapter is an improvement upon its predecessor. I am sure that old age is the best of Life, mismanaged though it usually is. I mean to manage mine and save it, as I used to food, for the last."

26

CARMEL CHARM

IF STEFFENS'S OLD age was indeed the best of life, much of the credit has to go to the beauty of the coastal town he chose as his final home: Carmel. He had always anticipated a permanent return to California; fifteen years earlier, Fremont Older had bought a large piece of land near Los Gatos, encouraging Steffens and others in their circle, including Heney, Darrow, Colonel Wood, and Whitlock, to embrace middle age by establishing a well-heeled, anarchist community featuring free speech and free love. Steffens's response was to suggest an even larger community, including his sister Laura. The radical venture never materialized, but Steffens had been easily charmed by Carmel and the California coast from previous visits. For the last stop on his life's long journey, Steffens felt that this was where he belonged. On August 3, only a few days after getting to Carmel and renting a house, Steffens told Allen, "I feel like staying here forever."

Long before Steffens arrived there, Carmel had already made its name as an upscale bohemia for those who were artistic, eccentric, or rich, often a combination of all three. Forty years earlier, Robert Louis Stevenson, just married in San Francisco, had found the Carmel seacoast appealing if still an outpost. In 1903, however, the future for Carmel was set when the Carmel Development Company enticed the Bay Area's successful artists and, more profitably, the sizable, well-endowed group of aspiring artists, to settle there. The San Francisco earthquake three years later hastened the retreat of artists south.

George Sterling, appropriately, led the procession down the coast. Known to his friends as the king of bohemia and "handsome as a Roman faun" to Mary Austin, Sterling had the paradoxical character of a hard-drinking poet mixed with a gentle soul and a cosmic imagination, but, unfortunately, quite earthly

talents. Following Sterling to Carmel were Austin, the San Francisco photographer Arnold Genthe, Jack London, Upton Sinclair, and a wildly eclectic cast of
now-forgotten characters.

Of course, Steffens recognized that he was settling into a very genteel, eccentric community "living upon its dividends and rents," although for much of his
recent life, his own income had arrived by the same route. Ella, feeling that she
"did not belong," was more taken aback. She vividly captured the town's color:

> There were the "arty" . . . parading up and down Ocean Avenue in their
> pants of purple toweling, or watching John Bovingdon dance nude
> in the rafters of somebody's cottage. The latest modern musician was
> explaining psycho-physical tonality; a poet published his theories in a
> slim volume called *Seed Ideas*, printed by hand and bound in purple
> by one of his devotees. And there was Mrs. Dickinson introducing a
> lecture by a swami from Los Angeles, with the warning, "Mr. X will
> now explain to us what we do not know in a language we do not
> understand."

Still, to Steffens, the peaceful, simple beauty of Carmel was compelling.
Rarely were trees cut or roads built. Three traffic police and one judge easily
maintained what little law and order was required. And the chance, finally, to
be settled with his family was more than enough to convince Steffens to stay.
The family first rented a cottage they called "The Sandbox" before, following
Steffens's wishes, purchasing a Carmel home on October 20. Ella, expecting that
their "vacation" in California to be just that, was stunned by the prospect of not
returning to Europe and remaining in a sunny playground where, she observed,
"something was always going on that seemed to me lunatic." Yet, Steffens was
undeterred, and Ella remained—happily, as the future passed—with him.

A short walk from the beach and bordered by sandy streets dotted with
large pine trees, the new home featured a sizable garden filled with flowers and
a smaller rock garden. From his room, Steffens could gaze past a towering pine
tree to the Pacific expanse beyond, often using the great pine and its scattered
cones and needles to help illustrate points to guests. Ella liked to write in the
spacious living room, where light from the bay windows flooded in, surrounded
by shelves of books. In the background, visitors would later hear Pete, as a
young boy, practicing on his violin.

The guardian of Steffens's writing time, Laura advised him not to invite
people too eagerly. But as Steffens hoped and as Ella feared, the home took
on a magnetic-like attraction as old friends, European and American, flocked

to Carmel in search of Steffens. Steffens told Laura herself about the home: "It's going to be yours and Doctor's in the sense that 850 [the Suggetts's San Francisco home at 850 Francisco Street] was always mine. I'd like it to be our family home."

In fact, the frequent gatherings in the living room were, one guest marveled, a "constellation of luminaries." Steffens's family had barely been in Carmel two weeks when word came that Hadley Hemingway, who had recently become the first member of Hemingway's club of ex-wives, would be along soon, with little Jack ("Bumby") to play with Pete. While Jack loved being there, his mother, understandably, took longer to adjust. "Hadley is looking well & is quite cheerful, tho she wasn't at first," Ella wrote Hemingway at the end of summer. "But the perpetual sun and breezes & Cypresses & blue sky of the last week or two have raised everyone's spirits." Indeed, Ella herself was so inspired by the weather that she declared Carmel had "more sun" than the Italian Riviera. Being on a trip to San Francisco at the time, Steffens missed part of Hadley's visit (and probably some of the sun as well), but Ella conveyed his sentiments: "Stef says to tell you that your baby is a great big brute and if society were properly managed in the interests of humanity it would never let a menace like that grow up."

Ella's letter to Hemingway included two enclosures that she thought he might appreciate. One was a letter from Frank Smith, the warden at San Quentin Prison; the other from a young inmate, Robert Joyce Trasker, both showing a side of Steffens that Hemingway and other friends knew well. Trasker devoted his prison time to writing, and Steffens, on a recent visit, had presented him with a copy of *The Sun Also Rises*. In gratitude, Trasker sent a letter to Smith: "When he [Steffens] was kind enough to call on me, I was compelled to admire him for his questions, and his answers to my questions were of a nature to indicate that he has a profound sympathy and understanding at least for the regenerative prisoner, and, I suspect, the same sympathy and understanding for all humanity." Smith forwarded Trasker's letter, along with his own note of thanks, to Steffens.

Others who would pass through Carmel included the tempestuous couple Sinclair Lewis and Dorothy Thompson. Lewis, who was considering a novel on labor, had good reason to consult the Steffenses and discuss the dynamiters, still a guilt-ridden topic for Steffens. Rhys Williams, back from seven years in Russia, gave Steffens a full account—all positive—of "the future." Among Steffens's permanent Carmel neighbors, standing above all was Robinson Jeffers, the reclusive, apocalyptic poet who was forever rolling stones up from the beach to build his own iconic tower, Tor House, on a rocky point above the bay. Jeffers had made his literary mark in 1924 with the publication of *Tamar and Other Poems*, after which callers frequently stopped by to hear a word or two from the bard, but as Steffens observed, Jeffers said it all in his poetry, which was as austere as his personality, and had little left to give to his admirers. Rarely did he venture into town, having inherited sufficient money to allow him the choice of hibernation, and less often did he seem to speak. Instead, he wrote, piled stones, and enjoyed the quiet life he had so carefully crafted with his beloved wife, Una, an intellectual and emotional soulmate who, by contrast, was quite vivacious (Ella compared her to "a rushing, bubbling brook"), and their twin boys.

Although Jeffers was a staunch conservative and a man of very few public words (poet Orrick Johns called him "the most silent man I have ever met"), Steffens and Ella soon were picnicking with the Jefferses, whom they met through Colonel Wood and Sara Bard Field. Steffens judged them right off to be "the real thing": "They know what they want, and how to live and get it out of life."

Steffens worked intermittently on the story of his own life, finding the task sluggish when he had to write of the muckraking years, as he himself no longer believed in the possibility of muckraking alone to produce substantive social changes. Ella also was unnerved at times by his "black moods," several days of total silence. While Steffens insisted that his distress had no connection to Ella, she felt vaguely—and inexplicably—responsible. Still, the autobiography was progressing.

Following a cross-country speaking tour in which he debated Darrow in Chicago and Ella back in Carmel, Steffens returned to his autobiography and wrote an article, "Becoming a Father at Sixty," for *American* magazine. He continued churning out letters, most of them enthusiastically reporting on the progress of Pete. A note to Gilman Hall, the former editor of *Everybody's* and *Ainslie's*, shows that Steffens, in barely three years, had surpassed any cure for paternal pride: "He is a charming child. He has no inferiority sense, and yet is not a prig; he is cautious, without any sense of fear; he is not obedient to commands, but very courteously considerate of requests; he is like a little gentleman, with exceptional manners."

One friend Steffens always enjoyed hearing from was Rhys Williams, who was at least as enthusiastic as Steffens about progress in Russia. Steffens pointed out to Laura that life had improved substantially there—no more breadlines, no unemployment, universal suffrage, and living conditions "better than over here." Williams and Steffens were not alone in thinking so, but among the American Left, particularly in view of the vicious implementation of Communism under

Lenin and the subsequent power grab by Stalin in the mid-1920s, they had less company than a decade earlier.

Some saw the warning signs but maintained a faltering hope that revolution was a series of phases, with the initial ones being exceedingly grim but necessary. Dreiser, for example, decried the poverty and oppressive surveillance in the name of state security that marked life in Russia, but maintained that its government was "likely to lead man away from ignorance and misery to knowledge and happiness." Although he had similar misgivings, John Dos Passos felt that "the mass of the people have infinitely more opportunities for leading vigorous and unstagnant lives than before the revolution." A more conservative but respected voice, Joseph Wood Krutch, emphatically made the case for liberalism, denouncing the rigid party line that even artists were expected to toe under Communism. And when Eastman, the socialist turncoat to many, came back to America in 1925, his political friends, true believers in Russia, now shunned him. "I was a traitor, a renegade, a pariah, a veritable untouchable, as far as the communists were concerned," he wrote.

The resolute faith of Steffens's left him increasingly grouped with the most radical elements on the American political spectrum, even though he had spent the better part of his accomplished career publishing in the mainstream press. Yet, that is where Steffens, quite deliberately and enthusiastically, placed himself as he entered old age.

Steffens found happiness nearly everywhere as 1928 passed, and he wanted others to share in his Carmel pleasure. Thus was born the nickname of his house overlooking the ocean: The Getaway. He had been telling Laura of how much Jane, now twenty-two, had appreciated his offer of the house as a place to which she could escape whenever she needed somewhere "to breathe and think and feel safe." That was an excellent purpose for the house, he thought—to serve as a welcome retreat for Jane and others. Steffens saw it as "a refuge for any poor s.o.b. in a jam." He displayed his own devotion to the home by assuming a somewhat surprising passion for yard work, meticulously caring for his flower garden and a small plot of lawn.

An appeal from Davidson, though, temporarily uprooted Steffens. Davidson had become enamored over the revolutionary approach put forward by the entrepreneur Ernest Marland. Like Filene, the liberal Marland could not understand why America accepted an economic system so burdened by inefficiency and unfairness. An immensely wealthy oil man who would go on to be a Democrat congressman and the governor of Oklahoma, Marland held a real passion not for oil or politics but for art and economic justice. Davidson

and Marland had quickly grown close; the sculptor, however, saw Marland as
a restless man, a "lonely soul," unable to truly enjoy the lap of luxury he lived
in. "He is another 'American Tragedy' that someone ought to write," Davidson
observed. "I wish I could. I want Steffens to know him." Steffens, of course, did
not need much coaxing to hear more from such an interesting figure, so in mid-
April, he boarded a train with Davidson to meet Marland at his estate in Ponca
City, Oklahoma.

Steffens found that Marland was nothing if not a big thinker. The oil magnate planned to construct a grand home, adorned by Davidson's statues, to
provide a creative paradise for artists and writers to work in comfortably and
undisturbed, apparently believing that Shangri-La was more likely than bohemia to inspire masterpieces. Here was a man, Steffens realized, who saw a future
that most Americans could not imagine.

During Steffens's visit, the two men had wide-ranging discussions. Marland
entertained Steffens with a delicious inside view of the American political system
that average voters never saw: the rigging of Harding's election, a governor's
being guided by an astrologer and a palmist, and the "bandits" who became
mayors, police chiefs, and chairmen. "It is amazing to me how easy it is to get
the facts," Steffens told Laura, claiming that he had made a friend for life "by
simply not laying down to him as his staff does. These bosses prefer and promote yes-men, but when they strike independent people who contradict them,
they come to life and like it."

Marland lavished so many facts upon Steffens that he was a bit dazed. In
an appreciative letter to Marland, Steffens admitted, "I am all stirred up; it's
as if I had travelled in a new country." American writers rarely touched upon
this "very stuff of American life," because they met the bosses only socially for
drinking and flattery: "It is absurd, and the results are ridiculous." People like
Marland had valuable experiences to share, and writers needed to hear them,
he felt. The respect was mutual. Davidson later informed Steffens of Marland's
desire "to hold on to that friendship."

In Carmel, Steffens and Ella were not shy about speaking their own minds
before the local citizenry. Ella, her usual whirlwind of energy, took over the
unpaid editorship of *The Carmelite* following a lengthy clash with previous editor Pauline Schindler. The paper was a small circulation weekly that featured an
eclectic blend of local and national news and achieved a certain cachet among
liberals nationwide, and she quickly had the two-room shop buzzing. One of the
printers, a "hard boiled union man," complained to Steffens, "You know how
Ella Winter runs,—she never walks anywhere,—always a dog trot. Fine for her.

But, God damn it, it's catching, and every once in a while I find myself trotting around like her, on a run. And, say, I draw the line at running. It's against the union rules and what t'hell. Why should I run?" The paper went on to become nearly a family operation when Steffens began contributing a regular column, pushing the radical side on both local and international issues but always with his trademark humor.

The paper's other contributors reflected the flavor of the town as well. Ella recalled that Schindler, a wealthy patron of the arts who, to her credit, had promoted the work of Jeffers, photographer Edward Weston, and Ansel Adams during her tenure, had come into work one morning and asked Ella, "Is the universe conscious? Harold and I were up all night arguing it." Poetry came from the wife of Orrick Johns, Caroline Blackman, who was devoting her life in Carmel to achieving "absolute poverty." After Johns assumed the paper's editorship a short time later, Steffens advised him to "enjoy your editorship," adding, "If you have a good time, your readers will."

In the fall of 1928, Steffens headed east for another lecture tour taking him through Denver and Chicago on his way to New York and Boston. He traveled alone, Ella remaining behind with Pete, who had a fractured leg. Far from being a neglected relic of a Red, Steffens was back in serious demand. "I have so much to do, so many people to see," he wrote Ella from New York, "and all I've done so far is to see and have a long, good,—a really amazing talk with Hemingway (talk about artists!) and Isaac McBride. I'm waiting now for Charlie Wood, the writer. I see Frank Polk this afternoon. And there's the Roes, the Howes, the editors,—you know the list. I can't do it all."

The highlight of the tour was his November talk at Ford Hall on Boston's historic Beacon Hill. The building was full, with many standing in the aisles. He spoke as well as ever, he told Ella, and he judged the evening "a triumph." Most satisfying to him were the questions that poured out for an hour from the "very quick" audience. "I must have been in fine fettle," he noted, pleased that a pointed speech on graft, Reds, and Mussolini from an old muckraker could still fill a hall and entertain a crowd for hours.

One of those most impressed by Steffens's talk was Granville Hicks, a young leftist instructor at Harvard. Hicks would go on to become an enthusiastic Marxist as literary editor of the liberal-radical magazine *New Masses* and one of America's leading men of letters. For some extra money, he had been heavily editing, if not rewriting, C. C. Regier's *Era of the Muckrakers*. His responsibilities included interviewing the leading members of the old cast. Hicks had spoken with Ida Tarbell, Ray Stannard Baker, Samuel Hopkins Adams, and others.

Steffens, though, with his constant travels, had eluded Hicks, and his presence at Ford Hall gave Hicks the opportunity he sought.

After listening to Steffens speak "brilliantly on dictatorship and democracy, heaping paradox upon paradox" before being "even more brilliant" at responding to the crowd's questions, Hicks sent a note to Steffens, and a meeting was arranged at Filene's home. Discussing graft, *McClure's*, and, of course, Pete, Steffens left a marked impression on Hicks. "Here, I felt at once, was a muckraker who had not grown tired and tame," Hicks wrote. "I was shocked by some of Steffens' ideas—by his willingness, for instance, to say a good word for Mussolini—but I was filled with admiration just the same. . . . Everyone, it seemed to me, ought to know about Lincoln Steffens."

After returning to Carmel, Steffens caught up with old friends, two of the most important being Colonel Wood and Sara Bard Field, who had built their own version of The Getaway on a hill in Los Gatos, a more exotic, stunning home nicknamed "The Cats," as two heroically sized white cats marked the driveway entrance. Amid music, poetry readings, art displays, and literary discussions, distinguished visitors came and went, most touched by the warm embrace of their hosts. As one guest observed, "When you walked into that home, you walked into love." Steffens and Ella went there in early 1929, a trip that left a deep impression. "I felt that I had been in a place of beauty," Steffens wrote to Wood. "I would like to feel often as I feel at The Cats. . . . As poets and priests, you are bound to realize yourselves that you and this creation of yours are greater than everything else that you have ever done. . . . You are, both of you, each one of you, beautiful works of art." The bond between the couples was as strong as ever.

The Marland estate remained no less fascinating to Steffens, so in February, he accepted an invitation from Davidson to return, this time along with Ella and Pete. While Steffens found the visit to be "another fine chapter in our lives," viewing the human mosaic of Ponca City and wondering "what Proust would have done with all that," Ella, still a bit dazed by her Carmel neighbors, was far less enthusiastic, referring to Ponca City as a "Western-movie city," where Indians, made wealthy by the oil Marland had extracted from their land, rode in "sleek limousines." What captured most of her attention, though, was Marland's extravagant tastes, which she found appalling. Marland's home was a "palatial" mansion, featuring a kitchen that had six huge refrigerators with "practically a whole slaughtered animal" in each, and a team of six cooks on duty. Outside, the grounds were modeled after St. Germain-en-Laye, Versailles, and the Petit Trianon, artificial lakes were stocked with Japanese ducks, and hundreds of ponies had been imported for polo games. "I was not exactly overwhelmed," Ella declared, although she conceded that "Stef was enchanted."

The spring of 1929 saw one of the most bizarre turns in Steffens's life, as well as highly questionable judgment on his part. Steffens and Ella, not because they loved each other too little but because they did too well, filed for divorce in a Salinas County courthouse. Officially, Ella charged Steffens with extreme cruelty. The divorce was meant to be private, known only to them and the court, and the rationale behind it reflected Steffens's thinking more than Ella's. In 1924, Steffens had already supported the idea of divorce, mainly on principle— that they would remain together because of love, not law. Acutely aware of their age difference, Steffens never wanted to feel that Ella, watching her husband grow old, would be bound to him by a legal snare. Five years of marriage was enough. If Ella still loved him, of course, that was a different and vital matter, but not one that required the chains of marriage.

In fact, Ella, who felt that their marriage "lacked nothing" and wished to have a second child with Steffens, was far more uncertain of the undertaking and went along rather reluctantly, wanting to get the deed done quickly and quietly, if Steffens insisted on doing it at all. And the episode would have remained a secret between the two had not a curious reporter happened to scan the court calendar and notice the names. The *New York Times* picked up the story and ran it on June 7, giving Steffens and Ella instant notoriety. Their friends around the world and nearly everyone in Carmel were stunned by the news and wondered what had happened.

The unanticipated publicity amused Steffens but scandalized Ella. "Stef laughed," she recalled. "He was used to attacks and disagreeable publicity and having the world on his tail, but it was my first dose and I shrank from it in hurt consternation. Carmel buzzed; I did not go out." When neighbors quizzed the family servant, Anna, about the affair, Steffens instructed her to tell everyone "that we have built a stone wall down the middle of the studio and that she lives on one side of it and I on the other."

What made the spreading story more difficult for them to manage was the unfortunate truth that quite soon, they would, in fact, be physically separated. Ella and Pete planned to go to her mother's home in London for the summer, while Steffens would remain behind in Carmel to write. Instead of enjoying relaxing summers, both parents, especially Steffens, faced some very awkward questions. Inquiring reporters and photographers descended on the Steffens home seeking an explanation from Steffens, who told them either nothing or whatever quirky reasoning struck him at the moment. Ella, traveling, met similar demands from friends. "My attempted explanations met incredulity; this was not something one played with," she wrote. "It wasn't, either, I concluded wryly." She felt some relief when a friend commented perceptively, "Only God and Freud can understand this Steffens business." Steffens and Ella, of course, had no wish whatsoever to be apart, which explains why their paper divorce, amid all the chaos, did not lead to an actual split.

In a clear, sympathetic letter on June 12 that went on for pages to Ella's mother, Steffens tried his best to explain the debacle, reviewing the entire family situation. He recalled that Ella had come to him not to be restricted in any way—in fact, to escape limits and to live freely, as she wished, and that she was "still young, very young; and thank the Lord, very interested in the world." He understood, he said, that she [Mrs. Winter] would be shocked by the news, and then he got to the heart of the matter: "I have seen what Peter wants to see, the world. I can sit here watching Pete and understand what is going on outside Carmel. Pete and Peter can't. And I can't, and I should not, tell them what it all is and what it all means. . . . I cannot give them what they may only *think* they want: their own comprehension of life; that they will have to get for themselves."

Their divorce, nevertheless, managed to accomplish just what Steffens must have originally hoped: their devotion to one another grew even stronger. Their love letters, one being an outpouring of twenty-one pages from Ella, crisscrossed the Atlantic all summer. Ella's words reminded Steffens of "the moonlight on the Seine," while Ella, despite feeling chagrin over the public ugliness of their act, believed the divorce gave them, once again, "the spring of love." While they felt a certain awkwardness over their "new" relationship, there was no doubt as to how their future would play out. A typical sentiment closed Steffens's August 6 letter: "Peter, you'll always have me, who wants you, and will be there always for you." He had initially feared a permanent separation, but by late September, he knew better, declaring, "We are married once more."

Steffens also used the lengthy letters to discuss labor and politics, offering abundant advice, solicited or otherwise, to Ella. To hear some fresh ideas, he prodded her to contact some "hip-thinkers." "Why not call on that editor of some weekly who is an economist—what's his name—Keynes. Talk to him." On another occasion, he chided her for using the word "profit" rather than "dividend," reminding Ella that the best, including Hemingway, "think it through to precision in words; just as sculptors or painters model up to an edge, to perfection."

Steffens, meanwhile, was on his own in Carmel, where his divorce had changed the social scenery considerably. The Getaway was no longer a friendly escape, so Steffens ventured out of Carmel often that summer. He saw Laura and Allen in San Francisco, the Hollisters at the ranch, and Bob La Follette Jr. in Los Angeles. In July, he traveled to Colorado to give a course of six lectures that went well, he thought, his only frustration being that he "didn't get it all out." Mabel Dodge, who had left New York behind in 1917 to seek "Change" and landed in Taos, invited Steffens to join Hutchins Hapgood and Neith Boyce for a visit. And as dedicated as he was to his autobiography, which he initially assumed would take a year or two of concentrated writing, progress was slow. "The key to my life is the *Life*," he confessed to Ella. "I must jam it through. I wish I could do it this summer and fall."

Instead, the work dragged on. He reported to Ella on August 20 that he expected to get writer's cramp before completing the chapter on his departure from *McClure's*, leaving still more than twenty years to cover. When Upton Sinclair asked Steffens if he could take a look at his own manuscript, Steffens had a quick reply: "Get ye behind me. . . . I must stick to my job." Both Steffens and Ella dreamed of the relief they would feel when the work, "that interminable *Life*, that big, too big book," would be put to rest.

Of course, most of all, the letters crossing the ocean focused on Pete. Although the boy had not yet seen his fifth birthday, Steffens already had college firmly in mind. He approved wholeheartedly of Ella's move to get Pete started in kindergarten, partly to prevent a repeat of the Hollisters' experience. Jack and Clinton Hollister, Dot's sons, had told Steffens that despite being raised in one of the wealthiest families in California, they felt that their parents had taken the matter of college preparation too lightly. Jane herself had dropped out of college and, in another shock to her parents but not to Steffens—"This generation is the open season for parents"—secretly married Joseph Wheelwright, who later became a psychologist, in September. Steffens, in this case, had seen the future and had no desire to repeat the mistakes with Pete. He told Ella that he could get Pete started on mathematics and spark the boy's enthusiasm for history and geography. "That's the parents' part: curiosity," he wrote Ella. "Let the schools satisfy it, and try to kill it. We'll open more holes in his head than they can ever fill up. And so with college."

To Steffens's delight, Ella, Pete, and their servant, Anna, returned in mid-fall, and by the spring of 1930, the completion of the *Life* was in sight as well. On April 24, he informed his publisher, Alfred Harcourt, that he had one chapter remaining and expected to finish the editing quickly with Ella's help, much to the relief of Harcourt, who had been announcing the arrival of Steffens's anticipated work for months, only to be told by him, "I've lived too long." The oversized work still lacked a title, although in a letter to Mabel Dodge Luhan, again remarried, Una Jeffers noted that they were considering *In Wonderland*, which Ella felt aptly described Steffens's colorful life. Steffens still held out for *My Life of Unlearning*.

He had hoped that the book would be completed by summer, for Ella had plans to be in Germany for a month and then, after some encouragement from Rhys Williams, in Russia to research the economy there, while Steffens and Pete would stay with the Davidsons in Bécheron. Again, though, Steffens misjudged the timing and had to bring the work with him to France, where in August he did indeed reach the end. He told Ella that even though the manuscript was unpolished, it said what had to be said. "The *Life* is me and my story as I see it and want it seen. And," he could not resist adding, "*it is not bad*."

Once more, Steffens and Ella exchanged a flurry of letters. Pete was weary of crisscrossing the ocean and had little interest in France or in learning French, Steffens reported, but Steffens had hired a French governess to help him along. An extended visit from H. G. Wells, who arrived with his mistress, Odette Keun, kept Steffens entertained for hours on end. Steffens and Wells had never met, although Ella knew Wells from managing his campaign for a Labor seat in Parliament a decade earlier. Their conversations ranged from Russia to America to literature and far beyond. "He . . . agrees with everything I say," Steffens bragged to Ella. Davidson, however, recalled that they agreed on very little but had a lively exchange in the process, particularly in a spirited debate over the merits of Dorothy Parker's latest novel, *Laments for the Living*. George Slocombe later paid a visit as well, informing Steffens of his recent journey to India and two long interviews with Gandhi. Steffens, however, was underwhelmed by the results, writing to Ella's mother, "He says Gandhi understands the English better than the English do. That's easy. Any foreigner can see the English better than the English can see themselves. Even I can see and say that much."

As Ella's letters arrived full of enthusiasm for all that she was observing in Russia, Wells retained doubts about the Russian experiment, but Steffens was overjoyed to see that Ella, unlike so many foreigners who had been to Russia, "got it." "Go on, dear, get it all," he urged her. "Let it lift and clear your mind. . . . Russia can put you forward centuries in civilization. It can jerk you up to where it has got, and then show you the future. And Pete will profit by it, and I will. Russia is just what the Dorothy Parker, Hem, Dos Passos and all the Youth school of writers lack and need."

He pushed her not to dwell on such divisive subjects as Trotsky and Stalin but to encompass the whole operation. Are people working hard without the incentive of high pay? Are they interested in self-government? What about relations between managers and owners? There was so much—he told her it would take a year to digest it all. And to Steffens, it seemed almost as important for Ella to get Russia as for the Russians themselves. When Ella returned to Bécheron, she talked incessantly about the progress she had witnessed in Russia—improved education and health care, free divorces, extensive counseling for new mothers (and legal abortions), growing industrialization—mixed with appalling inefficiency and poverty, all further proof to Steffens that Russia had not retreated from its painstaking but heartening march to the future.

The *Life* required Steffens to return to New York for the winter, and the family decided to settle temporarily at Croton-on-Hudson. By mid-December, Steffens had nearly finished examining most of the galley proofs, and Ella was editing and collecting illustrations for the book. The only sizable hurdle remained the elusive title. Steffens and Harcourt finally reached a bland compromise of *The Autobiography of Lincoln Steffens*, which, Steffens remarked, gave "a nice false impression of dignity and self-sufficiency" for a book that was supposed to show the failure of a life.

In the depths of the Depression that had now seized America, it was apparent that one aspect of Steffens's life that he had not mishandled was money. In fact, it had been years since he had earned any significant income from his work. But he had invested—and fallen in love—wisely. Ella and he continued to make travel plans and to live exactly as they wished.

From an economic distance, though, he tried to comprehend how the business world, which he still believed could carry America a lot farther with its modernization than any politician, had utterly failed. Hoover, of course, was being pilloried, and Steffens watched the public flailing of the president from New York, both puzzled and bemused. "The most unexpected phenomenon hereabouts is the detestation of Hoover," he wrote to Colonel Wood in February 1931. "It is so violent and universal that I began to have some sympathy for him, and the denunciation of him on Wall Street convinces me that there is something good in him, and I look and inquire, but no, nothing." And it was not at all clear, Steffens confessed to Wood, that business could revive itself any easier than Hoover in the short term. "I've been looking all the time as publicly as I could for that big business man who is going to think," Steffens wrote. "You heard the rumor: that if this depression keeps up much longer somebody in business will begin to think. It sometimes sounds like a mere empty threat, but gosh! It might happen and I'd like to get a scoop on that thought or that thinker. A world beat!"

Others in the New York literary crowd viewed the dismal situation across the country and were more eager to take action. One of the most vocal was Theodore Dreiser, a socialist (although never a party member) whose own work had been influenced decades earlier by the muckrakers and reformers. No stranger to dissent, Dreiser had already spoken out against the persecution of the IWW, the deportation of Emma Goldman, and the death sentence of Sacco and Vanzetti. Now he called a gathering at his ornate studio on West Fifty-Seventh Street and included Steffens and, Malcolm Cowley recalled, nearly everyone else in the literary world with an opinion on the economic debacle.

Dreiser, then fifty-nine and, according to some, well overdue for the Nobel Prize, had the stature and the determination, if not the oratorical skills—he spoke endlessly and with "a large sort of bumbling dignity," Cowley noted—to influence events. Direct action was needed, and he wanted it to come from the people before him. "The time is ripe," he declared, "for American intellectuals to render some service to the American worker." Following Dreiser's sincere if clumsy appeal, Steffens took his own turn and evidently was barely an improvement. Both Cowley and author Louis Adamic observed that Steffens, who had spoken so effectively to countless audiences over the years, merely rambled on about his past, offering dated tales of strike breakers and police beatings that silenced the gathering for the wrong reasons. His sartorial statement, however, opened some eyes. "Small, trim, with a little white chin-beard and a Windsor tie tucked loosely into his collar, Steffens looked like a cartoonist's notion of a dapper French artist, an Aristide Duval," Cowley recalled.

His reputation apparently rescued him, as soon afterward, a group of writers, including Sherwood Anderson and John Dos Passos, formed the National Committee for the Defense of Political Prisoners, choosing Steffens to be treasurer. The organization, strongly sympathetic to the Communist Party, aimed to recognize "the right of workers to organize, strike and picket, their right to freedom of speech, press, and assembly" according to its statement of purpose. If he could not be in Russia, Steffens was certainly willing to support such revolutionary work at home. The committee, however, despite its investigative and publicity efforts on behalf of oppressed workers, ultimately wielded far less influence than its founders envisioned.

27

FAME AND FORTUNE IN THE DEPRESSION

INCREASINGLY, STEFFENS'S AUTOBIOGRAPHY was bringing good news. By February, he had finished reading the proofs ("The darn book is done and out of my hands and off my blooming mind," he exclaimed to Colonel Wood), and as the spring of 1931 passed, the Depression must have seemed farther away than ever to Steffens. The *Autobiography of Lincoln Steffens* came out on April 9, with smashing success, surprising—and pleasing—no one more than Steffens. "I have never seen the critics so unanimous," he crowed to Ella's mother. In fact, there were so many rave reviews that Ella had difficulty sending them all to her mother. On its front page, the *New York Times Book Review* declared, "There are one or two books a season which no intelligent person can afford to miss: Mr. Steffens's is one of them." The *New York Herald Tribune* asserted, "It should be made compulsory reading for all Americans desiring to be called 'grownup.'" From his legendary perch at the *Emporia Gazette*, William Allen White wrote of his old friend, "He had a singular detachment, a merry, kindly, but deadly aloofness which gave him perspective among men and measures. . . . By being brave and wise and charitably honest he did what he could to make the angels win, knowing full well that many of them were destined to lose." Gertrude Stein's sentiments were of great significance as well to the aging Steffens: "Just read your book and I like it a lot, I liked the crime wave and I liked Roosevelt and I liked me, and I may say I liked it all, I liked it in itself and I liked it because it brought back my early days, best to you always." Later, President Franklin Roosevelt told Ella that this was the book to teach Americans about their own country.

It was like a rebirth for Steffens, who wrote to Anton Johannsen's wife, Margaret, "I wish you and Jo could be here to get the full force of the reception of my book and,—don't laugh, Jo,—and me. If I believed all that they say about me I'd be so swelled up that I'd never speak to Jo again." At the Ritz in New York, Filene gave an April 27 dinner for Steffens. Attended by eighty-five guests—"the damndest mixed company you ever saw," he told Margaret—the evening featured many of the book's main characters, including Fred Howe, Clarence Darrow, Ida Tarbell, Mark Fagan, Rudolph Spreckels, Abraham Cahan, and Max Eastman. "And what do you think they demanded of me? Another, a third volume," he wrote with delight. Telegrams came in as well from old muckraking warriors unable to attend, including McClure, aged but not vindictive, who called Steffens a "Columbus."

One invited guest who neither attended nor cabled his good wishes was Steffens's old friend, Ezra Pound, by now thoroughly disenchanted with American politics and literature. He replied to Harcourt from Rapallo:

The problem whether a country that does not provide me with $50 a month in regard to my literary work should be regarded as a country or a shit house is one that I cheerfully leave to posterity.

But I certainly shall not spend money on congratulatory cables until the situation has changed.

I have great respect for Mr. L. Steffens but until you or some of the god damned plods can run a publishing house that will use at least 1% of its profits in printing literature that I care to read I can not see that I need to assist you in your prandial celebrations.

But Steffens's celebration was richly deserved. Published in two volumes at the rather considerable price of $7.50, the first printing of the book nevertheless sold out quickly and went into a second printing within ten days. Forty thousand copies rolled off the presses in one run. The Literary Guild chose the book as a selection of the month and had sold 37,500 copies by November. One bookstore alone ordered 1,000 copies from Harcourt, and at public libraries, there were waiting lists of readers eager to check it out. The book was on best-seller lists through the fall and winter of 1931 and, by Christmas, had sold 65,000 copies. Invitations for Steffens to speak at bookstores, lunches, and various conferences flowed in. A year after publication, still in the darkest days of the Depression, the book continued to sell 300 to 500 copies a month. Harcourt told Steffens he was confident that the book would go on selling for a generation, while Upton Sinclair, who had experience with best sellers, told Steffens to inform his publishers that "if a more interesting book has ever been published in America, I would not know where to look for it." Brand Whitlock said it reflected Steffens's character perfectly because it did not say a bad word about anyone. Wryly recalling the California bookends of his life, Steffens concluded, "My spiral-like story ends as it began: by my being thrown out of bed by the shocks of an earthquake which has laid me out, not crying, however, but smiling."

For Steffens, who had never fully recovered from the staggering personal blow of the McNamara debacle and his subsequent challenges in getting published, the public praise heaped upon him was highly gratifying. Undoubtedly of special meaning to Steffens was a letter sent to Harcourt by James McNamara at San Quentin after receiving a copy of the book from Steffens. "I have paid a tremendous price to be called a friend of Lincoln Steffens—denied twenty years of freedom—and though the Christians and the Gods of finance and industry decree that it be twenty more I consider the price dirt cheap," he wrote, concluding by calling Steffens "a genuine friend of mankind."

Although the essence of Steffens's long account of unlearning was his rejection of liberalism, reform, privilege, and American "democracy" in favor of revolution, the book's warmth and humor combined with Steffens's contagious optimism to ensure that his words would be met largely with acclaim, not hostility. This was particularly true in the Depression, when a story as uplifting as that of Steffens reminded Americans, disillusioned by a world war, a decade of mad pleasure, and a financial crash, of the potential for greatness still inherent in their wounded country.

Other forces were at work in making the book a best seller, a significant one being the stunning breakdown of the American economy and the contrasting Five-Year Plan of the Soviet Union, where rapid industrialization had reportedly sent factory production surging. During the economic boom and social frivolity of the 1920s, most Americans had paid scant attention to events abroad. Now, however, it seemed to many that a fundamental societal change was under way, leading to a sudden increase in analyses of what exactly was causing the dramatic shift in fortunes. In his controversial article, "An Appeal to Progressives," which appeared in the January 14, 1931 issue of the *New Republic*, literary critic Edmund Wilson voiced concerns that were blatantly un-American but nevertheless shared by Americans ranging from intellectuals to the poor:

> During these last years our buoyancy, our hope, our faith has all been
> put behind the speed of mass production, behind stupendous campaigns
> of advertising, behind cyclones of salesmanship. . . . Money-making

and the kind of advantages which a money-making society provides for
money to buy are not enough to satisfy humanity—neither is a social
system like our own where everyone is out for himself and devil take
the hindmost, with no common purpose and little common culture to
give life stability and sense. . . . The Buicks and Cadillacs, the bad gin
and Scotch, the radio concerts interspersed with advertising talks, the
golf and bridge of the suburban household which the bond salesman
can get for his money, can hardly compensate him for daily work of a
kind in which it is utterly impossible to imagine a normal human being
taking satisfaction or pride.

Steffens's work essentially told an American story of a child, raised in the
freedom and vast open space of California, who grew to be a successful man,
one who had traveled the world, observed its ways, and now concluded that the
standard wisdom explaining the greatness of his own capitalist country—that
democracy was the bedrock of America—had been an untruth, causing him to
look elsewhere for a better path toward genuine democracy. In the frightening
days of 1931, it was hardly an outrageous approach; indeed, some saw it as
visionary.

Still, others wondered what all the commotion was about, none more
so than Steffens's disaffected friend, Max Eastman, who in his own memoir
rebuked the notion that Steffens in his long life had learned—or unlearned—
much at all. "It is a delightful tale warmly told," Eastman wrote, "and gives a
picture of certain phases of American life that only a very brilliant and boldly
inquiring reporter could give. To me, however, its contribution to wisdom lies
in the unconsciousness with which it portrays a sprightly and rather self-pleased
cork bobbing about on currents of which it had no understanding and upon
which it had no effect."

Another harsh critic was the ardent communist writer and wanderer,
Michael Gold, who, in the pages of *New Masses*, viewed the book as a typical look down at the ills of the world from a very comfortable liberal loft.
Gold compared the ever optimistic Steffens to "comrade Jesus," who "always
admired everybody," adding that Steffens possessed the "charming trait of toler-
ance one finds in people who have incomes, and do not have to slave in offices
or steel mills."

More pertinent was an exchange between Steffens and Orrick Johns, by
then an established poet and, like Steffens, an ardent communist supporter.
In Carmel, Johns asked Steffens why, in his lengthy account of Joseph Folk's

moral crusade in St. Louis, Steffens had not seen fit to mention the help both he and Folk received from Johns's father, George Sibley Johns, the crusading editor of the *Post-Dispatch*. Steffens acknowledged that the senior Johns had been of great help to him but noted that as he was working on a national scale at that time for *McClure's*, he received far more material than he could use. Then, according to Orrick Johns, Steffens was silent for a moment before adding, "You know, Orrick, it isn't true—no autobiography is *true*. It was the way I wanted to remember it."

Such a quote from Steffens, given his lifelong habit of mixing irreverence with seriousness and tempered outrage, sounds highly characteristic, and was. While working on his autobiography, he addressed the matter directly in a 1928 letter to Hemingway:

> What I am writing is what I remember, the way I remember it. And the way I remember it is the way I have been telling it for fun, for effect in conversations. That incident of T.R. and his denial I have told many times, once to T.R. himself when he was President; and he said it wasn't as bad as that, but also he remembered enough of it to laugh and admit that was like that. I shall be writing that too, later. But he knew as I do that we were brought up in a time and a school that did make stories of what needed no making, and you might as well know that you are profiting by our old fiction habit to make your new—fiction.

Steffens's autobiography, like any memoir written at the end of a long life, omitted some facts, enlarged some truths, and was sometimes guilty of inconsistency, all of which combined with his admitted enthusiasm for storytelling— Alexander Woolcott, in *The New Yorker*, referred to one anecdote as "folklore in the making"—and his obstinate fidelity to the revolution in Russia. Still, Steffens was a witness to much of what he described, and as all memoirists do, he filtered the history through his own personal lens of subjectivity. Even in the muckraking days, Walter Lippmann recalled, Steffens "used to deplore the frightened literalness with which some of his articles were taken." In the end, he provided a largely valid, fascinating rendition of history, and while he may not have had every detail correct, he got enough right to impress a national audience that included many of the main characters in his book.

The Steffens family separated again in early May 1931. Steffens headed to Chicago with Pete and Anna for some book promotions before moving on to Carmel, while Ella, with a six-month advance from Harcourt, went back to

Russia to work on a book and do some reporting for the Hearst papers, focusing on a trip Shaw made to Russia.

Steffens spent the summer with Pete at The Getaway and the Hollister ranch, deeply satisfied with the results of his memoir. In his usual tongue-in-cheek manner, he assured Yvonne Davidson that he had, once again, made his mark: "You don't have to tell me that it is great. I have it from all sides that it is a 'masterpiece,' written by a 'wizard,' a 'classic,' done with a 'smile,' . . . The long book that I got so tired of writing and expected so little of has won the applause of all sorts of people." Steffens's only regret was that he had not foreseen this gratifying slice of the future while he was writing. "I could have enjoyed it more and done it so much better," he wrote.

As he turned sixty-five and the Depression in the summer of 1931 entered its darkest days, Steffens (and other rejuvenated leftists) felt that the global economic decline was a sign of the inevitable collapse of capitalism itself. No longer hopeful that American businessmen had the solutions, Steffens observed that the economic system was unable to serve the needs of the masses, especially in such desperate times. He offered the example of a downturn in the stock market following a government report predicting increased wheat production. "Think of a civilization in which a good crop of breadstuff is bad news. And with breadlines waiting for bread," he commented. Later, he continued the lament. "We can't distribute an abundance," he wrote, "under a system founded upon a philosophy of scarcity. We kill pigs not to feed the multitude, as we think, but to continue the profits of the minority. We prepare for the war we all dread. All, I say, even the munitions makers. And we don't know what is the matter with us; we see—no, we refuse to see a way out."

To Steffens, the hopeful signs of collapse were everywhere. The stock market was in shambles. Miners "with their picks on their shoulders" were parading in protest through the streets of London. British bankers predicted that Communism was imminent. The Japanese incursion into China "may be the beginning of a Jap-Chink war." Large corporations, most notably General Electric, considered centralized management ("the plan Owen D. Young talked to me about last winter"). Increasingly, Steffens's approval of the tumultous changes was nothing short of enthusiastic, and some of his remarks on the Depression, even taken as they were intended, displayed the same callousness that Gussie, Josephine, and others knew too well. "I'll be glad to go East to hear more"; "I feel like a front-seater at a great play"; "To celebrate and take advantage of the probable fall of our stock prices today I ordered a purchase"; "Capitalism is breaking down. . . . There is something to sing"—all comments showing Steffens's pleasure in the upheaval. Yet, Steffens realized that nothing was permanent, particularly his own "knowledge" of anything. After all, the same man who wrote, "A great world in which everything is clear to me" followed it up six weeks later with "I am only wondering, thinking, and not at all sure."

Requests for articles, books, and lectures continued to swamp Steffens, including one from a group of New York school teachers who wanted Steffens to speak on the education of children. College professors made the autobiography required course reading. To capitalize on the book's momentum, Steffens made plans to lecture his way to New York in October and back home through Texas in December.

Meanwhile, Ella, after spending a month in Germany searching for material on the ominous political rise of Nazism, was making her way around Russia, absorbing as much as she could of the communist approach but never enough to satisfy Steffens. He was pleased to hear that she wanted to stay there through the winter, encouraging her to find a job and work on her book. Still, he hoped that Ella would accept the new Russia whole, as he himself had, and any hesitation on her part tried his patience. In September, he wrote to Jo Davidson that Ella was getting some "good stuff" over there that, unfortunately, "she can't quite master and digest." After hearing her say that she was a "near" communist, Steffens told her that if she would just look at the rest of the world, she would become "all" communist. "My surprise is that you have not done so already."

Ella was present for the arrival of Shaw, who was accompanied by Lady Astor and Lord Lothian, the former Philip Kerr who had assisted Lloyd George at the Paris talks. Shaw recalled her from their previous meeting, asking her how she had managed to find her way to Russia. More interesting to Steffens was her talk with Lord Lothian. Steffens wanted some historical clarification, asking Ella to inquire about the legitimacy of the controversial note that Bullitt had carried to Lenin. Lothian acknowledged that Lloyd George himself had suggested the questions, confirming what had been so publicly and emphatically denied twelve years earlier.

Ella saw enough in Russia—and heard enough from Steffens—to finish her book. *Red Virtue: Human Relationships in the New Russia*, came out the following year to favorable reviews and displayed her unyielding devotion to both her husband and Russia by beginning with Steffens's infamous comment about "the future."

By early November, Steffens was in New York, being lavished with praise by his publishing house—the company president down to the telephone operators were "crazy about it"—and finding that audiences were as eager as ever to hear what he had unlearned. "My humble lecture tour is developing into a triumph," he assured Dot. "Everybody seems to have read (*and bought*) my book and they most of them have an emotional sense of it." Steffens took the tour through Texas in December before returning to The Getaway later in the month. The talks had gone well, but the grinding travel schedule had left Steffens exhausted and with little time to see old friends. He vowed never to go through it again. Naturally, he was back at it within a year.

28

LEFT IS RIGHT

STEFFENS PASSED THE early months of 1932 relaxing in Carmel with the Jefferses, Edward Weston, and other friends. Through Una Jeffers, he stayed abreast of various friends, including the irrepressible Mabel Dodge Luhan. Having sent her third, and precarious, husband, the artist Maurice Sterne, off to Taos in 1917, Dodge soon followed him there, only to quickly fall under the spell of a tall, handsome, and married Pueblo Indian named Tony Luhan. He thoroughly charmed her with the simplicity of Native American life until he became her fourth husband, when he developed a fondness for driving her distinguished visitors, including D. H. and Frieda Lawrence, Willa Cather, Georgia O'Keefe, Ansel Adams, and Mary Austin, around in her Cadillac and helped her turn a three-room adobe home into a seventeen-room house with 8,400 square feet of living space. But Dodge was devoted to Luhan, and her immersion in Pueblo culture, seemingly the "Change" she sought, was genuine. As a result, she spent considerable energy defending and explaining the Native American ways to a skeptical outside world. Like so many others, the Luhans dropped by The Getaway whenever they were in Carmel. In character, Dodge worked up a fit of pique, Steffens observed, because Jo Davidson's statue of Jeffers, which had captivated everyone except her, had been sculpted in Steffens's home and not her own.

Steffens's own relationship with Dodge had cooled somewhat, as he explained to Una: "Mabel is all right to anyone she is winning, but to others she has won or doesn't want to win, she's not so nice, not nearly so nice. I've been both. Long ago when I was a key to Jack Reed, she was charming to me; now she is—herself. . . . When she isn't shining, she's a wet, cold, cloudy day." Steffens may have been on the mark. Dodge, who admittedly saw her years in

Europe as silly and those in New York as rather self-absorbed, endeavored to find a more meaningful life in the Southwest, but the devastation she had felt since 1930 over both the death of D. H. Lawrence—whom she deeply admired and probably loved—and her futile effort to replace the artist-god of Lawrence with Jeffers, made it hard for Dodge to shine on a regular basis. And Steffens was no longer the energetic, captivating host of the Evenings but an aging intellectual on the Far Left, a political position that Dodge, now focused on personal growth and oneness with her surroundings, found far from compelling.

Still, they remained friends and socially active throughout the Carmel years. Steffens recalled a day that Tony Luhan drove Steffens, Mabel, Una, and Jeffers's older brother, the astronomer Hamilton Jeffers, up to the nearby mountains for a picnic dinner before gazing through a large telescope at the moon and Mars. But Steffens was unimpressed, as he could see very little and noted that "there appeared to be no taxpayers on either heavenly body." The artist John O'Shea and his wife, Molly, hosted some memorable picnics for the Carmel arts circle along a secluded coastal spot just below a towering cliff. Ella Young, a poet, recounted one such affair attended by Steffens and Dodge:

> It is a gay party, as gay as the sunshine, as gay as the coloured stripes on the awning. . . . Sinclair Lewis is raying out the wittiest and most fantastic remarks. John O'Shea replies in kind. Lincoln Steffens is even more dazzling. So lightning-quick is thrust and riposte in this rapier play of wit that I find myself bewildered by it. Una Jeffers, at the other end of the table, is telling amusing anecdotes. Tony, tired of it all, is standing on a rock. He stands majestic in a scarlet serape. The sea curls in waves behind him.

Apart from the colorful social scene, Steffens wrote his local columns, answered fan mail, and kept in touch with friends. Fred Howe, whose own memoir had sold well but who had been badly bruised by Wall Street, told Steffens he thought that "the system" was finished. However, Steffens, upon hearing strong rumors that speculators were eager to invest heavily once the Wall Street malaise had run its course, saw another boom ahead. Filene, whose neglected crusade for reform now had outlasted a world war, a boom, and an international depression, prodded Steffens to cross the Atlantic one more time for another look at Europe. Steffens turned him down: "You are opposite to the world and most of its inhabitants: you are hopeless in principle but in fact all right."

A more serious letter exchange took place with John Reed's mother, who was hoping to enlist Steffens's support in preventing a number of American communist groups called John Reed Clubs—there were twelve nationwide—from appropriating his name. Ella, in fact, had organized one in Carmel, and Steffens had given a talk there. After offering Frank Heney's name for legal help, Steffens calmly explained the problem to Mrs. Reed. Her son, Steffens reminded her, was a hero—in Russia. In his last years, Reed "did go completely over" and "lived the life of a party communist," having been on speaking terms with Lenin and Trotsky and received a prestigious appointment to the Executive Committee of the Communist International just before his untimely death of typhus in Moscow in 1920. Several communist leaders, including Nicholas Bukharin, spoke at his funeral, and his body lay in state for a week before his burial under the Kremlin Wall. Steffens wrote in *The Freeman* at the time, "To a poet, to a spirit like Jack Reed, the communist, death in Moscow must have been a vision of the resurrection and life of Man." If anything, Steffens pointed out to Mrs. Reed, her son would have wished the John Reed Clubs to be more radical than they were.

And, Steffens had to acknowledge, his close relationship with Reed—the proud, seasoned mentor and the energetic, romantic poet—had ended badly. On a deserted side street under a "staring street lamp" in New York, Steffens had encountered Reed and greeted him pleasantly only to be met by a bruising response. His young friend, he recalled, "blew me up hard." Feeling annoyed and betrayed, Reed snapped at Steffens, "Why don't you join us? We are trying to do what you used to talk and write about." He challenged Steffens to drop what Reed saw as his lukewarm support of Russia. "Go on—the limit," he exclaimed. Steffens had promised Reed's father years ago that he would keep an eye on "the beautiful boy" at Harvard, but he now admitted that Reed had "frightened" him at times with his unrestrained embrace of "some cause." Once a poet searching for beauty and a better world, Reed, the committed communist, "didn't smile anymore." Steffens closed the letter to Reed's mother by conceding that there was not much comfort in his letter, but that he felt honesty was his only choice. He could not help her.

One possible use of his talents in Carmel, Steffens thought, was to assist young people with their unlearning, as he was doing so diligently with Pete. He spoke at a high school, where, he told Harcourt, the excited students came up "to the edge of their seats" and let him know that it was "the first time they had ever got it straight." Steffens later wrote to Robert Sproul, president of the University of California, to support students in the university's Social Problems Club, which had been been banned from meeting on the campus. He proudly recalled a student club he had formed with Lippmann at Harvard, noting that he had encouraged students all his life to be curious, ask questions, and express opinions. "I wish there had been a Social Problems Club at Berkeley in my day," he told Sproul. "It might have saved me years of fumbling."

Steffens's literary success continued into the summer of 1932. He did not receive the Pulitzer Prize as some critics had expected, but he was given awards by the Commonwealth Club of San Francisco and the New York Evening Post Association. Sales of his autobiography remained strong. The book's popularity partly sheltered Steffens from the relentless dive of stock values, which had chopped his income by two-thirds and done similar damage to his Carmel neighbors, all of whom, Steffens noted to Jo Davidson, were "nice people who don't do a thing."

Ella, meanwhile, was busy with her own lectures on Russia as well as scandalizing herself by promoting her John Reed Club—"a near-Communist organization for near-writers and near-artists" that did everything "from despising their neighbors to making money on cheap entertainments," Steffens told her mother. In his jibe, he conveniently chose to ignore the fact that the club's membership featured Jo Davidson, Rhys Williams, and Orrick Johns, while Langston Hughes and Joseph Freeman, a prominent American communist intellectual, were guest speakers. Ironically, even as Steffens himself gently chided Carmelites over their trivial pursuits, renowned California writer and satirist Carey McWilliams lumped Steffens in with the crowd, noting that he produced "blazing editorials" for *The Carmelite* and was "rather naively regarded by the citizenry as a radical thinker."

After Langston Hughes read his poems at the club, he paid a visit to Steffens's home, where the two writers had a practical reason for discussing Russia: Hughes was about to embark on a trip to Russia on a movie-making venture involving race relations in America. They passed an hour together, with Hughes receiving what he termed "good advice" from Steffens, who undoubtedly was more than willing to discuss the topic. Steffens, as usual, warned him to be prepared not to like what he found under Soviet Communism, particularly as an American accustomed to drugstores filled with everything from "mousetraps to waterproof watches." What he would need to bring with him, above all, Steffens admitted, was soap and toilet paper—"don't part with it!" he instructed. As Hughes left, Steffens displayed the folksy humor that had been his trademark for so many years. "I'm glad you're going to Russia," Steffens said. "It's time Negroes were getting around in the world. Can you tell me why in the hell they stay home so much?" When Hughes later met Karl Radek, editor of *Izvestia*, the Russian man's quick wit, short stature, and striking goatee reminded Hughes of the old muckraker.

Steffens was content to observe the political and economic landscape and to jokingly "campaign" for Hoover in the 1932 election, confident that "he and his backers will bring on the revolution." Otherwise, he pushed the communist line at every opportunity from the comfort of Carmel. In the turmoil of the 1932 campaign, nearly everyone in America, it seemed, had an answer to the nation's woes. More than two dozen alternative political parties, including Socialist-Labor, Farmer Labor, Independent, Liberty, Independent Liberty, Jacksonian, and, of course, Jobless, fought for votes. Wall Street wanted a Republican, Hoover or otherwise. Franklin Roosevelt sought support from Democrats all over, especially from the Catholics who had been so excited over Al Smith in 1928 only to be spurned at the Democratic Convention. Many intellectuals and leftists promoted Norman Thomas of the Socialist Party, although, particularly for writers who felt that only a dramatic social and economic upheaval would salvage the situation, even Thomas was insufficiently radical. "I should think that becoming a Socialist right now," Dos Passos commented, "would have about the same effect on anybody as drinking a bottle of near beer."

For such radicals, that left the Communist Party, whose ideals appealed to a group of fifty-three influential artists and intellectuals, including Steffens, Ella, Dos Passos, Dreiser, Anderson, Edmund Wilson, Langston Hughes, and Sidney Hook. The members of this group denounced the two major parties as corrupt and the socialists as stagnant. Associated with a leftist group known as the League of Professional Groups, they published an open letter, "Culture and the Crisis," to fellow artists, writers, scientists, teachers, engineers, and "all professional workers," stating that "the only effective way to protest against the chaos, the appalling wastefulness, and the indescribable misery inherent in the present economic system is to vote for the Communist candidates." Capitalism, they wrote, should be abolished through "the conquest of political power and the establishment of a workers' and farmers' government which will usher in the Socialist Commonwealth." And in those dark days of the Depression, there was a genuine feeling, sometimes euphoric, among the believers that revolution was inevitable and that workers could rise up and claim their rights.

Malcom Cowley, never a radical but a league member and keen observer, recalled the idealistic fervor of the times:

> The casting out of old identities, communion with the workers; life in a future world that the workers would build in America as they were building it in Russia; all those religious elements were present in the dream of those years. It made everything else seem unimportant,

including one's pride, one's comfort, one's personal success or failure, and one's private relations. There wasn't much time for any of these. Everything personal except marriage—and even marriage for many— was allowed to remain provisional until the glorious day when the bridge had been built and crossed.

But Cowley, unlike Steffens, also recognized the petty infighting, the obstinate factions, the frightening language of revolt, and the insistence on obedience and preaching the narrow party line—all these aspects that marked the movement. What Steffens cast off as growing pains and necessary stumbles were signals that alarmed many who wanted reform but not catastrophe. Unfortunately for the league and the devoted volunteers who spent exhausting days organizing in cramped offices and standing on city street corners handing out copies of the *Daily Worker*, the effort was largely in vain. William Z. Foster, the Communist Party presidential candidate and a man, Sidney Hook observed, who "knew how to organize a strike, although he did not have the eloquence to inspire one," landed briefly in jail in June before suffering a heart attack and resigning from the race, while Roosevelt entered the White House. The paltry 103,000 votes given to the Communist Party in 1932 would actually be its high-water mark in American electoral history.

Still, the American Left did not abandon Russia. The issue of formal diplomatic recognition by America had been debated for over a decade, although Hoover's visceral hatred of the Bolsheviks had muted the conversation. Upon the election of Franklin Roosevelt, who had expressed a willingness to reconsider the matter, public interest intensified, and the president's desk soon was covered with petitions signed by college presidents, economists, social activists, and others in support of Soviet recognition. Steffens, in his late sixties, joined the chorus by serving with William Allen White on the advisory council of the Independent Committee for the Recognition of Soviet Russia. The movement was rewarded when Roosevelt extended official recognition on November 17, 1933, a victory for liberals who felt vindicated for their steadfast belief in the revolutionary ideals of the communists.

Steffens maintained his faith that the stagnant economy would do its part to usher in a new age in his own country. "I'm a bear on our civilization but a bull on the market," he told Dot. Even after the collapse of Central Railroad of Georgia doomed his ten-thousand-dollar investment, he told Ella, "I'm glad, not sorry. I'm a bear all right." Yet the devastating economic swath that cut across the country ultimately touched Steffens as well and increasingly left him with debilitating losses. Joseph Steffens had been a director at the California National Bank of Sacramento and happily, no doubt, had passed on his shares to his son. But with those same shares now worth less than a third of their previous value and Steffens liable for the par value of the stocks, he was looking at an assessment of possibly twenty-five thousand dollars. "It gets on my nerves a little, more and more, in spite of the way I take it," he admitted to Ella. "I understand now better how my neighbors feel, with their similar losses . . . nobody talks much about it, but you feel it in the air." Still, he concluded his letter in typical style: "I tell you nobody in the world *proposes* anything basic and real, except the Communists."

While his fortune was shrinking, the limelight continued to shine on Steffens. In August, *Cosmopolitan* asked him to contribute to an article titled "But Will It Be the Same One Hundred Years From Now?" He agreed, joining Wells, Bertrand Russell, Amelia Earhart, and others in an article that appeared the following March. Two months later, *Cosmopolitan*, which had recently asked Steffens if he would consider muckraking Europe (he left open the possibility, despite his advancing age), published a Steffens story with the unabashed title "This World-Depression of Ours Is Chock Full of Good News." He declined another offer from a publisher to do a biography on La Follette.

Ella and Steffens had gone their own separate ways again in the fall of 1932. Ella headed back to New York for several months to deal with the publication of her book, a promotional lecture tour, and political organizing (she joined Joseph Freeman in forming a committee against Hitler). Steffens, meanwhile, spent a couple of weeks in November giving talks in Sacramento, San Francisco, and Los Angeles. In the capital, he addressed a rally in support of the infamous San Quentin prisoner Tom Mooney, an outspoken labor leader and former Wobbly who had been imprisoned since 1916 for the bombing deaths of nineteen people during a Preparedness Day parade in San Francisco. Mooney became an international hero to the Left when, on the basis of questionable testimony, he was convicted and sentenced to death. Under intense pressure from intellectuals, radicals, and even President Wilson, California Governor William Stephens spared Mooney's life but declared that Mooney would remain in jail permanently. Nearly two decades later, with the resurgence of the Left and a newsletter and a magazine devoted specifically to Mooney's case, Steffens continued to speak out in an effort to commute Mooney's sentence. After the rally, he met with California Governor James Rolph in mid-November and raised the issue of Mooney, to no avail.

About the same time, Steffens, joined by Ella, Dreiser, Orrick Johns, and the radical screenwriter Samuel Ornitz (later to be one of the Hollywood Ten investigated by the House Committee on Un-American Activities), drove to San Quentin to see the "bombing" prisoners: Mooney, James McNamara, and Matthew Schmidt. Upon arriving, Steffens, with his "jaunty tweed cape flowing from his shoulders," Johns recalled, went ahead and arranged the meeting. To Johns, the men all appeared to be in good spirits, probably a result of the public support that at least Mooney was receiving. When Steffens spoke with McNamara, however, the muckraker's eyes teared up, his past actions evidently weighing heavily as he faced the man who symbolized the failure of the Golden Rule. In a later letter to Secretary of Labor Frances Perkins, Steffens alluded to his critical misjudgment: "I personally would not trust . . . official promises by any business-like politicians; I did it once and there's a man in the penitentiary now paying with his life for my fool confidence."

In November, Steffens accepted an invitation from the Liberal Forum in Los Angeles to join a debate, "Can Capitalism Be Saved?" He took the negative side, of course, arguing before a sold-out auditorium of three thousand that Communism may not be desirable, yet was inevitable. Steffens felt that the debate, with Berkeley Mayor Stitt Wilson, was "a thriller," although he regretted leaning so far to the left that he might have carried only "the Communists in the top gallery." Continuing on the theme in a letter to Beverley Bowie, a Harvard student, Steffens reiterated his position but avoided the frightening issue to many—the brutality of the Russian government. "I am not a communist," he insisted. "I merely think that the next order of society will be socialist and that the Communists will bring it in and lead it. . . . Intellectually they are ahead of the Socialists in this, that they know that there is a job to do and that it has to be done. . . . As to violence in the transition, that depends upon the opposition. The old order will probably fight; it's a fighting order, so the Communists must be prepared to fight."

Reporting to Ella on his local lectures, Steffens wrote of an auspicious talk he had given in San Francisco in late January 1933 in front of another full house. Which of the political systems, he asked, was trying go all the way forward to eliminate war, graft, and tyranny? "Yes, I am talking Communism, Bolshevik Communism," he declared. At the close, waves of applause went on until Steffens had to reappear for a bow. Old radical friends told him it was his best effort ever. A restaurant owner took Steffens and his circle back for a free meal and drinks, and at the end of the night, a Standard Oil manager, of all people, gripped Steffens's hand. "You're all right, all right," he repeated. For

Steffens, sixty-six, a best-selling author (over ninety thousand copies of his auto-biography had been sold by February), and a speaker in demand in the midst of a capitalist meltdown, his faith in his own vision of the future had never been stronger.

A man who had once prided himself on his openness to all ideas in his ear-nest search for truth, Steffens had hardened his views by the time Hitler seized power in Germany. Steffens's urge to reform the future had now increasingly solidified into full support of total revolution. Steffens, fairly, pointed out simi-larities between the political systems of Hitler, Mussolini, and the West—just like capitalists, the dictators used wars and markets to fuel their economies and their dreams of empire. But the dictators, particularly Hitler, also shared a tragic belief with the Soviets that Steffens himself too easily accepted: that the only path forward was, as Reed had maintained, to go "the limit." Steffens's letters are a grim reminder that from the sunshine and safety of Northern California, he continued to see the use of terror as unavoidable in the struggle to produce genuine democracy.

Even when Ella, working with a group supporting the victims of German Fascism, asked Steffens for a public statement on the crisis, he could only look toward the ideal future of Communism that the present dark days, he was sure, would usher in. And while not a Nazi supporter, he gave an uncomfortably rational appraisal of their violence in a letter to the *New York World Telegram* on March 30:

> People who are incensed at the mishandling of the Jews and Reds in Fascist Germany should remember that moral violence is of the very essence of Fascism. Fascism is not only counter-revolutionary; it is counter-historical, too. It takes all one's force to go against the stream, as Hitler goes and Mussolini went. Hitler has to seize upon every prejudice, every passion in sight to counter the natural, the economic currents that make for the ending of the capitalist system and the beginning of Communism. He may be sincere in his hatred of Jews; the Germans he needs with him are. Anti-Semitism existed as a force for him to use and he had to use it. A must it was. His sincerity only caused the gross excesses that arouse the world outside. The world should learn, however, that Fascism, threatened everywhere, will and must always behave this way. Communism had anti-Semitism in Russia; it is very strong, very widespread. And that they did not avail of it was, not because they are gentler than the Hitler Germans, but because they

did not need it. On the contrary, they needed the Jews. They needed all peoples who could fall in with, help and function under the humanly understandable system called Communism.

It's too bad to miss in indignation, however just, the lesson Germany today is teaching: that Fascism will be fierce on Jews, Germans, Americans,—all economically civilized people. And that they will fit in with and be happily at home under Communism. It is not an outrage, it is a revelation that Fascist Germany is offering us.

In a letter three days later to Ella, again on the topic of Jews, he once more stressed the importance of clear thinking analysis, writing as if oppressed individuals always had the luxury of political choices under dictators:

> It's not Hitler, it's Fascism that has to be met. The Jews are intelligent enough to see that Fascism is a movement of defense against economic forces that make for Communism. The Fascists haven't got history with them, they must depend on existing psychological forces of prejudice and passion. Hitler has two such that he can use—anti-Semitism and anti-Red. Well, he cultivates, voices and puts in action both, and they form a wave he can ride on. Mounted upon them, loosing them recklessly, he can do other things that otherwise he could not do. We'll find in this country that something like it will be done. The passion here is against financiers; not Jews. But there is some anti-Semitism and, as Ford illustrated, a demagogue can mistake the hate of bankers for the hate of Jews.
>
> The big thing to bring out is that the Jews have to see, like the rest of us, that the choice is between Fascism and Communism, between Russia and Germany.

And the revolutionary bloodletting was, Steffens believed, "for the children." "I care what sort of world Pete's generation will have to live and fit in," he wrote. Earlier he had commented to Ella's mother, "I'd rather have it [the Depression and revolution] now while Pete's a child so that he can go out into a decent world. Not this, not this!"

Steffen's open support of violent revolution did not diminish his public standing—indeed, it may have increased the public wish to hear the words of the brilliant or wayward prophet, depending on one's point of view. He clearly stirred political passions on all sides. Communists could not accept his unwillingness to condemn Hitler, liberals criticized him over the Red Terror, and conservatives dismissed him as utterly misguided. But he was not ignored, and being in the fray was where Steffens had long felt most comfortable.

In the midst of his rebirth, he maintained his avid support for the labor movement, now a shell of its former self after the prosperity of the 1920s was followed by the current desperation of millions seeking any form of work. On July 15, Steffens took advantage of the Convention of State Governors, which was meeting in California. He wrote to President Roosevelt, encouraging him to take the bold step of declaring a "New Deal for Labor" and to instruct the governors to grant an amnesty to all the labor agitators still in prison. Referring to FDR as a "poet in action," Steffens noted that the president was always promoting a positive course, not assigning blame, and addressing the needs of the country, making this an excellent moment to move nobly in the direction of the prisoners.

Roosevelt, however, was content to ignore the dynamiters and political prisoners. Undeterred, Steffens next called on Governor Rolph on October 18. Rolph had surprisingly told the press of the meeting, so Steffens and his nephew Joseph, along for the visit were stopped by reporters outside the governor's mansion. What did he want to see the governor about? Flashing his old wit, Steffens announced that he was launching an investigation to find out if the governor had any sense of humor.

The governor greeted them warmly, but the meeting itself began slowly, at least for Steffens, as Governor Rolph seemed more interested in discussing the history of the mansion and Steffens's family connection to it than the dynamiters. Steffens finally brought the governor back to the uncomfortable subject of the laborers, contrasting how "strikers" continued to be sent off to prison while criminals "of our class" operated freely. Rolph, according to Steffens, could not deny it. After the meeting, Steffens felt encouraged: "Rolph *is* really tempted to do something."

The governor was not, however, tempted enough. The dynamiters remained behind bars, Schmidt even sending word to Steffens to cease his efforts, judging that Steffens was too radical to help. And Schmidt was undoubtedly correct. For two decades, Steffens's appeals had reached as high as the White House, to no avail. Old and in declining health himself, Steffens had little left to offer McNamara and the others.

Ella's book on Russia had come out in April. Steffens praised it yet acknowledged what Ella really wished for: "I hope it sells," he wrote to her, "but I pray that it may be read." For Steffens, approval of the book did not imply that it was perfect. He realized Ella was quite disturbed over the public skepticism aimed at what she saw as progress in Russia. Steffens advised her to calm down. "People can't be expected to 'get' all that," he told her. "It's too much, too new. And your unrealistic feelings about it will make you sick and useless if you don't look out. . . . The world is moving fast, faster than I ever expected it to, and you should sense that and let it reassure you."

In November, Steffens journeyed again to the East Coast, where he renewed ties with friends in Boston and New York. He dined with the wealthy entrepreneur Roger Babson, who looked into the future and saw "some sort of technocracy" ahead for America. Babson also mentioned that he had seen Thomas Edison just before Edison's death and suspected that his last words to Babson would delight Steffens in particular: "And remember, Babson, we don't know nothing about nothing." Steffens could not resist passing along the great inventor's parting words to Ella.

With a group of friends that included Filene—a Jew—Steffens took in a Nazi speech at a packed Ford Hall in Boston and later termed it "a really absurd or ignorant" talk. The German speaker was a professor who gave "a slow, dull, utterly uninspired" defense of the Nazi takeover and the mistreatment of only "bad" Jews. The talk was delivered so poorly that at a gathering at Filene's home later that night, Steffens commented that Moscow must have sent the professor over "to do the Hitlerites damage." A week later, he remarked to Ella concerning free speech for the Nazis, "If they have speakers like the one at Ford Hall, I say the more they appear the better."

The night after attending the Nazi speech, Steffens took his own turn at lecturing, across the Charles River. As he reported to Ella, "I have made better speeches, but I have never had a greater success than at Harvard." It was another capacity audience for Steffens, and he did not disappoint. A professor introduced Steffens as the best, most dangerous salesman in America, warning students to remain alert or, at Steffens's persuasion, they would run the risk of acquiring new ideas.

With his typical approach of tact, humor, and patience, Steffens fully engaged the audience. At the conclusion, he took more than an hour of questions and was ushered out with cheers. "There is no doubt that I accomplished something, cleaned the whole atmosphere," he told Ella. Beverley Bowie, the Harvard student whom Steffens had written to a year ago, supported his appraisal: "He was unmercifully brilliant to questioners. I never witnessed such slaughter." Harcourt evidently agreed, telling Steffens that he had gone far beyond the autobiography and that despite his age, another volume was certainly needed. In fact, two years later, Harcourt did bring out a slim volume of Steffens's work,

Boy on Horseback, the excerpt from his first autobiographical volume that had charmed so many readers, which went on to sell over four thousand copies.

From Boston, Steffens traveled to New York, where he kept up a hectic schedule, meeting Harcourt, the editors of *New Masses*, Max Lerner, and other writers. One day, he met Whittaker Chambers, whose stories in *New Masses* he had praised in a letter to Chambers five months earlier: "Whenever I hear people talking about 'proletarian art and literature,' I'm going to ask them to shut their minds and look at you. I hope you are very young, though I don't see how you can be. I hope, too, that you are daring, that you have no respect for the writers of my generation and that you know as well as I do that you can do it." In New York, Chambers thanked Steffens for his encouragement. "[Chambers] really appreciated it because nobody before had ever given him a hand," Steffens reported to Ella, agreeing with Chambers that lack of praise for others' work was a "Red fault" and more "warm spots" were needed in the party.

Steffens also had business of a more serious nature on his New York stay. Laura, his conscience and counselor through trying times and alway a faithful correspondent, had been suffering a tragic mental decline over the past few years. Passionate and idealistic, she had put tremendous energy into reforming the California library system over two decades, and although she was instrumental in helping to establish a statewide network of free county libraries and rose to become assistant state librarian, she became exhausted and embittered by the experience. In 1924, she poured her frustations into a small book, *The Beginning and the End of the Best Library Service in the World*. By the late 1920s, she had developed schizophrenia and, with the assistance of Jane Hollister Wheelwright, had several sessions with Carl Jung in Zurich in 1932. Now, she was in New York for more treatment. Steffens, with Allen, visited Laura's doctor in December, but did not receive hopeful news. In a letter to Dot, Allen relayed the bad news: "Dr. W. had a long talk with me in Lin's [Steffens's] presence to make it clear to me that I must be in as good condition as possible for I had a big job ahead of me." Sadly, Laura never recovered, with Allen devoted to his wife's care until her death in 1946. For Steffens, her steady voice of reason had been silenced.

29

"I Thought He Was Just My Daddy"

From New York, Steffens returned to Boston before moving on to Chicago, where, speaking without a microphone, he gave a rousing address on December 11 at the Hotel Sherman to a Rotary gathering that was "a whirl of a success" and "took the Rotarians by storm." Darrow, among the eight hundred attending, told Steffens that he was in the best form ever. For his efforts, Steffens earned two hundred dollars and sold and signed about thirty copies of his book. He also informed Ella of a reporter's view that Brandeis and Frankfurter were "the real power" behind President Roosevelt, encouraging her to renew her old ties with Frankfurter in an effort to aid Mooney.

Chicago, however, became a far different memory for Steffens, as his successful talk was given only under painful duress. "Something has happened,—is happening to my left leg," he wrote worriedly to Ella. "It weakens and gives me a terrifying tendency to go left. I have to hold on to somebody. I'm hoping it will pass, but I've had it two days and it gets worse, not better." Two days later he collapsed, doctors told Ella, from hardening of the arteries in his brain, with the possibility of progressive incapacity or paralysis looming. Steffens would not enter a hospital and chose instead to be carried on a stretcher aboard a train bound for California, where he would be confined to The Getaway indefinitely. Eager to work but fearful of a more debilitating attack, Steffens remained bedridden and, to Ella's great distress, again prone to significant mood swings.

From bed, Steffens continued to observe the world. Seeing labor again being maligned by landowners and law enforcement officials across the state, Steffens took on the whimsical but symbolically important task of purchasing a single typewriter to bolster the workers' cause. His support was given to the small but feisty Cannery and Agricultural Workers Industrial Union (CAWIU), which organized strikes of migrant fruit-pickers and other low-wage earners statewide. Representing workers who made as little as ten cents an hour, the CAWIU had obvious appeal for Steffens, as it had been created in 1932 by another union under the control of the American Communist Party (CPUSA). To publicize their efforts, union representatives, working tirelessly on a meager budget, relied on mimeograph copies, handmade posters, and campfire speeches to reach the transient-worker population.

Twenty-one-year-old Caroline Decker, the "tiny little labor agitator" who served as executive secretary of the CAWIU, had an unfortunate problem, Steffens learned: She had no typewriter. Decker undoubtedly attracted the attention of Steffens for some of the same reasons that Ella had in Paris. Extremely energetic, intelligent, and bravely outspoken in the cause of the workers, Decker (referred to as "Comrade Decker" in the union literature) was wholly devoted to her work. She was a former member of the Youth Communist League and, the previous October, had defiantly led the notorious California cotton strike of nearly twenty thousand pickers, the largest agricultural strike in the nation's history. Dramatically heading a parade of Mexican, Filipino, and other protesting workers marching on a courthouse in Visalia to speak out at a government hearing on the strike, the petite Decker must have resembled an agitated Shirley Temple. In a front-page headline on October 26, the *San Francisco Chronicle* blared, "Girl, 21, Laughs at Fear as She Directs Strike." And with impressive results: Decker's efforts eventually helped to secure concessions of more than a million dollars in increased wages. In a celebratory party at The Getaway after the strike, James Cagney, a close family friend of Steffens and Ella's, offered to teach Decker how to tap dance. So Steffens, appointing himself chairman, secretary, and treasurer of the Caroline Decker Typewriter Fund, applied his efforts to fund-raising.

One of his first targets was Governor Rolph. He explained to the governor the enormity of the challenge: "She thinks she can make consumers, citizens, and human beings out of these peon producers. An audacious experiment, as dubious as mine, and therefore worth boosting." He asked the governor to solicit funds from his staff as well and added that in the fortuitous event of excessive contributions, he would invest the difference in a second typewriter "if the first one should be wrecked in some righteous raid." Steffens also sought donations from others, including Filene, who eventually provided the machine that became a prized possession of Decker's. "I guessed that she was keeping it in good shape," Steffens teased Filene, "for the next raid by the Chamber of Commerce and the Law-and-Orderlies."

Ella, now a leading activist among leftist writers, was quite willing and able to assist the CAWIU as well, aggressively confronting judges in court and taking full advantage of the family connection to Cagney and Hollywood by raising bail money for strikers. At the same time, she involved herself in the ongoing and increasingly controversial case of the Scottsboro boys in Alabama, where state prosecutors were determined to see the young black defendants convicted of rape. In San Francisco, Ella, with help from Hughes, Cagney, and others, organized a successful art auction benefit. Between her open admiration for Russia and her dedicated work for social justice in California, Ella had become such a lightning rod for conservatives that Guy Hickok, in New York, sent her a recipe for removing tar and feathers.

Cagney's association with Steffens and Ella would cause him some uncomfortable moments. Having grown up on New York's Lower East Side and not afraid to side with the oppressed, Cagney had donated money in support of Ella's work for the cotton pickers, a fact that Sacramento district attorney Neil McAllister eagerly exploited in his efforts to identify communist sympathizers amid the labor strife. Citing Ella's own letters in which she gratefully acknowledged Cagney's help, McAllister declared that he would use Cagney's connection with Steffens and Ella to prove he was a communist, and obtain a court injunction preventing Cagney from lending any more financial support to their work. The case eventually fizzled, but the public image of Cagney as a communist would linger for years.

Although Steffens was largely confined to bed, the CPUSA apparently hoped that he would rise, Lazurus-like, at the prospect of a U.S. Senate campaign. The head of the California Communist Party, Sam Darcy, who occasionally visited Steffens to discuss labor issues, sent him a letter in April asking him to run as a Communist Party candidate, even though Steffens was not a member of the party. Flattered, Steffens nevertheless turned down the offer because, he wrote to Darcy, he was "a lifelong liberal with liberal instincts and habits of mind." And what the communists—or the world—did not require, he asserted in a pointed letter, was "the goodwill and fresh insight" of another liberal.

Darcy was so impressed by the rejection that he felt compelled to write to Steffens: "Your letter declining to join the Party only raises you in my estimation." He added that any voice "Comrade Steffens" could give to the movement would be "a tremendous help."

While Steffens convalesced, Ella did her best to shield him from the ongoing procession of young visitors who routinely showed up at the door in Carmel, hoping to get a word with the muckraking legend. One young man who needed no permission was Martin Flavin Jr., son of the playwright and later Pulitzer Prize–winning novelist who earlier had befriended Steffens. Flavin, encouraged by his parents and by Steffens, often stopped by to talk with the housebound Steffens, later recalling the appeal of the muckraker's presence: "There were a dozen or so people in Carmel, my father was one of them, who used to drop in any afternoon for a few minutes, and three or four of them would sit around and talk or argue. I was young enough then for it to seem perfectly natural, that people should gather not to drink cocktails or play bridge, but simply to talk. I see now that it was something quite unique. Something rather classical and far away. It was like a school, like people coming from far away to hear and see him."

Langston Hughes particularly enjoyed seeing Steffens in those days of recovery. On the poet's daily trips to the post office to pick up his mail—Carmel insistently had no paved roads or sidewalks, and no mail delivery—Hughes would pass by Steffens sitting on his porch, eager to disobey his doctor and chat with Hughes at every opportunity. The poet stopped often, sometimes staying for dinner, recalling that on one occasion, Steffens declared, "You tell the blacks to ask for *everything*, then maybe they would get *something*." Ella, Hughes observed, was a tireless and devoted hostess, friend, mother, companion, and, of course, a well-off radical with a touch of bohemia, greeting guests while wearing an elegant housecoat of red velvet over an old sweatshirt and jeans. Steffens, planted on the porch, "delighted to hold forth like a pert Socrates on a sunny afternoon." Quite comfortable in Carmel, Hughes became such good friends of Steffens's family, the Jefferses, Edward Weston, and others that he joked to Carl Van Vechten, "I am living so much like white folks that I'm washing my hair with Golden Glow [a popular shampoo]." He made no secret of his affection for Steffens: "Steffy, Peter, and Pete were among my best friends at Carmel," he wrote in his autobiography.

Steffens's letter writing, like his conversation, was restricted, as he was supposed to stay up for only two hours a day. He persisted at his writing, however. In mid-January 1934, he praised Marie Howe, who had been a devoted correspondent, as "the best of the letter writers" and gently nudged her to write even more, only to hear less than two months later of her passing. Fred Howe felt the loneliness of Marie's passing and sent a "long warm letter" that Steffens responded to in kind. He recalled their "comic heroes" of long ago—Tom Johnson, Bob La Follette, Teddy Roosevelt—all "in hell now," Steffens was sure, but "happy in there." Steffens had no doubt that he would follow them, yet for the moment he had every intention of pushing on. He told Howe, "It's tough on the rest of us, but we must all suffer till that old crowd is dead. We can't have a boom and a recovery too."

Part of the youthful crowd was Anna Louise Strong, who had established herself in both Russia and China in a way that Steffens could only envy. She had been Trotsky's English teacher, gained an interview with Stalin, befriended the elite Russian agent Mikhail Borodin, and married a Russian. Later, she would interview Chou En-lai and Mao Tse-tung. Frequently she returned home to lecture on Russian affairs at prominent schools such as Stanford and Wellesley while also briefing President Roosevelt at the request of Eleanor, who wrote often to Strong. The reporter, however, could not easily accept the wanton killings, the censorship of news, the abject poverty and massive inefficiency, and the strict obedience to the party, all of which stood in stark contradiction of a revolution supposedly liberating workers from tyranny and destitution.

Strong visited Steffens in Carmel in the early 1930s and, partly because of his suggestion, started on her autobiography, a book that reflected her ambivalence toward Russia. When she sent several chapters to Steffens in 1934 for his comments, he quickly noted the conflict within her. Calling her book "important," he insisted that the problem was not that she had seen too much of the revolution but that she had barely begun to absorb its full measure, despite having seen more than ten years of it: "The transition the Revolution is making in you, is not yet finished. You haven't made the grade, but I think that is all to the good; it makes your story more meaningful to the rest of us who are only on the way." He encouraged her to get "the notion of liberty" out of her head: "It is false, a hangover from our Western tyranny." Still, he noted his envy for all that Strong had taken from Russia. "I wished as I read you that I could see and have such talks with Borodin. He has so much to give and I have so much to get." Steffens expressed the hope that Strong would rummage through her "civilized mind" and "throw out the debris," ending, "For this keep up front in your head: you can write."

Steffens was too weak to respond fully to the torrent of energy Strong was pouring into the correspondence, but he continued to hammer away at the key point of party unity, using the example of Trotsky to illustrate the danger of dissent. "Your difficulties with Trotzky are the sign of your failure," he wrote in the fall of 1934. "Trotzky was a hero to me once too, but when he put 'right' above unity and broke our front to be right, I, from here,—I recognized that he was not of the New Day, but of the old. He says to the world what is only fit for the Party. I have things I would like to say or sound the Party on, but I can feel in my bones that I must not say them at this stage to the enemy. . . . Trotzky does not matter."

Journalism students from Stanford and Berkeley also stopped by regularly for talks with Steffens, seeking his insights on understanding and reporting the news. Predictably, he advised them to get off the campus and visit the farms, speak with the strikers, and give the public the truth. Unfortunately for the students, getting the story across to the readers was no small challenge, as most newspapers stood firmly opposed to the demands of farm labor. But despite his declining health, Steffens urged young people in particular to examine all sides, as he had done over his long career. He pressed the point in a sincere letter to a recent Dartmouth graduate:

> I had come to regard the New Capitalism as an experiment till, in 1929, the whole thing went over the top and slid down to an utter collapse. That was clear to all. I went to New York to hear the semi-scientific captains of industry say in words and facial expressions that they did not know what had happened or what was to be done about it. They did not understand their own experiment. Then—not till then—did I give up, and turned to see what else there was. Well, I had been to Soviet Russia and, as I looked us and the Russians over, I saw this that appealed to me: The Russian Revolution had abolished all those privileges which, in this country, balked all reforms. Gone! All gone.

By 1934, however, not only was privilege not gone, but daily tyranny and terror were already hallmarks of the Stalin regime that, seventeen years into the revolution, could not be easily dismissed as growing pains or a necessary part of the evolution of Communism. Disillusionment for some on the American Left had started as far back as the 1921 Kronstadt naval rebellion, when an uprising of Russian sailors protesting for the right of assembly, free speech, and the release of political prisoners was crushed by government forces, and hundreds were killed. At the same time, food shortages were so severe that riots among peasants and factory workers ensued, forcing Lenin to ease his stranglehold on the country in the guise of his "New Economic Policy" and allowing a small measure of capitalism to breathe some life into the moribund system and, far more importantly, enabling Lenin to retain power. Others, including Debs, found it impossible to accept the 1922 state prosecution of the opposition Socialist-Revolutionaries; the 1925 purge of Trotsky by the "Old Guard Bolsheviks" of Stalin, Zinoviev, and Lev Kamenev; or the brutal collectivization of the peasants in the early 1930s, when millions perished.

Yet, throughout the Soviet descent into dictatorship, Steffens simply commented, "Of course," always mindful that Lenin himself had said that liberty would take two or three generations to establish. Even the vicious Stalinist purges that followed the assassination of Politburo member Sergie Kirov on December 1, 1934, stirred only small doubt in Steffens's mind. He wrote to an uncertain Anna Louise Strong in January 1935, barely a year prior to his seventieth birthday, "It seems to me that I understand [the purges]. I am not sure or proud of it even now. . . . We are both in the same boat as far as understanding goes." In the meantime, the terror, Steffens felt, was a necessity.

In America, the result was that dissent among prominent names on the left, including Socialist Party presidential candidate Norman Thomas, spread throughout the 1930s. Dwight MacDonald would ask the relevant question: "Is it impossible to express [criticism] without being accused of counterrevolution and herded into an amalgam of anarchists, Mensheviks, and capitalist journalists?" One of those most disillusioned with the political situation in Russia was Max Eastman, whose recent book, *Artists in Uniform*, had detailed how Russian artists were forced to provide state-sponsored propaganda or face severe consequences. Ella in particular had lost all patience with Eastman, having written to Steffens the previous year, "It is unbelievable that anyone could turn so bad."

The result, at Ella's prodding, was Steffens's corrective book review, "Swatting Flies in Russia," which appeared in the *New Republic* on June 20, 1934. Steffens lamented the loss of "our Max," the "pre-revolutionary Revolutionary," noting that the young radical would have sought the full story and examined not only the hardships of artists but "the many devastations of the complete Change; and why; . . . We want to know that; Lenin once asked to know that. . . . There was a time when Max Eastman might have told us." He conceded, "There are lots of flies on Russia. It's lousy. The Russians are covered with these pests, as we Westerners are eaten up by millionaires. And there is danger that they will get used to their lice as we are used to and patient with ours. They need fly-swatters over there, but though we mass-produce these handy weapons, we haven't many swatters of our own flies." Steffens's advice was that "fine old liberals" like Eastman should go to Russia "to learn what the Russians can teach us, to the end that we may get out of our uniforms."

Eastman naturally responded, charging that Steffens had conveniently ignored his specific points of criticism and that Steffens himself had merely been "trotted out," like an old warhorse, by the radical Left to once more cite the virtues of the revolution and the importance of otherwise being silent.

In his reassuring way, Steffens replied with a long letter to the magazine expressing surprise over Eastman's volatile reaction: "When I hauled off and smote him affectionately on the wrist for enjoying for his own sweet sake— not art's—the misdirected joy and rage I have watched him arousing for about five years, I had no idea that I was delivering a 'mortal thrust.'" Referring to Eastman as his "favorite philosopher and friend," Steffens commented, "The only decay my fond eyes can detect is in his once so lively, lovely mirth."

In acknowledging that he was "trotted out" by his wife and not by unnamed conspirators in writing his review, Steffens declared, "That is all Stalin had to do with this particular persecution." He then turned serious to address the substance of Eastman's outrage: that Steffens, and many others, were willfully ignorant apologists for a dictatorship that stripped workers of rights and vehemently rejected the views of genuine socialists:

> Now I can't speak for the Stalinists (they wouldn't let me), but I have been watching some Communist leaders of the American working class out in the field and I have found them to be thoughtful, rather silent men and women, terribly overworked but poised in their manifold activities, loyal, uncompromising, daring and very understanding," he wrote. "As a mere political observer, I will report to Max Eastman and all my other old friends, that out here on the picket lines of the actual struggle there are Communist party leaders whom I can follow. I can't lead them, Max, but I can follow them with a satisfaction I have never felt before in all my professional career.

His unflagging support of the communist cause, particularly through the fierce 1930s, calls into question how much Steffens, in fact, knew of the actual Soviet conditions. Even a minimal awareness should have given him far more serious pause in his judgment, and it is clear from his letters that he possessed at least that. Unfortunately, his years of study in philosophy and psychology, along with his vast, intimate experiences as a journalist, all critical to his understanding of the complexities of political behavior, had been largely lost in old age. Steffens showed little willingness to consider the possibility that both systems—Leninism and capitalism—were deeply flawed and that his observations on the lack of democracy in America were valid, but that the terror was no substitute.

Two situations reassured Steffens that he was correct in siding with the communists and laborers against capital: the political monopoly in Washington and the worsening labor situation in San Francisco. The two-party system, Steffens

believed, was a myth. Both sides battled each other for the right to change . . .
nothing. "The old parties, Republican and Democrat, represent at bottom the
same thing—I might also say—the same damn thing. That Thing is business. The
emerging idea now is to have a second party that would represent another interest, like labor and farming, which are beginning to see that Business is not, but
only wants to be, the whole Thing. I might also say the whole damned Thing."

San Francisco was then still very much a tough, blue-collar city featuring
scores of saloons, gambling houses, and bordellos to serve the sailors, truckers,
dock workers, and other laborers that dominated the workforce. There, a longshoremen's dispute that crippled shipping along the Pacific Coast had developed
by summer into a full-blown general strike, halting everything from shipping to
streetcars across the city. Inflammatory rhetoric only increased the animosity on
both sides, with Steffens, predictably, offering his own home as a contribution
to the labor cause. On May Day, the local John Reed Club held an evening of
proletarian poetry readings at The Getaway, with Langston Hughes reading
two of his translations of Mayakovsky. On the capitalist side, a shipping company president blamed the strike on communists spreading propaganda along
the docks. The San Francisco mayor declared a state of emergency, and the governor of Oregon wired President Roosevelt that "armed hostilities" had pushed
the situation "beyond the reach of state authorities."

Near hysteria gripped Carmel as well. On July 2, 1934, the John Reed Club
hosted a spokesman for the longshoremen. The event set off alarming radio
reports that police would be questioning Steffens and other club supporters
regarding their sympathy for the strikers, while Ella was rumored to be overseeing a pipeline of strike money flowing from Moscow. The American Legion in
particular, convinced that Carmel's John Reed Club was a communist nest, saw
Ella as an imminent threat. Accordingly, the legion started monitoring the club's
meetings to the point of disrupting speakers and threatening the owner of the
meeting hall with a boycott. Carmel's village council ordered supplies of teargas,
while a local militia, backed by the American Legion, trained nearby.

The effort to infiltrate Ella's circle culminated in the comical Sharkey affair,
in which a certain Captain Charles Bakcsy, going under the name of Captain
Sharkey, appeared on the scene spouting communist rhetoric and throwing lavish parties for the local Left, at one point encouraging Ella to pose for a photo
with a machine gun he had pulled from a closet. (She demurred.) Sharkey later
left town after it was revealed that he had been hired by a San Francisco business
group to uncover Carmel's communist connection. His house had been amply
bugged to pick up any incriminating talk among Reds at his parties, but the only

result of his efforts was the loss of thousands of dollars that the businessmen squandered on his short-lived employment.

As the anti-Red fever grew, police raids in San Francisco and Sacramento resulted in hundreds of arrests, Caroline Decker among them on her way to a two-year jail sentence, although her typewriter, Steffens noted, survived intact. On July 19, barely a week before the general strike buckled under intense pressure in heated negotiations, Steffens fired off a scathing letter to Secretary of Labor Perkins, generally a sympathetic ear, in support of the movement:

> There is hysteria here, but the terror is white, not red. Business men are doing in this Labor struggle what they would have liked to do against the old graft prosecution and other political reform movements, yours included; they are sicking on the mob, which, mark you well, is all theirs. . . . Let me remind you that this widespread revolt was not caused by aliens. It takes a Chamber of Commerce mentality to believe that these unhappy thousands of American workers on strike against conditions in American shipping and industry are merely misled by foreign Communist agitators. It's the incredibly dumb captains of industry and their demonstrated mismanagement of business that started and will not end this all-American strike and may lead us to Fascism.

The final agreement saw concessions made by both sides, with the result being the continued emergence of an organized labor voice in California and nationwide, an achievement in which Steffens took some consolation. Perkins herself did not ignore Steffens, inviting him the following year to attend a San Francisco meeting of West Coast leaders "to consider a program of economic security and State labor legislation."

Steffens continued to be as active as possible, even while stationary. Each morning, he would prop up the newspaper on his bed table and type his own comments, as well as letters to friends. One letter went out in October to Fremont Older, who, Steffens was chagrined to learn, had recently suffered a heart attack. Employing his trademark humor, though, Steffens suggested from his sickbed, "Perhaps we can agree on a date and go together,—as we always have." Older, however, would be dead within six months.

Still, even as old friends passed, Steffens kept up his spirits. After stimulating visits from friends and strangers alike, Steffens would write to them punctually, expressing his enthusiasm for the visit. And he did receive a flock of guests from Hollywood, New York, Europe, and elsewhere, even while he was limited by his doctor to a half hour of conversation at a time, hardly enough for him. He enjoyed

Cagney in particular. "We have lots of visitors, correspondents and others who know the news, but none like you, Cagney. I wish you'd come up," he wrote.

At the same time, Steffens kept up the political fight from home with occasional long letters—against his doctor's orders—and commentary in a new weekly magazine titled *Pacific Weekly*. He contributed a column, "Lincoln Steffens Speaking," and along with Ella, who maintained her frantic pace of supporting strikes, writing articles, giving lectures, and raising Pete, Steffens radicalized a good number of their Carmel neighbors, although others deeply resented the Steffens family. Vigilantes, Steffens called them—their interference only strengthened his resolve. Legionnaires waited outside The Getaway, recording the license numbers of any visitors, and one legionnaire threatened to burn their house down. The local attacks were aimed at Ella as well, with one particularly provocative charge—arising from her close connection to Langston Hughes, a bachelor—that she had slept with twenty-nine black men. "Why not thirty?" Steffens quipped. An accusation that Steffens could not abide was leveled by a local newspaper: It claimed that he had failed as a parent, the incriminating evidence an alleged incident in which Pete urinated on school property to protest the education system. Steffens promptly denounced the attack.

Early in 1935, Steffens gave his name in support of the American Writers' Congress to be held in New York. Borne from the antifascist outrage of communists and leftists over the rise of Hitler, Mussolini, and particularly Franco, the congress reflected the growing strength of the international Popular Front opposing fascism. The movement was heavily promoted by the Soviet Union and naturally supported by Steffens, who, having now clearly chosen between Stalin and Mussolini, saw an inevitable and necessary choice between Communism and fascism on the near horizon. In a column, he declared where his own preference lay:

> I am for a United Front over here, if the Communists will lead it. I
> don't want the Republicans or the Democrats or us Liberals or Upton
> Sinclair or myself to lead it. I won't have anything to do with a United
> Front or even a strike that the Communist Party does not lead. And I
> can tell you why. We all will stop a revolution as we do a reform, as
> we always have stopped everything when we have got enough. And we
> already have so much graft, property, privileges—what you like—that
> we will get enough too soon, before we have got enough for all, before
> we have got ALL. In every revolution in history men have cried enough,
> when *they* got enough. This time we must go on until we have all.

Hoping to use the congress to form a League of American Writers in affiliation with the International Union of Revolutionary Writers (IURW), *New Masses* issued a call in its January 22 issue, written largely by literary editor Granville Hicks, for influential writers to explore "the most effective ways in which writers, *as writers*, can function in the rapidly developing crisis." The initial concept of the league had been put forward the previous year by the CPUSA, which intended to replace the John Reed Clubs with a more established group of writers to broaden their appeal. Ultimately, sixty-two writers and radicals, including Steffens, Ella, Dos Passos, Dreiser, Langston Hughes, and Richard Wright, signed the document. The Left's split over CPUSA leadership and political tactics was reflected in the makeup of the congress, as anti-Stalinist voices such as Max Eastman and Sidney Hook were not welcome by some, while the CPUSA itself feared that the congress might be "too red," diminishing its public impact. Steffens, of course, was most welcome but in no condition for a cross-country trip.

While four thousand people packed the congress at New York's Mecca Temple on April 26, Hicks later contended that most had come not to consider the revolutionary roles of writers but were sent in by the Communist Party to guarantee an overflow turnout. Despite its awkward start, the congress did lead to the formation of the League of American Writers and international gatherings that Steffens no doubt would have joined with enthusiasm, but how much he would have agreed with them is uncertain. The single point that rallied most of the participants was the importance of halting the spread of fascism throughout Europe, with the violent struggle in Spain shaping up as the key battleground. Aggressively raising relief funds for the Spanish war effort, the league donated an ambulance to support the Spanish Republican cause. Steffens sided with the Republican forces—he later wrote a sympathetic piece toward them for *New Masses*—but the same fascination he had shown with Mussolini as a strongman, a man of bold, decisive character, may have left him intrigued by Francisco Franco as well. At the very least, a younger Steffens would have been on Spanish soil to witness the future of Europe for himself.

What Steffens undoubtedly realized but refused to concede, even in old age, was the reality that American political life would prevent anything but the most meager semblance of Communism on its own soil. Socialism at its peak enjoyed measured success because millions of workers, particularly the immigrants flooding ashore and the masses of blue-collar Americans, supported better social and labor conditions out of impoverished necessity. In America, practicality mattered, and Americans saw very practical reasons for the rise and fall of socialism. Communism, however, had no legitimate hope of achieving popularity in a country where, despite all of the corruption Steffens and others had exposed, individuals accepted (and often embraced) a largely unregulated economic system that allowed them opportunities to succeed or fail in spectacular fashion, or more likely, in the depths of the Depression, to eke out a grinding existence. For most Americans, competition and self-reliance, unfair and brutal as they often were, had long ago been accepted as the most profitable economic model, and America was clearly a country more mindful of profit than equality. And, as Steffens should have seen, the communist model in Russia had produced little profit, while equality was seen only in the misery endured by millions of its oppressed masses.

Yet, contrary to Steffens's insensitive view of Russians was the heartfelt interest he could take in the lives of others. He had devoted most of his life to pursuing his own interests, yet he was no loner. Even in his final years, he patiently answered letters from young admirers and students invested in their own unlearning, and the youthful staff at the *Pacific Weekly* had an obvious admiration for their mentor.

One of his most devoted friends remained Filene, a liberal to the last and one of the few millionaires helping FDR to promote the New Deal. Filene planned to go to Russia in June and tempted Steffens with an offer of a final trip. Both knew that such a journey for Steffens was beyond serious consideration, but Steffens, still a dreamer, momentarily indulged himself, telling Filene how much he would relish the trip and that the moment could not have been better: "Russia just now is a sort of heaven, where humans have got rid of the great primitive problems of food, clothing, and a roof. And therefore of all the other mean problems that go with business for private profit. That leaves the Russians with minds for philosophy, art and science. Now civilization may begin."

For Steffens and Filene, however, there was a far more immediate and pressing concern. With financial woes from the bank failure continuing to haunt him, Steffens now faced a lawsuit filed in San Francisco. The charge was that he had transferred much of his wealth, including book royalties, property, stocks, and bonds, to Ella in order to avoid liability. On March 22, the *New York Times* publicized the financial troubles of Steffens and Ella's with the cutting headline "Sues Steffens and Wife; Bank Receiver Says They Have Fortune Despite Fight on Capitalism." From The Getaway, Steffens gave testimony, ultimately resolving the case by paying fourteen thousand dollars, Filene providing eight thousand of the amount. Steffens expressed his gratitude in a June 28 letter to Robert Cantwell, who had been working—unsuccessfully—on a Filene biography: "The bank business of mine is near a settlement, and the result is thanks to E. A. He saved me my home here. My health too. You don't got to be grateful, but I am."

His health declining from the arteriosclerosis—"I am getting tired of this bed," he complained to Filene—Steffens passed his last Christmas at The Getaway in 1935. Feeling physically weak but mentally robust, he found the energy to keep up his writing as best he could. In a January 1936 letter, he was pleased to tell Sam Darcy, who considered Steffens a true friend of the CPUSA, about his latest article, a piece on Lenin, titled, "The Greatest of Liberals." Two months later, Steffens again wrote to Darcy, effusively praising a young talent, a local writer and frequent visitor to The Getaway. After hearing Steffens and Ella ceaselessly promoting the cause of the farmworkers, the young writer had fixed his keen eye on the strife, telling the story of the bitter struggle—money, once more, against labor—that dominated the vast, profitable farmlands of the Central Valley:

> His name is John Steinbeck. His novel is called *In Dubious Battle*, the story of a strike in an apple orchard. It's a stunning, straight, correct narrative about things as they happen. Steinbeck says it wasn't undertaken as a strike or labor tale and he was interested in some such theme as the psychology of a mob or strikers, but I think it is the best report of a labor struggle that has come out of this valley. It is as we saw it last summer. It may not be sympathetic with labor, but it is realistic about the vigilantes.

Like Steffens, Steinbeck had childhood memories of horseback riding across the Salinas Valley, encountering fishermen, farmhands, tramps, rodeo riders, and others with stories to tell. At opposite ends of their writing careers, Steinbeck was naturally drawn toward Steffens in Carmel, although the efforts of Steffens and Ella's to promote Steinbeck's work the previous year had, for the intensely private Steinbeck, been ill advised. Steffens, writing with admiration of *Tortilla Flat* in the May 31, 1935, issue of *Pacific Weekly*, noted that Steinbeck was "rather wrecked emotionally" following the recent death of his father, adding, "An odd life, his. In an 'ivory tower' but not built of stone, like Jeffers', but of mountains, valleys and trails." Two days later, in the Sunday book page of the *San Francisco Chronicle*, Ella praised the novel as well but provided a strikingly intimate description of Steinbeck and his wife, Carol, focusing particularly on their lack of income. Steinbeck, annoyed, wrote to his literary agent that Ella had deceived him by "promising to lay off the personal and then pulling out all the stops."

Countering Steffens's praise of *In Dubious Battle* was Caroline Decker, who understandably objected to Steinbeck's impersonal impression given of the strikers: "When you're heart and soul and up to your ears involved in something as important as we were doing, you get very emotionally disturbed when someone has set forth a view that you think is inaccurate." Ella herself objected to the emphasis on discussions of violence among the strike leaders, claiming that she had never heard such talk.

Steinbeck's early association with Steffens did not go unnoticed by the U.S. government. In 1939, the House Committee on Un-American Activities provided files on Steinbeck to the FBI, at the time ever alert to the Red menace under the watchful eye of J. Edgar Hoover. When Steinbeck complained, Hoover denied any involvement on the bureau's part, ignoring the fact that the FBI, aware of Steinbeck's contribution to a Steffens memorial issue of the *Pacific Weekly*, had started its observations of Steinbeck three years earlier. The same committee questioned James Cagney about his association with Steffens. Silencing his interrogators with a response that undoubtedly would have pleased Steffens, the actor asserted that Steffens's "viewpoint was so contradictory . . . that you could not arrive at any conclusion regarding the man."

To the end, Russia was on Steffens's mind. He sent out his final letter to Sam Darcy, in Russia, on April 12, less than a week after Steffens had received a cascade of messages from well-wishers from around the world on his seventieth birthday. The letter was long, filled with thoughts of Russia—thoughts that clearly gave deep comfort to Steffens. He had received "the most amazing sheaf of cables" from Russian writers and other communists, including William Foster and the CPUSA, to celebrate his milestone, and the aging Steffens still harbored the illusion of one more trip to the future. An invitation from Jo Davidson to visit Bécheron was a standing offer, and from there Russia beckoned. Tempting him further was the knowledge that Dot and Jim Hollister would also be going to Russia that summer. Steffens noted the obvious possibility that if he went to Russia, he might die there, not that it disturbed him much. But his own frailty, he admitted, would likely keep him home.

More uplifting news was the publication of Granville Hicks's biography, which revived many fond memories of the Harvard and Greenwich Village days. *John Reed: The Making of a Revolutionary*, which Hicks dedicated to Steffens, perfectly captured the romantic, impulsive, idealistic poet, Steffens felt, and he sent an open letter to the *New Republic*, published in the May 13 issue, expressing his admiration of the work. "The marvelous Hicks book," he wrote, "really shows how a poet can and is bound to turn poetry into dire deeds, and a poet of our days is bound to turn into a hero." Steffens was all the more impressed because, he admitted, he "did not believe Granville Hicks the critic could do it." Hicks had assumed as much, he acknowledged in his memoir: "I suspected that Stef had always thought I was too solemn and academic to write a good book about Reed." So of all the positive reviews of the biography, "nothing pleased me more," Hicks wrote, than the praise from Steffens. Hicks, Steffens told Darcy, had used Reed's life to show that "all roads in our day lead to Moscow," a certainty in Steffens's mind that he would take with pleasure to his grave.

Through the summer, he attended to business as best he could, giving much of his time to overseeing an editorial revolution at the *Pacific Weekly*, with Steffens and Ella emerging as editors as well as fledgling financiers. "'We' have 'seized' the *Pacific Weekly*," he wrote with delight to Cantwell on June 15, encouraging Cantwell to submit stories pointing out "anything the world has overlooked anywhere." Paying the bills, however, was an ongoing challenge: After sending out a fund-raising letter in mid-June ("It will cost some little money, work, art, management, character, but it will be some fun too"), Steffens conceded to Dot that the magazine was "succeeding,—in vain." With few new subscribers, no advertisers or cash reserve, and hostile Carmelites eager to see it shut down, the magazine survived from issue to issue, owing largely to the dedication of Ella.

In April, Harcourt wrote to Steffens that his editors, seeing book potential in Steffens's Carmel columns, had already collected eighty-five pieces of writing in what Harcourt called a "first rate" manuscript. He urged Steffens—"here's the modern stuff and you know it"—to consider publishing them under the title *Lincoln Steffens Speaking*. Steffens agreed and was pleased to send the good news to Fred Howe, who had written to Steffens in January, "I'd rather see you than anyone else." Steffens's final response, "So long, Fred. I gotta quit enjoying myself," was the apt closing to the letter and to a relationship between two dissenters who had spent thirty years looking, always, ahead.

Steffens's mind remained sharp, focused, as ever, on politics. Throughout his letters to Howe, Filene, Darcy, and others, he offered a running commentary on the Roosevelt presidency, mixing wit and what he hoped was wisdom. "They [California businessmen] hate the President for trying to go ahead slowly. They prefer Fascism, and are looking for a Hitler"; "Well, if it [political debate] takes the form of reelecting Roosevelt, it's all right with me, although I am out for Hoover myself"; "That speech of acceptance he [Roosevelt] made was a corker, a classic"; "Roosevelt is going to win anyhow, I guess, but we Republicans can make it certain"; "Why do they [businessmen] hate him so? . . . Roosevelt told them the truth, told and he tells. They hate *that*," were typical observations from Steffens. To hasten the onset of full revolution, Steffens declared his wish to see the Republican Alf Landon in the White House.

In the planning stages at that time was a Western Writers Conference, organized by Carey McWilliams and to be held in San Francisco in November. Among the prominent sponsors were Steffens, Upton Sinclair, Kenneth Rexroth, Dorothy Parker, and Clifford Odets, with Steffens's name featured on congress letterhead. His name, though, was all the weakened Steffens would contribute to the cause.

Pete had gone to the Hollister ranch for the summer. Jane, now married and a mother, had come back from a stay in China and planned to accompany him to see his parents in August. In the meantime, Steffens peppered Pete with letters, the last, written on August 2, giving perhaps the truest wish of Steffens's for his son, not yet twelve. "You are learning about life," Steffens counseled. "As you will realize when you come to write, as you will." Six days later, reflecting on his heartfelt duty as a father, he wrote, "I thought I had to make my son at home in the strange world I had invited him to visit."

Ella and Steffens recognized Steffens's declining health without directly speaking of it, although Steffens saw his future clearly enough. "I've had my life. I'm ready to go," he remarked one day. "When people have fulfilled their lives, it's no tragedy." He counseled Ella to remarry, asking only that Pete be encouraged to remember him. "I don't like the thought of Pete calling another man Daddy," he conceded.

On the afternoon of August 9, one day after he had finished reading the proofs of *Lincoln Steffens Speaking*, Steffens complained of feeling worse than usual. As Ella and the doctor sat with him in his bedroom, he suddenly raised his arms and cried in pain, "No, no. I can't—" His head fell back on the pillow. Steffens was dead at seventy.

The Hollisters brought Pete back from the ranch the next day. Friends stopped by the house, offering tributes to Steffens while Ella observed silently and Pete stayed back in a corner, listening to the words praising his father. When John O'Shea told Pete that his father was a great man, Pete, rather surprised, replied, "Yes, I'm beginning to see that. I thought he was just my Daddy and wrote a book."

With no formal service, Steffens was buried next to his parents and sister Lou in San Mateo. Ella called the last three years of their life together "three full, rich years," years that were "so fulfilling, so satisfying, so rich with love." Fittingly, she organized a November 1936 memorial issue of the *Pacific Weekly*.

The issue featured contributions from Steinbeck, Jeffers, and William Saroyan and used the magazine to promote the Western Writers Conference, which was held in November and dedicated to the memory of Lincoln Steffens.

CONCLUSION

STEFFENS'S WELL-PRACTICED AND now infamous comment on the virtues of
Russian Communism has been used by critics for nearly a century to label
Steffens as a man who was either acutely naive or a card-carrying communist.
It was an unfortunate and misleading effort that distracts from his significant
influence on both the profession of journalism and the nature of government in
America.

Still, "I have seen the future" cannot be ignored, or easily understood, particularly in light of Steffens's sincere devotion to strengthening democracy in
his own country and abroad, even while countless people were dying in "the
future." In fact, it seems hardly possible to study the life of Steffens without
confronting the paradox in much of what he said and wrote. His tendency to
appear to be on two sides of an issue simultaneously, or to utter borderline
seditious or provocative remarks with a straight face, agitated his critics while
troubling even his friends at times, as Steffens could be open-minded and clever
in his analysis to the point of exasperation.

Many of Steffens's points, particularly in his muckraking days, were right
on target, even though his semantic games with language, such as his exchange
with Judge Bordwell in the McNamara trial, were understandably vexing to
some. Steffens certainly was sometimes muddled in his thinking—he acknowledged in his own letters how little he or any man truly knows, which is why he
focused on unlearning, for himself and Pete. But actively participating in the
public conversation, putting forward unproven but intriguing theories, making
scandalous declarations, and provoking reactions from audiences were all part
of his life's joyful path, as they have been for countless figures of fame, including Theodore Roosevelt. And remarkably, his easygoing manner and eagerness
to explore a disputed point at length allowed Steffens not only to strike up

friendships with an array of notable figures but also to keep their respect over decades. In the years between 1904 and 1924, for example, Roosevelt, Wilson, Debs, and La Follette all ran on different tickets for president, yet each was on reasonably cordial terms or better with Steffens, two while in the White House. Despite his rhetoric, Steffens was never a rabid member of any political party, preferring to observe, analyze, comment, and, to a limited degree, advocate. He was a journalist, not a policy maker—it was not his responsibility to find solutions, as much as he sought them.

Why he wholeheartedly supported the Russian Revolution in particular is perplexing and ultimately troubling as well. His road to becoming a supporter of radical political changes in general is clear and even admirable. Like no one before him, Steffens had gone to the cities and states of America to sound out the country's leaders—and betrayers (in some cases, the same people)—in his quest to find out how his government actually functioned, and why. As he painstakingly detailed in his remarkable writings, he discovered, in the process of unlearning, that true democracy was almost nonexistent throughout the land, and deliberately so. The obvious conclusion to be drawn was that American democracy was a myth, that an elite of wealthy, if not always particularly intelligent, leaders had contrived for years to maintain their undemocratic grip on power, and that the mass of people not only had little control of their own government but had barely any awareness of how far removed the government's priorities were from their own. Urban streetcar systems, for example, interested politicians not because of their value in transporting ordinary citizens but in the huge—and illegal—profits to be skimmed from the public purse year after year. Perhaps worst of all to Steffens, there was little indication that the future would be any different. The next step, naturally, was to seek a remedy, and for this Steffens looked to both American reformers and political conditions abroad, which led him to Mexico and, ultimately, Russia.

But that his unlearning would lead him to express enthusiastic support for the upheaval in Russia, which he fully knew involved the slaughter and misery brought on by Lenin's unswerving policies, is far more problematic. Even had there been a guarantee of democracy and freedom for the Russian people following the revolution, such a change was many years from happening and meanwhile would have necessitated a staggering number of deaths, mostly among the already battered peasants. But Steffens, of all people, should have known better, for he had personally seen the destructive consequences of the Mexican Revolution and had admitted that even there, even after so many deaths, an acceptable resolution was nowhere in sight. And Lenin, in his relentless determination to foment revolution in Russia and, if possible, abroad, dwarfed any dictator that might have arisen in Mexico. Steffens should have known early on that the carnage under Lenin would be shocking to much of the world, and in fact he lived long enough to be aware of the extent of the brutality that dominated daily life in Russia. Steffens certainly was not alone on the Left in his sympathies for the Russian communists, but, having examined the actual conditions as extensively as he had, he might have been expected to have shown far greater hesitation in his judgments.

So, why was Steffens infatuated with Russia? It certainly was not because he himself found any satisfaction in violence, or that Ella unduly influenced him (he had already fallen under the charm of Lenin long before he met her). Nor was it because he had no sympathy for the suffering masses (as far back as his reporting days on the Lower East Side, he had witnessed their plight with chagrin).

Several reasons are plausible, yet none fully justify Steffens in his views. He had no patience with the blatant hypocrisy of American leaders who patriotically preached democracy while profiting immensely precisely by engaging in whatever undemocratic and illegal behavior would benefit themselves the most. Their behavior was a national disgrace, as Steffens amply documented. So America had been going politically astray for so long that to Steffens, it was not unthinkable that another country, with a different perspective, might find a better way.

Also, with his direct personal experience with Lenin, having heard him speak to Russian crowds and meeting with him individually, Steffens was left with the conviction that Lenin had the boldness to take on the entrenched powers, conceived in privilege and graft, and see the fight through to a far better future, even if the human price for such progress was appalling. Lenin, quite obviously, also had dazzled Steffens with his demeanor—here was a man who would not be intimidated or deterred.

Age and location may have influenced Steffens as well. The Mexican Revolution had largely failed, and Steffens was aware that Russia might have been the last opportunity for any country to undertake such radical changes in his lifetime. He was most vociferous in support of the communists later in his life, and certainly had not supported such violence as a young man. He could barely tolerate the New York police clubbings of protesters in the Lower East Side. Also, the comfort of his Carmel home was far removed from the blood being spilled on Russian soil.

A final and not insignificant factor was undoubtedly the timeless romance of revolution itself, particularly if observed from a safe distance. In the case of Russia, the appeal of casting out the old, oppressive order and ushering in a new regime, especially one seeming to promote idealistic notions of peace, full employment, equitable land ownership and food distribution, abolition of the death penalty, and, ultimately, freedom, was like fresh air to many radicals and liberals alike, at least until the Bolsheviks seized firm control. And Steffens and others on the left, whose own visions of the just society that they hoped to see emerge in Russia were quite laudable, could not bring themselves to accept what would have been the crushing realization that Russia, even after centuries of harsh rule under Russian dictators, was not bringing about a new reality but only yet another chapter of government tyranny. It was an admission that Steffens, particularly as the future world of his beloved son was foremost in his mind, could not consider.

Steffens's life, however, involved far more than revolution in Russia, where he was at most an enthusiastic commentator. As a journalist, Steffens left an indelible mark on America, and it is largely on this basis that his legacy should rest. It is a testament to his intellect, charm, and remarkable, life-long dedication to setting America on a path toward legitimate democracy that so many sought his company and praised his efforts, controversial as they were. The doors of elected leaders from mayors to presidents were open to him, business magnates confided in him, and his Carmel home served as a kind of Mecca for liberals and reformers who wanted a cherished word with the aging muckraker. And his optimism undoubtedly carried a special appeal. At the close of his autobiography, he affirmed, with characteristic humility, "I have not lived in vain. The world which I tried so hard, so honestly, so dumbly, to change has changed me. It took a war, and a couple of revolutions to do it, but it is done. . . . My life was worth my living. And as for the world in general, all that was or is or ever will be wrong with that is my—our thinking about it."

Following his death, tributes flowed in from around the world, saluting his professional accomplishments, but perhaps most striking are the personal remembrances of Steffens the man, particularly those noting his humanity. These provide a clue to his unique success at extracting news from so many sources. Jo Davidson, a friend for nearly two decades, recalled, "Steff was a friend I could tell anything to. He had that rare faculty for listening—listening and understanding. . . . Steffens truly loved humanity with understanding." Martin Flavin echoed Davidson's words: "I know many people, artists that came and talked to him sometimes when they were really hopeless, and hadn't worked for a year perhaps, and when they went away they felt self-confident and worthwhile again. . . . Lincoln Steffens was one of the very few real humanitarians. . . . What he gave people, all of them, who came and talked with him, was self-confidence. He had it himself, unlimited."

Even Max Eastman, who had split so dramatically with Steffens over the course of Russian Communism, was moved to write to Ella "to express in some direction and some small measure my own sadness. But I . . . felt somehow embarrassed. His pleasure in my high spirits that last visit was tinged with sorrow and when he came to the door to watch us go I knew he was thinking it was probably the last time. I went away with a choking throat. He was sweet and true." Indeed, in his own memoir, Eastman conceded that Steffens's sincere effort to salvage Eastman's failing marriage to Ida Rauh was "so large a kindness that I feel compunction now for the harsh truths I spoke about him."

And Hemingway, despite his cruel words years earlier, remembered Steffens and his family fondly, writing to Ella, "The last time we were all together was up-stairs at Lipp's wasn't it? I haven't ever thought of Steff as dead. . . . Am pretty nearly through with a novel [*To Have and Have Not*] that he might have liked. . . . I hope you are well, Ella, and that your son Pete is fine. Anything that I can ever do—please contact me." (A month earlier, Ella had told Hemingway, "I'm so sorry you never got out here for a visit with Stef—he would have so appreciated it, as he so appreciated you.")

Lippmann, Bullitt, Cagney, and many others expressed similar regard for their friendships with Steffens. His knack for intimacy with such a broad range of people, dating back to his days as a cub reporter covering fires and crime scenes, was crucial to his success as a muckraking journalist and obviously led to many heartfelt, lasting relationships as well.

Most importantly, Steffens's fearless revelations of graft and corruption became synonymous with the muckraking era and government reform. After leaving *McClure's*, Steffens enjoyed continued success as an independent journalist, but his name would have meant little during those later years had he not played such a pivotal role in the muckraking frenzy. At the height of Steffens's popularity, millions of readers bought magazines because of his byline. Corporate and political leaders at the highest echelons of power, including William Randolph Hearst, Clarence Darrow, Louis Brandeis, Felix Frankfurter, Woodrow Wilson, and Theodore Roosevelt, confided in Steffens. Ida Tarbell, herself a muckraking pioneer, acknowledged Steffens's preeminence in the field. And the American government, exposed by the muckrakers, did reform itself in numerous ways, although never close to the extent that Steffens felt necessary.

Moreover, his professional approach to his work helped change the course of journalism. Steffens's method of combining diligent research; personal

interviews with figures on all sides of an issue; a patient, empathetic, and conversational manner; and factual articles that gripped the public imagination led the
way in transforming the role of journalists from collectors of news, often from
company or government cronies, to more professional investigators and liter-
ate reporters. As much as Sam McClure feared lawsuits over Steffens's intrepid
reporting, none ever materialized.

Steffens's life was marked by paradoxes that remain difficult to explain.
Perhaps Ray Stannard Baker, a sensitive man who was closer than many to
Steffens, particularly during their glory years at *McClure's*, best describes the
odd journey taken by Steffens. "Later in life," Baker wrote in his memoir, "he
seemed to me to have a kind of messianic complex. I always thought he was at
his best, doing his greatest work—in the sense of complete, self-fulfillment—in
the days when he was still the eager, observant, thirsty reporter, striving first
of all to understand." *Understanding* was always the goal of Steffens's efforts
at unlearning. Given the ultimate collapse of the Soviet Union and the ongoing
struggle for genuine democracy in the United States a full century after Steffens's
muckraking, maybe no amount of unlearning on Steffens's part would have
been sufficient to realistically envision a better way forward. In the end, Steffens
himself went too far. His acceptance of Lenin and Communism was extreme.
But his painstaking diagnosis of the central problem in his own country—the
deliberate suppression of democracy—and his courage in pursuing and revealing
this ugly truth helped to set America on a better course, rightfully establishing
the name of Lincoln Steffens as the greatest of the muckrakers.

Acknowledgments

Any biographical work on Steffens benefits greatly from what Steffens revealed about himself in his autobiography and the hundreds of letters he wrote, and my work is no exception. Initially, I knew of Steffens as a muckraking journalist associated with *McClure's Magazine*, Theodore Roosevelt, and, later, the Russian Revolution, but when I chose to read his autobiography, I was intrigued by the breadth of his experience. With a biography of Steffens in mind, I then turned to his letters, which span his adult life and show him chasing revolutions, elections, and corruption at the highest levels. The letters expressed his deep doubts over his own understanding of human behavior, his sharp wit (often aimed at himself), his close relationships with family members and a wide array of friends, and his detailed descriptions of the political landscape wherever he traveled. His memoir, more of an "outside" than an "inside" story, as Steffens put it, and certainly subjective in its telling, reveals a man connected to the great figures and events of his time, and one whose sometimes vexing uncertainties and joy of life never wavered. He left behind a fascinating account of a life well-lived, if not always wisely so.

A biography cannot be written in isolation, and I am pleased to acknowledge the support I received from many quarters that helped make my pursuit of Steffens a most satisfying and rewarding experience. I am especially grateful to Steffens's son, Pete, for his ready cooperation and warm support of my work. I regret that we have not yet had a chance to meet, but our correspondence has been a source of inspiration. I also wish to express my thanks to Valerie Alia, Pete Steffens's wife, for her support as well.

Steffens was quite fond of his niece Jane Hollister Wheelwright, and I am grateful to her daughter, Lynda Wheelwright Schmidt; her son, John Hollister Wheelwright; and her daughter-in-law, Betty Coon Wheelwright, for their enthusiasm and willingness to assist, particularly in providing permission to use family photos. Betty Coon Wheelwright's own biographical writings on her mother-in-law and on the Hollister and Steffens families provide a valuable and informed perspective.

Reading excerpts of the manuscript and offering generous comments were biographers Ronald Steel (on Walter Lippmann), Robert Rosenstone (on John Reed), Alice Wexler (on Emma Goldman), and Melvin Urofsky (on Louis Brandeis). Many thanks to Jill Seapker, a fellow unlearner, for an encouraging and perceptive reading of the entire manuscript, and to old friend Jim Stallings, always a reliable editor who, as Steffens would say, helps to clear the view. I am also indebted to Carole Thieme for a helpful reading of selected chapters and moral support on a daily basis, and to Liz Nicholson for her enduring interest in my work. And for generously sharing his astute observations on the ways of the publishing world, as well as his faith in my efforts at a critical juncture before a word of this book had been written, I want to acknowledge the late Peter Davison, poetry editor of the *Atlantic*.

The story of Steffens's life is spread across many archives that have been essential in my research. I am most grateful to the following individuals for their patience and diligence in responding to my requests for assistance: Jennifer Lee and Tara Craig, Butler Library, Columbia University; Lisa Marine, Wisconsin Historical Society; Ben Primer and Charles E. Greene, Princeton University Library; Peter Blodgett and Katrina Denman, Huntington Library; Maria Fernanda Meza, representing the Man Ray Trust; Marianne Leach and Kathleen Correia, California State Library; Jane Westenfeld, Pelletier Library, Allegheny College; and Suzanne Maggard, Archives and Rare Books Library, University of Cincinnati. I am also indebted to the following institutions for their kindly assistance: the Library of Congress; Houghton Library, Harvard University; Bancroft Library, University of California, Berkeley; Brandeis University Library; the Hemingway Archive, John F. Kennedy Presidential Library and Museum; the Boston Public Library; and the San Francisco Public Library.

I owe a very sizable debt to my agent, Paul Bresnick, whose firm belief in this project was uplifting. His experience, guidance, and ceaseless optimism were invaluable in seeing the book through to publication, and I am very pleased to acknowledge that fact.

At Counterpoint, my work benefited greatly from the experience and direction of Jack Shoemaker. He sees straight, to use Steffens's words, and I always appreciated Jack's insight, support and patience with my numerous inquiries. I am also very grateful to Laura Mazer for her enthusiastic and encouraging guidance through the editing process, as well as Roxanna Aliaga and Elizabeth Matthews for their assistance. I thank Patricia Boyd for a rigorous yet sensitive editing of the manuscript. Her keen eye for detail resulted in grammatical and stylistic changes that improved my work significantly.

My children, Julia and Timothy, both at the challenging age where they are trying to see their own futures, graciously read portions of the manuscript and offered helpful comments. My wife, Cristina, read the entire manuscript with care and intelligence and was a constant source of encouragement and support from start to finish. Her patience never wavered, despite having Steffens as a houseguest for years, and she gave the whole experience satisfaction and meaning that I deeply appreciate.

Finally, I am grateful for the influence of my father-in-law, Alfonso Mottola of Trieste, Italy, on this work. Although he did not live to see the book published, the many hours that we enjoyed together in discussions of history and politics, often late at night and in plumes of smoke from his well-used pipe, were always inspirational. The memory of his sincere and dedicated attention to my work lives on in this book and any others to follow.

Notes

Abbreviations

A	Lincoln Steffens, *The Autobiography of Lincoln Steffens* (New York, 1931)
AS	Allen Suggett
DH	Dorothy "Dot" Hollister
EW	Ella Winter
JS	Joseph Steffens
L	Lincoln Steffens, *The Letters of Lincoln Steffens*, vols. 1 and 2 (New York, 1938)
LAS	Laura Steffens
LS	Lincoln Steffens
LSP	Lincoln Steffens Papers, Rare Book & Manuscript Library, Columbia University in the City of New York

Introduction

1	"My story": *A*, 3.
1	"He cultivated": Sinclair, *Lifetime*, 50.
2	"For every illusion": *L*, xv.
2	"Europe is east": LS to Clinton Hollister, August 13, 1912, *L*, 306.

1: Boy on Horseback

3	"She not only knew": *A*, 4.
3	"the scrub": *A*, 5.
4	"conscious life": *A*, 7.
4	"ringing into town": *A*, 8.
4	"a gun-playing": *A*, 9.
4	"I didn't know why": *A*, 13, 14.

5   "a light to offer": LS to Marie Howe, February 8, 1926, *L*, 733–734.

6   "that Terror": *A*, 14.

6   "It interfered": *A*, 17.

6   "everybody that had anything": *A*, 16.

6   "All I want": *A*, 19.

7   "It covered": *A*, 23.

7   "Now I could ride": *A*, 26.

7   "the most active faculty": *A*, 27.

8   "I could cry": *A*, 37.

8   "the outsiders": *A*, 39, 40.

8   "And Charlie took it": *A*, 47.

9   "he did it very seldom": *A*, 92.

9   "My father's way": *A*, 93.

9   "I had never considered": *A*, 88.

10   "is one long search": *A*, 56.

10   "a mere matter": *A*, 72.

10   "Mrs. Neely never knew": *A*, 99.

10   "I became a drunkard": *A*, 101.

11   "It showed me": *A*, 107, 108.

11   "That book": *A*, 108.

11   "That's poppycock": *A*, 109.

12   "Their own motives": *A*, 111.

13   "Go to, boy": *A*, 113.

13   "my preparation for college": *A*, 114.

13   "established in me": *A*, 115.

13   "there was nothing": *A*, 118.

13   "specialists in football": *A*, 126.

14   "The professors' attitude": *A*, 119–120.

14   "It is possible": *A*, 124.

14   "I was the only rebel": *A*, 120.

2: To the Continent and Back

17   "understand and feel": *A*, 129.

17   "natural and unsound taste": LS to LAS, August 18, 1889, *L*, 10.

17   "I could see": *A*, 130–131.

17   "nothing but scorn": *A*, 131.

18   "He despised my degree": *A*, 132.

18   "I did not have to work": *A*, 133.

18   "very scarce.": LS to Lou Steffens, August 3, 1889, *L*, 7.

18   "both my woollen shirts": LS to Louisa Steffens, August 3, 1889, *L*, 5.

18   "Sunday evening": LS to LAS, August 18, 1889, *L*, 9.

18   "the richest men": LS to Louisa Steffens, October 1889, *L*, 18.

19   "Of all the privileged classes": LS to Frederick M. Willis, December 29, 1889, *L*, 37.

19   "You can scarcely realize": LS to Lou Steffens, August 25, 1889, *L*, 11.

19   "I know, too": LS to Frederick M. Willis, October 18, 1889, *L*, 20.

19   "a life of study": LS to Frederick M. Willis, December 8, 1889, *L*, 30.

20   "I am inclined to think": LS to Frederick M. Willis, December 22, 1889, *L*, 35.

20   "Your letter came yesterday": LS to Frederick M. Willis, October 18, 1889, *L*, 19.

20   "I think I am": LS to Frederick M. Willis, April 1, 1893, *L*, 95.

20   "the Americans whirled": LS to Louisa Steffens, November 30, 1889, *L*, 26.

20   "I have enjoyed a bliss": LS to Frederick M. Willis, October 18, 1889, *L*, 20.

21   "foolish": LS to Frederick M. Willis, February 23, 1890, *L*, 46.

21   "in as gentle a manner": LS to Frederick M. Willis, April 19, 1890, *L*, 47.

21   "without a word": LS to LAS, June 25, 1912, *L*, 300.

21   "brilliant young mind": LS to Frederick M. Willis, September 5, 1890, *L*, 50.

21   "poetical prose": *A*, 135.

21   "They could not agree": *A*, 139.

22   "a couple of good years": *A*, 139.

22   "I must leave the philosophers": *A*, 139.

22   "talked while they worked": *A*, 142.

22   "in psychology": *A*, 146.

22   "a working-girl": *A*, 147.

23   "almost all of the joy": LS to Frederick M. Willis, June 4, 1891, *L*, 61, 62.

23   "Lightly I say this now": *A*, 151.

23   "satisfying vanity": LS to JS, December 7, 1890, *L*, 56.

23   "give up the degree business": LS to JS, June 19, 1891, *L*, 64.

23   "glory of divine beauty": LS to Frederick M. Willis, January 29, 1891, *L*, 57.

24   "He demands": LS to Frederick M. Willis, April 19, 1890, *L*, 47.

24   "Your remembrance": LS to Louisa Steffens, July 31, 1891, *L*, 65.

24   "Her mind was alert": *A*, 156.

24   "dominating": *A*, 157.

25   "From a purely worldly standpoint": LS to Louisa Steffens, July 31, 1891, *L*, 65.

25   "Our agreement": LS to Harlow Gale, October 8, 1891, *L*, 67.

25   "make a noise": LS to JS, October 15, 1891, *L*, 68.

25   "sweet": LS to Louisa Steffens, February 4, 1892, *L*, 69.

26   "idyllic": *A*, 159.

26   "The French speak": *A*, 161.

26   "Obedient, unquestioning": *A*, 164.

26   "not what thinkers thought": *A*, 165.

26   "Italy is the worst governed country": LS to JS, April 22, 1892, *L*, 73, 74.

26   "The fame of cities": LS to Harlow Gale, October 8, 1891, *L*, 68.

27   "So soon as I felt": ibid., 67.

27   "in a sad and unaccountable way": LS to Harlow Gale, March 16, 1895, *L*, 113.

27   "means of the application": ibid., 113, 114.

28   "pleasure trips": LS to JS, May 20, 1892, *L*, 76.

28   "I have never felt": LS to JS, April 12, 1892, *L*, 74.

28   "American life": LS to JS, May 4, 1892, *L*, 75.

28   "I don't expect you": LS to JS, May 4, 1892, *L*, 75.

28   "all sorts of fashionable clothes": *A*, 166.

29   "By now you must know": *A*, 169.

3: MAKING HIS MARK

31   "from an editorship": *A*, 170.

32   "But": *A*, 171.

32   "My father was right": *A*, 171.

32   "I wish I could see": LS to JS, November 21, 1892, *L*, 85.

32   "the men of the day": LS to Frederick M. Willis, December 19, 1892, *L*, 87.

32   "bad government": *A*, 179.

33   "My notion is": Nevins, *Evening Post*, 458.

33   "Reporters were to report": *A*, 179.

33   "I do not want literature": N. Hapgood, *Changing Years*, 125.

33   "a remote deity": Nevins, *Evening Post*, 527.

33   "toe in the door": LS to JS, December 7, 1892, *L*, 86.

34   "regular and constant": LS to JS, January 18, 1893, *L*, 88.

34   "I have never since failed": *A*, 178.

34   "the joy I feel": LS to Frederick M. Willis, December 19, 1892, *L*, 87.

35   "the gentleman reporter": LS to JS, January 18, 1893, *L*, 89.

35   "Years of theory": LS to JS, March 18, 1893, *L*, 92.

35   "dazed": *A*, 181.

36   "The great Reading failure": LS to Harlow Gale, March 18, 1893, *L*, 93.

36   "an opportunity to see giants": *A*, 183.

37   "The falling, failing banks": *A*, 184.

37   "such and such a railroad": *A*, 185.

37   "As a study": LS to Harlow Gale, March 18, 1893, *L*, 93.

37   "are all": LS to Harlow Gale, March 18, 1893, *L*, 93–94.

38 "as brave as I was afraid": *A*, 190.

38 "Knows what he wants": *A*, 190.

38 "common practice": *A*, 191.

38 "what the world needs": *A*, 193.

39 "doubts and confusion": LS to JS, November 3, 1893, *L*, 97.

39 "That's why they put me": LS to JS, August 10, 1894, *L*, 104.

39 "It is beastly work": LS to JS, November 3, 1893, *L*, 98.

39 "a delightful way of life": Chamberlain, *Farewell*, 17.

39 "standing at Mulberry Bend": J. George Frederick to EW, November 6, 1936 (LSP).

40 "mixture of comedy": *A*, 243.

40 "Yom Kippur on the East Side, Scenes of Devotion and Mockery Among the Poorer Jews," *New York Evening Post*, September 17, 1896.

41 "Blessed is the man": I. Howe, *World*, 75–76.

41 "an abyss of many generations": *A*, 244, 245.

41 "You are more Jewish": *A*, 244.

42 "It dawned upon me": Parkhurst, *Forty Years*, 108.

42 "every step that we take": Parkhurst, *Forty Years*, 109–117.

42 "intemperate ravings": Sloat, *Battle*, 8.

42 "the most brutal": Parkhurst, *Forty Years*, 126–134.

43 "a lecher": Lardner and Reppetto, *NYPD*, 100.

43 "that it was possible": *A*, 198.

43 "calm, smiling, earnest": *A*, 198.

44 "filled the upper world": *A*, 201.

44 "His very manner": Jeffers, *Commissioner Roosevelt*, 9.

44 "no little dread": *A*, 199–200.

44 "There is more law": Jeffers, *Commissioner Roosevelt*, 11.

45 "He struck me": *A*, 201.

45 "shaggy-looking fellow": *A*, 203.

45 "He hated passionately": *A*, 203.

45 "I have read your book": "Jacob A. Riis Tells Of His Early Trials," *New York Times*, October 29, 1906, 7.

45 "You have started": *A*, 205.

46 "Many a morning": *A*, 207.

46 "the most exhaustive": LS to JS, November 24, 1893, *L*, 99.

46 "newspapers, literature": *A*, 215.

47 "good, prominent citizens": *A*, 219.

47 "dummy directors": *A*, 233.

47 "The real thing": H. Hapgood, *Types*, 57.

48 "sweet-faced": *A*, 235.

48   "A business man": *A*, 236.

48   "hard as nails": *A*, 238.

49   "It was the same picture": *A*, 250.

49   "singularly efficient": Sloat, *Battle*, 201.

49   "Oh God, yes": Jeffers, *Commissioner Roosevelt*, 49.

50   "remain here": "Mr. Croker Goes to Europe," *New York Times*, June 10, 1894, 5.

50   "painful labor": *A*, 292.

50   "You will always be loved": *A*, 292.

50   "There, I told you": *A*, 293.

52   "Like a thoughtless American": LS to Harlow Gale, January 13, 1895, *L*, 112.

52   "Money is not money": *A*, 310.

52   "Now I feel": LS to JS, October 18, 1894, *L*, 106.

4: ENTER TR

53   "pegged out": LS to JS, December 15, 1894, *L*, 107.

53   "mugwump or independent": LS to JS, October 18, 1894, *L*, 106.

53   "I feel that I have earned": LS to JS, August 10, 1894, *L*, 104.

53   "the disrepute": Stein, "Apprenticing Reporters," 12.

54   "I would literally": Morris, *Roosevelt*, 475.

54   "he knew nothing": *A*, 255.

54   "eminently satisfactory": LS to JS, November 8, 1894, *L*, 107.

54   "that the Republican officers": LS to JS, December 15, 1894, *L*, 108.

55   "the department is rotten": "Martin Gravely Accused," *New York Times*, December 22, 1894, 1.

55   "the most exciting strain": LS to JS, December 15, 1894, *L*, 107–108.

56   "I saw enough": *A*, 257.

56   "Mayor Strong": Riis, *Making*, 326.

56   "I think I could": LS to Harlow Gale, January 13, 1895, *L*, 113.

56   "Well, are you satisfied": *A*, 256.

56   "First or last": LS to JS, November 4, 1894 (LSP).

56   "the only voice": LS to JS, January 6, 1895, *L*, 108.

57   "deplorably ignorant": LS to JS, January 6, 1895, *L*, 109.

57   "Cyclone Hero": Bishop, *Roosevelt*, 28.

57   "Hello, Jake": *A*, 257.

58   "It was all breathless": *A*, 258.

58   "moral myopia": Jeffers, *Commissioner Roosevelt*, 156.

58   "the man who was closest": Roosevelt, *Autobiography*, 172.

58   "I loved him": Riis, *Making*, 328.

58   "a personal friend": Theodore Roosevelt to Horace Elisha Scudder, August 6, 1895, in Roosevelt, *Letters*, I, 472.

59   "I did feel immensely superior": LS to Marie Howe, June 25, 1927, *L*, 795.

59   "I have the most important": Morris, *Roosevelt*, 491.

60   "The public may rest assured": "New Police Board Meets," *New York Times*, May 7, 1895, 8.

60   "I am glad": Theodore Roosevelt to Anna Roosevelt Cowles, May 19, 1895, in Roosevelt, *Letters*, I, 458.

60   "When he asks": Jeffers, *Commissioner Roosevelt*, 76.

60   "Come on": *A*, 261.

60   "almost without words": *A*, 263.

60   "I shall move": Theodore Roosevelt to Henry Cabot Lodge, May 18, 1895, in Roosevelt, *Letters*, I, 458.

61   "We shall not soon": Riis, *Making*, 339.

61   "When Superintendent Byrnes retired": *A*, 261.

61   "We have four commissioners": Jeffers, *Commissioner Roosevelt*, 102.

61   "full of fight": Theodore Roosevelt to Henry Cabot Lodge, September 1895, in Roosevelt, *Letters*, I, 478.

61   "The policeman": Morris, *Roosevelt*, 485.

62   "Don't you dare": *A*, 259, 260.

5: A New Venture

63   "more and more deeply": LS to Harlow Gale, January 13, 1895, *L*, 110.

63   "a great deal": LS to Louisa Steffens, May 5, 1895, *L*, 116.

63   "Both of us": LS to JS, June 9, 1895, *L*, 118.

64   "What a handsome man": *A*, 266.

64   "His testimony": *A*, 273.

64   "You don't know": *A*, 268.

65   "No, no, no!": *A*, 275.

65   "the broom": *A*, 278.

65   "It worked": *A*, 264.

66   "What counted with them": *A*, 280.

66   "bold, intelligent bandits": *A*, 281.

66   "old-time confidence": LS to Louisa Steffens, October 26, 1895, *L*, 119.

66   "It seemed as though": LS to JS, January 12, 1896, *L*, 119.

66   "to make some studies": LS to JS, February 26, 1896, *L*, 120.

67   "It is idle to say": Morris, *Roosevelt*, 526.

67   "hours of profound depression": ibid., 527.

67   "I have no faith": LS to JS, November 9, 1896, *L*, 127.

67   "We were not so interested": LS to Harlow Gale, July 20, 1896, *L*, 122.

68   "I am sorry to say": LS to Frederick M. Willis, July 20, 1896, *L*, 124.

68   "busy, anxious": LS to JS, November 9, 1896, *L*, 126.

68   "I am working": LS to JS, November 6, 1896, *L*, 125.

68   "spent considerable": LS to JS, October 13, 1897, *L*, 128, 129.

69   "wretched old street-walker": *A*, 311.

69   "The Commercial Advertiser": Roy L. M. Cardell, "Notes Among the Newspapers," clipping, 1897 (LSP).

69   "a Park Row firetrap": Dunn, *World*, 9.

69   "My inspiration": *A*, 311–312.

69   "We probably": N. Hapgood, *Changing Years*, 125.

69   "Nobody is more cynical": H. Hapgood, *Types*, 102.

69   "a murder": *A*, 315.

69   "go on": *A*, 313.

69   "openly or secretly": *A*, 314.

70   "Care like hell": *L*, xv.

70   "I should become identified": Hartsock, *History*, 37.

70   "utterly inexperienced writers": *A*, 315.

70   "hand and glove": LS to JS, March 23, 1898, *L*, 130.

70   "He was almost": H. Hapgood, *Victorian*, 140.

70   "I'm city editor": Dunn, *World*, 9–16.

71   "There was almost nothing": H. Hapgood, *Victorian*, 140.

71   "would have long platonic conversations": H. Hapgood, *Types*, 109.

71   "He is a man": LS to Harlow Gale, July 20, 1896, *L*, 123.

71   "artists, bums, and thieves": *A*, 314.

72   "a very charming piece": H. Hapgood, *Victorian*, 149.

72   "like a wounded bird": *A*, 318.

72   "Neith Boyce was as romantic": *A*, 319.

72   "Of course": H. Hapgood, *Victorian*, 161.

72   "Well, of course": ibid., 284.

73   "That man": *A*, 317.

73   "It was a place": *A*, 317.

73   "picturesque Ghetto": *A*, 318.

73   "changed wonderfully": LS to JS, October 23, 1898, *L*, 132.

74   "The place for a war correspondent": *A*, 339.

74   "The end of the reign": "Mr. Roosevelt's Work," *New York Evening Post*, 1897 (LSP).

74   "no more backbone": Morris, *Roosevelt*, 610.

75   "He did not know": *A*, 344.

75   "looking as he often looked": *A*, 348.

75	"in identifying himself": Morris, *Roosevelt*, 518.
75	"Will I?" *A*, 346.
76	"bronzed and a trifle thin": "Roosevelt Meets Platt," *New York Times*, September 18, 1898, 1.
76	"Since I know": LS to JS, December 10, 1898, *L*, 133.
76	"He let me": *A*, 350.
77	"use up": *A*, 350–351.
77	"They want the earth": *A*, 351.
77	"I was delighted": Theodore Roosevelt to William Dudley Foulke, November 1898, in Roosevelt, *Letters*, II, 891.
77	"Of course": Theodore Roosevelt to Frank Moss, January 31, 1899, in Roosevelt, *Letters*, II, 926.
77	"dishonest lunatics": Theodore Roosevelt to Henry L. Sprague, January 26, 1900, in Roosevelt, *Letters*, II, 1141.
77	"It was a good excuse": *A*, 350.
77	"jim-dandy": S. S. McClure to LS, March 14, 1899 (LSP).
78	"We all feel": LS to JS, June 30, 1899, *L*, 133.
78	"noteworthy new book": "Letitia Berkeley, A.M.," *New York Times*, December 16, 1899, BR881.
78	"lecherous": *L*, 134, n. 1.
78	"prig": LS to JS, August 13, 1899, *L*, 134.
79	"I am trying to write": LS to JS, January 13, 1900, *L*, 135.
79	"the tale": LS to JS, August 27, 1901, *L*, 143.
79	"too long and unlovely": LS to JS, January 13, 1900, *L*, 135.
79	"they were a bit frightened": LS to JS, November 11, 1900, *L*, 136, 137.
79	"Stocks are booming": ibid., 136.
79	"I want to get rid of the bastard": Miller, *Roosevelt*, 335.
80	"I was emptied of energy": *A*, 353.
80	"strangely tired": H. Hapgood, *Types*, 111.
80	"The move contemplated": LS to JS, May 4, 1901, *L*, 138.
80	"We've got out of that man": *A*, 353.
80	"too artistic": Josephine Bontecou Steffens to JS, May 8, 1901 (LSP).
80	"far from a town": LS to JS, May 7, 1901, *L*, 138.
81	"What he does": LS to JS, June 20, 1901, *L*, 140.
81	"I must have put away": LS to William F. Neely, July 14, 1901, *L*, 142.
82	"It had better not circulate": LS to JS, September 4, 1901, *L*, 145.
82	"Either of us": LS to JS, September 4, 1901, *L*, 144.
82	"dreamless nights": *A*, 359.
82	"Don't you think": LS to Louisa Steffens, July 11 or 12, 1901, *L*, 141.

I HAVE SEEN THE FUTURE

6: The White House Beckons

83   "every conceivable symbol": Johns, *Time*, 138.

83   "Now look": "Theodore Roosevelt," *The American Heritage Book of the Presidents*, vol. 8, (New York: Dell, 1967), 665.

84   "Roosevelt as president": LS to JS, September 11, 1901, *L*, 146.

84   "It was like springing up": *A*, 359.

84   "The gift of the gods": *A*, 502.

84   "allowed his gladness": *A*, 503.

84   "a chamber of traitors": *A*, 504.

85   "to the hilt": *A*, 505.

85   "was a politician": *A*, 506.

85   "He takes counsel": "President's Development," *New York Mail and Express*, March 1, 1902.

86   "a Napoleonic belief": Sedgwick, *Happy Profession*, 139.

86   "embraced everything": ibid.

87   "If only I could have": R. S. Baker, *Chronicle*, 147.

87   "I did not want": ibid., 158.

87   "The most brilliant addition": Tarbell, *Day's Work*, 198.

87   "incredibly outspoken": ibid., 199.

88   "There was never any doubt": Brady, *Tarbell*, 136.

88   "He comes back to me": R. S. Baker, *Chronicle*, 221.

88   "Socratic skeptic": ibid.

88   "displayed all the impudence": Irwin, *Making*, 152.

88   "kindly, tolerant": Sullivan, *Education*, 200.

89   "a devoted friend": Sinclair, *Lifetime*, 50.

89   "Nobody will remain": LS to Belle Case La Follette, December 25, 1908, *L*, 214.

89   "brave effort": Tarbell, *Day's Work*, 199.

89   "He was a flower": *A*, 361–362.

90   "We had to unite": *A*, 363.

90   "A week in the McClure office": Sedgwick, *Happy Profession*, 142.

90   "hack-work": LS to JS, April 11, 1902, *L*, 155.

90   "a great, rambling, beautiful old accident": *A*, 436–440.

91   "lovely wilderness": LS to JS, December 29, 1901, *L*, 154.

91   "Meet people": ibid., 155.

7: Muckraking Sensation

93   "false alarm": *A*, 360.

94   "Do you think": Filler, *Crusaders*, 35.

94	"Obviously, the distribution of wealth": White, *Autobiography*, 181.
95	"I am glad to be called": Charles Edward Russell, letter to the editor, *Everybody's*, February 1909, 279.
96	"I'm going to do a series": Whitlock, *Forty Years*, 158.
96	"a very quiet": A, 365.
96	"His courtesy": Filler, *Crusaders*, 102.
96	"We were shut in": A, 367.
97	"being all slashed": A, 369.
97	"straddled the town": Johns, *Time*, 131.
97	"represents bribery": A, 371.
97	"Or—the best": A, 372.
98	"that political evils": A, 375.
99	"Where in the Constitution": Chamberlain, *Farewell*, 132.
99	"I hope the people": Brady, *Tarbell*, 139.
100	"We had a pretty hot fight": A, 375.
100	"protect, share with": A, 376.
101	"He was one of a group": A, 385.
102	"You have made": Lyon, *Success*, 204.
102	"Your articles": S. S. McClure to LS, November 10, 1902, in Cheslaw, "Intellectual," 75.
102	"Capitalists, workingmen": editorial, *McClure's*, January 1903.
103	"No hard-and-fast rule": Hofstadter, *Reform*, 205.
103	"Evidently": A, 392.
104	"The machinery of justice": A, 396.
104	"It might be": A, 399.
105	"I was afraid": A, 400.
105	"looked like hell": A, 401.
105	"Magee wanted power": Steffens, *Shame*, 106.
106	"I have been thinking": Lyon, *Success*, 218.
106	"after painstaking research": Steffens, *Upbuilders*, xxii.
106	"Your theory": A, 407.
107	"in desperation": A, 411.
108	"big, bad men": A, 417.
108	"The petty honest men": A, 418.
108	"That is why": A, 417.
109	"sensationally wicked story": A, 423.
109	"You are the man": A, 424.
110	"The New York Tenderloin": A, 425.
111	"pecuniarily honest": Steffens, *Shame*, 199.

8: THE SHAME OF THE CITIES

113   "all up in the air": *A*, 434.

113   "With all my growing contempt": *A*, 522, 523.

114   "Everything, everything goes well": LS to JS, December 13, 1903, *L*, 160, 161.

114   "little triumphs": LS to JS, October 17, 1903, *L*, 158.

114   "Of course you know": LS to Ray Stannard Baker, November 8, 1903, *L*, 159.

114   "If I am to have": LS to JS, December 13, 1903, *L*, 161.

114   "come around": LS to JS, October 17, 1903, *L*, 158.

115   "for a short confab": LS to JS, December 1903, *L*, 162.

115   "I believe we can do more": Lyon, *Success*, 220.

115   "Tell Folk": ibid.

115   "Maybe I can": LS to JS, January 26, 1904, *L*, 164.

115   "I am not for individual men": LS to JS, February 14, 1904, *L*, 165.

116   "The State was the unit": *A*, 443.

116   "governed by a railroad": LS to JS, December 1903, *L*, 162.

116   "The stream of pollution": Steffens, *Struggle*, 3.

116   "big boodlers": *A*, 446.

116   "ideal citizen": *A*, 447–448.

117   "I suppose": *A*, 449.

117   "the inability of the minds": *A*, 449.

117   "a system": Steffens, *Struggle*, 4–5.

117   "Interstate corporations": White, *Autobiography*, 345.

117   "The world must be weary": Riis, *Roosevelt*, 135.

117   "Nobody can realize": Steffens, *Struggle*, 7.

118   "I am sorry": Lawrence Godkin to LS, April 1, 1904 (LSP).

118   "being reviewed everywhere": LS to JS, April 10, 1904, *L*, 168.

118   "with a purpose": Steffens, *Shame*, 18.

119   "a big thing": LS to JS, February 14, 1904, *L*, 165.

120   "get a true insight": "On Mission for Roosevelt," *New York Times*, June 28, 1904, 1.

120   "seemed fair": *A*, 455.

120   "the story": *A*, 456.

120   "polite but reserved": La Follette and La Follette, *La Follette*, 182.

120   "The other day": Belle Case La Follette to Louis D. Brandeis, June 15, 1910, in Brandeis, *Letters*, II, 330, n.2.

121   "a dictator": *A*, 458.

121   "I had then": La Follette, *Autobiography*, 96.

121   "sincerity, his integrity": *A*, 458.

121   "No one": Lyon, *Success*, 228.

121   "a veritable bomb": La Follette and La Follette, *La Follette*, 185.

121   "Poor Payne": Theodore Roosevelt to Henry Cabot Lodge, October 2, 1904, in Roosevelt, *Letters*, IV, 965.

9: THE SHAME OF THE STATES

123   "the best established": *A*, 465.

123   "a fine old New England gentleman": *A*, 465.

123   "he had had himself admitted": *A*, 465.

124   "common knowledge": Steffens, *Struggle*, 127.

124   "the Democrats": ibid., 133.

124   "My town is all right": ibid., 128.

124   "good old American stock": *A*, 464.

124   "wherever the farmers": *A*, 469.

125   "There is no reform": Steffens, *Struggle*, 160.

125   "Aldrich article": Lyon, *Success*, 225.

125   "know nothing": Theodore Roosevelt to LS, June 24, 1905, in Roosevelt, *Letters*, IV, 1255.

125   "I believe the present reform": James Higgins to LS, October 6, 1906, in Shapiro, "Evolution."

126   "We must begin": Steffens, *Struggle*, 161–162.

126   "read a book": *A*, 475.

126   "socialist-anarchist-nihilist": Steffens, *Struggle*, 183.

127   "I continued in my business": T. Johnson, *Story*, 51.

127   "was not merely a good rich man": *A*, 477.

127   "It is privilege": *A*, 479.

127   "gone back on his class": *A*, 477.

127   "was an armed camp": T. Johnson, *Story*, xxiv.

128   "I pictured him": F. Howe, *Confessions*, 182.

128   "My estimate of muck-raking": ibid., 183.

128   "I think he and I": LS to Marie Howe, April 16, 1919, *L*, 466.

129   "The ideals of America": *A*, 494.

129   "Jersey shows": Steffens, *Struggle*, 252.

129   "the evening": LS to JS, January 26, 1904, *L*, 164.

129   "especially interested": Theodore Roosevelt to LS, June 24, 1905, in Roosevelt, *Letters*, IV, 1254–1256.

130   "absolutely": LS to Theodore Roosevelt, September 21, 1905, *L*, 170.

131   "Mr. President": LS to Theodore Roosevelt, September 21, 1905, *L*, 171.

131   "most emphatically": Theodore Roosevelt to LS, September 25, 1905, in Roosevelt, *Letters*, V, 36, 37, 38.

132   "It's hard": LS to JS, August 5, 1905, *L*, 169.

132   "Business with them": Shapiro, "Evolution," 158.

132   "our profession": McGerr, *Discontent*, 170.

132   "the likeness of the business graft": *A*, 529.

132   "sacred trusts": *A*, 530.

132   "If a public": *A*, 530.

132   "Cheerful idiots": Steffens, *Struggle*, 182.

133   "first in my heart": Steffens, *Upbuilders*, vii.

133   "The church": *A*, 500.

133   "There is a constantly growing class": Steffens, *Upbuilders*, 47.

134   "stirring up the people": Everett Colby to LS, October 20, 1905 (LSP).

134   "Ohio recognizes your message": Lyon, *Success*, 228.

134   "Why, that man's program": Whitlock, *Forty Years*, 164.

135   "the most advanced leader": LS to Brand Whitlock, November 8, 1905, *L*, 171.

135   "primarily an artist": F. Howe, *Confessions*, 187.

135   "Graft is not sporadic": "Where Graft Begins," *New York Times*, January 15, 1906, 5.

136   "He was not": *A*, 513.

136   "reacted like a democrat": *A*, 514.

136   "any officer or employee": *A*, 515.

136   "In Congress": Theodore Roosevelt to LS, February 6, 1906, in Roosevelt, *Letters*, V, 147, 148.

137   "among the first": "The Man with the Muckrake," *New York Times* (*Saturday Review of Books*), August 4, 1906, 487.

1 0: Goodbye to All That

139   "constant inspiration": R. S. Baker, *Chronicle*, 179.

139   "It is an unfortunate thing": Theodore Roosevelt to S. S. McClure, October 4, 1905, in Roosevelt, *Letters*, V, 45.

140   "The kind of work": Cheslaw, "Intellectual," 109.

140   "the most potent": Theodore Roosevelt to John St. Loe Strachey, October 25, 1906, in Roosevelt, *Letters*, V, 469.

140   "was not the best man": Chamberlain, *Farewell*, 140.

140   "Well, you have put an end": *A*, 581.

140   "poor old Chauncey Depew": *A*, 581.

140   "indignation": Theodore Roosevelt to George William Alger, March 20, 1906, in Roosevelt, *Letters*, V, 189.

140   "the satiety of the public": *A*, 581.

141   "who never thinks or speaks": "Roosevelt for Tax on Wealth," *New York Times*, April 15, 1906, 1.

141   "In speech after speech": Creel, *Rebel*, 94.

141   "all of our stories": Wilson, *McClure's*, 199.

142   "I don't object to the facts": Tarbell, *Day's Work*, 242.

142   "the letting in": R. S. Baker, *Chronicle*, 203.

142   "rewards an honest man": "Didn't Mean Me—Steffens," *New York Times*, April 17, 1906, 1.

142   "This is a point": LS to Theodore Roosevelt, March 6, 1907, *L*, 184.

142   "It was miraculous": Sedgwick, *Happy Profession*, 144.

142   "Nothing fails like success": *A*, 535.

143   "a Mormon": Wilson, *McClure's*, 170.

143   "I realized": *A*, 535.

144   "Political influence": *A*, 535.

144   "I resisted": *A*, 536.

144   "No man": LS to JS, June 3, 1906, *L*, 174.

144   "I feel that I should remain": Wilson, *McClure's*, 184.

145   "our friend": Lyon, *Success*, 299.

145   "He has lost his staff": LS to JS, June 3, 1906, *L*, 174.

145   "bleeding reformer": White, *Autobiography*, 388.

145   "and he is not": Brady, *Tarbell*, 180.

145   "We shall not only": R. S. Baker, *Chronicle*, 226.

146   "We really believed": ibid.

146   "Every man": LS to JS, June 3, 1906, *L*, 174.

146   "in a way": ibid., 175.

146   "a feast of fun": *A*, 536.

146   "I was ashamed": JS to Ray Stannard Baker, July 25, 1906, *L*, 177.

146   "It was certainly": R. S. Baker, *Chronicle*, 230.

147   "He could not make himself write": *A*, 537.

147   "He would talk about it": *A*, 538–539.

147   "Hearst's nomination": Theodore Roosevelt to Henry Cabot Lodge, September 27, 1906, in Roosevelt, *Letters*, V, 429.

147   "We come home at night": Dunne, *Mr. Dooley*, 243.

148   "We are pretty brutal": Ellis, *Mr. Dooley's*, 225.

148   "is so far ahead": *A*, 543.

148   "Some people": Steffens, "Hearst, the Man of Mystery," *American Magazine*, November 1906, 6.

148   "a great man": *A*, 541–542.

148   "has recently written an article": Theodore Roosevelt to William Howard Taft, November 8, 1906, in Roosevelt, *Letters*, V, 491.

149   "We can guarantee": "A People's Lobby to Watch Congress," *New York Times*, September 18, 1906, 6.

149   "The Congress stands": Cheslaw, "Intellectual," 94.

150   "California theory": *A*, 544.

150   "against every evil": A, 546.

151   "All of the 'reformers'": Creel, Rebel, 119.

151   "I saw my wife gasp": A, 547.

151   "Nobody could tell us": A, 548.

152   "My husband has become famous": Josephine Bontecou Steffens to W. Lorenz, December 17, 1907 (LSP).

152   "the crowd": "Under the Kremlin," in Steffens, Speaking, 312.

152   "to get rid of literary buzzards": Shapiro, "Evolution," 70.

153   "Mr. Heney has uncovered": Theodore Roosevelt to Charles William Fulton, May 13, 1905, in Roosevelt, Letters, IV, 1176, 1177.

153   "started it all": A, 553.

153   "the license and the easy money": A, 554.

153   "This was the beginning": Older, Story, 33.

153   "Nobody was ever secure": Steffens, "William J. Burns, Intriguer," American Magazine, April 1908, 615.

154   "a close and intimate advisor": Roosevelt, Autobiography, 387.

154   "a family of individuals": Steffens, Upbuilders, 249.

154   "had not learned": A, 554.

155   "Patrick Calhoun offered": Steffens, Upbuilders, 267.

156   "I was fifty years old": Wells, Older, 207.

156   "Ruef did not make those conditions": Older, Story, 162.

157   "That moment": A, 567.

158   "It seems to me": LS to Theodore Roosevelt, March 6, 1907, L, 182, 183, 184.

158   "It is not my business": Theodore Roosevelt to LS, March 12, 1907, in Roosevelt, Letters, V, 615.

159   "You and I do not agree": Theodore Roosevelt to LS, November 4, 1907, in Roosevelt, Letters, V, 829–830.

159   "cool harbor water": LS to JS, August 16, 1907, L, 185, 186.

159   "Hello, old man": LS to JS, August 27, 1907, L, 186, 187.

160   "His view": Brady, Tarbell, 183.

161   "Is that not": Tarbell, Day's Work, 298.

161   "love to all": LS to Belle Case La Follette, May 1, 1908, L, 189.

161   "All by myself": A, 576.

161   "I did not intend": A, 357.

161   "how little": A, 632.

162   "one of the most earnest": A, 632.

1 1: "If You Are Not a Socialist"

163   "gratification": LS to Robert La Follette, May 28, 1908, in La Follette and La Follette, *La Follette*, 257.

163   "I am often interested": Theodore Roosevelt to LS, June 5, 1908, in Roosevelt, *Letters*, VI, 1051, 1052, 1053.

164   "I want to see": LS to Theodore Roosevelt, June 9, 1908, *L*, 194–196.

165   "nice letter": Theodore Roosevelt to LS, June 12, 1908, in Roosevelt, *Letters*, VI, 1072.

165   "again the conservative party": LS to Theodore Roosevelt, June 20, 1908, *L*, 200.

166   "a sensitive, warm-hearted man": R. S. Baker, *Chronicle*, 37.

166   "There may have lived": Darrow, *Story*, 68.

166   "Don't choose": LS to Brand Whitlock, October 30, 1908, *L*, 209.

166   "You have written": Eugene V. Debs to LS, September 15, 1908, *L*, 203.

166   "I certainly am socialistic": LS to LAS, September 23, 1908, *L*, 202.

166   "I simply don't know": LS to LAS, September 23, 1908, *L*, 202.

167   "Both the old party": Shapiro, "Evolution," 206.

167   "The world is moving": LS to LAS, November 1, 1908, *L*, 211.

167   "call on my good old father": LS to Upton Sinclair, November 8, 1908, in Sinclair, *Lifetime*, 51.

167   "I couldn't vote": LS to LAS, November 1, 1908, *L*, 211.

167   "given up reading": Theodore Roosevelt to John Graham Brooks, November 13, 1908, in Roosevelt, *Letters*, VI, 1343.

168   "I can see you": LS to Theodore Roosevelt, March 21, 1909, *L*, 219.

168   "Down at the bottom": Theodore Roosevelt to William Allen White, August 10, 1908, in Roosevelt, *Letters*, VI, 1166.

1 2: Boston

169   "a cross between": G. Johnson, *Liberal's Progress*, 6.

170   "Instead of holding": "Brandeis Named for Highest Court; Will Be Opposed," *New York Times*, January 29, 1916, 1.

170   "He would make": LS to Edward A. Filene, June 28, 1908, *L*, 200.

170   "I am glad": Louis D. Brandeis to Henry Beach Needham, March 16, 1908, in Brandeis, *Letters*, II, 101.

171   "sat up till near midnight": Louis D. Brandeis to Alfred Brandeis, April 4, 1908, in Brandeis, *Letters*, II, 115.

171   "Having borne so patiently": Louis D. Brandeis to LS, December 10, 1909, in Brandeis, *Letters*, II, 300.

171   "the failure": *A*, 603.

171   "I really expect": LS to Edward A. Filene, July 15, 1908, *L*, 201.

171   "profoundly interesting": ibid.

172   "everything in my power": Edmund Billings to LS, July 23, 1908 (LSP).

172   "earnest, representative men": *A*, 613.

172   "I don't expect it": LS to Upton Sinclair, November 8, 1908, in Sinclair, *Lifetime*, 51.

172   "We have always wanted": *Boston Post*, October 9, 1908 (LSP).

172   "The most interesting immigrant": "Steffens Just a Glimpse" (LSP).

173   "heavy jaw": Ainley, *Mahatma*, 182.

173   "bad, cold, hard": *A*, 615.

173   "failure of democracy": *A*, 616.

173   "I gave it to him": Ainley, *Mahatma*, 183.

173   "He was honest": *A*, 617.

173   "pleasant": LS to Louisa Steffens, October 3, 1908, *L*, 204.

174   "beautifully": LS to Louisa Steffens, December 6, 1908, *L*, 212.

174   "How little": LS to LAS, December 13, 1908, *L*, 212.

174   "nothing like Scripps": Eastman, *Companions*, 11.

174   "life in all forms": *A*, 667.

174   "We are seeking": LS to E. W. Scripps, January 23, 1909, *L*, 216.

175   "I think": *A*, 618.

175   "had done wrong": *A*, 618.

175   "kicking like steers": *A*, 620.

176   "'hurrah boys' element": Kellogg, "Boston's Level Best," 383.

176   "It is like reforming drunkards": LS to LAS, May 31, 1909, *L*, 222.

176   "We know them": Ainley, *Mahatma*, 184.

176   "has sworn by me": LS to LAS, March 12, 1912, *L*, 291.

176   "Once named to me": Ainley, *Mahatma*, 184.

177   "Is it hope": Steffens, *Upbuilders*, vii.

177   "*Wherever the people*": Steffens, *Upbuilders*, vii.

177   "inspired millionaires": LS to LAS, April 9, 1910, *L*, 242.

177   "I believe": Fels, *Joseph Fels*, 195.

177   "I am using": Fels, *Life of Joseph Fels*, 149.

178   "as convinced a Single Taxer": Steffens, *Upbuilders*, xxvii.

178   "With money to use": *A*, 643.

178   "My conclusion": *A*, 643.

179   "think about": LS to Tom Johnson, September 1, 1909, *L*, 225.

179   "lack of courtesy": George Boke to LS, January 18, 1910 (LSP).

179   "in the midst of my book": LS to John Reed, September 25, 1909 (John Reed Papers, Harvard).

179   "We all hate it": LS to John Reed, October 8, 1909, *L*, 228, 229.

179   "I have felt the defeat": LS to Brand Whitlock, November 24, 1909, *L*, 231.

180   "I saw": Louis D. Brandeis to LS, November 9, 1909, in Brandeis, *Letters*, II, 295.

180   "I feel these things": LS to JS, November 13, 1909, *L*, 230.

180   "I know the cause": LS to Brand Whitlock, December 4, 1909, *L*, 233.

180   "It looks as if": LS to LAS, January 4, 1910, *L*, 236.

180   "Reform has got to come": LS to Fremont Older, February 21, 1910, *L*, 238.

180   "My dear Lincoln": Josephine Bontecou Steffens to LS, November 19, 1909 (LSP).

181   "Your letters": Victor Berger to LS, December 6, 1909 (LSP).

181   "And suddenly": *A*, 525.

181   "I haven't finished": LS to JS, May 24, 1910, *L*, 246.

182   "see what" *A*, 525.

182   "the biggest thing": LS to Louisa Steffens, December 21, 1909, *L*, 235.

182   "an adventure": *A*, 525.

182   "the doctrine of Jesus": "Moses in Red," in Steffens, *World*, 72.

182   "I never heard": ibid., 73.

182   "Every real reform": Steffens, "Into Mexico and Out," *Everybody's*, May 1916, 539.

13: A Death in the Family

183   "I appreciate your reflections": LS to LAS, April 9, 1910, *L*, 241.

183   "I thought": *A*, 586.

183   "where they really work": *A*, 586.

183   "A bourgeois uptown organization": Richwine, *Liberal Club*, 89.

184   "I did not want to feel": *A*, 587.

184   "The result": *A*, 587.

184   "swelling around": *A*, 587.

184   "to turn attention": LS to LAS, April 9, 1910, *L*, 242.

184   "long and well-trained": *A*, 592.

184   "the ablest mind": *A*, 593.

185   "What I have dreamed of doing": Steel, *Lippmann*, 33–34.

185   "I'll try to be square": ibid., 35.

186   "keen, quiet, industrious": *A*, 593.

186   "We found": Lippmann, *Preface*, 20.

186   "When Lippmann showed me": LS to LAS, January 28, 1924, *L*, 637.

187   "think what they themselves": *New Britain Daily Herald*, December 13, 1910 (LSP).

187   "been fighting": Erwin Edwards to LS, December 1910 (LSP).

187   "typical leading citizens": *A*, 597.

188   "two hours": LS to AS, March 6, 1911, *L*, 266.

188   "Of course": *Greenwich Press*, January 4, 1911 (LSP).

188   "too whimsical": Kaplan, *Steffens*, 178.

188   "Lord": Steel, *Lippmann*, 39.

188   "We have been": LS to Francis Heney, December 23, 1910, in Kaplan, *Steffens*, 178.

189   "They really deserve": LS to Brand Whitlock, April 25, 1910, *L*, 244.

189   "could have wished": LS to JS, August 29, 1910, *L*, 248.

189   "Josephine is still": LS to JS, October 22, 1910, *L*, 253.

189   "Hope is still held out": LS to LAS, December 25, 1910, *L*, 254.

189   "My poor girl died": Susan Bontecou diary, January 8, 1911 (LSP).

190   "My wife": *A*, 634.

190   "The whole thing": LS to Ray Stannard Baker, January 11, 1911, *L*, 258.

190   "The pathos": LS to Belle Case La Follette, January 11, 1911, *L*, 258.

190   "It was not alone": LS to Harlow Gale, February 7, 1911, *L*, 262.

190   "such a portrait": *A*, 635.

191   "I don't count": LS to Jane Hollister, February 25, 1913, *L*, 319.

191   "Only Lincoln here": Susan Bontecou diary (LSP).

191   "He was": H. Hapgood, *Victorian*, 277.

192   "I was lost": *A*, 635.

192   "I hardly know": LS to Harlow Gale, February 7, 1911, *L*, 263.

192   "I'd like to see if": LS to Brand Whitlock, January 21, 1911, *L*, 261.

193   "I love the little bruiser": LS to DH, March 20, 1911, *L*, 268.

193   "what had never been written": Steffens, "Mary Austin," *American Magazine*, LXXII, 1911, 180.

193   "the most God-awful hats": White, *Autobiography*, 370.

193   "been seeing": LS to LAS, December 25, 1910, *L*, 255.

194   "Steffy is saturated": Fink, *I—Mary*, 156.

194   "I thought": Austin, *Western Trails*, 233.

194   "You cannot imagine": Mary Austin to LS, March 24, 1911 (LSP).

194   "If you wish": Fink, *I—Mary*, 159.

195   "I suffered incredibly": Austin, *Woman*, 499.

196   "It appeared": Luhan, *Movers*, 68.

196   "This is the second time": Mary Austin to LS, undated letters (LSP).

197   "I killed a man": Langlois, "Mary Austin and Lincoln Steffens," 379.

197   "savage with irritability": LS to Lou Suggett and AS, September 23, 1911, *L*, 278.

198   "I count you a discovery": LS to AS, August 29, 1910, *L*, 248.

198   "wreck": LS to Lou Suggett and AS, September 23, 1911, *L*, 278.

198   "youth lived": *A*, 653.

198   "bourgeois pigs!": Wetzsteon, *Republic*, 20.

199   "I was afraid": Reed, "Almost Thirty," 333.

199   "nothing but a bundle": "Back from Russia," in Steffens, *Speaking*, 309.

199   "No ray of sunshine": "Under the Kremlin," in Steffens, *Speaking*, 313.

199   "I think and talk": Rosenstone, *Romantic*, 85.

199   "Get him a job": *A*, 653–654.

200   "I couldn't help but observe": Hicks, *John Reed*, 73.

200   "More than any other man": Reed, "Almost Thirty," 333.

200   "When you really fall in love": LS to John Reed, June 14, 1912, *L*, 296–297.

200   "Girls, plays, bums": *A*, 654.

200   "Write it down": Hicks, *John Reed*, 68.

201   "Nothing but revolution": *A*, 631.

201   "I believe in Free Speech": H. Hapgood, *Victorian*, 279.

201   "Any censorship": Steffens, "An Answer and an Answer," *Everybody's Magazine*, November 1911, 717–720.

14: Dynamite

203   "O you anarchic scum": Adamic, *My America*, 18.

204   "there was no such thing": Burns, *Masked*, 218.

204   "deep in the dregs": ibid., 13.

204   "an undoubting belief": *A*, 660.

204   "It's a delicate job": LS to JS, November 3, 1911, *L*, 278.

205   "The Bivouac": Adamic, *My America*, 14.

205   "well-backed": *A*, 660.

206   "the attorney for the damned": "That Man Darrow," in Steffens, *Speaking*, 143.

206   "organized injustice": Cowan, *People*, 41.

206   "more of a poet": *A*, 664, 666.

207   "to try this case": *A*, 661.

207   "That is why": *A*, 661.

207   "put on an air": *A*, 662.

207   "Oh, the fraud of it all": LS to DH, November 28, 1911, *L*, 279.

208   "I don't have to wait": LS to DH, November 28, 1911, *L*, 279.

208   "justifiable dynamiting": *A*, 663.

208   "I want to assume": LS to LAS, November 17, 1911, *L*, 280.

208   "these men": Scripps, *I Protest*, 401.

209   "I have come up": LS to Ermin Ridgway, *Everybody's Magazine*, November/December 1911, 717–720, 796–799, quoted in Cheslaw, "Intellectual," 161.

209   "political bosses": *A*, 671.

210   "big, bad men": *A*, 673.

210   "a creature who is vile": Mowry, *California*, 126.

210   "an honest man": Adamic, *Dynamite*, 205.

210   "a hard-headed": *A*, 674.

210   "My God": Tierney, *Darrow*, 243.

210   "I intended": Brian C. Ernst, "Joseph Scott, Upholder of American Justice in Los Angeles," April 21, 2003, available at www.lmu.edu/Page39949.aspx.

211   "What is this gink Steffens": Cowan, *People*, 227.

211   "Publicity would have meant": Darrow, *Story*, 181.

211   "They took it all in": LS to LAS, November 29, 1911, *L*, 281.

212   "idealists and reformers": *A*, 682.

213   "That court": *A*, 684.

213   "I am astounded": "Labor Denounces the M'Namaras," *New York Times*, December 8, 1911, 1.

213   "joins in the satisfaction": *San Francisco Examiner*, December 2, 1911.

213   "hostile fashion": *A*, 685.

213   "an old-maidish fuss budget": Eastman, *Enjoyment*, 431.

214   "of the olden days": LS to DH, December 3 or 4, 1911, *L*, 281.

214   "I see": LS to LAS, November 1911, *L*, 282.

214   "Watch out": *A*, 686.

215   "The sermons": *A*, 688.

215   "There is no denying": *Los Angeles Tribune*, December 12, 1911.

215   "You were wrong": *A*, 689.

215   "it would result": "Got Pleas to Show Need for Reforms," *New York Times*, December 3, 1911, 7.

216   "go-between": "M'Namaras Had to Tell or Die," *New York Times*, December 3, 1911, 1.

216   "I never knew him": "Confessions Forced by Bribery Plot," *New York Times*, December 4, 1911, 2.

216   "the court was not swayed": "Judge Denounces Lincoln Steffens," *New York Times*, December 6, 1911, 2.

216   "I would rather": ibid.

216   "a friend of mine": "Burns Wins Over a Hostile Audience," *New York Times*, March 8, 1912, 4.

217   "Since the startling outcome": Theodore Roosevelt, "Murder Is Murder," *The Outlook*, December 16, 1911, 902.

218   "Such people": Goldman, *Living*, 487.

218   "In the midst of our indignation": Louis D. Brandeis to Paul Underwood Kellogg, December 19, 1911, in Brandeis, *Letters*, II, 522.

218   "He understood": Darrow, *Story*, 186.

219   "guilty as hell": Cowan, *People*, 184.

219   "took very great cognizance": Fry, "Sara Bard Field," 263.

219   "Sure enough": LS to LAS, December 24, 1911, *L*, 285.

219   "all the homeless young poets": LS to Lou Suggett and AS, December 24, 1911, *L*, 286.

219   "no end of it all": LS to LAS, December 24, 1911, *L*, 285.

219   "For years after": Fry, "Sara Bard Field," 266.

219   "It doesn't matter": LS to LAS, December 24, 1911, *L*, 285.

15: THE WHITE HOUSE AGAIN

221   "For myself": LS to LAS, February 1, 1912, *L*, 288.

221   "I like to think": LS to JS, March 13, 1909, *L*, 218–219.

221   "with wild acclaim": "La Follette Wants No Limit on Recall," *New York Times*, January 23, 1912, 1.

222   "a damn, pig-headed blunderer": Mowry, *Roosevelt*, 108.

222   "You would laugh": Hofstadter, *Political Tradition*, 302.

222   "bully": LS to AS, January 24, 1912, *L*, 287.

222   "insane distemper": Cooper, *Wilson*, 154.

223   "to kill Lincoln Steffens": Mowry, *Roosevelt*, 225.

223   "New England is ready to blow up": LS to LAS, March 12, 1912, *L*, 292.

223   "There's none": LS to LAS, March 12, 1912, *L*, 291.

223   "approve of force": LS to DH, June 26, 1912, *L*, 304.

224   "courteous": LS to LAS, June 25, 1912, *L*, 300–302.

224   "I wish I could go": LS to LAS, May 17, 1912, *L*, 294.

224   "Hanging is none too good": Starr, *Endangered*, 34.

225   "dirty business": *A*, 664.

225   "is here to make sure": LS to DH, June 10, 1912, *L*, 296.

225   "not for an umpire": LS to LAS, June 25, 1912, *L*, 301.

225   "I was eager for the fray": *A*, 698.

226   "a terrible, useless cost": LS to James Hollister, June 6, 1912, *L*, 295.

226   "There was the typical lawyer": *A*, 700–701.

227   "elaborate, philosophical addresses": Shapiro, "Steffens and the McNamara Case," 407.

227   "gasp": Cowan, *People*, 385.

227   "Steffens pleads for use": (LSP).

227   "I wish you had gone": LS to LAS, July 20, 1912, *L*, 305.

227   "one of the great": Tierney, *Darrow*, 267.

227   "I am not on trial": Cowan, *People*, 421.

229   "come back": LS to Lou Suggett, AS, DH, and LAS, August 1912, *L*, 307.

229   "He dined with me": LS to LAS, October 3, 1912, *L*, 308–309.

229   "I want to be in the family": LS to LAS, May 24, 1912, *L*, 295.

230   "love illustrated": LS to Clinton and Jane Hollister, January 9, 1913, *L*, 314.

230   "He is a dear boy": LS to DH, October 17, 1912, *L*, 310.

230   "But I find it hard": LS to DH, September 19, 1913, *L*, 327.

231   "ball bat convention": Mowry, *Roosevelt*, 232.

231   "I hope your people": Theodore Roosevelt to William Howard Taft, September 5, 1908, in Roosevelt, *Letters*, VI, 1209–1210.

232   "If he does some fur will fly": LS to LAS, November 11, 1912, *L*, 312.

233   "It may be exciting": LS to Lou Suggett, February 22, 1913, *L*, 319.

233   "Anyhow, it was a good fight": *A*, 701.

233   "I've been in Boston": LS to DH, October 24, 1912, *L*, 311.

233   "You must be surely aware": Edmund Billings to LS, November 2, 1910 (LSP).

233   "I know you'll be glad": LS to Lou Suggett, July 6, 1913, *L*, 324, 325.

234   "darkest America": *A*, 605, 606.

234   "thrift, cunning, and possessions": *A*, 607.

234   "carried the practice of hypocrisy": *A*, 607, 608.

234   "heelers": *A*, 627.

16: Fun on Fifth Avenue

235   "taste and grace": *A*, 654.

235   "We have left everything": Hicks, *John Reed*, 96.

235   "one of the most attractive": Luhan, *Movers*, 47.

235   "spectators": H. Hapgood, *Victorian*, 348.

236   "rapier-keen mind": Luhan, *Movers*, 66.

236   "a refuge from the street": Rudnick, *Luhan*, 59.

236   "attract, stimulate, and soothe": Wetzsteon, *Republic*, 21.

236   "Why not organize": Luhan, *Movers*, 80.

236   "Poor and rich": *A*, 654–655.

236   "I wanted": Luhan, *Movers*, 84.

237   "that the minds of men": *A*, 655, 656.

237   "men are the victims": Wetzsteon, *Republic*, 19.

237   "No one felt": *A*, 655.

237   "Oh, I never listened": Winter, *Yield*, 135.

238   "A rich woman": Stansell, *Moderns*, 109.

238   "She does not create": Rudnick, *Luhan*, 88.

238   "Bohemian": LS to Jim Hollister, February 27, 1912, *L*, 289.

239   "Good-by, my darling": Rosenstone, *Romantic*, 146.

239   "You stay put": LS to John Reed, November 1913, *L*, 329.

240   "It has no dividends to pay": Eastman, *Enjoyment*, 421.

240   "a sort of cherishing godfather": Eastman, *Companions*, 7.

240   "sentimental rebels": Eastman, *Enjoyment*, 424.

241   "to hear Steffens talk": Johns, *Time*, 158.

241   "cook, waiter, dishwasher": Dell, *Love*, 23.

241   "I showed them": LS to LAS, November 1, 1913, *L*, 328.

242   "I need this triumph": LS to LAS, January 2, 1914, *L*, 333.

242   "set me up again." LS to Lou Suggett, January 4, 1914, *L*, 333, 334.

242   "inspired and inspiring": Avrich, *Modern School*, 185.

243   "What are these men to do": "Police Drive I.W.W. Crowd from Park," *New York Times*, March 6, 1914, 1.

243   "anything whatsoever": LS to LAS, March 1914, *L*, 337.

243   "Your toil made the wealth": "Anarchists Spread Alarm in 5th Avenue," *New York Times*, March 22, 1914, 1.

243   "a human boiling pot": Luhan, *Movers*, 118.

244   "I got the cops": LS to AS, March 23, 1914, *L*, 336.

244   "a professional lawbreaker": "Anarchy," *New York Times*, March 23, 1914, 10.

244   "so should Emma Goldman": Rabban, *Free Speech*, 59.

244   "many broken heads" "Police Use Clubs on I.W.W. Rioters," *New York Times*, April 5, 1914, 1.

244   "I've seen such things": LS to LAS, April 5, 1914, *L*, 337.

245   "destroy buildings": "'Dynamite' Cries Steffens," *New York Times*, January 13, 1914, 2.

245   "That's where he belongs": LS to DH, June 10, 1916, *L*, 374.

245   "I had been 'educated'": LS to LAS, July 2, 1916, *L*, 375.

245   "dead": LS to DH, June 6, 1914, *L*, 340–342.

246   "Your poor children": LS to DH, June 26, 1912, *L*, 303.

I 7: REVOLUTIONARY ROAD

247   "at the height of the season": LS to LAS, June 17, 1914, *L*, 343.

247   "They may be grafters": LS to LAS, June 29, 1914, *L*, 344.

247   "Only an Englishman": ibid.

248   "down to the last period": LS to DH, September 18, 1914, *L*, 345.

248   "the long expected": *A*, 712.

248   "How would one make": *A*, 710.

248   "the financiers of London": *A*, 712.

248   "looked around": *A*, 714.

249   "Something happened to me": LS to LAS, October 10, 1914, *L*, 347.

249   "I can tell you": LS to John Reed, November 19, 1914, *L*, 349.

249   "She had no right": Dearborn, *Queen*, 45.

249   "old gangs": LS to AS, November 4, 1914, *L*, 348.

250   "slow, peaceful voyage": *A*, 715.

250   "When does Stef go?": Luhan, *Movers*, 164.

250   "It's barbarism, savagery": "The Sunny Side of Mexico," in Steffens, *World*, 5.

250   "It's no use": LS to John Reed, November 19, 1914, *L*, 350.

250   "tremendous power": LS to LAS, December 5, 1914, *L*, 351.

251   "If all history": Walter Lippmann to John Reed, March 25, 1914 (John Reed Papers, Harvard).

251   "our grand democratic institutions": Hicks, *John Reed*, 139.

251   "with hate": *A*, 716.

252   "he took those murderous brigands": "The Sunny Side of Mexico," in Steffens, *World*, 5.

252   "had to import": "Making Friends with Mexico," in Steffens, *World*, 28.

252   "drunken crook": *A*, 726.

252   "I will not recognize": Link, *Wilson*, 109.

253   "going according to Marx": *A*, 717.

253   "the actual": N. Hapgood, *Changing Years*, 244.

253   "If I were a Mexican": LS to Edward M. House, July 31, 1915, *L*, 356.

254   "I cannot understand": LS to Edward M. House, August 7, 1915, *L*, 357, 358.

254   "don't know how": LS to Edward M. House, September 13, 1915, *L*, 359.

254   "The Mexicans know my interest": LS to LAS, November 4, 1915, *L*, 362.

254   "I'm putting ideas into the heads": LS to Lou Suggett and AS, December 10, 1915, *L*, 364.

255   "that beautiful revolution": LS to Upton Sinclair, October 15, 1915, in Sinclair, *Lifetime*, 52.

255   "the revolution is running over": LS to Lou Suggett and AS, December 25, 1915, *L*, 366.

255   "what I needed": LS to AS, April 30, 1916, *L*, 371.

255   "I never found": *A*, 735.

255   "had no love": *A*, 736.

256   "pull off some sort of colonial policy": LS to DH, March 2, 1916, *L*, 370.

256   "marvelous record": LS to AS, June 2, 1916, *L*, 373.

256   "silly note": *A*, 737.

256   "very valuable information": *A*, 739.

256   "No one knows": Robert La Follette to Charles H. Crownhart, July 8, 1916, in La Follette and La Follette, *La Follette*, 574.

257   "My plan for the settlement": LS to Lou Suggett and AS, July 16, 1916, *L*, 377.

257   "It's going my way": LS to LAS, July 28, 1916, *L*, 381.

257   "stopped a war": *A*, 740.

257   "a generation or two": LS to Edward M. House, September 25, 1916, *L*, 385.

257   "Only Mexico": N. Hapgood, *Changing Years*, 240.

257   "gleeful, malicious rejoicing": LS to DH, March 2, 1916, *L*, 370.

257   "The social problem": ibid., 369–370.

18: To Russia

259   "churchman": LS to DH, July 1, 1916, *L*, 375.

259   "Wall Street is for TR": LS to AS, June 2, 1916, *L*, 373.

259   "goes on about its business": LS to AS, October 3, 1915, *L*, 360.

260   "None of your other labors": W. L. Locke to Daniel Kiefer, December 1, 1916 (LSP).

260   "Our meetings yesterday": unknown correspondent to Daniel Kiefer, November 25, 1916 (LSP).

260   "He enjoyed his hate": A, 502.

261   "I feel": LS to Edward M. House, November 18, 1916, L, 387, 388.

261   "I'm off to Washington": LS to John Reed, January 5, 1917 (John Reed Papers, Harvard).

261   "cool and fresh": LS to John Reed, January 22, 1917, L, 391.

261   "There are eager business men": LS to Edward M. House, January 22, 1917, L, 390.

262   "Is the present war": Hofstadter, Reform, 277.

262   "It seems that": LS to AS, March 18, 1917, L, 391.

262   "I've been told": ibid., 392.

262   "Well, I guess this king business": LS to LAS, March 20, 1917, L, 394.

262   "But they don't know": ibid., 393.

263   "It was": Draper, Roots, 101.

263   "gifted journalist": Hook, Out of Step, 151.

264   "the very thing to do": LS to LAS, March 22, 1917, L, 395.

264   "We are not an expressive family": LS to Lou Suggett, January 12, 1917, L, 389.

264   "She is the most": LS to JS, November 21, 1892, L, 85.

264   "deeply shocked": LS to LAS, March 20, 1917, L, 393–394.

264   "One thought": LS to LAS, March 22, 1917, L, 395.

265   "Sorry to go now": LS to LAS, March 24, 1917, L, 396.

265   "I soon leave to go": LS to LAS, March 27, 1917, L, 396–397.

265   "It's a wound": LS to AS, April 2, 1917, L, 397.

266   "He was very kind": Luhan, Movers, 68.

266   "no tourists": A, 744.

266   "History?": A, 749.

267   "a stinking mob of delegates": A, 748.

267   "I was halted": A, 759.

267   "Responsibility without power": Kennan, Russia, 20.

268   "We hated it": A, 754.

268   "There they go again": A, 753.

268   "That was democracy": A, 754.

268   "menacing, empty": A, 747.

269   "crime against civilization": "Text of the President's Address: The War Resolution Now Before Congress," New York Times, April 3, 1917, 1.

269   "President Wilson": A, 742–743.

271   "It was": A, 758.

271   "He could but follow": A, 757.

271   "an absurdity": Lasch, Liberals, 142.

272   "firm, short, quiet message": *A*, 760.

273   "Japan": *A*, 768, 769.

273   "a silent, thoughtful man": *A*, 770–772.

274   "But the way he said it": *A*, 770.

274   "The revolution is very inconvenient": LS to Upton Sinclair, June 29, 1917, in Sinclair, *Lifetime*, 53.

19: SELLING PEACE

275   "Done all I promised": LS to LAS, June 27, 1917, *L*, 400.

275   "Every unpopular cause": LS to AS, June 30, 1917, *L*, 401.

275   "Rage is developing": LS to Robert La Follette, August 17, 1917, *L*, 401.

276   "all war": LS to Edward M. House, September 8, 1917, *L*, 402–403.

277   "absolutely no criticism": LS to AS, September 16, 1917, *L*, 404.

277   "pro-war": LS to LAS, September 26, 1917, *L*, 405.

277   "As soon as I": LS to AS, September 16, 1917, *L*, 404.

277   "I heard Lincoln Steffens": Helen M. Wayne, "Radicalism as a Fashionable Pose," *New York Times*, March 9, 1919, 76.

278   "Just a line": LS to AS, September 30, 1917, *L*, 405–406.

278   "I feel": LS to Robert La Follette, October 7, 1917, *L*, 406, 407.

278   "big scheme": LS to AS, October 20, 1917, *L*, 409.

278   "practice mercy": LS to Edward M. House, October 18, 1917, *L*, 1032.

279   "hundreds of socialists": Draper, *Roots*, 96.

279   "an act of clemency": LS to Edward M. House, October 18, 1917, *L*, 1032.

279   "substitute real defence": LS to AS, October 13, 1917, *L*, 409.

279   "Help us to crush": Ida Rauh, "The National Labor Defense Counsel," *International Socialist Review*, November 1916, 318.

279   "Please don't scorn my faith": LS to Edward M. House, October 18, 1917, *L*, 1034.

279   "I may be a fool": LS to AS, October 20, 1917, *L*, 410.

279   "impracticable": LS to AS, December 30, 1917, *L*, 415.

279   "like a pack of cards": Price, *Dispatches*, 102.

279   "worn out": Abraham, *Kerensky*, 134.

280   "had a plan": *A*, 767.

281   "We are so cocksure": LS to DH, January 5, 1918, *L*, 416.

281   "the broadest and friendliest": McFadden, *Alternative Paths*, 40.

281   "I have not lost faith": Weber, *Sovereignty*, 73.

281   "If the peoples": Carr, *Revolution*, vol. 3, 17.

282   "We're afraid to": *A*, 774.

283   "very gingerly": *A*, 774.

283   "My dear Mr. Steffens": Woodrow Wilson to LS, January 15, 1918, *L*, 417.

283 "clog in your peace machinery": LS to Edward M. House, February 1, 1918, *L*, 419.

283 "Steffens believes": Lasch, *Liberals*, 73.

284 "use any means open": LS to Edward M. House, February 1, 1918, *L*, 419.

284 "Don't return": LS and Louise Bryant to John Reed, February 25, 1918, *L*, 422.

284 "Trotzky making epochal blunder": LS to John Reed, February 25, 1918, *L*, 422.

284 "idiocy": Williams, *Journey*, 218.

284 "The news from Russia": LS to AS, February 24, 1918, *L*, 421.

285 "Important you designate": *Revolutionary Radicalism: Its History, Purpose, and Tactics*, report of the Joint Legislative Committee Investigating Seditious Activities, filed April 24, 1920, in the Senate of the State of New York (Albany: J.B. Lyon Company, 1920), 847.

285 "The whole heart": "Wilson's Message Cheered at Moscow," *New York Times*, March 19, 1918, 2.

285 "The Russian Socialist": Bonsal, *Suitors*, 16.

286 "Wilson's message": LS to AS, March 12, 1918, *L*, 424.

286 "pain on the faces": *A*, 775.

286 "This speaking is all very well": LS to AS, March 12, 1918, *L*, 424.

286 "As a matter of fact": LS to Edward M. House, May 8, 1918, *L*, 427.

287 "poison gas": *A*, 776.

287 "I think I should cancel": LS to Edward M. House, April 29, 1918, *L*, 426.

287 "distressed": Edward M. House to LS, May 14, 1918, *A*, 777.

287 "sinister": LS to W. H. Porterfield, May 11, 1918, *L*, 1039, 1041.

20: The Paris Power Game

289 "off over the hills": LS to John Reed, June 1, 1918, *L*, 427, 428.

289 "many times": John Reed to LS, June 9, 1918, in Rosenstone, *Romantic*, 319–320.

290 "I haven't much hope": LS to John Reed, June 17, 1918, *L*, 428.

290 "They are showing": ibid., 428–429.

291 "I am not of your opinion": John Reed to LS, June 19, 1918 (LSP).

291 "The American working class": Hicks, *John Reed*, 342.

291 "gaunt, unshaven": Eastman, *Heroes*, 223.

292 "imperialists": LS to DH, October 10, 1918, *L*, 430.

292 "The men who are in control": R. S. Baker, *Chronicle*, 353.

292 "sudden idea of peace": LS to Edward M. House, October 10, 1918, *L*, 430.

292 "could make more friends": McFadden, *Alternative Paths*, 137.

293 "so putrid": ibid.

293 "I have been sweating blood": Cooper, *Wilson*, 439.

293 "bargain his way": LS to AS, October 15, 1918, *L*, 431, 432.

294 "Again I warn you": ibid., 432.

294   "from all quarters": LS to LAS, October 16, 1918, *L*, 433.

294   "They wanted my ability": LS to AS, October 18, 1918, *L*, 434.

295   "fierce, but impotent": LS to AS, October 20, 1918, *L*, 435.

295   "practical, meaty": LS to LAS and AS, October 27, 1918, *L*, 436, 437.

295   "Peace vs. punishment": LS to LAS, October 28, 1918, *L*, 437.

295   "I am worried": LS to AS, November 5, 1918, *L*, 439–440.

296   "speeches in San Francisco": LS to LAS and AS, November 7, 1918, *L*, 440.

296   "I may have to publish": LS to AS, November 5, 1918, *L*, 440.

296   "is the greatest reporter": Davidson, *Sittings*, 147.

297   "Mr. Wilson has no authority": "League Opposition to Launch Attack on Wilson Tuesday," *New York Times*, September 8, 1919, 3.

297   "If you do that again": Davidson, *Sittings*, 135.

298   "I don't know": ibid., 141.

298   "moving, ever-changing play": LS to Etta Augusta Burgess, November 24, 1918, *L*, 444, 445.

298   "young, militant, progressive": McFadden, *Alternative Paths*, 309.

299   "spokesman of public opinion": *A*, 779.

299   "a few words": LS to Etta Augusta Burgess, December 19, 1918, *L*, 449.

300   "beyond anything": Heckscher, *Wilson*, 501.

300   "But then": LS to Etta Augusta Burgess, December 19, 1918, *L*, 449.

300   "careful to show them": LS to LAS, December 24, 1918, *L*, 451.

300   "hanging to his points": LS to AS, January 14, 1919, *L*, 455.

301   "the man who broke Wilson": *A*, 781.

301   "It was a struggle": *A*, 780.

301   "We are setting up a nation": LS to AS, January 14, 1919, *L*, 455, 457.

301   "Certainly": N. Hapgood, *Changing Years*, 247.

2 1 :   " I   H a v e   S e e n   t h e   F u t u r e "

303   "How I would like to be": LS to AS, January 14, 1919, *L*, 457.

304   "sometimes in politics": McFadden, *Alternative Paths*, 200.

304   "To arrest revolutionary movement": Brownell and Billings, *So Close*, 78.

305   "Talk of methods": J. M. Thompson, *Russia*, 182.

306   "semi-official": LS to Etta Augusta Burgess, February 22, 1919, *L*, 460.

306   "a pretty noisy secret mission": *A*, 792.

306   "there will be no hitch": LS to LAS and AS, March 3, 1919, *L*, 461.

307   "nobody in the dark": *A*, 792.

307   "I am certain": Brownell and Billings, *So Close*, 85.

307   "Soviet Russia": *A*, 795–796.

308   "There was no doubt": Brownell and Billings, *So Close*, 87.

308   "You must do your utmost": ibid., 88.

308   "open, inquiring face": A, 796, 797.

309   "however it is done": Service, Lenin, 373.

309   "Lenin was a navigator": A, 798.

310   "We were very successful": LS to his family, March 24, 1919, L, 461.

310   "We heard all their story": LS to Marie Howe, April 3, 1919, L, 462.

310   "There is more vision": LS to LAS, April 8, 1919, L, 465.

310   "Of all evenings in Paris": Shotwell, Paris, 230.

310   "I was asked to write": LS to Marie Howe, April 3, 1919, L, 462.

310   "the most autocratic": "The Bullitt-Steffens Mission to Russia—1919," in Steffens, World, 55–66.

311   "Russia to-day is in a condition": Bullitt Mission, 49, 50, 53, 54.

311   "It's an emergency": A, 800.

311   "at last I can see": Lasch, Liberals, 193.

312   "wished above all": Steed, Thirty Years, 302.

312   "Lincoln Steffens found conditions": Kahn, World, 222.

312   "The other reporters": LS to Marie Howe, April 3, 1919, L, 462.

313   "After the Bullitt incident": LS to Brand Whitlock, January 25, 1925, L, 684.

313   "the darkest annals": "British Publish New Evidence of Bolshevist Crime," New York Times, April 6, 1919, 1.

313   "Of all the many falsehoods": "The Bullitt-Steffens Mission to Russia—1919," in Steffens, World, 53.

313   "This is an amazing article": J. M. Thompson, Russia, 155.

314   "murderous tyranny": Brownell and Billings, So Close, 93.

314   "The invitation to lunch": LS to LAS, April 8, 1919, L, 464.

315   "Just start shipping!": McFadden, Alternative Paths, 29.

315   "bug-eyed with wonder": White, Autobiography, 562.

316   "I was one of the millions": Bullitt Mission, 96.

316   "was not to be mollified": A, 801–802.

317   "the proper policy": Lasch, Liberals, 198.

317   "an astonishing delusion": "Misjudging Russia": New York Times, April 6, 1919, 37.

318   "Candor compels me": McFadden, Alternative Paths, 258.

318   "I don't see why": LS to AS, September 14, 1919, L, 486.

318   "Russia is coming along all right": W. Johnson, America, 302.

318   "how beautifully things are working out": William C. Bullitt to LS, January 27, 1934 (LSP).

318   "When the last battalion": Knightley, Casualty, 167.

319   "The rest of us": Mee, Versailles, 62.

319   "We are going to have": LS to AS, April 13, 1919, L, 465–466.

319   "The failure here is complete": LS to LAS, June 18, 1919, L, 472.

320 "devilish": LS to AS, May 14, 1919, *L*, 468.

320 "We are Germans": Knightley, *Casualty*, 134.

320 "and, of course, informed": *A*, 789.

321 "I do not know": Edward House to LS, June 24, 1919 (LSP).

321 "There's nothing to do now": Young, *Art Young*, 369.

22: PETER

323 "She was as joyous": *A*, 812.

323 "avid tomboy": Winter, *Yield*, 9–11.

324 "dull, red-brick building": ibid., 34.

324 "such as I could have imagined": ibid., 43.

324 "Have you ever heard": ibid., 53.

325 "Felix giving another of his parties?": ibid., 54–64.

326 "What fascinated me": Steffens, *World*, viii.

326 "We are all here": LS to LAS, July 1, 1919, *L*, 475.

326 "policy of infinite compromise": LS to LAS and AS, July 26, 1919, *L*, 478.

326 "a good deal": LS to Etta Augusta Burgess, July 23, 1919, *L*, 476.

327 "he had seen a vision": LS to LAS and AS, August 2, 1919, *L*, 478.

327 "One conclusion after another": LS to DH, August 27, 1919, *L*, 482.

327 "Now I am a pacifist": LS to AS, September 14, 1919, *L*, 486.

328 "It isn't important": LS to Dan Kiefer, June 21, 1920, *L*, 545.

328 "my theory": "Moses in Red," in Steffens, *World*, 90.

328 "I've been tempted to answer": LS to LAS, October 25, 1919, *L*, 491.

328 "find and show the people": LS to LAS and AS, November 4, 1919, *L*, 491.

329 "meeting everybody": ibid., 491–492.

329 "All the time": Winter, *Yield*, 69.

329 "No goodbye is goodbye": LS to EW, December 8, 1919, *L*, 496.

330 "a kiss and the tears": LS to EW, December 10, 1919, *L*, 498.

330 "I don't want to tell": LS to EW, December 11, 1919, *L*, 500.

330 "Maybe I could be your friend": ibid., 499.

330 "a friend": LS to EW, December 12, 1919, *L*, 501.

330 "And you, Peter": LS to EW, December 22, 1919, *L*, 512.

331 "I was sorry for what I felt": H. Hapgood, *Victorian*, 415.

331 "Many of them": F. Howe, *Confessions*, 327.

332 "a forum for the preaching of Bolshevism": "Goldman Wrote 'Dear Fred Howe'; Had Friend Freed," *New York Times*, November 27, 1919, 1.

332 "humanity, sanity, and mercy": LS to AS, December 23, 1919, *L*, 513.

332 "Labor unions": LS to EW, December 16, 1919, *L*, 504.

332　"You are not a friend of Labor": LS to EW, December 20, 1919, *L*, 507–508.

332　"seems too horrible": LS to Marie Howe, December 28, 1919, *L*, 519.

333　"Our love doesn't want": LS to EW, December 22, 1919, *L*, 512.

334　"She knows about Us": LS to EW, January 1920, *L*, 528–529.

334　"It was, it is": LS to LAS, January 11, 1920, *L*, 529–530.

335　"We talked blockade-lifting": LS to EW, January 20, 1920, *L*, 530.

335　"Germany is depressing": LS to AS, January 30, 1920, *L*, 531.

335　"It was a terrible thing": LS to AS, February 10, 1920, *L*, 532.

335　"I mustn't quit this yet": ibid., 533.

335　"good": LS to Jack Hollister, February 21, 1920, *L*, 536.

336　"better, much better": LS to LAS, March 29, 1920, *L*, 540.

336　"a rich and suggestive": LS to AS, May 2, 1920, *L*, 541.

336　"I have got a deep respect": LS to AS, May 15, 1920, *L*, 543.

23: EXPATRIATE

337　"Arresting revolutionists": "Moses in Red," in Steffens, *World*, 76.

338　"Jehovah symbolizes Nature": LS to Gilbert Roe, April 16, 1925, *L*, 693.

338　"tired out, spiritless": "Moses in Red," in Steffens, *World*, 103.

338　"They must learn new ideals": ibid., 143.

338　"It had to be fought for": ibid., 150.

339　"They believe in evolution": ibid., 82.

339　"That is the point": ibid., 86.

339　"long lines": Winter, *Yield*, 73.

339　"We saw Wien": LS to the Steffens family, August 2, 1920, *L*, 548.

339　"It is not possible": Filene, *American Views*, 45.

340　"thinks straight": LS to Daniel Kiefer, August 20, 1920, *L*, 552.

340　"taught": LS to Daniel Kiefer, June 21, 1920, *L*, 544.

340　"She is used to me now": LS to LAS, January 2, 1921, *L*, 559, 560.

340　"was up against the System": LS to LAS, October 5, 1920, *L*, 554–555.

341　"You're dangerous": LS to AS, November 18, 1920, *L*, 557.

341　"he has nothing to think with": Cooper, *Wilson*, 589.

341　"If you nominate Harding": White, *Autobiography*, 597.

341　"clearer, firmer": LS to LAS, December 10, 1920, *L*, 558, 559.

342　"Never!": Strong, *I Change*, 88.

342　"It's Paris all over again": LS to AS, March 11, 1921, *L*, 563.

343　"It makes me laugh": LS to LAS, September 24, 1921, *L*, 569–570.

343　"As I look over an audience": LS to AS, November 1, 1921, *L*, 575.

344　"I have heard you say things": LS to Will H. Hays, November 1, 1921, *L*, 1043.

344   "We had": ibid., 1042–1043.

344   "raised the deuce": LS to LAS and AS, November 12, 1921, *L*, 575.

344   "that letter": LS to AS, December 5, 1921, *L*, 576–577.

345   "saw it all": LS to LAS and AS, December 16, 1921, *L*, 580.

345   "had the impulse": LS to LAS and AS, December 20, 1921, *L*, 581.

345   "I never met a man": Darrow, *Story*, 73.

345   "I am glad": LS to LAS and AS, December 23, 1921, *L*, 582.

346   "Well, they pardoned Debs!": Darrow, *Story*, 73.

346   "see and talk with Gandhi": LS to LAS and AS, December 23, 1921, *L*, 581, 582.

346   frankly communistic organizations": "Admits Political Motives," *New York Times*, February 11, 1922, 4.

346   "Heaven save us": "Says American Reds Embarrass Soviet," *New York Times*, February 18, 1922, 3.

346   "that the thing for him": LS to LAS and AS, December 16, 1921, *L*, 580–581.

346   "I have to watch the Reds": LS to DH, [February 1922], *L*, 583.

347   "the greatest gathering": C. Fink, *Genoa*, 152.

347   "There were sensational rumors": Slocombe, *Tumult*, 158.

348   "The sun, shining": Davidson, *Sittings*, 162.

348   "loafing along": LS to LAS and AS, [May 1922], *L*, 587.

348   "It seems that posing": Davidson, *Sittings*, 165.

348   "mostly we listened to Steffens": Seldes, *Witness*, 312.

349   "What a farce!": LS to LAS, May 16, 1922, *L*, 588.

349   "I can't finish it": LS to LAS and AS, June 17, 1922, *L*, 591.

349   "she still denounces the communists": LS to EW, June 13, 1922, *L*, 590.

350   "bed, study Italian, sleep": LS to LAS and AS, June 17, 1922, *L*, 592.

350   "The trouble down there": LS to LAS and AS, September 23, 1922, *L*, 598–599.

350   "she gave them all": *A*, 834.

350   "good revolutionary influence": *A*, 833.

351   "Ezra insisted on taking us": Colum, *Life*, 307.

351   "for the rebels to conspire": *A*, 833.

351   "Walking along the street with him": *A*, 834.

351   "You can": *A*, 835.

351   "He does it": LS to Alfred Harcourt, March 10, 1932, *L*, 919.

352   "utter honesty and hard labor": *A*, 835.

352   "I have been reading a book": LS to AS, October 17, 1922, *L*, 606.

352   "I hear that Joyce": LS to LAS, December 12, 1922, *L*, 610–611.

352   "very much better": LS to AS, August 28, 1923, *L*, 621.

24: The Future Revisited

354   "*Le Temps!*": *A*, 815.

354   "I hear Steff has at last decided": Ezra Pound to Upton Sinclair, January 30, 1935, in Sinclair, *Lifetime*, 373–374.

354   "How did you ever do it?": *A*, 816.

355   "Was that what": *A*, 813.

355   "They are doing little": LS to AS, November 25, 1922, *L*, 609.

355   "No": *A*, 834.

356   "because of Ernest's letters": Fenton, *Apprenticeship*, 196.

356   "I had never seen anyone": C. Baker, *Hemingway*, 135.

356   "3 years on the damn stuff": Ernest Hemingway to Ezra Pound, January 23, 1923, Hemingway, *Selected Letters*, 77.

357   "He specifically wanted to show": Diliberto, *Hadley*, 132.

357   "With his work destroyed": Cowley, *Flowering*, 62.

357   "I am afraid the stuff is lost": LS to Ernest Hemingway, December 9, 1922 (Hemingway Archive, John F. Kennedy Library).

357   "halt, lame and nerve shattered people": Davidson, *Sittings*, 175.

357   "I did not think": LS to Etta Augusta Burgess, December 17, 1922, *L*, 613.

357   "My conscience talks about it": LS to LAS, January 23, 1923, *L*, 613.

357   "a darned stinker": LS to Jo Davidson, April 9, 1923, *L*, 615, 616.

358   "a Radical and a Red": *L*, 617, n. 1.

358   "bully excursions": LS to LAS, July 27, 1923, *L*, 618, 619.

358   "Mussolini certainly did put": Brady, *Tarbell*, 239.

358   "She wants me to do": LS to LAS, July 27, 1923, *L*, 619.

359   "on a perfect train of Pullmans": LS to LAS, October 1, 1923, *L*, 625.

359   "best guest-house": LS to Etta Augusta Burgess, September 21, 1923, *L*, 622.

359   "the loneliest soul in Asia": LS to Matthew Schmidt, July 20, 1926, *L*, 758.

359   "a city come to life": LS to LAS, October 1, 1923, *L*, 624.

359   "The big points are": LS to Etta Augusta Burgess, September 11, 1923, *L*, 622.

359   "six weeks on the go": LS to LAS, October 1, 1923, *L*, 623.

360   "The brave new Thing": LS to Fremont Older, October 5, 1923, *L*, 626–628.

360   "a small devil in him": Luhan, *Movers*, 68.

361   "Louise is going to have": Winter, *Yield*, 96.

361   "Think of the baby": ibid., 101.

361   "somewhat bewildered": ibid., 100.

362   "the dirt as it appears": Ernest Hemingway to Ezra Pound, May 2, 1924, Hemingway, *Selected Letters*, 114.

362   "You heard of course": Ernest Hemingway to Ezra Pound, July 19, 1924, Hemingway, *Selected Letters*, 120.

362   "a conscious wish": "Radiant Fatherhood," in Steffens, *Speaking*, 3–5.

363   "the Supreme Court of Final Appeal": LS to AS, August 12, 1924, *L*, 656.

363   "You used to be a genius": Winter, *Yield*, 121.

363   "that London girl": LS to LAS, April 16, 1924, *L*, 640, 641.

363   "I don't seem to care": LS to LAS, May 23, 1924, *L*, 646.

363   "L has let me go": Etta Augusta Burgess to Laura Steffens, 1926 (LSP).

364   "I think that you and Sara": LS to Charles Erskine Scott Wood, August 30, 1922, in Hamburger, *Two Rooms*, 296.

364   "He's a remarkable proof": LS to LAS, March 16, 1921, *L*, 563.

364   "You two practically ushered in": Ella Winter to Sara Bard Field, February 14, 1944, in Hamburger, *Two Rooms*, 298.

364   "if the Democrats": LS to Edward A. Filene, April 30, 1924, *L*, 645.

364   "about like Tahoe": LS to AS, July 1924, *L*, 648.

365   "This winter I intend": LS to Edward A. Filene, July 21, 1924, *L*, 650.

365   "very good proposition": LS to LAS and AS, May 6, 1922, *L*, 585–586.

365   "moral turpitude": Winter, *Yield*, 104.

365   "cold and judicial": Fry, "Sara Bard Field," 268.

365   "She had it all pretty much": LS to EW, August 4, 1924, *L*, 653.

365   "she had her indictments": LS to LAS, August 5, 1924, *L*, 654.

366   "I love G": LS to LAS, October 18, 1924, *L*, 665–666.

366   "Steffens is in town": Ernest Hemingway to Gertrude Stein and Alice B. Toklas, August 9, 1924, Hemingway, *Selected Letters*, 121.

366   "Hutch": H. Hapgood, *Victorian*, 584.

367   "little paradise": LS to Jo Davidson, September 18, 1924, *L*, 659.

367   "It is to be the greatest": LS to Edward A. Filene, September 21, 1924, *L*, 660.

367   "courageous, hopeless": LS to Edward A. Filene, September 21, 1924, *L*, 660.

367   "to play with": LS to Frederic C. Howe, November 24, 1924, *L*, 675.

367   "laid down their arms": F. Howe, *Confessions*, 194.

367   "I think his religion": LS to Marie Howe, November 15, 1924, *L*, 667, 668.

368   "have every chance": ibid., 670.

368   "All the books tell you": Winter, *Yield*, 107.

25: FINALLY, A FATHER

369   "He will not be righteous": LS to AS, November 21, 1924, *L*, 673.

369   "No doubt other men": LS to Jo Davidson, November 26, 1924, *L*, 676.

369   "I can hear him crying": LS to Ernest Hemingway, November 21, 1924 (Hemingway Archive, John F. Kennedy Library).

369   "I gave him the two names": LS to AS, August 7, 1925, *L*, 703, 704.

370   "old, frivolous days": LS to Jo Davidson, November 26, 1924, *L*, 675.

370   "He was devoted to no person": H. Hapgood, *Victorian*, 584.

370 "Italy is the best place": "Radiant Fatherhood," in Steffens, *Speaking*, 10.

370 "the process of mind-fixing": ibid., 17–19.

370 "I find that it does not work that way": LS to LAS, January 26, 1925, *L*, 683.

371 "What *did* they teach you": Winter, *Yield*, 109.

371 "political genius": LS to LAS, January 1, 1925, *L*, 679.

371 "I am intensely interested": LS to LAS, January 26, 1925, *L*, 683.

371 "He never sucks his thumb": LS to LAS, January 5, 1925, *L*, 680.

371 "My papa says no grown-up": LS to Mrs. A. Winter, March 21, 1925, *L*, 689.

372 "my one and only last editor": LS to AS, May 26, 1925, *L*, 696.

372 "I put some money": LS to AS, February 17, 1925, *L*, 687.

372 "It was all romance": *A*, 820.

372 "two years of such happiness": *A*, 823.

372 "It hit me hard": LS to Belle Case La Follette, June 20, 1925, *L*, 700.

373 "The fight must be fought": Aaron, *Writers*, 126.

373 "from a sentimental rebel": ibid., 130.

373 "She is so intelligent": LS to LAS, July 23, 1925, *L*, 702.

373 "Sunshine in England!": LS to Pete Stanley Steffens, September 29, 1925, *L*, 709.

373 "the sun all day": LS to LAS, October 13, 1925, *L*, 713.

374 "Pete *solo*": "Education of a Father," in Steffens, *Speaking*, 45.

374 "What is the use": LS to LAS, October 13, 1925, *L*, 715.

374 "full of indiscretions": LS to Edward A. Filene, November 25, 1925, *L*, 718, 719.

374 "ignoramuses that are so sure": LS to Marie Howe, November 29, 1925, *L*, 721.

375 "One question I'd like to ask": LS to Frederic C. Howe, December 6, 1925, *L*, 721–722.

375 "was a subconscious expression": LS to Marie Howe, December 23, 1925, *L*, 722.

375 "I'm indifferent just now": LS to Frederic C. Howe, December 6, 1925, *L*, 722.

375 "But Fred": Winter, *Yield*, 113.

376 "not muckraking": LS to Hutchins Hapgood, February 7, 1926, *L*, 731.

376 "I was always naive": LS to Marie Howe, January 23, 1926, *L*, 727.

376 "bully story": LS to Upton Sinclair, May 19, 1926, *L*, 743.

376 "art, music, literary revolt": LS to AS, June 21, 1926, *L*, 750.

376 "It was a sight": LS to EW, June 20, 1926, *L*, 749.

377 Concert details are given in Ford, *Four Lives*, 42–45.

377 "promenaded a bit": LS to EW, June 20, 1926, *L*, 749.

377 "I decided to cut": LS to AS, June 21, 1926, *L*, 750.

377 "I am alone": LS to LAS, June 25, 1926, *L*, 755.

378 "have a game called tennis": LS to Pete Steffens, June 23, 1926, *L*, 754.

378 "Daddy, why do people listen": "Youth and Plenty," in Steffens, *Speaking*, 150.

378 "You will like it": LS to Matthew Schmidt, July 20, 1926, *L*, 757–760.

379   "positive and generous": Kaplan, *Steffens*, 283.

379   "all Mozart": Winter, *Yield*, 114.

380   "I have been made permanent": LS to Mrs. A. Winter, October 15, 1926, *L*, 768.

380   "no stir": LS to Jo Davidson, January 7, 1927, *L*, 776.

381   "you can improve man": Winter, *Yield*, 119.

381   "a conceited but secretly": *A*, 830.

381   "They coveted not our reformers": *A*, 837.

381   "a cleaning out of the Bunk": O'Neill, *Last Romantic*, 119.

381   "I wonder if that is not": *A*, 850.

382   "a reformer without politics": *A*, 853.

382   "quickly, easily": LS to Fremont Older, May 17, 1927, *L*, 789.

383   "If you feel very bad": LS to Clarence Darrow, August 24, 1927 (LSP).

383   "If the reformers are defeated": *A*, 847.

383   "It is a fascinating narrative": LS to Horace Liveright, February 1926, *L*, 731.

383   "conquered everyone here": LS to Mrs. A. Winter, June 7, 1927, *L*, 793.

383   "a bully long morning": ibid., 794.

384   "Life gets better and better": LS to Fola La Follette, June 1927, *L*, 792.

26: CARMEL CHARM

385   "I feel like staying here forever": LS to AS, August 3, 1927, *L*, 798.

385   "handsome as a Roman faun": Starr, *Americans*, 276.

386   "living upon its dividends": "Something New Under the Sun," in Steffens, *Speaking*, 74.

386   "did not belong": Winter, *Yield*, 138.

386   "something was always going on": ibid., 132.

387   "It's going to be yours": LS to LAS, October 20, 1927, *L*, 807.

387   "constellation of luminaries": Loftis, *Witnesses*, 47.

387   "Hadley is looking well": EW to Ernest Hemingway, August 26, 1927 (Hemingway Archive, John F. Kennedy Library).

387   "When he": Robert Joyce Trasker to Frank J. Smith, July 16, 1927 (Hemingway Archive, John F. Kennedy Library).

388   "the most silent man": Johns, *Time*, 311.

388   "the real thing": LS to AS, September 8, 1927, *L*, 800, 801.

388   "He is a charming child": LS to Gilman Hall, January 19, 1928, *L*, 812.

388   "better than over here": LS to LAS, March 26, 1928, *L*, 818.

389   "likely to lead man away": Aaron, *Writers*, 142.

389   "I was a traitor": Eastman, *Reflections*, 15.

389   "to breathe and think": LS to LAS, March 26, 1928, *L*, 819.

389   "a refuge for any poor s.o.b.": Winter, *Yield*, 129.

390   "lonely soul": Davidson, *Sittings*, 220.

390   "It is amazing to me": LS to LAS, April 20, 1928, *L*, 820–821.

390   "I'm all stirred up": LS to E. W. Marland, April 23, 1928, *L*, 821, 822.

390   "to hold on": Jo Davidson to LS, June 6, 1928 (LSP).

390   "a hard boiled union man": LS to Mrs. A. Winter, September 13, 1928, *L*, 826.

391   "Is the universe conscious": Winter, *Yield*, 140.

391   "enjoy your editorship": Johns, *Time*, 310.

391   "I have so much to do": LS to EW, November 16, 1928, *L*, 826–828.

392   "brilliantly on dictatorship": Hicks, *Truth*, 77.

392   "When you walked into that home": Dorothy Erskine, introduction to Fry, "Sara Bard Field," vi.

392   "I felt that I had been": LS to Charles Erskine Scott Wood, February 13, 1929, *L*, 828.

392   "another fine chapter": EW to Jo and Yvonne Davidson, March 22, 1929, *L*, 831.

392   "Western movie city": Winter, *Yield*, 136.

392   "palatial": ibid., 143.

393   "Stef laughed": ibid., 144.

394   "still young": LS to Mrs. A. Winter, June 12, 1929, *L*, 832–834.

394   "the moonlight on the Seine": LS to EW, June 28, 1929, *L*, 835.

394   "Peter, you'll always have me": LS to EW, August 6, 1929, *L*, 843.

394   "We are married once more": LS to EW, September 27, 1929, *L*, 856.

394   "hip-thinkers": LS to EW, August 12, 1929, *L*, 844.

394   "think it through": LS to EW, October 17, 1929, *L*, 859.

395   "didn't get it all out": LS to EW, July 22, 1929, *L*, 839.

395   "Change": Luhan, *Edge*, 6.

395   "The key to my life": LS to EW, July 10, 1929, *L*, 838.

395   "get ye behind me": LS to Upton Sinclair, December 5, 1929, *L*, 865.

395   "that interminable *Life*": LS to EW, August 20, 1929, *L*, 849.

395   "This generation": LS to Mrs. A. Winter, September 17, 1929, *L*, 852.

395   "That's the parents' part": LS to EW, September 26, 1929, *L*, 855.

395   "I've lived too long": Winter, *Yield*, 147.

396   "The *Life* is me": LS to EW, August 1, 1930, *L*, 874.

396   "agrees with everything": LS to EW, August 10, 1930, *L*, 877.

396   "He says Gandhi": LS to Mrs. A. Winter, August 28, 1930, *L*, 883.

396   "Go on, dear": LS to EW, August 16, 1930, *L*, 880.

397   "a nice, false impression": LS to Yvonne Davidson, December 1930, *L*, 884.

397   "The most unexpected phenomenon": LS to Charles Erskine Scott Wood, February 3, 1931, *L*, 888.

397   "I've been looking": ibid.

398   "a large sort of bumbling dignity": Cowley, *Dream*, 56–57.

398   "the right of workers": Aaron, *Writers*, 178.

27: Fame and Fortune in the Depression

399   "The darn book is done": LS to Charles Erskine Scott Wood, February 3, 1931, *L*, 887.

399   "I have never seen the critics": LS to Mrs. A. Winter, April 30, 1931, *L*, 891.

399   "There are one or two books": *New York Times Book Review*, April 12, 1931 (LSP).

399   "It should be made compulsory reading": *New York Herald Tribune*, April 9, 1931 (LSP).

399   "He had a singular detachment": *Emporia Gazette*, May 2, 1931 (LSP).

399   "Just read your book": Gertrude Stein to LS, n.d., *L*, 904.

399   "I wish you and Jo": LS to Margaret Johannsen, April 29, 1931, *L*, 891.

400   "The problem whether a country": Tytell, *Pound*, 226.

400   "if a more interesting book": Harris, *Sinclair*, 278.

401   "My spiral-like story": *A*, 873.

401   "I have paid a tremendous price": James McNamara to Harcourt, Brace & Company, June 2, 1931 (LSP).

401   "During these last years": Filene, *American Views*, 72.

402   "It is a delightful tale": Eastman, *Enjoyment*, 430.

402   "comrade Jesus": Aaron, *Writers*, 189.

403   "You know, Orrick": Johns, *Time*, 156.

403   "What I am writing": LS to Ernest Hemingway, October 11, 1928 (Hemingway Archive, John F. Kennedy Library).

403   "Folklore in the making": Alexander Woolcott, *The New Yorker*, April 2, 1932, n.p. (LSP).

403   "used to deplore": Lippmann, *Drift*, 24.

404   "You don't have to tell me": LS to Yvonne Davidson, July 25, 1931, *L*, 900, 901.

404   "Think of a civilization": Steffens, *Speaking*, 128.

404   "We can't distribute an abundance": "United Front," in Steffens, *Speaking*, 208.

404   "with their picks": LS to EW, September 17, 1931, *L*, 904.

404   "I'll be glad to go East": ibid.

404   "I feel like a front-seater": LS to Jo Davidson, September 19, 1931, *L*, 905.

404   "To celebrate": LS to Mrs. A. Winter, September 21, 1931, *L*, 906.

404   "Capitalism is breaking down": LS to Sara Bard Field, September 21, 1931, *L*, 908.

405   "A great world": LS to EW, September 27, 1931, *L*, 908.

405   "I am only wondering": LS to DH, November 8, 1931, *L*, 911.

405   "good stuff": LS to Jo Davidson, September 19, 1931, *L*, 905.

405   "near": LS to EW, September 27, 1931, *L*, 908.

405   "crazy about it": LS to DH, November 1, 1931, *L*, 909.

406   "My humble lecture tour": LS to DH, November 8, 1931, *L*, 910.

28: LEFT IS RIGHT

407   "Mabel is all right": LS to EW, December 24, 1932, *L*, 944.

408   "there appeared to be": LS to EW, March 5, 1933, *L*, 952.

408   "It is a gay party": Rudnick, *Luhan*, 298.

408   "You are opposite": LS to Edward A. Filene, April 5, 1932, *L*, 920.

409   "did go completely over": LS to Mrs. C. J. Reed, May 25, 1932, *L*, 921.

409   "To a poet": "Under the Kremlin," in Steffens, *Speaking*, 315.

409   "staring street lamp": "Back from Russia," in Steffens, *Speaking*, 307.

409   "blew me up hard": LS to Mrs. C. J. Reed, May 25, 1932, *L*, 921.

409   "Why don't you join us?" "Back from Russia," in Steffens, *Speaking*, 307.

409   "Go on—the limit": LS to Mrs. C. J. Reed, May 25, 1932, *L*, 922.

409   "the beautiful boy": ibid., 921.

409   "didn't smile anymore": "Under the Kremlin," in Steffens, *Speaking*, 314.

409   "to the edge of their seats": LS to Alfred Harcourt, March 10, 1932, *L*, 918, 919.

410   "I wish there had been": LS to Robert G. Sproul, September 29, 1933, *L*, 963.

410   "nice people": LS to Jo Davidson, June 3, 1932, *L*, 923.

410   "a near-Communist organization": LS to Mrs. A. Winter, August 10, 1932, *L*, 927.

410   "blazing editorials": Loftis, *Witnesses*, 69.

410   "good advice": Hughes, *I Wonder*, 66.

411   "he and his backers": LS to Mrs. A. Winter, August 10, 1932, *L*, 927.

411   "I should think": Cowley, *Dream*, 112.

411   "The casting out": ibid., 118.

412   "knew how to organize": Hook, *Out of Step*, 149.

412   "I'm a bear": LS to DH, November 1932, *L*, 932.

412   "I'm glad, not sorry": LS to EW, December 22, 1932, *L*, 942.

413   "It gets on my nerves": LS to EW, February 7, 1932, *L*, 949.

414   "jaunty tweed cape": Johns, *Time*, 320.

414   "I personally would not trust": LS to Frances M. Perkins, July 19, 1934, *L*, 989.

414   "a thriller": LS to EW, November 23, 1932, *L*, 937.

414   "I am not a communist": LS to Beverley M. Bowie, November 19, 1932, *L*, 934.

414   "Yes, I am talking Communism": LS to EW, January 29, 1933, *L*, 947, 948.

415   "People who are incensed": LS to the editor of the *New York World Telegram*, *L*, 954.

416   "It's not Hitler": LS to EW, April 2, 1933, *L*, 955.

416   "for the children": LS to Mrs. Gilbert E. Roe, April 30, 1933, *L*, 958.

416   "I'd rather have it": LS to Mrs. A. Winter, February 18, 1933, *L*, 952.

417   "poet in action": LS to Franklin D. Roosevelt, July 15, 1933, *L*, 962.

417   "strikers": LS to EW, October 19, 1933, *L*, 965, 966.

417   "I hope it sells": LS to EW, April 19, 1933, *L*, 956, 957.

418   "some sort of technocracy": LS to EW, November 1933, *L*, 966.

418   "a really absurd or ignorant": LS to EW, November 27, 1933, *L*, 968.

418   "If they have speakers": LS to EW, December 1, 1933, *L*, 972.

418   "I have made better speeches": LS to EW, November 28, 1933, *L*, 969, 970.

418   "He was unmercifully brilliant": Beverley M. Bowie to EW, n.d. (LSP).

419   "Whenever I hear people talking": LS to Whittaker Chambers, June 18, 1933, *L*, 961.

419   "Really appreciated it": LS to EW, November 1933, *L*, 971.

419   "Dr. W. had a long talk": AS to DH, December 11, 1933, in B. C. Wheelwright, "The Road to Zurich," 33.

29: "I Thought He Was Just My Daddy"

421   "a whirl of a success": LS to EW, December 11, 1933, *L*, 973, 974.

422   "tiny little labor agitator": LS to James J. Rolph, February 2, 1934, *L*, 975.

422   "She thinks she can make": ibid.

422   "I guessed": LS to Edward A. Filene, April 1, 1934, *L*, 979.

423   "a lifelong liberal": LS to Sam Darcy, April 28, 1934, *L*, 983.

423   "Your letter": Sam Darcy to LS, May 5, 1934 (LSP).

424   "There were a dozen": Flavin, "Conversations," 14.

424   "You tell the blacks": Rampersad, *Life*, 280.

424   "delighted to hold forth": Hughes, *I Wonder*, 283.

424   "I am living so much": Rampersad, *Life*, 280.

424   "Steffy, Peter, and Pete": Hughes, *I Wonder*, 283.

424   "the best of the letter writers": LS to Marie Howe, January 17, 1934, *L*, 974.

424   "long warm letter": LS to Frederic C. Howe, May 11, 1934, *L*, 985–986.

425   "important": LS to Anna Louise Strong, September 11, 1934, *L*, 995, 996.

425   "Your difficulties with Trotzky": LS to Anna Louise Strong, October, 1934, *L*, 1000–1001.

426   "I had come to regard": LS to Joseph R. Boldt Jr., September 10, 1935, *L*, 1007.

427   "Of course": Steffens, *Speaking*, 176.

427   "It seems to me": LS to Anna Louise Strong, January 10, 1935, *L*, 1002.

427   "Is it impossible": MacDonald, *Discriminations*, 357.

427   "It is unbelievable": EW to LS, July n.d., 1933 (LSP).

427   "our Max": Steffens, "Swatting Flies in Russia," *New Republic*, June 20, 1934, 47.

428   "When I hauled off": LS to the editor of the *New Republic*, July 1934, *L*, 988.

429   "The old parties": Steffens, *Speaking*, 224–225.

429   "armed hostilities": Starr, *Endangered*, 113.

430   "There is hysteria here": LS to Frances M. Perkins, July 19, 1934, *L*, 988–989.

430   "to consider a program": Frances Perkins to LS, March 8, 1935 (LSP).

430   "Perhaps we can agree": LS to Fremont Older, October 20, 1934, *L*, 999.

431   "We have lots of visitors": LS to James Cagney, October 9, 1935, *L*, 1008.

431   "Why not thirty?": Winter, *Yield*, 207.

431   "I am for a United Front": "United Front," in Steffens, *Speaking*, 209.

432   "the most effective ways": "Call for an American Writers' Conference," *New Masses*, January 22, 1935, 20.

433   "Russia just now": LS to Edward A. Filene, May 18, 1935, *L*, 1002.

433   "The bank business": LS to Robert Cantwell, June 28, 1935, *L*, 1004–1005.

434   "I am getting tired": LS to Edward A. Filene, October 26, 1935, *L*, 1010.

434   "His name is John Steinbeck": LS to Sam Darcy, February 25, 1936, *L*, 1015.

434   "rather wrecked emotionally": Loftis, *Witnesses*, 53.

435   "When you're heart and soul": ibid., 60–61.

435   "viewpoint was so contradictory": ibid., 172, 173.

435   "the most amazing": LS to Sam Darcy, April 12, 1936, *L*, 1019.

435   "The marvelous Hicks book": "Back from Russia," in Steffens, *Speaking*, 309.

436   "I suspected that Stef": Hicks, *Truth*, 141.

436   "all roads in our day": LS to Sam Darcy, April 12, 1936, *L*, 1020.

436   "'We' have 'seized'": LS to Robert Cantwell, June 15, 1936, *L*, 1021.

436   "It will cost some little money": LS to Prospective Supporters of the *Pacific Weekly*, June 16, 1936, *L*, 1022.

436   "succeeding,—in vain": LS to DH, June 25, 1936, *L*, 1023.

436   "here's the modern stuff": Alfred Harcourt to LS, April 8, 1936 (LSP).

436   "I'd rather see you": Frederic C. Howe to LS, January 15, 1936 (LSP).

436   "So long, Fred": LS to Frederic C. Howe, July 8, 1936, *L*, 1024.

436   "hate the president": LS to Edward A. Filene, October 26, 1935, *L*, 1010.

436   "Well, if it": LS to Edward A. Filene, March 23, 1936, *L*, 1016.

436   "That speech of acceptance": LS to Frederic C. Howe, July 8, 1936, *L*, 1023.

436   "Roosevelt is going to win": LS to Pete Steffens, July 13, 1936, *L*, 1026.

436   "Why do they": LS to Edward A. Filene, July 25, 1936, *L*, 1028.

437   "You are learning about life": LS to Pete Steffens, August 2, 1936, *L*, 1029.

437   "I thought I had to make": *L*, xiv.

437   "I've had my life": Winter, *Yield*, 211.

437   "Yes, I'm beginning to see that": ibid., 214.

437   "three full, rich years": ibid., 200.

Conclusion

442   "I have not lived in vain": *A*, 872–873.

442   "Steff was a friend": Davidson, *Sittings*, 293.

442   "I know many people": Flavin, "Conversations," 14, 39.

443   "to express in some direction": Max Eastman to EW, November 26, 1936 (LSP).

443   "so large a kindness": Eastman, *Enjoyment*, 575.

443   "The last time": Ernest Hemingway to EW, October 28, 1936 (LSP).

443   "I'm so sorry": EW to Ernest Hemingway, September 26, 1936 (Hemingway Archive, John F. Kennedy Library).

444   "Later in life": R. S. Baker, *Chronicle*, 223.

BIBLIOGRAPHY

Aaron, Daniel. *Writers on the Left: Episodes in American Literary Communism*. New York: Harcourt, 1961.

Abraham, Richard. *Alexander Kerensky: The First Love of the Revolution*. New York: Columbia University Press, 1987.

Adamic, Louis. *My America, 1928–1938*. New York: Harper, 1938.

———. *Dynamite: The Story of Class Violence in America*. New York: Viking, 1955.

Adams, Graham, Jr. *Age of Industrial Violence 1910–1915*. New York: Columbia University Press, 1966.

Ainley, Leslie G. *Boston Mahatma*. Boston: Bruce Humphries, 1949.

Andelman, David A. *A Shattered Peace: Versailles 1919 and the Price We Pay Today*. Hoboken: Wiley, 2008.

Armstrong, William M. *E. L. Godkin: A Biography*. Albany: State University of New York Press, 1978.

Arthur, Anthony. *Radical Innocent: Upton Sinclair*. New York: Random House, 2006.

Austin, Mary. *Earth Horizon*. New York: Literary Guild, 1932.

———. *No. 26 Jayne Street*. Boston: Houghton, 1920.

———. *A Woman of Genius*. Boston. Houghton, 1917.

———. *Western Trails: A Collection of Short Stories by Mary Austin*. Edited by Melody Graulich. Reno: University of Nevada Press, 1987.

Avrich, Paul. *The Modern School Movement: Anarchism and Education in the United States*. Princeton: Princeton University Press, 1980.

Baker, Carlos. *Ernest Hemingway: A Life Story*. New York: Avon, 1968.

Baker, Leonard. *Brandeis and Frankfurter*. New York: Harper, 1984.

Baker, Ray Stannard. *American Chronicle*. New York: Scribner's, 1945.

Bean, Walter. *Boss Ruef's San Francisco*. Berkeley: University of California Press, 1972.

Bishop, Joseph Bucklin. *Theodore Roosevelt and His Time*. New York, Scribner's, 1920.

Bonsal, Stephen. *Suitors and Suppliants: The Little Nations at Versailles*. New York: Prentice Hall, 1946.

Brady, Kathleen. *Ida Tarbell: Portrait of a Muckraker*. New York: Seaview/Putnam, 1984.

Brandeis, Louis D. *Letters of Louis D. Brandeis*. Edited by Melvin I. Urofsky and David W. Levy. Vols. 2–4. Albany: State University of New York Press, 1972–1975.

Brinton, Crane. *The Anatomy of Revolution*. 1938. New York: Prentice-Hall, 1965.

Brownell, Will, and Richard M. Billings. *So Close to Greatness: A Biography of William C. Bullitt*. New York: Macmillan, 1987.

The Bullitt Mission to Russia: Testimony Before the Committee on Foreign Relations United States Senate of William C. Bullitt. New York, Huebsch, 1919.

Burns, William J. *The Masked War*. New York: Doran, 1913.

Cantwell, Robert. "Lincoln Steffens' Voice." *New Republic* (November 18, 1936).

Cargill, Oscar. "Lincoln Steffens: Pied Piper of the Kremlin." *Georgia Review* (Winter 1951).

Carr, Edward Hallett. *The Bolshevik Revolution, 1917–1923*. 3 vols. New York: Macmillan, 1951–1953.

Cassella-Blackburn, Michael. *The Donkey, the Carrot, and the Club: William C. Bullitt and Soviet-American Relations 1917–1948*. Westport, CT: Praeger, 2004.

Chalmers, David Mark. *The Social and Political Ideas of the Muckrakers*. New York: Citadel, 1964.

Chamberlain, John. *Farewell to Reform*. New York: Liveright, 1932.

Cheslaw, Irving G. "An Intellectual Biography of Lincoln Steffens." PhD diss., Columbia University, 1952. Ann Arbor: University Microfilms, 1968.

Colum, Mary. *Life and the Dream*. New York: Doubleday, 1947.

Cooper, John Milton. *Woodrow Wilson: A Biography*. New York, Knopf, 2009.

Cowan, Geoffrey. *The People v. Clarence Darrow: The Bribery Trial of America's Greatest Lawyer*. New York: Times Books, 1993.

Cowley, Malcolm. *The Dream of the Golden Mountains*. New York: Viking, 1980.

———. *A Second Flowering*. New York: Viking, 1973.

Cramer, C. H. *Newton D. Baker: A Biography*. Cleveland: World, 1961.

Creel, George. *Rebel at Large: Recollections of Fifty Crowded Years*. New York: Putnam's, 1947.

Darrow, Clarence. *The Story of My Life*. New York: Grosset, 1932.

Davidson, Jo. *Between Sittings*. New York: Dial, 1951.

Dearborn, Mary V. *Queen of Bohemia: The Life of Louise Bryant*. New York: Houghton Mifflin, 1996.

Dell, Floyd. *Love in Greenwich Village*. Reprint. North Stratford, NH: Ayer, 2000.

Diliberto, Gioia. *Hadley*. New York: Ticknor, 1992.

Di Scala, Spencer M. *Italy: From Revolution to Republic*. Boulder: Westview, 1995.

Draper, Theodore. *American Communism and Soviet Russia*. New York: Viking, 1968.

———. *The Roots of American Communism*. New York: Viking, 1957.

Dreiser, Theodore. *A Book about Myself*. New York: Boni & Liveright, 1926.

Dunn, Robert. *World Alive*. New York: Crown, 1956.

Dunne, Finley Peter. *Mr. Dooley on Ivrything and Ivrybody*. Edited by Robert Hutchinson. New York: Dover, 1963.

Eastman, Max. *Enjoyment of Living*. New York: Harper, 1948.

———. *Good Companions*. New York: Farrar, 1959.

———. *Heroes I Have Known: Twelve Who Lived Great Lives*. New York: Simon and Schuster, 1942.

———. *Love and Revolution: My Journey Through an Epoch*. New York: Random House, 1964.

———. *Reflections on the Failure of Socialism*. New York: Devin-Adair, 1955.

Eisenhower, John S. D. *Intervention! The United States and the Mexican Revolution 1913–1917*. New York: Norton, 1993.

Ellis, Elmer. *Mr. Dooley's America*. New York: Knopf, 1941.

Fels, Mary. *Joseph Fels: His Life-Work*. New York: Huebsch, 1916.

———. *The Life of Joseph Fels*. New York: Doubleday, 1940.

Fenton. Charles A. *The Apprenticeship of Ernest Hemingway: The Early Years*. New York: Viking, 1954.

Ferlinghetti, Lawrence, and Nancy J. Peters. *Literary San Francisco*. San Francisco: City Lights, Harper, 1980.

Filene, Peter G. *Americans and the Soviet Experiment 1917–1933*. Cambridge, MA: Harvard University Press, 1967.

———. "The 'Secret Desire' of Lincoln Steffens." *Harvard Magazine* (September–October, 1985).

———. ed. *American Views of Soviet Russia*. Homewood, IL: Dorsey, 1968.

Filler, Louis. *Appointment at Armageddon: Muckraking and Progressivism in the American Tradition*. Westport, CT: Greenwood, 1976.

———. *Crusaders for American Liberalism*. New York: Collier, 1961.

Fink, Augusta. *I-Mary: A Biography of Mary Austin*. Tucson: University of Arizona Press, 1983.

Fink, Carole. *The Genoa Conference: European Diplomacy, 1921–1922*. Chapel Hill: University of North Carolina Press, 1984.

Flavin, Martin, Jr. "Conversations with Lincoln Steffens." *Harvard Advocate* (June 1938).

Foner, Philip S. *The AFL in the Progressive Era*. Vol. 5 of *History of the Labor Movement*. New York: International, 1980.

Forcey, Charles. *The Crossroads of Liberalism: Croly, Weyl, Lippmann and the Progressive Era, 1900–25*. New York: Oxford University Press, 1961.

Ford, Hugh. *Four Lives in Paris*. San Francisco: North Point, 1987.

Francis, David R. *Russia from the American Embassy: April, 1916–November, 1918*. New York: Scribner's, 1921.

Freeberg, Ernest. *Democracy's Prisoner: Eugene V. Debs, the Great War, and the Right to Dissent*. Cambridge, MA: Harvard University Press, 2008.

Fry, Amelia. "Sara Bard Field: Poet and Suffragist." Suffragists Oral History Project, Bancroft Library, University of California, 1979.

Gage, Beverly. *The Day Wall Street Exploded*. New York: Oxford University Press, 2009.

Geiger, Louis. G. *Joseph W. Folk of Missouri*. Columbia: Curators of the University of Missouri, 1953.

Gilbert, Martin. *The First World War*. New York: Holt, 1997.

Goldman, Emma. *Living My Life*. 2 vols. New York: Knopf, 1931.

Graham, Jane K. *Viola, The Duchess of New Dorp: A Biography of Viola Roseboro*. Reprint, Whitefish, MT: Kessenger, 2006.

Greenstein, Paul, Nigey Lennon, and Lionel Rolfe. *Bread & Hyacinths: The Rise and Fall of Utopian Los Angeles*. Los Angeles: California Classics, 1992.

Gunn, Drewey Wayne. "Three Radicals and a Revolution: Reed, London, and Steffens on Mexico." *Southwest Review* (Autumn 1970).

Halliday, E. M. *The Ignorant Armies*. London: Wiedenfeld, 1961.

Hamburger, Robert. *Two Rooms: The Life of Charles Erskine Scott Wood*. Lincoln: University of Nebraska Press, 1998.

Hapgood, Hutchins. *Types from City Streets*. New York: Garrett, 1970.

―――. *A Victorian in the Modern World*. New York: Harcourt, 1939.

Hapgood, Norman. *The Changing Years*. New York: Farrar, 1930.

Harris, Leon. *Upton Sinclair: American Rebel*. New York: Crowell, 1975.

Hartsock, John. *A History of American Literary Journalism*. Amherst: University of Massachusetts Press, 2000.

Heckscher, August. *Woodrow Wilson: A Biography*. New York: Scribner, 1991.

Hemingway, Ernest. *Selected Letters 1917–1961*. Edited by Carlos Baker. New York: Scribner's, 1982.

Hicks, Granville. *John Reed*. New York: Macmillan, 1936.

―――. *Part of the Truth*. New York: Harcourt, 1965.

Hillquit, Morris. *Loose Leaves from a Busy Life*. New York: Rand School Press, 1934.

Hodgson, Godfrey. *Woodrow Wilson's Right Hand: The Life of Colonel Edward M. House*. New Haven: Yale University Press, 2006.

Hofstadter, Richard. *The Age of Reform*. New York: Knopf, 1963.

―――. *The American Political Tradition*. New York: Vintage, 1974.

―――, ed. *The Progressive Movement: 1900–1915*. Englewood Cliffs, NJ: Prentice-Hall, 1963.

Hook, Sidney. *Out of Step: An Unquiet Life in the 20th Century*. New York: Carroll & Graf, 1988.

Horrocks, Sir Brian. *A Full Life*. London: Collins, 1960.

Horton, Russell M. *Lincoln Steffens*. Boston: Twayne, 1974.

Howe, Frederic. *The Confessions of a Reformer*. New York: Scribner's, 1925.

Howe, Irving. *Socialism and America*. New York: Harcourt, 1985.

―――. *World of Our Fathers: The Journey of the East European Jews to America and the Life They Found and Made*. 1976. Reprint, New York: Monticello, 1993.

Hughes, Langston. *I Wonder as I Wander: An Autobiographical Journey*. New York: Farrar, Straus, and Giroux, 1981.

Irwin, Will. *The Making of a Reporter*. New York: Putnam's, 1942.

Jeffers, H. Paul. *Commissioner Roosevelt*. New York: Wiley, 1994.

Johns, Orrick. *Time of Our Lives*. New York: Stackpole, 1937.

Johnson, Gerald. *Liberal's Progress*. New York: Coward-McCann, 1948.

Johnson, Tom L. *My Story*. New York: Huebsch, 1913.

Johnson, Walter. *William Allen White's America*. New York: Holt, 1947.

Juergens, George. "Theodore Roosevelt and the Press." *Daedalus* (Fall 1982).

Kahn, E. J., Jr. *The World of Swopes*. New York: Simon, 1965.

Kaplan, Justin. *Lincoln Steffens*. New York: Simon, 1974.

Kellogg, Paul U. "Boston's Level Best: The '1915 Movement' and the Work of Civic Organizing for Which It Stands." *The Survey* (June 5, 1909).

Kennan, George F. *The Decision to Intervene*. Princeton, NJ: Princeton University Press, 1958.

———. *Russia and the West Under Lenin and Stalin*. Boston: Little, 1961.

Knightley, Philip. *The First Casualty*. New York: Harcourt, 1975.

Koch, Stephen. *Double Lives: Stalin, Willi Münzenberg, and the Seduction of the Intellectuals*. New York, Enigma, 2004.

Kutulas, Judy. "Becoming 'More Liberal': The League of American Writers, the Communist Party, and the Literary People's Front." *Journal of American Culture* (Spring 1990).

La Follette, Robert M. *La Follette's Autobiography*. Madison: University of Wisconsin Press, 1963.

La Follette, Belle Case, and Fola La Follette. *Robert M. La Follette*. New York: Macmillan, 1953.

Lakoff, Sanford A. *Max Lerner: Pilgrim in the Promised Land*. Chicago: University of Chicago Press, 1998.

Langlois, Karen S. "Mary Austin and Lincoln Steffens." *Huntington Library Quarterly* 49, no. 4 (Autumn 1986).

Lardner, James, and Thomas Reppetto, *NYPD: A City and Its Police*. New York: Holt, 2000.

Larkin, Susan G. *The Cos Cob Art Colony: Impressionists on the Connecticut Shore*. New Haven: Yale University Press, 2001.

Lasch, Christopher. *The American Liberals and the Russian Revolution*. New York: Columbia University Press, 1962.

———. *The New Radicalism in America 1889–1963*. New York: Vintage, 1965.

Link, Arthur S. *Woodrow Wilson and the Progressive Era*. New York: Harper, 1954.

Lippmann, Walter. *Drift and Mastery*. 1914. Reprint, Madison: University of Wisconsin Press, 1985.

———. *A Preface to Politics*. 1914. Reprint, Ann Arbor: University of Michigan Press, 1962.

Loftis, Anne. *Witnesses to the Struggle: Imaging the 1930s California Labor Movement*. Reno: University of Nevada Press, 1998.

Luhan, Mabel Dodge. *Movers and Shakers*. New York: Harcourt, 1936.

———. *Edge of Taos Desert: An Escape to Reality*. New York: Harcourt, 1937.

Lynn, Kenneth S. *Hemingway*. New York: Simon, 1987.

Lyon, Peter. *Success Story: The Life and Times of S. S. McClure*. New York: Scribner's, 1963.

MacDonald, Dwight. *Discriminations: Essays & Afterthoughts*. 1974. New York: Da Capo, 1985.

Martinez, Elsie. "San Francisco Area Writers and Artists." Interview. Berkeley: Regional Oral History Office, Bancroft Library, University of California, 1969.

Mee, Charles L., Jr. *The End of Order: Versailles 1919*. New York: Dutton, 1980.

McClure, S. S. *My Autobiography*. New York: Ungar, 1963.

McDougal, Dennis. *Privileged Son: Otis Chandler and the Rise and Fall of the L.A. Times Dynasty*. Cambridge, MA: Perseus, 2001.

McFadden, David W. *Alternative Paths: Soviets and Americans, 1917–1920*. New York: Oxford University Press, 1993.

McFarland, Gerald W. *Inside Greenwich Village: A New York City Neighborhood, 1898–1918*. Amherst: University of Massachusetts Press, 2001.

McGerr, Michael. *A Fierce Discontent: The Rise and Fall of the Progressive Movement in America*. New York, Free Press, 2003.

Mellow, James R. *Hemingway: A Life Without Consequences*. New York: Houghton Mifflin, 1992.

Miller, Nathan. *Theodore Roosevelt: A Life*. New York: William Morrow, 1992.

Miraldi, Robert, ed. *The Muckrakers: Evangelical Crusaders*. Westport, CT: Praeger, 2000.

———. *The Pen Is Mightier: The Muckraking Life of Charles Edward Russell*. New York: Palgrave Macmillan, 2003.

Morris, Edmund. *The Rise of Theodore Roosevelt*. New York: Ballantine, 1979.

———. *Theodore Rex*. New York: Random, 2001.

Mowry, George E. *The California Progressives*. Berkeley: University of California Press, 1951.

———. *Theodore Roosevelt and the Progressive Movement*. Madison: University of Wisconsin Press, 1947.

Nasaw, David. *The Chief: The Life of William Randolph Hearst*. New York: Houghton, 2000.

Nevins, Allan. *The Evening Post: A Century of Journalism*. New York: Russell, 1968.

Nies, Judith. *Seven Women: Portraits from the American Radical Tradition*. New York: Penguin, 1979.

Older, Fremont. *My Own Story*. New York: Macmillan, 1926.

O'Neill, William L. *The Last Romantic: A Life of Max Eastman*. New York: Oxford University Press, 1978.

Palermo, Patrick. *Lincoln Steffens*. Boston: Twayne, 1978.

Parkhurst, Charles. *My Forty Years in New York*. New York: Macmillan, 1923.

Pease, Otis, ed. *The Progressive Years: The Spirit and Achievement of American Reform*. New York: Braziller, 1962.

Pethybridge, Roger, ed. *Witnesses to the Russian Revolution*. London: Allen, 1964.

Piott, Stephen L. *American Reformers, 1870–1920: Progressives in Word and Deed*: New York: Rowman and Littlefield, 2006.

———. *Holy Joe: Joseph W. Folk and the Missouri Idea*. Columbia: University of Missouri Press, 1997.

Pipes, Richard. *The Russian Revolution*. New York: Knopf, 1990.

Poli, Bernard J. *Ford Madox Ford and the Transatlantic Review*. Syracuse: Syracuse University Press, 1967.

Price, Morgan Philips. *Dispatches from the Revolution*. Durham, NC: Duke University Press, 1998.

Rabban, David M. *Free Speech in Its Forgotten Years*. Cambridge, UK: Cambridge University Press, 1997.

Raphelson, Alfred C. "Lincoln Steffens at the Leipzig Psychological Institute, 1890–1891." *Journal of the History of the Behavioral Sciences* 3, no. 1 (January 1967).

Rampersad, Arnold. *The Life of Langston Hughes: I, Too, Sing America*. Vol. 1. New York: Oxford University Press, 2002.

Reed, John. "Almost Thirty." *New Republic* (April 29, 1936).

Regier, C. C. *The Era of the Muckrakers*. Chapel Hill: University of North Carolina Press, 1932.

Riasanovsky, Nicholas V. *A History of Russia*. New York: Oxford University Press, 1977.

Richwine, Keith Norton. *The Liberal Club: Bohemia and the Resurgence in Greenwich Village, 1912–1918.* PhD diss. Ann Arbor: University Microfilms, Inc., 1969.

Riis, Jacob A. *The Making of an American.* New York: Macmillan, 1924.

———. *Theodore Roosevelt the Citizen.* New York: Outlook, 1904.

Rischin, Moses. "Abraham Cahan and the New York *Commercial Advertiser*" *Publications of the American Jewish Historical Society* (September 1953).

Roosevelt, Theodore. *The Letters of Theodore Roosevelt.* Edited by Elting E. Morison. 6 vols. Cambridge, MA: Harvard University Press, 1951.

———. *Theodore Roosevelt: An Autobiography.* 1913. Reprint, New York: Da Capo, 1985.

Rosenstone, Robert A. *Romantic Revolutionary: A Biography of John Reed.* New York, Knopf, 1975.

Rudnick, Lois Palken. *Mabel Dodge Luhan: New Woman, New Worlds.* Albuquerque: University of New Mexico Press, 1984.

Russell, Charles Edward. *Bare Hands and Stone Walls: Some Recollections of a Side-Line Reformer.* New York: Scribner's, 1933.

Schroeder, Theodore. *Free Speech for Radicals.* New York: Free Speech League, 1916.

Scripps, E. W. *I Protest: Selected Disquisitions of E. W. Scripps.* Edited by Oliver Knight. Madison: University of Wisconsin Press, 1966.

Sedgwick, Ellery. *The Happy Profession.* Boston: Little, 1946.

Seldes, George. *Witness to a Century: Encounters with the Noted, the Notorious, and the Three SOBs.* New York: Ballantine, 1987.

Service, Robert. *Lenin: A Biography.* Cambridge, MA: Harvard University Press, 2000.

Shapiro, Herbert. "Lasch on Radicalism: The Problem of Lincoln Steffens." *Pacific Northwest Quarterly* (January 1969).

———. "Lincoln Steffens: The Evolution of an American Radical." PhD diss. University of Rochester, 1964. Ann Arbor: University Microfilms, 1974.

———. "Lincoln Steffens: Light and Shadow on His Historical Image." *American Journal of Economics and Sociology* (July 1972).

———. "Lincoln Steffens and the McNamara Case: A Progressive Response to Class Conflict." *American Journal of Economics and Sociology* (October 1980).

———. "Lincoln Steffens: The Muckraker Reconsidered." *American Journal of Economics and Sociology* (October 1972).

———, ed. *The Muckrakers and American Society.* Lexington, MA: Heath, 1968.

———. "Steffens, Lippmann, and Reed." *Pacific Northwest Quarterly* (October 1971).

Shotwell, James T. *At the Paris Peace Conference.* New York: Macmillan, 1937.

Sinclair, Upton. *My Lifetime in Letters.* Columbia: University of Missouri Press, 1950.

Sklar, Dusty. "Radiant Fathers, Alienated Sons." *Nation* (October 2, 1972).

Sloat, Warren. *A Battle for the Soul of New York: Tammany Hall, Police Corruption, Vice and Reverend Charles Parkhurst's Crusade Against Them, 1892–1895.* New York: Cooper Square, 2002.

Slocombe, George. *The Tumult and the Shouting.* New York: Macmillan, 1936.

Stansell, Christine. *American Moderns: Bohemian New York and the Creation of a New Century.* New York: Holt, 2000.

Starr, Kevin. *Americans and the California Dream 1850–1915.* 1973. Reprint, Santa Barbara: Peregrine, 1981.

————. *Endangered Dreams: The Great Depression in California.* New York: Oxford University Press, 1996.

Steed, Henry Wickham. *Through Thirty Years.* Garden City: Doubleday, 1924.

Steel, Ronald. *Walter Lippmann and the American Century.* New York: Vintage, 1980.

Steffens, Lincoln. *The Autobiography of Lincoln Steffens.* New York: Harcourt, 1931.

————. *The Letters of Lincoln Steffens.* Edited by Ella Winter and Granville Hicks. 2 vols. New York: Harcourt, 1938.

————. *Lincoln Steffens Speaking.* New York: Harcourt, 1936.

————. *The Shame of the Cities.* 1904. Reprint, New York: Hill, 1963.

————. *The Struggle for Self-Government.* 1906. Reprint, New York: Johnson, 1968.

————. *Upbuilders.* 1909. Seattle: University of Washington Press, 1968.

————. *The World of Lincoln Steffens.* Edited by Ella Winter and Herbert Shapiro. New York: Hill, 1962.

Steffens, Pete. "The Identity Struggle of Lincoln Steffens—Writer or Reporter." *Journalism History* 2 (1975).

Stein, Harry H. "Apprenticing Reporters: Lincoln Steffens on the 'Evening Post.'" *Historian* (January 1, 1996).

————. "Lincoln Steffens: Interviewer." *Journalism Quarterly* 46 (1969).

————. "Lincoln Steffens and the Mexican Revolution." *American Journal of Economics and Sociology* 34, no. 2 (April 1975).

————. "Theodore Roosevelt and the Press: Lincoln Steffens." *Mid-America* (April 1972).

Stimson, Grace Heilman. *The Rise of the Labor Movement in Los Angeles*. Berkeley: University of California Press, 1955.

Stinson, Robert. *Lincoln Steffens*. New York: Ungar, 1979.

Strong, Anna Louise. *I Change Worlds*. New York: Holt, 1935.

Sullivan, Mark. *The Education of an American*. New York: Doubleday, 1938.

Tarbell, Ida. *All in the Day's Work*. New York: Macmillan, 1939.

Tebbell, John. *The American Magazine: A Compact History*. New York: Hawthorn, 1969.

Thompson, John A. *Reformers and War: American Progressive Publicists and the First World War*. New York: Cambridge University Press, 1987.

Thompson, John M. *Russia, Bolshevism, and the Versailles Peace*. Princeton, NJ: Princeton University Press, 1966.

Tierney, Kevin. *Darrow*. New York: Crowell, 1979.

Tuchman, Barbara. *The Proud Tower: A Portrait of the World Before the War 1890–1914*. New York: Bantam, 1981.

———. *The Zimmerman Telegram*. New York, Macmillan, 1966.

Tytell, John. *Ezra Pound: The Solitary Volcano*. New York: Doubleday, 1987.

von Mohrenschildt, Dimitri S. "Lincoln Steffens and the Russian Bolshevik Revolution." *Russian Review* 5, no. 1 (Autumn 1945).

Urofsky, Melvin I. *Louis D. Brandeis: A Life*. New York: Pantheon, 2009.

Wade, Rex A. *The Bolshevik Revolution and the Russian Civil War*. Westport, CT: Greenwood, 2001.

Walker, Franklin. *The Seacoast of Bohemia*. Santa Barbara: Peregrine Smith, 1973.

Weber, Cynthia. *Simulating Sovereignty: Intervention, the State, and Symbolic Exchange*. Cambridge: Cambridge University Press, 1995.

Weinberg, Arthur and Lila, eds. *The Muckrakers*. New York: Simon, 1961.

Weinberg, Steve. *Taking On the Trust: The Epic Battle of Ida Tarbell and John D. Rockefeller*. New York: Norton, 2008.

Wells, Evelyn. *Fremont Older*. New York: Appleton, 1936.

Wetzsteon, Ross. *Republic of Dreams*. New York: Simon, 2002.

Wexler, Alice. *Emma Goldman: An Intimate Life*: New York: Pantheon, 1984.

Wheelwright, Betty Coon. "A Common Life: Lincoln Steffens and Jane Hollister Wheelwright (1925–1927). *Jung Journal: Culture and Psyche* 4, no. 1 (Winter 2010).

——. "The Road to Zurich." *Jung Journal: Culture and Psyche* 3, no. 1 (Winter 2009).

Wheelwright, Jane Hollister. *The Ranch Papers*. San Francisco: Lapis, 1988.

White, William Allen. *The Autobiography of William Allen White*. New York: Macmillan, 1946.

Whitlock, Brand. *Forty Years of It*. New York: Appleton, 1914.

——. *The Letters and Journal of Brand Whitlock*. 2 vols. New York: Appleton, 1936.

Wilhelm, J. J. *Ezra Pound in London and Paris 1908–1925*. University Park: Penn State University Press, 1990.

Williams, Albert Rhys. *Journey into Revolution: Petrograd, 1917–1918*. Chicago: Quadrangle, 1969.

Wilson, Christopher. "The Era of the Reporter Reconsidered: The Case of Lincoln Steffens." *Journal of Popular Culture* 15 (Fall 1981).

Wilson, Harold S. *McClure's Magazine and the Muckrakers*. Princeton, NJ: Princeton University Press, 1970.

Winter, Ella. *And Not to Yield: An Autobiography*. New York: Harcourt, 1963.

——. *Red Virtue: Human Relationships in the New Russia*. New York: Harcourt, 1933.

Young, Art. *Art Young: His Life and Times*. New York: Sheridan House, 1939.

INDEX

CREDITS

PHOTOS

1. The Steffens's home in Sacramento. California History Room, California State Library, Sacramento, California

2. Steffens at twenty-eight. The Bancroft Library, University of California, Berkeley

3. Josephine Bontecou Steffens. The Bancroft Library, University of California, Berkeley

4. Ida Tarbell. The Ida M. Tarbell Collection, Special Collections, Pelletier Library, Allegheny College

5. The San Francisco graft prosecutors. The Bancroft Library, University of California, Berkeley

6. Steffens, *circa* 1915. Wisconsin Historical Society

7. Jo Davidson. Sylvia Beach Collection. Manuscripts Division. Department of Rare Books and Special Collections. Princeton University Library. ©2010 Man Ray Trust/Artists Rights Society (ARS), NY / ADAGP, Paris

8. Steffens with Jane Hollister. Lincoln Steffens Papers, Rare Book and Manuscript Library, Columbia University

9. Steffens and Ella with Charles Erskine Scott Wood. This item is reproduced by permission of The Huntington Library, San Marino, California

10. Art Young's view. *New Masses*

11. Steffens, Ella, and Albert Bender. San Francisco History Center, San Francisco Public Library

Cover Photo: Courtesy of Bancroft Library, University of California, Berkeley